# Informal International Lawmaking: Case Studies

Ayelet Berman, Sanderijn Duquet, Joost Pauwelyn, Ramses A. Wessel and Jan Wouters (editors)

2012
Torkel Opsahl Academic EPublisher
The Hague

This and other books in the Law of the Future Series may be openly accessed and downloaded from www.fichl.org. This site uses Persistent URLs (PURL) for all publications it makes available. Printed copies may be ordered through online distributors such as www.amazon.co.uk. This book was first published on 24 December 2012.



**ISBN 978-82-93081-84-5**

# PUBLICATION SERIES PREFACE

The Hague Institute for the Internationalisation of Law (HiiL) and the Torkel Opsahl Academic EPublisher (TOAEP) are pleased to include *Informal International Lawmaking* in the *Law of the Future Series* established in October 2012.

HiiL – an independent research and advisory institute – is the driving force behind this Publication Series, which aims at promoting future-oriented research in the field of law. Thanks to the close cooperation with TOAEP, it is possible to bring such innovative research to persons anywhere in the world who may be interested in it, using an online platform that is open and freely accessible to all.

The *Law of the Future Series* is premised on the assumption that prospective thinking about law and justice systems is not only desirable but also necessary, in order to ensure that they do not become obsolete, ineffective or unjust. The Series primarily features compilations of 'think pieces' about the law of the future and the future of law, but also includes other publications.

The first book in the Series brought together trends from different areas of law. The second book explores what you do with those trends: how does one get to strategise? Both used the same method: that of 'think pieces' by thought and practice leaders in different areas. This volume critically assesses the dangers inherent within informal international lawmaking concerning its accountability, transparency, and effectiveness.

As will be the case with all future volumes in the *Law of the Future Series*, this book can be freely read, printed or downloaded from www.fichl.org/law-of-the-future-series/. It can also be purchased through online distributors such as www.amazon.co.uk as a regular printed book. Firmly committed to open access, neither TOAEP nor HiiL will charge for this book. Questions and comments are welcomed and may be transmitted via toaep@fichl.org.

Sam Muller, Larry Catá Backer and Stavros Zouridis
*Publication Series Co-Editors*

# ABBREVIATIONS

| | |
|---|---|
| 3G or GGG | Global Governance Group |
| ABAC | APEC Business Advisory Council |
| ABTC | APEC business travel card |
| ACASH | Association for Consumers Action on Safety and Health (India) |
| ACS | Andean Community Secretariat (Andean Committee for the Defense of Competition) |
| ACT | Anti-Corruption and Transparency Experts' Task Force (APEC) |
| AFM | Stichting Autoriteit Financiële Markten (Authority for Financial Markets, Netherlands) |
| AGCARM | Association for Animal Health and Crop Protection (New Zealand) |
| AHC | APEC's Harmonization Centre (APEC) |
| AHI | Animal Health Institute (United States) |
| AHWP | Asian Harmonization Working Party |
| AMWG | Asset Management Working Group (UNEP) |
| ANVISA | National Health Surveillance Agency (Brazil) |
| ANZFA | Australia and New Zealand Food Authority |
| APEC | Asia Pacific Economic Cooperation |
| APIs | Active pharmaceuticals ingredients |
| APVMA | Australian Pesticides and Veterinary Medicines Authority |
| ASEAN | Association of the South East Asian Nations |
| ASEAN PPWG | Association of Southeast Asian Nations Pharmaceutical Product Working Group |
| AU | African Union |
| BACEN | Banco Central do Brasil (Central Bank of Brazil) |
| BCBS | Basel Committee on Banking Supervision |
| BIAC | Business and Industry Advisory Council (OECD) |
| BIS | Bank of International Settlements |
| BMC | Budget and Management Committee (APEC) |
| BPNI | Breastfeeding Promotion Network (India) |

| | |
|---|---|
| BTR | Breaking the Rules-report (IBFAN) |
| CAC | Codex Alimentarius Commission |
| CAD | Company Affairs Directorate (OECD) |
| CAHI | Canada Animal Health Institute |
| CDS | Credit default swaps |
| CEN | European Committee for Standardization |
| CIC | China Investment Corporation |
| CMN | Conselho Monetário Nacional (National Monetary Council, Brazil) |
| COMIECO | Council of Ministers of Economy of Central America |
| CSWB | Central Social Welfare Board (India) |
| CTD | Common technical document |
| CTI | Committee on Trade and Investment (APEC) |
| CVM | Comissão de Valores Mobiliários (Securities and Exchange Commission, Brazil) |
| DDA | Doha Development Agenda (WTO) |
| DG | Directorate-General (EU) |
| DG | Director-General (EU) |
| DNB | De Nederlandsche Bank NV (Central Bank, Netherlands) |
| DRAs | Drug regulatory authorities |
| DRC | Democratic Republic of the Congo |
| DRR | Disaster risk reduction |
| EAC | East African Community |
| EB | Executive board |
| EC | European Commission (EU) |
| EC DG SANCO | Directorate General for Health and Consumers (EU) |
| EC FVO | Food and Veterinary Office (EU) |
| ECGI | European Corporate Governance Institute |
| ECN | European Competition Network (EU) |
| eCTD | Electronic common technical document |
| EFPIA | European Federation of Pharmaceutical Industries' Associations |
| EFSA | European Food Safety Authority (EU) |
| EMA | European Medicines Agency (EU) |
| EMDCs | Emerging markets and developing countries |

| | |
|---|---|
| ESG | Environmental, social and corporate governance |
| EU | European Union |
| FAO | Food and Agriculture Organization (UN) |
| FATF | Financial Action Task Force |
| FDA | Food and Drug Administration (United States) |
| FDI | Foreign direct investment |
| FMR | Financial market regulation |
| FOPREL | Forum of Presidents of Legislative Branches in Central America and the Caribbean |
| FSANZ | Food Standards Australia-New Zealand Agency |
| FSAP | Financial Sector Assessment Program (IMF – World Bank) |
| FSB | Financial Stability Board |
| FSF | Financial Stability Forum |
| FTA | Free trade agreement |
| GAL | Global administrative law |
| GATT | General Agreement on Tariff and Trade (WTO) |
| GC | Global Compact (UN) |
| GCC | Cooperation Council of Arab States of the Gulf |
| GCC-DR | Gulf Central Committee for Drug Registration (GCC) |
| GCG | Global Cooperation Group (ICH) |
| GCGF | Global Corporate Governance Forum (OECD – World Bank |
| GCP | Good clinical practice |
| G-FMR | Global financial market regulation |
| GFSI | Global Food Safety Initiative |
| GHS | Globally Harmonized System of Classification and Labeling of Chemicals (UN) |
| GHTF/IMDFR | Global Harmonization Task Force/International Medical Devices Regulators Forum |
| GLOBALG.A.P. | Global Partnership for Good Agricultural Practice |
| GMDN | Global Medical Device Nomenclature |
| GMOs | Genetically modified organisms |
| GNDR | Global Network for Disaster Reduction |
| GPEG | Government Procurement Experts' Group (APEC) |
| G-SIFI | Global systemically-important financial institutions |

| | |
|---|---|
| HFA | Hyogo Framework for Action (UNISDR) |
| HiiL | The Hague Institute for the Internationalization of Law |
| HTF | Health Task Force (APEC) |
| IADB | Inter-American Development Bank |
| IAP | Individual action plan (APEC) |
| IASB | International Accounting Standards Board |
| IBEF | Brazilian Institute of Finance Executives |
| IBFAN | International Baby Food Action Network |
| ICCW | Indian Council for Child Welfare |
| ICDC | International Code of Marketing of Breastmilk Substitutes Documentation Centre (IBFAN) |
| ICGN | International Corporate Governance Network |
| ICH | International Conference on the Harmonization of Technical Requirements for Registration of Pharmaceuticals for Human Use |
| IEC | International Electrotechnical Commission |
| IFAH | International Federation of Animal Health |
| IFAH–Europe | European Federation for Animal Health |
| IFIs | International financial institutions |
| IFPMA | International Federation of Pharmaceutical Manufacturers and Associations |
| IFSWF | International Forum of SWFs |
| IGE | Intergovernmental Group of Experts (UNCTAD) |
| IGPA | International Generic Pharmaceutics Alliance |
| ILO | International Labour Organization |
| IMDRF | International Medical Device Regulators Forum |
| IMF | International Monetary Fund |
| IMFC | International Monetary and Finance Committee (IMF) |
| IMS | Infant Milk Substitutes, Feeding Bottles and Infant Foods Act (India) |
| INDECI | National Institute of Civil Defence (India) |
| INDECOPI | National Institute for the Defense of Competition and Intellectual Property Protection (Peru) |
| INFACT | Infant Formula Action Coalition (United States) |
| INFOSAN | International Food Safety Authorities Network (WHO) |
| IN-LAW | Informal international lawmaking |

| | |
|---|---|
| IOs | International organizations |
| IOSCO | International Organization of Securities Commissions |
| IPEG | Intellectual Property Rights Experts' Group (APEC) |
| IPR | Implementing rules and regulations |
| ISDA | International Swaps and Derivatives Association |
| ISDR | International Strategy for Disaster Reduction (UN) |
| ISO | International Organization for Standardization |
| ISSBs | International standard-setting bodies |
| IWGSWF | International Working Group of Sovereign Wealth Funds |
| JMHLW | Japanese Ministry of Health, Labor and Welfare |
| JPDMA | Japanese Pharmaceuticals and Medical Devices Agency |
| JPMA | Japanese Pharmaceutical Manufacturers Association |
| JVPA | Japanese Veterinary Products Association |
| KP | Kimberley Process Certification Scheme |
| LAHWP | Latin American Harmonization Working Party |
| MDGs | Millennium Development Goals (UN) |
| Mercosur | Common Market of the South |
| MNCs | Multi-national corporations |
| NAFTA | North American Free Trade Agreement |
| NDCC | National Disaster Coordinating Council (The Philippines) |
| NDRRMC | National Disaster Risk Reduction and Management Council (The Philippines) |
| NEN | Nederlands Normalisatie-instituut (Normalisation Institute of the Netherlands) |
| NEPAD | New Partnership for Africa's Development (AU) |
| NGOs | Nongovernmental organizations |
| NMPB | National Movement for the Promotion of Breastfeeding (The Philippines) |
| NPs | National Platforms for Disaster Risk Reduction |
| NZFSA | New Zealand Food Safety Authority |
| OAA | Osaka Action Agenda (APEC) |
| OECD | Organisation for Economic Cooperation and Development |

| | |
|---|---|
| OIE | World Animal Health Organization |
| OTC | Over the counter |
| OUP | Oxford University Press |
| PAHO | Pan American Health Organization |
| PANDHR | Pan American Network on Drug Regulatory Harmonization |
| PFA | Prevention of Food Adulteration Act (India) |
| PhRMA | Pharmaceutical Research and Manufacturers Association of America |
| PRIA | Principles for Responsible Investment Association (UN) |
| PRIAC | Principles for Responsible Investment Advisory Council (UN) |
| RASFF | Rapid Alert System for Food and Feed (EU) |
| RHIs | Regional harmonization initiatives |
| RTA | Regional trade agreement |
| SADC | South African Development Community |
| SAICM | Strategic Approach to International Chemical Management (UN) |
| SCE | Senior Officials' Meeting (SOM) Steering Committee on Economic and Technical Cooperation (APEC) |
| SEC | Securities and Exchange Commission (United States) |
| SICA | Central American Integration System |
| SIECA | Central American Economic Integration Subsystem |
| SINADECI | National System for Civil Defence (Peru) |
| SOE | State-owned enterprise |
| SOM | Senior Officials' Meeting (APEC) |
| SPS | Sanitary and Phytosanitary Measures Agreement (WTO) |
| SRI | Sustainable and responsible investment |
| SWF | Sovereign wealth fund |
| Swissmedic | Swiss Agency for Therapeutic Products |
| TBT | Technical Barriers to Trade Agreement (WTO) |
| TFEP | Task Force for Emergency Preparedness (APEC) |
| TPR | Transnational private regulation |
| TPRM | Trade policy review mechanism |

| | |
|---|---|
| TRSN | Transnational regulatory safety net |
| TUAC | Trade Union Advisory Council (OECD) |
| UK | United Kingdom |
| UN | United Nations |
| UNCTAD | United Nations Conference on Trade and Development |
| UNEP FI | United Nations Environment Programme Finance Initiative |
| UNEP | United Nations Environment Programme |
| UNICEF | United Nations Children's Fund |
| UNISDR | United Nations International Strategy for Disaster Reduction Secretariat |
| UNPRI or PRI | United Nations Principles for Responsible Investment |
| UNSG | United Nations Secretary-General |
| US | United States of America |
| USKPA | United States Kimberley Process Authority |
| VHAI | Voluntary Health Association of India |
| VICH | International Cooperation on Harmonization of Technical Requirements for Registration of Veterinary Medicinal Products |
| WHA | World Health Assembly |
| WHO | World Health Organization |
| WSMI | World Self-Medication Industry |
| WTO | World Trade Organization |

# TABLE OF CONTENTS

PART II:
FINANCE AND COMPETITION

# Introduction and Key Issues Surrounding Informal International Lawmaking

**Ayelet Berman,* Sanderijn Duquet,** Joost Pauwelyn,*** Ramses A. Wessel† and Jan Wouters‡**

## 1. The Rise of Informal International Lawmaking and Accountability Concerns

The current architecture of global governance includes a variety of different forms of bilateral and multilateral cooperation. At the global level,

---

* **Ayelet Berman** is a Ph.D. Candidate in the International Law Unit at the Graduate Institute of International and Development Studies in Geneva and a Research Associate at the Centre for Trade and Economic Integration (CTEI). Before her Ph.D. studies, Berman was an Associate at Herzog, Fox and Neeman in Tel Aviv, Israel, and at Sidley Austin LLP in Geneva. Previously, she also held teaching and research assistantship positions in constitutional and administrative law at the Hebrew University of Jerusalem, Israel. She holds a LL.B. magna cum laude from the Hebrew University of Jerusalem, and a D.E.A. in International Law from the Graduate Institute.

** **Sanderijn Duquet** (Master of Laws, Ghent U. and LL.M. International Legal Studies, American U. Washington College of Law) is a Ph.D. candidate at the Leuven Centre for Global Governance Studies and the Institute for International Law, University of Leuven, Belgium, where she works as a research fellow of the Policy Research Centre on Foreign Affairs, International Entrepreneurship and Development Cooperation for the Flemish Government.

*** **Joost Pauwelyn** is Professor of International Law at the Graduate Institute of International and Development Studies in Geneva. He is also Co-Director of the Centre for Trade and Economic Integration (CTEI) and Senior Advisor with the law firm of King and Spalding LLP.

† **Ramses A. Wessel** is Professor of the Law of the European Union and other International Organizations and Co-Director of the Centre for European Studies, University of Twente, the Netherlands.

‡ **Jan Wouters** is Professor of International Law and International Organizations, Jean Monnet Chair Ad Personam EU and Global Governance. He is Director of the Leuven Centre for Global Governance Studies and of the Institute for International Law at the University of Leuven, Visiting Professor at Sciences Po (Paris) and at the College of Europe (Bruges), member of the Royal Academy of Belgium for Sciences and Arts, *Of Counsel* at Linklaters (Brussels), and President of the Flemish Foreign Affairs Council.

alongside the more traditional way to create international law through the conclusion of treaties or customary law, for a number of decades now there has been a tendency to engage in alternative methods to generate international agreement.[1] Indeed, although for most pressing trans-boundary issues such as trade, investment, health, finance and human rights, institutional frameworks have been established for many years and are fully operational, regulators have simultaneously been looking for less institutionalized forms of rule-making. One of the most commonly heard justifications for this observation is the search by States, sub-state entities and private actors to engage in interaction across national borders that results in more desirable, detailed and effective regulation in technical or highly political matters.[2] It is this understudied category of international rule-making, which we have coined as *informal international lawmaking* (IN-LAW) that is the object of research in this book. The book aims to make an empirical contribution to the debate of international lawmaking in the 21st century by analyzing entities that have been playing a role in international or transnational normative processes in a variety of policy areas.

A central criticism of informal international lawmaking has been that it falls outside of the strictures of both international law and domestic law, and that it consequently suffers from an accountability deficit. The objective of this book has, hence, not only been to provide an 'objective' overview of cases of informal international law, but also to approach and assess these cases from an accountability perspective.

## 2. The IN-LAW Project

This book is one of the many fruits of a research project entitled *Informal International Lawmaking,*[3] launched in November 2009 for a two-year period and sponsored by the Hague Institute for the Internationalization of

---

1 Kal Raustiala, "Form and Substance in International Agreements", in *American Journal of International Law*, 2005, vol. 99, no. 3, pp. 581–614.

2 See Joost Pauwelyn, Ramses A. Wessel and Jan Wouters, "The Exercise of Public Authority through Informal International Lawmaking: An Accountability Issue?", Jean Monnet Working Paper 06/11, available at http://centers.law.nyu.edu/jeanmonnet/papers/index.html, last accessed on 26 February 2012; Charles Lipson, "Why Are Some International Agreements Informal?", in *International Organization,* 1991, vol. 45, p. 500.

3 For further project information, see http://www.informallaw.org, last accessed on 28 June 2012.

Law (HiiL). Together with the academic promoters, researchers of the three participating institutes – the Graduate Institute of International and Development Studies in Geneva, the University of Twente and the Leuven Centre for Global Governance Studies/Institute for International Law at the University of Leuven – engaged in a prolific cooperation that has resulted in an edited volume published with Oxford University Press (OUP),[4] five workshops bringing together more than 40 scholars and practitioners, and a show case event at the 2011 HiiL Law of the Future Conference in The Hague. From the outset, the project aimed to be empirical and solution-oriented: selected IN-LAW activity was mapped based on in-depth case study research, publicly available primary sources and interviews. The aforementioned OUP book, *Informal International Lawmaking,* sets out the IN-LAW framework and methodology.

## 3. The Methodological Framework of IN-LAW

When writing chapters, contributors have examined their cases from an IN-LAW and accountability perspective. These notions have been defined, for the purpose of this project, as follows.

### 3.1. The Definition of Informal International Lawmaking

The term 'informal' international lawmaking is used in contrast and opposition to 'traditional' international lawmaking. More concretely, IN-LAW is informal in the sense that it dispenses with certain formalities traditionally linked to international law. These formalities may have to do with the *process, actors and output* involved.[5] It is along these three criteria that we define Informal International Lawmaking: first, in terms of 'process', international cooperation may be 'informal' in the sense that it occurs in a loosely organized network or forum rather than a traditional treaty-based international organization. Such process informality does, however, not prevent the existence of detailed procedural rules, permanent staff or a physical headquarter. Nor does process informality exclude IN-LAW in the context or under the broader auspices of a more formal organization,

4 Joost Pauwelyn, Ramses A. Wessel and Jan Wouters (eds.), *Informal International Lawmaking*, Oxford University Press, Oxford, 2012.

5 Joost Pauwelyn, "Informal International Lawmaking: Framing the Concept and Research Questions", in Joost Pauwelyn, Ramses A. Wessel and Jan Wouters (eds.), *Informal International Lawmaking*, Oxford University Press, Oxford, 2012, pp. 13–34.

Second, in terms of 'actors' involved, international cooperation may be 'informal' in the sense that it does not engage traditional diplomatic actors (such as heads of state, foreign ministers or embassies) but rather other ministries, domestic regulators, independent or semi-independent agencies (such as food safety authorities or central banks), sub-federal entities (such as provinces or municipalities) or the legislative or judicial branch. While the focus is on cooperation among governmental actors, it can also include private actors and/or international organizations. Third, in terms of 'output', international cooperation may be informal in the sense that it does not lead to a formal treaty or any other traditional source of international law, but rather to a guideline, standard, declaration or even more informal policy coordination or exchange.[6]

On the basis of this methodological framework, we aim to highlight elements of normative global processes that *prima facie* fall outside the traditional scope of 'law' but may nevertheless be seen as forming part of a law or rule-making process. All contributors to this book use this terminology and build on this definition.

### 3.2. The Definition of Accountability

Accountability has many definitions, but we can generally distinguish between a broad and a narrow definition.

Bovens defines 'accountability' as "[a] relationship between an actor and a forum, in which the actor has an obligation to explain and to justify his or her conduct, the forum can pose questions and pose judgment, and the actor may face consequences".[7] This definition is narrow. When operationalized, the definition limits us to examining mechanisms that provide judgment *after* (*ex post*) a decision or action has already been taken. It also limits us to looking at mechanisms that have a sanctioning element. Examples of such accountability mechanisms are electoral, hierarchical, supervisory, fiscal and legal.[8]

---

6 Pauwelyn, 2012, see *supra* note 5, pp. 15–20.

7 Mark Bovens, "Analysing and Assessing Public Accountability: A Conceptual Framework", in *European Law Journal*, 2007, vol. 13, no. 4, p. 450.

8 Richard Stewart, "Accountability, Participation, and the Problem of Disregard in Global Regulatory Governance", Draft paper, January 2008, available at http://www.iilj.org/courses/documents/2008Colloquium.Session4.Stewart.pdf, last accessed on 28 June 2012.

A broader definition of accountability, which is common in international relations scholarship, refers to it as 'responsiveness' to the people,[9] or put negatively, 'disregard' of the people.[10] This definition is broader because when we operationalize it, we can look at a broader set of measures that promote accountability, and are not limited to accountability mechanisms in the narrow sense. The attention goes to criteria such as transparency, participation of stakeholders, decision-making rules *et cetera* – criteria that arguably promote accountability too, but fall short of accountability mechanisms in the strict sense. Moreover, rather than being limited to *ex post* oversight, the timeline of the broader approach is longer and includes examination of measures at all stages: *ex ante* (before a decision has been made), ongoing (during the decision making process), and *ex post* (after a decision has been made).

Another relevant question is accountability to whom? To whom should informal international lawmaking bodies be held accountable? Here, too, we distinguish between two categories: internal and external stakeholders. First, accountability can be owed to actors who entrust the makers of IN-LAW with the power to set norms (think of participating countries, responsible ministers in those countries or the people/parliament who elected those ministers). These are the internal stakeholders. Second, accountability can be owed to actors that are affected by an IN-LAW body and its output (think of non-member countries, industries and consumers). These are external stakeholders.[11]

Furthermore, typically composed of domestic actors, accountability measures can exist at both the international and domestic level.

In line with the project's problem oriented approach, we take a broad approach to accountability. This means that in examining IN-LAW bodies, we are interested in accountability mechanisms in the narrow sense (such as courts), as well as accountability promoting measures (such as transparency, decision-making rules, and participation of stakeholders). These accountability measures may be before, during or after a decision

9 Anne-Marie Slaughter, "Agencies on the loose? Holding government networks accountable", in George Bermann, Matthias Herdegen and Peter Lindseth (eds.), *Transatlantic Regulatory Cooperation, Legal Problems and Political Prospects,* Oxford University Press, 2001, p. 523.

10 Stewart, 2008, p. 1, see *supra* note 8.

11 Ruth W. Grant and Robert O. Keohane, "Accountability and Abuses of Power in World Politics", in *American Political Science Review*, 2005, vol. 99, no. 1, p. 38.

has been taken. They may also be at the international or domestic level. The project is also interested in the extent to which IN-LAW bodies are accountable towards both internal and external stakeholders. This broad analytical framework is the framework within which the contributors to this book have worked, and each of the case studies addresses or focuses on specific aspects of accountability within this framework. The case studies analyze whether – and to what extent – IN-LAW bodies are subject to some form of accountability and, if so, in what form and at what level. The assessments at the case study level also include the search for the most suitable mechanisms and venues to hold the relevant actors accountable at the international and domestic levels.

These challenges are further complicated by the search for effectiveness in cross-border cooperation. Many of the IN-LAW bodies in fact are considered well-equipped to perform coordination functions across functional divides, to set more coherent policies and action, and to effectively tackle the cooperation problems where formal forms of lawmaking failed. Yet, it should be kept in mind that a certain tension may exist between accountability and effectiveness. Strengthening domestic or international accountability measures may for example come at the cost of effectiveness of the IN-LAW process. Some of the case studies, accordingly, consider this tension in their respective contexts and discuss when and whether the enhancement of accountability is beneficial for the effectiveness of the body and vice versa.

## 4. Relation Between this Book and the OUP Informal International Lawmaking Book

Both the OUP book *Informal International Lawmaking* and this book bring together efforts to solve the above-mentioned problems in a way that can assist policymakers and stakeholders. Their starting point is, however, different. The present volume reflects the core of the research effort undertaken and is to be seen as the bundling of *empirical studies* on the organization and effects of non-traditional international lawmakers. The omnipresence in the international spectrum of IN-LAW, and its impact in topics as diversified as financial, investment and competition policy, as well as in areas of health, food, social and human rights regulation, are assessed. The contributions to the OUP book on the other hand assembled overall lessons from certain issue areas at a more conceptual level. All of the chapters in *Informal International Lawmaking* were written with the case studies presented in this book in mind; they cross-refer to them and take advantage of the empirical data uncovered during the entire IN-LAW project. Therefore, the editors considered it important for a good understanding of the overall theory to also publish these case studies as they are the result of in-depth research by experts in a variety of regulatory fields.

## 5. Case Study Selection

This volume bundles case study research on a selection of IN-LAW, all of which bear the potential to directly impact on national regulators and private actors. The editors aimed to generate information on IN-LAW bodies active in a significant number of policy fields in order to draw on comprehensive datasets in the second, theoretical, phase of the project to proceed to a controlled comparison of selected cases.

The selection criteria applied at the start of the project to identify informal international lawmaking networks as object of our research still stand. The focus is on cross-border cooperation related to the global economy that should, preferably, be considered 'informal' in all three senses (output informality, process informality and actor informality). While most case studies are indeed informal in all three senses, we have also included several cases that do not cumulatively fulfill all three levels of informality and are informal at only one or two levels (for example WHO food standards).[12]

Furthermore, being a legally focused project, IN-LAW bodies that were selected had acquired some level of institutionalization (in the form of a website, address, formal meeting place *et cetera*), and created normative output beyond mere meetings or exchange of information (such as declarations, standards or guidelines). The selection of the case studies on different topics enabled us to address the question to what extent informal lawmaking is more successful in some policy fields than in others and why.

The case studies compiled in this book only cover part of the IN-LAW story. The present book does not aim to, nor can it, offer a full view on IN-LAW mechanisms. Rather, a balance was sought between the editors' aim to enable the reader to survey the omnipresence and heteroge-

[12] Pauwelyn, 2012, see *supra* note 5, pp. 32–34.

neity of IN-LAW (horizontally) and the need to present results of thorough research on specific specialized networks (vertically).

All fourteen case studies selected for this volume apply the IN-LAW methodological framework to a number of informal international lawmaking mechanisms. As we collected data in a broad range of policy fields, we explored variation in the studied levels of IN-LAW and related key issues such as accountability and effectiveness. Informality in lawmaking indeed raises these additional questions both at the domestic and at the international level.

## 6. Structure of the Book

The structure of this volume is as follows. Fourteen self-standing case studies were categorized in three thematic parts.

In **Part I, Regional and Country Specific Case Studies**, four case studies were selected to discuss domestic and regional elaboration and implementation of IN-LAW. In *Chapter 1* Jan Wouters and Dylan Geraets discuss a relatively new yet highly influential informal actor on the world stage, the *Group of Twenty* or G20. Although membership of the G20 comprises five continents, two-thirds of the world's population and approximately 80% of world trade, it remains by invitation only and therefore exclusive. Informal rules are upheld that limit membership in this 'club' to a selected number of countries that are considered 'systemically important' in international economic and financial matters. Furthermore, as Wouters and Geraets argue in their contribution, the G20 was never aimed to be a universal network or to become the forum for negotiations to reach a binding treaty. Amongst others for these reasons the authors consider it one of the most wellknown IN-LAW bodies, which despite its restrictive membership has considerable impact at the global level.

*Chapter 2* by Takao Suami offers insights in the activities of the regional Asia Pacific Economic Cooperation or *APEC*. The author analyzes the extent to which APEC resulted in liberalizing trade in goods and services as well as in facilitating foreign investment in the Asia-Pacific region while relying on informal processes and producing informal output. The use of informality in lawmaking is far from uncommon on the Asian continent. Yet, APEC serves as an atypical example of IN-LAW, mainly because the author considers its activities policy-making rather than lawmaking. In particular, the author's argument that APEC cannot be incontestably labeled lawmaking *per se* was of great significance in the development of other case studies and in the further refinement of the overall IN-LAW theory.

The other two chapters of Part I focus specifically on the impact, elaboration and implementation of IN-LAW at the domestic level in selected countries. In *Chapter 3*, Leonard Besselink argues that international law's effect is increasingly to be located within the national legal orders and subsequently looks for the concrete manifestations thereof in the Netherlands. The author examines the status and implementation of the output of informal international lawmaking in a monist EU Member State. This is highly relevant to the IN-LAW discussion since monist States premise themselves on the unity of international and national law and consequently consider (duly consented) international obligations to be part of the 'law of the land'. Besselink also links his assessment of the modes of entrance of non-traditional international law to the manners in which the constitutional bodies of government and parliament, as well as stakeholders, are involved in the creation and implementation of informal international law. The author furthermore contributes to the conceptualization of issues of accountability and democratic legitimacy in the Dutch, European and global context.

In *Chapter 4* Salem Nasser and Ana Mara Machado take the reader to Brazil to answer the question of how IN-LAW is dealt with in a local context that differs considerably from the one discussed in the previous chapter. Brazil can be considered a 'moderate monist country': although treaties in principle automatically enter the Brazilian domestic legal order upon ratification, Brazilian courts have consistently held that for this to happen, the Presidency has to issue a decree promulgating the treaty, as would be the case in a dualist country. The authors consider two levels of lawmaking: first, the international, by analyzing Brazil's participation in specific IN-LAW networks, and, second, the national by analyzing the implementation of selected IN-LAW regulations and output. The reader is provided with a complete overview of the different stages of the IN-LAW timeline: from the reasons for creating it to its specific impacts. Here, too, as in Besselink's contribution on the Netherlands, accountability, legitimacy, and the rule of law in the sphere of Brazil's relatively young democracy are discussed.

In **Part II, Finance and Competition**, international financial and competition rules are analyzed which have become articulated through informal accords. A range of trans-boundary market and institutional mechanisms, regulators and funds that have shaped the international financial and competition architecture are discussed in detail. Informal international lawmaking has been employed for decades in international financial regulation, which has developed into an IN-LAW area of research par excellence.[13] In *Chapter 5*, Shawn Donnelly takes an overview approach to financial market regulation and zooms in on a large number of regulators and standard-setters, amongst others the Basel Committee on Banking Supervision, the International Organization of Securities Commissions, the OECD's Committee on Corporate Governance, the Financial Stability Board, the Financial Action Task Force, and the G7/G20. Donnelly argues that the world has seen an increase of IN-LAW in financial regulation and focuses on specific accountability problems related to this trend. Highly interesting in this regard is the author's overview of the networks in analytical categories of various degrees of institutionalization, their respective level of formality and accountability.

*Chapter 6* by Maciej Borowicz takes a considerably different starting point and analyzes the roles of IN-LAW and of transnational private regulation (TPR) in global financial regulation specifically to avoid and address market failures. Multi-level governance theories are used to review transnational regulatory safety nets, that is, arrangements designed to protect societies from paying for losses that financial institutions may incur, taking both public and private perspectives. The author's thesis is concretized in comprehensive research on the International Swaps and Derivatives Association ISDA (in the news recently as the institution with the authority to decide whether Greece's March 2012 bailout package amounted to a 'credit event'), as an example of TPR, and the Basel Committee on Banking Supervision, as an example of IN-LAW. Complementing the research effort undertaken in the previous chapter, the contribution delves into the debate on private governance of market regulation and its effects on IN-LAW.

*Chapter 7* looks at IN-LAW answers to regulating sovereign wealth funds (SWFs), the government controlled investment vehicles engaging in

13 See David Zaring, "International Law by Other Means: The Twilight Existence of International Financial Regulatory Organizations", in *Texas International Law Journal*, vol. 33, pp. 281–330. Zaring describes international financial "regulatory organizations as acting secretly and neither promulgating treaties or laws nor having the bureaucracies in place to monitor or insure the implementation of their promulgations".

foreign direct investment and/or portfolio investment. Elissavet Malathouni examines whether the International Forum of Sovereign Wealth Funds (IFSWF) can be classified as an informal international public policy-making forum and whether it suffers from an accountability deficit. Special attention is given throughout the chapter to the Santiago Principles, a set of 24 voluntary standards on best practices for the operation of SWFs, promulgated by the International Monetary Fund and the International Working Group of Sovereign Wealth Funds. More concretely, their unclear status under international and national law and the effectiveness of this voluntary code of conduct is assessed.

Megan Smith discusses the global framework for responsible investment in inclusive finance in *Chapter 8* on the United Nations Principles for Responsible Investment (UNPRI), which she considers 'an excellent example of IN-LAW'. She furthermore links responsible finance, competition and trade governance to the topic of informal lawmaking in the context of the United Nations, which as a global international organization is for obvious reasons assimilated with formality in cross-border cooperation. Yet, despite its connection with the UN, most actors involved in UNPRI are 'informal', as they are not central State representatives. Moreover, businesses and industries play a double role as they are one of the governing actors in UNPRI and at the same time constitute the 'targets of regulation' of this informal regulatory initiative. This observation is of importance as the Principles rely on the market, via reputational accountability, to be effective. Challenges observed are, first, the need to increase – and maybe even formalize – committed membership and, second, to uphold current standards of transparency, accountability, and enforcement.

In *Chapter 9,* the final contribution to the finance and competition part, Pierre M. Horna analyzes how accountability and effectiveness go hand in hand in two Latin American competition networks, the Central American Group of Competition and the Andean Committee for the Defense of Free Competition. This case study relies on the use of primary sources, questionnaires and interviews to assess Latin American cross border cooperation which arguably suffers from an accountability deficit and network effectiveness. A core point for discussion taken up by the author is whether networks profit from the opportunities offered to them by past failures and successes and how they can use past experience to adapt accordingly in order to fully realize the learning dimension of accountability.

**Part III, Health, Food and Social Standards,** turns to the topic of health, food and social standard-setting in an IN-LAW context. The reader becomes acquainted with a wide variety of public and private regulations that all ultimately aim to enhance global safety and justice. Although somewhat controversial, the authors address the respective social standards under review in light of global and regional trade regulation.

Ayelet Berman in *Chapter 10* investigates medical products regulation bodies that meet the three IN-LAW criteria of process, output, and actor informality: the International Conference on the Harmonization of Technical Requirements for Registration of Pharmaceuticals for Human Use (ICH), the International Cooperation on Harmonization of Technical Requirements for Registration of Veterinary Medicinal Products (VICH), the Global Harmonization Task Force, and the International Medical Devices Regulators Forum. This chapter analyzes common features, such as governance structures and decision-making procedures, shared by informal networks that promulgate technical, scientific guidelines on different subject matters of human health and animal health.

In *Chapter 11,* questions of harmonization of technical requirements for products and processes are also addressed by Sanderijn Duquet and Dylan Geraets in their chapter on food safety standards. The authors provide an overview of the current food safety governance regime, which is characterized and influenced by the multi-actor context in which the phenomenon of standard-setting on this subject takes place. Their case study involves both public and private trans-boundary networks which set standards: bilateral networks, Mercosur, the EU, the Codex Alimentarius Commission, the World Health Organization (WHO), the International Organization for Standardisation (ISO), the Global Partnership for Good Agricultural Practice and the Global Food Safety Institute. A fundamental question answered by the authors is how these actors, and more specifically the public and private food safety standard-setters, coexist and what role the IN-LAW framework plays in enhancing food safety cooperation.

In *Chapter 12,* Ina Verzivolli studies in-depth from an IN-LAW perspective the WHO's International Code of Marketing of Breastmilk Substitutes, which regulates marketing practices of breastmilk substitutes. The author links the global framework to domestic practices, by evaluating the implementation level and strength of overall measures adopted by

India, Malaysia, and The Philippines and by including this in her general assessment of the effectiveness of the Code in the aforementioned countries.

In *Chapter 13,* Luca Corredig addresses the IN-LAW components of schemes of global resilience against disasters. He argues in favor of enhanced vertical interaction between the international, national and community levels as well as of horizontal cooperation across the different actors operating at each level. The International Strategy for Disaster Reduction (ISDR) represents an interesting example of network-based informal international cooperation and arguably even lawmaking. Like other authors, he focuses on how accountability impacts upon effectiveness. However, unlike other authors, Corredig stresses that overall IN-LAW, within the specific context of the ISDR system, should not raise major concerns in relation to the question of accountability deficit.

*Chapter 14* contains a case study by Victoria Vidal on the Kimberly Process (KP) on 'blood diamonds'. In her analysis, the author raises two different kinds of accountability questions: first, she analyzes accountability and legitimacy of the network itself; in a second step, the focus is on the accountability of the KP owed to external stakeholders. These questions are to be distinguished from the equally important assessment of the effectiveness of IN-LAW in the case of the KP. The chapter concludes with a section on the strengths and weaknesses of IN-LAW answers to prevent the trade in diamonds that fund conflict, and offers potential solutions.

## 7. Carrying the Debate Further

The plethora of case studies makes the present volume an original and noteworthy contribution to the understanding of significant transformations in international lawmaking. The ubiquity of IN-LAW in numerous regulatory fields is reflected in the essays that cover a vast range of substantive matters. From these case studies it transpires that, over the years, the rise of globalization processes in the economic and technological field has demanded ever-growing international governance responses. The present book analyzes non-traditional normative processes, how and to what extent these are used, as well as the driving forces behind the networks and the extent to which these *de facto* may have similar effects as traditional legal rules.

A great asset of all case studies is that they address concerns relating to the democracy, legitimacy and accountability of informal lawmaking. Bearing in mind the vague legal status of most norms and standards covered, when evaluating the implementation of IN-LAW output, researchers consider principles of good governance, the rule of law, and traditional checks and balances systems. Next to this, and although 'purely' private cooperation falls outside the scope of the project, participation of private actors in IN-LAW bodies otherwise populated by public officials is another very present theme. For the sake of comparison, a number of authors also describe private networks, which provides useful insights. Indeed, IN-LAW can benefit from private experiences and often hinges on private participation for its success. As shown in Chapter 5 on financial market regulation as well as in Chapter 11 on food safety standards, the expertise of a large pool of regulators and other actors can lead to more dynamic regulation, sensitive to global and regional changes and evolutions. The contributors to this volume are all concerned with the question of whether informal cooperation at the international level effectively promotes change at the international, national and sub-national levels, as this is what is generally aimed for in most networks. Drawing from these case studies, it can be observed that IN-LAW bodies generally are well-equipped to grasp certain complex global trends and the resulting uncertainty and rapid changes that come with them.[14] In financial market regulation as well as standard-setting in health, food safety and human security, IN-LAW bodies provide a large number of much needed flexible norms and guidelines, that are grounded in practical experience, consensus-building and expertise. An important overall feature is the possibility to continuously correct IN-LAW, taking into account new developments and learning. This being said, some caution is still due. The contributors to this book judged the level of accountability differently depending on the IN-LAW body or regulation under review. In Chapter 13 on disaster risk reduction practices, for example, accountability has not been considered a major issue, whereas many other authors, when assessing the same issue, remain critical and formulate ways to improve responsiveness and

[14] See also: Joost Pauwelyn, Ramses A. Wessel and Jan Wouters, "Informal International Lawmaking: An Assessment and Template to Keep It Both Effective and Accountable" in Joost Pauwelyn, Ramses A. Wessel and Jan Wouters (eds.), *Informal International Lawmaking*, Oxford University Press, Oxford, 2012.

inclusiveness, in order for the IN-LAW bodies to become fully accountable.[15]

In short, by compiling and structuring the research efforts of experts in a great variety of regulatory fields the present book provides the reader with insightful views on informal international lawmaking. The case studies substantiate the IN-LAW theory and indicate the extent and complexity of the outstanding issues. As indicated above, while encompassing and detailed, the present volume cannot and does not aspire to offer a full view on IN-LAW mechanisms. However, through the carefully selected 14 contributions compiled in this volume, we have attempted to grasp in a practical way the manner in which international lawmaking is evolving and to contribute to elucidate and carry further the academic debate on the fascinating IN-LAW phenomenon.

15 See, *e.g.*, Chapter 1 on the G20, Chapter 5 on financial market regulation and Chapter 9 on competition networks in Latin America.

# PART I

# REGIONAL AND COUNTRY SPECIFIC CASE STUDIES

# 1

# The G20 and Informal International Lawmaking

**Jan Wouters[*] and Dylan Geraets[**]**

## 1.1. Introduction

In the past years global governance has witnessed the emergence of a relatively new actor on the world stage. After the financial crisis hit the global economy in the second half of 2008, President George W. Bush convened a meeting of the 'Group of 20' (or G20) in November 2008. The Group had in fact already been created in September 1999, spurred by the Asian banking crisis, yet at that time only at the level of Ministers of Finance and Central Bank Governors.[1] After the first two summits at Heads of State and Government level, the focus of the G20 gradually shifted from

---

[*] **Jan Wouters** is Professor of International Law and International Organizations, Jean Monnet Chair Ad Personam EU and Global Governance. He is Director of the Leuven Centre for Global Governance Studies and of the Institute for International Law at the University of Leuven, Visiting Professor at Sciences Po (Paris) and at the College of Europe (Bruges), member of the Royal Academy of Belgium for Sciences and Arts, *Of Counsel* at Linklaters (Brussels), and President of the Flemish Foreign Affairs Council.

[**] **Dylan Geraets** is Research Fellow at the Leuven Centre for Global Governance Studies and Institute for International Law, Leuven University.

[1] At the time, finance ministers and central bank governors of the Group of Seven countries (the G7), announced their intention to 'broaden the dialogue on key economic and financial policy issues among systemically significant economies and promote cooperation to achieve stable and sustainable world economic growth that benefits all.' See G7, "Communiqué – G20 Finance Ministers and Central Bank Governors", Berlin, 15–16 December 1999. For the purpose of this chapter, when reference is made to the term G20, we refer to G20 at Heads of State and Government level (post-2007). There are many publications on the evolution from the G7 to G20. For example, G20, "The Group of Twenty: A History", available at http://www.g20.utoronto.ca/docs/g20history.pdf, last accessed on 17 March 2012; Claudia Schmucker and Katharina Gnath, "From the G8 to the G20: Reforming the Global Economic Governance System", in Christoph Herrmann and Jörg Terhechte (eds.), *European Yearbook of International Economic Law*, vol. 2, Springer, Berlin, 2011, pp. 389–402; or Gordon S. Smith, "G7 to G8 to G20: Evolution in Global Governance", CIGI G20 Papers, No. 6, May 2011, available at http://www.cigionline.org/sites/default/files/G20No6.pdf, last accessed on 17 March 2012.

enacting measures against the worst effects of the financial crisis, to topics ranging from the reform of the international monetary system to climate change and commodity price volatility.[2] Compared to traditional international organizations, the G20 resembles a loosely organized network or informal gathering. Meetings take place in different locations, there are no procedural rules and its output is anything but a treaty or any other form of traditional international law. The first objective of this chapter is to assess whether the G20 can easily be placed within the proposed IN-LAW framework. The second purpose is to determine the extent to which problems often associated with informal types of international cooperation, also materialize with regard to the G20.

The structure of this chapter is as follows: first, we briefly set out the basic characteristics of 'Informal International Lawmaking' and the methodological framework in which processes of informal international law making are placed (1.2.). Throughout the chapter, the G20 will be considered in light of this framework. In the following section the G20 as a relatively new international phenomenon will be situated, including its history, general nature, composition and objectives (1.3.). The workings of the G20 will then be examined in more detail (1.4.). How does the policy-making process work, who is involved in agenda-setting, what actors play a dominant role? 'Traditional' international organizations, such as the International Labor Organization (ILO), the World Bank, the International Monetary Fund (IMF), the Organization for Economic Co-operation and Development (OECD) and the World Trade Organization (WTO) are increasingly involved in the G20's work; to what extent does this impact the latter's legitimacy? Subsequently, the output of the G20 will be addressed (1.5.). Last but not least, the G20 will be scrutinized from an accountability and effectiveness point of view (1.6.). In the conclusion (1.7.) the main findings will be wrapped up.

## 1.2. The Concept of Informal International Lawmaking

IN-LAW consists of three constitutive elements: informality, international and lawmaking. The Project Framing Paper uses the term '"informal" international lawmaking' in contrast and as opposed to "traditional" international lawmaking. IN-LAW is 'informal' in the sense that it dispenses with certain formalities traditionally linked to international law.

2 See *infra*, at 1.3.

These formalities may have to do with output, process or the actors involved.[3] In traditional international lawmaking, the result is usually a treaty or any other classical source of international law. Output informality can be described as outcomes that do not fall under such sources, for example guidelines, standards or declarations. Process informality should be understood as the way in which meetings of the 'network' are convened. Compared to traditional international organizations, informal international cooperation may be organized more loosely with different venues for each meeting. Actors involved in international cooperation may be 'informal' in the sense that they do not engage only traditional diplomatic actors (such as heads of state, foreign ministers or embassies), but also other ministries, domestic regulators, independent or semi-independent agencies (such as food safety authorities or central banks), sub-federal entities (such as federated states, provinces or municipalities) or the legislative or judicial branch.[4] The 'international' element of IN-LAW means that international cooperation must include actors from two or more different countries, and may also include cooperation between international organizations. Lawmaking is defined in the Project Framing Paper as "norm-setting or public policy making by public authorities", and law is thus used in a broader sense that also includes guidelines or standards. This leads to the following working definition of 'informal international lawmaking':

> Cross-border cooperation between public authorities, with or without the participation of private actors and/or international organizations, in a forum other than a traditional international organization (process informality), and/or as between actors other than traditional diplomatic actors (such as regulators or agencies) (actor informality), and/or which does not result in a formal treaty or legally enforceable commitment (output informality).[5]

3 Joost Pauwelyn, "Key Issues Informal International Lawmaking: Framing the Concept and Research Questions", in Joost Pauwelyn, Ramses A. Wessel and Jan Wouters (eds.), *Informal International Lawmaking*, Oxford University Press, Oxford, 2012, p. 3.

4 Pauwelyn, 2011, p. 7, see *supra* note 3.

5 Pauwelyn, 2011, p. 11, see *supra* note 3.

### 1.3. Origins and Evolution of the G20

The G20 can best be characterized as a 'network'.[6] Members depend on each other when they try to reach agreements by diplomatic means in a culture of reciprocity.[7] Unlike 'traditional' international organizations which are typically made up of sovereign States and which usually have permanent headquarters,[8] the G20 is an informal forum or 'club.' Moreover, not being a traditional international organization with conferred powers, the G20 can focus on activities such as agenda-setting, policy coordination, consensus-building and the distribution of tasks across existing institutions.[9] Its history starts in 1999, when finance ministers and central bank governors met for the first time in response to the Asian financial crisis of the late 1990s. Up and until 2008 the G20 kept meeting regularly in this constellation, despite repeated calls that there should be meetings at the leaders' level.[10] These calls were mostly fuelled by a wish to see the G8 meetings replaced by meetings with more representative participa-

6 Leonardo Martinez-Diaz and Ngaire Woods, "The G20 – the perils and opportunities of network governance for developing countries", 2009, p. 1, available at: http://www.globaleconomicgovernance.org/wp-content/uploads/G20_PolicyBrief.pdf, last accessed on 17 March 2012. Martinez-Diaz and Woods characterize a network as a forum where participants are involved in repeated and enduring relations. There is no delegation of authority to the network to make decisions. There is also no dispute settlement mechanism that can solve disputes when they arise. Networks can be distinguished from formal organizations in that they have no formal rules of membership, or structure of representation. There are no formal decision-making rules, and there is no authority to make, implement or enforce rules. Networks are typically used for agenda-setting, consensus-building, policy coordination, knowledge production and exchange and norm-setting and diffusion.

7 Anne Mette Kjær, *Governance (Key Concepts)*, Polity Press, London, 2004, p. 41; Kjær compares markets, hierarchies and networks as systems of governance and notes that networks are based on reciprocity and trust.

8 Such as, for example, the United Nations, the World Trade Organization and the European Union.

9 Ngaire Woods, "The Impact of the G20 on Global Governance: A History and Prospective", in Colin I. Bradford and Lim Wonhyuk (eds.), *Global Leadership in Transition – Making the G-20 More Effective and Responsive*, Korea Development Institute and the Brookings Institution, Washington, 2011, p. 37.

10 One of the main proponents of this idea was Paul Martin, the Canadian Finance Minister at the time. For his views on the matter, consult Paul Martin, *Hell or High Water: My Life in and Out of Politics*, McLelland and Stewart, Toronto, 2008.

tion.[11] Again spurred by a moment of crisis in late 2008, the United States convened the 'Group of 20 Summit on Financial Markets and the World Economy' on 14–15 November 2008 in Washington D.C., in response to the global financial crisis. It was attended by the leaders of the members of the G20 Finance Ministers and Central Bank Governors Meetings. At the third G20 Summit in Pittsburgh in 2009, the leaders designated the G20 as 'the premier forum for international economic cooperation'.[12]

The G20 is currently made up of seven advanced economies, twelve emerging economies and the EU.[13] The membership thus comprises five continents, two-thirds of the world's population, roughly 85% of global GDP and approximately 80% of world trade. Unlike many traditional organizations, the G20 does not have any formal criteria for membership, which already highlights a substantial degree of informality. It is said that countries and regions that are of 'systemic importance' to the international financial system, were deemed important to be included in the membership.[14] However, as Jokela shows, "economic weight does not automatically translate into a seat in the G20".[15] In the first five meetings some important agreements were reached between the members. In Washington the G20 decided on the implementation of economic stimulus measures. Its members also agreed not to pursue protectionist policies by way of

[11] Mark Beeson and Stephen Bell, "The G-20 and International Economic Governance: Hegemony, Collectivism, or Both?" in *Global Governance*, 2009, vol. 15, no. 67, p. 77; John Kirton, "Toward Multilateral Reform: The G20's Contribution" in John English, Ramesh Thakur and Andrew F. Cooper (eds.), *Reforming from the top: A Leaders' 20 Summit,* United Nations University Press, New York, 2005, p. 143. For a more elaborate discussion on the history see Smith, 2011, see *supra* note 1.

[12] G20, "Leaders Statement, The Pittsburgh Summit", 24–25 September 2009, para. 19, available at http://www.g20.org/images/stories/docs/eng/pittsburgh.pdf, last accessed on 17 March 2012.

[13] The 19 countries are (alphabetically): Argentina, Australia, Brazil, Canada, China, France, Germany, India, Indonesia, Italy, Japan, the Republic of Korea, Mexico, Russia, Saudi Arabia, South Africa, Turkey, the United Kingdom and the United States.

[14] "The Origins and Evolution of the G20", available at http://www.g20.org/index.php/en/the-origins-and-evolution-of-the-g20, last accessed on 21 November 2012.

[15] Juha Jokela, "The G-20: A Pathway to Effective Multilateralism?", Chaillot Papers, April 2011, Institute for Security Studies (ISS), p. 20, available at http://www.iss.europa.eu/uploads/media/The_G20_-_a_pathway_to_effective_multilateralism.pdf, last accessed on 17 March 2012.

creating new barriers to investment or trade in goods and services.[16] Furthermore, they agreed to refrain from imposing new export restrictions for the coming 12 months. In the second meeting in London on 2 April 2009 further expansionary fiscal measures were agreed upon.[17] Additionally, a declaration was issued on strengthening the financial system and the upgrading of the Financial Stability Forum to a Financial Stability Board (FSB).[18] In hindsight, the second G20 Summit in London can be seen as the point at which the most effective cooperation materialized.[19] In Pittsburgh, during the third meeting on 24–25 September 2009, members agreed to hold the meeting annually. Agreement was reached on the need for strengthening international coordination in macroeconomic policies while preparing for the eventual exit strategies from the emergency fiscal measures. Again, the need for strengthened financial regulations and the importance of discouraging protectionism were emphasized.[20] However, it is now recognized that at this point diverging views on financial regulation had started to become clear.[21] The fourth meeting in Toronto on 26–27 June 2010 was characterized by an agreement on a set of principles for fiscal consolidation in the context of 'The Framework for Strong, Sustain-

16 G20, "Declaration – Summit on Financial Markets and the World Economy", 15 November 2008, paras. 5, 13, available at http://www.canadainternational.gc.ca/g20/summit-sommet/g20/declaration_111508.aspx?view=d, last accessed on 28 June 2012.

17 G20, Leaders Statement: "The Global Plan for Recovery and Reform", London, 2 April 2009, available at http://www.bundesregierung.de/Content/DE/StatischeSeiten/Breg/G8G20/Anlagen/G20-erklaerung-london-en.pdf?__blob=publicationFile, last accessed on 28 June 2012. Paragraph 5 of the statement states: "The agreements we have reached today, to treble resources available to the IMF to $750 billion, to support a new SDR allocation of $250 billion, to support at least $100 billion of additional lending by the MDBs, to ensure $250 billion of support for trade finance, and to use the additional resources from agreed IMF gold sales for concessional finance for the poorest countries, constitute an additional $1.1 trillion programme of support to restore credit, growth and jobs in the world economy".

18 G20, "Declaration on Strengthening the Financial System", London, 2 April 2009, available at http://www.g20.org/images/stories/docs/eng/london.pdf, last accessed on 28 June 2012.

19 Woods, 2011, p. 40, see *supra* note 9.

20 G20, "Leaders Statement", The Pittsburgh Summit, 24–25 September 2009, paras. 19, 48, 50, available at http://www.g20.org/images/stories/docs/eng/pittsburgh.pdf, last accessed on 28 June 2012.

21 "Biden asks G20 Protestors: Give us a Chance", EuroNews, 29 March 2009; and "Indonesia Warns on Over-regulation", Financial Times, 4 March 2009.

able and Balanced Growth'.[22] G20 leaders also agreed to speed up the process of IMF reform.[23] This reform was agreed upon during the Meeting of the Finance Ministers and Central Bank Governors held on 23 October in Gyeongju, Republic of Korea, which preceded the fifth G20 Meeting in Seoul on 11–12 November 2010.[24] The Seoul Summit Document reaffirmed the commitment to reform the IMF. The need to resist protectionist policies was emphasized and again the strong wish was expressed to bring the Doha Development Agenda in the WTO to a successful conclusion. Strong differences between China and the United States about exchange rate policies however overshadowed the fifth G20 Summit.[25] The Korean presidency was also credited with placing issues such as global financial safety nets and development on the agenda in a way that requires future summits to follow-up on them.[26] Prior to the sixth G20 Heads of State Summit in Cannes in November 2011, this broadening of the agenda was also reflected in the fact that G20 meetings now take place not only at the level of Heads of State or ministers of finance, but also at the level of specialized ministries. In June 2011, Ministers of Agriculture of the G20 countries met for the first official G20 Agriculture Ministerial, during which they discussed biofuels, high and volatile food prices as well as other issues related to food security.[27] Finance, development and

[22] G20, "The G20 Toronto Summit Declaration", 26–27 June 2010, Annex 1, p. 10, available at http://canadainternational.gc.ca/g20/assets/pdfs/g20_declaration_en.pdf, last accessed on 28 June 2012.

[23] G20, "The G20 Toronto Summit Declaration", para. 29, see *supra* note 22.

[24] G20, "Communiqué Meeting of Finance Ministers and Central Bank Governors", Gyeongju, Republic of Korea, 23 October 2010, para. 5, available at http://www.mof.go.jp/english/international_policy/convention/g20/g20_101023.pdf, last accessed on 28 June 2012.

[25] G20, "The G20 Seoul Summit Leaders Declaration", 11–12 November 2010, paras. 8–10, available at http://www.g20.org/images/stories/docs/eng/seoul.pdf, last accessed on 28 June 2012; see also G20, "The G20 Seoul Summit Document", 12 November 2010, available at http://www.g20.utoronto.ca/2010/g20seoul-doc.pdf, last accessed on 17 March 2012.

[26] G20, "The G20 Seoul Summit Leaders' Declaration", 11–12 November 2010, Annex I and II, available at http://www.g20.utoronto.ca/summits/2010seoul.html, last accessed on 28 June 2012; Smith, 2011, p. 6, see *supra* note 1.

[27] G20, Ministerial Declaration, "Action Plan on Food Price Volatility and Agriculture", Meeting of G20 Agriculture Ministers Paris, 22 and 23 June 2011, available at http://www.g20.utoronto.ca/2011/2011-agriculture-plan-en.pdf, last accessed on 28 June 2012.

labor ministers also met in September 2011. The proliferation of sectoral ministerial meetings increases the degree of actor informality within the G20 setting. In the run-up to the sixth G20 Summit held in Cannes on the 3 and 4 November 2011, the French Presidency presented six priorities which included the combating of commodity price volatility and the 'strengthening of the social dimension of globalization'.[28] Other items on the agenda were the phasing out of fossil fuel subsidies, anti-corruption and innovative financing for development.[29] Very little was achieved on these topics as growing fears concerning the European sovereign debt crisis and a possible default of Greece overshadowed most other agenda items of the sixth summit. However, this does not mean that the Cannes Summit was a complete failure, as some commentators have suggested.[30] One of the decisions agreed upon was the strengthening of the resources and governance of the FSB. To this end, G20 Leaders equipped the FSB with a stronger political mandate, greater financial autonomy and legal personality.[31] In itself, this decision can be seen as an example of the formalization of processes and structures that had many informal characteristics themselves.[32] It appears that, after a number of summits with an increasingly broad agenda, G20 has managed to reposition itself as 'a concentrated crisis committee in global affairs'.[33]

---

28 The other priorities were "reforming the international monetary system (IMS)", "strenghtening financial regulation", "fighting corruption" and "working on behalf of development". See official website of the French G8-G20 Presidency, "What are the priorities for the French presidency of the G20 in 2011?", available at http://www.g20-g8.com/g8-g20/g20/english/priorities-for-france/the-priorities-of-the-french-presidency/the-priorities-of-the-french-presidency.75.html, last accessed on 17 March 2012.

29 G20, Cannes Summit Final Declaration, "Building Our Common Future: The Renewed Collective Action for the Benefit of All", 4 November 2011, available at http://www.g20.org/images/stories/canalfinan/docs/cannes_summit_final_declaration.pdf, last accessed on 17 March 2012.

30 Financial Times, "Markets Hit by G20 Failure To Tackle Crisis", 4 November 2011; see also: CNN, "For world leaders, G-20 an enormous waste of time", 7 November 2011.

31 G20, Cannes Summit Final Declaration, 2011, para. 38, see *supra* note 29.

32 For a more elaborate discussion on the FSB and Financial Regulation in general, see Shawn Donelly, Chapter 5.

33 Andrew F. Cooper, "The G20 Returns to Crisis Committee – With Positive and Negative Implications", 4 November 2011, available at http://www.cigionline.org/publications/2011/11/g20-returns-being-crisis-committee-%E2%80%94-positive-and-

The objectives of the G20 have changed and continue to change over time. During the peak of the financial crisis of 2008–2009, emphasis was placed on economic stimulus, whereas later strategies were thought out to exit from the fiscal stimulus without crippling the weak economic growth in some countries. The need to abstain from adopting protectionist measures appears to have been, and continues to be, an important objective of the G20.[34] After five G20 Summits in the past three years, the role of the G20 appears to have evolved from providing a forum for the immediate international response to the global financial crisis to a forum for international cooperation in multiple policy areas.[35] The European sovereign debt crisis forced G20 Leaders to return to their core objective of being 'the premier forum for international economic cooperation'.

## 1.4. Functioning and Policymaking Process of G20

Khanna draws a striking analogy between the functioning of the G20 and the latest in thinking about decentralized management. He sees the G20 as an organization with "twenty hubs and no HQ".[36] This accurately captures

negative-implications, last accessed on 17 March 2012; John Kirton, "Cannes 2011: A Summit of Substantial Success", 4 November 2011, available at http://www.g20.utoronto.ca/analysis/111104-kirton-cannes-perf.html, last accessed on 17 March 2012.

34 WTO Secretariat, "Report on G20 Trade Measures (May to Mid-October 2011)", available at http://www.unctad.org/en/docs/unctad_oecd2011d6_report_en.pdf, last accessed on 17 March 2012. Nevertheless, the report notes "disappointingly weak growth in some G20 countries and continuing macroeconomic imbalances globally are testing the political resolve of many governments to abide by the G20 commitment to resist protectionism, as reaffirmed by the G20 Leaders at their last Summit Meeting in Seoul. Over the period under review, there is no indication that recourse to new trade restricting measures by the G20 as a group has slackened nor that efforts have been stepped up to remove existing restrictions, particularly those introduced since the onset of the financial crisis".

35 This change was noted by the organizers of the G20 Seoul International Symposium "Toward the Consolidation of G20 Summits: From Crisis Committee to Global Steering Committee" which was held in Seoul 27–29 September 2010. For a report on the symposium, see C.I. Bradford and Lim Wonhyuk (eds.), "Toward the Consolidation of G20 – From Crisis Committee to Global Steering Committee", available at http://www.kdi.re.kr/kdi_eng/database/report_read05.jsp?1=1&pub_no=11568, last accessed on 17 March 2012.

36 Parag Khanna, *How to Run the World*, Random House, New York, 2011, p. 54. See also Coimbatore K. Prahalad and Hrishi Bhattacharyya, "Twenty Hubs and no HQ", in *Strategy and Business*, 2008, issue 50, pp. 1–6.

the essence of the G20 as a prime example of network-style governance. Compared to international organizations such as the United Nations (UN), the OECD, IMF, World Bank or WTO, the G20 does not have a permanently staffed secretariat of its own.[37] Rather, it is an informal club without permanent representatives of its members that was designed to provide a forum for debate and consensus-seeking.[38] Its chair rotates between members, and is selected from a different regional grouping of countries each year.[39]

> The chair is part of a revolving three-member management Troika of past, present and future chairs. The incumbent chair establishes a temporary secretariat for the duration of its term, which coordinates the group's work and organizes its meetings. The role of the Troika is to ensure continuity in the G20's work and management across host years.[40]

The final declaration of the G20 Summit in Cannes notes that the G20 "is a leader-led and informal group and it should remain so".[41] Nevertheless, the declaration also notes that the Troika will be formalized in order to better coordinate the work of G20.[42] Part of this formalization lies in the fact that as of 2015 the annual presidencies will rotate between a number of regional groups.[43] As the G20 meets in different locations, funding of those meetings is arranged by the host State. With regard to the use of experts from private institutions and non-governmental organizations (NGOs), the G20 provides the possibility to invite them on an *ad*

37 The French Presidency proposed the establishment of a permanent G20 Secretariat as it would "strengthen the expertise of G20 and ensure the internal consistency and continuity of action". See French G8-G20 Presidency, "What are the priorities", *supra* note 28. However, as will be seen, this idea was rejected at the Cannes Summit.

38 Jokela, 2011, p. 23, see *supra* note 155.

39 The Republic of Korea was chair in 2010, in 2011 it was France and in 2012 it will be Mexico.

40 About G20, "What Is The G20?", available at http://www.g20.org/index.php/en/what-is-the-g20, last accessed on 17 March 2012.

41 G20, Cannes Summit Final Declaration, 2011, para. 91, see *supra* note 29.

42 G20, Cannes Summit Final Declaration, 2011, para. 92, see *supra* note 29.

43 G20, Cannes Summit Final Declaration, 2011, para. 94, see *supra* note 29. Up and un til 2015, the presidencies will be as follows: as of 1 December 2011, Mexico (with a meeting in Los Cabos, Baja California in June 2012). In 2013, Russia. In 2014, Australia. In 2015, Turkey. After 2015, the system of presidencies from rotating regional groupings will commence with the Asian Regional Grouping (China, Indonesia, Japan, Korea).

*hoc* basis to meetings "in order to exploit synergies in analyzing selected topics and avoid overlap".[44] All of this leads to a high degree of what is called 'Process Informality' in the IN-LAW framework.

The G20 members themselves play the biggest role in the agenda-setting process, with a particular role for the chair of the meeting. The chair will usually host an 'agenda-setting meeting' a couple of months in advance of the actual meeting of the G20. During this meeting deputy finance ministers and senior central bank officials will discuss what the most prominent issues are that need to be on the agenda for the meeting at ministerial level.[45] The chair will have the final say in the adoption of the agenda, although pressure will be exerted from all delegations to get desired topics on the agenda. NGOs are absent from these meetings and thus have no direct influence on the agenda-setting process. However, they will try to influence the chair. NGOs organize amongst themselves from time to time in order to have a stronger voice.[46] Details of the G20's meetings and its work program are posted on a dedicated website by the country currently chairing the G20.

> Although participation in the meetings is reserved for members, the public is informed about what was discussed and agreed immediately after the meeting of ministers and governors has ended. After each meeting of ministers and gov-

44 About G20, "Interaction with other international organizations", see *supra* note 40. The French Presidency of the Cannes G20 Summit invited Bill Gates to the Summit, to "report on financing for development". See http://www.g20-g8.com/g8-g20/g20/english/news/news/programme-of-the-g20-cannes-summit.1509.html, last accessed on 17 March 2012, and Bill Gates, "Innovation with Impact: Financing 21st Century Development", November 2011, available at http://www.thegatesnotes.com/~/media/Images/GatesNotes/G20/G20-Documents/g20-report-english.pdf, last accessed on 17 March 2012.

45 The Korea Times, "Meeting shows hassle in G20 agenda setting", available at http://www.koreatimes.co.kr/www/news/special/2010/08/176_66750.html, last accessed on 17 March 2012, for an insightful look into the agenda-setting process for the G20 Summit in Seoul, Korea in November 2010; and http://english.yonhapnews.co.kr/national/2010/09/05/8/0301000000AEN20100905001600320F.HTML for a report on the concluding agenda-setting meeting, last accessed on 17 March 2012.

46 See for example: "NGO Leaders Challenge G20 Summit to Expand Scope", available at http://www.huffingtonpost.com/2009/04/02/ngo-leaders-challenge-g-2_n_182381.html, last accessed on 17 March 2012; Amnesty International, Greenpeace, Oxfam, Care International and Save the Children joined forces to focus G20 leaders attention on issues such as poverty and climate change.

ernors, the G20 publishes a communiqué which records the agreements reached and measures outlined.[47]

Interesting in this respect are the suggestions by some, which, if followed, would lead towards a substantial degree of formalization of the G20. The argument has been made that the G20 needs formal authority, processes and institutions if it is envisaged as an important decision-making mechanism.[48] Although not as far-reaching as establishing a formal G20 Secretariat, UK Prime Minister David Cameron also indicated that a certain degree of formality would be necessary to expand the G20's capacity.[49] He proposes a small secretariat that should be based in the country of the presidency. As discussed *supra*, in Cannes G20 leaders decided to formalize the Troika but rejected the idea of establishing a G20 secretariat.[50]

Another important aspect of the G20's functioning lies in the way it interacts with other international organizations. Cooperation is close with a number of international organizations, such as the IMF, WTO and OECD, "as the potential to develop common positions on complex issues among G20 members can add political momentum to decision-making in other bodies".[51] Director-Generals and heads of traditional organizations take part in G20 Summits. Former Managing Director of the IMF, Dominic Strauss-Kahn has been present at all G20 Summits (his successor Christine Lagarde attended the Cannes Summit), whilst WTO Director-General Pascal Lamy, World Bank President Robert Zoellick, ILO Director General Juan Somavia and OECD Secretary General Angel Gurria have also attended multiple G20 summits after the first one in Washington. UN Secretary-General Ban Ki-moon has also been present at every G20 Summit, except for the one in Washington. In June 2011 the UN

47 About G20, "External communication", see *supra* note 40.

48 Lan Xue and Yanbing Zhang, "Turning the G20 Into a New Mechanism", in Colin I. Bradford and Lim Wonhyuk (eds.), *Global Leadership in Transition – Making the G20 More Effective and Responsive*, Korea Development Institute and the Brookings Institution, Washington, 2011, p. 58.

49 David Cameron, "Governance for Growth – Building Consensus for the Future", November 2011, p. 18, available at http://www.g20.utoronto.ca/2011/2011-cameron-report.pdf, last accessed on 17 March 2012.

50 Kirton, Cannes 2011, see *supra* note 33. Kirton notes that this idea was wisely rejected as a G20 Secretariat would transfer ownership of the club from the most powerful leaders in the world to international bureaucrats claiming to act in their name.

51 About G20, "Interaction with other international organizations", see *supra* note 40.

General Assembly held an informal thematic debate on the role of the UN in global governance.[52] In response to UN General Assembly resolution 65/94 on 'The UN in Global Governance', the Secretary-General prepared a report in which it was suggested that there should be "predictable and consistent engagement" between the UN and G20.[53] Until now there has not been a decision by which the G20 invites the UN Secretary-General systematically. The presence of heads of international organizations further indicates the high degree of actor informality that is present in G20. A prominent example of cooperation between international organizations upon request of the G20 are the semi-annual trade reports that are compiled by the WTO, OECD and UNCTAD, and which monitor the compliance of G20 members with their commitments to resist protectionism.[54] Reference can also be made to the report on price volatility in food and agricultural markets that was compiled by the FAO and OECD upon request of the G20 leaders.[55] Other international groups and organizations the G20 works with include the FSB and the Basel Committee on Banking Supervision.

---

52 UN, Informal Thematic Debate of the General Assembly on "The United Nations in Global Governance", New York, 28 June 2011, Informal Summary by the Secretariat, available at http://www.un.org/esa/ffd/economicgovernance/InformalSummary.pdf, last accessed on 17 March 2012.

53 UN General Assembly, "The United Nations in global governance", Resolution adopted by the General Assembly, 28 January 2011, A/RES/65/94; UN General Assembly, "Global economic governance and development", Report by the Secretary-General, 10 October 2011, A/66/506, para. 67.

54 WTO Secretariat, "Report on G20 Trade Measures", see *supra* note 34. In the Seoul Summit Document (see *supra* note 25) G20 leaders reaffirmed the extension of their standstill commitments until the end of 2013 as agreed in Toronto, committed to rollback any new protectionist measures that may have risen, including export restrictions and WTO-inconsistent measures to stimulate exports, and asked the WTO, OECD, and UNCTAD to continue monitoring the situation and to report publicly on a semi-annual basis.

55 FAO and OECD, "Price Volatility in Food and Agricultural Markets: Policy Responses", 2 June 2011, available at http://www.oecd.org/dataoecd/40/34/48152638.pdf, last accessed on 17 March 2012. The introduction notes: "The preparation of this report, coordinated by the FAO and the OECD, has been undertaken in a truly collaborative manner by FAO, IFAD, IMF, OECD, UNCTAD, WFP, the World Bank, the WTO, IFPRI and the UN HLTF. We, the international organisations, are honoured to provide you with this joint report and look forward to continuing collaboration within the G20 framework to further elaborate and, as appropriate, implement the recommendations of the international organisations that it contains".

The linkages between these traditional international organizations and the G20 are not undisputed. Woods puts forward that the Toronto summit saw a much wider participation of non-G20 countries (including Algeria, Colombia, Egypt, Ethiopia (NEPAD), Malawi (African Union), the Netherlands, Nigeria, Spain and Vietnam (ASEAN)) in response to the growing concerns that the G20 would start to conclude agreements with these organizations without consulting non-G20 countries. These concerns became particularly pressing as the G20 started to give direct instructions to international organizations, such as the IMF, "thereby bypassing the properly constituted decision-making process of those organizations".[56] This attitude is also prevalent within the OECD, where non-G20 members have voiced concern about the fact that, as a substantial part of its work is now carried out upon request of the G20, some of the OECD's output has bypassed the formal decision-making process. Moreover, the assignments conducted for the G20 take up a considerable part of the resources of the OECD, which also include contributions of non-G20 Members. Finally, the Council of the OECD never formally agreed to the increased cooperation between G20 and the OECD.[57]

Business Summits (B20) held prior to leaders' G20 Summits bring together the heads of some 120 of the world's leading companies from 34 developed and developing countries.[58] As from the sixth G20 Summit in Cannes in November 2011, there is also an L20, which brings together trade union organizations of the G20 countries. For the Cannes Summit, the French Presidency invited the Chair of the African Union (AU), the

---

56 Woods, 2011, pp. 42–43, see *supra* note 9.

57 Jan Wouters and Sven Van Kerckhoven, "The OECD and the G20: An Ever Closer Relationship?", in *George Washington International Law Review* 2011, vol. 43, p. 373. The authors note that the G20 benefits from this collaboration, since the OECD has an enormous pool of knowledge and expertise in many different issue areas and the G20, as a global playmaker, increasingly taps from this pool: "Currently, the OECD supports the G20 on matters related to bribery, development, employment, environment and energy, financial sector reform, green growth, international monetary system, investment and trade, taxation, and consumer protection. Accordingly, G20 communiqués and declarations increasingly refer to, and call upon, the OECD".

58 Nancy Alexander, "Introduction to the G20", Heinrich-Böll-Stiftung, available at http://www.boell.org/web/134-651.html, last accessed on 17 March 2012. "The Business Summit met for two-days prior to the Summit and issued a call for G20 countries to take actions to support free trade, bolster foreign investment, facilitate green growth, nurture small- and medium-sized enterprises (SMEs), improve energy efficiencies, and increase youth employment".

Chair of the New Partnership for Africa's Development (NEPAD), Singapore as representative of the Global Governance Group (3G), and the Chair of the Cooperation Council of Arab States of the Gulf (GCC).

It has been suggested that the G20 will have three distinct effects on international organizations.[59] First, a 'complementary effect' will generate political support for the decision-making process in international organizations, thereby pressurizing them to accelerate their initiatives. For example, a sound often heard in the corridors of the WTO is that for the Doha Development Agenda (DDA) to be completed, what is really needed is the political will to reach an agreement. The required technical work itself has been completed years ago. In theory, the complementary effect of the G20 should help the decision-making process move forward. In reality, however, G20 leaders have not been able to provide the political backing for an agreement. On the contrary, at the Cannes Summit, G20 leaders for the first time acknowledged that the DDA negotiations, as they have been conducted to this point, would not bring the desired results.[60] Second, there is a 'competitive effect', whereby certain formal bodies such as the International Monetary and Finance Committee (IMFC) of the IMF and the Development Committee of the World Bank now compete with the G20 as the latter tries to gain authority on these matters.[61] Third, the G20 leaders' network may have a 'rebalancing effect' in global governance and international organizations. It brings emerging economies into agenda-setting and coordination discussions. Furthermore, it may serve "as a catalyst for reform of formal international organizations".[62] This has most recently been highlighted by the decision on IMF reform that was taken during the Seoul Summit in November 2010.[63] In addition to these three effects, highlighted by Martinez-Diaz and Woods, it now seems there might be a potential fourth effect, which could be called the 'replacement effect'. Now that the G20 includes emerging economies such as China, India and Brazil, it has been put forward that the IMFC should be replaced

59 Martinez-Diaz, Woods, 2009, p. 1, see *supra* note 6.

60 G20, Cannes Summit Final Declaration, see *supra* note 29.

61 Prior to the fifth G20 Summit in Seoul, November 2010, a G20 High-level Development Conference was organized on 13 October 2010 in Seoul. The Seoul Summit Document included a paragraph entitled "The Seoul Development Consensus for Shared Growth", which included a "Multi-year Action Plan on Development".

62 Martinez-Diaz, Woods, 2009, p. 3, see *supra* note 6.

63 See *infra* note 64, case study on IMF reform.

by the Ministers of Finance of the G20.[64] In reality, however, it appears that these proposals have not acquired sufficient support and that one cannot (yet) speak of any formalized or institutionalized linking of the G20 to the IMF. On the contrary, the Cameron Report (see *supra*) seemed to suggest a reinforcement of the IMFC rather than its replacement.[65]

## 1.5. G20 Output

G20 summits do not result in a formal treaty or any other type of classical international law instruments. As shown above, the outcome of a G20 Summit is written down in a 'communiqué', 'a declaration' or 'a statement', which is then made available to the wider public.[66] The type of document released depends on the kind of G20 meeting. G20 summits at leader's level typically result in a Communiqué and a Final Declaration or Summit Document. G20 meetings at ministerial level are usually concluded with a Ministerial Declaration.[67] Although the outcomes of a G20 Summit qualify as political decisions at the international level, they do not have the form of a binding legal instrument under international law and

64 A report authored by former IMF managing directors Michel Camdessus and Horst Koehler as well as former U.S. Federal Reserve Chairman Paul Volcker and commissioned by French President Nicolas Sarkozy, puts forward recommendations for G20 reform. These include a major overhaul to bring G20 more in line with how the IMF operates. Most importantly, the report proposes that G20 finance ministers form a council that would take strategic decisions concerning the international monetary system, replacing the International Monetary and Financial Committee. Palais-Royal Initiative, Reform of the International Monetary System: A Cooperative Approach for the 21st Century, 8 February 2011, available at http://global-currencies.org/smi/gb/telechar/news/Rapport_Camdessus-integral.pdf, last accessed on 17 March 2012. See also: Financial Times, "Reform blueprint gives G20 authority over IMF", 8 February 2011, available at http://www.ft.com/cms/s/0/02dfb954-33af-11e0-b1ed-00144feabdc0.html?ftcamp=rss#axzz1DSPsaNJX, last accessed on 17 March 2012; and Wall Street Journal, "G20 ponders more inclusive governance", 7 February 2011, available at http://online.wsj.com/article/BT-CO-20110207-703352.html, last accessed on 17 March 2012.

65 Cameron, 2011, p. 22, see *supra* note 49.

66 G20, "Documents", available at http://www.g20.org/index.php/en/documents, last accessed on 29 June 2012.

67 Note that the G20 Labour and Employment Ministers issued "Conclusions" after their meeting in Cannes in September 2011. The G20 Meeting of Agriculture Ministers resulted in a Ministerial Declaration containing an "Action Plan on Food Price Volatility and Agriculture". G20 Finance Ministers' meetings usually result in a "Communiqué".

can therefore be considered to fall under the category of 'output informality'. The question to ask within the IN-LAW framework, however, is whether these communiqués, declarations, guidelines and summit documents constitute law or merely coordinated policies. Law is to be understood in a broad sense, namely "norm-setting or public policy making by public authorities" whereby the result of these processes must 'have legal effects or fit in the context of a broader legal process.'[68] Understood in this sense, G20 certainly makes 'law': the declarations, communiqués and summit documents may not be law *stricto sensu* as they are not formal treaties under international law.[69] However, they do on some occasions have legal effects and they do certainly fall within "a broader legal or normative process".[70]

As said, the G20's output materializes in the form of communiqués or declarations. Concretely these documents set out the policies and plans that have come out of a particular meeting. In his aforementioned report with suggestions for G20 improvements, Cameron notes under the heading 'G20 output and accountability':

> The main summit products should be regularised to maximise consistency and comparability, and comprise a short summary of key decisions taken, accompanied by a longer annex that records in detail the specific measures agreed by Leaders. To improve the general public's understanding of the G20's work, the Presidency should produce, on its own authority, a short and accessible factsheet setting out the key achievements of the year and progress made against past commitments.[71]

This partially addresses the concerns that G20 commitments are often not measurable and hard to define. G20 output certainly does not resemble traditional international law. However, the coordinated policies that are agreed upon and incorporated in communiqués or declarations are of great importance and warrant further attention. The proposal to some extent aims to make G20 commitments more measurable and transparent. It, however, also indicates once more the inherent problems associated with output informality, namely, the difficulty of determining the effec-

68 Pauwelyn, 2011, p. 11, see *supra* note 3.

69 Article 2.1 (a) Vienna Convention on the Law of Treaties, 23 May 1963, Vienna.

70 Pauwelyn, 2011, p. 11, see *supra* note 3.

71 Cameron, 2011, p. 17, see *supra* note 49.

tiveness of the G20's output and holding G20 leaders to account based on general commitments instead of specific targets (see *infra*, 1.6.2.).[72]

In the three years since its re-invigoration, G20 has produced significant output (see *supra*, 1.3. Origins and Evolution). It would go beyond the scope of this chapter to discuss all policies agreed upon, but one very illustrative example is the reform of the IMF that was decided in the autumn of 2010.

On 22–23 October 2010, the Finance Ministers and Central Bank Governors held a meeting in Gyeongju, Republic of Korea that preceded the fifth G20 Meeting of 11–12 November in Seoul. Issues discussed included financial repair regulatory reforms and the move to make exchange rate systems more market-determined. One of the most striking decisions came however in the notice that agreement had been reached on an ambitious set of proposals to reform the IMF's quota and governance.[73] This reform of the IMF forms part of the wish to address perceived representational imbalances in international financial institutions (IFIs). Together with the reform of the World Bank, IMF reform should lead to more inclusive governance in those institutions. Elements of the agreement to reform the IMF include a shift in quota shares to dynamic emerging markets and developing countries (EMDCs) and to underrepresented countries of over 6%. Furthermore, it was decided that EMDCs would be granted greater representation at the Executive Board of the IMF through two fewer advanced European chairs and the possibility of a second alternate for all multi-country constituencies. The reform was confirmed at the fifth G20 Summit in Seoul. According to the Summit Document released afterwards, the goal of modernized IMF governance is "a more legitimate, credible and effective IMF", which can be achieved "by ensuring that quotas and Executive Board composition are more reflective of new global economic realities, and securing the IMF's status as a quota-based institution, with sufficient resources to support members' needs".[74] The doc-

72 See *infra*, at 1.6., Accountability and Effectiveness.

73 Former IMF Managing Director Dominic Strauss-Kahn stated that this decision constitutes the "biggest reform ever in the governance of the institution"; available at http://www.bloomberg.com/news/2010-10-23/strauss-kahn-says-officials-at-g-20-agreed-on-biggest-reform-ever-of-imf.html, last accessed on 17 March 2012.

74 G20, "Seoul Summit Document", para. 16, released 12 November 2010, see *supra* note 25.

ument called upon G20 members to urgently and promptly conclude the 2008 IMF quota and voice reforms.

The decision to grant greater representation in the IMF's Executive Board to EMDCs, at the cost of two fewer advanced European chairs, sparked quite a bit of controversy. Currently, France, Germany and the United Kingdom are all represented by an Executive Director on the board of the IMF. Furthermore, there are so-called multiple-State constituencies that are represented by one Executive Director who speaks on behalf of a number of IMF Member Countries.[75] European countries that lead a constituency are the Netherlands, Belgium, Spain, Italy, Switzerland and Denmark. To achieve a cut of two European chairs, some proposals have already been tabled. Belgium co-chairs its group with Turkey, which amounts to half a chair. The same applies for Spain, which co-chairs with Mexico. The decision needs to be implemented within two years, which gives European nations two years to work out exactly how the shift in Board seats will take place.[76] Inevitably this decision affects many countries, not in the least the Netherlands and Belgium. Arguably as a sign of gratitude for its efforts in the war in Afghanistan and the network established by former Prime Minister Jan Peter Balkenende, the Netherlands had been invited to all four previous G20 meetings. After the installation of a new coalition government in October 2010, headed by Prime Minister Mark Rutte, the Netherlands was no longer invited to the table in Gyeongju and Seoul nor to any subsequent G20 meetings at ministerial and leaders' level.[77] During those meetings, decisions were made that may have far-reaching consequences for The Netherlands. The question is how this relates to the concept of accountability in a network such as G20. Prior to the meetings in Gyeongju and Seoul, Dutch Treasury Minister Jan Kees de Jager already expected that it would be difficult to defend the

---

75 Belgium, for example, heads a constituency that consists of Austria, Belarus, Belgium, Czech Republic, Hungary, Kazakhstan, Luxembourg, Slovak Republic, Slovenia and Turkey; the Netherlands heads a constituency that includes Armenia, Bosnia and Herzegovina, Bulgaria, Croatia, Cyprus, Georgia, Israel, Macedonia (former Yugoslav Republic of), Moldova, Montenegro, the Netherlands, Romania and Ukraine.

76 IMF, "G20 Agreement on Quotas and Governance", available at https://www.imf.org/external/np/exr/faq/quotasgov.htm, last accessed on 17 March 2012.

77 Peter Debaere, "The Output and Input Dimension of the European Representation in the G20", in *Studia Diplomatica*, 2010, vol. 63, no. 2, p. 146.

Dutch chair, as The Netherlands would not be present at the meetings.[78] The G20 Seoul Preparation Committee's Deputy Chief Rhee Chang-yong was quoted as saying "it might be perplexing to The Netherlands. We feel a bit sorry for them. But the Sherpas of the G20 member nations have finally agreed that we needed to have a better geographical balance. There was a consensus that a certain region had been over-represented".[79] In the subsequent meetings the decision on IMF reform, as described above, was taken without one of the countries expected to be affected being present.

This case study illustrates one of the problems often associated with informal international lawmaking mechanisms: key stakeholders are not directly involved in the decision-making process, as they fall outside of the network, but bear the direct consequences.[80] The next section addresses the question as to whether this lack of inclusiveness is problematic from an accountability perspective.

## 1.6. Accountability and Effectiveness

On the one hand, when G20 leaders in Pittsburgh designated the G20 as "the premier forum for international economic cooperation",[81] this created annoyance with smaller emerging economies that are not included in the G20. On the other hand, questions relating to effectiveness of the G20 can equally be asked. Kirton has rightly observed that "the principle of openness will ensure the G20's effectiveness long after the crisis that created it has passed".[82] The question is how to best reconcile (perceived) inadequacies when it comes to accountability with the desire of having effec-

[78] Financieel Dagblad, "Nederland Stap Dichterbij Zetelverlies IMF-Bestuur", 10 October 2010.

[79] The Korea Times, "Five non-G20 nations invited to Seoul Summit", available at http://www.koreatimes.co.kr/www/news/biz/2010/09/301_73469.html, last accessed on 17 March 2012.

[80] Pauwelyn, 2011, p. 2, see *supra* note 3.

[81] G20, "Leaders' Statement: The Pittsburgh Summit", 25 September 2009, para. 50.

[82] John Kirton, "The G8: Legacy, Limitations, and Lessons", in Colin I. Bradford and Lim Wonhyuk (eds.), *Global Leadership in Transition – Making the G-20 More Effective and Responsive*, Korea Development Institute and the Brookings Institution, Washington, 2011, p. 33. It is Kirton's view that "as the values of social and political openness have global appeal, their reinforcement will enhance the G20's legitimacy in the eyes of the "G172" citizens left out. They therefore should guide the G20's policy prescriptions to its own members and its choice of who should lead and join the group".

tive platforms for cooperation. To what extent should accountability be searched for at the international level? What about internal and external accountability; is the network only accountable to its members, or is there a way for external stakeholders to exert influence? This last question is closely related with the question of effectiveness. Bradford and Lim have identified the "trade-off between achieving legitimacy as a representative body and achieving legitimacy as an effective body" as one of three key challenges to make the G20 "a more enduring, inclusive, and credible form of summitry for the twenty-first century".[83] The question is how G20 governance can be structured in a way that includes third-parties' interests, whilst not losing the effectiveness associated with informal ways of cooperation.

### 1.6.1. Accountability, Legitimacy, Responsiveness and Inclusiveness

Networks like the G20 have inherent advantages as they tend to empower the actors that are part of the network. By the same token, however, they exclude actors that are not part of the network. Kjær notes that

> networks may be efficient in conceiving new policy ideas and realizing them, but they may also impede a democratic process. The democratic problem is that networks usually only serve some interests, and not the aggregated interest: the common will.[84]

In the words of Slaughter, networks, such as the G20, are inherently different from traditional international organizations, as their essence is a process rather than an entity, thereby making it difficult to subject them to traditional forms of accountability.[85] Keohane noted that

---

83 Colin I. Bradford and Lim Wonhyuk, "Introduction: Toward the Consolidation of the G20: From Crisis Committee to Global Steering Committee", in Colin I. Bradford and Lim Wonhyuk (eds.), *Global Leadership in Transition – Making the G-20 More Effective and Responsive*, Korea Development Institute and the Brookings Institution, Washington, 2011, p. 3. See also UN General Assembly, Letter dated 3 October 2011 from the Permanent Representative of Singapore to the United Nations addressed to the Secretary-General – Annex: Global Governance Group (3G) inputs to the G20 on global governance', A/C.2/66/3, 5 October 2011, para. 2. The 3G identified the legitimacy and effectiveness as two competing principles which have to be balanced in order to achieve a sustainable global governance architecture.

84 Anne Mette Kjær, *Governance*, Polity Press, London, 2004, p. 57.

85 Anne-Marie Slaughter, "Agencies on the loose? Holding government networks accountable", in George Bermann, Matthias Herdegen and Peter Lindseth (eds.), *Trans-*

> we need urgently to seek innovative ways to hold potential abusers of power, at a global level, to account; otherwise, we risk discrediting global governance and fostering a reversion to national sovereignty, with disastrous consequences for co-operation, for peace, and for our own prosperity and personal security.[86]

At this point it is necessary to examine how the G20 deals with the issue of accountability as part of a democratic process.

In the context of the IN-LAW project, and inspired by the work of Bovens,[87] the following definition of accountability is used:

> A relationship *(at the domestic or international level)* between an actor *(exercising public authority in the context of IN-LAW)* and a *forum (internal to the IN-LAW process or an external stakeholder)*, in which the actor has an obligation *(in particular, but not exclusively, expressed in legal rules or procedures)* to explain and to justify his or her conduct *(ex ante leading up to a decision or ex post in the implementation of a decision)*, the forum can pose questions and pose judgment, and the actor may face consequences *(in particular, but not exclusively, so as to enhance the democratic nature of the IN-LAW)*.[88]

Accountability of IN-LAW raises questions and offers possible solutions at both the international and the domestic level.

#### 1.6.1.1. Accountability at the International Level

On numerous occasions G20 leaders have expressed their intention to hold themselves accountable for their commitments. The preamble of the G20 Toronto Summit Declaration notes: "we are determined to be accountable for the commitments we have made".[89] In the Cannes Summit Final Declaration, with respect to the fight against corruption, G20 leaders

*atlantic Regulatory Cooperation, Legal Problems and Political Prospects,* Oxford University Press, 2001, p. 525.

86 Robert Keohane, "Accountability in World Politics", in *Scandinavian Political Studies,* 2006, vol. 29, no. 2, p. 78.

87 Mark Bovens, "Analysing and Assessing Public Accountability: A Conceptual Framework", in *European Law Journal*, 2007, vol. 13, no. 4, p. 450.

88 Pauwelyn, 2011, p. 21, see *supra* note 3.

89 G20, "The G20 Toronto Summit Declaration", para. 6, see *supra* note 22.

stated: "we hold ourselves accountable for our commitments and will review progress at our next Summit".[90] Furthermore, they noted that "the G20 must remain efficient, transparent and accountable".[91] That the need is felt to express this so explicitly indicates that G20 leaders are aware of the possibility of an accountability deficit arising from the lack of formal mechanisms.

Two types of G20 accountability mechanisms at the international plane can be distinguished. First, making use of the concept of peer review, G20 leaders hold each other to account for the promises and pledges made at previous G20 summits.[92] One could refer to this as 'internal accountability' of the IN-LAW process. One example of the use of 'peer review' can be found in the Financial Stability Board's 'Coordination Framework for Monitoring the Implementation of Agreed G20/FSB Financial Reforms'.[93] As de Hoop Scheffer has rightly noted, the question remains of course to what extent more autocratic or semi-democratic G20 Members will be willing to reveal their domestic financial policies.[94] To prevent the risk of 'peer-protectionism', Subacchi and Pickford have argued for the relevant international organizations to serve as independent audit mechanisms.[95]

Second, academics and NGOs monitor the commitments made by G20 leaders and assess whether they stick to those commitments.[96] This

---

[90] G20, "Cannes Summit Final Declaration", 2011, para. 89, see *supra* note 29. Similar statements were made in the Seoul Summit Document: "The G20 will hold itself accountable for its commitments", G20, Seoul Summit Document, para. 71, see *supra* note 25.

[91] G20, "Cannes Summit Final Declaration", 2011, para. 92, see *supra* note 29.

[92] G20, "Toronto Summit Declaration", paras. 16, 22 and 32–36, see *supra* note 22.

[93] FSB, "A Coordination Framework for Monitoring the Implementation of Agreed G20/FSB Financial Reforms", 18 October 2011, available at http://www.financial stabilityboard.org/publications/r_111017.pdf, last accessed on 17 March 2012.

[94] Jaap de Hoop Scheffer, "Opkomst G20: een bedreiging voor gevestigde instituties?" [The Rise of the G20: A Threat to Traditional Institutions?], in *Internationale Spectator*, January 2011, p. 10.

[95] Paola Subacchi and Stephen Pickford, "Legitimacy vs Effectiveness for the G20: A Dynamic Approach to Global Economic Governance", Chatham House Briefing Paper, IE BP 2011/01, October 2011, p. 8, available at http://www.chathamhouse.org/sites/default/files/1011bp_subacchi_pickford.pdf, last accessed on 17 March 2012.

[96] G20 Research Group, "2010 Seoul G20 Summit Final Compliance Report – 13 November 2010–19 October 2011", 6 November 2011, available at http://www.g20.

could be seen as some form of 'external accountability'. However, what these mechanisms have in common and what distinguishes them from the accountability mechanisms of traditional international organizations, is that there are no formal rules of procedure. In essence they are voluntary mechanisms without formal backing. This stands in stark contrast with, for example, the Trade Policy Review Mechanism (TPRM) used in the WTO.[97] There, WTO Members' trade policies are subjected to the scrutiny of the whole membership so as to assess compliance with the obligations under the covered WTO Agreements. Here, however, one should point to important differences with an informal mechanism such as G20. WTO Members can be subjected to such stringent review because they have signed up to defined commitments and obligations upon joining the organization.[98] By contrast, the commitments made by G20 leaders are often broad and in need of further elaboration. Thus, it is the very nature of the G20 output that renders it difficult to hold G20 actors to account. This does not mean that G20 leaders should not strive for accountability. After all, we do not necessarily need more, but *better* accountability.[99] The G20 should strive to offer more inclusive discussions and outreach to non-G20 countries and those 'who are not on the table', instead of aiming for very legalistic mechanisms. The G20 has faced and still faces criticism for its lack of what could be called 'stakeholder-involvement'. NGOs can only passively participate in G20 meetings, by way of accreditation. They cannot voice their opinion during meetings, and their responses afterwards seem to indicate uncertainty about the role of the G20 in global governance.[100] Civil society groups have asked the G20 to hold thematic 'Civil

---

utoronto.ca/compliance/2010seoul-final/2010seoul-final-all.pdf, last accessed on 17 March 2012.

97 WTO, "Agreement Establishing the World Trade Organization", Annex 3: Trade Policy Review Mechanism.

98 Ruth W. Grant and Robert O. Keohane, "Accountability and Abuses of Power in World Politics", in *American Political Science Review*, 2005, vol. 99, no. 1, p. 39. "The WTO represents one of the few attempts in world politics to formalize legal and supervisory accountability over the actions of sovereign states".

99 Joost Pauwelyn, "The Rise and Challenges of Informal International Law-Making", in Sam Muller, Stavros Zouridis, Morly Frishman and Laura Kistemaker (eds.), *The Law of the Future and the Future of Law*, Torkel Opsahl Academic EPublisher (TOAEP), Oslo, 2011, p. 137.

100 Movimiento Mundial por la Infancia, "NGO reactions to G20 Summit", available at http://www.gmfc.org/es/noticias/world-news-on-child-rights/662-ngo-reactions-to-g20-summit-show-overall-disappointment-, last accessed on 15 December 2012, for a

G20 meetings' prior to its summits, akin to the way in which the G8 holds Civil G8 meetings. It cannot be denied, however, that the G20 has a tradition of 'outreach'. From the very first summit in 2008, to which Spain and the Netherlands were invited as non-member countries, to the summit in Cannes in 2011, the number of 'external' participants has increased steadily.[101] As indicated above, under the French presidency invitations were sent to the AU, 3G, NEPAD and GCC. Additionally, France hosted B20 and L20 Summits in parallel with the G20 Leaders' Summit in Cannes. Some have argued that formal outreach mechanisms should be put in place to answer concerns that in the long run the G20 may not always continue to recognize non-member countries' interests.[102]

Transparency within the G20 has always been an issue, and will continue to be so. As we have seen above, one of the decisions taken to address the transparency issue is the posting of the Group's meetings and work program on a dedicated website, which is done by the country chairing the G20; afterwards communiqués are released which contain information on what has been discussed and decided.[103] Other proposals have focused on agreeing on more concrete objectives for the G20. This, in combination with making G20 Summit commitments fully transparent, should enable NGOs and civil society to better monitor and assess the implementation record of G20 member countries.[104]

### 1.6.1.2. Accountability at the Domestic Level

Accountability mechanisms at the domestic level of each of the G20 members are very diverse and beyond the reach of this chapter. It would appear that the role of domestic institutions, in holding G20 as a network

list of NGO responses to the G20 Summit in Toronto, Canada. The NGOs seem to be unsure what to make of the G20 so as a result their reactions are more about future G20 agenda items or the gap left by the G8 from yesterday.

[101] International Organisations Research Institute, "G20 Outreach", available at http://www.hse.ru/en/org/hse/iori/G20_outreach, last accessed on 17 March 2012.

[102] Yulius P. Hermawan, "Formalizing the G20 regional outreach contact groups and civil G20", in Thomas Fues and Peter Wolff (eds.), *G20 and Global Development – How Can The New Summit Architecture Promote Pro-Poor Growth and Sustainability*, German Development Institute, Bonn, 2010, p. 40, available at http://www.yorku.ca/ycar/GDI_G20_Korea.pdf, last accessed on 17 March 2012.

[103] G20, "External communication", see *supra* note 40. The current chair often hosts a dedicated website.

[104] Subacchi and Pickford, 2011, p. 8, see *supra* note 95.

to account, is rather limited. To a large extent this can of course be explained with the fact that foreign policy traditionally is a prerogative of the executive branch of government, rather than the legislative branch. Presidents, Prime Ministers or other civil servants representing their country in G20 meetings act on behalf of their constituencies. The only influence domestic institutions can exert lies in the fact that they can hold their leaders accountable in parliament. This can be '*ex ante*', by sending the leader away with a list of objectives or goals to be achieved during the meeting, or '*ex post*', when a leader is questioned regarding the results achieved in a meeting. In this sense it is the leaders of G20 members who are accountable as diffuse actors, rather than the network itself. Each G20 member has a domestic agenda and is held to account by its domestic institutions on that basis alone. At the domestic level one can speak of 'hierarchical' and 'supervisory' accountability.[105] Accountability will largely be based on the type of relationship between the national institutions on whose behalf leaders, civil servants and diplomats exercise authority in G20 meetings and those leaders, civil servants and diplomats themselves. Broadly speaking, national institutions will only be concerned about national interests. Since there are a large number of actors involved in G20 decision-making, there is also a multitude of constituencies to whom they may be accountable. Most likely this will happen through what Grant and Keohane describe as 'delegation' mechanisms.[106] One of the prerequisites for parliamentary accountability is of course the existence of an independent parliament representative of the people of the State in question.

Based on a brief assessment of the practice of a number of G20 members' parliaments, we have not been able to conclude that there is indeed an institutionalized form of reporting on G20 Summits by the representatives of a particular G20 member. Rather we found that national parliaments occasionally request their respective governments to pursue certain policies in the context of G20 ('*ex ante*' control).[107] Similarly, the practice to request governments to provide parliaments with information on the positions taken during those summits also displays *ad hoc* charac-

[105] Grant and Keohane, 2005, p. 36, see *supra* note 98.

[106] Grant and Keohane, 2005, p. 37, see *supra* note 98.

[107] See for example: Assemblée Nationale, "Résolution Européenne sur l'Union européenne et le G20", 20 November 2011, available at http://www.assemblee-nationale.fr/13/pdf/ta/ta0759.pdf, last accessed on 17 March 2012.

teristics.[108] Only in the United Kingdom there appears to be a routine where either the Prime Minister or the Chancellor of the Exchequer makes a statement on the outcome of a G20 Summit in the House of Commons.[109] However, we have not been able to establish whether this practice has been institutionalized in any significant manner. Research by others has shown that parliaments from emerging economies such as India and South Africa are also unable to exercise effective foreign policy oversight.[110]

In this respect it is interesting to assess domestic accountability at the EU level. The EU is represented at G20 leaders' level by European Commission President Barroso and European Council President Van Rompuy. However, as four of its Member States (France, Italy, Germany and the United Kingdom) also take part in G20 meetings in their own right, coordination is essential. Preparation for the G20 takes place in the European Council, where the EU position is coordinated.[111] For the Washington Summit in 2008, the London Summit in 2009 and the Pittsburgh

[108] See for example: Deutscher Bundestag, "Grosse Anfrage Umsetzung der Ergebnisse im Bereich der Wirtschafts- und Finanzpolitik der G8- und G20-Gipfel durch die Bundesregierung", 19 May 2010, available at http://dipbt.bundestag.de/dip21/btd/17/017/1701796.pdf, last accessed on 17 March 2012; Assemblée Nationale, Débat sur les conclusions du sommet européen du 26 octobre et du G20 des 3 et 4 novembre 2011, 9 November 2011. Transcript available at http://www.assemblee-nationale.fr/13/cri/2011-2012/20120048.asp, last accessed on 17 March 2012.

[109] See: House of Commons, Daily Hansard – Debate 'G20', 07 November 2011. Transcript available at http://www.publications.parliament.uk/pa/cm201011/cmhansrd/cm111107/debtext/111107-0001.htm#1111073000001, last accessed on 17 March 2012; House of Commons, Daily Hansard – Debate 'G20 Summit', 15 November 2010. Transcript available at http://www.publications.parliament.uk/pa/cm201011/cmhansrd/cm101115/debtext/101115-0001.htm#10111511000002, last accessed on 17 March 2012; House of Commons, Daily Hansard – Debate 'G20 Summit, 2 April 2009. Transcript available at http://www.publications.parliament.uk/pa/cm200809/cmhansrd/cm090402/debtext/90402-0016.htm#09040254000003, last accessed on 17 March 2012.

[110] Michael Hammer, "The Time Is Now: Parliaments need to assert their role in ensuring the G20 members deliver on the Washington and London programme of work", One World Trust Briefing Paper No 118, April 2009, London.

[111] For a more elaborate discussion on the EU's representation in G20 see: Dermot Hodson, "The Paradox of EMU's External Representation: The Case of the G20 and the IMF", 2011 EUSA Paper, available at http://www.euce.org/eusa/2011/papers/6e_hodson.pdf, last accessed on 17 March 2012; Wouters and Van Kerckhoven, 2011, see *supra* note 57; Debaere, 2010, see *supra* note 77.

Summit in 2009, this resulted in 'Agreed Language'.[112] The European Council of 23 October 2011 resulted in a coordinated position for the sixth G20 Summit in Cannes.[113] Prior to the European Council meeting that discussed the preparation for the Cannes G20 Summit, the President of the European Commission attended the plenary debate in the European Parliament (EP). However, he only mentioned the G20 once, in the context of the EU's proposals on how to implement the G20 commitments to establish a system of financial regulation. He was not interpellated by any of the MEPs on the issue of G20.[114] Interestingly, there is no recurring practice of either the President of the Commission or the President of the European Council reporting back to the EP on the issues discussed during a G20 Summit. After the G20 Summits in Washington, London and Seoul, either the President of the Commission or a Member Commission defended the outcome of these summits in the European Parliament.[115] However, no such debates were held after the summits in Pittsburg and Toronto, although both G20 summits were preceded by a preparatory de-

[112] See European Council Presidency Conclusions, "Agreed Language", Informal Meeting of EU Heads of State or Government, 7 November 2008; European Council Presidency Conclusions,19–20 March 2009, Annex 1: Agreed language with a view to the G20 Summit in London, 7880/1/09 REV1; European Council Presidency Conclusions, "Agreed Language for the Pittsburgh G-20 Summit", Informal Meeting of EU Heads of State or Government, 17 September 2009.

[113] European Council Presidency Conclusions, Part. II. "G20", 23 October 2011, EUCO 52/11.

[114] European Parliament, "Preparation for the European Council meeting (23 October 2011)", 12 October 2011, Brussels. Transcript available at http://www.europarl.europa.eu/sides/getDoc.do?type=CRE&reference=20111012&secondRef=ITEM-014&format=XML&language=EN, last accessed on 17 March 2012.

[115] See: European Parliament, "EU response to the world financial crisis: follow-up of the informal European Council from 7 November and of the G20 Summit from 15 November 2008 – Commission's legislative and work programme for 2009 (debate)", 18 November 2008, Strasbourg. Transcript available at http://www.europarl.europa.eu/sides/getDoc.do?pubRef=-%2F%2FEP%2F%2FTEXT%2BCRE%2B20081118%2BITEM-011%2BDOC%2BXML%2BV0%2F%2FEN, last accessed on 17 March 2012; European Parliament, "Conclusions of the G20 Summit (debate)", 23 April 2009, Strasbourg. Transcript available at http://www.europarl.europa.eu/sides/getDoc.do?type=CRE&reference=20090423&secondRef=ITEM-013&language=EN, last accessed on 17 March 2012; European Parliament, "Results of the G20 summit (debate)", 24 November 2010, Strasbourg. Transcript available at http://www.europarl.europa.eu/sides/getDoc.do?pubRef=-%2F%2FEP%2F%2FTEXT%2BCRE%2B20101124%2BITEM-007%2BDOC%2BXML%2BV0%2F%2FEN, last accessed on 17 March 2012.

bate in the European Parliament at which either the President of the Commission or one of the Members of the Commission would defend the EU's position at the upcoming summit.[116] Hence, there is no institutionalized form of '*ex post*' accountability in the EU with respect to the outcomes of G20 summits. In order to ensure effective control over the positions taken by the representatives of the EU at G20 level, it seems to us that the European Parliament can, and indeed should, use its powers to hold EU representatives to account on a more structural basis.[117]

### 1.6.1.3. Towards Inclusiveness and Responsiveness

The question is to what extent the fact that accountability of the G20 is far from self-evident, is problematic. The G20 is not, and does not pretend to be, a global regulator. Throughout this chapter we have emphasized its informal nature and consequently, its lack of legally binding outcomes. Rather, it is a forum where world leaders meet and discuss global issues. Accordingly we have to ask ourselves whether it would not be more helpful to ensure that the voices of those who are not at the table are heard, than to strive for very legalistic accountability mechanisms, akin to those present in traditional international organizations. Steven Slaughter has argued that "it is ultimately unhelpful to claim that the G20 should be accountable for its decisions and actions in moral or even judicial terms". Instead, he argues that more emphasis should be placed on 'responsiveness' rather than direct judicial accountability.[118] In this context, several institutional

116 See: European Parliament, "G20 Summit in Pittsburgh (24–25 September) (debate)", 16 September 2009, Strasbourg. Transcript available at http://www.europarl.europa.eu/sides/getDoc.do?type=CRE&reference=20090916&secondRef=ITEM-004&language=EN, last accessed on 17 March 2012; European Parliament, "4. Preparations for the European Council meeting (17 June 2010) - Preparations for the G20 summit (26–27 June) (debate)", 16 June 2010, Strasbourg. Transcript available at http://www.europarl.europa.eu/sides/getDoc.do?pubRef=-%2f%2fEP%2f%2fTEXT%2bCRE%2b20100616%2bITEM-004%2bDOC%2bXML%2bV0%2f%2fEN, last accessed on 17 March 2012.

117 Kolja Raube, 'The European External Action Service and the European Parliament *The Hague Journal of Diplomacy*, 2012, vol. 7, pp. 65–80 at 79; de Hoop Scheffer, 2011, p. 13, see *supra* note 94.

118 Steven Slaughter, "Promising the World? The G20, Public Accountability and Global Environmental Governance", Draft Paper Presented at the ANU Democratizing Climate Governance, 15 and 16 July 2010, p. 7, available at http://deliberativedemocracy.anu.edu.au/Content/pdf%20files/conference%20papers/SLAUGHTER%20Promising%20the%20World.pdf, last accessed on 17 March 2012.

innovations for consultation and outreach have been proposed.[119] The proposal by Wonhyuk and Park includes outreach to organizations such as the UN, ASEAN and AU. The relationship between the G20 and the UN certainly warrants further attention.[120] We firmly believe that the practice of inviting the UN Secretary-General to G20 summits should be institutionalized. Furthermore, we support the proposed creation of a 'G20-subgroup' within the UN, as it could contribute to greater transparency.[121] Its function would be to communicate with non-G20 UN Member States and enable those States to have their voices heard in the preparatory phase of an upcoming G20 summit. Strengthening the linkages between the G20 and the UN system will enhance the degree of responsiveness G20 displays towards non-members.[122] Moreover, we are of the opinion that institutionalizing essential parts of G20's outreach to non-members will prove essential in ensuring the network's future.

### 1.6.1.4. G20: Legitimate Global Governance

Legitimacy is a typical problem associated with informal networks such as the G20. The claim has been made that networks only serve the interests of those included in the network, whilst disregarding the interests of those that are not included. From the perspective of 'input legitimacy', and compared to older forms of informal global cooperation, such as the G8, the G20 is certainly more legitimate in the sense that it includes a number of emerging markets, comprises countries from all five continents and represents 85% of global GDP. Nevertheless, there are concerns that the interests of the "G173" are not adequately represented.[123] Vestergaard

---

[119] Lim Wonhyuk and Yumi Park, "Institutional Innovations for Consultation and Outreach: Making the G20 More Responsive and Effective", Korean Development Institute (KDI), Paper Prepared for the Presidential Committee of the G20 Summit, November 2010.

[120] See Paul Heinbecker, "The United Nations and the G20: Synergy or Dissonance?" in Colin I. Bradford and Lim Wonhyuk (eds.), *Global Leadership in Transition – Making the G-20 More Effective and Responsive*, Korea Development Institute and the Brookings Institution, Washington, 2011, p. 236.

[121] de Hoop Scheffer, 2011, p. 9, see *supra* note 94.

[122] UN General Assembly, 2011, A/66/506, para. 52, see *supra* note 53.

[123] Jakob Vestergaard, "The G20 and Beyond – Towards Effective Global Governance", DIIS Report 2011:04, Copenhagen, 2011, p. 25, available at http://www.diis.dk/graphics/Publications/Reports2011/RP2011-04-G20-and-beyond_web.pdf, last accessed on 17 March 2012. Vestergaard is extremely critical of G20 which he sees as

puts forward that the G20 is not representative enough and furthermore "undermines the existing system of multilateral cooperation in institutions such as the IMF, the World Bank and the UN". In his view, problems such as climate change, global imbalances and rising poverty, should not be discussed in an informal forum such as G20, but in a "truly multilateral framework".[124] These concerns become apparent when addressing specific examples, such as the case study on IMF reform (see *supra*), but also when listening carefully to the statements of groupings such as the 3G (Global Governance Group). The 3G, led by Singapore, is an informal grouping of a number of small and medium-sized UN Member States.[125] The grouping started its operations in 2009 [126] and in March 2010 sent a document to the UN Secretary-General entitled 'Strengthening the Framework for G20 Engagement of Non-Members'.[127] Gradually the group has increased its influence, culminating in an invitation from the French presidency to the Cannes Summit in November 2011.[128] Prior to the Cannes Summit, the 3G issued a press release in which it noted that "while the G20 has a key contribution to make in enhancing global economic governance, the UN system must remain the cornerstone of global governance, in recognition of the universality and unquestioned legitima-

"a self-selected and illegitimate group of countries which – by permanently excluding 173 countries from key deliberations on global economic governance – is undermining a system of multilateral cooperation that it has taken more than sixty years to build".

124 Vestergaard, 2011, p. 25, see *supra* note 123.

125 Its 29 members are: Bahamas, Bahrain, Barbados, Botswana, Brunei Darussalam, Chile, Costa Rica, Finland, Guatemala, Jamaica, Kuwait, Liechtenstein, Malaysia, Monaco, Montenegro, New Zealand, Panama, Peru, Philippines, Qatar, Rwanda, San Marino, Senegal, Singapore, Slovenia, Switzerland, United Arab Emirates, Uruguay and Viet Nam.

126 Iftekhar Ahmed Chowdhury, "The Global Governance Group ('3G') and Singaporean Leadership: Can Small be Significant?", ISAS Working Paper No. 108, 19 May 2010, p. 6, available at http://www.boell.org/downloads/ISAS_3GThe_Global_Governance_Group_19052010134423.pdf, last accessed on 17 March 2012. Chowdhury provides insightful background information to the inception of this grouping.

127 UN General Assembly, "Letter dated 11 March 2010 from the Permanent Representative of Singapore to the United Nations addressed to the Secretary-General", A/64/706, 11 March 2010.

128 See G20, "Invitation to non-members of the G20 to the G20 Summit of Cannes on November 3 and 4, 2011", Press Release, Paris, 12 February 2011, available at http://www.g20-g8.com/g8-g20/g20/english/for-the-press/news-releases/invitation-to-non-members-of-the-g20-to-the-g20.929.html, last accessed on 17 March 2012.

cy of the UN".[129] After the Summit, the 3G commended the G20 for the Cameron Report on Global Governance and "the G20 Leaders' commitment to pursue 'consistent and effective' engagement with non-members and for the G20 to accept contributions from non-members, international institutions and others, when appropriate".[130] 3G's main concerns are related to the issue of representational legitimacy. According to some, "the lack of a formal legal mandate, such as that underpinning most, if not all, traditional international organizations, is problematic at times when the G20 appeared to be moving from a crisis committee to a global steering committee".[131] At this point, the G20 certainly has not attained the level of legitimacy that traditional international organizations with almost universal membership, such as the UN, have. As Wonhyuk and Nicolas correctly observe, because of its informal and *ad hoc* nature, the G20 "faces an inherent legitimacy problem".[132] However, they argue that as the G20 shows its relevance and effectiveness, concerns about legitimacy will become less pressing. Here they refer to the fact that G20 will gain 'output legitimacy' through effective policies. According to them, the best way to increase the legitimacy of G20 is to make it more effective.[133] Zhang has argued that "the output legitimacy of G20 based on its effectiveness has been proven by the G20's positive performance in dealing with the global financial crisis".[134] We agree with this analysis, yet, as a result, the G20's future legitimacy depends to a large degree on the extent to which it can successfully address the problems being posed to it in a globalized context.

---

129 3G, "Press Statement by the Global Governance Group (3G) on the G20 Summit in Cannes", 3–4 November 2011, para. 5, available at http://app.mfa.gov.sg/2006/press/view_press.asp?post_id=7399, last accessed on 17 March 2012.

130 3G, "Press Statement by the Global Governance Group (3G) on the outcomes of the G20 Summit in Cannes", 3–4 November 2011, para. 7, available at http://app.mfa.gov.sg/2006/lowRes/press/view_press.asp?post_id=7431, last accessed on 17 March 2012.

131 Lim Wonhyuk and Françoise Nicolas, "The G20 From Seoul to Cannes – Towards a Global Governance Committee", KDI and IFRI, p. 7, available at http://www.ifri.org/downloads/ifriifrireportasianstudiesg20.pdf, last accessed on 17 March 2012.

132 Wonhyuk and Nicolas, 2011, p. 6, see *supra* note 131.

133 *Ibid.*

134 Haibing Zhang, "G20 and global governance: Challenges and impacts", in Thomas Fues and Peter Wolff (eds.), *G20 and Global Development – How Can The New Summit Architecture Promote Pro-Poor Growth and Sustainability*, German Development Institute, Bonn, 2010, p. 61.

### 1.6.2. Effectiveness

In the context of the informal international lawmaking project, 'effectiveness' is characterized as follows: "(1) does cooperation materialize; (2) does it stick; (3) does it solve the problem; (4) does it solve the problem in a cost-effective way".[135]

The question is first what is expected from the G20 as a network. As discussed above, the G20's output consists of coordinated policies contained in summit documents and communiqués. How does one assess effectiveness 'as such'? Kirton signals "a gap between how [effectiveness] is conceptualized in the ideal, ideational, cost-free world and how it is actually operationalized in the real world where resources are required to measure and monitor what is done".[136] Often, commitments made in a setting such as the G20 are treated rather literally. "Assessment focuses on the manageably measurable first-order compliance of implementing action by those making the commitment, rather than the extended outcomes of what they do".[137] In examining the way in which effectiveness is measured, Kirton distinguishes between legalized international organizations such as the WTO and informal, multilateral institutions without a secretariat such as the G8 and G20. In the WTO, the reports of Panels and Appellate Body provide "systematic, well-used evidence of which countries are complying with their commitments under the governing treaties".[138] With respect to the G20, "measurement of effectiveness concentrates more broadly on the overall ongoing commitments by the highest level political authorities that make them".[139] Evenett has cautioned against the danger of seeing the G20 as an institution that makes and complies with transpar-

---

[135] Pauwelyn, 2011, p. 23, see *supra* note 3.

[136] John Kirton, "Enhancing Effectiveness through Improved Accountability Assessment", p. 2, available at http://www.g20.utoronto.ca/biblio/kirton-princeton-2011.pdf, last accessed on 17 March 2012. In his vision, 'effectiveness' is often reduced to compliance with the commitment by those that made it or their targets outside, their implementation through commitment-consistent action and their progress toward achieving the specified goals.

[137] *Ibid.*, p. 3.

[138] *Ibid.*, Kirton notes the advantages of this approach: comprehensibility and credibility coming from its legalization and its close relationship with "enforcement" action for redress or deterrence.

[139] *Ibid.*

ent policy commitments.[140] One of the main benefits attached to the informality of G20 is that world leaders have the opportunity to discuss issues in a setting that fosters trust. As Smith indicates, "the greater the number of leaders around the table, the more challenges it presents in developing empathy and personal relationships – imperative in generating consensus. Personal trust among leaders allows for the candid discussion of sensitive issues without political posturing. To engage the leaders in discussions, there need to be fewer people in the room, and the heads of international organizations should only be present for relevant agenda items".[141]

On the other side of the spectrum, Vestergaard and Wade are critical of the G20 not only because of its alleged lack of input legitimacy, but also because they consider it ineffective and therefore lacking output legitimacy.[142] In Vestergaard's view it makes no sense to see the G20 as an effective global steering committee, as it has so far failed to reach agreement on reform of the World Bank as well as on stricter international financial regulation.[143] Instead it is argued that the problems that the world leaders have to deal with require binding agreements instead of informal dialogue. Vestergaard rejects the notion that an informal mechanism such as G20 can contribute to solving these problems, "as it lacks an institutional framework of a formal and binding nature which can enable negotiation and arbitration".[144] As an alternative, they propose a global economic council that would act as a steering committee of the global econo-

[140] Simon J. Evenett, "What Can We Realistically Expect from the G20?", 12 November 2010, available at http://www.voxeu.org/index.php?q=node/5777, last accessed on 17 March 2012. He notes that "just because the G20 doesn't appear to be suited to making and sticking to transparency policy commitments, does not mean that, overall, it is useless. The trap to avoid here is the logic "if-it-isn't-nailed-down-in-precise-legalese-it-won't-work". This apparent logic hasn't stopped governments during the crisis from routinely circumventing clear obligations at the WTO and, quite probably, in the case of bailouts (subsidies) and stimulus packages (government procurement in WTO parlance) outright violations of existing international trade law".

[141] Smith, May 2011, p. 7, see *supra* note 1.

[142] Jakob Vestergaard and Robert Wade, "The G20 Has Served Its Purpose and Should be Replaced", DIIS Policy Brief, October 2011, p. 1, available at http://www.diis.dk/graphics/Publications/Policybriefs%202011/The%20G20%20has%20served%20its%20purpose%20and%20should%20be%20replaced.web.pdf, last accessed on 17 March 2012.

[143] Vestergaard, 2011, p. 28–29, see *supra* note 123.

[144] Vestergaard, 2011, p. 52, see *supra* note 123.

my.[145] Other, more moderate proposals for the reform of the G20 increasingly also include aspects of what could be called re-formalization (see *supra*, 1.4.). As Wonhyuk and Nicolas put forward:

> While the G20 summit process has relied so far on a revolving three-member management mechanism (the so-called troika system), the preparation, organization and management of the G20 Summits is an increasingly daunting task, and effective logistical, administrative and technical support for the G20 would certainly help make the whole process more effective.[146]

Clearly, this statement does not suggest that the G20 should turn into a traditional international organization with a founding charter, permanent Secretariat and permanent location. Nevertheless, what it hints at is a certain formalization of the process. The Cameron Report sees the establishment of a permanent policy Secretariat as an over-reaction and only suggests a small secretariat to support the Troika. However, even this proposal was rejected during the Cannes Summit.[147] We do not consider a formalization of the G20 or the establishment of new multilateral institutions, such as a global economic council, as solutions to the deficiencies of the G20. Although another organization with (quasi-) universal membership may have more input legitimacy, we fail to see how it would be more effective than an informal constellation such as the G20.

Turning back to the question as to what can be expected from the G20 as a network, we emphasize the opportunities for cooperation it can offer between world leaders and its role as a forum where political guidance for more formal institutions can be created.[148] The G20 was never intended to provide detailed international agreements on complex issues such as trade or climate change, and as such they are not the outcomes we can realistically expect from it. What we can expect, however, are more detailed commitments and action plans instead of the communiqués and declarations that have been issued so far. G20's effectiveness should be measured both on the extent to which its commitments are implemented

145 Vestergaard and Wade, 2011, p. 1, see *supra* note 142.

146 Wonhyuk and Nicolas, 2011, p. 18, see *supra* note 131.

147 G20, 2011, see *supra* note 29.

148 Alex Evans, Bruce Jones and Steven David, "Confronting the Long Crisis of Globalization. Risk Resilience and International Order", Brookings/CIC, 26 January 2010, p. 38–39, available at http://globaldashboard.org/wp-content/uploads/2010/Long_Crisis.pdf, last accessed on 17 March 2012.

as well as on the basis of the extent to which it is capable of providing the political impetus needed in the existing multilateral institutions of this world. To this end the strengthening of the linkages between G20 and institutions such as the UN, the IMF, the World Bank and the WTO can only be welcomed.

## 1.7. Concluding Remarks

G20 summits take place on a yearly basis, at different locations and are chaired by different hosts. The G20 is not based on any treaty, nor are there any procedural rules on decision-making. Furthermore, the objective of the G20 has never been to be the forum for negotiations to reach a binding treaty. Given these characteristics, the conclusion that the G20 is an IN-LAW mechanism is warranted. The G20 brings together leaders of the twenty systemically most important economies to discuss global issues in an informal setting. As a network it does not have the formal decision-making procedures and rules of procedure that characterize traditional international organizations. As a result of the informal decision-making process and the output that takes shape in the form of communiqués and declarations, there are a number of problems associated with holding G20 as a network to account. The mechanisms that are in place are largely voluntary and have not been formalized in any significant way. In order to strengthen the legitimacy of the G20, effective policies and the willingness to reach out to those that are not in the network are needed. To this end, the proposals to engage with stakeholders in a more structured manner can only be encouraged. Similarly, continuing the dialogue with non-G20 countries would enhance its legitimacy. The G20 is one of the few fora in which world leaders can informally discuss global issues. In a setting that stimulates trust rather than suspicion, points of view can be exchanged without leaders immediately being bound by legal commitments. The benefit of being able to have these dialogues outweighs the perceived, and real, deficiencies G20 displays in terms of accountability and legitimacy.

# 2

# Informal International Lawmaking in East Asia – An Examination of APEC

**Takao Suami***

## 2.1. Introduction

IN-LAW (Informal International Lawmaking) may become a useful mechanism to organize regional policy as well as international policy beyond any particular region. This chapter will focus on the role of IN-LAW at the regional level, in particular within East Asia. It is generally believed that countries in this region have preferred non-binding measures and thus East Asia is characterized by dependence on soft legislation.[1] This preference is apparent in the fact that, unlike in other regions including Europe, there are fewer ordinary international organizations in East Asia. While there is ongoing regional cooperation, most cooperative frameworks are organized as informal networks or forums, whose outputs are not implemented by legally enforceable means. It is therefore not difficult to find a good example of IN-LAW among such regional networks or forums, and one can reasonably presume that an analysis of them will be meaningful for further study of IN-LAW in general.

Among regional forums in East Asia, this chapter will mainly examine the 'Asia Pacific Economic Cooperation' (APEC). Primarily, APEC has features which can be categorized under the heading of IN-LAW. It is not an international organization founded on an international treaty and has not produced any legally binding treaties. In addition, many sub-groups, which deal with various policies, are organized under the auspices of APEC, and non-governmental stakeholders including businesses, academics and research institutions as well as domestic regulatory officials have been participating in discussions within the forum. Secondly, with a history that extends over 20 years, APEC is now the most inclu-

* **Takao Suami** is a Professor of Law at Waseda University, Japan.

1 Miles Kahler, "Legalisation as Strategy: The Asia-Pacific Case", in Judith L. Goldstein, Miles O. Kahler, Robert Keohane and Anne-Marie Slaughter (eds.), *Legalisation and World Politics*, MIT Press, 2001, pp. 165–167.

sive forum in East Asia in terms of both the number of participating countries and the broad scope of policy areas it covers. Recently however, due to the ineffectiveness of APEC, the center of regional cooperation seems to have moved from APEC to other regional forums such as ASEAN (Association of the South East Asian Nations) plus Three (China, South Korea and Japan) or ASEAN plus Six (China, South Korea, Japan, Australia, New Zealand and India). Several regional frameworks now coexist and compete against each other in East Asia, and it is against this background that we conduct an examination of whether or not APEC has been successfully functioning for the purpose of IN-LAW.

This chapter, first, briefly gives an overview of APEC and, second, examines how APEC meets IN-LAW requirements. Third, it identifies APEC's 'informal international instruments' as reflected in each policy area. Fourth, it further examines whether or not those instruments have had legal effects on the domestic laws of APEC members. Finally, it considers why the question of accountability deficit has not become a large issue in the context of APEC.[2] Even in East Asia, informal policy-making does not necessarily suit all kinds of regional issues. This chapter will, on the whole, reveal limitations in APEC's IN-LAW and present brief remarks regarding the notion of IN-LAW from the viewpoint of APEC.

## 2.2. Overview of APEC

### 2.2.1. Birth of APEC[3]

APEC was established in 1989 just before the fall of the Berlin Wall at the initiative of both Australia and Japan. In November 1989, the First APEC Ministerial Meeting was held in Canberra, Australia with 12 partic-

[2] These examinations are based upon information which the author obtained mainly from the website of APEC (see http://www.apec.org/, last accessed on 29 June 2012) and an interview with a public official in charge of APEC in the Ministry of Economic and Industry of Japan.

[3] Lorraine C. Cardenas and Arpaporn Buranakanits, "The Role of APEC in the Achievement of Regional Cooperation in Southeast Asia", in *Annual Survey of International and Comparative Law*, 1999, vol. 5, issue 1, pp. 52–54; Merit E. Janow, "Assessing APEC's Role in Economic Integration in the Asia-Pacific Region", in *Northwestern Journal of International Law and Business*, 1996, vol. 17, no. 2, pp. 951–952; Kenneth W. Abbott and Gregory W. Bowman, "Economic Integration for the Asian Century: An Early Look at New Approaches", in *Transnational Law and Contemporary Problems*, 1994, vol. 4, pp. 208–209.

ipants. These countries discussed how to advance the process of regional economic cooperation among themselves.[4] During that period, many countries in East Asia and the Pacific were seriously concerned that the emergence of trade blocks in North America (NAFTA) and Europe (in particular the Internal Market program of the EC) would have the effect of excluding their industries from those markets.[5] In order to protect their economic interests, these countries were, therefore, forced to strengthen their intra-regional economic cooperation. In addition, the slow progress of the GATT Uruguay Round negotiations compelled them to search for an alternative to multi-lateral trade negotiation. The growing intra-regional trade and investment in the 1980s also constituted an economic incentive for the establishment of APEC.

Since its first ministerial meeting, APEC has held annual ministerial meetings. Simultaneously, since 1993, within the framework of the annual APEC Economic Leaders' meeting (a summit meeting of APEC members), the heads of APEC member governments have been meeting, too.

### 2.2.2. APEC's Activities and Membership

#### 2.2.2.1. Trade and Investment Liberalization

As its name indicates, the core objective of APEC has always been to strengthen regional economic cooperation. In order to achieve this objective, APEC has aimed at liberalizing trade in goods and services, in addition to facilitating foreign investment in the Asia-Pacific region. The 'Bogor Declaration' by APEC economic leaders in 1994 clearly established APEC's long-term goal of free and open 'trade and investment' by 2010 for industrialized members and by 2020 for developing members. Subsequently, both the Economic Leaders' Meeting and the 7$^{th}$ Ministerial Meeting in Osaka, Japan led to the adoption of the Osaka Action Agenda (OAA) for the purpose of attaining those goals.[6]

---

4 The First APEC Ministerial Meeting, Joint Statement (Canberra, Australia, 6–7 November 1989).

5 Abbott, Bowman, 1994, pp. 209–210, see *supra* note 3.

6 Thomas C. Fischer, "A Commentary on Regional Institutions in the Pacific Rim: Do APEC and ASEAN Still Matter?", in *Duke Journal of Comparative and International Law,* 2003, vol. 13, no. 2, pp. 343–344; Janow, 1996, pp. 960–967, see *supra* note 3; "APEC Economic Leaders' Declaration of Common Resolve" (Bogor, Indonesia, 15 November 1994); "APEC Economic Leaders' Declaration For Action" (Osaka, Japan,

One of the major features of APEC is that the attainment of these goals is wholly dependent upon 'voluntarism', a fundamental principle of the forum. For instance, in terms of the Bogor Declaration, each member would voluntarily adopt its own action plan for trade and investment liberalization in accordance with the general principles and within the framework of the OAA.[7] The system of peer review by other APEC members would also be conducted to assess implementation of these plans.[8] However, the submission of action plans is also voluntary, and some of the members have not submitted their Action Plans yet.

In relation to non-members, APEC has never aimed for a closed trade bloc. Its main slogan is 'open-regionalism'. APEC leaders and ministers repeatedly emphasized firm opposition to the creation of an inward-looking trading bloc among its members.[9] Therefore, APEC does not support the introduction of discrimination between members and non-members in terms of trade and investment. In line with this policy, APEC has consistently expressed its strong support for the multilateral trading system.

#### 2.2.2.2. Expansion of APEC's Activities and Membership

From its foundation, APEC has gradually developed its sphere of activities and expanded its membership.[10]

As regards to its activities, liberalization of trade and investment remains a central pillar of APEC's activities. All of APEC's main objectives, as embodied in the Seoul APEC Declaration of 1991, were of economic nature.[11] However, with the turn of the century APEC has begun

---

19 November 1995); "APEC Economic Leaders' Meeting", The Osaka Action Agenda, Implementation of the Bogor Declaration (Osaka, Japan, 19 November 1995); The Seventh Ministerial Meeting, Joint Statement (Osaka, Japan, 16–17 November 1995).

7 The "Seventh Ministerial Meeting", para. 9, see *supra* note 6.

8 The "Osaka Action Agenda", Part One, Section B: Framework for Liberalization and Facilitation, see *supra* note 6.

9 The "First APEC Ministerial Meeting", see *supra* note 4; "APEC Economic Leaders' Declaration of Common Resolve", para. 6, see *supra* note 6; "APEC Economic Leaders' Declaration for Actio"n, para. 4, *supra* note 6.

10 Fischer, 2003, pp. 342–345, see *supra* note 6.

11 The "Third APEC Ministerial Meeting", Joint Statement, Annex B-Seoul APEC Declaration (Seoul, Korea, 12–14 November 1991); Cardenas and Buranakanits, 1999, p. 60, see *supra* note 3.

attaching more importance to non-economic issues and has been aiming at human security, anti-terrorism and responding to climate change. For example, the 17th Economic Leaders' Meeting in 2009 expressed its concern over enhancing human security, fighting corruption and improving governance and transparency.[12] Following the 11 September attacks in 2001 APEC members have also discussed anti-terrorism at recent APEC meetings.[13]

Not only has APEC expanded its activities, it has also accepted new members. As mentioned before, APEC started with 12 members only. At the moment, APEC consists of 21 members including 19 countries (China, South Korea, Russia, seven ASEAN countries, Canada, US, Mexico, Papua New Guinea, Peru, Chile, Australia, New Zealand and Japan) and two regions (Hong Kong and Chinese Taipei) in Asia and the Pacific. It is noteworthy that China, Hong Kong and Chinese Taipei are working together within the framework of APEC. APEC members do not participate in APEC as states, but as a member economy. It is interesting that this formulation has enabled both China and Taiwan to join APEC together.

### 2.2.3. APEC's Organizational Structure and Decision-Making Process

#### 2.2.3.1. Multilevel Meetings

APEC is not formally classified as an international organization (IO) under public international law.[14] Nevertheless, it has a similar hierarchical institutional structure. Major institutions of APEC are classified into the following categories:

(a) Annual Economic Leaders' Meeting,

---

12 The 17th APEC Economic Leaders' Declaration, "Sustaining Growth, Connecting with the Region" (Singapore, 14–15 November 2009).

13 Anti-terrorism is one of the key priority subjects of APEC: see Jaemin Lee, "Juggling Counter-Terrorism and Trade, the APEC Way: APEC's Leadership in Devising Counter-Terrorism Measures in Compliance with International Trade Norms", in *University of California Davis Journal of International Law and Policy,* 2006, vol. 12, pp. 262–266.

14 This is indicated by the fact that most textbooks of international law do not mention APEC at all (Malcolm D. Evans, *International Law*, Oxford University Press, 2006; Malcolm N. Shaw, *International Law*, Cambridge University Press, 2008; Ian Brownlie, *Principles of Public International Law*, Oxford University Press, 2008).

(b) Annual Ministerial Meeting,
(c) Senior Officials' Meeting,
(d) Committees, Sub-Committees and Working Groups,
(e) APEC Secretariat,
(f) APEC Business Advisory Council.

As this structure shows, APEC provides its members with multi-level forums for discussion. Within this hierarchy, APEC's 'informal international instruments'[15] are normally prepared in lower level meetings, and then endorsed or recognized in higher-level meetings.

#### 2.2.3.2. Economic Leaders' Meeting and Ministerial Meeting

The Economic Leaders' Meeting is located at the top of this structure, which is in fact an APEC Summit Meeting. Under the Leaders' Meeting, there is a 'Ministerial Meeting' and several 'Sectorial Ministerial Meetings'. The former draws both one minister of foreign affairs and one minister of economy and industry for each member economy. The latter meeting is organized on a sector-by-sector basis, and ministers in charge of each particular policy area have their respective meetings. Those Sectorial Meetings include, for example, a trade ministers' meeting, a finance ministers' meeting, an education ministers' meeting and so on. Each year APEC appoints a President among its members. For example, Japan was appointed as President for 2010.

#### 2.2.3.3. Other Types of Meetings and the APEC Secretariat

Within the Ministerial Meeting, there is a 'Senior Official's Meeting' (SOM), and under the control of SOM, four committees are organized. They include the 'Economic Committee' (EC),[16] 'Committee on Trade

[15] For this IN-LAW research project, "informal international instrument" is defined in the sense that "it does not lead to a formal treaty or any other traditional source of international law, but rather to a guideline, standard, declaration or even more informal policy coordination or exchange" by Prof. Pauwelyn in: Joost Pauwelyn, "Informal International Lawmaking: Framing the Concept and Research Questions", in Joost Pauwelyn, Ramses A. Wessel and Jan Wouters (eds.), *Informal International Lawmaking*, Oxford University Press, Oxford, 2012, p. 15.

[16] The EC was established in 1994 and aims at removing the structural and regulatory obstacles that inhibit cross-border trade and investment.

and Investment' (CTI),[17] 'SOM Steering Committee on Economic and Technical Cooperation' (SCE) and 'Budget and Management Committee' (BMC). Under each Committee, except for the BMC, many working groups or sub-committees are organized for the purpose of discussing each specific subject.

Although it is not a formal IO, APEC has its small secretarial office in Singapore. Under the authority of a Secretary-General, there are approximately two dozen diplomats seconded from APEC members and as of 2005, about twenty local staff work there.[18]

### 2.2.3.4. APEC Business Advisory Council (ABAC)

From the viewpoint of IN-LAW, it should be noted that APEC members' business societies are closely associated with APEC's activities through their incorporation into its organizational structure. The key institution is the 'APEC Business Advisory Council' (ABAC) established by the Ministerial and Summit Meeting in Osaka 1995. It is an official advisory organ and has the task of monitoring APEC activities and advancing necessary suggestions from the business point of view to the Leaders' Meeting and the Ministerial Meeting.[19] A small number of business leaders (for example, the heads of big enterprises) are appointed by each APEC member in order to provide APEC with advice on the implementation of the OAA and to offer a business perspective on certain key issues.[20] In its annual dialogue with the APEC Economic Leaders, the ABAC presents recommendations on how to improve business and investment environments in the Asia-Pacific region. The ABAC representatives also attend the SOM, the Annual Ministerial Meeting and the Sectorial Ministerial Meet-

---

17 The CTI was established in November 1993. The scope of CTI's work was expanded and clarified by the OAA in 1995.

18 Greg J. Bamber, "How Is The Asia-Pacific Economic Cooperation (APEC) Forum Developing? Comparative Comments on APEC and Employment Relations", in *Comparative Labor Law and Policy Journal*, 2005, vol. 26, no. 4, p. 442.

19 In 1996, the Manila Summit Meeting affirmed that the central role of the business sector in the APEC process is the contributions of ABAC (APEC Economic Leaders' Declaration, Subic Declaration – From Vision To Action (Subic, Philippines, 25 November 1996)). ABAC have held four general meetings per year in recent times.

20 Fischer, 1996, p. 348, see *supra* note 6; for example, in the case of Japan, former presidents of Mitsui Trading Company, Toshiba Co., Bank of Tokyo-Mitsubishi-UFJ were appointed as the ABAC members.

ing.[21] Furthermore, representatives from the private sector are often invited to join APEC working groups and expert groups.[22]

#### 2.2.3.5. APEC Decision-Making

Within the framework of APEC, all decisions are made by consensus. To put it differently, each member is granted veto power to prevent decision-making.[23] Besides its decision-making rule, the substance of APEC's decisions is also noteworthy. Such decisions usually only include principles and certain exceptions to them.[24] Since APEC does not aim to advance legal integration through legally binding instruments, those decisions are drafted in quite a different manner as compared to ordinary legal texts.

### 2.2.4. APEC and Legal Measures

#### 2.2.4.1. APEC and International Organizations

From a legal point of view, APEC is different from other regional organizations such as the EU and NAFTA in that there is no formal founding agreement or treaty binding upon its members. Therefore, the APEC agreement is of a political nature. In the same light, with no founding treaty APEC responds to neither a legitimate supranational institution nor a judicial mechanism to resolve disputes or enforce obligations. In other words, APEC has no interpretative, enforcement or adjudicative powers.[25] The APEC's official website explains that "APEC is the premier Asia-Pacific economic forum" and that the "Asia-Pacific Economic Cooperation (APEC) operates as a cooperative, multilateral economic and trade

---

[21] APEC Business Advisory Council, available at http://www.apec.org/Home/Groups/Other-Groups/APEC-Business-Advisory-Council.aspx, last accessed on 26 June 2012.

[22] For example, a representative of the ABAC joins the Market Access Group under the CTI as a member, see http://www.apec.org/About-Us/How-APEC-Operates/Stakeholder-Participation.aspx, last accessed on 26 June 2012.

[23] Cardenas and Buranakanits, 1999, p. 61, see *supra* note 3; Abbott and Bowman, 1994, p. 214, see *supra* note 3.

[24] Fischer, 1996, pp. 341–342, see *supra* note 6.

[25] Cardenas and Buranakanits, 1999, p. 51, see *supra* note 3.

forum".[26] The wording of 'forum' implicitly indicates that there is a difference between APEC and an ordinary international organization.[27]

In conclusion, APEC remains an informal organization from a legal point of view.[28] This character of APEC derives partly from the fact that East Asian members appear to have considerable antipathy toward firm and binding legal commitments codified in formal agreements.[29] These members maintain that APEC cannot be a place for negotiation on legal commitments, but a place for voluntary cooperation.

### 2.2.4.2. APEC and Legal Obligations

As a result, even if consensus is reached on a specific issue, APEC never requires its members to assume legally binding obligations.[30] Accordingly, for example, the targets of the Bogor Declaration cannot be regarded as legally binding upon APEC members. Despite the absence of legal obligation, they are expected to voluntarily make their best efforts to achieve the agreed targets. In short, APEC is not based upon the idea that legal integration is indispensable to materialization of regional economic integration. Likewise, APEC does not pay much attention to binding norm-setting activities. However, this does not mean that it completely excludes norm-setting from the sphere of its activities. This point will be further examined later.

In any case, APEC rarely became a subject of legal study in the past, and legal scholarship on APEC is more limited than any other regional organization. The shortage of legal analysis on APEC derives mainly from the circumscribed role of law in the APEC framework.[31]

---

26 APEC, "Mission Statement", available at http://www.apec.org/About-Us/About-APEC/Mission-Statement.aspx and http://www.apec.org/About-Us/How-APEC-Operates.aspx, last accessed on 26 June 2012.

27 It should be noted that APEC began as an informal ministerial-level dialogue group, see Bamber, 2005, p. 428, see *supra* note 18.

28 Abbott and Bowman, 1994, p. 213, see *supra* note 3. Even if we assume that it can be considered as an international organization, it is a very loose organization.

29 Janow, 1996, p. 1009, see *supra* note 3.

30 Fischer, 1996, p. 343, see *supra* note 6.

31 Janow, 1996, p. 948, see *supra* note 3.

## 2.3. The Notion of IN-LAW and APEC

In light of the brief review of APEC in the previous section, this section will examine APEC from the viewpoint of IN-LAW. According to Joost Pauwelyn, the notion of IN-LAW consists of three elements: 'Informal', 'International' and 'Lawmaking'.[32] Therefore, before starting the examination of APEC instruments, this section will consider whether or not APEC's decision-making process meets these requirements for IN-LAW.

### 2.3.1. Informality

First of all, IN-LAW must be 'informal'. The notion of informality is defined "in the sense that it dispenses with certain formalities traditionally linked to international law" from three different viewpoints including 'output', 'process' or 'the actors involved'.[33] It follows from the examination in the previous section that APEC has fully satisfied those requirements of IN-LAW.

#### 2.3.1.1. Output Informality

First, 'output informality' means that international cooperation does not lead to a formal treaty or any other traditional source of international law, but rather to a guideline, standard, declaration or even more informal policy coordination or exchange. This is exactly the case of APEC. As mentioned before, APEC does not aim to negotiate an international treaty or agreement and has never produced any legally binding treaties. Instead, it has published many guidelines, principles and model measures, all of which are not legally binding upon its members.

#### 2.3.1.2. Process Informality

Secondly, 'process informality' means that international cooperation does not occur in a traditional international organization, but in a loosely organized forum. This also corresponds to the reality of APEC. APEC is not based upon any founding international treaty and is not equipped with any detailed procedural rules on decision-making. In fact, APEC can be considered as a loosely organized forum for discussion and cooperation

32 Pauwelyn, 2012, p. 13, see *supra* note 13.
33 *Ibid.*

among its members on various policy subjects. APEC can also be distinguished from informal negotiations for conclusion of treaties. Although APEC has, to a certain extent, been institutionalized as a forum for discussion, it has never been considered as based on a binding treaty. Therefore, APEC clearly meets this requirement.

### 2.3.1.3. Actor Informality

Thirdly, 'actor informality' means that international cooperation does not engage traditional diplomatic actors such as ministers of foreign affairs, but rather other ministers, domestic regulators and private actors in its process. This requirement is also fully satisfied by APEC. In terms of actors involved, APEC does not only include in its discussions traditional actors, but also other non-traditional actors such as ministers other than foreign ministers, and private actors. In particular, APEC has been positively accepting participation of various stakeholders including the "business sector, industry, academia, policy and research institutions, and interest groups".[34] This practice is clearly indicated by the establishment of the ABAC, which is working as the highest level consultative body. Other non-governmental actors have also been involved in discussions at the various levels of APEC.[35] In this context, the 'Guidelines on Non-Member Participation' are crucial.[36] Under the Guidelines, non-members including non-member economies (which are usually countries), other regional or international organizations, business/private sector representatives, academic bodies and other experts are allowed to participate in APEC meetings (such as APEC Committees, SOM Task Forces or Working Groups) as guests. The Guidelines stipulate detailed procedures for their participation.[37]

---

34 Stakeholder Participation, available at http://www.apec.org/About-Us/How-APEC-Operates/Stakeholder-Participation.aspx, last accessed on 26 June 2012.

35 *Ibid.*; for example, through "APEC Study Centers (ASC) Consortium" comprising some 100 universities and research institutions in the region, APEC members actively engage academic and research institutions in the APEC process (see http://www.apec.org/Groups/Other-Groups/APEC-Study-Centres-Consortium.aspx, last accessed on 26 June 2012).

36 Revised Consolidated Guidelines on Non-Member participation in APEC Activities (Approved by the 20th Ministerial Meeting, Joint Statement – A New Commitment to Asia-Pacific Development (Lima, Peru, 19–20 November 2008)).

37 Under the Guidelines (*Id.*), any non-member who wishes to participate in a specific APEC meeting will first submit its application to the APEC secretariat, and then each

### 2.3.2. International

The second requirement is that IN-LAW must be 'international'. This means that international cooperation 'must include two or more actors in different countries'.[38] It is easy to conclude that APEC meets this requirement. Since many countries in the Asia-Pacific region are APEC members, there is no doubt that APEC includes two or more actors in different countries. Since various ministers other than foreign ministers participate in APEC meetings, they cooperate in a trans-governmental context as regulators or agencies of their countries.

### 2.3.3. Lawmaking

The third requirement is that IN-LAW must be 'lawmaking'. 'Lawmaking' is defined as "norm-setting or public policy making by public authorities".[39] Prof. Pauwelyn explains that the term 'law' is used in a broader sense including statements or guidelines. However, it is notable that those statements or guidelines must "have legal effects or fit in the context of a broader legal process".[40]

Contrary to the first and second requirements of IN-LAW, it is still an open question whether or not APEC has engaged in such lawmaking activities. Without examining each informal instrument of APEC, it would be difficult to reach a definitive answer to this question. So far, APEC has adopted a number of principles, guidelines and model measures. In terms of their substance, these APEC informal instruments have some relevance to the domestic lawmaking of its members. Howev-

forum will consider the application and may approve on an *ad hoc* basis by consensus. Guest status given by the decision will be valid for three years including the calendar year in which the application is made. It should be kept in mind that authorization of participation in a particular forum does not imply any endorsement of future participation. To put it differently, permanent observer status cannot be given to any non-members. Although guests are allowed to participate in discussions with the agreement of the Chair, they will be excluded from the decision-making procedure. The Chair may also convene closed sessions excluding guests. The same procedure will apply to proposed invitations to non-member guests. However, details of their participation have not been made public yet.

38 Pauwelyn, 2012, p. 20, see *supra* note 15.

39 Pauwelyn, 2012, p. 21, see *supra* note 15.

40 Pauwelyn, 2012, p. 21, see *supra* note 15.

er, it seems that these instruments cannot be automatically regarded as instruments having legal effects.

This is because these instruments do not necessarily propose to regulate or control details of domestic legislation. In practice, APEC meetings will discuss and agree to certain policy targets (for example, five percent reduction of trade related costs within five years) or a certain direction of policy making (for example, regulatory reform). Then each APEC member will voluntarily decide to commit itself to such targets or policy direction, and will take voluntary measures in order to domestically implement them. In the process of implementation, APEC will introduce best practices of a certain member to other members in order to encourage them to adopt similar measures. Accordingly, it is not likely that those targets or directions will have direct impact upon domestic regulations.

APEC is based on an idea that a legal measure is not essential to harmonization of domestic regulations. In the context of its activities, APEC always tries to encourage its members to adopt similar policies for various agendas. This is because if they hold similar policy ideas, it is likely that they will inevitably adopt similar rules by and large. As long as they have the same idea, therefore, it is no longer absolutely necessary to set legal norms at international or regional levels. This has been a regional cooperation strategy adopted by APEC. Under such a strategy, which does not prioritize formal instruments which would clearly require the amendment of domestic law, it is less clear what the impact is on domestic laws of an APEC informal instrument. Therefore, it has to be carefully examined on a case-by-case basis whether or not each APEC instrument can be considered a legal measure. This examination will be made in the following sections.

## 2.4. Informal Lawmaking in APEC: APEC Guidelines, Principles, Codes and Model Measures

### 2.4.1. Overview

APEC has already produced a great deal of instruments such as guidelines, principles, codes and model measures. This section will list major APEC measures to be further examined in terms of their legal effect. Since informal international instruments must have certain effects upon domestic lawmaking, only measures which could affect the domestic laws of each APEC member will be listed hereafter.

In this context, it should be kept in mind that APEC instruments are normally regarded as "indicative references that may be useful to members" when they improve domestic regulations.[41] However, many of them explicitly add that they are not designed to change existing laws.[42] Their purpose is not to harmonize national laws. This chapter does not take these assertions for granted, but assumes that despite the official intention of APEC members, these instruments can actually influence domestic laws, and are able to have legal effects on them.

### 2.4.2. Trade and Investment Liberalization

As already mentioned, the main purpose of APEC is to liberalize trade in goods and services, and foreign investment. APEC members expressed their intention to remove trade barriers on many occasions. For this purpose, APEC has established the following principles, guidelines and model measures.

#### 2.4.2.1. Mobility of Business Persons

First of all, APEC members believe that mobility of business people is a key factor of free and open trade in this region. In order to promote such mobility, APEC members committed themselves to streamline immigration procedures for business travelers, and have implemented the 'APEC Business Travel Card' (ABTC) scheme since May 1997. Pursuant to suggestions by ABAC, the ABTC scheme gives genuine business travelers carrying an ABTC issued by each APEC member both "visa-free travel on their short-term stay" and "expedited airport procedures" when visiting other APEC members.[43]

---

41 Good examples are the "APEC Model Guidelines to Reduce Trade in Counterfeit and Pirated Goods" and "Model Guidelines to Protect against Unauthorized Copies".

42 *Ibid.*; likewise, many of the APEC informal instruments explicitly declare that some are not expected to have impact upon domestic laws. For example, the preamble in "APEC Principles on Disaster Response and Cooperation" pronounces that "they will not, in any way, affect the rights, obligations or responsibilities of member economies under international and domestic law" (2008/CSOM/020; "Concluding Senior Official's Meeting", 16–17 November 2008).

43 In other words, business travelers are able to enjoy exemption from individual visa applications for short-term business stays (as long as the card is valid, a card holder can always enter into participating members) and expedited procedures through special APEC lanes at major airports when visiting other members of APEC.

In the 1996 Summit Meeting three members agreed to initiate a preliminary ABTC scheme on a trial basis, and other members gradually joined this scheme. As a result, all APEC members are currently taking part in this scheme. This is a successful example of introducing a common system into APEC.

### 2.4.2.2. Free Trade Agreements and Regional Trade Agreements

APEC considers Free Trade Agreements (FTAs) or Regional Trade Agreements (RTAs) important tools for the promotion of liberalization in trade and investment. Therefore, it introduced a number of measures to encourage the establishment of RTAs and FTAs.

#### 2.4.2.2.1 APEC's Best Practice

Primarily, in 2004, the APEC Ministerial Meeting endorsed the 'Best Practice for RTAs/FTAs in APEC'.[44] Whereas 'best practice' is usually a tool for the diffusion of the best experience among APEC members to other members,[45] this code specifies conditions which RTAs/FTAs involving APEC members should satisfy (for example, consistency with APEC Principles and Goals, and consistency with WTO). In this sense, its substance is in fact similar to principles or guidelines.

#### 2.4.2.2.2 Model Measures for RTAs/FTAs

The aforementioned Best Practice document was drafted in a general or abstract manner. Therefore, APEC needed to further develop instruments for RTAs and FTAs. In the 2005 Busan Declaration, the APEC economic leaders recognized the promotion of high-quality RTAs and FTAs as an element of the Busan Roadmap aimed at achieving the Bogor Goals,[46]

---

44 See Document 2004/AMM/003 of the 16th APEC Ministerial Meeting, Santiago, Chile, 17–18 November 2004, available at http://www.apec.org/Groups/Other-Groups/~/media/D3CEA02503D04FB49D9859EA10D29520.ashx, last accessed on 29 June 2012.

45 For example, "APEC Economies' Submissions for: Best Practices Paper on Innovative Techniques for IPR Border Enforcement" (22 August 2007) provides APEC members with information on innovative techniques which are in use by a part of APEC members.

46 The 13th APEC Economic Leaders' Meeting, Busan Declaration (Busan. Korea, 18–19 November 2005).

calling for the development of model measures by 2008. In this Declaration, model measures were proposed, including commonly accepted RTA/FTA chapters, in order to create high-quality RTAs/FTAs in the region. Then, pursuant to this schedule, the Committee on Trade and Investment (CTI) completed its drafting work on model measures,[47] and those measures were accepted by the Economic Leaders in November 2008.[48] These Model Measures provide non-binding guidance for APEC members when concluding RTAs or FTAs.[49]

With 15 chapters, the Model Measures cover most subjects that should usually be included in ordinary RTAs/FTAs, and encourage the harmonization of regional RTAs/FTAs.[50] The chapeau of the Measures explains that with respect to APEC's principle of voluntarism, they are in principle not drafted in legal language that might be used in an agreement. Nevertheless some chapters are actually drafted in a manner that can easily be transformed into a legal text. In particular, the Customs Administration and Trade Facilitation chapters are drafted in a form, which is similar to legal text.[51] Likewise, some chapters set out very detailed definitions of

---

47 Committee on Trade and Investment, "2008 Annual Report to Ministers", Appendix 2 – APEC Model Measure for RTAs/FTAs, available at http://www.apec.org/Home/Groups/Other-Groups/~/media/441C73DB54E746E4835F883BF7154612.ashx, last accessed on 29 June 2012.

48 The 16th APEC Economic Leaders' Declaration, Lima Declaration – A New Commitment to Asia-Pacific Development (Lima, Peru, 22–23 November 2008).

49 For example, the chapter on Trade Facilitation is based upon the Best Practices for RTAs/FTAs adopted in 2004. The Measures are also based upon previously adopted non-binding principles. For example, the chapter on Government Procurement is built upon the APEC Non-Binding Principles on Government Procurement and Transparency.

50 Chapeau, see *supra* note 47; they cover subjects including Safeguards, Competition Policy, Environment, Temporary Entry for Business Persons, Customs Administration and Trade Facilitation, Electronic Commerce, Rules of Origin and Origin Procedures, Sanitary and Phytosanitary Measures, Trade in Goods, Technical Barriers to Trade, Transparency, Government Procurement, Cooperation, Dispute Settlement and Trade Facilitation. It is noteworthy that the Customs Administration and Trade Facilitation chapter was submitted by the ABAC.

51 Another example is the chapter on Electronic Commerce.

some notions to be included in RTAs/FTAs.[52] A couple of provisions also give exact time limits to customs authorities (Articles 3(2), 8 and 11(2)).[53]

The major motivation to adopt the Measures lies in the minimization of the 'spaghetti-bowl effect' arising from discrepancy among APEC members' RTAs/FTAs. The Measures, however, have not succeeded in fully harmonizing the substance of the agreements as some chapters allow a choice of options.[54]

### 2.4.2.2.3 Rules of Origin

Rules of origin are essential elements of RTAs/FTAs. The CTI has also worked towards harmonization of rules of origin among APEC members in order to alleviate the impact of the 'spaghetti-bowl effect'. It is noteworthy that business people have joined this discussion through both industry dialogues (the Automotive Dialogue and the Chemical Dialogue) and ABAC. At the time of writing, three measures have been adopted by APEC.

First, the Trade Ministers' meeting in 2007 endorsed the model chapter on "Rules of Origin and Origin Procedures" [55] and in 2008 it was integrated into the aforesaid Model Measures. The model chapter includes several interesting provisions such as accumulation/cumulation among APEC members, *de minimis*, treatment of accessories, spare parts and tools, and packaging materials and containers. Like other chapters, the model chapter is expected to become a reference point when APEC members negotiate RTAs and FTAs. Second, the 'APEC Pathfinder Initiative for Self-certification of Origin' was launched in 2009, and aims to intro-

---

52 For example, the chapter on Temporary Entry for Business Persons provides for the classification of business people wishing to gain temporary entry and a detailed definition of each category of them.

53 In addition, the Measures give advanced suggestions to APEC members. For example, it is recommended that they will set out an institutional framework such as an environment committee to facilitate the implementation of the environment chapter.

54 For example, the chapter on safeguards provides three options for the exercise of safeguards measures. The chapter on trade in goods also presents three options for the use of anti-dumping measures including non-use of AD between the parties to RTA. However, these measures are not enough to completely exclude discrepancy among APEC members.

55 The chapter on "Rules of Origin and Origin Procedures" in APEC Model Measures was agreed by the Trade Ministers in 2007 (Committee on Trade and Investment, pp. 78–81, see *supra* note 47).

duce self-certification practice for participating members.[56] Third, the 'APEC Elements for Simplifying Customs Documents and Procedures Relating to Rules of Origin' was adopted by the Market Access Group and the Sub-Committee on Customs Procedures in 2009.[57] This instrument proposes to simplify documentation and procedures relating to rules of origin. For this purpose, it presents several principles such as period of documents validity and waiver of document requirements for low value goods.

#### 2.4.2.3. Trade in Services and Investment

Several instruments were adopted for the purpose of liberalizing trade in services and investment.

##### 2.4.2.3.1 Non-Binding Investment Principles

First, APEC aims at promoting not only trade liberalization, but also investment liberalization. For this purpose, in 1994 the Ministerial Meeting reached a consensus on the formulation of "APEC Non-Binding Investment Principles".[58] This instrument outlines basic principles for regional investment on the basis of liberalization and fairness.[59] In particular, in line with the principle of open-regionalism, it stipulates that non-APEC investors should be treated equally to domestic APEC investors under the principle of 'Non-Discrimination between Source Economies'.

---

56 APEC Pathfinder Initiative for Self-certification of Origin, available at http://www.apec.org/Home/Groups/Committee-on-Trade-and-Investment/~/media/Files/Groups/ROO/App1_09_cti_rpt_Self-Cert%20of%20Origin.ashx, last accessed on 26 June 2012.

57 APEC Elements for Simplifying Customs Documents and Procedures Relating to Rules of Origin, available at http://www.apec.org/Home/Groups/Committee-on-Trade-and-Investment/~/media/Files/Groups/ROO/App3_09_cti_rpt_Simplifying%20Procedures.ashx, last accessed on 26 June 2012.

58 APEC, "1994 APEC Ministerial Meeting", available at http://www.apec.org/Meeting-Papers/Ministerial-Statements/Annual/1994/1994_amm.aspx, last accessed on 26 June 2012; The Sixth APEC Ministerial Meeting, Joint Statement (Jakarta, Indonesia, 11–12 November 1994).

59 Cardenas and Buranakantis, 1999, p. 58, see *supra* note 3; they include, for instance, transparency, non-discrimination (Most Favored Nation treatment and National Treatment), non-relaxation of social regulations to encourage foreign investment and minimization of performance requirements.

By and large, these Principles do not seem to contain any radical provisions. Their substance is rather modest.[60] One can argue, therefore, that these APEC Principles afford no degree of meaningful legal protection to investors from arbitrary and capricious actions of governments. Accordingly, the business society was not fully satisfied with them and, in October 1996, ABAC called for an expansion of the Principles.[61] In fact, most of those Principles were subsequently incorporated into investment protection treaties within the Asia-Pacific region.[62]

### 2.4.2.3.2 Menu of Options for Liberalization

Second, the Investment Experts Group compiled 'Options for Investment Liberalization and Business Facilitation' in 1998.[63] These Options provide APEC members with a number of specific choices. APEC members can choose one among these options when determining their individual Action Plans. The Options include guiding principles, which influence domestic law-making.

The APEC Group on Services adopted another instrument in 2001 concerning trade and investment.[64] This instrument demonstrates the basic principles which APEC members are expected to respect (such as Most-Favored-Nation Treatment, National Treatment, Market Access and De-regulation). It also provides an indicative list of measures which are to be included in individual action plans. Many of these principles overlap with

60 For example, they do not prohibit APEC members from making use of performance requirements. Instead, they only recommend that they minimize such requirements.

61 ABAC Meeting in Manila, Philippines 1996, List of Recommendations, 1996; Janow, 1996, p. 985, see *supra* note 3.

62 For example, they are incorporated into the Agreement between Japan and The Lao People's Democratic Republic for the Liberalisation, Promotion and Protection of Investment.

63 Options for Investment Liberalization and Business Facilitation to Strengthen the APEC Economies – For Voluntary Inclusion in Individual Action Plans, available at http://www.apec.org/Home/Groups/Committee-on-Trade-and-Investment/~/media/Files/Groups/IEG/03_cti_ieg_optionbizlib.ashx, last accessed on 26 June 2012.

64 Menu of Options for Voluntary Liberalization, Facilitation and Promotion of Economic and Technical Cooperation in Serviced Trade and Investment (20 August 2001), available at http://www.apec.org/en/Groups/Committee-on-Trade-and-Investment/~/media/Files/Groups/GOS/01_cti_gos_menu.ashx, last accessed on 26 June 2012.

obligations under WTO agreements, but they were important for some APEC members who had not joined the WTO in 2001.

### 2.4.2.3.3 Principles on Services Trade

Third, a trade-in-services specific instrument was also established. In 2009, APEC Leaders endorsed the 'APEC Principles for Cross-Border Trade in Services'.[65] This document recognizes many principles which have direct impact upon domestic regulations. These include the prohibition of requiring foreign service-suppliers to maintain local presence, and the prohibition of imposing a quantitative restriction on the number of foreign suppliers. However, they do not require APEC members to apply these prohibitions to all sectors at the same time, accepting their right to regulate and to introduce new regulations on cross-border services for policy reasons. Finally, their preamble explicitly indicates that they are non-binding principles.

### 2.4.2.4. Chemical Regulation

The APEC Chemical Dialogue was established at the beginning of the 21st century. In this forum, regulatory officials and industry representatives of APEC members discuss issues including chemical sector liberalization and chemical trade facilitation. Its activities have mainly been aimed towards promoting the implementation of UN regulations including the 'United Nations Globally Harmonized System of Classification and Labeling of Chemicals' (GHS) and the 'UN's Strategic Approach to International Chemical Management' (SAICM). In the latter context, in 2008, APEC Ministers endorsed guidelines entitled the 'Principles for Best Practice Chemical Regulation'.[66] The Principles explain that they aim at providing a framework for APEC members when they develop and implement regulatory measures. Accordingly, they are expected to have a certain impact upon domestic regulations. Since they guarantee a considerable margin of appreciation to APEC members, it is difficult to assess how much impact they will have on domestic regulations.

---

65 The 17th APEC Economic Leaders' Declaration – Sustaining Growth, Connecting The Region (Singapore, 14–15 November 2009).

66 See Document 2008/SOM2/CTI/024att2 (22 May 2008); for example, the first principle is that chemical regulations should be the minimum required to achieve their stated objectives.

### 2.4.2.5. Intellectual Property

Protection of intellectual property is crucial for most business activities nowadays. The CTI founded the Intellectual Property Rights Experts' Group (IPEG) in 1997. In 2005, the APEC Trade Ministers' Meeting endorsed the 'APEC Anti-Counterfeiting and Piracy Initiative'. Since then, the IPEG has adopted a series of Intellectual Property (IP) Rights Model Guidelines within the framework of this Initiative.

In particular, in 2005, the APEC Ministerial Meeting endorsed three model guidelines on anti-counterfeiting and piracy prepared by the IPEG.[67] Those guidelines are (1) 'APEC Model Guidelines to Reduce Trade in Counterfeit and Pirated Goods', (2) 'Model Guidelines to Protect against Unauthorized Copies', and (3) 'Model Guidelines to Prevent the Sale of Counterfeit and Pirated Goods over the Internet'. The IPEG has encouraged APEC members to domestically implement those guidelines. On the one hand, these guidelines emphasize respect for domestic laws of each member and expect to have no impact upon its existing laws, but on the other hand, they include many elements that might possibly affect future domestic laws. Therefore, it is anticipated that APEC members will modify their domestic laws in order to enhance the protection of IP Rights.[68]

### 2.4.2.6. Competition and Regulatory Reform

Reduction of tariff barriers encourages APEC members to pay more attention to domestic regulations. In this context, the APEC Economic Leaders' Meeting approved the 'APEC Principles to Enhance Competition and Regulatory Reform' in 1999.[69] These principles include non-discrimination, comprehensiveness, transparency and accountability. They

---

67 Three Model Guidelines: APEC Anti-Counterfeiting and Piracy Initiative, 2005/AMM/002anx4rev1 (The 17th APEC Ministerial Meeting, 15–16 November 2005).

68 For example, the first Model Guidelines make clear that effective enforcement regimes should include imposing criminal and/or administrative penalties sufficient to deter trafficking in counterfeit and pirated goods, and adequate civil remedies (3.(b)).

69 The Auckland Challenge - Attachment, Open and Competitive Markets are the Key Drivers of Economic Efficiency and Consumer Welfare (Auckland, New Zealand, 13 September 1999), see http://www.apec.org/Meeting-Papers/Leaders-Declarations/1999/~/media/Files/LeadersDeclarations/1999/1999_LeadersDeclaration.ashx, last accessed on 26 June 2012.

reflect basic principles that constitute the basis of domestic laws, and indicate specific policy directions. However, in addition to their non-binding nature, they do not necessarily lead to modification of national competition laws, since they are expressed in a general and abstract manner.

In 2002, the Economic Leaders also affirmed a series of transparency standards in several policy areas, including 'Transparency Standards on Competition Law and Policy'.[70] These Standards are not inclusive, and deal with only two issues: the availability of competition law information and the right to be heard before being subject to sanctions. They have not had any impact upon what type of conduct should be legally prohibited.

#### 2.4.2.7. Government Procurement

Opening up of a market for government procurement is an important element of market liberalization. The 'Government Procurement Experts' Group' (GPEG) was established in 1995 and developed a set of "Non-binding Principles on Government Procurement", which include value for money, open and effective competition, fair dealing, accountability and due process, and non-discrimination.[71] The Ministerial Meeting endorsed these principles in 1999.[72]

### 2.4.3. Non-Economic Subjects

APEC instruments have gradually expanded their scope beyond APEC's original focus on trade and investment, and are now also concerned with non-economic subjects.

---

70 "APEC Economic Leaders' Statement to Implement APEC Transparency Standards" (Los Cabos, Mexico, 27 October 2002).

71 Government Procurement Experts' Group, "Review of the APEC Non-Binding Principles (NBPs) on Government Procurement" (2006/SOM3/GPEG/005) (Government Procurement Experts' Group Meeting, Hoi An, Viet Nam, 8–9 September 2006).

72 The Eleventh APEC Ministerial Meeting, "Joint Statement" (Auckland, New Zealand, 9–10 September 1999).

#### 2.4.3.1. Anti-Corruption

Corruption may prejudice the proper functioning of a market economy, and some APEC members have serious corruption problems.[73] Although corruption does not necessarily have direct relationship with trade and investment, it has nevertheless become an APEC subject without any objection on behalf of its members. APEC economic leaders first endorsed the 'Santiago Commitment to Fight Corruption and Ensure Transparency' in 2004.[74] Then the 'Anti-Corruption and Transparency Experts' Task Force' (ACT) was established in 2005 for the purpose of coordinating the implementation of the Santiago Commitment. The ACT meetings are open to anti-corruption experts, law enforcement officials of APEC members, APEC Observers, ABAC and the APEC Secretariat. The ACT has already developed several documents: (1) 'APEC Conduct Principles for Public Officials', and the (2) 'Code of Conduct for Business: Business Integrity and Transparency Principles for the Private Sector', both of which were endorsed by APEC Economic Leaders in 2007.[75]

In terms of substance, the Principles are aligned with the 'UN Convention against Corruption' as well as the 'UN International Code of Conduct for Public Officials', and only stipulate basic principles which must constitute the basis of domestic laws.[76] The Code provides rules which private enterprises should respect. Unlike the Principles, the rules

[73] For example, it was reported that Viet Nam has such a problem (IAP Peer Review Report 2008 – Viet Nam (2009/SOM2/015anx2), at 11–12).

[74] The 12th APEC Economic Leaders' Meeting, Santiago Declaration "One Community, One Future" (Santiago, Chile, 20–21 November 2004).

[75] Complementary Anti-Corruption Principles for the Public and Private Sectors (2007/SOM3/012attB1rev1), The Third Senior Officials' Meeting, Cairns, Australia, 3 July 2007; Anti-Corruption and Transparency Experts' Task Force 2007 Deliverables (2007/AMM/008), The 19th APEC Ministerial Meeting, Sydney, Australia, 5–6 September 2007; The Fifteenth APEC Economic Leaders' Meeting, "Strengthening Our Community, Building A Sustainable Future" (Sydney, Australia, 9 September 2007).

[76] For example, "a public official shall use his or her public position only in furtherance of the public interest and not for purposes of gaining unwarranted advantages for him- or herself or for others".

in the Code are drafted in more detail as well as in a more statute-like style.[77]

### 2.4.3.2. Emergency Preparedness

Various natural disasters (including tsunamis and earthquakes) have frequently hit the Asia-Pacific region in recent times. Therefore, emergency preparedness has become one of the key issues in APEC's human security agendas. In order to respond to such disasters, APEC Senior Officials established the 'APEC Task Force for Emergency Preparedness' (TFEP) in 2005. The TFEP's main task is to coordinate emergency preparedness among APEC members. The TFEP also adopted the 'APEC Principles on Disaster Response and Cooperation' in 2008, which were endorsed by the SOM.[78] These Principles consist of 26 concrete policy suggestions to APEC members.[79]

### 2.4.3.3. Fishery

Fishery is an important industry for many APEC members. The first APEC Ocean-Related Ministerial Meeting adopted the 'Seoul Oceans Declaration' in 2002.[80] By introducing guiding principles, the Declaration clarifies ideal domestic and regional measures of APEC members in the field of fishery. In 2005, APEC Ocean-Related Ministers further endorsed the 'Bali Action Plan' to implement the commitments of the Seoul Declaration.[81] The Bali Plan was drafted in more detail on the basis of the Seoul Declaration, and it stresses promotion of cooperation among APEC members. There are some elements that encourage APEC members to modify

---

77 For example, those rules include the definition of bribery which shall be prohibited, Complementary Anti-Corruption Principles for the Public and Private Sectors, see *supra* note 75.

78 APEC Principles on Disaster Response and Cooperation, 2008/CSOM/020, Concluding Senior Officials' Meeting, Lima, Peru, 16–17 November 2008.

79 For example, the first principle suggests that disaster risk management should be incorporated into the process of policy-making by an individual member.

80 The First APEC Ocean-related Ministerial Meeting, "Seoul Oceans Declaration" (Seoul Korea, 22–26 April 2002).

81 Bali Plan of Action towards Healthy Oceans and Coasts for the Sustainable Growth and Prosperity of the Asia-Pacific Community, available at http://aimp.apec.org/Documents/2005/MM/AOMM/05_aomm_jms_1.doc, last accessed on 26 June 2012.

their domestic regulatory frameworks,[82] but most elements remain policy suggestions. The Bali Plan also pays much attention to capacity building of APEC developing members. The importance of capacity building reflects the wide discrepancy among APEC members in terms of their capability to implement any policy.

#### 2.4.3.4. Environmental Protection

APEC has been discussing environmental protection since its inception.[83] In 1994, the APEC Environmental Ministers' meeting already discussed two documents entitled the 'APEC Environmental Vision Statement' and the 'Framework of Principles for Integrating Economy and Development in APEC'.[84] The Statement emphasizes the need to integrate environmental considerations into other policies. In response to this emphasis, the framework sets out nine principles for sustainable development. These principles offer the basis for regional environmental governance, as long as they are taken into consideration by APEC members.[85] These principles include the principle of sustainable development, internalization of environmental costs, the use of economic instruments, and the precautionary approach. They are aligned with the 'Rio Declaration on Environment and Development' and can serve as a guide to the national environmental legislation of APEC members.

---

82 For example, in the context of protection of coral reefs and other vulnerable areas, they suggest addressing destructive practices such as reef bombing and cyanide fishing. However, they never propose prohibition of such practices (I.b. Managing the marine environment sustainably in Bali Plan of Action, see *supra* note 81).

83 In the environmental area, one author concluded in 1997 that APEC had focused on building common norms and developing the management capacities of its poorest members; see Lyuba Zarsky, "The Asia-Pacific Economic Cooperation Forum and the Environment: Regional Environmental Governance in the Age of Economic Globalization", in *Colorado Journal of International Environmental Law and Policy*, 1997, vol. 8, p. 356.

84 APEC, "1994 APEC Environment Ministerial Meeting on Sustainable Development, available at http://www.apec.org/Meeting-Papers/Ministerial-Statements/Environment/1994_environment.aspx, last accessed on 26 June 2012.

85 *Ibid.*; Zarsky, 1997, p. 348, see *supra* note 83.

#### 2.4.3.5. Public Health

The potential emergence of pandemics has increased the necessity for regional cooperation. In 2007, the 'Health Task Force' (HTF) meeting adopted 'APEC Guidelines: Functioning Economies in Times of Pandemic', which aim at promoting international assistance for combating pandemics.[86] This occurred in line with the APEC's Action Plan, which was adopted in the 2006 Ministerial Meeting.[87] In 2007, the SOM also established 'Guidelines for APEC member economies for creating an enabling environment for employers to implement effective workplace practices for people living with HIV/AIDS and prevention in workplace settings'.[88] The Guidelines include minimum requirements that should be satisfied by domestic legislation.[89] They also impose on APEC members many conditions for implementation with regard to their domestic health care, social security and health insurance institutions.[90]

## 2.5. APEC Informal Instruments and their Impact upon APEC Members' Domestic Law

### 2.5.1. Issues Relating to APEC IN-LAW

As the previous section reveals, APEC has already produced a great deal of 'informal international instruments' (informal instruments) such as principles, guidelines and model measures. Therefore, it seems at first glance that APEC's IN-LAW has been very active and fruitful. It is doubtful, however, whether or not all of those informal instruments can be rightly classified as 'lawmaking'.

As IN-LAW does not lead to the adoption of legally binding instruments under international law, an informal instrument has weaker in-

---

86 Health Task Force Meeting, Document 2007/HTF/004, Sydney, Australia, 5–6 June 2007.

87 APEC Action Plan on the Prevention and Response to Avian and Influenza Pandemics (Ministerial Meeting on Avian and Influenza Pandemics, Da Nang, Viet Nam, 4–6 May 2006).

88 Third Senior Officials' Meeting, Document 2007/SOM3/013, Cairns, Australia, 3 July 2007.

89 *Ibid.*, pp. 2–3: Legal and Policy Framework; for example, prohibition of mandatory HIV testing in the context of employment is included here.

90 *Ibid.*, p. 5: Health Care, Social Security and Insurance.

fluence over domestic laws than formal international law instruments. Nevertheless, it is presumed that in the context of IN-LAW, such informal instruments must have legal effects on domestic legal orders. In other words, if the informal instruments are not able to promote coordination of domestic laws in line with them to a minimum extent, they cannot be called "law" at all. In conclusion, some of APEC informal instruments meet this requirement, but it is difficult to prove that most of APEC instruments meet it.[91] In spite of the large volume of its instruments, one cannot definitively conclude that APEC has been functioning well as a tool for IN-LAW. This point will be further examined hereinafter.

### 2.5.2. Positive Examples of APEC IN-LAW

#### 2.5.2.1. ABTC Scheme

A few APEC measures certainly meet IN-LAW requirements. The most evident example is the ABTC scheme, which harmonizes national immigration regulations of APEC members. For example, Japan joined this scheme in April 2003, and has issued 1,715 ABTC's as of end-August 2006.[92] In order to join this scheme, the Japanese Ministry of Foreign Affairs issued a new ministerial decree in 2003.[93] Japan's participation in the ABTC scheme has produced visible changes at major airports in Japan, such as a special APEC lane for cardholders (similar to lanes for EU citizens at EU Member States' airports). There are currently over 80,000 active cardholders throughout APEC.

[91] According to an official of the Japanese Government, generally speaking, the impact of APEC's informal instruments upon Japanese laws has been very minimal. There are few cases in which Japanese laws were forced to modify themselves because of APEC informal instruments.

[92] Study Report of the Individual Action Plan (IAP) Peer Review of Japan (2007/SOM1/007anx2), First Senior Officials' Meeting, Canberra, Australia, 18 January 2007, p. 85.

[93] The Japanese Ministry of Foreign Affairs Decree No.7 on Business Travel Cards which is in operation within the framework of Asia Pacific Economic Cooperation (2004), available at http://www.mofa.go.jp/mofaj/gaiko/apec/btc/btc_04.html, last accessed on 26 June 2012.

### 2.5.2.2. Model RTAs/FTAs Measures

APEC instruments on RTAs/FTAs, in particular the Model Measures for RTAs/FTAs are other positive examples. Although many of APEC's informal instruments provide general and basic principles only, these RTAs/FTAs instruments are drafted subject-by-subject, and lay down detailed rules governing RTAs/FTAs. They influence the substance of RTAs/FTAs to a considerable extent. This is evident in the fact that some APEC members have changed their practices regarding RTAs/FTAs after the adoption of these measures. Most notably, rules of origin have been the subject of such influence.

#### 2.5.2.2.1 Model Measures and Previous RTAs/FTAs

First, the Model Measures derive from APEC members' past practice and aim at improving it. For instance, the inter-governmental negotiation on the ASEAN-Japan Economic Partnership Agreement (EPA) was concluded in November 2007. Since the model chapter on rules of origin was endorsed at the level of the Trade Ministers in 2007 as well, it was not likely that the model chapter would influence negotiations within the framework of the ASEAN-Japan EPA. Nevertheless, ASEAN-Japan EPA's chapter on rules of origin has a similar basic structure to the model chapter. However, several subjects recommended by the model chapter were not included in the ASEAN-Japan EPA.[94] These unincorporated subjects are not necessarily relevant to a basic structure of origin rules; although they are technical they have the potential to contribute to an improvement in the transparency of origin rules. Since the model chapter was drafted on the basis of APEC members' practice, it makes sense that there is similarity between the ASEAN-Japan EPA and the model chapter in terms of its basic structure. Nevertheless, the model chapter was more advanced than the previous RTAs/FTAs in other respects.

---

94 For example, they are the methods for determining whether accessories, spare parts and tools are originating goods, the method for determining whether sets of goods are originating goods, how packaging materials for retail use are to be considered, how indirect materials are to be treated, criteria for the treatment of material that is self-produced, the rules for transit and transshipment goods, and exceptions to certification requirements. The ASEAN-Japan EPA did not set them out. Available at http://www.mofa.go.jp/policy/economy/fta/asean/agreement.pdf, last accessed on 26 June 2012.

### 2.5.2.2.2 Model Measures and Subsequent RTAs/FTAs

After the endorsement of the Model Measures in 2008, their impact on APEC members' RTAs/FTAs is clear and visible. However, one cannot conclude that all of the recent RTAs/FTAs in this region are fully consistent with the Model Measures.

First, Chapter 4 (Rules of Origin) of the China-Singapore FTA (CSFTA), signed in October 2008 after the endorsement of the model chapters on rules of origin, includes 13 articles.[95] A few suggestions by the Model Measures (for example, rules on accessories, spare parts and tools, as well as fungible products and materials) were incorporated into these articles; but like the ASEAN-Japan EPA, the Model Measures' impact is only discernible, and not fully visible.

Second, in contrast with CSFTA, the Model Measures' influence is more evident in EPAs concluded by Japan than in the CSFTA. For example, Japan officially signed an EPA with Viet Nam in December 2008, which came into force in October 2009. The main part of a chapter on Rules of Origin (Chapter 3) is almost identical to that in the ASEAN-Japan EPA, but the Japan-Viet Nam EPA added six additional articles, all of which are directly derived from the Model Measures.[96] Those articles were drafted in accordance with the relevant part of the chapter on Rules of Origin in the Model Measures, and some of those articles use exactly the same wording as the Model Measures, but for small modifications.[97]

95 CSFTA came into force at the beginning of 2009, available at http://www.fta.gov.sg/csfta/chapter4_rulesoforigin.pdf, last accessed on 26 June 2012.

96 Agreement between Japan and the Socialist Republic of Viet Nam for an Economic Partnership, available at http://www.mofa.go.jp/region/asia-paci/vietnam/epa0812/agreement.pdf, last accessed on 26 June 2012. Those are Article 32 (Packaging Materials and Containers), Article 33 (Accessories, Spare Parts, Tools and Instructional or Other Information Materials), Article 34 (Indirect Materials), Article 35 (Identical and Interchangeable Materials), Article 36 (Operational Certification Procedures) and Article 37 (Sub-Committee on Rules of Origin).

97 For example, Article 32, para. 3 is a good example. It stipulates that "if a good is subject to an LVC-based rule of origin, the value of the packing material and containers in which the good is packed for retail sale shall be taken into account as originating or non-originating materials, as the case may be, in calculating the LVC of the good". On the other hand, the Model Measures state that "if a good is subject to a regional value content requirement, the value of the packaging materials and containers for retail sale is taken into account as originating or non-originating, as the case may be, in

A Japanese EPA is not an exception in APEC. The strong influence of the Model Measures is also found in RTAs/FTAs of other APEC members. For instance, the Singapore-Peru FTA, concluded in 2008, is strongly influenced by the Model Measures in terms of origin rules.[98] The New Zealand-Malaysia FTA, signed in October 2009, follows the Model Measures too.[99]

Third, it seems however, that the Model Measures' influence has not reached APEC members' RTAs/FTAs with non-APEC members. As regards rules of origin, for example, the Japan-Switzerland EPA, concluded in February 2009, did not follow the Model Measures,[100] and neither did the EU-Korea FTA, officially signed in October 2010.[101] These facts indirectly indicate that APEC members have actually respected their consent to the Model Measures.

It follows from the above examination that, as far as RTAs/FTAs concluded between APEC members are concerned, the Model Measures have considerable power to influence their content and have contributed to the harmonization of their substance to a certain extent at least. Therefore, it makes sense to argue that the Measures can be considered an instrument of informal lawmaking.

calculating the regional value content of goods". Clearly, these two provisions are almost identical.

98 Rules of Origin, available at http://www.fta.gov.sg/PeSFTA/04_rules_of_origin_final_2008_05_26.pdf, last accessed on 26 June 2012. They are articles on "Accessories, Spare Parts and Tools", "Sets and Assortments of Goods", "Packaging Materials and Containers For Retail Sale", "Fungible Goods and Materials", "Indirect Materials Used in Production", "Transit Through Non-Parties" and "Consultation and Modifications" (Articles 4.9–4.16).

99 New Zealand-Malaysia FTA came into force in August 2010, available at http://www.mfat.govt.nz/downloads/trade-agreement/malaysia/mnzfta-text-of-agreement.pdf, last accessed on 26 June 2012.

100 Japan-Switzerland EPA came into force in September 2009, available at http://www.mofa.go.jp/region/europe/switzerland/epa0902/agreement.pdf, last accessed on 26 June 2012.

101 Protocol Concerning the Definition of 'Originating Products' and Methods of Administrative Cooperation, available at http://trade.ec.europa.eu/doclib/docs/2009/october/tradoc_145192.pdf, last accessed on 26 June 2012.

### 2.5.3. Negative Examples of APEC IN-LAW

#### 2.5.3.1. Doubt About APEC IN-LAW

As regards to many other APEC informal instruments however, it is dubious whether they fall under the notion of law. This is because, although their substance has some relevance to domestic laws, it is not fairly certain that they have had any practical impact or effect upon existing or future domestic laws of APEC members. Even assuming that they do have some impact, it is difficult to prove causality between the endorsement of these instruments by APEC members, and amendments to their domestic laws. The next part will present some cases which place doubt on APEC IN-LAW.

#### 2.5.3.2. APEC IN-LAW and Domestic Laws in the Context of Peer Review

##### 2.5.3.2.1 Peer Review and Informal International Instruments

First, it appears noteworthy in the context of peer review that APEC does not have much interest in actual implementation of these APEC instruments. An Individual Action Plan (IAP) submitted by each APEC member is a core measure in the process of achieving APEC goals, and in order to encourage APEC members to satisfy their own IAPs, APEC has a system of peer review by other members. The peer review is mainly exercised on the basis of questions submitted by appointed experts and other APEC members. Finally the results of the peer review are published in individual country reports which are available on the APEC website. The country reports include overall assessments on each member's developments mainly in the light of commitments in its IAP.

##### 2.5.3.2.2 Individual Country Peer Review Reports – Australia and Japan

A couple of recent peer review reports invoked APEC informal instruments for the purpose of assessing its members' progress. The typical example is Australia's review report. The peer review of Australia made an assessment of Australia's progress in light of the 'APEC Non-Binding Investment Principles' and the 'Menu of Options for Investment Liberalization and Business Facilitation'.[102] In particular, the Study Report on Australia evaluated the investment regime of Australia on the basis of non-binding principles of non-discrimination, national treatment, and minimization of performance requirements referred to in these Principles and Options.[103] In the field of government procurement, the Study Report also evaluated Australia's procurement framework in light of the 'APEC Non-Binding Principles on Government Procurement'.[104]

In addition to Australia, Japan's peer review affirmed that Japan's investment policy regime was compatible with 'APEC's Non-Binding Investment Principles' and 'Menu of Options for Investment Liberalization and Business Facilitation' too.[105] The Study Report on Japan furthermore mentioned the implementation of both 'Principles to Enhance Competition and Regulatory Reform' and 'Transparency Standards for Competition Law and Policy'. It briefly examined recent amendments to the Antimonopoly Act and regulatory reform in Japan, in light of these principles and standards.[106]

#### 2.5.3.2.3 Informal Instruments as Reference Points

As far as these instruments are concerned, therefore, it seems at first glance that they function as a reference point in the framework of peer review, except for the degree of their effect upon domestic laws. However, this conclusion cannot be definitively confirmed.

---

[102] Report of the Individual Action Plan (IAP) Peer Review of Australia (2007/SOM1/008), First Senior Officials' Meeting, Canberra, Australia, 18 January 2007; Study Report on Australia's 2006 Individual Action Plans (IAP) (2007/SOM1/008anx2), First Senior Officials' Meeting, Canberra, Australia, 18 January 2007.

[103] Study Report, see *supra* note 102; The Study Report is attached to the Peer Review Report as an annex.

[104] Study Report, see *supra* note 102; furthermore, it confirmed consistency between the Australia-United States Free Trade Agreement (AUSFTA) and APEC Best Practice guidelines on FTAs/RTAs.

[105] Individual Action Plan (IAP) Peer Review of Japan (2007/SOM1/007), First Senior Officials' Meeting, Canberra, Australia, 18 January 2007; Study Report of the Individual Action Plan (IAP) Peer Review of Japan (2007/SOM1/007anx2), First Senior Officials' Meeting, Canberra, Australia, 18 January 2007, p. 37.

[106] Study Report, pp. 69–70, see *supra* note 102; the Report also referred to Anti- Counterfeiting and Piracy measures including guidelines adopted in 2005 (*Ibid.*, p. 58).

First of all, although it appears that some APEC instruments have been used as standards to assess domestic laws, the Peer Review's references to them are generally very simple and concise without any in-depth examination. The outcome of the Study Reports only confirms compatibility between these instruments and domestic laws of APEC members concerned. It is not possible to obtain information from these Reports on how those instruments have been implemented by APEC members, and it is questionable to what extent the Reports seriously examine compatibility of domestic laws with them.

Second, certain legal approaches can be found in the peer reviews of both Australia and Japan. However, there are other types of peer review reports which do not pay any attention to the informal instruments. A good example is the peer review of Viet Nam. The Peer Review Report of Viet Nam recognized that the Vietnamese Government considered APEC guidelines developed by GPEG when designing new domestic legislation,[107] but unlike the reviews of Australia and Japan, this Report did not make reference to any other instruments at all. This fact reveals that there is no consensus in APEC on how the informal instruments should be treated in the context of the peer review system.

Finally, APEC instruments referred to in the peer review reports vary and entirely depend upon the respective peer review. These reports randomly refer to several instruments without justification. It is not clear at all why one report picked some instruments up and did not take up others. Such arbitrariness may cast a shadow on the assumption that the instruments referred to in the reports come under the notion of law. This is because arbitrary use of these instruments is contrary to the essential nature of law which intends to achieve uniform application, although the degree of its real achievement may vary. Wide discrepancy among the peer review reports seems to reflect the fact that these instruments have not been functioning as norms or standards uniformly applicable to all APEC members.

Therefore, it is not possible to preclude serious doubts about a conclusion that those informal instruments come under the notion of law.

---

[107] Report of Viet Nam's IAP Peer Review (2009/SOM2/015), Second Senior Officials' Meeting, Singapore, 19 July 2009; IAP Peer Review Report 2008 - Viet Nam (2009/SOM2/015anx2), Second Senior Officials' Meeting, Singapore, 19 July 2009, p. 25.

#### 2.5.3.3. Other Instruments Not Mentioned in Peer Reviews

Most APEC informal instruments have not been mentioned in these peer review reports. The influence or effect of these instruments on domestic laws still has to be determined, because it cannot be assumed that the peer review examined all instruments. In addition, even if the informal instruments do not play a major role in the peer review process, it would be theoretically possible that they have been actually governing domestic laws and regulations in APEC. In order to prove the actual effect of these instruments, comprehensive research on domestic laws must be conducted for each APEC member. Due to limited time and space, it is not possible to undertake such research in this article. However, it is not inferred from the analysis in the reports that all of the non-referred instruments can be considered as having legal effects in domestic legal orders.

One example supports such a hypothesis. In the field of anti-corruption, APEC Leaders endorsed the 'APEC Code of Conduct for Business' in 2007. The Code prohibits enterprises from bribing public officials. In particular, the Code provides that enterprises should not make any contributions to political parties, party officials, candidates, organizations *et cetera*. In Japan, political contributions by private enterprises are not legally prohibited,[108] but it has become a political issue since 2009, whether political contributions by enterprises should be legally prohibited.[109] Nevertheless, the Code has not influenced the present discussion in Japan. To the author's knowledge, both sides of argument have never invoked the APEC Code. It seems that the Code has been totally ignored in Japan.

---

108 The Supreme Court of Japan recognized such political contributions by private enterprises as lawful in its judgment of 24 June 1970; see Supreme Court of Japan, *Claim to Pursue the Responsibility of Directors*, Judgment, 24 June 1970, Minshu vol. 24-6, p. 625.

109 For example, a group of constitutional law professors started a public campaign to ask Japanese political parties to support the adoption of legislation prohibiting political contributions by private enterprises, available at http://blog.livedoor.jp/nihonkokukenpou/archives/51313328.html, last accessed on 26 June 2012. The ruling Democratic Party of Japan officially takes a position of prohibiting political contributions by private enterprises (Manifesto for the Upper House Election in 2010), available at http://www.dpj.or.jp/special/manifesto2010/data/manifesto2010.pdf, last accessed on 26 June 2012.

### 2.5.4. Overall Analysis of APEC Informal Instruments

#### 2.5.4.1. Introductory Remarks

It can be concluded from the previous examination in this chapter that some of the APEC informal instruments such as ABTC and the Model Measures for RTAs/FTAs may fall under the notion of law. However, it is still uncertain whether or not other informal instruments can be considered as law in the context of IN-LAW. Several APEC instruments have tried to harmonize domestic laws, in particular standards of its members. For example, the Bali Action Plan suggests that APEC instruments would improve production and post-harvest practices by harmonizing standards to ensure healthy and safe seafood products in the context of sustained economic benefits from oceans.[110] If they have the actual impact of modifying domestic regulations, they can be understood as a product of IN-LAW, but it is difficult to reach any definitive conclusion about their effect upon domestic laws.

There are several difficulties which constitute obstacles in reaching such a conclusion. These difficulties will be further examined one by one hereinafter.

#### 2.5.4.2. Practical Difficulty to Monitor

First, it is actually difficult to monitor how APEC members have implemented these informal instruments. Since, as previously mentioned, the peer review reports have not made use of many instruments as standards, they publish a very limited amount of information on the domestic implementation of informal instruments. Other information sources are not easily available to the general public.

#### 2.5.4.3. General, Abstract, Modest and Allowing Exceptions

Second, in addition to the practical difficulty of monitoring implementation, there are other difficulties in assessing the impact of APEC instruments on domestic legal orders. These difficulties are inherent in the instruments themselves. This means that many instruments are drafted in a

[110] Bali Plan of Action, see *supra* note 81.

more general and abstract manner than ordinary legal texts.[111] They are likely to have certain impacts upon policy making, but their vagueness makes it difficult to assess domestic laws in light of them. This is because such ambiguity or lack of precise definition in these instruments gives APEC members a wide margin of discretion in their implementation. This feature of APEC instruments derives mainly from an inherent element of APEC itself, which is dissimilarity among its members. There are large differences among APEC members in many aspects, such as the level of economic and social development, culture and religion. In order to achieve its common goals, APEC takes into account such differences among its members and respects their diverse, social, economic and cultural frameworks.[112] As a result, in APEC, progress in regional cooperation does not automatically lead to approximation of domestic laws. In this context, it should be noted that APEC has been emphasizing capacity building of its developing members in many policy areas. Capacity building and technical assistance are also emphasized in many instruments.[113] The importance of capacity building implicitly indicates that not all APEC members are able to apply the same norms at the same time.

#### 2.5.4.4. Reliance on International Rules

Third, full reliance of APEC on international rules also makes it difficult to distinguish the impact of APEC instruments from that of internationally agreed standards.

---

111 For example, "APEC Principles to Enhance Competition and Regulatory Reform" only states "Transparency in policies and rules, and their implementation" in terms of transparency (see *supra* note 69). This is very similar to a political slogan.

112 Preamble of "APEC Blueprint For Action on Electronic Commerce", attached to APEC Economic Leaders Declaration: Strengthening Foundation for the Growth (Kuala Lumpur, Malaysia, 18 November 1998), available at http://www.apec.org/Meeting-Papers/Leaders-Declarations/1998/1998_aelm/apec_blueprint_for.aspx, last accessed on 26 June 2012.

113 For example, the 1994 "Framework of Principles for Integrating Economy and Development" provides for the strengthening of capacity building through exchanges of scientific and technical knowledge (see *supra* note 84). Capacity building has also been emphasized in the area of food safety standards and practices (Draft Implementation Plan for Strengthening Food Safety Standards Practices in APEC Economies for 2008–2011 (2008/SOM1/SCSC/007) (First Sub-Committee on Standards and Conformance Meeting, Lima, Peru, 25–26 February 2008)).

As regards to harmonization of standards, APEC has been mindful that differing standards and conformity procedures can distort trade and investment flows within the Asia-Pacific region. The EU has produced a number of regional standards in the process of completing the Internal Market. Unlike the EU, however, APEC has not been active in establishing its own regional standards. Instead, in order to harmonize standards, APEC has preferred the promotion of international standards or multilateral instruments over its own standards. For example, the Implementation Plan on Food Safety Standards aims at harmonizing food safety standards of APEC members, to the extent possible with international standards (such as Codex, OIE, and IPPC).[114] Among international standards, WTO standards have been particularly important. For example, the IPEG works for the full implementation of the TRIPS Agreement. Their guidelines on IP Rights take note of consistency between domestic laws and TRIPS.[115] In one sense, APEC can be considered as a complement to the WTO. This is because some APEC members have not joined the WTO yet. It is speculated that their implementation of WTO standards have the effect of accelerating their preparation for WTO membership. From the viewpoint of the WTO, APEC's attitude towards them must be welcome. However, from the viewpoint of this article, it has become more difficult to discern an impact of APEC instruments upon domestic laws, as far as APEC members being WTO members are concerned. Since these APEC members assume legal obligations to observe WTO standards, any impact of APEC instruments cannot be distinguished from the impact of WTO standards. For example, such difficulty can be found in terms of tariff re-

[114] Draft Implementation Plan, see *supra* note 112; there are many other examples of adoption of international standards. For example, Seoul Oceans Declaration by the APEC Ocean-related Ministers also facilitates the adoption and implementation of international instruments relating to maritime safety, marine pollution, compensation and liability for environmental damage from ships, and the use of harmful anti-fouling paints (see *supra* note 80). The Bali Action Plan also encourages APEC members to ratify or adhere to UNCLOS, UNFSA and FAO Compliance Agreement (p. 5, see *supra* note 83). The Guidelines on HIV suggest that APEC members should consider ratifying and implementing the UN Conventions (such as the UN Conventions on the Elimination of all Forms of Discrimination against Women and the UN Convention on the Rights of the Child) and the ILO Convention (such as the ILO Minimum Age Convention) (p. 4, see *supra* note 88).

[115] For example, APEC Model Guidelines to Reduce Trade in Counterfeit and Pirated Goods and Model Guidelines to Protect against Unauthorized Copies, in Three Model Guidelines APEC Anti-Counterfeiting and Piracy Initiative, see *supra* note 67.

ductions.[116] This problem also arises in the context of other international standards and rules.

It should be kept in mind that the lack of interest in setting original standards or norms on a regional basis is inherent in APEC's structure. Unlike the EU, APEC does not have much momentum to search for regional standards among its members. If anything, in APEC, in particular among East Asian members, it is more difficult to establish regional consensus on any issue than to participate in a global or multinational system such as the WTO and the United Nations. Political, economic and cultural diversity among East Asian countries will often become an obstacle to consensus building for the adoption of regional legal rules. In contrast to this, within global organizations, their diversity will become relatively minor owing to participation of other countries outside East Asia. Therefore, APEC has been playing a role in connecting international rules with East Asian countries, and no tension has arisen between APEC instruments and international rules.[117] In this sense, APEC can be considered as being embedded in other international systems beyond the Asia Pacific region.

To sum up, instead of establishing its own rules, APEC has been inclined to accept international rules as much as possible. This tendency composes another obstacle to discerning the legal effects of APEC instruments.

### 2.6. APEC and Accountability Deficit

#### 2.6.1. Transparency in APEC

The IN-LAW process is often accompanied by accountability problems. In order to solve the accountability deficit, the accountability of the IN-

---

[116] It is reported that average tariffs in APEC members have been reduced from 16.9% in 1989 to around 6.2% in 2009 (see http://www.apec.org/Groups/Committee-on-Trade-and-Investment.aspx, last accessed on 26 June 2012). In addition, APEC's total trade (goods and services) has increased from 3.1 trillion US Dollars in 1989 to 16.8 trillion US Dollars in 2009 (*ibid.*). However, it is not entirely clear how much APEC has contributed to such changes.

[117] Kikuchi Tsutomu, "Chiki-Seido to Gurobaru-Gabanansu" [Regional System and Global Governance], in Yuichi Morii (ed.), *Chiiki-Togo to Gurobaru-Chitsujyo* [*Regional Integration and Global Order*], Shinzan-sah, Japan 2010, pp. 232–234 and 262.

LAW process may be pursued at both the international and domestic levels.[118]

APEC economic leaders repeatedly affirmed APEC's transparency principles in the 'Shanghai Accord' in 2001. Additionally, other APEC instruments also contain the transparency provisions.[119] These principles and provisions affect the domestic procedures of APEC members, and there has been little concern about transparency at the APEC level. To the author's knowledge, however, there has not been any argument at all about an accountability deficit in APEC itself. Why has APEC not been subject to any accountability deficit related criticism yet? It seems that the answer to this question is related to the subject of APEC's activities.

### 2.6.2. ABTC Scheme

As the issuance of a new ministerial decree in Japan indicates, the ABTC scheme can have actual legal effects upon domestic laws and determine how passport control procedures at major airports of APEC members should be organized. When joining the ABTC scheme, Japan did not amend its parliamentary legislation. Instead, the Ministry of Foreign Affairs issued a new ministerial decree. Nevertheless, the question of accountability deficit has not become a domestic issue in APEC. This seems to derive from the nature of the ABTC scheme. The ABTC scheme does not require any essential modification to the structure or substance of immigration regulations of APEC members. It only streamlines immigration procedures for genuine business travelers in APEC. Therefore, any ensuing modifications to domestic law are only technical in nature. It is quite usual that the discretion for making technical changes to domestic regulations is given to administrative authorities. Accordingly, the introduction

---

[118] Pauwelyn, 2012, p. 22, see *supra* note 15.

[119] APEC Economic Leaders' Declarations, Appendix 1, (Shanghai, China, 21 October 2001); the 10th APEC Economic Leaders' Meeting 2002, Leaders' Statement to Implement APEC Transparency Standards (Los Cabos, Mexico, 27 October 2002); the 11th APEC Economic Leaders' Meeting 2003, Leaders' Statement to Implement APEC Transparency Standards (2003/AELM/PIC/2) (Bangkok, Thailand, 21 October 2003); the 12th APEC Economic Leaders' Meeting 2004, Leaders' Statement to Implement APEC Transparency Standards (2004/SOM3/ACE/015)(Santiago, Chile, 21 November 2004).

of the ABTC scheme to APEC members can be exempt from criticism of the accountability deficit.[120]

### 2.6.3. Model Measures on RTAs/FTAs

Recent FTAs/EPAs between APEC members have generally followed the Model Measures on RTAs/FTAs. They have really restrained the discretion of APEC members. Despite such impact, accountability has not become an issue. The major reason may be that affected measures are not part of domestic legislation, but part of international treaties. As FTAs or EPAs are international treaties, the Model Measures never have direct effect upon domestic legal orders. They have actual effect upon RTAs/FTAs, but they have to overcome other hurdles in order to have effect on domestic laws. First, such a trade agreement normally has to be ratified by national parliaments before coming into force. Second, even after its entry into force, national parliaments are given a chance to deliberate and approve domestic laws to implement RTAs/FTAs. Since parliamentary approvals are needed twice, there is substantial distance between the Model Measures and domestic laws, and the intervention of national parliaments alleviates the extent of the accountability deficit. As long as national parliaments are guaranteed opportunities to discuss the implementation of international treaties as well as their ratification, accountability deficit will not appear as a serious problem.

### 2.6.4. Other Informal Instruments

Unlike both ABTC and the Model Measures, it is questionable whether or not other informal instruments have actually reduced the discretion of APEC members. These instruments have certain relevance to the substance of domestic laws, and are able to influence public policy-making of APEC members to some extent. However, it is another issue whether or not they are able to influence lawmaking at the domestic level. On the one hand, if these instruments would considerably restrict or limit APEC members with respect to domestic lawmaking, the accountability deficit argument would inevitably appear. On the other hand, as long as they only

[120] In Japan, a ministerial decree is subject not to *ex ante* parliamentary control, but *ex post* judicial control. The fact that there is no necessity to modify parliamentary legislation in Japan reveals the technical nature of this scheme, and such nature justifies the conferral of the power on the Japanese government to adopt the scheme.

guide APEC members' policy, an accountability issue does not necessarily appear as serious. This is because policy-making will not automatically determine the law-making process. Lawmaking before national parliaments requires autonomous procedures which are distinct from political policy-making by any government, although it is difficult to draw a clear-cut line between law-making and policy-making in the context of IN-LAW.

Accordingly, the non-appearance of the accountability deficit argument in APEC understandably indicates that many of APEC's informal law instruments have not produced real constraints upon domestic laws, or that citizens of APEC member states have not been aware of such real constraints. In principle, the effectiveness of informal law instruments is proportional to the necessity of accountability. If these instruments do not have real power on domestic lawmaking, it will not be necessary to discuss their accountability. Since these APEC instruments are not as meaningful as legal rules, they do not require a high level of accountability both at the international and domestic levels.

## 2.7. Concluding Remark: The Notion of IN-LAW

APEC has produced a great deal of informal law instruments, but it might not be a typical example of IN-LAW as this chapter shows. Alternatively, it is probable that APEC's experience offers a good opportunity to examine the notion of IN-LAW.

The original purpose of APEC was not to create legal norms or set standards, but to facilitate trade and investment policy coordination among its members. Accordingly, APEC activities have been leaning towards policy coordination from its foundation, but have also included elements for legal harmonization to the extent that such harmonization is indispensable to policy coordination. However, it is not easy to draw a clear line between norm-setting and policy-coordination, namely between law-making and policy-making. This distinction is an issue of degree in terms of effect on domestic laws. It is clear that if there is no impact upon domestic laws, establishing APEC instruments cannot be considered as IN-LAW. However, most instruments have more or less some effect upon domestic lawmaking as well as policy-making. The issue must be what extent or degree of effect is necessary for such an instrument to be regarded as a legal instrument. It is difficult to answer this question definitively. Assuming that the degree of such an effect may be low, many APEC instruments will be classified as law. If not, only a few APEC instruments will be regarded as law. In any case, a further study of APEC's IN-LAW process could contribute to determining how the notion of law should be defined in the context of IN-LAW.

# 3

# Informal International Lawmaking: Elaboration and Implementation in the Netherlands

**Leonard F.M. Besselink***

## 3.1. Introduction

Informality is the hallmark of present-day globalization. Formal distinctions such as those between public and private are not decisive if we are to capture the nature of globalization. Actor informality, process informality and output informality epitomize globalization. Informal international lawmaking as defined in the IN-LAW project is, then, essentially a phenomenon of globalization. In turn, it is in the nature of globalization that it takes place in 'a space in which the strict dichotomy between domestic and international has largely broken down'.[1] As many authors have submitted, international law no longer takes its primary effect in international

* **Leonard F.M. Besselink** is Professor of European Constitutional Law at the University of Utrecht. This paper was finalised while H.G. Schermers Fellow of The Hague Institute for the Internationalisation of Law (HiiL) at the Netherlands Institute for Advanced Studies (NIAS). This chapter began as a conceptual paper on constitutional parameters of the status of informal decision-making output in national legal systems, which was discussed at an IN-LAW research group meeting at Geneva, June 2010; next, it was discussed in a version focusing more on aspects of implementation and effects in domestic law, discussed at the IN-LAW group meeting at the NIAS in March 2011. The author is grateful to the participants and the editors of these volumes for their remarks and input. Special thanks are owed to Owen Neuteboom, who provided important research assistance, as well as doing most of the 'fieldwork' on implementation of IOSCO standards in the Netherlands, and drafted sections on IOSCO in this chapter.

1 Nico Krisch and Benedict Kingsbury, "Introduction: Global Governance and Global Administrative Law in the International Legal Order", in *European Journal of International Law*, 2006, vol. 17, issue 1, p. 1.

relations but aims at effectiveness within the domestic legal order.[2] International law's objective is increasingly its realization within the domestic legal order, and its effect is increasingly located within the national legal orders. 'The global is local', as the saying goes, hence the importance of examining the manners in which informal international lawmaking takes effect in the domestic legal order.

This chapter focuses on the status and implementation of the output of informal international lawmaking in the Netherlands, and looks at the manner in which certain types of informal international lawmaking in the field of the financial sector are implemented from the perspective of its consequences for accountability both in a broad social sense ('responsiveness'), as well as in a political and legal sense.[3] It looks at the constitutional explanations and implications this has.

The choice for the Netherlands is explained by the fact that it is a country with a typically monistic system as regards the relation between international law and national law, while it is also an EU Member State, which can have an impact on implementation. An initial hypothesis researched within the overall project was whether in monist countries, the reception of the products of informal international lawmaking would be different from and presumably easier than in dualist countries. This chapter corroborates the hypothesis that the Netherlands easily takes on board the relevant output within the legal system. This, however, is not due so

---

2 Jean-Bernard Auby, "Globalisation et droit comparé", in *European Journal of Law*, 2006, p. 48 : "Si l'on y regarde bien, on découvre que c'est de plus en plus au travers du droit interne que les normes internationales - en croissance, certes -, produisent leurs incidences. Ce qui est déterminant, c'est le fait que, notamment au travers des mécanismes d'effet direct, les normes internationales viennent trouver dans le sein des mécanismes juridiques nationaux - et notamment des mécanismes judiciaires- les ressorts d'une efficacité qu'elles ont bien du mal à trouver au niveau international. [...]Si l'on regarde bien, on observe que ce droit international dont le poids se fait de plus en plus sentir dans le droit interne, a une tendance croissante à s'éloigner des préoccupations internationales pour s'intéresser de plus en plus abondamment à des questions internes"; Jean-Bernard Auby, "Is legal globalisation regulated? Memling and the business of baking camels", in *Utrecht Law Review*, 2008, vol. 4, issue 3; Paul Schiff Berman, "From International Law to Law and Globalization", in *Columbia Journal of Transnational Law*, 2005, vol. 43, pp. 486–556.

3 See Joost Pauwelyn, "Informal International Lawmaking: Framing the Concept and Research Questions", in Joost Pauwelyn, Ramses A. Wessel, Jan Wouters (eds.), *Informal International Lawmaking*, Oxford University Press, Oxford, 2012, pp. 13–34.

much to its monist system as such. In the course of the research undertaken for this chapter, moreover, it emerged that other factors may provide more crucial clues to explaining the manner in which and the degree to which informal international law is part of the legally relevant sources in domestic practice. Apart from certain elements specific to the relevant informal international law output, broader explanations are found in the constitutional culture of the country which creates the 'fit' between informal international lawmaking and the domestic order.

We shall find that classic constitutional institutions of democracy and accountability are used to a limited extent to oversee the entrance of informal international law into the domestic setting, but almost necessarily these are quite limited and seem to that extent eclipsed by others. If this is true and can be generalized, it would mean that, instead of the widely propagated 'constitutionalization' thesis, international law is in a sense 'de-constitutionalized' in the framework of informal international law.

In this case study of the Netherlands, we limit ourselves, as far as the empirical material is concerned, to how output in the financial sector as produced by the Basel Committee on Banking Supervision and by the International Organisation of Securities Commissions (IOSCO), including both IOSCO Principles and the standards produced by the International Accounting Standards Board (IASB) fared.[4]

The structure of this chapter is determined as follows. The topic of giving effect to the output of informal international lawmaking in the do-

4 On the financial sector and these organisations in particular, see Chapter 5 by Shawn Donnelly, "Informal International Lawmaking: Global Financial Market Regulation, On the Basel Committee"; see Pierre Hugues Verdier, "U.S. Implementation of Basel II: Lessons for Informal International Lawmaking", in Joost Pauwelyn, Ramses A. Wessel, Jan Wouters (eds.), *Informal International Lawmaking* Oxford University Press, Oxford, 2012, pp. 437–467; David Zaring, "Informal Procedure, Hard and Soft, in International Administration", in *Chicago Journal of International Law*, 2005, vol. 5, p. 547; Michael S. Barr and Geoffrey P. Miller, "Global Administrative Law: The View from Basel", in *European Journal of International Law*, 2006, vol. 17, no. 1, pp. 15–46. The IASB is briefly introduced and further literature provided on by Maurizia De Bellis, "International Accounting Standard Setting and the IASC Foundation", in Sabino Cassese, Bruno Carotti, Lorenzo Casini, Marco Macchia, Euan MacDonald, Mario Savino (eds.), *Global Administrative Law: Cases, Materials, Issues*, 2008, Institute for International Law and Justice, pp. 9–15, and De Bellis, "Global Private Standards and Public Law: The EU Approach to Accounting Harmonization", *ibid.* pp. 15–19.

mestic legal order is essentially about determining the 'fit' (or 'misfit') between the two. This necessitates us first to describe aspects of both the relevant international lawmaking and of the relevant domestic legal order which could provide that 'fit'. Next, we examine how some of the output of the financial sector institutions mentioned is endorsed within the Netherlands legal order. On the basis of this analysis we draw some conclusions on the parameters of the domestic effects of informal international lawmaking. We next return to the issue of accountability and democratic legitimacy which has been haunting the informality of international lawmaking.

### 3.2. Informal International Law in Domestic Law: In Search of Elements of 'Fit'

It is not easy to say anything meaningful about the legal status of a phenomenon which precisely because of its intended informality also intends to escape from having any formal legal status. The 'output informality' of the decision-making of organizations and networks with which this book is concerned, makes determination of its legal status problematic. Fortunately, what is 'informal' in one context can become 'formal' in another. It is at this crossing point from informality to formality, from non-status to status, that we are to examine issues of accountability and legitimacy in this chapter. In doing so, we must examine the manner in which a 'fit' exists – or is lacking – between the informal nature of the output and the particular legal order in which it is 'received', implemented and elaborated. Highlighting some general characteristics of informal lawmaking and the correspondent characteristics of the domestic system, which provide a potential 'fit', should clear the path to studying more concretely the manner in which particular forms of informal international law enter the domestic legal order with its attendant forms of accountability.

#### 3.2.1. Functional Governance

One crucial aspect of nearly all informal international lawmaking is that it constitutes a form of functional governance as opposed to territorial political government. States, however, are territorially based political communities. Its purpose and objective is not a specific 'functional' interest but the 'general' interest, which in turn is conceived as a political category in terms of the relevant territorial entity. Functional forms of government within the state can be quite controversial and often sit uneasily with traditional, territorially organized representative democracy. Functionally organized government within the state is easily associated with forms of corporatism, neo-corporatism or consociationalism, which are often criticized for their potential of undermining the 'general' interest formulated on the basis of political democracy.

From the point of view of a territorially organized political democracy, the 'specificity' of functional interests can be legitimately served only to the extent that these can be aggregated into a perceived 'general' interest as determined by that territorially organized political community. Most Western states have succeeded in doing so, because functional governance has existed within all such state legal orders, though to quite different degrees.

Recognizing that most forms of informal international decision-making are forms of *functional* governance can explain some of the questions and issues that arise concerning legitimacy and accountability, as these stem particularly from the national constitutional frames of thought rooted in territorial political communities.

### 3.2.2. Ways in Which International Decisional Output Enters the National Legal Order: Formal International Law and Domestic Constitutional Arrangements

Our frame of thought as to the manner in which informal international lawmaking acquires effect in the domestic legal order, takes its starting point in the traditional manner in which *formal* international law does so. This should make it possible to examine how *informal* law compares to these methods.

Of the various forms of classic international law, the categories of treaties and decisions of (formal) international organizations under public international law are next of kin to informal international lawmaking as defined in this project. We focus on these in this section.

As concerns national constitutional systems on how international law enters the domestic legal order, *treaties* are the traditional form of international decision-making and in this matter precise rules and practices have existed at least since the 19$^{th}$ century. Constitutions link treaties to legislation and take their alleged legislative nature as the benchmark for the national procedures which allow treaties into the national legal order.

This has determined the accountability framework for the incorporation of treaties into the national setting.

From the international law perspective, treaties are – as far as the legal nature of the international obligations is concerned which they engender – outside the sovereign remit of each of the single parties; they exist inter-subjectively between the parties to the treaty.[5] But as to their conclusion, they must be viewed as the product of governments: they are classically concluded by government representatives.[6] Besides the similitude of a treaty to legislation, this is the other reason for subjecting this form of decision-making to parliamentary oversight. To the extent that national constitutional treaties consider treaty obligations equivalent to legislation, they require specific parliamentary approval; and to the extent that they do not, governments act in this regard under general supervisory and accountability rules of a parliamentary systems, such as the general concept of ministerial responsibility.[7]

A *caveat* is in place regarding the concept of a 'treaty'. When use is made of instruments which create legal obligations *not* having formal treaty status under *national* law, these may still be for all intents and purposes 'treaties' under *international* law.[8] These may take the form of 'executive', 'governmental', 'ministerial' international agreements, memoranda of understanding and so forth. Even though they are 'treaties' under public international law, in most countries these agreements do not require parliamentary approval under national law. Instead they may need a form of governmental approval, typically by the council of ministers, but

---

5 See International Court of Justice, *Case concerning Maritime Delimitation and Territorial Questions between Qatar and Bahrain*, ICJ Reports 1994, 14 at para. 27; Jan Klabbers, *The Concept of Treaty in International Law*, The Hague, Kluwer, 1996.

6 Article 7 of the Vienna Convention on the Law of Treaties.

7 We are here speaking in broadly comparative terms. This is not to deny that in some countries treaties which are not legislative in terms of binding citizens, affect their rights or impose obligations on state entities in the internal legal order. Thus, we shall see that in the Netherlands in principle all treaties (in the sense of public international law) require parliamentary approval. Moreover, in non-parliamentary systems of government, matters within the constitutional remit of the executive are usually excluded from parliamentary oversight, as is typically the case for presidential powers in the USA.

8 See Jan Klabbers, "Impact of Informal International Law before International Courts and Tribunals", in Joost Pauwelyn, Ramses A. Wessel, Jan Wouters (eds.), *Informal International Lawmaking*, Oxford University Press, Oxford, 2012, pp. 219–240.

this is not always and everywhere a rule of constitutional law. In the domestic context, in most constitutional orders with a parliamentary system of government,[9] accountability for these instruments is only through ministerial responsibility towards parliament.

For national legal orders, the specific substance of a treaty influences the particular form of entry into the national legal order. When a treaty concerns rights of citizens or otherwise affects existing legislation, the general principle in continental European countries is that parliaments need to approve such treaties before they can become effective within the national legal order.[10] The rationale is that such treaties are considered equivalent to legislation; they are in a sense legislative treaties. Interestingly, this requirement exists both in monist and dualist systems. This brings us to the conclusion that as to their validity within the national legal order, there is therefore no essential difference between monist and dualist systems with regard to this category of treaties: in both systems they require formal parliamentary endorsement before they can have legally binding force. This is an important accountability guarantee.

The legal status of decisions of (formal) international organizations is in the main determined by the treaty by which they are established. In the domestic legal order, the legal status of these decisions is as a general rule governed by the status which those empowering treaties have in the domestic order. This is also true in the Netherlands, which is one of the very few countries which mentions in its Constitution 'decisions of inter-

9 The US presidential system of government may be part of an explanation why in US legislation (which is the exclusive power of the parliament, Congress) there are relatively many provisions on participation of US bodies in institutions of informal international lawmaking, as this provides both legitimacy to that activity as well as a grip of Congress over such activity in the course of reviewing the relevant legislation; thus as regards the Basel Committee, *e.g.*, International Lending Supervision Act of 1983, section 902b, codified as 12 USC § 3901(b); see also *infra* Ayelet Berman, "Informal International Lawmaking in Medical Products Regulation", Chapter 10. For the other part of the explanation (the Federal Reserve being outside the separation of powers), see Barr and Miller, 2006, p. 33, see *supra* note 4.

10 This is at any rate the situation in, *e.g.*, the Czech Republic, Belgium, Denmark, Germany, Finland, France, Greece, Italy, Luxemburg (a general requirement for treaty approval), Norway, Poland, Spain, Slovakia, Sweden. For a treaty to effect citizens' rights within the UK it in principle needs transformation by act of parliament. In the Netherlands there is a general principle that all treaties require prior approval, but the legislative exceptions that can constitutionally be made to this do not guarantee that all treaties changing citizens' rights and obligations need parliamentary approval.

national organizations under public international law' alongside 'treaties'.[11] In the context of the European Union we find in several other Member States mention of EU decisions, but not of decisions of other international organizations.

It should be pointed out that treaties which 'delegate' traditional powers to exercise public authority to international entities usually require parliamentary approval. In many countries such treaties, at least with some forms of delegation of powers, require the approval by a qualified majority, and under certain circumstances this requires procedures equivalent or identical to those for constitutional revision or a referendum. Such procedures provide constitutional legitimacy to attributions or transfers of power beyond the state. They can be found in both monist and dualist systems.[12]

We now turn to the distinction between 'monist' and 'dualist' national systems. By these terms we mean legal systems in which international law forms part of a domestic legal system once a particular international obligation becomes binding on the relevant state, versus systems in which international obligations become an integral part of domestic law only through a separate national act by which they are incorporated into the domestic legal system respectively. Often the terms 'monism' and 'dualism' are used in an overly generalized manner so as to refer also to the priority or inferiority of international obligations in relation to national legal obligations in cases in which they collide, which is common in text books on public international law but, to say the least, a confusing use of terminology. Below we shall see that in the Netherlands, for instance, we have a monist system but not all international law has priority over conflicting national law. Monism and dualism are even mistakenly identified by absence or presence of the requirement of parliamentary approval.

In monist systems, as we just defined them, treaties form part of the national legal order from the moment that they become binding under public international law for the relevant state, irrespective of whether parliamentary approval took place or not.[13] Therefore even executive agree-

[11] Articles 93 and 94, *Grondwet*.

[12] Dualist: *e.g.*, Denmark, Germany, Ireland, Sweden; monist: Austria, Greece, Latvia, Luxembourg, Spain.

[13] But also in monist systems there may be a requirement of parliamentary approval for international engagements, as we will see is the constitutional principle in the Netherlands.

ments which are not 'treaties' in the national sense and hence do not need parliamentary approval form part of the national legal order. In dualist systems, parliamentary approval and adoption is usually the prerequisite for treaties to become part of national law, so this type of executive treaty would need formal parliamentary endorsement in the form of passing statute law before it can acquire binding legal effects in the national legal order and can be invoked as a standard of review in court. Treaties, whether encompassing executive agreements, memoranda of understanding or not, which have not been adopted into the national order by some act of incorporation, remain outside the legal system, although courts in dualist countries have of old found techniques of interpreting national law in conformity with unincorporated treaty obligations, for example, by relying on the assumption that the government cannot be presumed to have concluded a treaty conflicting with national legislation, or on the presumption that the legislature cannot be presumed to have legislated in conflict with the country's international obligations.

As to the *validity* of treaties and the output of the international institutions set up by them as part of national law, there is no difference between monist and dualist systems once the latter have approved the constitutive treaties in accordance with domestic constitutional requirements.

One can conclude that treaty approval by parliaments is the main form of endorsing formal international obligations. This tends to be *ex post* accountability in terms of the content of the treaty, but *ex ante* as to its operation. So if a treaty is the basis for further international decision-making, parliamentary approval of the empowering treaty provides a mandate for such decision-making. If treaties do not require parliamentary approval, parliaments have as a rule only the general instruments over executives they normally have, which in parliamentary systems of government is, for example, the rule of ministerial responsibility.

### 3.2.3. Informal International Decision-Making in the National Legal Order

The previous section concerned international law proper and the manner in which treaty law enters into national legal orders. We must now look at the manner in which informal lawmaking, which does *not* have the objective of creating rights and obligations *per se* under international law, enters the domestic legal order.

We first make some remarks on IN-LAW as an international (that is, inherently multilateral) phenomenon, on monism and dualism, and next look at possible forms of unilateral endorsement.

By definition, informal international law does not constitute treaty obligations and cannot therefore enter the domestic legal order in the manner described in the previous section. In terms of public international law, there might at least theoretically be other manners in which it acquires legal significance. For instance, consistent international behavior on the part of an actor has a certain promissory effect. Under the doctrine of *estoppel* such behavior may under circumstances prevent the actor from subsequent contrary behavior, as otherwise he would act in conflict with the principle of international good faith ('soft law'). This phenomenon is described in the text books on public international law with regard to state representatives, but it might also occur with regard to public and even private actors in the process of informal international decision-making. The principle of good faith could *in nuce* be or lead to the creation of a transnational legal principle of a constitutional nature applying to informal decision making. That is a point that may be relevant to the overall IN-LAW project, but outside the remit of this chapter.

Informal international decisions do not as such require parliamentary approval in any Western state this author knows of. Only in the context of national parliamentary scrutiny of EU documents, certain forms of decision-making that do not *per se* aim at creating legal rights or obligations would need to pass parliament. Also here this is a form of *ex ante* accountability which only has the most general sanction attending to ministerial responsibility; put differently, parliament may scrutinize European informal lawmaking, but only if it concerns a matter which would lead to a loss of confidence would parliament attach any sanctions.[14] Outside EU law no similar arrangements exist for the type of informal international law we are dealing with in this chapter.

It can be hypothesized that in practice, at the stage of the actual making of informal international law, it will by and large depend on whether these international instruments are related to other governmental

[14] For a recent description of the situation in the EU country with the strongest regime of document based parliamentary scrutiny, the UK, see Davor Jančić, "National Parliaments And European Constitutionalism: Accountability Beyond Borders", available at http://igitur-archive.library.uu.nl/dissertations/2011-1004-200607/UUindex.html, last accessed on 26 June 2012, pp. 233–300.

policy issues whether it needs dealing with in the national council of ministers in the form of cabinet approval or otherwise and whether they may draw the attention of parliament in its trail. But this plays a role as well as regards parliamentary accountability at the stage at which the informal law has already been made and needs national application or implementation in some form or another.

The status of the output of international decision-making as not creating rights and obligations under international law, might give rise to the thought that in dualist states these would not have any legal relevance, whereas in monist systems they might somehow. This conclusion would be dismissing 'dualist' systems too quickly. As we already pointed out, the classic manner in which in dualist countries courts dealt with non-incorporated international law has been that of 'consistent interpretation' on the basis of the assumption that the national legislature or executive would not have intended to act in contravention of international commitments they have previously engaged in. This kind of approach reduces the perceived differences between dualist and monist systems considerably when we are dealing with formal, hard law. But this is all the more a conclusion as regards informal law. After all, both in monist and in dualist countries, informal law, in as much as it is not *per se* creating rights and obligations in the way in which legislation does so, is not used as the primary legal standard, but can be used as a fact which acquires legal significance in the particular context of the case, just as other facts may do.

What seems more important is that in monist systems as well as under dualist systems the relevant international decisions can be accepted and dealt with unilaterally, since this is not dealing with such international output *qua* international norm. Precisely because the informal international output is not a treaty or in other ways legally binding law, the manner in which it is used in national contexts cannot be bound to whatever the implications of 'monism' or 'dualism' might be. It is to this unilateral endorsement which we now turn to.

Informal international output as defined in this project does not as such impose a legal obligation to take any particular steps to apply, implement or elaborate it nationally. If it is given any of these effects, this is not in order to comply with an international obligation to do so. This implies that giving such effect is an autonomous unilateral act. It is what German scholars have of old called 'self-binding' (*Selbstbindung*). Informal output which is not as such legally binding is unilaterally attributed normative value within one's own domestic setting.

Often some form of endorsement in national law of the informal outputs will take place in this approach, rendering informal output effective in the domestic legal order:

- passing relevant legislation;
- references in legislation to relevant international standards (for example ISO, NEN-EN, CEN, International Accounting Standards, IOSCO principles, *et cetera*);
- non-legislative policy measures with the status of 'quasi-legislation' as they exist in many administrative law systems, with similar legal effect as *estoppel* in international law, often based on legal principles of good faith or legitimate expectations;
- compliance by public officials based on discretion under existing legislation;
- by way of functional governance of either formal or informal nature: leaving it to relevant functional bodies or to actors on the market to adopt codes of behavior and other forms of self-regulation without further formal endorsement.

Each of these manners of endorsing informal international law has its own accountability aspects, which range from parliamentary accountability to sectorial responsiveness (responsiveness to 'stakeholders').

Finally, it is important to draw attention to a particular juridical technique for taking informal international law into account. This is endorsement of an informal norm or standard as a legally relevant fact without it having been transformed into a national legal norm of any kind. Although this can be done in a non-legal and unofficial context – factual compliance by, for instance, a market operator because he thinks it is fit to do so, for example, as he believes ultimately to profit from compliance – it is of special significance in judicial settings in which courts take into account informal international norms as legally relevant facts.[15] We will come across examples of this below.

[15] This phenomenon suggests that the ambiguity of the law/fact relationship is not always dichotomous. See Dick W.P. Ruiter and Ramses A. Wessel, "The Legal Nature of Informal International Law: A Legal Theoretical Exercise", in Joost Pauwelyn et

### 3.3. The Netherlands: Monism, Openness to the International Order and the Evolutionary Constitution

The Netherlands has generally been characterized as a 'monist' system. Many text books are imprecise as to the meaning of the term, and it is therefore often unclear if this judgment focuses on international law's forming part of the national legal order or on the superior rank of international law. The Netherlands is monist on the first point. On the basis of consistent case law since 1919, it is a well-established rule of constitutional law that both written and customary international law that is binding on the Netherlands under public international law, forms an integral part of national law. For treaties, this is independent from the question whether it has been submitted to parliamentary approval.[16]

The issue of the rank of the respective sources of international law is more complicated. Leaving aside some of the details, the situation is as follows. Since a constitutional amendment of the early 1950s which purported to facilitate European integration, the *Grondwet* (Constitution) provides that directly effective provisions of treaties and decisions of international organizations under public international law have priority over conflicting national law. In case of a collision of these norms the national provisions cannot be applied.[17]

However, in case of conflict between an international legal norm not being a directly effective provision of a treaty or of a decision of an international organization, national law prevails over international law.

al. (eds.), *Informal International Lawmaking*, Oxford University Press, Oxford, 2012, pp. 162–184.

16 As pointed out in footnote 13 above, in the Netherlands all treaties in principle need prior parliamentary approval (Art. 91 (1) *Grondwet*). Exceptions are made on the basis of the Act for the Realm on the Approval and Publication of Treaties (*Rijkswet goedkeuring en bekendmaking verdragen*), which includes secret treaties (which must be approved *a posteriori* once the reasons for secrecy no longer apply), treaties implementing earlier treaties which have been approved by parliament and short term treaties which do not involve high cost for the state.

17 Article 94 *Grondwet*: "Statutory regulations in force within the Kingdom shall not be applicable if such application is in conflict with provisions of treaties or of decisions by international organisations under public international law, which can bind everyone".

National law also prevails over customary international norm and general principles of international law.[18]

As regards European Union law, the constitutional provisions on the priority of decisions of international organizations had the very purpose of guaranteeing the priority of directly effective European law over conflicting national legislation. After 1983, the larger part of the constitutional and European doctrine has taken the stance that these constitutional provisions do not apply with regard to European law, as the EU's legal effect in the national legal order is taken to be determined autonomously by EU law.[19]

On the basis of the sketch of the state of affairs so far, the conclusion may be that the output of informal international decision-making can only clarify that it can never overrule statutory provisions, unless EU law would attribute such superior rank to informal norms. The constitutional rules do not seem to guarantee that informal international law is part of the national legal order. The legal rule on monism is, after all, restricted to legally binding international norms. But it does not prevent them to acquire any effect either. In order to search for the possibilities of a 'fit' between the Netherlands' legal order and informal international law, we need to look for other elements.

One of these elements is the underlying openness to the international legal order of which 'monism' and the superior rank of directly effective international law is but an expression. This openness coincides with the natural interests of the Netherlands viewed from the geo-political and economic point of view. The Netherlands is a relatively small country, but for centuries it possessed important overseas territories and as a seafaring nation was for a while a superpower on the world scene. Its size has to a considerable extent been compensated for by its location in the delta of main continental rivers, the Rhine and Meuse, which made large parts of

---

[18] This has been established by the Netherlands Supreme Court, *Hoge Raad*, 6 March 1959, *Nyugat*, Nederlandse Jurisprudentie 1962, 2 and re-confirmed in *Hoge Raad*, 18 September 2001, *Bouterse*, available at http://www.rechtspraak.nl, LJN-number: AB1471.

[19] For a brief discussion, see Leonard Besselink, "The Netherlands Constitutional Law and European Integration" in *European Public Law*, 1996, vol. 2, no. 1, pp. 34–39; more elaborately, Leonard Besselink, "An Open Constitution and European Integration: The Kingdom of the Netherlands" in *SEW Tijdschrift voor Europees en economisch recht*, 1996, vol. 44, no. 6, pp. 192–206.

the European continent into Holland's hinterland, while its North Sea coast opened up the country to other parts of the world. Its economic potential, as well as its colonial empire, was based on its sea power as well as its favorable location for international trade, and to a large extent it still is. Politically, its international orientation was to a large extent westward (North-Atlantic), but at the same time in favor of supranational integration of Western Europe. In this respect, the economic and trade interest has been dominant. This exposure to international relations has been reflected in constitutional history, even to the level of concrete constitutional provisions, which can be traced to international historical developments.[20]

This openness to international relations fits in well with the type of constitution the Netherlands has. If we distinguish between the revolutionary blue-print constitutions which claim to govern and modify the fate and future of the political community on the one hand, and the evolutionary constitutions which take on board whatever political settlement has been reached in practice in an incremental long-term fashion, the Netherlands' constitution belongs to the latter. It is not like most continental European constitutions that are rooted in post-French Revolutionary ideas of sovereignty, the nation and the *pouvoir constituant*. In fact, like the British constitution, it is impossible to say what legally the 'original' Netherlands constitution was, and those of 1814, 1815, 1840 and 1848 as well as that of 1983 are considered milestones, though for instance the latter has been adopted in accordance with the rules of amendment, while some of the others were not. Unlike continental constitutions like the French, German and Italian ones, there is no strong constitutional theory of sovereignty (a concept with which one has constitutionally dispensed in this part of the Low Lands since the end of the 16th century, initially for political reasons[21]). This facilitates incoming international norms.

So it is arguable that it is not monism which makes for the openness of the Netherlands' legal order to international law and order, but the constitutional openness of the Netherlands that has been expressed in its monism.

---

20 See for a description Leonard Besselink, "Grundstrukturen staatlichen Verfassungsrechts: Niederlande", in Armin von Bogdandy, Pedro Cruz Villalón, Peter M. Huber (eds.), *Handbuch Ius Publicum Europaeum, Band I: Nationales Verfassungsrecht*, C. F. Mueller Verlag, Heidelberg, 2007, pp. 327–388, paras. 1–60.

21 See also Besselink, "An Open Constitution and European Integration: The Kingdom of the Netherlands", 1996, pp. 192–195, see *supra* note 19.

The absence of a strong notion of the nation, the people and popular or other sovereignty that we mentioned, has also meant that there is no constitutional theory of the ultimate source of law and political authority. This means that in the Netherlands there is no problem in recognizing the legal relevance and authority of norms which have been generated outside the state system in the strict sense.

This is confirmed by the 'new' doctrine of the autonomous effect of EU law in the Netherlands' legal order, which is now held to be *praeter constitutionem*. Although there are dissenting views on this matter, the majority view proves the constitutional openness in accepting heteronomy, that is to say, law stemming from sources outside the constitutionally recognized ones, from external legal orders, as part of the national legal order, even with overriding legal rank.

Also, state sources and non-state sources of public authority outside that of the national state are acknowledged. The Constitution (*Grondwet*) itself confirms that public authority may be exercised by autonomous bodies of territorially decentralized government with an original power to legislate their own affairs (municipalities and provinces), as well as a broad range of other bodies which include Waterboards (*waterschappen*, who govern water levels (and some qualitative aspects) of surface and underground water by legislation, executive and taxation powers).[22] But also 'public bodies for the professions and trades and other public bodies' with legislative, executive and taxation powers, of which a plethora have been established by act of parliament, almost all of which govern specific sectors of the economy, and play a crucial role in, for instance, the conclusion of collective labor agreements, and provide fora for economic factors of labor and enterprise to consult and coordinate with representatives of the political system.[23]

Such a broad inclusion of the public and actors within the public domain has been favored by the social structure of the country, which historically has been made up by religious denominational minorities which needed to strive to consensus in order to make the political and social system work. In the period of the last quarter of the 19th century till the end of the 1960s, this translated into the 'pillarized society' which was both socially and politically organized along denominational lines: each group

[22] Art. 133 *Grondwet*.

[23] Art. 134 *Grondwet*.

had its own sports clubs, trade unions, leisure societies, newspapers and broad casting associations and political parties. 'Consociationalism' was the principle on which the country functioned.[24]

Functional government has been part of the constitutional habitus, even if it involves major 'private' actors. The General Administrative Law Act thus defines as 'public authority' not only institutions, bodies and organs established under public law, but also "any other person or body corporate which is invested with the exercise of any public authority".[25]

Democracy in the Netherlands is therefore also a much broader notion than one which identifies it with the constitutional institution of parliament. Even parliamentary democracy is conceived differently from that in some other continental countries in the sense that political parties are strictly private law entities, which are not governed by public law. Social and economic participatory structures are as much part of democracy in the Netherlands.

It is hypothesized that both in the openness to international law and international relations and in the constitutional open culture, a 'fit' can be found which allows informal international law to enter into the domestic order.

### 3.4. Output of Informal International Decision-Making: Some Findings Concerning the Financial Sector

In this section we turn to a brief discussion of how output of the Basel Committee, the International Organisation of Security Commissions (IOSCO) as well as the International Accounting Standards Board (IASB) has fared in the course of implementation in the Netherlands legal order, in particular from the point of view of 'accountability'. In order to do so we have to briefly introduce the 'counterparts' of these international institutions in the Netherlands, that is to say the institutions which ultimately have to apply the output.

---

[24] See the work of Arend Lijphart, *The Politics of Accommodation. Pluralism and Democracy in the Netherlands*, University of California Press, Berkeley, 1968; *Democracy in Plural Societies: A Comparative Exploration*, Yale University Press, New Haven, 1977; *Patterns of Democracy: Government Forms and Performance in Thirty-six Countries*, Yale University Press, New Haven, 1999.

[25] General Administrative Law Act, (*Algemene wet bestuursrecht*), Article 1:1, para. 1.

First, it is useful to point out that supervision in the financial sector follows a 'twin peak' model. The prudential and systemic oversight is fully concentrated in the central bank, *De Nederlandsche Bank NV* (DNB) while the 'conduct of business' supervision is concentrated in the Financial Market Authority, *Autoriteit Financiële Markten* (AFM). The Nederlandsche Bank both participates in the Basel Committee and plays a main role in the elaboration, implementation and application of its output. The AFM is a main player for the Netherlands in IOSCO, though the central bank is also represented in IOSCO.

### 3.4.1. The Basel Committee on Banking Supervision, the Netherlands Central Bank and Accountability

The Netherlands belongs to the 25 countries with the most interconnected economies in the world. According to the IMF, the Netherlands is financially the seventh most interconnected country.[26] It is one of the eight largest global common lenders (together with Switzerland, US, UK, France, Germany, Spain, Japan).[27] Traditionally, the Netherlands has played an active role in the Bank for International Settlements. Until recently, the President of the Netherlands Central Bank, DNB, Nout Wellink, was chair of the Basel Committee on Banking Supervision.

DNB has the legal form of a public limited company established under private law, of which all shares are owned by the State of the Netherlands. All its powers, however, derive primarily from a series of acts of parliament, of which the *Wet financieel toezicht* (Act on Financial Supervision) and *Bankwet 1998* give the most important institutional provisions and guarantee their independence. As we have mentioned, under Dutch administrative law the exercise of its authority brings DNB into the same category as public authorities established under public law.[28] As a consequence, all general provisions of administrative law apply in principle to their operation and decisions, including legal protection against their acts.

---

26 IMF, The Netherlands Financial Sector Assessment, available at http://www.imf.org/external/np/ms/2010/121410.htm, last accessed on 26 June 2012.

27 IMF, Understanding Financial Connectedness, Supplementary Information, 5 October 2010, p. 8.

28 *Algemene wet bestuursrecht*, Art. 1:1(1).

The functions (and members of) these institutions in the international network or in other organizations like the Basel Committee and IOSCO are not regulated by national law.

The elaboration of rulemaking by the Basel Committee has overall not been accompanied by national procedures which more broadly involve political institutions. The central bank does involve stakeholders in the national elaboration of policy measures and standards under standard procedures of notice and comment, even though the Dutch General Administrative Law Act does not make such procedures compulsory.

DNB published its policy approaches, partly in the form of quasi-legislation ('*Beleidsregels*') on its website, most of which are notified in one of the official journals, the *Staatscourant*. With a view to implementation of the Basel II package, consultations, information and training were organized for the sector. The Ministry of Finance also consulted the sector with regard to the implementation legislation.

Both during the negotiations of the Basel II and III packages, the government in the person of the Minister of Finance as well as (the President of) the Central Bank kept the Lower House informed on the Basel Committee.

The Lower House of the States General (*Tweede Kamer*) was informed about the progress of the Basel II process by three letters of the Minister of Finance (2001 and 2002) and by a technical briefing by *De Nederlandsche Bank* (June 2001). The letters were discussed in a parliamentary committee with the minister. Most critical was one remark by the Green Left MP on the alleged devolving of responsibility to the banks themselves, by the introduction of the internal rating system in Basel II. In similar fashion, parliament has been kept abreast of the elaboration of Basel III, both by the Minister of Finance and through briefings by *De Nederlandsche Bank*, one of which was conducted by the president of the Bank himself (who as we mentioned was then also chairing the Basel Committee).

Domestic legal implementation of the output of the Basel Committee is often mediated by EU legislative measures if it comes to turning it from non-law, informal or soft law into hard, formal law. This is particularly the case with the Basel packages.

Thus, EC-Directives 2006/48, Banking Directive or Capital Requirements Directive, and 2006/49, implemented the Basel II Accord.

These directives were not intensively scrutinized by either of the two Houses of Parliament, but merely taken notice of. This was offset by the fact that the process of implementation of the directives by legislation had started some months before the Directives were actually adopted, for reason of the relatively short implementation period and the importance of timely implementation.

The draft EU legislation adopting the Basel Accord III was scrutinized by the Upper House (*Eerste Kamer*). Major issues were the desire expressed by parliament to turn the directives which implemented Basel I and II into a regulation. This was related to the desire to avoid member states reverting to 'gold plating' over and above minimum rules, that is to say add extra requirements for specific situations within the relevant member state because EU law only establishes minimum standards. While the Swedish parliament has on this point issued a reasoned opinion in the framework of the EU subsidiarity mechanism, arguing that member states should have such discretion with a view to the stability of the national financial system, the Dutch feared that this would upset the 'level playing field'.[29]

In the Netherlands the Directives which turned Basel II into formal law, were implemented by an Act of Parliament entitled *Wet implementatie kapitaalakkoord Bazel II*, of 20 November 2006, amending the *Wet financieel toezicht*, as well as through an Order in Council (*algemene maatregel van bestuur*) *Besluit prudentiële regels Wft* (also known as *Amvb 5*).[30] The Netherlands' financial institutions had to implement Basel II per 1 January 2008 at the latest. Not only the Bill for the relevant Act but also the draft Order in Council was submitted to and discussed in Parliament.[31]

The scope for autonomous policy choices were limited, and on the whole avoided. The *Raad van State* (Council of State) criticized the initial choice in the bill implementing the Directives to regulate elements from the 'third pillar' of Basel II by Order in Council instead of Act of Parliament, because of the principle that important elements should be incorpo-

---

29 Relevant documents can be retrieved through http://www.ipex.eu/IPEXL-WEB/dossier/document/COM20110453.do#dossier-COD20110203, last accessed on 29 June 2012.

30 *Staatsblad* [Official Journal of the Kingdom of the Netherlands] 2006, p. 662.

31 *Kamerstukken* [Parliamentary documents], Tweede Kamer [Lower House], 29 708, no. 31 with annexes, as well as the parliamentary documents under that file number.

rated into the Act rather than in delegated legislation. The criticism led to changes in the Bill before it was introduced in parliament.

Parliamentary concerns were voiced. Some major points of concern were whether implementation should not go beyond what the Directives requires ('gold plating'), the alleged risk that there was change in approach from a 'principle based' to a 'rule based' approach. Both criticisms were rejected, though the second point was not argued in great detail.

Whereas some of the accountability practices indicated so far concern *a priori* accountability towards parliament, there is also a somewhat limited form of *ex post facto* accountability in which the Basel Committee and its output were involved. This was mainly in the aftermath of the financial crisis of 2008, in which one Dutch bank, DSB, went bankrupt, as did the IceSave, under which name the Icelandic Landsbanki Íslands bank operated very actively in the Netherlands; the 2008 crisis also necessitated major interventions including the nationalization of ABN. This gave rise to more attention by the political actors towards the supervisory institutions and to some extent the Basel Committee.

The President of the central bank *DNB* (and chair of the Basel Committee), in a hearing during a first parliamentary investigation[32] into the financial crisis in the Netherlands, declared during his witness that lobbying does not immediately take place at the Basel Committee, although before and after sessions of the Committee, exchanges of views take place with representatives of the Committee, but this is not the real lobbying; this takes place, he submitted, at the national level with the supervisors of the banks (*id est*, presidents of central banks). Other witnesses testified that severe lobbying takes place in Washington, and that it is 'general knowledge' that the presidents each meet with CEO's of the most important international banks regularly.[33]

Criticism was expressed by the parliamentary committee of investigation as to the lack of transparency regarding the existence and role of

32 A second parliamentary investigation, with powers to hold hearings in which (compulsory) witness is taken under oath, focusing on the role of parliament and the alleged inadequate accountability towards parliament during the crisis, with special attention to the nationalization of ABN, was decided on 16 November 2010, see *Kamerstukken* 2010–2011, Tweede Kamer, 31 980, no. 15. Hearings began in Autumn 2011, but at the time this chapter was finalized, it was still fully active.

33 *Kamerstukken*, Tweede Kamer, 2009–2010, 31 980, no. 3–4, pp. 126–127.

lobbies in Basel. This deficit was greater, in the opinion of the committee, than that in the EU context where at least a register is kept.[34]

In its final report, entitled 'Credit Lost' (*Verloren Krediet*), the parliamentary committee investigating the financial crisis assembled criticism of the parliamentary control over and the role of the Basel Committee. Among testimony of members of parliament, the MP for the Green Left (*Groen Links*) was the only one to be critical of the parliamentary scrutiny of Basel II. He vented his view that the coming about of Basel II was the low-tide of parliament's willingness to exercise its political supervisory powers and powers of scrutiny. Effectively, he submitted, the matter was negotiated between central bankers, with a lobby of international banks in their vicinity. The former Minister of Finance declared that the standards of the Basel Committee are brought about outside the influence of national governments and without European Union influence.[35]

Since the report of the first parliamentary committee of investigation on the financial crisis, parliament has not introduced formal procedures of scrutiny for international decision-making concerning the financial sector as they exist for EU decision-making.

### 3.4.2. International Organization of Securities Commissions (IOSCO) and the *Stichting Autoriteit Financiële Markten* (AFM)

In the International Organization of Securities Commissions (IOSCO) most of the Security Commissions in the world are represented. IOSCO consists *inter alia* of a Presidents' Committee (meeting yearly), an Executive Committee (meeting regularly), a Technical Committee and an Emerging Markets Committee. Through these Committees many standards have been published which are relevant to the sector.

The *Stichting Autoriteit Financiële Markten*, generally known under the acronym AFM, is a main player for the Netherlands in IOSCO, though the central bank is also represented in IOSCO. AFM's director Hans Hoogervorst was Chairman of the most important of IOSCO's commit-

34 *Ibidem*, p. 134.
35 *Kamerstukken*, Tweede Kamer, 2009–2010, 31 980, no. 3–4, pp. 124–126.

tees, the Technical Committee, from June 2010 [36] to June 2011, after having been its vice-chairman in the two previous years (he became full-time chairman of the IASB in June 2011). The AFM takes the form of a non-profit foundation under private law.

Like the DNB and the Ministry of Finance, the AFM conducts public consultations of the sector, while information and training is provided on a regular basis to stakeholders and representative sector members or organizations by the AFM on new policies. During the research it transpired that in this regard the AFM website is considerably more transparent and open to the public than that of the DNB.

Roughly the IOSCO standards can be distinguished into three categories: first, Memoranda of Understanding, second, the Objectives and Principles of Securities Regulation and third, Technical Principles. Here, only the last two will be discussed. The *Objectives and Principles of Securities Regulation* is the seminal document of IOSCO.[37] This document has been published in 2003 and revised in 2010 and consists of 38 principles a good Security Commission should adhere to. They are based upon three objectives of securities regulation: protecting investors, ensuring that markets are fair, efficient and transparent and reducing systemic risk. These principles have a high degree of abstraction. They include principles relating to the regulator (their goals and independence), self-regulation, enforcement of securities regulation (powers of securities commissions) and cooperation in regulation. Some more technical principles are included in these Objectives and Principles as well: principles concerning auditors, credit rating agencies, collective investment schemes and market intermediaries.

The Technical Committee of IOSCO produces the Technical Principles. There has been a steady flow of these Principles over the last years. Examples are the Principles for Dark Liquidity, Principles on Point of Sale Disclosure, Principles for Periodic Disclosure by Listed Entities and Principles for the Valuation of Hedge Fund Portfolios.[38]

---

[36] IOSCO, "Hans Hoogervorst appointed Chairman of IOSCO's Technical Committee", available at http://www.iosco.org/news/pdf/IOSCONEWS184.pdf, last accessed on 26 June 2012.

[37] The latest edition of *Objectives and Principles* can be obtained on the IOSCO-website.

[38] Also accessible via the IOSCO online public library.

### 3.4.2.1. Input Legitimacy and Accountability

The input (or *a priori*) accountability for the making of the IOSCO principles is largely that of the members of the committee's members. For the Netherlands there is no clear mechanism for mandating the members, either formally (there is no relevant legislation) or informally. Although the president of AFM meets a few times a year with the Minister of Finance, there are no indications that during these the former's input in IOSCO's Technical Committee has ever been discussed. According to our spokespersons at AFM, quite a few of the technical principles already existed in the Dutch practice before they were formulated at IOSCO level. It is felt important that IOSCO principles reflect existing practice.[39] In turn, most existing supervisory practices and the principles on which these are based, are a result of regular (but informal in the sense that these are always followed but are not legally compulsory) procedures of publication and consultation with stakeholders. These rounds of consultation are always published on the AFM website.

In practice, there is no central role for the lawyers at AFM in the application and implementation of IOSCO standards. Knowledge is decentralized to the relevant operative departments within AFM.

### 3.4.2.2. Legal Basis

The principles drafted by IOSCO can enter the legal order in many different ways. The principles can acquire a legal status either under national law directly or via European law. They can, however, also be applied independently of such a legal basis by the Financial Markets Authority as a relevant standard in its exercise of discretionary powers. Furthermore, it is possible that the principles acquire the status of legally relevant norms in the interaction between market parties. The way in which the principles enter the national legal order influences the accountability of IOSCO.

[39] Interviews at AFM on 26 May 2011, with Mr Gert Luiting (Manager, Public and International Affairs) and Mr. Niels de Kraker (Senior Officer, Public and International Affairs).

### 3.4.2.3. National and European Legislation

The first accountability mechanism is through adoption by a national or international legislature. In this case the focus of accountability shifts to another level, from IOSCO to the relevant legislature.

References to IOSCO principles in national law have, however, been scarce. There is only one reference to IOSCO principles in national statute law, *id est*, section 5:9 of the Financial Supervision Act. This section (based on Article 20 of the Prospectus Directive) provides that the Financial Markets Authority (AFM), in determining whether a prospectus may be issued, has to make sure it complies with "international standards drafted by international organisations of securities commissions". From the Parliamentary Documents we know that the IOSCO standards are meant.[40] This provision, however, concerns only prospectuses of issuing entities having their seat *outside* the EU. If the seat is inside the EU, the EU Prospectus Regulation, and the standards included therein, is applicable.

Some of the IOSCO principles have been included or referred to in EU legislation. This applies for instance to the Prospective Directive, which dynamically refers to IOSCO standards. One of the most prominent references can be found in the Prospectus Directive. Recital 22 of this directive states that

> [b]est practices have been adopted at international level in order to allow cross-border offers of equities to be made using a single set of disclosure standards established by the International Organisation of Securities Commissions (IOSCO); the IOSCO disclosure standards will upgrade information available for the markets and investors and at the same time will simplify the procedure for Community issuers wishing to raise capital in third countries.[41]

In Article 7 the power to take measures concerning more detailed specific information which must be included in a prospectus, is delegated to the Commission. These, according to Article 7 paragraph 3 of the Directive, "shall be based on the standards in the field of financial and non-

---

40 *Kamerstukken*, Tweede Kamer, 2005–2006, 29 708, no. 19, p. 53.

41 Recital 22 of the preamble of the Prospectus Directive, Directive 2003/71/EC of the European Parliament and of the Council of 4 November 2003 on the prospectus to be published when securities are offered to the public or admitted to trading.

financial information set out by international securities commission organisations, in particular by IOSCO […]".

Another major piece of EU legislation which is actually closely related to the IOSCO technical principles is the 'Markets in Financial Instruments Directive' (MiFID).[42] In the Netherlands, this is implemented through the *Wet financieel toezicht*, as well as through an Order in Council (*algemene maatregel van bestuur)* that is based on it.[43]

As with the Basel Committee's output, here informal law enters the national legal orders via the route of the European Union. A comparison of the *ex ante* scrutiny by the national parliament of the draft Directive with the legislation implementing the directive again shows that parliament's role in the latter is overall more active than in the former. The draft Directive was only taken note of without further deliberation, debate or memoranda in committee or plenary, but parliamentary involvement in passing implementing legislation was intensive. No particular mention was made, however, of Article 7 of the Directive or the IOSCO standards to which it refers. The focus of accountability is therefore not on the underlying IOSCO output but rather on how to give effect to it, though it is unclear to what extent the relevant legislation is consciously considered to be based on IOSCO standards.

### 3.4.2.4. Upward Internal Accountability: The IMF FSAP-Program

A second form of accountability, relates to the application of the *Objectives and Principles*' part on supervisory principles. This is the IMF's assessment of the financial sector as part of the Financial Sector Assessment Program (FSAP). This concerns accountability to the international finan-

---

[42] Directive 2004/39/EC of the European Parliament and of the Council of 21 April 2004 on markets in financial instruments amending Council Directives 85/611/EEC and 93/6/EEC and Directive 2000/12/EC of the European Parliament and of the Council and repealing Council Directive 93/22/EEC, as amended several times; a proposal for recasting the Directive and a new Regulation on Markets in Financial Instruments was adopted by the Commission in the autumn of 2011, see http://ec.europa.eu/internal_market/securities/isd/mifid_en.htm, last accessed on 26 June 2012, which also provides much information on implementation and the Commission's consulting stakeholders and experts on MiFID and its reviews.

[43] This was done through legislation (Wet implementatie richtlijn markten voor financiële instrumenten, 30 October 2007; in *Staatsblad* 2007, p. 406 and by a Decision (Besluit gereglementeerde markten Wft, 30 October 2007; in *Staatsblad* 2007, p. 407).

cial cluster of organizations which spawned IOSCO – in a sense 'upward' accountability. In its country report in the framework of the FSAP, the IMF evaluated the stability of the financial sector in the Netherlands and the extent to which the supervision in the country complies with international supervision standards. The international supervision standards that are used for the capital market are mainly IOSCO's *Objectives and Principles* as well as the Basel Committee's standards on banking supervision. The supervision by the Financial Markets Authority has been assessed twice, the first time in 2004 and the second time in 2011.[44] In both these assessments the supervision by the Financial Markets Authority scored high. Most of the relevant *Objectives and Principles* were fully implemented, some of them were broadly implemented and only a few were considered partly or not implemented. An interesting recommendation is that the Financial Markets Authority needs more regulatory powers to adopt technical measures that apply broadly.[45] Also, the IMF recommends the adoption of legislation providing "explicit legal protection to DNB and the AFM against lawsuits for actions taken in good faith while discharging their duties, provided they have not demonstrated willful negligence".[46] The issue of legal liability of supervising agencies is a hotly debated issue among lawyers, but has not been resolved. At the moment, they do not enjoy legal immunity in any manner. Limiting their liability would reduce possibilities for private actors to hold them to account legally.

### 3.4.2.5. Downwards Political Accountability at the National Level

Related to the IMF's assessment is the Minister of Finance's political accountability towards the Parliament for the results of this assessment. This again is not primarily accountability of IOSCO and can best be seen in letters sent to the Parliament about this assessment. In a letter sent to the Lower House on 15 December 2010 the preliminary results of the FSAP-assessment are communicated.[47] In a letter sent to the Lower House on 22

44 Netherlands: Financial System Stability Assessment, IMF Country Report No. 11/144, June 2011, available at http://www.imf.org/external/pubs/ft/scr/2011/cr11144.pdf, last accessed on 26 June 2012.

45 *Ibid.*, pp. 19–20, paras. 25–27.

46 *Ibid.*, p. 20.

47 *Kamerstukken*, Tweede Kamer [Lower House], 32 432, no. 13.

June 2011, the final results of the FSAP-assessment are communicated.[48] In this last letter not only the assessment of the financial sector by the IMF is discussed, but also the recommendations made by the IMF. With regard to the recommendation that the Financial Markets Authority does not have enough powers to create technical regulation, the Minister explains that there should be parliamentary control on the creation of new legislation that contains choices regarding the policy to be followed. This legislation should be drafted by the Minister of Finance. Yet, the view expressed on technical legislation is more important: drafting technical rules to supplement legislation could be done by the Financial Markets Authority and the Central Bank itself. Based *inter alia* on the recommendation of the IMF there is a discussion with the Financial Markets Authority and the Central Bank whether an extension of their powers to create technical rules is necessary and possible.

### 3.4.2.6. Multiple Forms of Implementation and Application

The IOSCO technical standards are often put into practice along multiple routes, often embedded in legislative rules as well. Nevertheless, it has been remarked by spokespersons in the AFM that many of the technical principles are not so much applied because of the IOSCO having set them, but antedate the IOSCO principles, either because they were already part of the national and European legal framework, or because they were already part of the supervisory practice. Also, it should be remembered that supervision remains to a large extent principle based instead of rule based, so beyond the legislative norms, the principles form a background against which practices evolve under the influence of trading and market developments.

Thus, for instance, the Principles on Outsourcing by Markets[49] are covered, as far as regulated markets are concerned, by Article 39 of MiFID,[50] and have been implemented in Article 5:31 *Wet financieel toezicht*

48 *Kamerstukken*, Tweede Kamer [Lower House], 2010–11, 32 013, no. 16.

49 IOSCO, "Principles on Outsourcing by Markets", Final Report, available at http://www.iosco.org/library/pubdocs/pdf/IOSCOPD299.pdf, last accessed on 26 June 2012 .

50 See also the requirements set in the Commission Directive 2006/73/EC of 10 August 2006 implementing Directive 2004/39/EC of the European Parliament and of the Council as regards organizational requirements and operating conditions for investment firms and defined terms for the purposes of that Directive.

and Articles 27 and following the *Besluit prudentieel toezicht Wft*. Also the Principles for Dark Liquidity[51] are applied on the basis of rules contained in the *Wet financieel toezicht*, which in turn incorporates the EU MiFID rules.

The Principles on Point of Sale Disclosure[52] on the other hand reflect what has been part of the rules and practices as they have been applied in the Netherlands already years before they were adopted in the form of the national requirement of a 'financial information leaflet'. This is also the case with, for instance, the Principles for the Valuation of Hedge Fund Portfolios.[53] Retail hedge funds, just like other financial institutions, have domestically been under AFM supervision for a long time and subject to the application of valuation standards.

### 3.4.2.7. Some Other Forms of Accountability: Liability for Standard Setting and Legal Accountability on the Basis of Standards

There are three other accountability-mechanisms possibly relevant to IOSCO, although they are all three usually considered an indirect form of accountability.

A first aspect would seem to be preliminary to the use of informal principles and standards as legally relevant or binding, which is the aspect of the constitutional and legal requirements such informal output has to live up to before it can at all become legally relevant or binding. In the Dutch case law, these questions have recently arisen but are not definitively settled at the time of writing. These questions arise in case of legislative referral to an informally set norm or standard: does this standard itself acquire a legislative character? If so, must it live up to constitutional requirements for legislative acts, in particular as regards its publication and public availability? In the Dutch context, the matter arose with regard

[51] IOSCO, "Principles for Dark Liquidity", Final Report, available at http://www.iosco.org/library/pubdocs/pdf/IOSCOPD353.pdf, last accessed on 26 June 2012.

[52] IOSCO, "Principles on Point of Sales Disclosure", Final Report, available at http://www.iosco.org/library/pubdocs/pdf/IOSCOPD310.pdf, last accessed on 26 June 2012.

[53] IOSCO, "Principles for the Valuation of Hedge Fund Portfolios", Final Report, available at http://www.iosco.org/library/pubdocs/pdf/IOSCOPD253.pdf, last accessed on 22 June 2012.

to national private standard setting institutions and legislative references to such standards.[54]

A case was brought by a company engaged in building consultancy, *Knooble*. Pursuant to Article 3 of the Netherlands Housing Act, delegated legislation can refer to standards "published by a professional, independent institute, in which the demands that must be met for construction material or constructions are defined in whole or in part, or in which a description is given of a testing method, measurement technique or calculation method". Relevant delegated instruments refer to building material and building technique standards, mainly as set by the NNI in its so-called NEN-standards. These can be bought at fairly high cost at the NNI, which is to a large extent dependent for its income on the sale of its standards, and can be consulted at the library of the NNI. *Knooble* complained in court that by legislative reference the relevant NEN-standards became binding on private citizens, but have not been published in conformity with the Constitution and organic legislation on the publication of legislative acts, and hence were not binding on it. It also submitted that no intellectual property rights could be exerted over NEN-standards since this would be an infringement of fundamental constitutional principles of accessibility of legislation and of the Copyright Act 1912. At first instance the District Court of The Hague held that indeed the relevant standards became legislation and hence would need to be published in accordance with the relevant constitutional and legislative provisions, in the absence of which they cannot be binding.[55] On appeal, the Court of Appeal of The Hague reversed this. It considered that the references in the applicable legislation did not render the standards absolutely binding in as much as

[54] On private and hybrid standard setting in the Netherlands (and its elation to international and European standard setting by ISO and ESO) Cees Stuurman, *Technische normen en het recht* [Technical Standards and the Law], Kluwer, Deventer, 1995; Guido J.M. Evers, *Blind vertrouwen? Een onderzoek naar de toepassing van certificatie ten dienste van de handhaving van wettelijke voorschriften* [Blind Trust: a Study of the Use of Certification and Standardization for the Enforcement of Legal Requirements], Boom Juridisch Uitgevers, Den Haag, 2002; Guido J.M. Evers, "Een normalisatienorm is geen algemeen verbindend voorschrift" in *Nederlands Juristenblad*, 1999, vol. 38, pp. 1814–1815; Cees Stuurman, Hugo S.A. Wijnands, "Legal Aspects of Standardisation in the Netherlands", in Josef Falke, Harm Schepel (eds.), *Legal Aspects of Standardisation in the Member States of the EC and EFTA*, Volume 2, Country Reports, Office for Official Publications, Luxemburg, 2002, pp. 557–624.

[55] Rechtbank [District Court] of The Hague, 31 December 2008, LJN: BG8465.

compliance with the NEN-standards creates a presumption of conformity, but also other methods than compliance with the NEN-standards are legally allowed if it has equivalent results. More generally it held that the NEN-standards have not been set by a body pursuant to a legislative power attributed or delegated to it by the Constitution or an act of parliament, and are hence not legislative acts which need to comply with the applicable rules on publication and accessibility of a legislative act. This, the Court of Appeal held, does not change if a competent legislative authority refers in its legislation to a standard set by such a standards body.[56] The Netherlands' *Raad van State* [Council of State] reached a similar conclusion in a case decided in February 2011.[57] The judgment of the Court of Appeal, however, has been appealed to the Supreme Court, where the matter is pending; a judgment is not expected to be handed down before the summer of 2012.

Nevertheless, these lawsuits have forced the Netherlands' government to clarify its position, particularly the fact that legislative references to 'non-public law' standards do not require compulsory application of such standards, but merely intend to establish a presumption of conformity with legal requirements if the standard is applied.[58] Legislative references should not be 'dynamic', that is to say, they may not incorporate later amendments to the text of a standard, but may only refer to a text in a specific form. The justification for such limitation is to create legal certainty. Should the reference be dynamic, then each amendment to the standard must be notified in the *Staatscourant*, one of the two official journals of the Netherlands.[59] Also, the government has now come to hold the view that in case a legislative reference leads to compulsory application of the standard, such standards should be accessible, its sources should be notified and should be available to the public at 'not unreasonable' cost. It has also announced that compulsory standards must be available for free as of 1 January 2014. Further, it will take this position in Eu-

56 Gerechtshof [Court of Appeal] of The Hague, 16 November 2010, LJN: BO4175.

57 Raad van State, 2 February 2011, LJN: BP2750.

58 This has been codified in the Ninth Amendment to the Prime Ministerial Instructions for Legislation, *Aanwijzingen voor de regelgeving*, of May 2011, Article 91a.

59 *Aanwijzingen voor de regelgeving,* Article 92, second paragraph.

ropean decision-making whenever EU legislative acts refer to informal standards with compulsory effect.[60]

As far as the IOSCO standards are concerned, these are accessible through its open access website. This is not an official publication, however, under national law, which would require formal status of IOSCO and its decisions.[61] So the open references to IOSCO standards, if these were to be strictly binding and applied in compulsory fashion, would not live up to the requirements for similar standards imposed by a national legislative act. Clear examples of such binding references, which have the effect of incorporating IOSCO standards turning them into hard law, do not yet exist, mainly because these standards are either made compulsory through their substantive inclusion in European or national legislative acts, or do not apply as strictly binding but as principles or guidelines only, as we saw in previous sections.

A further mechanism of legal accountability is the liability of the authority creating the norms. In this case, this could be IOSCO or the Financial Markets Authority (when it makes certain IOSCO principles ob-

---

60 Dutch Government Position Paper on "Accessibility of Standards and Standardisation", *Kabinetsstandpunt Nota Kenbaarheid Normen en Normalisatie, Kamerstukken* 27 406, no. 193. This 'position paper' is a government response to a memorandum produced by a typically Dutch 'forum' composed of trade unions, employers organisations, consumer organisations and some public officials under the auspices of the Ministry for Economic Affairs, on Standards and Standardisation. It also contains the government's response as to the participation of stakeholders in the decision-making of standards. A recent communication by the EU Commission on Standards promotes the development of private standards, but does not mention any accessibility requirements these must live up to beyond availability at reduced cost for small companies, possibly because it rigorously adheres to the view that such standards should be voluntary, but overlooks that also in EU law private standards (in the sense of standardisation – which as far as thir substantive nature concerns, become in reality hard to distinguish from some of the standards discussed in this chapter) are referred to in EU legislative acts and thus acquire legal significance; *A strategic vision for European standards: Moving forward to enhance and accelerate the sustainable growth of the European economy by 2020*, Communication from the Commission to the European Parliament, the Council and the European Economic And Social Committee, Brussels, 1 June 2011, COM(2011) 311 final.

61 The *Rijkswet goedkeuring en bekendmaking verdragen*, [Act for the Realm on Approval and Publication of Treaties], requires the publication of decisions of international organisations under public international law (which IOSCO presumably is not) in the official journal the *Tractatenblad*, or pursuant to a treaty published therein; these requirements cannot be met by IOSCO or its output.

ligatory). It is useful to first have a quick look at liability on the part of standards bodies or of the State for standards bodies as has been discussed by Schepel and Falke.[62] This might give us interesting information about the liability of IOSCO or the Financial Markets Authority. Spindler puts it this way: "If [standard setting bodies] pass 'bad' standards or if they do not adjust them, they should be deemed to have played a part in the chain of causation for a damage that has occurred due to a 'badly' designed product".[63] While litigation about this has only occurred in a few countries, it is interesting to see that standard setting bodies such as the BSI, AENOR, DS and NSF have taken liability insurance. The situation in France is interesting; the standards that AFNOR creates are seen as part of their public mission. As a consequence of this approach, challenges against standards need to be made before an administrative court. This means that courts will apply administrative discretion. In Portugal, challenges against the standards bodies are challenges against the State. In Spain, the state is responsible for the standard setting body except for liability that the body may incur. The standards' body of Northern Ireland has the power to sue and be sued in its own name. This all means that (except in Portugal) "the State could only be challenged for standards rendered mandatory – *in which case the normal rules for civil liability of the public authorities in the exercise of their public law powers apply*".[64] Schepel and Falke distinguish between unwanted errors, like misprints, and more fundamental errors (blatantly wrong standards). For liability in the latter case, "the mere fact of a Standards Body publishing a standard which subsequently proved to be dangerous, is unlikely to be considered a sufficient basis for liability".[65]

Time will tell whether this can be applied to IOSCO and the Financial Markets Authority. With regard to the IOSCO Principles, the Financial Markets Authority participates in IOSCO, yet also exercises state power and decides which IOSCO-principles to apply (sometimes, though, embedded in legislation). The issue of civil liability for IOSCO is beyond the scope of this paper, although it raises important questions which test both its own informality and the 'informality' of the standards it produces. Liability would thus seem to fall on the Financial Markets Authority if it

[62] Falke, Schepel, 2002, see *supra* note 54.

[63] *Ibid.*, p. 238.

[64] *Ibid.*, p. 239.

[65] *Ibid.*, p. 241.

renders rules mandatory or otherwise decides to apply them. Liability for supervisors is rather uncommon in the Netherlands, although recently authoritative legal scholars have argued for such liability.[66]

Another form of accountability is legal accountability on the basis of the standards set. This will occur if the judiciary uses principles as legally relevant rules to be applied to adjudicate the lawfulness of a particular situation or behavior. It is an implicit form of accountability: there is always a risk that the judiciary stops short of considering them legally binding. A good overview of how private norms can be applied judicially in the Netherlands is given by Giesen.[67]

He discerns the following lines.

> In the case law of the lower courts the results are mixed. Sometimes private norms are considered legally binding, sometimes they are not. In the case law of the *Hoge Raad* (the Netherlands Supreme Court), private norms are used and given a legally binding character, but never quite explicitly.[68]

The question arises whether these findings could also apply to IOSCO-standards. Here the difference with the previous form of accountability becomes obvious. While the previous form dealt with liability of the standards body (*id est*, IOSCO), this one deals with the question whether the private norms (*id est*, IOSCO-principles) can establish liability between two private parties. Whether the judiciary will take up IOSCO-principles as legally binding norms in liability cases will depend on how much they become part of socially applicable norms determining standards of legally enforceable propriety. No case law is available as re-

---

66 See Ivo Giesen, "Regulating regulators through liability. The case for applying normal tort rules to supervisors", in *Utrecht Law Review*, 2006, vol. 2, issue 1, p. 31.

67 Ivo Giesen, "De omgang met en handhaving van 'meervoudigheid van maatschappelijke normstelsels'; een analyse van recente rechtspraak", in *Weekblad voor Privaatrecht, Notariaat en Registratie*, 2008, p. 6772. A case concerning the liability of the DNB as successor to the supervisory agency *Verzekeringskamer*, is Hoge Raad, C04/279HR 13-10-2006, LJN: AW2077, in which it concludes to a marginal form of review, taking into account the discretion of the supervisor. The Advocate-General in this case explicitly referred to the first of the Basel Committee's "Core Principles for Effective Banking Supervision", concerning 'legal protection' for the supervisors as a starting point for the assessment of liability.

68 *Ibid.*

gards securities law in which IOSCO principles were used in such a manner, however, so the matter remains moot.

### 3.4.3. International Accounting Standards Board (IASB)

Another example of international standard setting by the type of 'informal' international body to which the overall research project is devoted, is the International Accounting Standards Board (IASB), whose work is highly important to the IOSCO and its affiliated national supervisory bodies. We mention these standards separately because within the group of informal international lawmaking in the financial sector, they seem to have the strongest position in the domestic legal order.

Since 2005, the IASB's standards, the so-called International Financial Reporting Standards (IFRS), have been turned into law by Regulation (EC) No 1606/2002 of 19 July 2002 on the application of international accounting standards (the 'Regulation'), through a comitology procedure (the 'regulatory procedure'), which as a matter of fact has meant that most IASB standards have been adopted as applicable standards within the EU. This Regulation enforces IFRS accounting standards on all publicly traded companies in the EU if the relevant IFRS has been adopted in the comitology procedure. Prior to the enactment of this Regulation the situation was governed by Directives which essentially allowed partly diverging national legislations of Member States to co-exist. As of 2005, and thanks to the adoption of the Regulation, this system of national generally accepted accounting principles was put to an end.

The Regulation on international accounting standards may be one of the most open and important manners in which informal international standards have become adopted by means of formal law. Moreover, according to the preamble in Recital 16, the basis for member states' obligation to comply with international standards can be found in the duty of Community loyalty. It sets out that:

> A proper and rigorous enforcement regime is key to underpinning investors' confidence in financial markets. Member States, by virtue of Article 10 of the Treaty [since Lisbon Art. 4 (3) 1 TEU], are required to take appropriate measures to ensure compliance with international accounting standards.

This would seem to be giving quite a strong position to the international standards of IASB. Potentially, Article 10 EC could give overriding effect to EU law and here, via EU law, to informal international standards. As a matter of fact, the national case law in the Netherlands is not quite clear on this question on overruling effect, and of what were in effect informal IASB formulated standards, but it does attach great legal importance to them.

At any rate, the legal status of the Regulation implies that domestic implementing legislation, transforming the international standards into national law, is not required. That said, in line with the quoted opening recital of the Regulation, a domestic enforcement mechanism is in place.[69] This allows competent bodies, as a rule the AFM, to request the competent court to order a company to rectify its annual account and report if these do not comply with the international accounting standards as adopted under the Regulation.

The importance given in the Dutch case law to the IFRS is in line with the European Court of Justice case law. Already in 2003, in *BIAO*, the ECJ indicated that the Fourth Directive on annual accounts of certain companies entails certain assessments that need to be made at the national level, but which must be made "in the light of international accounting standards".[70] In *ENDESA* the European Court of First Instance assumed the binding nature of the IFRS which have been, as of 2005, adopted via the procedure of the Regulation. That said, it did not decide on the precise legal nature of the IFRS involved, which was made easier by the fact that the case concerned mainly an inter-temporal situation.[71]

---

[69] See the Netherlands Civil Code, Book 2, Article 447.

[70] European Court of Justice, *Banque internationale pour l'Afrique occidentale SA (BIAO) and Finanzamt für Großunternehmen in Hamburg*, Case C-306/99, 7 January 2003, para. 118: "As for the questions seeking to obtain clarification as to the criteria for assessing the degree of likelihood of a risk, the legitimacy of taking 'country' risk and the risk of insolvency into account simultaneously, and the ways of avoiding risks being taken into account twice over, it is sufficient to point out that the Fourth Directive merely sets out general principles without seeking to regulate all their possible applications. In the absence of such particulars, that assessment is a matter for national law, read where appropriate in the light of the international accounting standards (IAS) as they applied at the time of the facts in the main proceedings, provided always that the general principles set out by the Fourth Directive, as referred to in paragraphs 72 to 75 of this judgment, are fully complied with".

[71] European Court of Justice, *Endesa v Commission of the European Communities*, Case T-417/05, 14 July 2006.

As we mentioned in the previous section, there is not a lot of Dutch case law referring to international standards in the financial sector. That said, while we have not found any cases concerning IOSCO principles, there are several cases that refer to other international standards in the financial sector. For example, in a case before the *Hoge Raad* the advocate general *referred to* a 1998 Basel Committee standard that sets out minimum capital requirements for calculating the assets size of a bank for the purpose of calculating a profit tax.[72] Again, the IASB accounting standards (IFRS) have been treated more directly as relevant standards, even by the *Hoge Raad*, which as a court of cassation can only interpret 'law', *id est*, legislative of customary law not having the nature of fact.[73]

In its judgment of 24 April 2009 it went very far in interpreting the IAS/IFRS standard 1.31, holding that AFM's request to have a company revise its yearly accounts because these were not in conformity with the IAS/IFRS standard was rightly dismissed. It determined that although it had been established in the lower instance that there were a number of inaccuracies and divergences on details, the overall aim of a reliable overall account as set out by the international standards was complied with.

This judgment leaves some uncertainty as to whether the international IAS/IFRS standard, as incorporated under EU law (by Regulation 1606/2002), was the actual legally binding rule, or whether it was a factual standard of legally non-binding nature which was reasonably assessed by the lower court. Here the 'principle based' nature of the international standards also seems to interfere with an unambiguous determination of the standards as 'law' which the Netherlands Supreme Court can interpret and apply.

## 3.5. Conclusions and Epilogue

### 3.5.1. Some Conclusions

The previous materials lead us to the following conclusions.

- 'Monism' as such does not seem to provide a major explanation for the role of informal international law in the Netherlands. This is

[72] Hoge Raad, 25 November 2005, LJN: AU2275.

[73] Hoge Raad itself in HR 24-04-2009, LJN: BG8790; references, sometimes elaborately, by the advocate general in HR 13-11-2009, LJN: BG5866; HR 16-11-2007, LJN: AZ7371.

mainly due to the fact that the international standards we have studied do not have the formal status of international law under national constitutional law. It is neither customary international law, nor takes the form of treaties or decisions of international organizations under public international law. Although there is some national case law regarding international informal standards in the sense of our project, none concerns a (potential) conflict between such a standard and domestic law. Hence the question of priority does not really arise.

- There are two manners in which informal international law acquires entry into domestic legal orders. One is by turning them into 'hard' law; another is by simply applying them or taking them into account directly in appropriate circumstances. Both are practiced in the Netherlands.
- Turning informal international law into hard law in the domestic context usually takes the route via the European Union, as far as the financial sector is concerned. Important international standards as developed by the Basel Committee, IOSCO and the IASB have been incorporated in EU Directives or Regulations. The Capital Requirement Directive, the Prospective Directive, the Markets in Financial Instruments Directive and the International Accounting Standards Regulation are good examples. These are next implemented or directly applied domestically. This reduces for EU member states whatever differences there might otherwise exist in the effect given to international standards. This is notably the case with the IAS Regulation, which by adopting the IFRS intends to harmonize the financial reporting standards across Member States, eliminating previously diverging national legislation. The application of these standards by the DNB and AFM do not seem to create problems or conflicts with domestic norms. The relevant standards are generally accepted and even promoted by the relevant authorities in the sector without any noticeable problem with their originally informal nature.
- As far as the informal international output is not mediated through EU law, the constitutional rules determining *formal international law's* position in the national legal order are not really applicable, and hence 'monism' is as such not the most significant explanatory factor. Other explanations must be found for the smooth manner in

which informal international standards are accepted and applied. We hypothesize that these must be sought in the features which underlie the adoption of the monist approach to formal international law: the constitutional openness towards international society, international decision-making which goes along with openness to non-national state sites of political, administrative and social authority. This openness in turn is not independent from the interests served by such openness. In this regard, we can point to the Netherlands' geo-political and geo-economical position. Compliance with informal international decision-making in the financial sector is closely related to the interests served by doing so; the Netherlands has a highly open economy which is largely dependent on international trade in goods and services. The banking sector is dominated by large, internationally active banks.

- A further explanation is more mundane. There is an inherent and desired informality in the financial sector, which finds its expression in the outspoken preference for a 'principle-based' rather than a 'regulation-based' approach. The financial sector prefers a principle-based approach, as it allows for the flexibility that is needed within a market economy. Such a principles-based approach leaves room for market supervisors and regulators to follow trends and developments among market actors and across markets. Regulation (like 'gold plating') is, moreover, viewed as exposing the relevant sector in a particular country at least potentially to a relative disadvantage. This leaves the fact that one is aware of the relative 'informality' of the applicable standards even after their incorporation into legislative complexes. The case law does not consider the principles to be hard and fast rules, but rather principles that are capable of suffering exceptions. The AFM and DNB, within the discretionary powers of their supervisory role, also rely on them as policy principles and objectives. These domestic agencies also tend to refer to them as they increase their independent regulatory power, as was notably the case in the recent IMF report on the Netherlands.

### 3.5.2. An Epilogue on Accountability and De-Constitutionalization

In the previous sections, we have tried to highlight the manner in which the constitutional bodies of government and parliament have been involved with informal international law in the financial sector. We saw that parliament had been kept regularly informed of the (negotiations on) the second and third Basel packages, through letters by the government and briefings by central bank officials and the President himself, who was chair of the Basel Committee at the time. This has not been the case with regard to the technical IOSCO and IASB standards. That said, the parliament was updated on the IMF's evaluation of the application of IOSCO and the Basel Committee's supervisory principles to national supervisory agencies. The parliament was informed of the Draft report and heard the government's view on the draft report, and was also informed of the final report.

Generally, the Netherlands views positively its participation in such international standard setting fora. The recent appointment of a Dutchman as chair of an essentially private body like the IASB was reason for its present employer, the AFM, not only to congratulate the person involved but the Netherlands as well.[74] Altogether, the major role which the President of DNB and the President of AFM played until recently in the Basel Committee, IOSCO and IASB was found important and a matter of satisfaction. The accountability of organizations like the Basel Committee, IOSCO and IASB has not been considered highly problematic by relevant actors. That said, in the aftermath of the 2008 banking crisis some criticism was voiced in parliament which can be understood as an expression of dissatisfaction with the lack of accountability of the Basel Committee to political institutions like parliament itself. The accountability of an international organization like IOSCO is, however, not based on the classical constitutional system of political accountability, ultimately towards institutions representing the electorate. It is based much more on transparency and participation of stake-holders, which are of paramount importance and are more or less consciously aimed to compensate for the 'democratic' deficit of these institutions.

We saw that the parliament's involvement with relevant standards was mainly in the context of national implementation if this was required by EU law, but their transformation from soft into hard law at the European Union level was not intensively scrutinized. The emphasis was at the national level, but criticisms were voiced as regards minimum harmoniza-

[74] AFM, "Hans Hoogervorst wordt voorzitter International Accounting Standards Board" [Hans Hoogervorst becomes Chairman of the International Accounting Standards Board], available at http://www.afm.nl/nl/professionals/afm-actueel/nieuws/2010/okt/hoogervorst-voorzitter-iasb.aspx, last accessed on 26 June 2012.

tion directives and the threats of gold plating, thus suggesting one would prefer the international standard to be transformed into firm norms which would not allow for all kinds of national variety.

All in all the parliamentary involvement with the international informal norms was marginal. This can be explained because of the highly technical nature of much of the international informal law in the financial sector. As long as the relevant sector finds the technical output important and workable, which is verified through notification and consultation practices by DNB and AFM, the matter is left to the sector and the sectoral supervisory agencies, who themselves are the 'national' representatives in the informal international lawmaking networks.

To a large extent this means that the classic constitutional institutions of government and parliament are eclipsed. This implies that classic constitutional understandings of accountability and legitimacy are eclipsed as well. In this respect a certain 'de-constitutionalization' is occurring, which can be considered typical for much of present-day globalization.

From the perspective of classic democratic constitutionalism the phenomena of informal international lawmaking are hence viewed with suspicion, which inspires much of the literature on what in this project is referred to as informal international lawmaking and accountability. This is caused by the prevalent continental European constitutional tradition in which democratic legitimacy is determined in terms of political 'delegation' from the electorate to parliament and from parliament to government. Accountability is then the feedback from government to parliament, ultimately to the electorate, with sanctioning options along the way: parliament being able (in parliamentary systems) to sanction government through votes of confidence or no confidence, and the electorate being able to sanction parliament through elections. This is reflected in many 'principal – agency' studies of governance.

Beyond this threefold chain of actors, delegation and accountability become problematic. If the government sets up agencies with some form of independent powers, and these agencies in turn set up formal or informal international decision-making institutions or networks, the chain of delegation becomes long and thin, and so does accountability.[75]

The alternative approach is indeed a concept of accountability which is based on transparency and broad stake-holder participation. This is a way of creating 'democratic' legitimacy within the circle of those directly affected, and is a kind of reaching out to the classic democratic institutions, which can act upon the information which is available to them. This requires a broader concept of democracy than is usual within the continental European constitutional tradition (like France, Germany, Italy, Spain and most other continental European countries), but which can be found at least to some extent in other European constitutional traditions which are not as strongly based on the French revolutionary ideas (such as the British, Dutch and Scandinavian constitutional systems), and which have a greater openness to societal influences and developments. The Dutch constitutional system certainly fits into the latter category. There has always been a non-exclusive democratic notion which is not strictly state-related. The role of the state has mostly been to encapsulate the various social spheres and groups, rather than assimilate them into a solid state-people. This has left ample room for social democracy rather than state democracy even within the context of lawmaking.

This might provide an avenue for conceptualizing issues of accountability and democratic legitimacy in the context of globalization. But it will not eliminate some of the problems which the Westphalian model solved: at what level to aggregate the general interest, to balance conflicting interests, to allocate responsibility and organize accountability. These questions are not always acute in much of the technocratic, expertise based issues addressed by informal international lawmaking, but even there they arise, particularly because of the backlash which the impact of compliance (or non-compliance) with informal standards can have in the classic political realm of democratic states. We see many examples of this around us, which vary from the prohibition of vaccination of animals against certain diseases (with massive slaughtering as a consequence of the outbreak of virulent animal diseases) to the consequences of failing capitalization standards and trading standards of financial derivates and

[75] The same applies, of course, when governments set up international organisations, which in turn set up informal decision-making institutions or networks which produce informal international law.

other financial instruments in the financial crisis besetting Europe since 2008.

# 4

## Informal International Lawmaking and Accountability in Brazil

**Salem H. Nasser*** **and Ana Mara França Machado****

### 4.1. Introduction[1]

The general question 'how does Brazil deal with informal international lawmaking (IN-LAW) products?' contains in itself several other questions and presupposes some answers. The first presupposed answer concerns the nature or the legal status of the informal lawmaking products. The answer is a negative one, in the sense that there is a refusal to settle upfront the question of whether such products are or are not law. This question is left open for further scrutiny.[2] We shall not reopen this debate for two reasons: first, it seems to have been satisfactorily resolved for the participants in the IN-LAW research project and in a way that responds to the project's needs. Second, it does not appear to be necessary for the purposes of this chapter, as it is to find its place within the project.

However, the very fact that this project decided to speak of informal *lawmaking* where the project's tender[3] spoke of informal *public policy making* is heavy of potential consequences and invites the necessity of further scrutiny. Furthermore, the framing paper opens four basic possibil-

---

* **Salem H. Nasser** is Professor of International Law at Direito GV (The São Paulo Law School of Fundaçao Getulio Vargas), Brazil.

** **Ana Mara França Machado** is a Ph.D. Candidate in Law at the University of São Paulo, Brazil.

1 Special thanks are due to Luciana Dias, Viviane Muller Prado, Otavio Yazbek, Bruno Salama, Jairo Saddi, Alkimar Moura, Pedro Gomes Pereira, Fernanda Terrazas, Ana Paula Soares Jucá da Silveira e Silva and Leandro Teixeira de Morais for their help in our efforts to understand the domestic regulatory space and the ways it is influenced by these three networks. The responsibility for any shortcomings and remaining errors is exclusively ours.

2 Joost Pauwelyn, "Informal International Lawmaking: Framing the Concept and Research Questions", in Joost Pauwelyn, Ramses A. Wessel and Jan Wouters (eds.), *Informal International Lawmaking*, Oxford University Press, Oxford, 2012, p. 15.

3 Pauwelyn, 2012, p. 13, see *supra* note 2.

ities about the status of the outcomes, namely that: they may be law; they may be regulated by law; they may participate in law-creation; they may have legal effects.[4] All things added it becomes evident that the question of the legal status is crucial. Even if one admits the general, theoretical, possibility that the output can be or not be law, the fact is that the question cannot be dispensed with when dealing with every particular output since, in all certainty, its legal status will have clear consequences on its implementation and on the accountability mechanisms attached to it. This, therefore, should be a guiding element in and for the case studies.

Other than that, it is our belief that the question concerning the legal status of a prescription or set of prescriptions can be considered in two diverse manners. One could be termed the essentialist take: whether something is, by nature, in essence, law. The other is more useful and easier to ask: whether the prescriptions are part of a legal system.

In order to answer this second question, one has to adopt the internal point of view of the legal system, look at it and see it as it sees itself.

In this context, the framing chapter offers us two precious pieces of information that will help us organize the discussion to come. The first is that the characterization of the outputs under consideration is done by reference to and in comparison with public international law, not domestic law.[5] This is to be expected, since the object is *international* lawmaking. The second is that the output does not come about through one of the traditional sources of international law.[6]

Therefore, looking at such outputs from the point of view of international law the answer is clear: they are not part of traditional international law – we will suspend any discussion on what it means to be regulated by law, to participate in norm creation and to produce legal effects. Looking at the outputs from the point of view of most domestic legal orders, we can safely assume that the answer would be the same: they would not be seen, by domestic law, as part of international law.

We undertake the task of assessing Brazil's participation in specific networks and its implementation of certain regulations, certain outputs, having in mind these conclusions which, we think, organize and illuminate the discussion. Accordingly, let us turn to the questions contained in

---

4 *Ibid.*

5 *Ibid.*

6 *Ibid.*

the general proposal. 'How does Brazil deal with the informal international law produced in and by a certain number of networks?' is a question that can in effect be translated and broken down into several others. Some of them concern, as it should be expected, Brazil:

1. Is Brazil, or are Brazilian bodies, part of the network?
2. How does Brazil's or the Brazilian parties' participation in the networks work? Do they have a say in the regulation produced and do they exercise this faculty?
3. Are the regulatory products of these networks implemented in Brazil? What does implementation mean in the Brazilian case?
4. Does internal implementation of the international informal regulatory products require domestic actors to have powers that are different from those needed for the production of the domestic regulation?
5. Do accountability mechanisms that apply to the creation and implementation of informal international law, if they exist, differ from those applying to domestic regulation by the same actors in the same sector?
6. Do these mechanisms differ from those applying to the creation and implementation of domestic law or regulation proper?
7. Do they differ from those that apply to the implementation of public international law?
8. Do they need to be thought of in relation to an overall assessment of some kind of standard of accountability in the legal system?

These questions relating to Brazil can only be answered, for the networks under consideration or any other, if they are put in relation with other questions concerning the network and the informal outputs they produce. These can be construed as follows:

1. How many and what are the informal law regulations or products of each network that need to be considered? In other words, which are the instruments whose implementation we are considering?
2. What do these products do? How do they, or how are they supposed to, perform their regulatory action? This includes the nature of the instrument and the language of the prescriptions.
3. Why are the outputs there?
4. Why does Brazil implement them?

We will try to offer some answers to these questions, where and when possible, with regards to each of the networks under consideration in this exploratory chapter, and see whether some general conclusions can be drawn from there. We will be economic in the description of the networks as this has already been the object of more detailed work within the research project.[7] We will try to refer only to what we feel will make Brazil's involvement and its implementation of the regulatory products more understandable.

We will start by discussing the ways Brazilian law deals with the conclusion of treaties and with the incorporation of international law (4.2.). This will be followed by a discussion of Brazil's relation with the Basel Committee and its outputs (4.3.); with the International Organization of Securities Commissions – IOSCO (4.4.); and with the International Conference on Harmonisation of Technical Requirements for Registration of Pharmaceuticals for Human Use – ICH (4.5.). The study of some specific traits of the incorporation and implementation of outputs by two financial international networks and one health network will allow us to offer some brief general conclusions (4.6.).

## 4.2. Brazilian Rules on the Conclusion of International Agreements and on the Incorporation of International Law

### 4.2.1. Formal International Law

According to the Brazilian Constitution, the President of the Republic is the competent authority to conclude international treaties, *ad referendum* of the National Congress.[8]

This means, firstly, that the initiative and the final decision to express Brazil's consent to be bound by an international treaty (the word is used in its most general sense: an agreement submitted to international law and binding on the parties who are either states or intergovernmental organizations) rests ultimately with the President and, by extension, with those parts of the Executive Branch of government which, according to international law, have the power to engage the state before other states or international organizations: the Minister of Foreign Affairs and chiefs of

[7] See Joost Pauwelyn, Ramses A. Wessel, Jan Wouters (eds.), *Informal International Lawmaking*, Oxford University Press, Oxford, 2012 and other chapters in this volume.

[8] Federal Constitution of Brazil, Article 84, VIII.

diplomatic missions. Of course, the President may authorize persons to negotiate and adopt specific treaties and express Brazilian consent to be bound by them.

Such presidential final decision is however, in principle, dependent on an authorization by the National Congress, which must approve any agreement that may represent an onus to the national treasury.[9] It would seem that this last condition, referring to the impact on the treasury, was inserted in the constitutional text promulgated in 1988 to make sure that agreements, for example, with the International Monetary Fund (IMF), of which Brazil had signed a few in the previous years, without congressional approval, would have to pass through the scrutiny of deputies and senators. Some argued that, in reality, the initiative aiming at more rigor could paradoxically be read as a limit to the kinds of agreements that would need to be approved in parliament.

The consensual interpretation, however, combining both articles, says that all international agreements, all treaties, should undergo the dual process by which the National Congress must approve all treaties, whether they require ratification or not, either before or after the negotiating process has been concluded. Once a treaty is entered into by Brazil it should be incorporated *as is* in the Brazilian domestic legal order. In principle, when it enters into force for Brazil in the international legal order it should also come into force in the domestic one. Brazilian courts have been consistently deciding that for this incorporation to happen, the Presidency has to issue a decree promulgating the treaty – similarly to what happens with federal statutes – giving it publicity.

According to this settled jurisprudence, the absence of such a decree or its delay could bring about a situation in which a treaty by which Brazil is bound internationally will be considered not to be in force in the domestic order. Of course, the same could take place if Brazil expressed its consent to be bound internationally without having the approval of the National Congress.

Despite the general acceptance of the principle that all agreements should go through the approval procedure, the fact is that in reality many do not, even when they are properly binding treaties according to international law. Some are entered into by the President or the Foreign Ministry and others are concluded by other branches of government – other minis-

9 Federal Constitution of Brazil, Article 49, I.

tries, agencies, *et cetera*. The first, more superficial explanation for this situation is the impracticability, in terms of time and procedures, to have every single agreement undergo the approval path.

Substantially, as elsewhere, there are attempts at differentiating between executive agreements and treaties in due form, or between simplified treaties and solemn ones, basically separating the ones that demand ratification from those that do not.

The critical moment would come when and if Brazilian courts are called upon to decide whether any of these binding agreements, whose inobservance would entail Brazil's international responsibility, are part of the Brazilian domestic law and may produce legal effects on the territory.

In any case, many of these agreements that bypass the congressional procedure would qualify as what one would have the tendency to call, in Brazil, administrative agreements, meaning that the substance of what is negotiated and agreed upon falls within the regulatory powers of the Brazilian agent or within its discretionary power for action. As we will see below, the IN-LAW outputs may be accompanied by or preceded by an agreement, between the state agents or the regulators, to implement them. Such agreements could fall into this category.

In what concerns customary international law, only a quick word is needed, if it is indeed. Brazilian courts may and do apply recognized principles of international law which, because they are not necessarily included in a treaty, do not undergo the above described procedure of internalization or incorporation. They are nevertheless, in principle, recognized as being part of the Brazilian domestic legal order. Which principles are recognized as such is, by the very nature of custom, a question to be decided in every concrete case.

### 4.2.2. Informal Outputs

This general picture of the ways in which international law is incorporated in Brazil would not be likely to offer very clear answers concerning the incorporation of what has been termed IN-LAW. As we have said before, the answer, a negative one, comes rather from the side of IN-LAW itself, from its own self-characterization, specifically from the characterization of its output, its products. These are indeed, as we have seen, doubly defined as (in most cases) non-binding and as not arising from the traditional sources of international law.

Because and to the extent they do not spring from its traditional sources they are not recognized, by international law, to be a part of international law (in the sense that they are not legal normative prescriptions). Because they are not binding, disconformities between actual and prescribed behavior cannot be viewed as illegal and, in as far as the addressed behavior is that of the states, they cannot entail international responsibility.

A conservative legal system as Brazil's tends not to call international law what is not recognized by international law as being an integral part of it. Because they are neither treaties nor part of customary law, IN-LAW products may not undergo the same incorporation or recognition processes.

Of course, someone could very well take issue with what could in thesis be called an agreement concluded by the Brazilian state. That would be an agreement undertaken by any of Brazil's representatives or sub-governmental units which are not supposed to represent it for international law purposes and determine Brazil's future actions without going through the channels of appropriate congressional approval. This by definition would be an accountability issue.

But this general idea has to be broken down into more specific and clear questions.

Let us take the notion, central to the accountability focus of the project and to its rationale, of public authority as "action by public entities which unilaterally 'determines' or 'reduces the freedom of' others".[10] Some possibilities are opened in relation to each of the elements of the definition. Public entities may be, in our context, either the states or the network. The actors who are 'determined' or whose freedom is reduced are either the states or other, non-state, actors, directly or through implementation by the states.

Thus, if we have in mind the determination of the state, its freedom will be reduced either by a unilateral action of the network or by its own acceptance of such a reduction – and in this case the criteria of unilateral determination is harder to demonstrate. It goes without saying that this determination does not flow from any legally binding character, which is inexistent. It is a consequence of some other consideration of prudency, interest, lack of options, *et cetera*.

---

[10] Pauwelyn, 2012, p. 21, see *supra* note 2.

If the determination is unilateral, it may touch states that are part of the network and those that are not. If it springs from the agreement, then it can only apply, as such, to the members of the network. Of course, a combination is possible, in which some states are determined by agreement and others are determined by other considerations.

If, on the other hand, we have in mind the determination of other actors, this may take place by the unilateral action of the network, directly, or by the unilateral action of the state or its authorities. We will not concentrate here on the possible operation of the informal output as it determines directly the behavior of other actors, without the intermediation of the state. Of course, the networks we are dealing with are by definition composed at least partially by state authorities, so the states will always be participants in the creation of the regulation. But this does not necessarily mean that any state's implementation action will be needed.

So, domestically, some could take issue with the fact that some agreements – even if not legally binding – made by the state in its international relations, by which it agrees to participate in a network or by which it agrees to implement all or some of the outputs produced by the network, do not undergo any kind of congressional or other control.

First of all, then, one has to verify whether the state is part of the agreement that has formed the network – or of the agreements that have created, modify and regulate its functioning – and to verify whether there is an agreement to incorporate and implement in some way the outputs of the network, and verify, finally, whether the output is itself an agreement.

If the output consists in or includes an agreement, and the agreement is, by definition, not legally binding, but, because it potentially determines the actors by reducing their freedom, is necessarily binding in some other, non-legal sense, then the question is whether Brazil or any other country, has a system by which agreements which are not binding but end up determining the state's behavior have to undergo approval or control procedures.

Such procedures could exist for this kind of agreements in general or for agreements relating to specific issues or regulatory areas. At this point, for Brazil, only the general question can be answered with safety and it is that Brazil has no such system requiring approval or control for non-binding agreements.

One could conceive, however, of an output that is not or does not include a clear agreement, or at least not an agreement that would call for any further action by the state or by its agencies.

In any case, the agreement, if there is one, is to be differentiated and distinguished from the normative substance of the output instruments. For example, a regulator, holding some measure of the state's public authority, agrees at an international forum to implement certain regulatory standards in the field comprised by its regulatory powers; the agreement is not binding, but the regulator may feel that it is under some kind of obligation to perform as agreed. This is one thing that may or may not undergo control.

Of course, such control, if it exists, will take into account the substance of what is to be implemented. But the substance, the sector's regulation in this case, is implemented by the regulator, according to its legal powers, and this is a second, different thing, that may or may not undergo a different kind of control that relates to the regulatory activity on the domestic plane and has no necessary relation with the fact that the origin of the substantive regulation is an international non-binding agreement.

In other words, in the absence of an agreement or when a state is not part of the network, the internal control, if it exists, touches the internal measures or regulations and can have two separate or concomitant contents: the substance of the measures or regulation and/or the fact that such content originates in the international network. But both things may be considered as one and the same basic question: *why* is that *specific measure or regulation* being adopted or implemented?

In the following sections we take a closer look at two informal networks that are active in the financial area – the Basel Committee on Banking Supervision (BCBS) and the International Organization of Securities Commissions (IOSCO) – as well as at one example of an informal network in the health area – the International Conference on Harmonisation of Technical Requirements for Registration of Pharmaceuticals for Human Use (ICH).

### 4.3. Basel Committee on Banking Supervision (BCBS)

#### 4.3.1. Overview of the Brazilian Financial System

The highest regulatory body of the Brazilian Financial System (*Sistema Financeiro Nacional* – SFN) is the National Monetary Council (*Conselho Monetário Nacional* – CMN), created in 1964.[11] It is responsible for establishing the general directives of the monetary, exchange and credit policies; for regulation of the constitution, and for functioning and supervision of financial institutions. Today its members are the Minister of Finance, as president, the Minister of Planning, Budget and Administration and the President of the Central Bank.[12]

The Central Bank (*Banco Central do Brasil* – BACEN) and the Securities Commission (*Comissão de Valores Mobiliários* – CVM) are the supervising bodies of the Financial System. We will deal with the CVM in more detail in the section dedicated to IOSCO. In this section, we will concentrate on BACEN and its role in the regulation of the banking system. It is important to keep in mind, however, as we study each of the two institutions, that they are both subject to the CMN and bound by its decisions concerning the regulation of the financial environment in Brazil. As we will see, the regulatory powers are exercised in different manners by BACEN and CVM, and through different mechanisms.

The Central Bank is a state company linked to the Ministry of Finance. Its competences are defined in the Constitution, in the federal statute that created it and in complementary legislation.[13] BACEN is, according to Brazilian law, responsible for establishing relations, on behalf of the Brazilian government, with foreign and international financial institutions[14] and, as we will see, responsible for representing Brazil in the BCBS.

---

11 Law (Federal Statute) 4595 of 31 December 1964.

12 Over time, there were changes in the structure and composition of the CMN, with the participation of ministries, federal banks, representatives of private and working classes, such as the Minister of Industry and Trade, the President of the National Economic and Social Development Bank (BNDES), the President of the Bank of Brazil, the Minister of Agriculture and members appointed.

13 Federal Constitution of Brazil, Article 164; Internal Rules of BACEN (Regimento Interno do Banco Central), Article 2.

14 Law 4595 of 31 December 1964, Article. 11, I.

The Central Bank is charged with implementing the measures and regulations of the CMN. It is indeed the main executor of CMN's determinations, contained in instruments called Resolutions. These Resolutions are made public by the Central Bank and, as it implements them, it does so through a series of regulatory instruments: (i) *Circulares*, issued by the Board of Directors, the top decision-making body of BACEN, responsible for formulating policies and guidelines;[15] (ii) *Cartas-circulares* and (iii) Communiqués (*Comunicados*), issued by the departments and dealing with operational aspects of the CMN's Resolutions and BACEN's *Circulares*.

BACEN is not what could be called a regulatory agency. It still follows the model of the traditional state company structure. It is not totally independent administratively, it is not free from hierarchical subordination, it does not have fixed serving time for its directors and president and it is not financially autonomous.[16] As far as the letter of the law is concerned, BACEN appears, therefore, as an institution lacking independence and autonomy. It has, however, acquired throughout its history a fair amount of both in practice. In relation to its regulatory powers, the more relevant theme for the purposes of our discussion, it is true that BACEN merely implements the regulation decided by CMN, but it is also true that the CMN is composed of only three members, of which the president of the Central Bank is one.

### 4.3.2. Background to Brazil Joining the Basel Committee on Banking Supervision

Brazil was not a party to the creation of the Basel Committee on Banking Supervision (BCBS).[17] It came to join it only in March 2009 when membership was expanded to include other than Brazil, Australia, China, In-

15 Internal Rules of BACEN, Articles 5–8.

16 In Europe, the Central Bank of Germany is an example of an independent administrative authority, that in Brazil we call agency. But the Brazilian case is different; the directors of the Central Bank have no fixed serving time. See Bruno Salama, "Como interpretar as normas emitidas pelo BACEN e CMN? Uma resposta a partir da evolução do modelo de Estado brasileiro", in *Revista de Direito Bancário e do Mercado de Capitais*, 2009A, no. 46, p. 114.

17 For an overview of the BCBS, please see Chapter 5 by Shawn Donnelly, "Informal International Lawmaking: Global Financial Market Regulation".

dia, Mexico, Russia and South Korea.[18] A simple explanation for not becoming a member before is that Brazil had not been invited in until after the 2008 financial crisis. In this sense, the background to its joining the BCBS is that of the well-known context of the crisis and the combination of lack of effectiveness of the regulation produced by the former club members, as well as the newly perceived lack of legitimacy of the regulatory network as it was until then constituted.

As far as Brazil is concerned, however, it is arguable that it would have certainly joined the club before. And this would have a very natural explanation, namely the BCBS being the forum in which the essential players of the global financial market discuss the rules of the game. Regardless of the nature of the rules discussed and produced in this forum, and regardless of their binding character or effective implementation, no player in this market would like to be kept out.

It is arguable as well that this did not present itself very strongly until recently. In part, this would be due to the fact that Brazil's opening of its economy did not begin until the early 90s and, in what regards specifically the banking sector, it is not yet a very open one. In part, this is related to the fact that the stabilization of the Brazilian monetary system did not take place until the mid-90s. In this context, much energy had been focused on holding the economy together on the domestic front.

The newly attained status of member of the club is the recognition that Brazil, especially as an important member of the G20 and of the increasingly relevant BRICS group[19] and its Central Bank, is a global player who must have a voice in the regulation of the sector, that is, as mentioned, undergoing a deep legitimacy and credibility crisis. This procures and at the same time recognizes both domestic and international prestige. It also shows that Brazil has a good history concerning banking regula-

18 The adhesion of Brazil to the BIS was concluded with the publication of the Legislative Decree No. 15 of 19 March 1997, which ratified and promulgated the agreement establishing the body. The Central Bank of Brazil, completing the final stage of accession, deposited on 25 March 1997, U.S. $ 35,877,696.37, for the 3,000 shares offered in Brazil, corresponding to the payment of the portion of payment (paid-in) BIS capital plus premium release. BACEN is, as said, the formal representative of Brazil before the BCBS.

19 The BRICS group is formed by the emerging economies Brazil, Russia, India, China and South Africa.

tion.[20] The essential gain, however, is the actual participation in the ordering of the global banking market. These gains are perceived, however, by concerned actors and by technically informed participants of the specific sector, and not by the general public who are distant from this debate.

As for Brazil's participation in the norm production process within the network, the very short time that has elapsed since its incorporation makes it very difficult to offer an assessment. Brazil did not participate in the elaboration of Basel I and II Agreements. With respect to Basel III, or the collection of measures taken in 2009, after Brazil's entry into the Committee, measures the approval of which came also from the G20 and from the Financial Stability Board (FSB), Brazil was certainly one of the participants to the discussion and negotiation. How active an actor it was remains to be seen. In any case, given the sense of urgency that governed this tentative response to the 2008 crisis, combined with the technical and closed character of the financial sector and its regulation, this Brazilian participation did not get previous approval nor was it informed by a previous consultation process. Rather, Brazilian participation was certainly informed by the resilience demonstrated by domestic financial institutions during the crisis, which made Brazil an authoritative voice.

### 4.3.3. Brazil's Reliance on Basel Standards Prior to and Since Membership

In 1988 the BCBS released the document *International Convergence of Capital Measurement and Capital Standards*, known as the first Basel Capital Accord, or Basel I, in order to create minimum capital requirements for financial institutions as a way to cope with credit risk.

All accounts of Brazilian implementation of Basel I and other outputs of the BCBS put the beginning of the process at the year 1994. Basel I's implementation was decided by CMN Resolution 2.099/94. Here it may be useful to clarify a point: despite the fact that BACEN is the formal Brazilian representative at BCBS, the incorporation of the latter outputs happens most often through Resolutions issued by the previously mentioned National Monetary Council (CMN), to which the Central Bank is

[20] For a picture of the development of financial regulation and alternatives for reformulation after the 2008 crises see: Bruno Meyerhof Salama, "De onde viemos? Inovação e resposta regulatória na indústria bancária no pré-crise", in *Revista Direito GV*, vol. 5, no. 2, 2009B, pp. 325–342.

subjected. BACEN, once again, is responsible, in the internal regulatory process, for executing and making public CMN decisions which are binding on BACEN, on other official bodies and on the regulated actors.

Brazil's decision to implement Basel I and the timing of the decision have some relation with Brazil's membership in Mercosur (Southern Common Market). Mercosur is an economic and political agreement between Brazil, Argentina, Paraguay and Uruguay created in 1991. It has established the coordination of macroeconomic policies between State Parties.[21] In 1993 Mercosur countries decided to incorporate[22] in their financial systems the principles and ground rules established by the Basel I agreement.

However, as it implemented the standard, Brazil opted, as it does often, for a more conservative regulation than what is agreed internationally. The Basel I agreement set a minimum capital standard of 8%. Brazil first adopted the 8% standard and then chose to establish the minimum at 11%.

Prudential regulation of the banking sector is said to have been launched in Brazil only with CMN Resolution 2.099 that implemented Basel I agreement, and its annexes, being virtually non-existent before 1994.[23] This resolution dealt with conditions for financial institutions to enter the National Financial System, with minimum capital and liquid equity, and with the obligation of maintaining a compatible ratio between equity and risk of the operations. The decision, however, of establishing a higher capital than that decided by the BCBS, was taken by BACEN as it has some autonomy while discharging itself of the obligation to implement CMN resolutions.

---

[21] Legislative Decree No. 350 of 21 November 1991, Article 1.

[22] MERCOSUR/CMC/DEC. No. 10/93.

[23] Marques cites CMN Resolution 1065 of 1985, Circular 1273 of 29 December 1987 and CMN Resolution 1970 of 2 October 1992 (Newton Ferreira da Silva Marques, "Quatro décadas de atuação do Banco Central do Brasil na fiscalização e supervisão bancária", in *Revista de Direito Bancário e do Mercado de Capitais*, 2005, no. 30, p. 260). See also Sergio Darcy da Silva Alves and Tatiana Muniz Silva Alves, "A experiência brasileira de regulação: um caso de sucesso?", in Fabio Giambiagi, *Risco e regulação*, Elzevier, Rio de Janeiro, 2010.

Resolution 2.099 has been followed by several others that are said to be inspired by Basel I.[24] Many more CMN Resolutions, as well as *Medidas Provisórias*,[25] federal laws,[26] BACEN's *Circulares* and Communiqués,[27] and one Complementary Law[28] have implemented Basel I, such as regarding Minimum Standards,[29] the Supervision of Cross-Border Banking,[30] Core Principles,[31] the Framework for Internal Control Systems,[32] the Prevention of Criminal Use,[33] the Principles for the Management of Credit Risk[34] and the Sound Practices for Managing Liquidity.[35] All of the mentioned instruments of domestic law and regulation are binding. CMN Resolutions have been mentioned before, as have *Circulares* and Communiqués issued by the Central Bank in order to implement the former. *Medidas Provisórias* are emergency and temporary laws passed by the

24 CMN Resolution 2399/97 that created the capital requirement for risk in swap and established a method of consistent evaluation in determining the values at risk; CMN Resolution 2692/99 on exposure to interest rate, laid down a standard of capital requirements based on a value of risk methodology (VaR); CMN Resolution 2837/2001 (initially CMN Resolution 2543/98) that defined the regulatory capital as Heritage of Reference with two levels, Tier 1 and Tier 2; CMN Resolution 2892/01 determined the operational limits and capital requirements for foreign exchange exposure.

25 Provisional Measures no. 1182/95 and no. 2008/99.

26 Federal Law no. 9447/97 and no. 9613/98.

27 BACEN Circular no. 2784/97 and no. 2852/98.

28 Complementary Law no. 101/00.

29 Provisional Measure (Medida Provisória) 1182/95. The Minimum Standards of Banking Supervision were a response to the crisis originated by the bankruptcy of the Bank of Credit and Commerce International (BCCI). The Standards were discussed not only by the G-10 countries, but also by Brazil and others.

30 CMN Resolution 2302/96.

31 Brazil has adopted the Core principles for effective Banking Supervision, originally published in September 1997, as those were endorsed by the Brazilian government in the same year (CMN Resolution 2390/97). However, in 2006, Brazil did not participate in the review of the principles and therefore did not formally endorse them. Salama, 2009B, p. 334, see *supra* note 20.

32 CMN Resolution 2554/98 and subsequent amendments. An example of accuracy in the adoption of Basel guidelines is the creation of internal controls at banks, which largely mirrored the guidelines of the Framework for Internal Control Systems in Banking Organizations, published by the Committee in early September 1998. Salama, 2009B, p. 331, see *supra* note 20.

33 BACEN Circular 2852/98 and Law 9613/98.

34 Provisional Measure (Medida Provisória) 2008/99.

35 *Ibid.*

Presidency. They tend to be later transformed into statutes and are binding. Complementary laws are at a higher hierarchical level than Federal statutes and, as the name shows, they complement the constitutional text. They are, of course, binding, and in the case of financial regulation, they play a key role, since the 1988 Constitution expressly foresaw the need of such laws in the field. Federal statutes or laws are binding as well.

In 2004, BCBS released the revision of the Basel Capital Accord, 'International Convergence of Capital Measurement and Capital Standards: A Revised Framework', known as Basel II, in order to get a more accurate measure of the various risks faced by internationally active banks. The Brazilian Central Bank, through Communiqué 12,746 of 9 December 2004,[36] established the procedures to be adopted for the implementation of Basel II with an implementation schedule ending in 2011.[37]

Before the forecasted end of Brazil's process of implementing Basel II, the BCBS released the Basel III Agreement. The implementation is going to be a long process, and is only in its beginnings, for Brazil as well as for others.

### 4.3.4. Accountability Mechanisms

BACEN is the domestic actor that integrates the Basel Committee. This competence to participate in international cooperation arrangements is provided for in the laws and regulations of the SFN.[38] No special supplementary authorization is needed or asked for. No domestic consultation or authorization processes exist for participating in the rule production within the network.

The decisions to implement BCBS recommendations or guidelines are almost always taken by the CMN, of which the BACEN's President, as must be recalled, is one of only three members, alongside two Ministers. Since BACEN is the responsible body both for the implementation of monetary policy and for the supervision of the banking sector, it may de-

36 Subsequently amended by Communication 16137 of 27 September 2007 and Communiqué 19028 of 29 October 2009.

37 The complete list of the Central Bank's regulation on Basel II can be accessed in English on the Brazilian Central Bank's website: http://www.bcb.gov.br/?BAS2NORVIGING, last accessed on 5 January 2012.

38 Law no. 4.595 of 31 December 1964, Article 11.

cide to implement the standards if it deems that by doing so it will be implementing the policies decided by the CMN. When the recommendations or guidelines are incorporated by Complementary laws, by Federal statutes or by Provisional Measures, this happens usually because such incorporation is seen as compatible with other political decisions contained in the normative instruments. The instruments undergo the usual prescribed procedure for them to come into force, either the parliamentary route and presidential approval, for the first two, or a presidential decision for the third.

Neither of the decision-making processes requires any special authorization besides the general competence given by the law for these bodies to regulate the financial and banking sectors. This is to be expected, first because the regulatory products, the BCBS outputs, are not binding and are incorporated and implemented on a voluntary basis; second because implementation must happen through domestically produced regulation and, at least in principle, any domestic consultation or authorization process would come into play if and when the incorporation into domestic regulation or implementation takes place; and finally, any such supplementary procedures would take place only if they are necessary for the production of domestically initiated regulation that is not aimed at implementing international standards.

No specific procedures of exchange with actors of the banking sector is mandatory before the incorporation and implementation of the Basel recommendations and it would appear as well that they do not turn out to be necessary for a good implementation. It suffices that the domestic regulatory authority decides to act according to its powers in order to regulate the sector in accordance with international standards. There is, however, exchange of information with the financial institutions, in order to guarantee adherence, but such exchange does not seem to be very different from what would happen in the case of purely domestic regulation.

The BACEN has been recently increasing transparency in its operations. But we are unable to establish a relationship of cause and consequence with international influence. It would rather seem that the concern with transparency flows from an internal path of democratic evolution that, by most accounts, led to a Brazilian financial environment that is more transparent than those of developed countries.

As it faces a dilemma between efficiency and legitimacy, and realizing that in order to be effective it is important to be perceived as legitimate, the BACEN has been adopting the practice of publishing proposed regulations, including those which are inspired by the policies of BCBS, for public discussion on its web site, where specific timelines for the proposed reforms can be found. It does so even though it is not legally required to.

Draft regulations are also discussed at public hearings. Interested parties may submit suggestions and comments. Such comments can be submitted via the email link in response to the notice published on the BACEN Internet site or by mail to the Department of Financial System Regulation Standards (Denor). The public hearings are not mandatory and are not conducted in all cases; BACEN is free to decide when and if they are to happen.

Pursuant to Communiqué No. 9187 of 16 January 2002, comments and suggestions submitted will be available to the general public on the website. Interested parties who do not want their comments and suggestions to be disclosed should clearly indicate this option in the text track. Even though holding public hearings is not an obligation, making available the comments and suggestions is mandatory upon the BACEN, by force of the Communiqué.

Since 1996 there were four public hearings about draft standards inspired by Basel Committee recommendations: 25/2006,[39] 26/2006,[40] 31/2009,[41] 32/2009.[42] The first two public hearings concerned draft rules

---

39 Concerned drafts of resolutions and circulars aimed at improving the definition of the Reference Equity (Patrimônio de Referência – PR), which aims mainly to align the definition of capital of the institutions of the SFN with the recommendations of Basel, both with respect to the constituent elements and the deductions to be made, as well as to simplify the process of authorization for the borrowing instruments that comprise the eligible Tier II of PR.

40 Resolution regarding the Required Shareholders Equity (Patrimônio de Referência Exigido – PRE), Resolution establishing limits for exposure to foreign exchange risk, for adjusting the threshold for exposure in gold, foreign currency transactions and exchange rates established by resolution 2606 of 1999; *Circular* detailing the specific procedures for calculation of the PRE shares.

41 Concerns two drafts of *Circulares*, the first establishes the minimum requirements and procedures for calculating the PRE dealt with in Resolution No. 3490 of 29 August 2007, and the second setting out, in a complementary way, the procedures to be followed in requesting permission to use internal models for market risk for the calculation of regulatory capital for the market risk.

42 Draft *Circular* providing for disclosure by the financial institutions and other authorized institutions of information regarding risk management, the assets of (PRE) in

about Phase I of the implementation of Basel II in Brazil. The parties that submitted suggestions and comments were basically Banks, Companies and Group entities. We could not establish the specific impact, if any, the suggestions and comments had on the resulting rules. The impression that one gathers from the literature, however, is that there is a good degree of sensibility to the views of the regulated and other interested bodies and a fair amount of communication.

### 4.3.5. An Assessment of the Accountability and Legitimacy of Banking Regulation

The legislation that has created the SFN is from the mid-60s. However, in order to understand the present state of the system and the domestic legal framework, one has to bear in mind two historical processes that took place in the mid-90s which have influenced all of the financial regulation: the transition relating to the state model and the return to democracy.

The landmark of the democratic transition is the 1988 Constitution. The political context imposed a tension between the need of limiting and overcoming the economic crisis of the time and moving towards economic development. This led the Executive to take a series of measures that were seen as conducive to effective governance but possibly in contradiction to a strict reading of legality. In the realm of financial regulation tension arose between governability and legal-rational legitimacy of the measures adopted by the Brazilian state.[43]

In the new Constitution, the role to be played by the state undergoes some changes. The economic model to be built is one in which the state is less of an entrepreneur and planner, and more of an inducer and organizer of the economic activities that are to be performed mainly by private actors.

In this context, starting in the 90s, regulation as a theme became an integral part of the legal discourse. This period is one of institutional learning and reform of the state under a democratic regime.[44] It is during this time that privatization processes, the fight against monopoly and the

Resolution No. 3490 of 29 August 2007, and the adequacy of the Reference Equity (PR) that treats Resolution No. 3444 of 28 February 2007.

43 José Eduardo Faria, *Direito e Economia na Democratização Brasileira*, Malheiros, São Paulo, 1993, p. 22.

44 Salama, 2009A, pp. 103–128, see *supra* note 16.

creation of regulatory agencies start taking place.[45] This scenario ensured the emergence of decentralized regulation and economic activities.

The previously alluded to tension between efficacy and legitimacy of the banking regulation takes place and is a consequence of this general picture. In fact, many point to the fact that the subordination of the BACEN to CMN opens doors to the direct influence by the Presidency of the Republic which is dependent only on political considerations and not on legal constraints.[46]

But, besides the possibility of this kind of direct intervention, the declared technical character of the banking regulation is seen by some as a means to escape legal and political legitimate control.[47] The efficacy/legitimacy dilemma was dealt with extensively in Brazilian tribunals over the last 20 years. The discussions concerned the legality and constitutionality of regulatory instruments in view, for example, of the constitutional limit to interest rates. The economic efficiency argument has won the day in almost all cases.[48]

We have mentioned the fact that BACEN is a state company with little formal independence, especially because of the precarious status of its president and directors and because of the possible influence of the political process over the technical regulation. It is true, however, that in practice and over time, as previously mentioned, it has acquired a fair degree of autonomy and independence which have allowed it to become, and be perceived as, an effective regulator. Such effectiveness does not spring from a perfect adhesion to international regulatory standards. To a great extent, there was adherence to guidelines such as those of the BCBS, but the quality of the Brazilian regulation seems to be due, with hindsight, to the parts that went beyond or were different from what was applied elsewhere.

We spoke above of a dichotomy between legitimacy and efficacy but one cannot disregard the fact that in what concerns the prudential regulation aimed at preventing systemic failures, effectiveness is also a

---

45 For an overview of the process of state reform towards a "regulatory" approach see: Paulo Todescan Lessa Mattos, *O novo Estado regulador no Brasil: eficiência e legitimidade*, Singular, São Paulo, 2006, p. 138.

46 Salama, 2009A, p. 114, see *supra* note 16.

47 *Ibid.*

48 Ademir Antonio Pereira Junior, "Legitimidade e governabilidade na regulação do Sistema Financeiro", in *Revista Direito GV*, vol. 4, no. 2, 2008, pp. 517–538.

measure of legitimacy. In the Brazilian case, features of legitimacy are part of the equation, such as transparency and accountability that have been contributing factors to the effectiveness of the regulation.

The fact that Brazilian courts have usually supported economic efficiency against what was perceived as being a bad legal framework could be construed either as an instance of lack of legitimacy and a poor degree of rule of law, or as a strong argument for the necessary independence of the regulator to produce good results.

In any case, when the regulation is challenged, this has usually no relation with whether it was inspired by international standards. Whatever oversight the banking regulation undergoes it is the same for purely domestic and for internationally produced rules.

Finally, it should be mentioned that we live a very specific historic moment in which the quality of the standards produced internationally is put in question, their legitimacy is being eroded by the fact that they do not seem capable of avoiding systemic risks, and that regulators from countries like Brazil are being called upon, not to endorse the existing rules but to rescue the legitimacy of the regulatory network by helping it transform itself.

## 4.4. International Organization of Securities Commissions (IOSCO)

### 4.4.1. Overview of the Brazilian Securities Market and Domestic Legal Framework for Rule Elaboration

As mentioned before, the main structures of the Brazilian Financial System (CMN and BACEN) were created in 1964. The legal basis for the development project that was being conceived by the newly installed military regime was thus launched. There were, however, more market institutions to create. A 1965 law tackled the task of stimulating long-term investments by developing a national capital market.[49] The intention was to migrate from a bank-oriented towards a market-oriented model.[50]

The law, which set the ground norms for professional intermediation and for regulating the capital market, until then a task undertaken by

[49] Federal Law 4728 of 14 July 1965.

[50] Otavio Yazbek, *Regulação do Mercado financeiro e de capitais*, Campus Jurídico, São Paulo, 2008, pp. 268–269.

the BACEN,[51] was the formal starting point of the securities distribution system in the country.

However, only in 1976 did Brazil enact a corporation's law,[52] conceived at that time as a necessary step to tackle the growing number of problems rising in an under-regulated field.[53] The law disciplines the functioning of the securities market and the performance of its protagonists, such as classified, open companies, financial intermediaries, investors, and others.

At the same time, and in conjunction with this measure, another law[54] created a specialized regulatory and supervisory body for the securities market, the previously mentioned CVM (the Securities Commission).

It may be relevant to note the fact that financial regulation at that point in time, in Brazil, was intimately connected to a national development model. One author sustains that "[…] the regulatory structures were not dedicated to the typically 'corrective' ends of regulation […] but rather to creating a true market in the country".[55]

This instrumental use of the securities market rules, aimed at creating the conditions for the development of a market, has had a long life in Brazilian recent history, starting during the military regime and surviving through the hard times of financial crises and high inflation. More than that, in the face of the challenge to contain inflation, regulation of the market took a secondary importance. Only with the monetary stabilization that took place in the mid 90s and with Brazil's entry, as an emerging country, into the world financial order, was the restructuring of the regulatory structures seen as a real necessity.

---

51 *Ibid.*, p. 269.

52 Law 6404 of 15 December 1976 (Lei das Sas).

53 Yazbek, 2008, p. 270, see *supra* note 50.

54 Law 6385 of 7 December 1976. CVM's functioning is also directly ruled by the previously mentioned Law 6.404/76 and by Law .457/97, Law 10.303/01 and Law 10.411/02.

55 "(…) Regulatory frameworks did not face typically "corrective" purposes of regulation (i.e. regulation as an affront to market failures), but rather intended to create a genuine single market in the country, seeking to shape the structures that would be part of it. The new legislation gave special emphasis on activities that stimulate and promote the domestic market, which also charged the regulators, which is evident in several provisions of diplomas, enacted in the period." Yazbek, 2008, p. 271, see *supra* note 50.

CVM is a state company, as is the case of BACEN, but it was created to function under a special regime. Law 6385 establishes that CVM has its own legal personality and equity, is administratively independent, enjoys financial and budgetary autonomy and its executives, chosen by the President of the Republic, have fixed mandates and cannot be fired except for very limited circumstances. This makes it different, in terms of autonomy and independence, at least as far as the letter of the law is concerned, from the BACEN. This may be explained by the difference in the timing of the creation of the institutions, the BACEN being older by more than a decade, and by the political sensibility over the theme of Central Bank independence in the Brazilian context. As we have mentioned, however, the BACEN has acquired a large degree of autonomy that in some respects erases this formal differences with the CVM's own independence.

As we have seen, both bodies are linked to the Ministry of Finance[56] and are subordinated to the CMN. They are both bound by the CMN's resolutions and mandated with the task of implementing them. CVM does so by issuing Instructions, Deliberations, Opinions and Explanatory Notes.[57] At this point another precision concerning the different ways in which the BACEN and the CVM perform their tasks is useful. The instruments of which the BACEN disposes are always necessarily aimed at implementing the CMN's decisions or policies. The CVM, on the other hand, enjoys a real regulatory power, meaning it can create regulation within the powers bestowed on it. Once again, this difference may be somewhat compensated by the fact that the BACEN has one of the three seats at the CMN.

Article 10 of Law 6385 establishes CVM's competence to conclude international agreements with other countries or with international entities, in order to better control and investigate lack of compliance with its regulations. Complementary Law 105 contains a similar language, allowing both BACEN and CVM to enter agreements, with the same kind of specific purpose. CVM's acceptance of IOSCO's Multilateral Memorandum of Understanding, to be discussed below, as well as its conclusion of several bilateral Memoranda of Understanding, flow from this competence. CVM's participation in IOSCO however, would rather seem to flow from its Internal Regiment (internal rules) enacted by the Ministry of

56 Created by Federal Law 6.385 of 7 December 1976

57 Respectively: *instruções, deliberações, pareceres, notas explicativas*.

Finance, to which CVM is institutionally submitted. This instrument authorizes CVM to "[…] establish relationships with any public or private entities, in the country and outside, with the objective of exchanging experiences and of information […]".[58]

### 4.4.2. Membership and Level of Involvement

CVM was one of the founders of IOSCO, when, in 1983, it was created with the decision to switch from an inter-American regional association (created in 1974) into a global cooperative body.[59] Brazil hosted two annual conferences, in 1979 and in 1987. CVM signed some cooperation agreements such as the 1995 Windsor Declaration, the 1996 Boca Raton Declaration ('Declaration on Cooperation and Supervision of International Futures Markets and Clearing Organizations') and the Multilateral Memorandum of Understanding concerning Consultation and Cooperation and the Exchange of Information on 21 October 2009.

CVM today is an ordinary member,[60] and member of IOSCO's Executive Committee. It has twice been responsible for the Presidency of the Inter-American Committee (1995–1996 and 2002–2004) and for the Working Group on Improvement of Standards for Investment Funds. It is also represented at the six working groups on the Technical Committee.

Several self-regulated bodies, the São Paulo Securities, Commodities and Futures Exchange ('*Bolsa de Valores, Mercadorias e Futuros*' – BM&F Bovespa) and the Central of Custody and Financial Settlement of Securities ('*Balcão Organizado de Ativos e Derivativos*' – CETIP) are members of the Advisory Committee. BM&F Bovespa, Brazilian Financial and Capital Markets Association (ANBIMA), CETIP and BM&F Bovespa Market Supervision (BSM) are affiliate members.

[58] Internal Regiment (*Portaria* n. 327 of 11 July 1977), Article 10, VIII.

[59] "IOSCO Historical Background", available at http://www.iosco.org/about/index.cfm?section=background, last accessed on 5 January 2012. For an overview of IOSCO, please see Chapter 5 by Shawn Donnelly, "Financial Market Regulation and Informal International Law Making".

[60] This category is open to a securities commission, or a similar government or statutory regulatory body that has primary responsibility for securities regulation in its jurisdiction.

Currently, the Executive Committee is presided over by the president of CVM, Maria Helena dos Santos Fernandes de Santana.[61] This fact alone signals the consistent history of Brazilian participation in the network and of the implementation of its outputs, as we will see below. More recently, Brazil's role has acquired a more substantial and important weight. Similarly to what happened in the BCBS context, after 2008's financial crises, Brazil's conservative approach has become well appreciated, and Brazil's role has grown. A very concrete example of its newly acquired status is Brazil's entry, following a peer review process, into the Appendix A group of countries.[62]

Following the 2008 events, IOSCO expanded the group of relevant countries and included new actors in the debate. Brazil, as well as India and China were invited to become parties to the Technical Committee, which up until that point had been a very closed group. This process illustrates the growing recognition of the different institutional approaches to financial regulation and reflects the understanding that there is a need to better guarantee the efficacy and the harmonization of these different institutional settings.

In this context, and before we move on to speak of Brazil's implementation of IOSCO outputs, it is interesting to note that some of the Brazilian practices concerning the securities market which were previously criticized by the market players are now increasingly being copied and praised. One example of this phenomenon is Brazil's practice of identifying the final clients in the stock market, rather than only the intermediaries. Brazil was one of only a few countries to adopt this measure, as part of a general policy on transparency, a policy deemed necessary as Brazil was recovering from its period of economic instability. What was before the object of criticism is now recognized as a worthy example of a legitimate specificity of the Brazilian system.

Other examples could be called upon to illustrate a general trend. Brazil's specificities relate to at least two related traits: the conservative tendencies of the Brazilian regulator and the insistence on what some

[61] Maria Helena took office on 21 April 2011 at the end of the Annual Conference in Cape Town, and its mandate will end in 2012, when the constituent committees of the organization will be integrated into the Board of Directors of IOSCO.

[62] Regulators that, in accordance with the procedures set forth in Appendix B, have signed the MOU, will be invited by IOSCO, subject to a peer review process, to be a signatory and to sign Appendix A of the MOU.

would view as excessive transparency. An example is the fact that contrary to the general tendency in world markets, it is estimated that 90% of the derivatives in the Brazilian market are negotiated in the stock exchange rather than in the over-the-counter market. The fact that Brazil has such clear information on the actors' exposures in the market is seen as an upside of the transparency trend.

Concerning the level of CVM's involvement in IOSCO, it is noteworthy, that even before the last crisis and the consequential important changes that have been taking place, Brazil has made considerable efforts, during the last decade or so, to be a very active participant in IOSCO and to influence its outputs – if not for any other reason, than at the very least to ensure that the outputs do not conflict with its own regulatory choices and do not negatively impact its market. This ambition, fairly successful so far, is supported by the fact that Brazil has one of the largest and most extensively regulated security markets in the world.

### 4.4.3. Implementation of IOSCO's Outputs

IOSCO has three main outputs: the 'Objectives and Principles of Securities Regulation', the 'Methodology for Assessing Implementation of the IOSCO Objectives and Principles of Securities Regulation' and the 'Multilateral Memorandum of Understanding'.

As we have seen, CVM signed the Memorandum of Understanding in 2009 and is now a party to its Appendix A. This entry into a select group of countries, which we have alluded before, and which was dependent on a peer review process, is proof of Brazil's total adherence to the IOSCO principles. Total adherence here does not mean that the CVM's regulation covers all aspects contemplated in the principles, but it means that all of the securities regulation in Brazil is in conformity with IOSCO standards, guidelines and principles, in as far as the latter contemplate the subject matter of the regulation. The incorporation and implementation is done on the basis of Instructions ('*Instruções*') issued by CVM and which legally bind the market actors.

For illustration purposes, we look at two IOSCO principles that the CVM has implemented as CVM instructions.

In the first case, the CVM adopted a registration model that is inspired by what IOSCO refers to as the 'shelf registration system'. According to this model, all information regarding the emitter of securities – such as activities, risk factors, administration, equity structure, financial data, *et cetera* – are gathered in a single 'shelf document'. This document must be filed with the regulator and kept up to date. CVM considers the 'shelf registration system' to be desirable and compatible with Brazil's market reality. It is expected that such a model will improve the conditions for investors and professionals to evaluate the securities issuers, as it will make good quality information permanently available.

In the second case, the CVM, according to IOSCO's principles that require adequate disclosure concerning the remuneration of administrators, has enacted an instruction that commands the disclosure of the remuneration paid to board members, directors and the fiscal council.[63]

As mentioned, whenever Brazilian securities regulation concerns a subject matter for which there are IOSCO principles, the CVM aims for total adhesion to the principles. This is asked for and welcomed by the market players that operate in the Brazilian environment. In some instances, issues that are the object of IOSCO principles are not regulated by CVM. Until recently this was the case concerning rating agencies, for which an Instruction is now under way, and is still the case of the so-called dark pools which are simply prohibited in Brazil.

### 4.4.4. Accountability Mechanisms

The first stage in the rule elaboration by CVM is one of market analysis and of comparative law studies. Once these studies are completed, a draft of the norm is prepared and discussed at the regulations committee. At least for the last five years, CVM has been organizing public hearings in which every rule under consideration is discussed.

CVM is not under a legal obligation to hold public hearings or consultations but it is authorized by Law 6385 to publish drafts of regulation to be enacted in order to receive suggestions from interested parties and to summon any person it deems capable of contributing to the betterment of the rules to give information or opinions.[64] The same authorization is contained in CVM's Internal Regiment, along with details on how public consultations should be conducted.[65] All the documents and information

[63] CVM Instruction no. 480, Annex 24.

[64] Law 6385 of 7 December 1976, Article 8.

[65] Internal Regiment, Article 26.

about the ongoing public hearings and the ones that have been concluded are available at CVM's website.[66]

In general, suggestions received from market players do not tend to challenge the contents inspired by IOSCO principles. Most usually, the participants in the audiences are entities that have multinational presence and are already subject to IOSCO guidelines in other jurisdictions. There are, however, cases in which regulation inspired by IOSCO may be seen as having a different impact on the local environment as compared to other markets. In such cases, there are more challenges to the regulation, as was the case for administrators' remuneration mentioned above.

In the case of the implementation of the principle regarding the remuneration of administrators, the issue reached the courts.[67] In that instance, a professional association (IBEF)[68] succeeded in suspending the applicability of a part of the CVM's resolution. They thereby succeeded in precluding the possibility that administrators (or the corporations to which they belong) be subjected to any sanctions for not complying with the disclosure obligations set by CVM.

IBEF argued that the command to disclose the remuneration violated the legality principle, since it was a new rule, non-existent in previous law, being created via a mere regulatory instrument, contradicted previous legal dispositions contained in the corporations law, violated the right to the protection of one's privacy, intimacy and secrecy of personal data, violated the principle of proportionality and, finally, was likely to endanger the safety of people whose earnings would be made public.

CVM, on the other side, argued that the disclosure would elevate the transparency of information available to investors to what was internationally recognized as being the minimum standard, and that Brazil ran the risk of being regarded as lagging behind in its market regulation and, finally and maybe more relevantly for our purposes, that the measure was

---

66 CVM, Securities and Exchange Commission of Brazil, available at http://www.cvm.gov.br/, last accessed on 26 June 2012.

67 5th Federal Court of the Judicial Section of Rio de Janeiro (5ª Vara Federal da Seção Judiciária do Rio de Janeiro), Civil Action (Ação Ordinária) n. 2010.5101002888. At the latest stage, the first instance's decision was upheld by the Superior Court of Justice (Superior Tribunal de Justiça - STJ) (Preliminary Injunction (Medida Cautelar) n. 17.350-RJ, 7 Octobe 2010). It has not reached the Supreme Court yet.

68 Brazilian Institute of Finance Executives (*Instituto Brasileiro de Executivos de Finanças* – IBEF).

implementing an agreement undertaken by Brazil at G20 meetings and within IOSCO.

This example is useful to illustrate some features of the debate on implementation of guidelines through domestic regulation and on the legitimacy and accountability of such regulation. Firstly, it shows that challenges to regulation, especially if they take place before the courts, will try to be comprehensive in the legal argumentation by pointing to all possible instances of lack of conformity with the constitutional, legal and regulatory framework. It is also for this reason that the challenging party in this case did not underline or even consider the fact that the regulation in question had been inspired by international guidelines.

Secondly, it illustrates the Brazilian regulator's tendency towards transparency to which the international guideline is only a complementary stimulus. In the Brazilian context, the defense argument of compliance with an international standard is relatively weaker than those arguments concerning the strict legality and even those relating to good prudential regulation.

Finally, it shows the exceptional circumstances in which Brazilian prudential regulation, generally perceived as very good, which is both successful in effectively regulating the market as well as fairly legitimated by a good degree of transparency and accountability, needs to be adapted to the specific concerns of domestic societal considerations.

To the just mentioned degree of effectiveness, legitimacy, transparency and accountability that Brazilian prudential regulation is believed to feature, the fact that the domestic regulator seeks adherence to internationally agreed guidelines like IOSCO's and to other commonly recognized national good practices is just one of the contributing factors. Adherence to international guidelines is not absolute and this is due to the specific traits of the Brazilian market that make some regulatory contents inappropriate or inapplicable to the national context.

### 4.5. International Conference on Harmonization of Technical Requirements for Registration of Pharmaceuticals for Human Use (ICH)

In this part of the chapter we move away from networks active in the financial area and take a look at a network active in the health area – the International Conference on Harmonization of Technical Requirements for Registration of Pharmaceuticals for Human Use (ICH).

### 4.5.1. Overview and Legal Framework

The 1988 Constitution and a 1990 Federal Law established that the functions of sanitary surveillance[69] are an integral part of the Single Health System (*Sistema Único de Saúde* – SUS).[70] A 1998 Provisional Measure (that was later converted into a 1999 Federal Law) instituted a National System of Sanitary Vigilance and created the National Health Vigilance Agency (ANVISA).[71]

ANVISA is one of several regulatory agencies created in Brazil after the mid-90s as part of a general effort by the Brazilian state to decentralize its public administration. This effort was in line with Brazil's decision to adapt its governance practices to international standards. ANVISA is also a state company. It functions under a special regime, which means it is administratively independent, its directors serve for pre-established terms and it enjoys financial autonomy. In this sense, it is closer to the model adopted for CVM than to the one under which BACEN functions.

ANVISA is functionally connected to the Health Ministry and is responsible for promoting and protecting public health through sanitary control of the production and trade of medical products and services. This includes the environment, the processes, the raw materials and technologies employed. It is also responsible for the control of ports, airports and borders and, in cooperation with the Ministry of Foreign Affairs, for interacting with foreign bodies in international matters related to sanitary vigilance.[72]

---

[69] Law 8080 of 19 September 1990, article 6, § 1: "It is understood as a set of sanitary surveillance actions that can eliminate, reduce or prevent health risks and intervene in health problems resulting from the environment, production and circulation of goods and services of interest to health, including: I - control of consumer goods that directly or indirectly relate to health, including all the stages and processes, from production to consumption, and; II - control of the services that relate directly or indirectly to health".

[70] Law 8080 of 19 September 1990.

[71] The provisional measure 1791/98 was converted into Law no. 9.782, of 26 January 1999.

[72] Law 9782 of 26 January 1999, Article 7, III.

The regulations produced by ANVISA take most usually the form of Collegiate Board Resolutions. These regulatory instruments are legally binding but this does not preclude the agency from issuing guidelines. These and other instruments can serve as vehicles for recommendations, for clarifications *et cetera*.

### 4.5.2. Brazil's Participation in the ICH

ANVISA purports to consider very highly the importance of international cooperation. It has an organ responsible for international relations and, in its publicly available information, discusses the importance of cooperation efforts in the international arena and Brazil's growing concern and importance in these efforts. Law 9782 gives ANVISA the competence to pursue its objectives including through international cooperation.[73] In what concerns sanitary matters, it presents its cooperation agreements and exchanges with other relevant national agencies and also with international organizations or bodies as part of a more general trend and effort. ICH is one of such listed bodies but there is little public information on the level and nature of the relationship.

The information is not much more abundant from the side of the ICH itself. What is known is that ANVISA, being Brazil's drug regulatory authority (DRA), was invited to join the Global Cooperation Group (GCG) of ICH in 2007. At that time the ICH invited drug regulatory authorities from countries with a history of ICH guideline implementation and/or where major production and clinical research are done. Alongside ANVISA, drug regulatory authorities from Australia, China, Chinese Taipei, India, Republic of Korea, Russia and Singapore were invited too.[74]

### 4.5.3. Implementation of ICH Guidelines

ANVISA does not adopt ICH guidelines *per se*. The guidelines are used as input or as a benchmark when ANVISA develops domestic regulations, usually through the previously mentioned Collegiate Board Resolutions. ANVISA then adapts ICH guidelines and takes them into account together with other inputs, such as international standards issued by other inter-

[73] Law 9782 of 26 January 1999, Article 7, XXIII.

[74] For more information about the Global Cooperation Group and ICH more generally, see Chapter 10 by Ayelet Berman "Informal International Law-Making in the Drug and Medical Devices Field".

national multilateral agencies[75] and other foreign, country-specific regulations as well as the opinions of CATEME (Technical Chamber of Medicines, ANVISA).

Within ANVISA there are specific technical divisions that are responsible for different subject-matters. These divisions analyze and scrutinize international guidelines. If needed, these divisions may ask for an evaluation of the Collegiate Board.

There are only very few examples of ANVISA regulatory documents that explicitly recognize their reliance on ICH guidelines. One 2003 resolution established that pharmacovigilance data should be presented in accordance with the Periodic Safety Update Report (PSUR/ICH).[76] A 2004 resolution established a new guide for stability testing and refers to an ICH quality guideline.[77]

Further, in March 2010 ANVISA released a Guide concerning non-clinical safety studies. The Guide is based on "documents from agencies recognized in the field of pharmaceutical sanitary vigilance (FDA, EMEA), and from institutions interested in the field (ICH, OECD, NCI, WHO)." It also goes on explicitly to say that "its aim is a greater harmonization with international scientifically reliable regulation".[78]

### 4.5.4. Accountability Mechanisms

ANVISA has developed, as it is authorized to do by its Internal Regiment,[79] a process of public consultation that takes place before it enacts each technical regulation. For the purposes of the consultations, the proposed texts of Resolutions of the Board (RDC) are published. The exist-

75 For medications, primarily World Health Organization (WHO) and Pan American Health Organization (PAHO).

76 RDC Resolution no. 136 of 29 May 2003.

77 ANVISA Resolution n. 398 of 12 November 2004, repealed by ANVISA Resolution n. 1 of 29 July 2005.

78 ANVISA, *Guia para a condução de estudos não clínicos de segurança necessários ao desenvolvimento de medicamentos*, p. 5, available at http://portal.anvisa.gov.br/wps/wcm/connect/30dd7a0047457fa68b53df3fbc4c6735/GUIA+PARA+A+CONDU%C3%87%C3%83O+DE+ESTUDOS+N%C3%83O+CL%C3%8DNICOS+DE+SEGURAN%C3%87A+NECESS%C3%81RIOS+AO+DESENVOLVIMENTO+DE+MEDICAMENTOS.pdf?MOD=AJPERES, last accessed on 5 January 2012.

79 *Portaria* 354 of 11 August 2006, Article 51.

ence and terms of each public consultation process is given publicity in the Official Gazette (DOU) and also on the Internet site of ANVISA.[80]

Any interested actor can comment and submit suggestions during a period most commonly of 60 days. The Agency evaluates all comments and, depending on the analysis, incorporates them into the process. According to the Agency, at the end of the consultation process, once it consolidates the results, the public can verify ANVISA's comments on the evaluation of the suggestions received. The consultation processes, which ANVISA is at liberty to conduct, apply to any kind of regulation to be produced and there are no specific or different procedures when the regulation is inspired by international bodies or guidelines.

In parallel to national public consultations, very often the proposed regulation undergoes an international process of scrutiny as ANVISA notifies the World Trade Organization's committees, under the Sanitary and Phytosanitary Measures Agreement (SPS) and the Technical Barriers to Trade Agreement (TBT) on the proposed regulations that fall under the scope of these agreements.

The open domestic consultation process and the international notification and consultation procedures seem to illustrate very well the Agency's efforts to provide accountability and legitimacy to its regulatory work. The consultations provide transparency to its work and provide stakeholders with the opportunity to intervene in the process. Through its participation in international networks, its pro-international cooperation discourse and its reliance on international standards, the Agency legitimizes its own work, as it presents it as proof of Brazil's belonging to the group of responsible regulators, and as the result of state of the art research that is collectively produced and scrutinized. Brazil's reliance on ICH standards and the Agency's explicit reference to them is part of this legitimizing effort.

Looking at the interaction between ANVISA and the ICH, on one hand, and at the interplay between Brazilian regulation on pharmaceuticals and ICH guidelines, on the other hand, one is left with a sense that there is very little to be grasped. This is due, in part, to the fact that Brazil is both a new and a marginal (with a very unclear role) member of the

[80] ANVISA, Legislação Sanitária, available at http://portal.anvisa.gov.br/wps/portal/anvisa/anvisa/legislacao and Consultas Públicas, available at http://portal.anvisa.gov.br/wps/portal/anvisa/anvisa/consultapublica, last accessed on 5 January 2012.

network. It is also due to the fact that ANVISA has many competences, among which regulation of pharmaceuticals is only one. And finally, it may be due as well, in part, to the fact that as an international standard setting body whose guidelines ANVISA may take into consideration, the ICH also faces the competition of other like bodies with which ANVISA concerns itself.

## 4.6. General Conclusions

The three networks we have dealt with in this chapter have served as illustrations, as tests, to a description, that could not in any way be exhaustive or comprehensive, of the ways in which Brazil deals with the outputs of informal international lawmaking networks.

At the outset of the chapter, we have offered some questions as guiding lights for our investigation. We will now use them as guides for our conclusions.

Brazil entertains different levels and different qualities of involvement with each of the networks. It has very recently joined the BCBS and its entry is very much a consequence of very relevant changes taking place in the international financial scene and regulation. It was always a member of IOSCO and, at least for the last decade, a very relevant one. The recent crisis that has prompted Brazil's participation in the BCBS has also increased its relevance as an influent participant in IOSCO. It is not a formal member of ICH, but has been called upon to integrate one of its bodies, because it is considered a relevant actor in the field. To conclude, where Brazil had until recently no voice in the outputs of the networks, it begins to be heard. Where it had already one, it is now more audible.

The incorporation or implementation of the outputs by Brazil, as it is the case for other actors in respect to these specific networks, needs some kind of regulatory action by the state, by the domestic regulator. As it incorporates these outputs, and it does so up to a certain extent, the Brazilian regulator takes the outputs mostly as an inspiration for the regulation it produces. Where local regulation deals with subject matters that are the object of IN-LAW outputs it adheres to the spirit of the guidelines, principles and standards, but this adherence does not change the fact that the local regulator is exercising its own regulatory powers and deciding the content and the language of the regulation.

More relevant to the accountability focus of the analysis in the Brazilian case is that the domestic regulator does not need – in order to implement international informal outputs – any powers other than those it has to produce domestically inspired regulation. Further, any accountability mechanism that applies to regulation that implements international informal outputs applies to any regulatory action of the domestic regulator. We have seen that, in all three cases, the Brazilian regulator has a concern with transparency and with procedures of consultation and response.

Very often, reliance on international standards or principles is a legitimizing factor for domestic regulation. Regulation is then presented as being proof of international prestige, because of Brazil's growing importance in the networks. It also presented proof of the good quality of the standards, as they rely on state of the art expertise and due to their harmonization nature.

When the regulation is challenged, and this happens most often in the financial and securities sectors, usually it is not the international origin of the regulatory content that is put into question. What is questioned is the overall regulatory power of the efficiency driven regulator, as this power is seen as a possible escape from legal control. The concerns are therefore related to a more comprehensive problem regarding the place of regulation, especially financial regulation, within the debate on the rule of law in the Brazilian legal system.

It is almost unnecessary to say that informal international lawmaking springs, naturally, from the need to offer answers to specific problems, answers that traditional law is unable to provide. IN-LAW is more flexible in its production procedures and is more flexible in it normative strength and contents. Its legitimacy may be questioned and judged as it is produced in the international sphere and it may be questioned and judged a second time, as it enters the domestic legal and regulatory environment.

The involvement of a domestic regulatory body with IN-LAW must also be evaluated at both these moments, considering whether it participates or not in the international decision-making process and whether, if it does participate, it does so transparently and accountably, and considering how accountable it is as it transfers into the domestic field the products of the international networks.

Since IN-LAW is here to stay and since it relates to the needs of a society in which Brazil is an important player, it is important that Brazil actively participate in the networks, being thereby more capable of influencing the outcomes that will likely affect it in one way or the other. This participation is less problematic from the point of view of democratic accountability as long as it is seen as a means to influence outcomes in ways that are compatible with Brazilian interests rather than as an unauthorized engagement of the country's will and interests. This is especially true since IN-LAW outputs are thought to be non-binding.

A more critical moment for the legitimacy of the regulator's involvement with IN-LAW networks is that of the internalization or of the domestic implementation of the outputs. At this point, we have been able to see that the behavior of the Brazilian regulators, as they implement outputs of all three networks we have looked at, have done so in responsible ways and with a fair degree of transparency and accountability. Even if this general conclusion were to be challenged, the challenge would not concern in a special way the IN-LAW outputs, but would rather be directed at the quality of the rules and at the quality of the regulatory process in general.

Brazil is a young democracy and there are numerous ways in which the rule of law is an ideal yet to be attained. This may also be true for the regulatory work that is also, but not exclusively, influenced by the work of international informal networks. We believe that the best way to ensure legitimacy of the regulation that is inspired by IN-LAW outputs is by making sure that the process at the international level is legitimate and takes into account Brazil's real needs and includes Brazil as one of the decision-makers. This will not automatically solve the problem of legitimacy or accountability of the domestic regulatory process, but will take away at least part of the complicating factor involved when domestic regulation is inspired by international guidelines.

# PART II

# FINANCE AND COMPETITION

# 5

# Informal International Lawmaking: Global Financial Market Regulation

**Shawn Donnelly***

## 5.1. Introduction

How much informal international lawmaking exists in financial market regulation (FMR)[1] and what drives its development? FMR at the global level was so weakly institutionalized before April 2009 that it neither constrained nor demanded much of national governments, regulators and legislators. Since then, however, it has undergone changes so significant that financial market regulators should be considered instances of informal international lawmaking. This means that global standard-setters for FMR generate output that is intended to be binding – regardless of the fact that it is not traditional international law and regardless of the fact that it is generated outside of official international organizations (IOs) – involving the participation of government officials and stakeholders outside national foreign ministries.[2] This development is not made directly through inter-

* **Shawn Donnelly** is Assistant Professor of European Economic Governance in the Department of Public Administration, School of Management and Governance at the University of Twente, the Netherlands.

1 Financial market regulation (FMR) can be described as the regulation of actors who participate in financial market transactions, which constitutes any activity related to the buying, selling or transfer of financial instruments. Financial instruments include currency, company shares, bonds (both corporate and sovereign) and a wide variety of financial derivatives. The activities covered extend not only to actors who are directly involved in financial transactions such as banks, insurance companies, hedge funds and stock brokers (either on a personal or institutional capacity) but also to the wide circle of actors who provide and process information based on which these actors buy or sell financial instruments. It therefore extends to accountants responsible for preparing financial reports, financial reporting boards within companies, credit rating agencies and even members of the press who provide assessments of the financial prospects of shares, bonds, and other financial instruments.

2 J. Pauwelyn, "Informal International Lawmaking: Framing the Concept and Research Questions", in Joost Pauwelyn, Ramses A. Wessel and Jan Wouters (eds.), *Informal International Lawmaking*, Oxford University Press, Oxford, 2012, pp. 14–34.

national standard-setting bodies (ISSBs) themselves, but through the establishment of a new body, the Financial Stability Board (FSB) that brings regulators together and insists that its members adopt its standards domestically. This is a significant introduction of political obligations on member governments to adjust national laws in compliance with international consensus. Furthermore, there are plans to extend the effective obligation of compliance to all countries globally, through pressure applied by the International Monetary Fund (IMF) and the World Bank. The G20 imposed this new form of informal international lawmaking on national governments in April 2009.

This chapter is structured as follows. Section 5.2. establishes the analytical reference points of informal international lawmaking as outlined by Pauwelyn, Wessel and Wouters, and provides a more fine-tuned analytical framework for operationalizing varying degrees of informal international lawmaking. Section 5.3. outlines briefly how the institutional features of the international financial architecture generate obligations for national governments in the absence of formal international law. Section 5.4. provides details of the institutional developments and legal standards that shed light on the legal informality of actors, institutions, process and output. Section 5.5. discusses accountability mechanisms. Section 5.6. discusses and draws conclusions.

## 5.2. Institutional Development and Reform

A key issue in this volume is distinguishing the nature of informal international lawmaking, and then of accountability. As stated by Pauwelyn elsewhere,[3] informal international lawmaking (IN-LAW) for the purpose of legal scholars is characterized in the first instance by:

> Cross-border cooperation between public authorities, with or without the participation of private actors and/or international organizations, in a forum other than a traditional international organization (process informality), and/or as between actors other than traditional diplomatic actors (such as regulators or agencies) (actor informality) and/or which does not result in a formal treaty or traditional source of international law (output informality).

[3] *Ibid.*, p. 22.

Additionally, IN-LAW recognizes that the obligation for national governments, regulators and legislators to comply by adopting internationally-generated standards must be added to the definition to make the connection between international activity and domestic practice.[4] The presence or absence of obligation allows us analytically to set aside situations in which networks of actors work across national borders, without the benefit of a formally institutionalized environment to guide their behavior[5] and keep them accountable,[6] and to focus on those areas where there is a material consequence to those activities, seen in the confluence of institutionalized activity generating standards for legislation that robs traditional participants in the lawmaking process of their participation in the process. The analytical framework outlined below uses the degree of institutionalization within international standard-setting bodies, and the degree of obligation attached to membership as the threshold of identifying what can be considered informal international lawmaking. This allows us to approach the issue of IN-LAW from a practitioner's perspective, with a view to the *materiality* of the institution,[7] reinforced by *a political or effective obligation* to national actors, rather than *legal obligation.*

To this end, Table 1 draws a distinction between various degrees of national and international institutionalization, providing information on how the relevant components of each policy system are best understood.

4 Dick W.P. Ruiter and Ramses A.Wessel, "The Legal Nature of Informal International Law: A Legal Theoretical Exercise" in Pauwelyn, Wessel and Wouters, 2012, see *supra* note 2, pp. 162–184.

5 Anne-Marie Slaughter, *A New World Order*, Princeton University Press, Princeton 2005.

6 Frank Vibert, *Democracy and Dissent: the challenge of international rule-making*, Edward Elgar, Cheltenham, 2011; Margaret Keck and Kathryn Sikkink, *Activists Beyond Borders: advocacy networks in international politics*, Cornell University Press, Ithaca, 1998; Burkard Eberlein and Edgar Grande, "Beyond delegation: transnational regulatory regimes and the EU regulatory state", in *Journal of European Public Policy*, 2005, vol. 21, no. 1, pp. 89–112.

7 For a discussion of institutions in international relations, see Barry Buzan, *From International to World Society? English School Theory and the Social Structure of Globalisation*, Cambridge University Press, Cambridge, 2004; Stephen Krasner, *International Regimes*, Cornell University Press, Ithaca, 1983; Robert Keohane, and Joseph Nye, *Power and Interdependence: World Politics in Transition*, Little, Brown and Co., Boston, 1977; Susan Strange, *States and Markets*, Continuum, London, 1988; and Shawn Donnelly, *The Regimes of European Integration: constructing governance of the single market*, Oxford University Press, Oxford, 2010.

This incorporates the main actors, their motivations, the structure of relations between them, their rights and responsibilities (in a constitutive sense, that affect the structural relations between them), and the procedural features of their interaction (in a regulative sense, that confirm and give substance to the constitutive rules and norms of the policy area).[8] In the table, the key to identifying informal international lawmaking is finding what is labeled as international institutional governance. This kind of international relations extends beyond networks, which lack detailed agreements that could be construed as law, and beyond the voluntary agreement to pursue best practice in the context of national law. It involves more sophisticated institutionalization to handle output, and a sense of obligation to the participating countries, and perhaps others as well.

[8] For a discussion of constitutive and regulative rules and norms, see John Searle, *The Social Construction of Reality*, Free Press, New York, 1995.

| Governance Type | National | International Network Governance | International Institutional Governance | Supranational Governance |
|---|---|---|---|---|
| **Actors** | National executives, lawmakers, regulators | National specialists | Specialist representatives of Member States working in the context of international institutions | IOs and Member States (generalist ambassadors) |
| **Motivation** | Coherence, effectiveness and accountability of national policy | *Ad hoc* cooperation without codified institutionalization, even if iterated<br>Prevention of regulatory arbitrage by transnational private actors through state cooperation | Regularized cooperation with codified institutionalization<br>Prevention of regulatory arbitrage by transnational private actors through common regulatory standards | Collective action on the basis of an agreed policy agenda<br>Prevention of regulatory arbitrage by transnational private actors through common regulatory standards |
| **Structure** | Central control domestically, anarchy internationally (internal and external sovereignty) | Horizontal networks of disaggregated state actors take policy initiatives | Vertically-integrated networks of disaggregated state actors and international bodies outside of formal IOs | Vertically-integrated structure of supranational law and national implementation |
| **Rights** | Standard rights of a functioning democracy<br>OR<br>Effective state rights (in dictatorships) | None. All cooperation and interaction may be altered by central national authorities | Institutions insist on application of decisions by member States | IO right to authoritative decision-making.<br>* May include application of standards developed elsewhere |

| | | | | |
|---|---|---|---|---|
| **Responsibilities** | Obligations under rule of national law (To the extent that a democracy is under investigation) | Standard operating procedures across jurisdictions as gentlemen's agreements | Political obligation of members to implement framework agreements and standards, subject to open method of coordination and review | Legal obligation of Member States to implement in good faith |
| **Process** | Policy formation takes place either by liberalism, corporatism, statism or elitism (models of public policy) | Informal agreements, and standard operating procedures, Memoranda of Understanding | Technical committees do research and policy development, normally with ministerial oversight | Unanimity / consensus of the Member States OR less frequently, qualified majority vote |
| **Accountability** | Central government authorities responsible to parliament (on laws); Regulatory authorities responsible to government, parliament or both; Some use of independent regulatory authorities limits accountability | Central government authorities in theory supervise and intervene where they disapprove; Parliaments may not be adequately informed or consulted | Institution is accountable to Member States, Member States accountable to parliament, domestic constituencies at implementation phase | Member States rights to vote; NGO rights to information and consultation |

| **Outcomes** | Wide variety of legal doctrines and instruments.<br>Institutional diversity<br>Output high | Practical accommodation of (perhaps otherwise incompatible) legal doctrines and instruments<br>Voluntary institutional isomorphism<br>Output moderate | Convergence on legal doctrines and instruments. Fine details vary, but remain functionally equivalent Guided, collective institutional isomorphism<br>Output high | Convergence on legal doctrines and instruments. Fine details vary, but remain functionally equivalent<br>Institutional diversity<br>Output low |
|---|---|---|---|---|
| **Governance Architecture** | Formal description of FMR | Horizontal networks within ISSBs to determine principles, guidelines<br>Networks to engage in mutual learning, forward planning, in context of experimental governance<br>Competing national principles, instruments retained | Sector-specific standards by ISSBs<br>Applied vertically since 1999 for emerging market countries and developing countries (partially) through IMF/World Bank<br>Since 2009 integrated system for developed countries as well as through FSB | UN Global Compact sets benchmarks only |

**Table 1:** The categories Actors and Motivations correspond broadly to what Pauwelyn refers to as actor informality. The categories Structure, Rights, Responsibilities, and Process refer to various aspects of process informality. The category output refers to output informality, and the category Governance Architecture binds the various categories together to provide an overall assessment of the impact that the governance form has on national law and regulation.

### 5.3. Institutional Features and Obligation

The row contrasting actors underlines the distinction made above between networks operating in the absence of institutions, which was not the primary form of cooperation in financial market regulation after 2009, and networks working within them, which was more generally the case, particularly after 2009. Materially, and with an eye to the question of whether and to what extent there is informal international lawmaking, the second is also far more important than the first, since the raised status and complexity of the institution provides means by which to make points of agreement on policy a generally accepted or recognized principle or practice, and moreover the benchmark from which peer pressure can be applied to national administrations that are unenthusiastic about application. This is even more so when it is expected that being a member in good standing requires compliance with all of the collective decisions. Since this is the case with regard to the global FMR, this feature is a mechanism that enables political or effective obligation. This distinction in institutional ethos is also reflected in the row setting out motivational characteristics. More ambitious attempts at common regulatory standards go hand in hand with institutional development and the intent to accept membership obligations of standard transposition. It is this triad of institutional development, standard development and political or effective obligation that makes IN-LAW a force to be reckoned with.

A distinctive aspect of both international networks and international institutionalized governance is the importance of *specialist actors as foreign representatives*, and the contrast it makes with the national and supranational poles. Both network governance and institutionalized international governance put technical expertise and efficiency high on the list of prized principles and prerequisites of good collective action. Indeed, the notion that the protocols of formal IOs, and principles of internal and external sovereignty should be followed and given priority over all other considerations, particularly the presence of foreign ministers and ambassadors, is not only seen as inappropriate, but a sign of poor state socialization, development, regulatory capacity and general upbringing into the club of developed nations.[9] Inappropriate socialization, based on a frame of international law rather than international technocracy, leads in turn to a concomitant lack of influence within the organization. Indeed, it is diffi-

[9] Interview with staff member of one of the studied organisations.

cult to imagine that a foreign minister would have the requisite competence to negotiate appropriate agreements. It remains to be seen whether the admission of new countries to the institutions of global financial market regulation that have authoritarian political systems and therefore stronger centralized control will change this culture, and if so, by how much.

Another important factor that varies between the various public policy models is the structure of relations between the various participating actors. Structure refers first and foremost to the degree of equality or hierarchy between the participating actors within the governance architecture. It is therefore of critical importance in identifying one of the key characteristics of informal international lawmaking, with a stress on obligation for national actors. Of key importance is the mix of horizontal and vertical relationships that denote either a degree of authority and codification (in a vertical relationship), or a degree of freedom, equality, informality and voluntarism (in a horizontal relationship). Changes in global FMR in 2009 moved away from purely horizontal relationships to ones, as will be seen with regard to the FSB, that involve a modicum of vertical direction, held together for as long as and to the extent that political obligation lasts.

In the context of informal international lawmaking, the vertical-horizontal structure distinction is an important one, as horizontal relationships indicate that national policymakers are being influenced by what is going on outside their jurisdictions, but by their own volition, and that the authoritative decisions they do make remain their own choice. The strategic nature of the situation these participants face strengthens the assessment that horizontal contacts are benign for the purposes of domestic law and accountability. This assessment is by virtue of the argument that horizontal cooperation in the absence of institutions allows countries to win back regulatory capacity that they would otherwise lose through regulatory arbitrage by transnational private actors and the regulatory competition and race to the bottom between States that otherwise would result. Horizontal cooperation, whether seen as governance beyond the state,[10] is therefore a rescue of the legal and regulatory systems of countries and the accountability mechanisms attached to it rather than a threat. The same

[10] David Held and Anthony McGrew (eds.), *Governing Globalization: Power, Authority and Global Governance*, Polity, Cambridge, 2002; Michael Greven and Louis Pauly (eds.), *Democracy Beyond the State: the European Dilemma and the Emerging Global Order*, Rowman and Littlefield, Oxford, 2000.

argument has been made in the case of strong institutionalization,[11] even though institutionalization brings with it a stronger sense of responsibility for the members. As Slaughter argues, horizontal structures also ensure that accountability functions at the place where policy is codified and implemented, where it is entirely compatible with national legal standards of accountability.[12]

The rest of this chapter focuses almost exclusively on international institutions that lack the legal status of IOs, the networks of actors within them and the kinds of standards they produce. Meeting in such fora has become the norm in international financial market regulation, and has been for at least 20 years. What has changed in the last five years, however, is that the institutions have transformed from bodies that made broad recommendations on how to build regulations - which did not really constitute something we would recognize as informal international lawmaking - to bodies that make specific recommendations on how to regulate financial market participants and how to construct and operate regulation. This is what is meant above by materiality. In other words, they not only generated much more important output, but became themselves much more institutionalized in the process, both of which indicate a stronger tendency toward informal international lawmaking.

## 5.4. Informal International Lawmaking in Financial Market Regulation

In the field of international political economy, the international financial architecture comprises both formal IOs, like the IMF and the World Bank, as well as specialist international standard-setting bodies (ISSBs) that institutionalize global governance by national governments but are not formal IOs, and private ISSBs. The FSB brings these bodies together for the purpose of improving the regulation of financial stability since 2009. Within this interconnected web, different bodies perform different functions in developing standards and generating obligation. The ISSBs are more directly focused on regulation standards, and are populated by policy experts. The FSB ensures that those standards are adopted through political agreements by its members. The IMF and the World Bank are not

[11] Alan Milward, *The European Rescue of the Nation State*, Routledge, London, 1992.

[12] Anne-Marie Slaughter, *A New World Order*, Princeton University Press, Princeton, 2005.

direct regulators as much as providers of finance to the countries that cannot draw on private markets for their needs. They apply FSB standards through the review of countries outside the FSB. This section deals primarily with this second group, but addresses the others as well as part of understanding how ISSBs have developed the informal capacity to put pressure on national regulators and legal systems in this way.

A key feature of the international financial regulatory architecture, at least until 2009, was its fragmented and uneven nature, and the comparative weakness of its standards and institutions. An international regulatory institution was established for banks in the 1970s, for securities markets in the 1980s, and for corporate governance and illicit cross-border financial transactions in the 1990s. For the most part, their regulatory output was very modest until the late 1990s and limited then primarily to either standards about what kinds of resources and powers regulatory bodies should have, or very general principles of financial market regulation. Those general principles, building on a broad consensus of developed countries, posed no adaptation pressures or legal or other obligations on the latter. They therefore posed no real difficulties in terms of accountability. Substantive policy, politics and legislation remained national, and were merely networked internationally to varying degrees.

The standards developed there did, however, pose adaptation pressures on other countries in emerging markets from 1999 onward. That was the year in which the consensus of the G7 was established that a financial crisis that started in Thailand in 1997 and then went viral throughout the global financial system was the result of poor regulation in emerging markets, requiring better standards and application in those countries. It is only since 2009 that the same pressures to adapt have been extended to developed economies as well, which originated, amplified and tried to deal with the consequences of the current financial and economic crisis.

The rest of this section discusses each of the fields of financial market regulation in the chronological order of their establishment, from 1974 to the present day. It elaborates on how the nature of global activity on financial market regulation has developed in that time, and what makes its current manifestation so indicative of informal international lawmaking. It starts with individual standard-setters, covering banking, securities, and corporate governance, and then adds the FSB, which binds them together and provides the crucial element of political obligation to developed countries in the international financial system.

### 5.4.1. Banking

Global financial market regulation began in the 1970s, in banking, as a response to economic difficulties that had local epicenters but generated international shockwaves. Initially, the primary method of collective action was informal in almost every sense, based on collective interaction and occasionally, horizontal coordination of national authorities. The collapse of Herstatt Bank in 1974 led to the development of the Basel Committee on Bank Supervision within the Bank for International Settlements (BIS). The Committee at that time was not yet the standard-setter it would later become nor was it a central command for directing a war on financial contagion, but rather a forum and network for information sharing, mutual learning, and from time to time, supporting collective action in time of a credit event that could spread into a broader financial crisis.

The development of the Basel Committee, even in this weakly institutionalized form, made sense as central bankers, who were responsible at the time for both regulatory oversight and lender of last resort facilities in case of insolvency, could only fulfill their roles properly during a crisis if they shared information and acted collectively with a minimum of delay and interference. As the interventions since 2008 remind us,[13] these interventions must be completed within a matter of hours. Delays result in a possible collapse of the global financial system. The free movement of capital across national borders, and the cross-holdings between banks that made them dependent on one another for their good health and survival, would have otherwise had to be terminated in the name of prudent regulatory oversight, or terminated periodically for purposes of financial quarantine in the absence of a collective action supporting body like the Basel Committee.

Beyond the pressing need for central banks to intervene on their own authority during a crisis, there were knowledge factors that spoke for them taking the lead on regulation in between crises. Central banks have intimate knowledge of the banks they regulate, and specialized knowledge of financial markets that are essential to monitoring bank activity, establishing and operating early warning systems and modeling the impact of regulatory interventions that are the product of both long-term skill investment and direct contact with the regulated. Their role cannot be repli-

[13] The two collective interventions took place in December 2008 and December 2011 respectively.

cated equivalently by other governmental bodies. This is visible in the Committee's first official agreement in 1975 on dealing with bank collapses that cross national borders, the so-called Concordat.[14] Due to the existential urgency of acting swiftly and decisively during an international credit event, the Basel Committee remains the most cohesive and important international body establishing international rules on national financial regulatory standards. Before 1989, the Basel Committee was as informal a grouping as one can imagine, considered in terms of actors, process or output. Basel claims that it intends neither enforceability[15] nor great detail in its standards, but with the exception of the United States (US), which did not adopt Basel II, adoption, implementation and enforcement is considered an important step in assuring markets that the banking system is properly run and stable.

The Committee's output includes the Basel Accords on Capital Adequacy (known as Basel I, Basel II and soon Basel III),[16] the Core Principles for Effective Banking Supervision (1997) and the Core Principles Methodology (1999).[17] The latter two were developed for assessment following G7 calls at the Lyon Summit of June 1996 to help improve supervision in emerging markets. Both were revised in 2006. All have been under review since 2008 in realization that they did not work sufficiently well in developed markets.

The upgrading of Basel's work has raised questions not only of accountability, but of whether decision-making within the Committee would benefit from new participants in the process. Unlike standards issued by other ISSBs, which are principle-based rather than rule-based and therefore provide a degree of flexibility and adaptation, the Accords have hard numerical targets that banks and lawmakers are asked to comply with, regardless of whether or not they are members.

---

14 Maartje van Putten, *Policing the Banks: accountability mechanisms for the financial sector*, McGill-Queens University Press, Montreal, 2008, p. 165.

15 Dieter Kerwer, "Rules that many use: standards and global regulation", in *Governance*, 2005, vol. 18, no. 4, pp. 611–32.

16 Basel I was established in 1988 in response to a wave of bank failures in the US, mostly in savings and loan banks, whilst Basel II was established in 2004 after the 1997–8 crisis that began in Southeast Asia and spread to the US via Russia and Latin America.

17 Bank for International Settlements, *About the Basel Committee*, 2010, available at http://www.bis.org/bcbs/, last accessed on 30 June 2012.

The adoption of Basel standards remains voluntary, even for members of the Committee, if one disregards the new demands of FSB membership, discussed below. The US Government did not adopt Basel II (2004, for implementation 2008), for example, and is only adopting Basel III in the context of other political commitments it has made on the FSB. Even then, it did not do so without a significant degree of bellyaching and debate within the Board. Other Committee members adopted the accords as official policy within the rather long transition periods that the Committee arranged. These long transition periods were the result of unofficial negotiations with regulated banks over the time required to adjust capital structures. Assessments of Basel's influence have been correspondingly lukewarm. Bryce Quillin's study of Basel I underlines that the Accord indeed set minimum standards for capital adequacy, but that it is not very reliable during difficult times,[18] which underlines that international commitments do not tie the hands of domestic policymakers. Duncan Robert Wood suggests that Basel is capable of 'limited success' where powerful countries wish it, where the private sector cooperates, and where the goal is to avoid strong conflict across jurisdictions.[19] There remains current skepticism about the capacity of responses to the crisis to be sufficient,[20] despite the fact that the Committee's output now extends into corporate governance principles for banks, which largely draw on OECD principles of corporate governance[21] as well as its voluntarism.

The Basel Committee incorporated two other elements of selective access to global economic governance which are relevant to the discussion of agency accountability. The Committee is known unofficially as a G10 committee, which reflects the dominance of the G10 in its composition. The G10 reflected what at the time of the Basel Committee's establishment were the world's largest financial centers. Within this group, however, was an even smaller group of five countries representing the

---

18 Bryce Quillin, *International Financial Cooperation: political economics of compliance with the 1988 Basel Accord*, Routledge, London, 2008, p. 173.

19 Duncan Wood, *Governing Global Banking: the Basel Committee and the politics of financial globalization*, Ashgate, Aldershot, 2008.

20 Mathias Dewatripont, Jean-Charles Rochet and Jean Tirole, *Balancing the Banks: global lessons from the financial crisis*, Princeton University Press, Princeton, 2010.

21 Bank for International Settlements, *Principles for enhancing corporate governance issued by Basel Committee*, 16 March 2010, available at http://www.bis.org/press/p100316.htm, last accessed on 30 June 2012.

world's most important financial centers, whose agreement was required for the work of the Committee to make progress. The influence of this group, known as the 'Senior Supervisors Group', is not formally codified anywhere, and relies solely on self-selection, but nevertheless serves as a practical veto player in the policy-making process.

From an informal international lawmaking perspective, the Basel Committee's limited scope of policy management and voluntarism is typical of international networking within an organization, rather than truly international institutional governance with a high degree of obligation. This was the typical way of dealing with the tension between the desire for international governance and the desire for accountability to domestic constituencies. Although there is no formal requirement or institutionalization of the practice, the Basel Committee also meets periodically with large banks to confer on the potential impact of its practices.

Having said this, there are some areas of bank regulation where the Basel Committee tends to devote little attention to matters that affect financial stability through risk management and corporate governance laws and institutions at the national level. The three-pillar of risk management under Basel II serves to illustrate that an official Basel policy can legitimate practices that are otherwise known to be unsafe: the use of financial derivatives as the core capital of a bank, the associated use of credit rating agencies as external, private regulators of the quality of those derivatives, and the reliance on financial reporting by the banks themselves to ensure market discipline in the use of such instruments.[22] Basel's insistence on retaining these corporate governance mechanisms and focusing solely on capital adequacy standards, whilst simultaneously refusing to discuss corporate governance matters of banks generally, despite calls for change, underline a problem of limited responsiveness to critique.

Overall, the Basel Committee is an important international standard-setter with global implications, and hard rules, yet consisting of a rather limited number of participants and having no direct accountability to political actors, not even to the G20. As is the case for central banks, its members are informal actors. The concluded accords and promulgated directives remain informal output, unattached to any formal IO. The procedures are also informal, with the result that the Committee remains the

[22] Paul Langley, "Sub-prime mortgage lending: a cultural economy", in *Economy and Society*, 2009, vol. 37, no. 4, pp. 469–494.

most selective and discrete ISSB populated by public sector actors, today. No move has been made to change that status.

### 5.4.2. Securities

The next sub-section of financial market regulation after banking to be organized internationally by public sector actors was in the securities field in 1983. The securities field consists of stock exchanges, commodity and derivative markets and a variety of financial market participants that are neither banks nor insurance companies, plus related financial products. It includes the activity of hedge funds, credit rating agencies, other financial analysts, investment banks and so on. Unlike the Basel Committee, the policy and regulatory agency in this field, the International Organization of Securities Exchanges (IOSCO), was established in the absence of crisis, and in the absence of a mission to ensure systemic stability.[23] Its primary purpose at the time of its establishment was to lobby national governments to open up their financial systems to the kinds of actors and financial instruments mentioned above. IOSCO itself would then serve as a forum in which national regulators could discuss market trends and exchange experiences in regulation for the purpose of mutual learning. Actors, processes and output were extremely informal and institutionalization was low.

The organization and membership of IOSCO reflected until recently this existence as an open forum for securities regulators. To this day, there are nearly as many members as officially recognized countries. During the 1990s, the 'Technical Committee' (TC) was established and rose in importance, to discuss and develop broad principles of financial market regulation for hedge funds and later credit rating agencies at the request of the G20. This was IOSCO's first venture into substantial output, but it served primarily to promote the institutional capacity and resources of regulators themselves. Therein lay a key incentive for even weak regulators to join the organization: it strengthened their calls for resources within their domestic policy environments, awakened the perception that there were standard operating procedures for financial market regulators that could ensure financial stability as securities markets were being promoted

23 David Zaring, "International law by other means: the twilight existence of international financial regulatory institutions", in *Texas International Law Journal*, 1998, vol. 33, p. 281.

by the private and public sectors as a means of securing investment in national economies. It therefore played an enabling role in pushing for a certain degree of institutional isomorphism across countries. Although the idea of opening up national financial markets and regulating in a similar fashion had to take place through national governments, this background of regulators made the transition easier. One of the most visible effects of this during the 1990s was the widespread switch from separate regulators for banking, insurance and securities to single financial service regulators. Beyond these general principles that regulators should have investigatory and supervision powers and resources sufficient to carry out these tasks, there was very little of substance that committed national regulation in any particular way. The informal contacts generated little demand for specific legal innovations that required clear accountability in terms of legislation and policy development.

IOSCO has transformed since 2008 from an organization that promotes discussion about regulatory practice to one that increasingly generates principles-based regulation for national and global bodies. It remains the world's most open ISSB, with over 180 national securities regulators as *ordinary members*, who have full discussion and voting rights. A smaller group of *associate members* represents sub-national securities regulators and a few derivative regulators, whilst a third group of *affiliate* members provides IOs (the IMF, the OECD and the World Bank) and financial market participants (exchanges) with consultation rights. Other financial market participants are included via the Self-Regulatory Organizations' Consultative Committee and the Emerging Markets Advisory Board.

Most of IOSCO's work is conducted by the Technical Committee. It generates official research and reports, particularly principles of good governance and other guidelines for a wide variety of national regulators.[24] Annual Technical Committee conferences tackle both specific questions and the 'overall financial regulatory framework'.[25] The 'Emerging Markets Committee' and four 'Regional Committees' (one each for

[24] Examples of policies handled are disclosure and accounting standards (for multinational corporations particularly), regulation of secondary markets, regulation of financial intermediaries, regulation of asset management firms, regulation of credit rating agencies and protocols for cross-border regulatory enforcement.

[25] IOSCO Technical Committee, Conference Communique, Basel, 7–9 October 2009.

the Americas, Europe, Middle East/Africa and Asia) add to the opportunity for exchange.

Agenda-setting, proposing strategic direction and oversight is led by the 19-member 'Executive Committee', which contains the Chairs of the Technical, Emerging and Regional Committees, plus members elected by the Regional and President's Committees (plenum).

Until the financial and economic crisis that started in 2007 blew up in 2008, IOSCO was primarily about interaction and mutual learning.[26] There had been a limited number of reports issued on security market participants – the only notable ones were for credit rating agencies and for hedge funds. The other code that IOSCO produced was the 'Principles for Securities Regulation' of 1999, which set out the independent powers and resources that a financial markets regulator should ideally have, and the role that it should play in supervising fair play in accordance with national securities law. Indeed, that focus on fair play reflects the original purpose of IOSCO, and until 2009, its continuing principal mission, which was to ensure a level playing field across countries for international investors, located at the time almost entirely in the US and Europe.

In the intermediate phase, between 1999 and 2009, IOSCO's principle work on standards consisted of more detailed guidance provided by the organization's Technical Committee on how regulators could go about implementing the general principles on sound regulation. The emphasis was not only on best practice, but on mutual learning, and knowledge dissemination from developed economies to emerging markets.[27] This squared with the dominant attitude after the East Asian Crisis of 1997–1998 that standard and institutional development was a necessity primarily outside of the OECD. As was the case with membership, however, IOSCO proved to be far more open and receptive to calls for inclusive participation and communication with the Technical Committee.

In the phase since 2009, IOSCO has made the full transition from discussion forum and generator of quite general principles to a more institutionalized body providing much more detailed research, analysis and regulatory advice about financial market participants and the development of regulatory policies and tools. Again, the most important of its tasks have dealt with credit rating agencies and with hedge funds, but also with

26 Interview with IOSCO staff member.

27 *Ibid.*

new possible solutions to the last financial crisis that rely on more highly developed securities markets, such as the question of whether risky financial operations such as short-selling[28] should be restricted, either entirely or simply during financial emergencies.

IOSCO's increased role in generating principles and codes has led to a few of these changes and an overall change in the nature of the organization. The Technical Committee now plays a central role in the impact that IOSCO has on global economic governance, at the invitation of the FSB. The interest of private associations to have input through the new form of affiliate membership has grown accordingly. IOSCO has specialized in particular in those business entities that were previously unregulated, for which no other IO previously had responsibility.

Whilst the Technical Committee is responsible for deciding on standards, it solicits a great deal of input in regional conferences and by holding its regular meetings in various parts of the world. The intention has been to ensure that to the extent IOSCO has patterns of communication that are not entirely horizontal, that they are as much bottom-up as they are top-down. This means not only participation by emerging markets, but also by financial market participants. The public interest sector is not involved, in contrast.

The result of these developments is that while IOSCO fulfills all of the criteria of informality set out in this study in all respects, it has evolved away from a body supporting a horizontal network into a highly-institutionalized body attracting specialists in a wide variety of financial market participants and practices. Indeed, IOSCO, backed by the G20 and the FSB, has become involved in discussions to regulate nearly everything that was unregulated before the current crisis. Although its guidelines remain formally voluntary, they are being granted much more bite by virtue of being used as criteria for membership in good standing of the FSB, and by their use by the IMF and the World Bank in their assessment of the quality of financial market regulation in recipient countries.[29]

---

28 Short-selling occurs when a financial market participant contracts to sell financial instruments at a point in the future without having the instruments.

29 This takes place in the context of Article IV negotiations of the IMF, as part of the Financial Services Assessment Programme.

### 5.4.3. Corporate Governance

Corporate governance regulation, which encompasses the rules governing how companies are structured and operated, has also attracted attention in the context of the financial crisis, although it was already on the radar screen in the early 1990s. At the end of the 1980s, serious corporate collapses that threatened the health of the UK financial system led to a review of corporate governance regulation and practice, and lead to a series of private initiatives by the City of London, known as the Corporate Governance Codes.[30] As similar corporate collapses occurred in other developed countries, the OECD adopted the UK practice of adopting private codes. Many embellished them with hard company law, but the key is that the OECD established its own Principles of Good Corporate Governance in 1999, and revised them in 2006. This relationship between national initiatives and international ones is therefore the reverse of that in securities regulation: in the case of corporate governance, international rules follow and are embedded in national ones, rather than the other way around.

The Principles themselves do not constitute hard law, but they were sufficiently influential to generate significant institutional isomorphism, even in countries that had grave misgivings about the possible implications of a voluntary corporate governance code. This was the case in Germany, for example, which introduced such a code in 2002, and stated explicitly that it was not intended to substitute voluntarism for the hard obligations of company managers, and the rights of various stakeholders and shareholders in German companies. The Principles dictate that there should be sufficient information and voting rights for shareholders over company managers and company policies, so that they can effectively control the company, and that they can do so over the objections of block holders (sometimes state block holders, with a significant public interest justification for wielding a veto over company decisions, might hold a blocking minority of votes under special national regulations.).

---

[30] Shawn Donnelly, *Regimes of European Integration: constructing governance of the single market*, Oxford University Press, Oxford, 2010; Shawn Donnelly, "Corporate governance and the Company Law Review in Britain", in Bjong-Man Ahn, John Halligan and Stephen Wilks (eds.), *Reforming Public and Corporate Governance: management and the market in Australia, Britain and Korea*, Edward Elgar, Cheltenham, 2002, pp. 195–214.

In principle, one should expect that this would put significant pressure on member States to change their domestic laws to conform. In practice, OECD negotiations and rule adoption practices ensure that the Principles reflect the lowest common denominator, and the staff of the Company Affairs Directorate (CAD) at the OECD was very aware that certain political sensibilities about the nature of company law and corporate governance had to be respected in whatever principles and interpretations thereof were put forward to the Ministerial level for adoption.[31] These differences boil down to a collision between shareholder-oriented systems of corporate governance, which identify most corporate failures as rooted in insufficient shareholder control over managers, and stakeholder systems of corporate governance, which identify corporate collapses as rooted in insufficient balancing between shareholder interests, which tend to bleed companies dry of sufficient resources to operate properly, and other interests, which are interested in the long-term vibrancy of the company, as employees, bondholder-investors, and so on.[32]

The OECD remains much different than the other two institutions in how it deals with decision-making and accountability, but there are some parallels. The distinctions lie in the OECD's more formal nature, with actual government ministers in attendance for the adoption of any agreements that their ambassadors have worked out, and the requirement of consensus on any measures adopted. The similarities are located in the technical work of the CAD, which has its own staff of 16 and operates regional and OECD-wide events on the state of corporate governance and company law. The CAD in this sense operates much like the Technical Committee of IOSCO, with the important distinction that CAD's work is far more sensitive to the political side of the standards they are promoting discussion on, and that the scope of stakeholders who attend such meetings is much more spread across the political spectrum. Although business interests dominate, union, gender and environmental NGOs are present at the discussions, infusing debate with demands and suggestions that are not present elsewhere. This is also true at the OECD-wide meetings when the Ministerial level discusses adoption. The two main organized social partners within the OECD are regular interlocutors on the quality and con-

31 Interview with OECD staff member.

32 Shawn Donnelly, "Public interest politics, corporate governance and company regulation in Germany and Britain", in *German Politics*, 2000, vol. 9, no. 2, pp. 171–94.

tent of both the Principles, and on regular reports on their functioning and application in the member States.

Although measures to promote good corporate governance are considered essential to combating corporate collapse which could undermine general confidence and even the systemic stability of financial markets, there remains a clear demand on the part of both members and non-members to keep the Principles flexible and voluntary:

> It was agreed that the revision should be pursued with a view to maintaining a non-binding principles-based approach, which recognizes the need to adapt implementation to varying legal economic and cultural circumstances.[33]

Member States are therefore not legally bound to do anything, but the political commitment that is required to approve the Principles has led all OECD member States to adopt private, voluntary Corporate Governance Codes, which express best practice. The relationship between the Codes and company law varies greatly, however. In the UK, the Code is the primary source of reference within limits set by the Companies Act, and is observed on a comply-or-explain basis. In Germany, the Code's voluntarism is understood to ensure the supremacy of company law over any competing principle.[34]

The OECD's 'Steering Group on Corporate Governance' was renamed the 'Corporate Governance Committee' in 2010. It is supported by the Corporate Affairs Division in the OECD Directorate for Financial and Enterprise Affairs, which serves as a research unit, secretariat, and organizer of outreach events.[35] In addition to Ministerial Representatives, it includes key IOs as observers as well: from the World Bank, the BIS, the IMF on an ongoing basis, and from the FSB, the Basel Committee, and IOSCO on an *ad hoc* basis.

The Committee is not as open as IOSCO due to the OECD's smaller membership, but its *modus operandi* is to make documentation of re-

[33] OECD, *Principles on Corporate Governance*, Paris, 2004.

[34] Donnelly, 2010, see *supra* note 30.

[35] OECD, "Corporate governance principles", available at http://www.oecd.org/document/42/0,3343,en_2649_34813_2048554_1_1_1_37439,00.html, last accessed on 26 June 2012.

search and background notes as open as possible,[36] and to include non-member States, business and labor interests via Regional Roundtables in the policy process.

Comments are solicited as well from two official advisory bodies to the OECD – the 'Business and Industry Advisory Council' (BIAC) and the 'Trade Union Advisory Council' (TUAC). Beyond these groups, OECD policy is discussed and commented on from the public sector by the 'European Corporate Governance Institute' (ECGI), which is an organization of public sector regulators and academics; and by the 'Global Corporate Governance Forum' (GCGF), which is part of the World Bank's International Finance Corporation. The GCGF supports measures improving corporate governance in low-to-mid income countries in the context of national reform programs. The private sector, particularly the financial services sector (investment) is represented as well by the 'International Corporate Governance Network' (ICGN). The GCGF and ICGN are more oriented to voluntary issues of corporate social responsibility, whereas the ECGI deals with issues of law and regulation, including self-regulation.

### 5.4.4. Combating Illicit International Financial Transactions

The Financial Action Task Force (FATF) has many of the same implications as the FSB does in the realm of combating illicit international financial transactions – particularly that it strongly encourages institutional and policy isomorphism in the member States (the FATF is hosted by the OECD), and that the G7 strongly encourages and even pressures countries that are not members to comply or face pressure. A key difference in general power patterns, however, is that whilst the US is somewhat of a reluctant participant in the mandatory application of standards through the FSB, it is the primary driving force in the case of the FATF.

The actual reasons behind illicit finance have changed over the years. In the early years of the FATF, during the 1990s, the US was interested in clamping down on financial transactions related to the drug trade as part of its domestic War on Drugs policy. In the context of the attacks of September 2001, an additional goal was introduced that eclipsed the

36 A notable restriction that applies throughout the OECD as a whole is that research documents, whilst easily accessible online in PDF format, are not free of charge as they are in many other IOs.

first one, which was suppressing finance of terrorist activity. That policy remains in the forefront, but has since been joined, to a must smaller degree, by the desire to clamp down on tax evasion, primarily by US citizens.

To do this, the US pursued and secured a Multilateral Memorandum of Understanding through the FATF that committed signatories to sharing information on any and all financial transactions and cooperating in pursuing investigations, arrest warrants and prosecutions. It also secured, in 2000, an agreement that the FATF should blackmail non-compliant countries, whether or not they were members. Blackmailing would have first been a labeling exercise that would then have extended into collective financial transaction embargoes of the country involved by the members of the FATF. Although the FATF signed on to this, without the benefits of ministerial representation, the ratification failed, so that the US was denied the advantage of having forceful informal international law in this area.

Although the FATF is a world apart from the rest of what we see in international financial market regulation, it does provide an interesting parallel with what the FSB is trying to do. Both are doing what they can to not only generate broad principles, as the OECD does, or detailed rules as IOSCO and the Basel Committee do to differing degrees, but to push them down into the national level where they will affect the real laws and institutions that are at the sharp end of regulation and policy-making, with strong isomorphism as a result. Both also require consensus, but the dynamic of decision-making makes them relevant and forceful, to the extent that the Member States concur. The real problems occur when a country is not a member state, and when a member state is irrelevant due to the power dynamics within the organization. This is separate, of course, from the fact that parliamentary assemblies are only consulted once a national government is presenting a concluded agreement for ratification and implementation, and of the question of stakeholder participation in the decision-making process. Both the FSB and the FATF are officially closed, but in practice the FSB cultivates a dialogue with the financial institutions they regulate that is more two-directional than is the case with the FATF. Although the consequences of systemic risk are enormous, there is a military culture within the FATF that sets it apart from the other institutions. Real private sector input does not fit in there.

### 5.4.5. Systemic Risk

In 1999, the first global institution was established to deal with the risk of a global financial collapse, after a two-year crisis that came close to resulting in precisely that. The Financial Stability Forum was called into being by the G7, with the support of a wider consultative group known as the G20, to serve as a means of overcoming fragmentation across ISSBs in banking, corporate governance, securities, financial reporting (through a private body known as the International Accounting Standards Board) and insurance (through a public body known as the International Association of Insurance Supervisors). Based in Basel, the FSF had little power of its own to do its own research on the causes of the financial crisis, nor did it attempt to do so. Basic research on the cause of the financial crisis and the best means of repeating such a crisis was undertaken by what was then a five-member country organization known as the 'Senior Supervisors' Group' (SSG). Before the SSG, which originally was limited to the UK, US, France, Japan and Switzerland, could have any significant impact on global financial market regulation, either directly or through the FSF, political discourse within the G7 over the causes of the crisis shifted from regulation issues to global macroeconomic imbalances. In short, the G7 identified the source of the crisis not in the poor regulation of banks, (despite initial complaints of crony capitalism in South-East Asia), but as excessive borrowing in East Asian emerging market countries, and prescribed higher rates of saving to fuel future economic growth. With the initial regulatory agenda pushed aside, there was very little for the Forum to do until the next crisis arose in 2007. The result was very weak institutionalization, limited network development beyond a very small circle on financial stability, and no independent standard development or encouragement. It did not constitute informal international lawmaking.

A side effect of the Forum's weakness was that regulatory standards issued by individual ISSBs were not designed to challenge the pre-crisis regulatory *status quo* prevalent in developed countries, particularly in the G7 countries. Since the latter had, for the most part, participated in writing those standards, and because the standards generally respected lowest common denominators, they posed little problem for these countries, were the largest financial markets were located.

For emerging markets the situation was somewhat different. Those countries that came out of the 1997–1998 crisis unscathed[37]or that rebounded quickly and replenished their capital reserves were not directly affected by regulatory standard development by ISSBs. They were not members of the organizations involved, at least in ways that would force them to adopt those policies to remain members in good standing. The countries most affected were those that had emerging or developing markets, but which wanted a stamp of approval from the IMF and the World Bank that investing in their countries was safe for international investors. The G7 exploited this vulnerability by assigning the IMF and World Bank the duty of investigating countries that might receive either disbursements or stand-by agreements for contingent aid (something like a line of credit for a country which is considered very useful in the event of a speculative run on the country's resources or currency). The two institutions jointly ran two programs: the 'Financial Sector Assessment Programme' and the 'Review of Standards and Codes', which provided or denied such a seal of approval.

The weaknesses of ISSBs and the FSF for countries hosting core financial markets were revealed in the financial crisis that began in 2007 and spun out of control in 2008. The Forum was deemed to have been useless in predicting such a crisis, dealing with it, or in having promoted the kinds of financial market regulation that could have prevented it in the first place. For that reason, the G7, together with the G20 again, called the FSB into being, which was designed to provide more institutional power behind a global regulatory effort. Whereas the Forum was not directly intended to generate what we might understand as informal international lawmaking (yet did so for the majority of the planet's countries not part of the OECD), the FSB most certainly was. The details of that body and its relationship with ISSBs and national governments and regulators will help us evaluate to what extent.

The FSB succeeded the Financial Stability Forum in April 2009, adopting a larger number of representatives of countries, key ISSBs, the IMF and World Bank as members, with the purpose of improving on financial reporting and regulation standards.[38] Global standards would have

---

37 Linda Weiss, *The Myth of the Powerless State*, Cornell University Press, New York, 1998.

38 G20, "Leaders Statement", 15 November 2008, available at http://www.cfr.org/financial-crises/statement-g-20-summit-november-2008/p17778, last accessed on 30

to apply not only to emerging markets,[39] but to developed markets as well, where risk management had failed.[40] The FSB's focus would be to ensure not only better standards, but greater consistency and systematic cooperation between countries, and as the US Treasury stated:

> promote international financial stability by facilitating better-informed lending and investment decisions, improving market integrity, and reducing the risks of financial distress and contagion.[41]

The FSB is designed to counter systemic risk through three main mechanisms. The first is to enhance the quality and coherence of standards set elsewhere: particularly at IOSCO,[42] the Basel Committee and the IAIS,[43] as well as their use by the IMF and the World Bank. The IMF incorporates standards through the Financial Sector Assessment Programme (FSAP) and the World Bank through the Review on Standards and Codes, which is a much wider-ranging exercise than the FSAP.

---

June 2012; Enrique Carrasco, "The Global Financial Crisis and the Financial Stability Forum: The Awakening and Transformation of an International Body", in *Transnational Law and Contemporary Problems*, 2006, vol. 19, pp. 203–20.

39 Alan Greenspan, "*Risk management in the global financial system*", Speech before the Annual Financial Markets Conference of the Federal Reserve Bank of Atlanta, Miami Beach, 27 February 1998, available at http://www.federalreserve.gov/boarddocs/speeches/1998/19980227.htm, last accessed on 30 June 2012. See also Geoffrey Underhill, Jasper Blom and Daniel Mugge, "Introduction: the challenges and prospects of global financial integration", in Geoffrey Underhill, Jasper Blom and Daniel Mugge (eds.), *Global Financial Integration Thirty Years On*, Cambridge University Press, Cambridge, 2010; Paul Langley, "(Re)politicizing global financial governance: what's 'new'about the 'New International Financial Architecture'?", in *Global Networks*, 2004, vol. 4, no. 1, pp. 69–87; Susanne Soederberg, "On the contradictions of the *New* International Financial Architecture: another Procrustean bed for emerging markets?", in *Third World Quarterly*, 2002, vol. 23, p. 4; Jacqueline Best, "From the top-down: the new financial architecture and the re-embedding of global finance", in *New Political Economy*, 2003, vol. 8, no. 3.

40 Alan Greenspan, "*International financial risk management*", Speech before the Council on Foreign Relations, 19 November 2002, available at http://www.federalreserve.gov/boarddocs/speeches/2002/20021119/default.htm, last accessed on 26 June 2012; Alan Greenspan, "*World finance and risk management*", Speech at Lancaster House, London, UK, 25 September 2002.

41 FSB. Why are Standards Important?, available at http://www.financialstabilityboard.org/cos/wasi.htm, last accessed on 30 June 2012.

42 International Organisation of Securities Commissions.

43 International Association of Insurance Supervisors.

The second mechanism is the supervisory college, which has the mission of looking at concrete developments in global systemically-important financial institutions (G-SIFIs). In other words, it sets up groups of regulators, central banks and finance ministers who may be involved in saving a specific G-SIFI if it threatens to collapse. A SIFI is any firm whose collapse could cause a cascade effect that undermines the liquidity or solvency of the financial system:

> The body will establish a supervisory college to monitor each of the largest international financial services firms. It will monitor a firm's financial and operational structure, and any contingency funding arrangements, amongst others. It will act as a clearing house for information-sharing and contingency planning for the benefit of its members.[44]

The third mechanism consists of peer reviews. FSB member States must undergo an assessment of their regulatory frameworks on the basis of the FSAP/ROSC assessments conducted by the World Bank and the IMF. The Board's concrete goal is to promote a general convergence of financial market regulation to standards that prevail within the most important member States,[45] raising the bar up to the level that both the US and Europe agree on.[46]

The FSB focuses on particular themes and particular countries in any given year, and devotes the Board's reviews and reporting on that before moving on to the next themes and countries. The Chairperson suggests to the Plenum what these focal points should be and the results are tabled before the Plenum, which adopts the findings on the Board's behalf by consensus.[47] This could be important, as reviews frequently recommend changes to laws and institutions.

Italy, Mexico and Spain were the first countries scheduled to be assessed on the basis of the IMF's FSAP. In late 2010, the report for Mexico[48] had been approved for release. In February 2011, the reports for Ita-

---

44 "The Financial Stability Board: how it will work", The Guardian, 4 April, 2010.

45 Interview with FSB member, January 2011.

46 Indeed, cooperation between the two parties is sometimes desired to prevent standards from truly being set 'somewhere else', *i.e.* by new members of the FSB. Discussion with European Commission staff, November 2010.

47 FSB, "FSB announces future peer reviews", 30 March 2010.

48 FSB *Country Review of Mexico*. 27 September 2010.

ly[49] and Spain[50] were released. Important to note here is that the FSB recommended institutional changes that would strengthen the regulatory powers of the respective institutions in these countries in the name of combating systemic risk.

Member States of the FSB may have between one and three representatives. The first representative is the monetary authority (the Central Bank). The second represents the government from the portfolio of the treasury ministry. The third, if present, represents a further specialized financial services regulator. Countries with one seat in the plenary are Argentina, Hong Kong, Indonesia, Saudi Arabia, Singapore, South Africa and Turkey; countries with two seats in the plenary are Australia, Mexico, the Netherlands, South Korea, Spain and Switzerland; countries with three seats in the plenary are Brazil, Russia, India, China, Canada, France, Germany, Italy, Japan, United Kingdom and the US. The number of seats is not up to the member state, nor are the criteria formalized: representation is decided collectively and politically based on economic importance and internal regulatory diversity of the country involved.[51]

In addition to this, the FSB Charter provides for the body to consult with the private sector and 'non-member authorities' on an *ad hoc* basis on account of being important stakeholders in the policy process.[52] The Board has also discussed the possibility of regional outreach programs beyond this membership.[53]

Decisions in the FSB are taken by the entire membership, which meets three times per year, by consensus. The work of the Board is supported by a Secretary General, a Secretariat, a Steering Committee made of up members elected by the full membership, three standing committees and working groups located within them.[54] The three Standing Commit-

---

49 FSB, *Peer Review of Italy*, 7 February, 2011, available at http://www.financialstabilityboard.org/publications/r_110207b.pdf, last accessed on 30 June 2012.

50 FSB, *Peer Review of Spain*, 7 February 2011, available at http://www.financialstabilityboard.org/publications/r_110207a.pdf, last accessed on 30 June 2012.

51 Stephany Griffith-Jones, Eric Helleiner and Ngaire Woods (eds.), *The Financial Stability Board: an effective fourth pillar of global economic governance?*, Centre for International Governance and Innovation, Waterloo, 2010.

52 FSB Charter, Art. 8. *Representation and Attendance*.

53 Mario Draghi, Speech on the occasion of the FSB's inaugural meeting, April 2009.

54 Griffith-Jones et al., 2010, p. 7, see *supra* note 51.

tees are the main institutional innovation through which the FSB is able to push the development of international standards that might constitute informal international lawmaking. The 'Vulnerabilities Assessment Committee' is responsible for undertaking research on the sources of potential economic crises in the future, with a practical view to dealing with so-called early warnings of possible financial trouble. The 'Supervisory and Regulatory Cooperation Committee' is responsible for working out mechanisms and protocols that bind together national regulators not only in time of crisis, but during routine oversight and supervision work. This is not so much writing national regulations as ensuring that the means of exchanging information are available in a complete and timely way. This is particularly the case for the working of supervisory colleges, which group together the regulatory supervisors for specific financial institutions that are considered too big to fail. However, the SRCC does see as part of its remit the need to ensure that level playing fields are ensured in the regulatory sphere, which normally means ensuring that minimum standards are respected. The 'Standards Implementation Committee' is the body that organizes and conducts the peer reviews of the FSB member States.[55] Standards from the ISSBs regarding institutional and legal design are bundled together and evaluated, one country at a time. It is here that the possible materiality of informal international lawmaking is strongest.

What is currently unclear is whether political input that restrains the Board or technocratic work that enhances its powers will win out over the long run. Despite the Board's introduction of committees with a clear mission, the influence of the committees is more subject to the countervailing influence of political judgment than one finds in the ISSBs. Political negotiations over the Board's Chair, the Board's mandate and output are ultimately decided by the G20, to which the Board reports. Items which do not enjoy consensus support within the G20, with the Chair, and across the Plenum's members, therefore never develop momentum. This allows the member States to ensure that they do not lose control of the process.[56]

The result of this dichotomy is that sweeping changes to financial market regulation that might collide with the prior practices of the member States may be safely considered unlikely. The same is true for ques-

[55] FSB, 27 June 2009, Basel.

[56] Interview with FSB official.

tions that the Board might pose about the soundness of financial market practices in terms of consequences for financial stability. The Board announced in September 2009, for example, that it would pursue 'relaunching securitization on a sound basis' and bringing out derivatives trading into the open on exchanges.[57] This was remarkable given the central role that securitization played in the financial bubble that preceded the crisis, and numerous calls to restrict it in the wake of the collapse of 2008.

Nevertheless, the FSB's current slate of issues on regulation now includes compensation, bank capital and liquidity, reducing moral hazard, enhancing cross-border resolution, accounting standards (IASB increasing technical studies of standards).[58] However, progress still awaits on a set of issues that could be described as technical, but actually requires political judgment to address a set of critiques about how finance operates. The G20 Communiqué noted that reporting gaps between two kinds of financial reporting standards: US-GAAP[59] and IFRS,[60] used in the US and the rest of the world respectively, would have to be addressed regarding off balance-sheet exposures,[61] but changes have not been forthcoming.

Assessments of the FSB's power range from the strong interpretation of an international institution[62] to a loose network of policy makers[63] to an advisory group.[64] The FSB lacks any formal power or legal personality and operates on the basis of political support from the G20. Its capacity to generate obligation is nevertheless present, however. Beyond

---

57 FSB 15 September 2009, Paris.

58 FSB, January 2010.

59 US-Generally-Accepted Accounting Practices.

60 International Financial Reporting Standards, issued by the International Accounting Standards Board. For this and the relationship between IFRS and US-GAAP, see Shawn Donnelly, "The International Accounting Standards Board", in *New Political Economy*, 2007, vol. 12, no. 1; Sebastian Botzem and Sigrid Quack, *Contested Rules and Shifting Boundaries: international standard setting in accounting* Discussion Paper SP III 2005-201; and FASB, "Progress report on IASB-FASB convergence work", 21 April 2011.

61 These refer to the special investment vehicles of the shadow banking system where much of the systemically risky activity was undertaken, above all in the US.

62 Tony Porter, "The G-7, The Financial Stability Forum, the G20, and the Politics of International Financial Regulation", available at http://www.g8.utoronto.ca/g20/biblio/porter-isa-2000.pdf, last accessed on 30 June 2012.

63 Griffith-Jones et al., 2010, see *supra* note 51.

64 The Guardian, 2009.

the business of working on the quality of regulations by the ISSBs, the FSB is involved in both horizontal and vertical measures that increase the sense of *political obligation* by member States, and eventually *effective obligation* by others. Horizontally, the FSB establishes supervisory colleges for the world's 28 largest financial institutions. These supervisory colleges typically bring together financial supervisors from the countries where a particular country does the most business to share information that could be relevant for an impending collapse, including briefings on daily business events and the organization of periodic stress tests. They are responsible for considering all of the factors that could lead to contagion across sub-sectors of financial markets and across countries. At the end of the day, the FSB theoretically has the power to directly regulate a financial institution in this way, but it remains in practice up to the financial service regulator in the country where the company has its headquarters to implement regulations. If it refuses, or takes a lighter approach than that proposed by its colleagues, there is precious little that the others can do. Decision-making at the FSB is by consensus.

The other method that the FSB uses is effectively a vertical relationship, even if it is formally a horizontal one. Using the open method of coordination developed by the OECD, member States of the FSB prepare reports on their legal and regulatory policies, institutions and practices and submit them to their colleagues at the board for peer review. At the time of writing, the peer review process had been used for Mexico, Spain, Italy and Australia, all of which were advised to provide more resources and powers to financial service regulators, so that they could adequately engage in early warning and crisis control at any given time. Although it would be difficult to force such a demand, it would be difficult to refuse it either. The FSB therefore establishes significant pressure on member States to view the standards of ISSBs, with all of the attendant recommendations on institutional and policy change, as authoritative and necessary. For non-member States, the accountability situation is different than for members, as the G20 supports applying FSB standards to non-member States as well through the FSAP/ROSC programs of the IMF and World Bank. The FSB's development therefore points to the development of informal international lawmaking within the context of a political consensus that is set by the G20.

## 5.5. Accountability

In the context of global financial market regulation, accountability claims from outside the organizations have been highly normative in nature, with procedural concerns forming part of that critique. Accountability claims from within the organizations have been highly focused on reporting-based procedural mechanisms that ultimately flow back to a recognized instance of political authority, which today is the G20. This is fitting (in a technical rather than normative sense) in that many of the new institutions of the international financial architecture are not formal IOs, but bodies whose legitimacy is founded on political consensus outside the international legal system. In contrast, accountability is not intended to end in the hands of stakeholders, in the sense that they should be in a position to formally ratify or veto decisions. In none of these bodies does a parliamentary assembly exist. Decision-making and accountability remain executive affairs, supplemented by consultation and reporting of results. Reporting here should not be confused with transparency, not least because, although these bodies tend to equate the two, the publishing of negotiating minutes, which is an acid test for transparency, happens nowhere in the new global financial architecture.

The One World Trust uses a four-stage means of accountability assessment as part of its Global Accountability Project. Accountability begins with transparency, then extends to participation of stakeholders in decision-making that affects them, complemented by regular, on-going self-evaluation and adjustment of the organization, and finally, complaint and response mechanisms by which stakeholders can express demands and have them responded to.[65]

One can say that the institutions reviewed above have gone through a process of self-evaluation and adjustment in the wake of the crisis that responds to certain critics. As a result, global financial market regulation has changed in terms of institutions, policies and the implications that they have for national governments. The legal status of the institutions and of the principles that they generate has not changed, while the character of the institutions and of the standards they generate has. Institutions have become more internally structured and formal, whilst standards have become more numerous and detailed. There remain many obstacles to de-

[65] Monica Blagescu, Lucy de las Casas and Robert Lloyd, *Pathways to Accountability: A short guide to the GAP framework,* One World Trust, London, 2005.

termine how exactly a country pursues particular standard-induced goals: the uncertainty is no longer on whether they will actually do so, but how they will implement the details.

Moreover, the degree of transparency and stakeholder input that accompanies it continues to vary greatly. The Basel Committee, the FSB and the FATF limit transparency to reports approved for release by the organizations' leadership. On the other hand, the OECD and IOSCO involve stakeholders in the deliberative process that leads up to formal decision-making by the member States.

The greatest impetus for self-evaluation and adjustment deals with the question of which countries participate in the rule-making process, in the pursuit of legitimacy. Decision-making in these international bodies is taken by consensus; the core group of countries that is involved in standard-setting has increased beyond the traditional set of advanced economies to include a number of emerging market countries, particularly the politically important BRIC countries. Other emerging markets are being consulted in one way or another in all of these bodies with the exception of the FSB, and market participants are as well. The standard-setters themselves have willingly expanded the scope of involved actors to ensure a sense of legitimacy about what they do that extends beyond the main claim to legitimacy, which is the technical expertise of the established economies. This is not accountability in the sense that there is political control, and that standard-setters can be forced to take actions that critics demand. Indeed, getting the bodies to do anything at all requires a consensus of the national governments and/or regulators and central banks involved, which mitigates against anything but moderate and incremental change. This has a great deal to do with why Global Financial Market Regulation (G-FMR) continues to focus on technical means of collecting information on financial market participants and ensuring good business practice rather than more assiduously restricting certain risky kinds of behavior that were surmised to be at the heart of the last crisis. Those voices must continue to place their hopes on lobbying national governments, in the hope that they will find acceptance at the international level.

Another trend that existed before the onset of the crisis, but which became more pronounced since then, is the consultation of Non-Member States, of market participants and of interested NGOs in regional roundtables. These roundtables serve the functions of encouraging regional discussion of how best to deal with the organization's standards and enticing discussion of how appropriate the standards are. The OECD and IOSCO set the global best practice in this form of providing legitimacy and accountability to stakeholders, with the OECD exerting more effort to incorporate not only business representatives, but also union representatives.

A key dynamic that deserves attention in these standard-setting bodies is the close interconnection between participation and ensuring legitimacy of what the bodies do. This dynamic means that the accountability process is not truly separated from the decision-making process, but incorporated into it in the executive decision-making process. Mutual recognition of how national jurisdictions apply the common standards is not automatic, but *politically managed* in most of the organizations studied here, at least for the members. The peer review process is the means by which national policies are reviewed and deemed to sufficiently implement international standards or even reflect best practice. It is passing muster with peer review in the WTO that may motivate those countries that must adjust their policies to do so. At the very minimum, remaining a member in good standing of the club requires interpreting, implementing and enforcing the standards that have been collectively decided on.

Therefore, the first incentive to adopt and implement standards is derived from the desire to participate in rule making. The second incentive is for non-club members to have a say in club standards, when club members or other organizations apply some form of *conditionality* to non-members in return for delivering something else of value. In the case of financial market regulation, the terms of this exchange are either that public financial or development assistance will be made available contingent on compliance with international standards, or that certification of compliance is necessary to secure private investment flows or prevent capital flight. Examples of direct conditionality are found in Reports on Standards and Codes (World Bank) and reports of the Financial Services Assessment Programme (IMF) that are used to determine official development or financial assistance. Examples of norm diffusion without direct conditionality are found in the negotiation of credit from the IMF (stand-by facilities) as both deterrent mechanisms/default buffers against speculation and quality signals to investment markets.

There is also a desire of those affected by standards to have an impact on norm development through *consultation*. This takes place in diverse ways, but with two main variants: in a centralized and in a decentralized fashion. In the centralized form, feedback is sought by and provided directly to the main IO. This is sometimes done through the mechanism of an advisory council, where non-voting members have the right to be informed and have their say about standard development. It is also sometimes done through the open consultation process, in which the organization releases consultation documents to the public with a request for feedback before an official policy proposal is tabled. In the decentralized form, regional organizations or roundtables serve both as a vehicle for transmitting decided norms to non-voting members, and for eliciting feedback from those non-voting members on prospective standard development. These non-voting members cover both public national bodies and private interest groups that have a stake in standard development.

Despite this, there is a trend within the FSB to not only tie together all standards relating to systemic risk, but to develop the institutional infrastructure that makes a substantive improvement of supervision and enforcement possible. This can be seen in the adoption and development of advanced typologies (studies of risky behavior on the part of financial market participants), methodologies (counter-measures that can be employed by supervisory and enforcement agencies) and protocols for cross-border exchange of information and enforcement cooperation.

To the extent that governments are participating in the development of the standards and rules that apply to them, that decisions are taken by unanimity of the members, and that the government representative works within the confines of a legal mandate,[66] accountability issues are minimal. The problem only becomes acute when these conditions are not in place. As discussed above, there is a real problem for emerging market economies that have been subject to international standards that they did not participate in developing, and from which they have no real capacity to extract themselves. This problem emerged from 1999 onward, after the G7 insisted that the IMF and World Bank tie financial disbursements to

[66] A legal mandate may be *ex ante* or *ex post facto*. *Ex ante* mandates are delegations of authority to the representative in question before it enters negotiations within institutional settings. *Ex post facto* mandates are ratification by the appropriate national legislative body. Where the national representative is not a foreign minister, but the representative of a government with majority control of the legislature, as is the case in all parliamentary democracies, the *ex post facto* method is easiest to use.

emerging markets to standard implementation in recipient countries.[67] The sting of this imposition was softened in 2009 when key emerging markets were brought into the bodies that set these standards and insisted on their adoption (the G20 and the FSB), but it has not gone away. It remains a problem in the context of accountability in national law.

## 5.6. Conclusion

The world has witnessed two global economic crises within the last 15 years. The result has been an expansion of global financial market regulation, in terms of organizational capacity and obligations to national governments. It constitutes an increase in the practice of informal international lawmaking.

The method chosen for establishing international FMR standards before the crisis (between the late 1990s and 2007) was to make them principle-based and voluntary, so that ultimate responsibility for fleshing out hard rules would remain with national governments. This formula meant that international standard-setting bodies could generate expert-informed regulation standards whilst rejecting critiques that they were imposing mandatory rules without the benefit of accountability to or input from stakeholders. Their internal organization remained light, since workload remained light and consequences of their actions were not profound.

In practice, this combination of instruments and assumptions meant that OECD countries sometimes failed to practice what they preached to others on financial market regulation, or to critically reflect on whether their regulations were fit for purpose. Their sense of obligation was low. Corporate governance standards remained unevenly transposed into national company laws, banking regulation retained a light-handed approach in Basel II, accounting standards continued to allow shadow banking off the balance sheets, and important countries like the US refused to undergo IMF and World Bank compliance reviews, whilst non-OECD countries were subjected to Financial Sector Assessments by those two bodies. This state of affairs resulted in a corresponding critique of the methods and motives of international standards and questions about the legitimacy of

67 For a general overview of the methods that the IMF and World Bank use to link aid and approval to the application of policies, see Ngaire Woods, *The Globalizers: The IMF, the World Bank and their Borrowers*, Cornell University Press, Ithaca, 2006, p. 82.

the decision-making process. The complacency could be fuelled by the Asian source of the 1997–8 crisis, and by the belief that securitization had successfully engineered risk out of the economy in countries with advanced financial markets.

What accompanies the institutional changes since 2009 is a heightened insistence on obligation of national governments to implement commonly-agreed standards that enhance financial stability. The most important change in thinking that increases that sense of obligation towards international standards is that advanced economies have realized that they can no longer be considered role models and rule makers who can make good financial market regulation. They need to accept the possible role of being rule takers from a collective whole. This shift can be seen through differences in membership before and after the 2007 crisis. Many of the global institutions devoted to financial market regulation were characterized until then by small memberships of OECD countries, a focus on modest codes of good governance as international standards, and a high degree of consultation with financial market participants, but not the wider stakeholder spectrum. The dominant expectation after 1997 was that this small group of countries would effectively see other countries adopt their standards as well or be sidelined in the growth of the world economy. This combination, known as the 'New International Financial Architecture', was itself underpinned by a Washington Consensus that improving poor governance and institutions in emerging markets showed the best promise of preventing systemic collapses in those countries and contagion to developed market countries.

This pattern of strengthening international standard setting and obligation to it can be seen as international standard-setting bodies and the new FSB enhance their missions, as detail is added to the standards they issue, and as they develop mechanisms to make demands on national governments and regulators, even beyond their own membership. Within the field of financial market integration, international standard development and mandatory national adoption on a universal scale is what the G20 is promoting, even for countries that do not participate in standard-setting. The G20, which is a political grouping and not a formal organization, drives institutional development and serves as the key political principal to which these bodies are accountable (rather than all of the affected Member States and the social partners). It therefore takes place outside the environment of the United Nations and other formal IOs, and outside any further accountability mechanisms.

Since 2009, as part of this process, the key ISSBs have developed complex, formalized institutional structures to manage a high workload and generate specific rules intended to apply to national regulations, whilst the FSB focuses on weaving those standards into a seamless web, encouraging standard-setters to close the gaps left behind, and pushing national regulators to adopt those standards and upgrade their institutions to increase their regulatory bite. G-FMR remains formally broad and voluntary if one looks at the individual standard setters, but increasingly less so in practice if one looks at what the FSB is doing with their work. The obligations of membership, and the effective obligations imposed on non-members by the IMF and the World Bank, are real enough to matter to domestic governments, regulators and legislators.

Obligation in global financial market regulation today is one that rests on prevailing political consensus rather than law, but it is nevertheless material for domestic lawmakers and regulators. In all cases the rules generated are voluntary until they are adopted into national law and regulation, but the degree of pressure on both Member States in the standard-setting bodies to adopt and implement them as a condition of membership in the rule-making club, as recognition of *political obligation*, and on Non-Member States, as signals of market worthiness, and as recognition of *effective obligation,* are strong. Peer review, based on the OECD's open method of coordination,[68] is the mechanism used to keep up the

[68] The OMC promotes norm and policy development at the international level and diffusion again at the national level through three interdependent mechanisms: by a club of countries setting common benchmarks or standards; by demanding transparency on compliance with those benchmarks from the member States within the club; and by applying peer review to the way that individual members interpret, implement, enforce the common standards. See Dermot Hodson and Imelda Maher, "The open method as a new mode of governance: the case of soft economic policy co-ordination", in *Journal of Common Market Studies*, 2001 , vol. 39, no. 4, pp. 719–46; Susan Borras and Kerstin Jacobsson, "The open method of coordination and new governance patterns in the EU", in *Journal of European Public Policy*, 2004, vol. 11, no. 2, pp. 185–208; Francesco Duina and Tapio Raunio, "The Open Method of Coordination and National Parliaments: Further Marginalization or New Opportunities?" in *Journal of European Public Policy*, 2007, vol. 14, no. 4, pp. 489–506; Martin Heidenreich and Jonathan Zeitlin, *Changing European Employment and Welfare Regimes. The Influence of the open method of coordination on national reforms,* Routledge, 2009; Jonathan Zeitlin, and Philippe Pochet with Lars Magnusson (eds.),

pressure on States who are members of these bodies. IMF and World Bank assessments are the mechanisms for other countries. Whilst the degree of peer review varies depending on the ISSB involved, the FSB, IMF and World Bank serve as backstops, applying pressure and ensuring obligation where the standard-setters do not. As always with the open method, the degree to which national rules may vary and various political demands can be accommodated through the democratic process is a function of how detailed the rules are, regardless of their voluntary nature. The level of obligation and of detailed prescriptions backed by the FSB, though not legal, is significant and rising.

The degree to which national governments need to be concerned about the implications also varies asymmetrically across countries. In practice, the FSB, which is responsible for deciding the extent of obligation, is populated by the central bank, finance ministry, and financial service regulator representatives of 24 different jurisdictions that may only decide formally by consensus. Although this is not always as constraining as it sounds, because the countries representing the dominant financial centers have a high degree of expertise and unwillingness to contemplate radical change to their financial systems, it does ensure that what the core does not want, the FSB does not do, and national governments do not have to worry about. This is not fair or equal in the legal sense, but is simple political fact. There is nothing about the FSB, despite its high profile, that constitutes a legal charter, a legal personality, any legal independence or a detailed mission independent of what the G20, and particularly the G7 that takes much of the initiative, wants. At the same time, core membership has expanded and consultation has increased, but largely for the financial market participants being regulated. Other stakeholders who are affected by the regulations are often absent, raising questions of whether the call for accountability in G-FMR has generated capture rather than a broader public interest.

Overall, the development of financial market regulation at the international level increases informal international lawmaking, precisely because this is what the G20 countries believed was necessary. Accountability concerns are not very strong for them, because they are participants in

---

*The Open Method of Co-ordination in Action: The European Employment and Social Inclusion Strategies*, Peter Lang, Brussels, 2005; Thomas Christiansen and Simona Piattoni (eds.), *Informal Governance in the European Union*, Edward Elgar, Cheltenham, 2004.

the process. What is missed is input and legitimation by countries that are not part of the process, and by stakeholders that are not part of the global consultation process.

# 6

## Financial Markets, Regulatory Failures and Transnational Regulatory Safety Nets: The Building of a Policy-Making Metaphor

**Maciej Konrad Borowicz***

### 6.1. Introduction

After years of neglect, financial markets again top the regulatory agenda.[1] Among the biggest questions on that agenda is how to avoid and address market failures. The ongoing turbulence triggered, back in 2008, by the collapse of Lehman Brothers, casts some doubt on the effectiveness of administrative formal legal measures in addressing financial markets failures.[2] Even a combination of *ex ante* and *ex post* legal interventions may

* **Maciej Konrad Borowicz** is a Ph.D. Candidate in law at the European University Institute (Florence, Italy). This is an expanded version of a paper presented by the author at the IN-LAW Workshop held at the Netherlands Institute for Advanced Study in the Humanities and Social Sciences in Wassenaar on 17–18 March 2011. All mistakes are the responsibility of the author.

1 See Sarkis J. Khoury, *The Deregulation of the World Financial Markets*, Quorum Books, New York, 1990 (for a comprehensive examination of "the deregulation of financial markets that began in the United States in the mid-1960s and has by early 1990s reached global proportions"). See also Alexandros-Andreas Kyrtsis (ed.), *Financial Markets and Organizational Technologies. System Architectures, Practices and Risks in the Era of Deregulation*, Palgrave Macmillan, 2010 (for an account of the role of technology in the progressive financial deregulation, following the abolishment of the Breton Woods system). For an illustrative story concerning the attitudes towards financial regulation in the late 2000s world see, *e.g.*, Yochai Benkle, "From Greenspan's Despair to Obama's Hope: The Scientific Bases of Cooperation as Principles of Regulation", in David Moss and John Cisternino (eds.), *New Perspectives on Regulation*, The Tobin Project, 2009.

2 When we speak of financial markets failures, we generally mean either the problem of (i) natural monopoly, (ii) externalities or (iii) information asymmetries. See Forrest Capie, "Some historical perspective on regulation", in David G. Mayes and Geoffrey E. Wood (eds.), *The Structure of Financial Regulation*, Routledge, 2007, p. 70. For a critique of reliance on administrative law-like measures see Lawrence G. Baxter, "Adaptive Regulation in the Amoral Bazaar", Twelfth Oliver Schreiner Memorial Lecture, School of Law, University of the Witwatersrand, Johannesburg, South Afri-

be insufficient insofar as the celebrated goal of making financial markets more efficient and safe is concerned.[3] What is missing from the agenda is the question: how can we avoid *regulatory* failures? In other words, what should we do if a regulator fails to deliver? This chapter explores the complementary role of informal international lawmaking (IN-LAW) and transnational private regulation (TPR) in the construction of an efficient and safe architecture of global financial markets, in particular by focusing on their role in addressing regulatory failures.

There are two strands of literature that can be helpful in conceptualizing the role of IN-LAW and TPR in global financial markets. The first one relates to multi-level governance (MLG) as a theory of public administration. Both IN-LAW and TPR build on the MLG literature, which emphasizes the increasingly frequent and complex interactions between government actors and the increasingly important dimension of non-state actors that are mobilized in cohesion policy-making.[4] The MLG literature

ca, 20 October 2010, in *South Africa Law Journal*, 2011, vol. 128, pp. 253–272, (describing the 'orthodoxy' of the theoretical underpinnings of modern administrative law, which rest on a "static, hierarchical model that has long captured our understanding of the Rule of Law and the principle of legality in a democratic state".).

3 The recognition that even a first-best regulatory regime cannot prevent every failure, and consequently a mixture of both *ex ante* and *ex post* law measures is needed to comprehensively address at least some of the failures associated with financial markets, is shared by both legal scholars see, *e.g.*, Steven L. Schwarcz, "Ex Ante Versus Ex Post Approaches to Financial Regulation", in *Chapman Law Review*, 2011, vol. 15, pp. 258–269 (Symposium "From Wall Street to Main Street: The Future of Financial Regulation" 28 January 2011) and economists, see, *e.g.*, Edward J. Kane, "Financial Safety Nets: Reconstructing And Modeling a Policymaking Metaphor", in *NBER Working Paper Series*, April 2001, Working Paper 8224, Cambridge, MA.

4 This is true of both multi-level governance in the EU and in the US. In the US, the notion of regulatory safety nets is used by some authors as synonymous with the notion of overlapping jurisdictions. For example, Kirsten Engel suggests that they "empower government to better address social ills through the combined application of state and federal law and resources to a particular social, economic, political or environmental problem." Kirsten H. Engel, "Harnessing the Benefits of Dynamic Federalism in Environmental Law", in *Emory Law Journal*, 2006, vol. 56, p. 159. Professor Erwin Chemerinsky, in particular, endorsed the concept of MLG in the context of US constitutional law by claiming that: "[t]he genius in having multiple levels of government is that if one fails to act, another can step in to solve the problem". Erwin Chemerinsky, "Empowering States: The Need to Limit Federal Preemption", in *Pepperdine Law Journal*, 2005, vol. 33, p. 69. See also Joseph J. Norton, "A Perceived Trend in Modern International Financial Regulation: Increasing Reliance on Public-Private Partnership", in *International Law*, 2003, vol. 37, p. 43.

plays up the regulatory capabilities of multiple regimes that can be combined to deliver better regulatory outputs, and so do IN-LAW and TPR.[5]

Another strand of literature that will be of relevance looks for patterns of commonalities between regulatory regimes. At the core of transnational regulatory networks[6] or global administrative law (GAL)[7] scholarship, for example, are questions concerning accountability and effectiveness of these individual bodies.[8]

These are also the sort of questions that are of interest to scholars associated with IN-LAW and TPR.[9] Whereas the former are predominantly concerned with public, informal regulatory arrangements, the latter focus on the role of private actors and their regulatory initiatives. From a methodological standpoint, these two perspectives share their respective point of departure: they begin with research clusters centered around a particular sector, which are then, through systematic case studies, meant

---

5 This is a perspective on regulation, which largely conceives of it as a product. See Colleen M. Baker, "Regulating the Invisible: The Case of Over-The-Counter Derivatives", in *Notre Dame Law Review*, 2010, vol. 85, no. 4, and the literature referred to therein, in particular Erin O'Hara, Larry E. Ribstein, *The Law Market*, Oxford University Press, 2009; Jeffrey L. Dunoff and Joel P. Trachtman, "Economic Analysis of International Law", in *Yale Journal of International Law*, 2009, vol. 1; Symposium, Economic Analysis of International Law, in *International Review of Law and Economics*, 1996, vol. 16, no. 1; and Symposium, Public International Law and Economics, in *University of Illinois Law Review*, 2008, p. 1.

6 See, *e.g.*, Anne-Marie Slaughter, *A New World Order*, Princeton University Press, 2004; David Zaring, "International Law by Other Means: the Twilight Existence of International Regulatory Organizations", in *Texas International Law Journal*, 1998, vol. 33, p. 281; and Pierre-Hughes Verdier, "Transnational Regulatory Networks and Their Limits", in *Yale Journal of International Law*, 2009, vol. 34, p. 113.

7 Benedict Kingsbury, Nico Krisch, Richard Stewart, "The Emergence of Global Administrative Law", in *Law and Contemporary Problems*, 2005, vol. 68, no. 3–4.

8 Global administrative law has been defined as "comprising the mechanisms, principles, practices, and supporting social understandings that promote or otherwise affect the accountability of global administrative bodies, in particular by ensuring they meet adequate standards of transparency, participation, reasoned decision, and legality, and by providing effective review of the rules and decisions they make". *Ibid.*

9 Both TPR and IN-LAW are multidisciplinary research projects funded by the Hague Institute for the Internationalization of Law. The TPR project is lead by Fabrizio Cafaggi (European University Institute) and IN-LAW is lead by Joost Pauwelyn (Graduate Institute, Geneva). For information on both projects, see HiiL, available at http://www.hiil.org, last accessed on 3 July 2012.

to prove or disprove the initial hypothesis concerning the accountability and effectiveness of individual regimes.

This essay is, in part, one such case study, even if a somewhat selective one. It juxtaposes both IN-LAW and TPR perspectives by looking at the International Swaps and Derivatives Association ('ISDA') as an example of TPR, and the Basel Committee for Banking Supervision ('BCBS') as an example of IN-LAW.

As this essay argues, what this juxtaposition tells us about those regimes is that they do not exist and should not be perceived in isolation. Not unlike the MLG literature, it points to the interfaces that exist between these regimes, for example, in terms of standard setting, monitoring and enforcement. But it also distinguishes itself from that literature, for example, by rejecting the notion of 'levels'.[10]

At the same time, unlike the literature which tries to align the perspectives on accountability and effectiveness among private and public actors/individual regimes (for example GAL), it suggests a way of thinking about those regimes, which not only acknowledges the differences in accountability and effectiveness mechanisms between IN-LAW and TPR, but also considers the possibility of accountability and effectiveness being a function not of individual regimes, but of the entire transnational regulatory safety net ('TRSN').

It should be made clear from the outset that the notion of TRSN will be used here as a metaphor. As Edward Kane once noted

> the heuristic value of the safety-net metaphor of financial regulation is determined by its 'redescriptive power': *i.e.*, by how well it simultaneously simplifies and approximates the cost-benefit issues with which regulators regularly contend.[11]

---

[10] "The very idea of levels is imbued with hierarchical implications. However, different levels or social spaces often interact or cut across with one another in complex ways that are not strictly hierarchical. To what extent can 'levels' be identified at all? The notion that international bodies constitute a discrete level of authority and governance is contestable. International regulatory networks may not be separate sources of authority but instead represent the reconstitution of state authority and the pursuit of state-level governance by other means. While territorial levels make sense when we are referring to public forms of authority, they seem less compatible with private and market forms of authority." David Andrew Baker, Richard Woodward Hudson (eds.), *Governing Financial Globalization: International Political Economy and Multi-Level Governance*, Routledge, 2005, p. 15.

[11] Kane, 2005, see *supra* note 3.

The TRSN metaphor suggests that, when thinking about addressing regulatory failures (*id est,* failures of some regimes to be accountable or effective), policy-makers should take into account a broader picture, including the role that IN-LAW and TPR regimes can play in that regard. This essay in fact provides evidence that policymakers actually do that already. Hence the purpose of this metaphor is to allow them to think about it in a more systematic way.

The TRSN metaphor can also be revealing for IN-LAW or TPR scholars in suggesting that it is not always appropriate to take a singled-out regime as a unit of analysis. Rather, accountability and effectiveness can be thought of as a collective endeavor of all actors involved, a function of particular TRSN's features.

## 6.2. Thinking in Transnational Regulatory Safety Nets

When we think about safety nets, about *what* they are, we generally think of ways in which a society safeguards individuals and/or organizations from falling beneath a certain threshold of a living standard or, in the case of organizations, beneath a certain threshold of economic viability of the organizations' working. The reasons for which these individuals or organizations may have found themselves in that condition may vary, but they are generally the consequence of the risks they have undertaken or simply the result of some arbitrary misfortunes. Safety nets thus, as the term is conventionally used, provide security against misfortune or difficulty.[12]

When we think about *why* we have safety nets in the first place, or in other words what is the justification for establishing safety nets in a society, we are, sooner or later, likely to come to think about moral justifications. From that point of view, the establishment of safety nets is justified if there are better reasons for having them than not having them, and those reasons are deemed to be good reasons, which people can agree on. These reasons can be based, for example, on the conception of justice as fairness. The conception of justice as fairness has been most famously formulated by John Rawls in his book, *A Theory of Justice*. In his book, Rawls uses a social contract argument to show that justice, and especially distributive justice, is a form of fairness.[13] We can envisage that from the

12 This is how Webster's dictionary defines a 'safety net'.

13 John Rawls, *A Theory of Justice*, Belknap Press of Harvard University Press, 1999. Rawls famously proposes the notion of a veil of ignorance that denies agents'

point of view of justice as fairness, we will favor the existence of safety nets, because we will be unwilling to assume the risk that one day we might turn out to be those whose existence will be threatened by falling beneath a certain threshold. We will rather have, for example, social or financial safety nets in place to protect us.

*Social* safety nets, generally speaking, are transfer programs seeking to prevent the poor or those vulnerable to shocks and poverty from falling below a certain poverty level. They can be provided by the public sector (the state and aid donors) or by the private sector (NGOs, private firms, charities, and informal household transfers). Safety net transfers, as the World Bank's website enumerates, include: cash transfers, food-based programs, in-kind transfers, conditional cash transfers, price subsidies for food, electricity, or public transport *et cetera.*[14]

*Financial* safety nets are conventionally understood as arrangements designed to protect the society for paying for losses that financial institutions may incur. They also find their moral justification in terms of fairness. Here fairness plays a justificatory role to the extent that the goal of financial safety nets is to protect borrowers and depositors, specifically by making sure that they do not suffer from a limited availability of credit or from losses of deposits.

Social and financial safety nets are the two most common ways in which the term 'safety net' has been used. The TRSN metaphor builds on these formulation of safety nets, but it is also departs from them, both in terms of *why* and *what*. Firstly, TRSN here-proposed leaves out the distributional effects aspect of regulation.[15] In other words, when we use the

---

knowledge of their personalities, social statuses, moral characters, wealth, talents and life plans, and then asks what theory of justice we would choose to govern our society when the veil is lifted, if we wanted to do the best that we could for ourselves. The decision-in-ignorance models fairness, because it excludes selfish bias.

14 World Bank, "Safety Nets", available at http://web.worldbank.org/WBSITE/EXTERNAL/TOPICS/EXTSOCIALPROTECTION/EXTSAFETYNETSANDTRANSFERS/0,,menuPK:282766~pagePK:149018~piPK:149093~theSitePK:282761,00.html, last accessed on 5 September 2012.

15 The purpose of this metaphor is not to explain how regulation can deliver justice. Compare Karl-Heinz Ladeur, "Der "Eigenwert" des Rechts – die Selbstorganisationsfähigkeit der Gesellschaft und die relationale Rationalität des Rechts", in Christian J. Meier-Schatz (ed.), *Die Zukunft des Rechts*, 1999, quoted in Lars Viellechner, "The Network of Networks: Karl-Heinz Ladeur's Theory of Law and Globalization", in *German Law Journal*, 2009, vol. 10, no. 4, pp. 516–36 (arguing that the role of law

TRSNs metaphor we are not *predominantly* concerned with the issue of distributing resources, opportunities, profits and advantages, responsibilities, taxes and burdens, or in other words, with questions of distributive justice.[16] Instead what we are concerned with are regulatory failures: situations in which regulatory resources (such as accountability and effectiveness) are not allocated in an optimal way. The question that the TRSNs metaphor is thus meant to help answer is how to optimally distribute accountability and effectiveness across a particular TRSN.[17]

Secondly, the notion of TRSN, as it will be used here, is also different from how the two other notions of safety nets are used, in terms of *what* it denotes. It is fair to say the safety nets are all concerned with failures. Social safety nets are concerned with failures of individuals (agents) or organizations. The term denotes a set of arrangements that a society has in place to alleviate the suffering that is normally associated with these failures. Financial safety nets are concerned with market failures (of financial organizations). Here the term denotes a set of arrangements that a society has in place to mitigate the consequence of failures of financial institutions.

TRSNs, in turn, are concerned with regulatory failures (or failures of regulators/regulatory regimes). The notion of a safety net is used here to explain how some regulatory regimes can "catch" or better address regulatory failures that other regimes miss, and perhaps most importantly, how to use a mixture of instruments to make that possible.

---

under modern conditions of uncertainty is to ensure favorable conditions for coordination of expectations to stay productive, *i.e.*, geared to innovation, thus preventing that creation of social capital will be distorted. Karl-Heinz Ladeur envisages this role for non-state, de-territorialized, self-organized networks beyond public decision-making and argues that they need to be strengthened and combined with various public forms of guaranteeing learning capacity and the enabling and enhancing of self-observation and observation of others within a global "network of networks."). It that sense, the notion of regulation is narrower here than the notion of regulation as it is often used in the literature (see, *e.g.*, Joseph Stiglitz, "Regulation and Failure", in Moss and Cisternino, 2009, see *supra* note 1, pp. 11–23. This has implications especially for accountability requirements.

16 John Finnins, *Natural Law and Natural Rights*, Oxford University Press, 1980, p. 166.

17 This is not to say that the standards that the regimes that are part of the TRSN do not have distributive consequences. To the contrary. But the TRSN metaphor largely remains agnostic towards them.

As such, the notion of a TRSN may be useful as a policy-making metaphor. Its value as a policy-making metaphor is related to the recognition that it brings to the debate concerning the role of non-legal-regulatory instruments, and in particular of the role of IN-LAW and TPR in achieving efficient and safe operation of financial markets. This recognition can be summed up to say that accountability and effectiveness are not necessarily a function of a particular regime, whether legal, or other. Instead it is possible to combine the regulatory capabilities of many regimes in order to achieve their greater accountability and effectiveness. Law for example, is generally deemed to enjoy, what we can call, a strong regulatory capability in terms of accountability.

> For lawyers, the administrative governance of social and economic activities is to be conducted under legislative authority that emanates from a democratically elected legislature and executive. These organs of government are themselves the creations of constitutions that have been accepted as politically legitimate, and by rules, principles and doctrines developed by courts and jurists over many years.[18]

At the same time, law's effectiveness can be enhanced by IN-LAW and TPR, both of which can be more flexible and more adaptive with respect to the goals that regulation is meant to achieve. In turn, accountability of IN-LAW and TPR regimes' can be improved when they work side by side with public regimes. Courts, for example, can endow them with greater accountability whenever they create avenues for having the IN-LAW and TPR rules (and regimes) reviewed.

### 6.3. TRSNs and the Concepts and Questions in the IN-LAW and TPR Framework – Finding Common Ground

How is the TRSN metaphor relevant for the discussion of IN-LAW and TPR, these two emerging paradigms of transnational regulation? TRSNs, as a way of looking at a complex of regulations designed to watch for and to address regulatory failures, consider both IN-LAW and TPR as complements to public regulation.

At the same time, this metaphor does not disregard the possibility that these regimes may conflict, impeding their respective regulatory ca-

[18] Baxter, 2011, p. 255, see *supra* note 2.

pabilities.[19] Certainly if we take *interests* as the central variable in explaining why these regimes emerge, we are likely to find out that in the real world different actors may have different interests concerning the same issue and consequently different regimes, shaped by those interests, are likely to emerge.[20]

### 6.3.1. Informal International Law-Making and Transnational Private Regulation: Complements or Alternatives?

IN-LAW has been preliminarily defined as

> cross-border cooperation between public authorities, with or without the participation of private actors and/or international organizations, in a forum other than a traditional international organization (process informality), and/or as between actors other than traditional diplomatic actors (such as regulators or agencies) (actor informality) and/or which does not result in a formal treaty or traditional source of international law (output informality).[21]

Transnational Private Regulation (TPR) has been defined as:

> constitutes a new body of rules, practices and processes, created primarily by private actors, firms, NGOs, independent experts like technical standard setters and epistemic communities, either exercising autonomous regulatory power or implementing delegated power, conferred by international law or by national legislation.[22]

---

19 See Gregory C. Shaffer, Mark A. Pollack, "Hard vs. Soft Law: Alternatives, Complementarities and Antagonists in International Governance", in *University of Minnesota Law School, Legal Studies Research Paper*, 2010, no. 09-23 (for a discussion of how hard law and soft law can act not only as complements but also as antagonists).

20 This is one of the hypotheses of Shaffer and Pollack's argument. "Where powerful states agree on a common policy, hard and soft law are more likely to work as complements in an evolutionary manner". On the other hand "[w]hen powerful states disagree on policy, we are likely to see hard law and soft law work in opposition to each other". *Ibid.*, pp. 765–767. See also Fabrizio Cafaggi, "The Architecture of Transnational Private Regulation", *EUI Working Papers (LAW)*, 2011, no. 12, p. 3.

21 Joost Pauwelyn, "Informal International Law-making: Mapping the Action and Testing Concepts of Accountability and Effectiveness", in Joost Pauwelyn, Ramses A. Wessel and Jan Wouters (eds.), *Informal International Lawmaking*, Oxford University Press, Oxford, 2012, p. 22.

22 Fabrizio Cafaggi, "New Foundations of Transnational Private Regulation", *EUI Working Papers (RSCAS)*, 2010, no. 53, p. 1.

The major difference in the outlook of these two perspectives is that, bluntly speaking, whereas IN-LAW uses the term 'law', TPR does not. In IN-LAW, the term 'law' is used to "connote the involvement of public authorities in the process, as opposed to what is often referred to more broadly as 'regulation'".[23] IN-LAW can include private actor participation, but excludes cooperation that only involves private actors. The term is also used in a broader sense "including statements or guidelines that may not, strictly speaking, be part of law but merely have legal effects or fit in the context of a broader legal or normative process".[24]

Another major difference concerns 'informality'. There are at least two dimensions of informality in IN-LAW. First, there is 'output informality'. IN-LAW rarely results in a formal treaty or some other traditional source of international law. More often the regulatory product is a guideline, a standard, a declaration, or an even more informal policy coordination or exchange. Second, there is 'process informality'. Much of IN-LAW occurs in a loosely organized network or forum rather than a traditional treaty based international organization.

TPR to a greater extent relies on formal mechanisms, especially contracts, which bear on both legitimacy and effectiveness of TPR regimes (especially with regard to enforcement).

Notwithstanding the dissimilar actor-orientation (public vs. private actors), and the resulting commitment to the term law, both perspectives have a lot in common. Most importantly, they emphasize the relationships between private and public actors. Both, being concerned with regulation and governance, recognize the practicability of the use of a combination of instruments to achieve certain objectives. Also, both recognize the role of non-state regulators at the transnational level.[25] Both seem to acknowledge that the differences between private and public have not been canceled, but force a reconsideration of their functions and the boundaries between the two spheres.[26]

In particular, in the TPR project framing paper, Fabrizio Cafaggi makes the claim that the public and the private spheres are mutually influential in at least two ways: (i) the distribution between hard and soft law

[23] Pauwelyn, 2012, p. 21, see *supra* note 21.

[24] *Ibid.*

[25] *Ibid.*, p. 19.

[26] Cafaggi, 2010, p. 3, see *supra* note 22.

within the public domain affects the functions of TPR; and (ii) the choice among different regulatory models, implying different regulatory relationships, reflects but also affects the nature of the public international regime.

> When hard law, including international treaties, is in place, private regulation acts as a complement to specify rules, tailoring them to specific markets, and frequently, formal or informal, delegation takes place. When soft law is chosen, private regulation mainly operates as a vehicle to harden soft law, providing binding force. In the former case it increases effectiveness, in the latter it confers higher legitimacy. Obviously there are TPR regimes that operate independently from any public regime and they seek legitimacy on different grounds.[27]

Both IN-LAW and TPR have yet another thing in common – the lack of a legal framework.

> While international public law is composed of a general part, applicable to all states and international organizations, and a specific part binding only on the signatory states, TPR lack, so far, a common legal framework, and tends to be sector specific and influenced by domestic private law regimes.[28]

Similarly can be said of IN-LAW. It seems therefore that these two perspectives can complement each other to a great extent and much mutual learning can be achieved. Much learning can be achieved also because both projects use similar methodologies (at least at a general level). They both try to identify mechanisms of accountability and effectiveness (broadly understood, as encompassing quality, efficiency and enforcement). In other words, both IN-LAW and TPR ask similar questions concerning regulatory failures, in particular what does it mean for a regime to be accountable and effective.

### 6.3.2. Accountability

Accountability is a concept in governance with several meanings. It is often used synonymously with concepts such as responsibility, answerability, liability, and other terms associated with the expectation of account giving. As a term related to governance, accountability has been difficult

---

27 *Ibid.*, p. 17.

28 *Ibid.*

to define.[29] It is frequently described as an account-giving relationship between individuals.

Both IN-LAW and TPR acknowledge the difficulty in defining the term and have generally refrained from defining it *ex ante*. Rather, they look for mechanisms of accountability broadly understood with the view to refine its meaning as they go along the investigation of the different regimes.

Notwithstanding these difficulties, and repudiating most conceptions of accountability that are associated with formal, public regulation, both perspectives have a good grasp of what it is that they are after. For example, they look for accountability to both *internal* and *external* actors (including broader societal interests and countries outside the network, but where network output is *de facto* implemented).[30] Also, both emphasize the distinction between accountability at the international and domestic level, accepting "that traditional checks and balances ad democratic mechanisms under domestic law cannot simply be replicated at the international level".[31]

From the perspective of IN-LAW the question of accountability only arises to the extent that public authority or power is being wielded under IN-LAW.[32] Since TPR does not, in principle, entail the exercise of public power, it primarily looks at how private actors achieve acceptance among members of the industry and the general public.

29 Richard Mulgan, "Accountability: An Ever-Expanding Concept?", in *Public Administration*, 2000, vol. 78, no. 3, pp. 555–573.

30 In the context of TPR see, *e.g.*, Fabrizio Cafaggi, "Contractual Networks and contract theory: a research agenda for European contract law", in Fabrizio Cafaggi (ed.) *Contractual Networks, Inter-Firm Cooperation and Economic Growth*, Edward Elgar, Cheltenham (UK) and Northampton, MA (USA), 2011, pp. 66–110.

31 Pauwelyn, 2012, p. 12, see *supra* note 21.

32 Compare Armin von Bogdandy, Philipp Dann and Matthias Goldmann, "Developing the Publicness of Public International Law: Towards a Legal Framework for Global Governance Activities", in *German Law Journal*, 2010, vol. 9, no. 11, p. 1376 (making the point that legal acts of global administrative bodies often involve an exercise of unilateral authority, thereby challenging the principle of individual freedom. As the authors argue, "any kind of governance activity by international institutions, be it administrative or intergovernmental, should be considered as an exercise of international public authority if it determines individuals, private associations, enterprises, states, or other public institutions.").

In short, from the perspective of both projects, the question of accountability demands at the very least answers to the following sub-questions:

- To whom? Internal (principal-agent) v. external;
- Why? Functions (democratic, constitutional, learning);
- How? (mechanisms of accountability, preconditions, other responsiveness-promoting measures);
- When? (*ex ante*/ongoing/*ex post*).

### 6.3.3. Effectiveness

As Joost Pauwelyn notes in the IN-LAW framing paper, one of the main attractions of IN-LAW as opposed to traditional, formal international lawmaking is that it offers "a device for minimizing the impediments to cooperation, at both the domestic and international levels. Enhancing the chances for international cooperation to occur is one crucial element of what we understand with effectiveness".[33] Another element of effectiveness that IN-LAW plans to examine relates to "how this cooperation – once it has been established – is actually implemented or complied with".[34] These four dimensions of effectiveness could be summarized as follows:

- Does cooperation materialize?
- Does it stick?
- Does it solve the problem?
- Does it solve the problem in a cost-effective way?

TPR brings us yet a different perspective on effectiveness. It focuses on the choice of governance structures and tries to determine whether the nature of the regulatory relationship – one that includes the beneficiaries – redefines the nature of responsiveness and the means through which effectiveness of the regulation should be measured. "Effectiveness does not only measure regulatees' compliance but looks at the effects of the

33 Pauwelyn, 2012, p. 15, see *supra* note 21.

34 *Ibid.*

regulatory process on the final beneficiaries”.[35] As such, it combines and interrelates the questions of effectiveness and legitimacy/accountability.

### 6.3.4. TPR, IN-LAW and Global Administrative Law (GAL)

To the extent that accountability and effectiveness are the core criteria that these projects use in the evaluation of the regimes they look at, it is apparent that the ultimate benchmark for their performance is not whether the objectives that the regime has set for itself have been met, but whether it takes into account and is shaped by some more general, societal interests as well. This is evident if we consider that both projects look at mechanisms of accountability to external actors as well as effectiveness towards third parties.

At the same time, these two projects do not seem to consider these informal and private regimes as functionally equivalent to formal public ones. Rather, the purpose of the exercise they are engaged in is to try to capture the characteristic of each regime. Given the heterogeneity of actors involved, actors with different incentives and goals as well as equipped with different regulatory tools, they preserve the distinction between public and private in the analysis even within a common set of principles concerning democracy and the rule of law.[36]

This is also where the difference between these two projects and the Global Administrative Project (‘GAL’) that has been initiated at New York University School of Law becomes apparent. First of all, by defining its activities in such a broad way, GAL removes the public/private distinction from the picture. Secondly, even if many of the problems are the same and the questions asked alike (accountability), the solutions are different. As Joost Pauwelyn notes in the IN-LAW framing paper,

> whereas the very idea of GAL is to describe and/or impose formal, legal strictures analogous to those found in domestic administrative law, the raison d’être and perceived problem of IN-LAW is exactly the avoidance of formal, legal strictures under domestic and/or international law.[37]

[35] See Cafaggi, 2010, p. 9, see *supra* note 22.

[36] *Ibid.*, p. 3 (footnote 14).

[37] Pauwelyn, 2012, p. 31, see *supra* note 21.

In this sense, GAL is a particular, law-based solution; IN-LAW is a perceived problem where actors move away from law. TPR, too, is not a law-based solution.

## 6.4. TPR and Financial Markets: The International Swaps and Derivatives Association

### 6.4.1. The International Swaps and Derivatives Association (ISDA) and the ISDA Master Agreement

ISDA is a good example of a TPR regime (TPRER). It brings together a wide variety of members – all participants in the over-the-counter (OTC) derivative markets.[38] It has over 825 member institutions from 57 countries,[39] most of which are end-users of derivatives: the world's major financial institutions and corporations. A number of transnational law firms also participate in the association as members.[40]

ISDA's role in financial markets consists of, but is not limited to, developing standardized documentation used by most OTC market participants. Through its standardized documentation, ISDA – as Colleen Baker points out – has created the 'global rules' of the OTC derivative markets.[41] These rules are contained in the ISDA Master Agreement (ISDA MA – the current version is the 2002 ISDA Master Agreement). The ISDA MA is a boilerplate contract used by the majority of dealers in derivatives transaction. It is 28 pages long, with an eight-page Schedule and

38 A 2010 EC impact assessment study notes that the use of derivatives has grown exponentially over the last decade. Most of this growth was driven by OTC transactions. The OTC market is the most common market where derivatives are traded, by means of bilateral contract, with the exchange market enjoying only a fraction of derivatives trading. At the end of December 2009, the size of the OTC derivatives market by notional value equaled to approximately $615 trillion, a 12% increase with respect to the end of 2008. See European Commission, "Impact Assessment – Accompanying document to the Proposal for a Regulation of the European Parliament and the Council on OTC derivatives, central counterparties and trade repositories" SEC(2010) 1058/2, available at http://ec.europa.eu/internal_market/financial-markets/docs/derivatives/20100915_impact_assessment_en.pdf, last accessed on 5 September 2012.

39 ISDA, available at http://isda.org, last accessed on 21 November 2011.

40 ISDA, "ISDA Primary Members", available at http://www.isda.org/membership/isdamemberslist.pdf, last accessed on 21 November 2011.

41 Baker, 2010, p. 1359, see *supra* note 5.

serves as a 'governance umbrella' for one or more subsequent derivatives transactions that parties enter into in the course of their relationship.

Both the Agreement and the Schedule specify, among other things, the obligations and representations of each party, and the relevant events of default and termination. Functionally, they serve the purpose of mitigating risks, most importantly credit and operational, as well as, of course, legal risks. They do that by allowing a certain degree of up-front risk assessment.

> For example, counterparties may assess the riskiness of the other party prior to the initiation of a transaction by requiring both representations and documents concerning credit risk as well as representations concerning legal risks. Also, the agreements may facilitate "ongoing" risk assessment following the initiation of the transaction by requiring, for example, the periodic provision of documents, the maintenance of covenants, and the use of collateral and market-to-market margining. These provisions help alleviate potential information asymmetries between counterparties and facilitate monitoring.[42]

In addition, the ISDA MA contains a 'close-out' provision. 'Closing-out' is the right of counterparty to unilaterally terminate contracts under certain specified conditions. As such it is an *ex post* risk control mechanism which allows a party to a transaction to limit exposure caused by the occurrence or discovery of specific events. Early termination protects parties from the risk of significant credit and legal developments arising from factors that may or may not be within the control or the fault of the counterparty (event risk protection) or that may result from *ex post* opportunism by counterparties (moral hazard).

But ISDA's role in regulation does not end with the ISDA Master Agreement. It has also developed highly effective and rapid 'legislative' reform processes through its protocols, self-help mechanisms through its collateral practices, and increasingly – in response to the crisis – global adjudicative mechanisms through Credit Derivative Determination Committees. In that regard

> as a global private actor, ISDA has replicated in varying degrees the basic jurisdictional powers-prescriptive, adjudica-

---

42 See Robert J. Schwartz, Clifford W. Smith (eds.), *Derivatives Handbook. Risk Management and Control,* John Wiley and Sons, 1997, p. 441.

> tory, and enforcement of government actors. Therefore, ISDA is more than just an industry trade association. It performs a very important private law making and governance function in the OTC derivative markets.[43]

To illustrate this point, consider an example fiercely discussed in the financial press at the time of the writing of this essay (summer of 2011). The example concerns Greece. After 15 consecutive years of economic growth, Greece entered recession in 2009. By the end of 2009, the Greek economy faced the highest budget deficit and government debt to GDP ratio in the EU. The 2009 budget deficit stood at 15.4% of GDP. This and rising debt levels (127% of GDP in 2009) led to rising borrowing costs, resulting in a severe economic crisis.[44]

It is hardly surprising that under these circumstances many investors and banks that purchased Greek sovereign bonds also purchased Greek sovereign credit default swaps (CDS) to protect themselves against the risk of default. These CDS that many entered into pursuant the ISDA MA are not unlike insurance contracts. In a CDS, the buyer of protection pays a fee to obtain indemnification against the risk of default of a borrower (for example, Greece) and any resultant loss from a protection seller. Payment is triggered by a "credit event", technically defined as failure to pay interest or principal, debt moratorium or repudiation, or restructuring. But there is currently a lot of uncertainty among Greek CDS holders concerning what 'restructuring' really means. Would voluntary restructuring – which would entail that lenders agree with Greece to exchange existing bonds and loans with ones with different terms (longer maturity, different rates) – be considered a credit event under the CDS?[45]

The final arbiter of whether the Greek CDS has been triggered will be the Credit Determinations Committee. Ten bankers and five investors will come to the table and decide on the interpretation of that provision. Unless backed by a supermajority of 12 out of 15 members, a committee of "independent experts" externally reviews its decisions. As one commentator for the *FT* remarked: "while perfectly legal, the ability of a pri-

---

43 Baker, 2010, p. 1360, see *supra* note 5.

44 Satyajit Das, Final arbiter in Greek saga is untested, private body, Financial Times, 22 June 2011.

45 *Ibid.*

vate body of financiers and lawyers to determine whether or not there has been 'default' is unusual and legally untested".[46]

### 6.4.2. ISDA and Its Regulatory Failure: Accountability and Effectiveness

To say that "while perfectly legal, the ability of a private body of financiers and lawyers to determine whether or not there has been 'default' is unusual and legally untested" is a rather genteel way of saying something about ISDA's accountability, or rather lack thereof. Given that derivatives were at the core of the 2008 financial meltdown it was hardly surprising to see ISDA become a somewhat toxic word in Washington and Brussels in the late 2000s.[47] But what does ISDA's regulatory failure exactly consist of?

First, there is the accountability dimension of ISDA as a TPRER. As noted above, there are some differences between the role of accountability in TPR and IN-LAW regimes. In particular, whereas in IN-LAW the question of accountability only arises to the extent that public authority or power is being wielded under IN-LAW, TPR looks at the issue of accountability by examining how private actors achieve acceptance among members of the industry and the general public. Thus, when looking at the ISDA, TPR scholars will not be so much interested in direct accountability of the ISDA, but rather in its role in endowing the market with an acceptable degree of legitimacy, for example, by ensuring relative transparency of transactions concluded therein or simply by providing output effectiveness. In other words, insofar as ISDA is concerned, the question of accountability and effectiveness may be intertwined.

---

46 *Ibid.*

47 See, *e.g.*, Gillian Tett, Calls for radical rethink of derivatives body, Financial Times, 26 August 2010 ("I think ISDA will need more deft repositioning, if it ever wants to remove the "toxic" political tag – let alone regain real clout. It is clear that the financial industry does need some trade group for derivatives, if nothing else to exchange ideas; but it would make far more sense for ISDA to clearly widen its mandate beyond the OTC world, to cover exchanges too and swap execution facilities, say. It would also be sensible to encourage far more investor involvement (just four of the 24 outside directors are from the buyside").

OTC derivatives markets were designed to be non-transparent.[48] Moreover, as opposed to trading on exchanges, which have a clear physical presence in a particular jurisdiction, bilateral OTC derivatives are transacted across jurisdictional boundaries and are primarily governed by the contractual relations between the parties. Is then the criticism of ISDA concerning the failure to endow the market with a degree of legitimacy that would justify its prominent role in the financial markets misdirected?

There is something to be said about the positive role of ISDA's documentation, which has governed both the settlement of credit default swaps as well as the liquidation of perhaps one million derivative contracts of defaulting counterparties during the period of financial stress in the late 2000s.[49] But its regulatory failure is apparent and it consists of its inability to provide information on positions and exposures in the market. This lack of transparency is usually identified among the most important problems that led to the spread of the crisis within the financial market and beyond.[50] As a result, market participants took insufficient measures to mitigate the potential adverse outcomes of, for example, counterparty credit risk.[51]

---

48 In fact, these markets are deemed so non-transparent, especially in comparison to derivatives traded on exchanges, that it lead some authors to label the OTC regulatory challenges as "regulating the invisible". Baker, 2010, see *supra* note 5.

49 See Letter from Mr. Conrad P. Voldstad, "Working hard to make markets safer", Financial Times, 2 September 2010.

50 In other words, risk transfer in itself is not bad, but can have dire consequences when the regulators lose track of how much risk has actually been transferred. See Steven Schwarcz, "Marginalizing Risk", in *Washington University Law Review*, 2012, vol. 89, no. 3.

51 As the Commission's Impact Assessment notes: counterparty credit risk is most often managed by bilateral collateral agreements. According to the results of the 2010 ISDA Margin Survey, in 2009, almost 172,000 collateral agreements were in place, covering 70% of OTC derivatives trades. The survey further estimates that approximately \$3.2 trillion of collateral was used in connection with OTC derivatives transactions, covering 69% of credit exposure. Finally, the survey reports that the dominant form of collateral was cash (82% of collateral received and 82% of collateral delivered), with government securities a distant second (10% and 14% respectively). As these numbers illustrates, the amount of collateral was, on average, too low compared to the level of counterparty credit risk associated with OTC derivatives exposures. Based on the ISDA survey, approximately \$1.4 trillion of exposures in OTC derivatives remained uncollateralized. Impact Assessment, 2010, p. 19, see *supra* note 38.

## 6.5. IN-LAW and Financial Markets: Basel II

### 6.5.1. The Basel Committee on Banking Supervision

It is difficult to imagine a better example of an IN-LAW regime in the realm of financial markets than the Basel Committee on Banking Supervision (BCBS), at least to the extent that the lack of formal existence or permanent staff are indicative of informality.[52] The BCBS provides a forum for regular cooperation on banking supervisory matters between regulators coming from 27 countries.[53] Issues related to banking supervision are discussed in those meetings held occasionally in the headquarters of the Bank for International Settlements in Basel, Switzerland.[54]

### 6.5.2. BCBS and Its Regulatory Failure: Accountability and Effectiveness

The regulatory failure of the BCBS is much less profound than that of the ISDA, at least insofar as accountability is concerned. This can be, in part, attributed to the fact that the BCBS is essentially a public body. As a result, its relative publicness has been more easily achieved, as compared with the ISDA, by modeling its decision-making process after two administrative law-like processes used in decision-making at the domestic and European level – notice and comment, and comitology.[55] Notice and

[52] The Committee's Secretariat is staffed mainly by professional supervisors on temporary secondment from member institutions. In addition to undertaking the secretarial work for the Committee and its many expert sub-committees, it stands ready to give advice to supervisory authorities in all countries.

[53] The Committee's members come from Argentina, Australia, Belgium, Brazil, Canada, China, France, Germany, Hong Kong SAR, India, Indonesia, Italy, Japan, Korea, Luxembourg, Mexico, the Netherlands, Russia, Saudi Arabia, Singapore, South Africa, Spain, Sweden, Switzerland, Turkey, the United Kingdom and the United States. Bank for International Settlements, "About the Basel Committee", available at http://www.bis.org/bcbs/about.htm, last accessed on 26 June 2012.

[54] Shawn Donnelly in his contribution to the book – "Informal International Lawmaking: Global Financial Market Regulation", chapter 5 – provides a description of the BCBS thus it would be futile to do it here as well.

[55] Compare Michael S. Barr and Geoffrey P. Miller, "Global Administrative Law: the View from Basel", in *European Journal of International Law*, 2006, vol. 17, no. 1 (for the notice and comment perspective) and Edward J. Kane, "Basel II: a Contracting Perspective", in *NBER Working Paper*, 2006, no. 12705 (for the comitology perspective).

comment ensures a certain degree of *ex ante* accountability towards external stakeholders, such as financial institutions or consumers' organizations. Comitology, on the other hand, ensures ongoing accountability of regulators sitting in Basel as agents towards their principals – their constituencies at home – including political constituencies and industries.[56]

The regulatory failure of the BCBS is much greater in terms of effectiveness, in particular, output effectiveness.[57] Basel II has been heavily criticized in the aftermath of the late 2000s financial crisis. The criticisms concerned many aspects of the framework, with the strongest criticism challenging the underlying philosophy of risk-calibrated capital, which lies at its heart.[58] The framework authorized banks to use their own estimates of risk as inputs for calculation of capital requirements. Many of the estimates, especially those relating to derivatives transactions entered into by banks, were off target and lie at the core of the undercapitalization of banks, which became evident after Lehman's Brothers' collapse and entailed the injection of taxpayers money into the banking system.[59]

## 6.6. TRSNs and Financial Markets: The Building of a Policy-Making Metaphor

The above analysis, however limited, provides us with some insights into how accountability and effectiveness work (or do not work) in IN-LAW and TPR regimes. First of all, we see that the mechanisms of accountability are not the same for IN-LAW and TPR regimes. Private regimes, in principle, do not exercise public power and hence, they do not embrace a

56 Still much of what has been written about BCBS's accountability deficit focused on the BCBS's informal status. In response to these calls, the Basel process has also become increasingly transparent in particular by developing its website which does not include the minutes of the meeting, but is constantly updated with speeches, working papers and other outputs of the BCBS's meeting. Bank for International Settlements, "Basel Committee on Banking Supervision", available at http://www.bis.org/bcbs, last accessed on 3 July 2012.

57 The story is different when we look at the effectiveness of the regulatory process itself. Basel II is often viewed as an unprecedented exercise in international regulatory coordination and harmonization. And for good reasons. Given the complexity of the issues at stake, the BCBS proved to be an effective forum for cooperation and one of lasting importance. Barr and Miller, 2006, see *supra* note 55.

58 See, *e.g.*, Martin Hellwig, "Capital Regulation after the Crisis: Business as Usual?", in *Preprints of the Max Planck Institute for Research on Collective Goods*, 2010, no. 31.

59 *Ibid.*

direct kind of accountability. It is with regard to public regulators (IN-LAW) that accountability is, or can be, designed in terms of mechanisms strictly defined and institutionalized. In the context of private regulators, there will inevitably be more emphasis on information sharing, transparency, participation rights as well as other measures that promote responsiveness.

Secondly, viewed against the backdrop of the financial crisis, which had banks and derivatives at its core, both the BCBS and ISDA can be easily accused of being terribly ineffective. To be clear, both have arguments to their defense and these are not bad arguments. But they merely account for part of the fault that can be attributed to these regimes. To the extent that fault can be identified with their regulatory failure, the most important reason for their ineffectiveness was their narrow focus.

In the context of Basel II, for example, it has been pointed out that it insufficiently accounts for risks arising from correlations of credit risks in mortgage or mortgage-backed securities and other derivatives in banking portfolios.[60] In the context of ISDA, it has been argued that it should extend its regulatory outlook beyond OTC markets into, for example, exchanges and swap execution facilities.[61] That said, in practice, how far can either of these regimes reach out? Is not a somewhat narrow outlook an inherent characteristic of any regulatory regime?

The bottom line to which that analysis points is that there are limits to how much accountability and effectiveness these regimes can achieve on their own.[62] This is where the TRSN metaphor comes into the picture. What it tells us is that these regimes do not exist in isolation. There is a great deal of interfaces in terms of norms production, monitoring and enforcement between IN-LAW, TPR and public law regimes. But what it al-

---

60 In these markets, risk was dispersed from owners of assets to investors in securities backed by those assets (ABS) and to other market participants. Banks generally did not take into account the fact that when ABS investments backed by subprime mortgage loans began defaulting, other investments backed by other types of assets began defaulting too. "Few had seen the correlation between the subprime mortgage loans and those other assets." Schwarcz, 2012, see *supra* note 50.

61 Compare Gillian Tett, 2010, see *supra* note 17.

62 In particular, from a post-crisis perspective, regimes such as the ISDA and the BCBS are themselves changing the self-governing rules by which they abide, allowing for more transparency and quality, and they are also increasingly subject to public scrutiny. But nonetheless, it remains modest at best and the question arises what can be done about it.

so points to is that there also exist interfaces and complementarities between these regimes in terms of accountability and effectiveness. In other words, as this metaphor suggests, accountability and effectiveness is often a collective endeavor of all actors involved, a function of a particular TRSN's features.

### 6.6.1. Interfaces in Terms of Norm Production, Monitoring and Enforcement

Markets are constructed by the interaction of public and private actors, also in terms of norm production, monitoring and enforcement. Consider the following examples.

First, when Basel II was negotiated back in the early 2000s, the ISDA was heavily involved in the notice and comment process. It provided the most substantive comment after the second consultative paper had been published. In a 150-page document, entitled *ISDA's Response to the Banking Committee on Banking Supervision's Consultation on the New Capital Accord* (2001), it made extensive suggestions concerning both the overall conceptual framework as well as the more detailed provision relating to the use of the internal rating based approach to credit risk and the advanced measurement approach to operational risk.

Second, ISDA sought to have enabling legislation recognized in various jurisdictions. In particular, it managed to secure exemptions of financial collateral arrangements from statutory and court ordered stays on the realization of collateral. Its endeavors have been rewarded in many jurisdictions, including in the European Union, where the Collateral Directive has been adopted in 2002.[63]

Third, as the most important actor in the derivatives industry, ISDA also collects data concerning activities in the market. When the European Commission announced its proposed rules for derivatives market in 2010, it heavily relied on the data provided by the ISDA.

Fourth, the Commission also relies on the ISDA in terms of monitoring. As we read in the legislative proposal: "[e]x-post evaluation of all new legislative measures is a top priority for the Commission [...] [f]or

[63] Directive 2002/47/EC of the European Parliament and of the Council of 6 June 2002 on financial collateral arrangements.

monitoring the progress in terms of contract and process standardization, existing sources could be used, such as the various ISDA surveys".[64]

Finally, enforcement of important aspects of the Basel Accords depends on private actors. This is why it is often referred to as 'enforced self-regulation'. When drafting Basel II, the BCBS remarked that it was prepared to "allow an unprecedented amount of flexibility to banks in choosing how to measure operational risk and the resulting capital requirement". Under the advanced measurement approach, banks were permitted to choose their own methodology for assessing operational risk, so long as it is sufficiently comprehensive and systemic.[65]

### 6.6.2. Interfaces in Terms of Accountability and Effectiveness

Even if we rely only on these few examples, we can still point to important complementarities, or what we may call interfaces, in terms of norm production, monitoring and enforcement. The question is whether these interfaces have consequences for accountability and effectiveness. In other words, can accountability and effectiveness be thought of and designed as 'dispersed', rather than associated with a particular regime?

As this section will argue, accountability and effectiveness can be designed and understood as cutting across different regimes, both public and private. Courts, for example, can help endow an IN-LAW or TPR regime with a certain degree of accountability (and sometimes effectiveness). On the other hand, it is also possible for private actors, for example, clearing houses or financial institutions, to help both public and private regimes achieve greater accountability and legitimacy.

#### 6.6.2.1. TRSNs and Courts

What is the role of courts in TRSNs? Courts can, in particular, enhance the accountability, and to some degree the effectiveness of particular elements of the TRSN, such as the IN-LAW and TPR regimes.

Does the role of court differ with regard to IN-LAW and TPR regimes? There is one apparent difference, which concerns the informality of IN-LAW regimes. Simply put, IN-LAW regimes, or their direct regulatory output, are unlikely to be subject to any litigation, precisely in virtue

64 Impact Assessment, 2010, p. 87, see *supra* note 38.

65 BCBS, "Overview Paper for the Impact Study", 2002, no.10, pp. 7–8.

of their informality. That is why we have never seen a case concerning the Basel Accords directly. It is not unlikely however, that these regimes, once implemented, can become a subject matter of litigation.

The case may be different with TPR, which is largely contract based. Here litigation and the role of courts will be much more substantial, and substantive.[66] Whenever a court's decision is out of alignment with commercial perceptions, this is usually followed by debate and refinement of standard form documentation or corrective legislative action.

Consider the following example. In the early 2000s, several cases were decided by the US Federal Court for the Southern District of New York involving ISDA Master Agreement-based credit default swaps that were written on Argentinean debt. After Argentina defaulted on its sovereign debt in December 2001, several creditors had a hard time enforcing certain provisions of the ISDA MA, which were designed with corporate rather than sovereign entities in mind. In response to these developments, the ISDA quickly revised the definition as well as formed a committee devoted to issues related to derivatives on sovereign debt.[67]

In such a case, the court does not directly change the standard, or in other words, the court does not get involved with the TPRER in question. To the extent that it does make a difference from the perspective of the standard users, it is only through clarifying the scope of the standard in a particular jurisdiction.[68]

66 See also Eyal Benvenisti, "The Role of National Courts in Reviewing Transnational Private Regulation", *Robert Schuman Centre for Advanced Studies (Discussion Paper)*, 2010, on file with author ("[i]n fact national courts are in a position to serve as the last national line of defense against skewed or unfair TPRs. Even when the national political branches and bureaucratic institutions are circumvented or compliant with the TPR, it would still be possible to approach NC to resist or challenges a TPR standard for specific measure"). Benvenisti points to a set of tools that national courts have a their disposal in reviewing TPR. They are tools of both substantive law (public law doctrines, laws regulating markets and doctrines applicable in private law) and procedural norms.

67 These cases are described in greater detail in Stephen J. Choi, G. Mitu Gulati, "Contract as Statue", in *Michigan Law Review*, 2005–2006, vol. 104, p. 1129.

68 Benvenisti, 2010, see *supra* note 66.

#### 6.6.2.2. TRSN, Central Counterparties and Trade Repositories

Not only public bodies, such as courts, can play an important role in endowing accountability to IN-LAW and TPR bodies. Private actors can do the same, especially if they are regarded as independent third parties.[69] For example, central counterparties and trade repositories.

Central counterparties, such as clearing houses, are financial institutions that provide clearing and settlement services for financial and commodities derivatives and securities transactions. They reduce counterparty or settlement risk – either by netting offsetting transactions, by requiring collateral deposits, or by providing independent valuation of trades and collateral. They can also perform important monitoring functions.

A trade repository is a

> centralized registry that maintains an electronic database of the records of open OTC derivatives transactions. The primary public policy benefit of a trade repository stems from the improved market transparency facilitated by its record keeping function, the integrity of information it maintains and effective access to this information by relevant authorities and the public in line with their respective information needs.[70]

Over the past years, and especially after the financial turmoil of the late 2000s, there have been many initiatives to establish clearing houses and trade repositories. Generally, on both sides of the Atlantic, regulation

---

69 Lack of independence is often perceived as the main problem in the discussion of legitimacy of credit rating. Independence in the private sectors, just as in the public sector, can be a critical dimension of legitimacy.

70 Bank of International Settlements, the International Organization for Securities Commission, Committee on Payment and Settlement Systems, Considerations for trades repositories in OTC derivatives markets, May 2010. ("In the absence of a trade repository, transaction data is maintained by individual counterparties and possibly other institutions providing services to market participants (*e.g.*, prime brokers, central counterparties (CCPs), trading platforms and custodians), often stored in proprietary systems in various formats with different data fields. Thus an important benefit of a TR is that it helps to promote standardization and provides a level of consistency in the quality and availability of transaction data."). The only TR that existed before the crisis was the Warehouse Trust Company LLC, a subsidiary of DTCC Deriv/SERV LLC. The Warehouse Trust is regulated as a member of the U.S. Federal Reserve System, and as a limited purpose trust company by the New York State Banking Department.

now requires that information on outstanding OTC derivatives contracts be reported to trade repositories (or if that is not possible, directly to supervisors) and that aggregated data on OTC derivatives be published for the benefit of the general public. These are requirements imposed by the financial reform-legislation of the early 2010s, but we find similar requirements imposed by the IN-LAW regime (in Basel III[71]) and by the ISDA as well.[72]

These initiatives have already led to substantial increases in the transparency of credit and interest rate derivatives. Both trade repositories currently hold information about the great majority of outstanding contracts and are being actively accessed by regulators in search of information. Since the information is collected at a central point, this facilitates the regulators job, as it spares them from having to compile individual information on their own. Furthermore, since both repositories publish aggregate data (with quite detailed breakdowns), the transparency for the general public has increased as well. That said, these repositories are not without their shortcomings, such as limited scope, issues relating to data protection and their non-binding nature.[73]

---

71 See BCBS, Basel III: A global regulatory framework for more resilient banks and banking systems, June 2011. "This document also introduces measures to strengthen the capital requirements for counterparty credit exposures arising from banks' derivatives, repo and securities financing activities. These reforms will raise the capital buffers backing these exposures, reduce procyclicality and provide additional incentives to move OTC derivative contracts to central counterparties, thus helping reduce systemic risk across the financial system." *Ibid.*, para. 13.

72 Craig Pirrong, "The Economics of Central Clearing: Theory and Practice", in *ISDA Discussion Paper Series*, no. 1, 2011.

73 In the US, the derivatives legislation is set forth in Title VII of the Act (entitled "Wall Street Transparency and Accountability") of the Dodd-Frank Wall Street Reform and Consumer Protection Act. However, provisions under other titles of the Act, such as Title VI on banking organizations, also have the potential to significantly affect the OTC derivatives market. In particular, the so-called "Volcker Rule" will ban the proprietary trading of derivatives by bank holding companies and their affiliates and, therefore, could materially affect the derivatives activities of banking organizations that are subject to regulation by U.S. governmental authorities. See "The Volcker Rule". Other provisions of Title VI, such as the inclusion of derivatives exposures under bank lending limits, also could affect the conduct of derivatives businesses by banking organizations. See Skadden, Apps, "Regulation of Over-the-Counter Derivatives Under the Dodd-Frank Wall Street Reform and Consumer Protection Act", available at http://www.skadden.com/newsletters/FSR_A_Regulation_of_Over-the-Counter_Derivatives.pdf, last accessed on 5 April 2011.

What is interesting about these reforms is that, both in the US and in the EU, the measures rely on private corporations to enhance accountability and effectiveness of the ISDA. The most important clearing houses and trade repositories are private corporations.[74] In Europe, one of the reasons why the Commission decided not to go for the option, which requires reporting directly to public regulators, is because it would, in its opinion, lead to a fragmentation of information for regulators. Moreover, to the extent that different information (or information in different format) would be reported to different regulators, piecing together a complete picture would become a challenging task. This problem would be particularly acute for market regulators and systemic risk regulators, but could also prove significant for prudential regulators of large groups active in multiple jurisdictions.

## 6.7. Conclusions

Every case study conducted under the IN-LAW and TPR projects brings with it new perspectives on what accountability and effectiveness mean; and how to improve them, so that these improvements do not come at the expense of one over the other. But every case study also brings a realization that there are limits and important constraints on the accountability and effectiveness of individual IN-LAW and TPR regimes. This essay suggested that these limits could be overcome by looking at regulation through the lens of the TRSN metaphor.

It argued that thinking about regulation in terms of TRSNs is useful, both analytically and practically, because insofar as non-legal-regulatory regimes are concerned, they will inevitably, perhaps necessarily, be deficient in these precious regulatory assets of accountability and effectiveness. The bottom line is that if we ask whether, for example, the ISDA is deficient in terms of accountability (and/or effectiveness); the answer will be a resounding yes. But if we focus on the direct accountability of the

[74] Both clearing houses and trade repositories are commercial firms. In Europe, the largest clearing houses are EMCF, LCH.Clearnet, SIX x-clear and EuroCCP. In the US, the largest ones are The Depository Trust and Clearing Corporation (DTCC) and Clearing House Interbank Payments System (CHIPS). Trioptima in Stockholm houses a global interest rate repository and DTCC Derivatives Repository Ltd in London houses a global equity derivatives repository and maintains global credit default swap data identical to that maintained in its New York based Trade Information Warehouse.

ISDA we will, more likely than not, miss the point. The ISDA is just one source of a complex of interlocking rules at different levels, dealing with different aspects of financial markets regulation. When looking at the ISDA, we also have to look at the role that courts and legislators can play in making the derivatives market more transparent, what role can be envisaged for public regulators, how the ISDA's regulation affects the operation of other aspects of the TRSN (and hence its relative importance in the TRSN), what complementarities exist between ISDA and other private regimes and actors (lawyers, accountants, bankers *et cetera*), and what role academics can play in shaping the regimes' accountability and effectiveness. TRSN, as a policy-making metaphor, is an exercise in understanding the shared responsibility for the efficient and safe operation of financial markets.

# 7

# The Informality of the International Forum of Sovereign Wealth Funds and the Santiago Principles: A Conscious Choice or a Necessity?

**Eliza Malathouni**[*]

## 7.1. Introduction

Sovereign Wealth Funds (SWFs) are government controlled investment vehicles engaging in foreign direct investment (FDI) and/or portfolio investment. Although SWFs do not constitute a novel phenomenon – the first SWF was set up in Kuwait in 1953 – it is only from 2005 onwards that they have attracted considerable attention from policy makers, academics and practitioners.[1] This renewed interest can be attributed to their sovereign nature in combination with the exponential growth that SWFs have been undergoing since 2000. The fact that SWFs constitute investment vehicles belonging to and controlled by the government of a country realizing or attempting to realize investments in the territories of other countries has been a characteristic of SWFs since their inception. However, what is alarming is that there has been a boom both in the establishment of new funds and in the size of the existing ones. Keeping in mind that there are approximately fifty SWFs in the world, almost thirty of them have been established since 2000.[2] Moreover, it is estimated that

* **Eliza (Elissavet) Malathouni** is a Ph.D. Candidate at the Faculty of Law of Maastricht University and a Ph.D. fellow with the Institute for Globalization and International Regulation (IGIR). She is also a Research Affiliate at the Sovereign Wealth Fund Initiative at the Center for Emerging Market Enterprises at the Fletcher School of Tufts University. The author would like to thank Dr. Denise Prèvost for her support and useful comments.

1 Contrary to widespread belief that Kuwait set up the first SWF, Gramlich reports that the first SWF was the French Caisse des Depots et Consignations, set up in 1816. Ludwig Gramlich, "An International Normative Framework for Sovereign Wealth Funds?", in C. Herrmann and J.P. Terhechte (eds.), *European Yearbook of International Economic Law*, Springer-Verlag, Berlin, Heidelberg, 2011, p. 49.

2 Ashby H.B. Monk, "Recasting the Sovereign Wealth Fund Debate: Trust, Legitimacy, and Governance", in *New Political Economy*, 2009, vol. 14, no. 4, pp. 451, 456.

SWFs hold approximately 5 trillion US $ in assets. Their volume is about nine times larger than that of private equity funds. Whereas proponents of SWFs view their size as a sheer benefit, especially in times of financial crisis, SWF critics voice serious concerns regarding SWFs' objectives.

SWFs are oftentimes portrayed in the media as either friends or foes of the countries in which they are to invest. In particular, in times of need for financial liquidity, SWF investments are thought to be capable of revitalizing national economies. This relief brought by SWF investments is however, not decoupled from fears on the part of recipient states – that is, the states receiving the investment – regarding the true motives of the SWFs' investment policies. SWFs are often perceived as instruments of the governments of the holder states – that is, the states controlling the SWFs – to pursue a geo-political agenda in the recipient state under the guise of commercial activity. In response, recipient states frequently adopt protectionist measures against investments by SWFs, thereby depriving themselves of much needed foreign investment and depriving holder states of interesting investment opportunities. The attempted investments have often failed on grounds of national interest erected by SWF-recipient countries.

Fears of the true objectives pursued through SWFs investments were voiced at the 2007 Economic Davos meeting and SWF recipient countries called for increased transparency as well as a code of conduct for SWFs. To address climbing pressure, SWF holder countries set up the International Working Group of SWFs (IWGSWF) under the aegis of the International Monetary Fund (IMF). In a short period of time the IWG-SWF produced a voluntary code of conduct, the 'Generally Accepted Principles and Practices', otherwise known as the 'Santiago Principles'. In 2009, the IWGSWF dissolved and was succeeded by the International Forum of SWFs (IFSWF). The aim of this chapter is to examine whether the IFSWF can be classified as an informal international lawmaking forum (IN-LAW) and whether the IFSWF suffers from an accountability deficit. Additionally, the chapter purports to assess whether the Santiago Principles, as currently formulated, promote the accountability of SWFs. The chapter is structured as follows: the *second part* will introduce the notion of SWFs and present the concerns they have raised. The *third part* will offer a review of the coming into being of the International Forum for Sovereign Wealth Funds (IFSWF). The *fourth part* will investigate whether the IFSWF can form part of the IN-LAW process. *Part five* will discuss the relevant principles contained in the Santiago Principles pertaining to accountability and transparency and will place them within the IN-LAW framework attempting to identify to whom SWFs should be accountable. The *sixth part* will examine the efficiency of the Santiago Principles and their effect on the practice of specific SWFs. To this end, the Report prepared by the IFSWF Sub-Committee on 'IFSWF Members' Experiences in the Application of the Santiago Principles' will be examined, providing feedback on the accountability of SWFs through the Santiago Principles at a domestic and international level. The seventh part concludes.

## 7.2. Sovereign Wealth Funds

### 7.2.1. Defining Sovereign Wealth Funds

This section will define SWFs and briefly explain the main concerns associated with them. The term SWFs – or more accurately Sovereign Wealth Managers – was first coined by Andrew Rozanov, a senior financial analyst. His proposed definition was a negative one, in that he stated what SWFs are not. According to Rozanov, SWFs are not prudential monetary reserves and they are not traditional pension funds. They are however managed by sovereigns, that is, states.[3] Since 2005, numerous definitions have been advanced by academics, practitioners, state officials, the European Union (EU) and the IMF, in an attempt to reach a commonly accepted definition for SWFs. They have unfortunately to date proven futile.[4] A common point of departure for all the proposed defini-

3 Andrew Rozanov, "Who Holds the Wealth of Nations?", in *Central Banking Journal*, May 2005, vol. 15, no. 4, p. 1.

4 For an overview of the most authoritative definitions advanced for SWFs see Andrew Rozanov, "Definitional Challenges of Dealing with Sovereign Wealth Funds", in *Asian Journal of International Law*, 2011, vol. 1, no. 2, p. 249; Edwin M. Truman, *Sovereign Wealth Funds: Threat or Salvation?*, Peterson Institute for International Economics, Washington DC, September 2010, pp. 9–33; Stephen Jen, "Currencies the Definition of a Sovereign Wealth Fund", available at http://www.morganstanley.com/views/gef/archive/2007/20071026-Fri.html, last accessed on 28 November 2011; Anne Gelpern, "Sovereignty, Accountability, and the Wealth Fund Governance Conundrum", in *Asian Journal of International Law*, 2011, vol. 1, no. 2, pp. 289–294; Monk, 2009, pp. 451–457, see *supra* note 2; International Monetary Fund, "Balance of Payments and International Investment Positions Manual, 6$^{th}$ ed. (BPM6)", 2009, available at http://www.imf.org/external/pubs/ft/bop/2007/pdf/bpm6.pdf, last accessed on 28 November 2011; Commission of the European Communities, Communication from the Commission to the European Parliament, the Council and the Economic and

tions is that SWFs are investment vehicles owned and/or controlled by a government. But this is probably the only element that the proposed definitions have in common. The practitioners' definition tends to emphasize the economic nature of SWFs, whereas the state officials, the IMF and the EU definitions underline the sovereign nature of the funds' owner. Academic definitions vary. The difficulty of agreeing on a common definition for SWFs emanated from their vast heterogeneity in terms of constitution in law and pursued macroeconomic policies or objectives. It is commonly said that there is no such thing as a typical SWF. The purpose of this chapter is not however to examine the preciseness of the various definitions nor to propose a commonly accepted definition. It will therefore proceed on the basis of a compromise definition provided for in the Santiago Principles and developed by SWFs themselves. The Santiago Principles define SWFs as:

> […] special purpose investment funds or arrangements, owned by the general government. Created by the general government for macroeconomic purposes, SWFs hold, manage, or administer assets to achieve financial objectives, and employ a set of investment strategies that include investing in foreign financial assets. The SWFs are commonly established out of balance of payments surpluses, official foreign currency operations, the proceeds of privatizations, fiscal surpluses, and/or receipts resulting from commodity exports.[5]

A few clarifications are in order regarding the type of government, the investments undertaken by SWFs, the funding of SWFs and the purposes pursued by SWFs. First, the Santiago Principles explicitly mention that the term government is to include both central and sub-national government.[6] Second, SWFs are only those investment funds or arrangements that invest abroad, that is in the territory of another state, and not domesti-

Social Committee and the Committee of the Regions, "A Common European Approach to Sovereign Wealth Funds", COM (2008) 115 provisional, available at http://ec.europa.eu/internal_market/finances/docs/sovereign_en.pdf, last accessed on 28 November 2011.

5 International Working Group of Sovereign Wealth Funds, "Sovereign Wealth Funds: Generally Accepted Principles and Practices, Santiago Principles", October 2008, p. 27, available at http://www.iwg-swf.org/pubs/eng/santiagoprinciples.pdf, last accessed on 28 November 2011. [IWGSWF, "Santiago Principles"].

6 IWGSWF, "Santiago Principles", 2008, p. 27, see *supra* note 5.

cally in the territory of the SWF holder country. Third, regarding the sources of funding, SWFs are typically funded by excess foreign exchange reserves, surpluses in the balance of payments, the proceeds of privatizations and fiscal surpluses. However, there are other sources of funding, such as the proceeds from natural resources. These different sources of funding have led to the classification of SWFs as non-commodity and as commodity SWFs respectively.[7] Fourth, the returns through SWFs investments can be used for a variety of purposes and have led to a five-tier classification of SWFs, namely stabilization funds, pension reserve funds, savings funds, reserve investment corporations and development funds.[8] Stabilization funds are used to insulate the economy and the budget from volatile commodity prices. Pension reserve funds build assets to cover an identifiable liability often related to an aging population. Savings funds focus on intergenerational equity and transfers. They have a dual aim of spreading commodity wealth over generations and of sustaining future income from the extraction of non-renewable resources. Reserve investment corporations aim to enhance returns on reserves and development funds allocate resources for funding priority socioeconomic projects. Fifth, SWFs are not state-owned enterprises (SOE), public pension funds, foreign exchange reserves nor hedge funds.

### 7.2.2. Concerns Related to Sovereign Wealth Funds

Although it is a widespread belief that SWFs have to date behaved as model investors, SWFs recipient countries have raised considerable con-

---

7 Steffen Kern, "How to Spend it: Commodity and Non-Commodity Sovereign Wealth Funds", Deutsche Bank Research, Working Papers Series, Research Notes 28, 18 July 2008, available at http://www.oecd.org/dataoecd/62/33/41212577.pdf, last accessed on 28 November 2011.

8 Peter Kunzel, Yinqiu Lu, Iva Petrova, Jukka Pihlman, "Investment Objectives of Sovereign Wealth Funds: a Shifting Paradigm", in Ubaidir S. Das, Adnan Mazarei, Han Van der Hoorn (eds.), *Economics of Sovereign Wealth Funds: Issues for Policymakers*, International Monetary Fund, 2010. Also available as an IMF Working Paper, WP/11/19, January 2011, p. 3, available at http://www.imf.org/external/pubs/ft/wp/2011/wp1119.pdf, last accessed on 28 November 2011. See also Ubaidir Das, Yinquin Lu, Christian Mulder, Amadou Sy, "Setting Up a Sovereign Wealth Fund: Some Policy and Operational Considerations", IMF Working Paper, WP09/179, 2009, pp. 9–10, available at http://www.imf.org/external/pubs/ft/wp/2009/wp09179.pdf, last accessed on 28 November 2011.

cerns relating to their activities.[9] These concerns can be based on two of the characteristics of SWFs, namely: first, because SWFs are linked through ownership or control to a sovereign and second, because SWFs accumulate large amounts of money.[10] Amongst the concerns voiced is the alleged claim that SWFs are solely interested in the transfer of expertise and technology from the company they invest in and not in the investment itself or that SWF investments are capable of disrupting capital markets, distorting competition or even causing the demotion of national champions.[11] The following paragraphs will present the most significant concerns attached to SWF investment. Examining these concerns is not only relevant to improve our understanding of SWF investments but also enables us to evaluate whether the accountability and transparency mechanisms contained in the Santiago Principles are capable of successfully addressing these concerns.

A great deal of literature is dedicated to identifying and explaining the risks attached to SWFs investments.[12] The arguments advanced can be categorized in two main categories; namely, first, that SWFs pose a systemic risk and a risk to economic security, and; second, that SWFs pursue strategic investments. The first category attempts to explain all economic

[9] Bradford DeLong and Stephen S. Cohen, *The End of Influence: What Happens When Other Counties Have the Money*, Perseus Books Group, New York, 2010, p. 114.

[10] Gerald Lyons, "State Capitalism: the Rise of Sovereign Wealth Funds", in *Law and Business Review of the Americas*, 2008, vol. 14, no. 1, p. 5; Donghyun Park and Gemma Esther Estrada, "Developing Asia's Sovereign Wealth Funds: the Santiago Principles and the Case for Self Regulation", in *Asian Journal of International Law*, 2011, vol. 1, no. 2, p. 384.

[11] Ronald J. Gilson and Curtis J. Milhaupt, "Sovereign Wealth Funds and Corporate Governance: A Minimalist Response to the New Mercantilism", in *Stanford Law Review*, 2008, vol. 60, no. 5, pp. 1360–1362; Richard A. Epstein and Amanda M. Rose, "The Regulation of Sovereign Wealth Funds: the Virtues of Going Slow", in *The University of Chicago Law Review*, 2009, vol. 76, no. 1, pp. 123–128.

[12] Amy Keller, "Sovereign Wealth Funds: Trustworthy Investors or Vehicles of Strategic Ambition – An Assessment of the Benefits, Risks and Possible Regulation of Sovereign Wealth Funds", in *The Georgetown Journal of Law and Public Policy*, 2009, vol. 7, no. 1, pp. 342–345; Paul Rose, "Sovereign Wealth Fund Investment in the Shadow of Regulation and Politics", in *Georgetown Journal of International Law*, 2009, vol. 40, no. 4, pp. 1207–1238; Paul Rose, "Sovereigns as Shareholders", in *North Carolina Law Review*, December 2008, vol. 87, no. 1, pp. 93–99; Jennifer Cooke, "Finding the Right Balance for Sovereign Wealth Fund Regulation: Open Investment vs. National Security", in *Columbia Business Law Review*, 2009, vol. 2009, no. 2, pp. 736–743; Epstein and Rose, 2009, pp. 123–128, see *supra* note 11.

concerns related to SWFs, whereas the second category attempts to muster all political arguments against SWF investment. We take a closer look at these arguments next.

#### 7.2.2.1. Economic Concerns

Several main economic concerns have been raised against SWFs.

First, SWFs have been criticized for posing a systemic risk. This concern relates to SWFs posing a twofold threat to the capitalistic system. One of the main characteristics of the capitalistic system is that it is profit oriented and that is precisely the goal of the market participants. Should SWFs not pursue a profit maximization goal – as the other market participants do – but instead pursue strategic goals, then SWFs would tamper with the predominant economic system and render it inefficient.[13] Furthermore, SWFs being government-owned or controlled investment vehicles distort the notion of a free market economy, where the role of the government is restricted to the enforcement of property rights. SWFs have also given rise to the debate of whether the predominant economic system is transforming itself into one of state nationalism.

Second, SWFs are said to pose a risk to the economic security of SWF recipient countries. SWFs have allegedly had the ability to cause microeconomic distortions in markets through influencing the behavior of the firm in which they have invested so as to attract benefits for the SWF holder country.[14] This fear can however easily be appeased, keeping in mind that to date SWFs mainly restrict themselves to acquiring small, non-controlling shares of the companies in which they invest and are therefore seemingly unable or disinterested in influencing the decision-making of the companies in which they invest.[15]

---

13 Christopher Cox, "The Rise of Sovereign Business", Gauer Distinguished Lecture in Law and Policy at the American Enterprise Institute Legal Center for the Public Interest, available at http://www.sec.gov/news/speech/2007/spch120507cc.htm, last accessed on 28 November 2011; Epstein and Rose, 2009, p. 123, see *supra* note 11, criticize the validity of the argument as farfetched.

14 Epstein and Rose, 2009, p. 124, see *supra* note 11.

15 Reality and practice however do not demonstrate a future stable behavior and it might well be that SWFs will go for larger equity stakes in the future. It comes in handy, therefore, that most SWF recipient countries have legislation in place subjecting large takeovers by SWFs to regulatory review.

Third, SWFs can cause the collapse of the market that they invest in. SWFs have been fiercely criticized of allegedly jeopardizing the position of ordinary investors in the SWF recipient country market by taking advantage of information asymmetries. SWFs, being closely related to the government of the SWF holder country, might have access to information not widely available to the public and to ordinary investors. Actual or presumable knowledge of insider information being available exclusively to SWFs might cause ordinary investors to behave in panic and affect their investment behavior in such ways that would discredit the financial system and even cause its collapse.[16]

#### 7.2.2.2. Political Concerns

Apart from the economic concerns that SWFs allegedly pose, political concerns have also been attributed to SWF investments.

First, SWFs have been accused of pursuing strategic rather than profit-maximization investments. This would in essence mean that SWFs allegedly constitute the 'long-arm of the SWF holder governments' and would serve their respective governments as an alternative route for exercising political power. Arguments have been advanced that SWF holder countries can use SWFs investments as a means to reinforce their leverage in diplomatic negotiations. One needs only to remember the example of the Russian state-owned company, Gazprom, which cut off the supply to Ukraine a couple of years ago, to understand the origin of this argument. What needs to be stressed here is that SWFs are not tantamount to State Own Enterprises (SOEs), yet because both entities are controlled or owned by a government, it is easy to draw an analogy and extend the fear related with SOEs to SWFs.

Second, supporters of the view that SWFs pursue strategic investments also stress that the underlying motives of a SWF investment might be to gain access to technology or to transfer expertise from the company in which they invest back to the SWF holder country. Such an ulterior motive – if proved substantial and true – could lead to the distortion of competition not only in the SWF recipient country market but also in the global market. Furthermore, by transferring sensitive technology and/or expertise from the company in which SWFs invest back to their own

[16] Cox, "The Rise of Sovereign Business", see *supra* note 13; Keller, 2009, p. 343, see *supra* note 12.

country, SWFs could be capable of stripping off the company of its competitive advantage in the market and thus succeed in deposing a national champion.

Third, SWFs also raise concerns of corruption – albeit of lesser significance than the aforementioned concerns. Keeping in mind that SWF investments entail a large amount of assets, critics fear that the persons in charge of handling the investment could abuse the economic commercial power or even use it for their own personal gain.[17]

Fourth, American academics have also identified and commented on the risk of conflict of interest when it comes to SWF investments, as the SWF holder government holds simultaneously the dual role of both the regulator and the regulated.[18] When it comes to cross-border investments, the US authorities, and more specifically the Securities and Exchange Commission (SEC), often find themselves in the position of requesting additional information from the government of the entity wishing to invest in US soil. Issues of conflict of interest could arise when it comes to SWF investments as the government of the SWF holder country would be essentially asked to provide the US information on its own activities. Previous cases have shown that where a foreign government has an interest in the person or entity under SEC investigation, the extent and nature of cooperation with the foreign government is compromised.[19]

Whether justified or not, the above mentioned concerns are only reinforced by the lack of transparency surrounding SWFs and their investments. As a response, SWF recipient countries often bar the realization of SWF investments on the pretense of national security and other societal values claiming that what SWF investments are actually pursuing is mainly a geo-political agenda. Hence, recipient countries contend that SWF investments are based primarily on geo-political criteria, and not on sound management criteria, as would have been expected. For this reason, the issue of investment through SWFs takes a political twist. To this end, SWF recipient countries bar SWF investments from their territory on grounds

17 Keller, 2009, p. 343, see *supra* note 12.

18 *Ibid.*

19 Linda Chatman Thomsen, "Testimony on Sovereign Wealth Funds and Public Disclosure Before the U.S.-China Economic and Security Review Commission", 7 February 2008, available at http://www.uscc.gov/hearings/2008hearings/written_testimonies/08_02_07_wrts/08_02_07_chatman_thomsen_statement.pdf, last accessed on 28 November 2011.

of societal values, thereby depriving themselves of much needed FDI and SWF holder countries of investment opportunities.

### 7.2.2.3. Dealing with these Concerns

Various proposals have been advanced in order to counter the fears raised by SWFs and to enjoy the benefits of receiving and of engaging in foreign investment. These proposals cover a whole spectrum ranging from the one extreme of wholly restricting SWF investment to the other extreme of granting SWFs a *carte blanche*. Along this spectrum and in the middle one can find a variety of proposals.[20] Some advocate in favor of permitting SWF investment solely through intermediaries. Others propose allowing SWFs to merely invest in global index funds.[21] Others advance the view that SWFs be treated as a category of special shareholders, where the shares they acquire are stripped of their voting rights, only to regain voting powers once they are to be re-sold.[22] There are also those who advance the view that SWFs should be forbidden from acquiring controlling stakes in domestic companies and those who are of the opinion that SWFs should be subjected to mandatory disclosures and governance rules.[23] Another option to regulate SWFs would be through the adoption of codes of conduct. A double effort through the auspices of the IMF and the Organization for Economic Cooperation and Development (OECD) has led to the adoption of best practices for SWF recipient and holder countries. This chapter focuses on the Santiago Principles that are a code of conduct for regulating SWF holder country behavior.

What one can discern from the above analysis is that what underlies the above mentioned concerns are the lack of information due to limited transparency, the problem of asymmetric information and the fear of SWF

---

20 For a general discussion on the regulation of SWFs, Epstein and Rose, 2009, pp. 119–120, see *supra* note 11.

21 Joshua Aizenman and Reuven Glick, "Sovereign Wealth Funds: Stumbling Blocks or Stepping Stones to Financial Globalization?", in Federal Reserve Bank San Francisco Economic Letter, 2007, no. 38, available at http://www.frbsf.org/publications/economics/letter/2007/el2007-38.pdf, last accessed on 28 November 2011.

22 Gilson and Milhaupt, 2008, pp. 1362–1368, see *supra* note 11.

23 Edwin M. Truman, "A Blueprint for Sovereign Wealth Fund Practices", Policy Brief Number PB08-3, Peterson Institute for International Economics, April 2008, available at http://www.iie.com/publications/pb/pb08-3.pdf, last accessed on 28 November 2011; Truman, 2010, pp. 69–120, see *supra* note 4.

recipient countries of losing power. Most of these concerns might be overcome through the establishment of accountability processes and transparency mechanisms. To some extent such processes and mechanisms have been incorporated in the Santiago Principles, which we discuss below.

Having examined the economic and political concerns that SWF investments instill in SWF recipient countries, the following section turns to the establishment by SWF holder countries of the IWGSWF and the IFSWF. This development reflects their coordinated response to calls by SWF recipient countries for greater transparency and accountability.

## 7.3. The Road Towards the IWGSWF and the IFSWF

As a response to the concerns of SWF recipient countries, SWF holder countries were 'forced' to coalesce in an informal forum, the IWGSWF initially and the IFSWF eventually. The aim of this section is to provide an overview of the events leading to the establishment of the IWGSWF and the IFSWF.

### 7.3.1. IWGSWF

Amidst the outbreak of the financial crisis, SWFs started injecting huge amounts of capital to save financial institutions. Such investment moves sparked competing reactions: some hailed SWFs as 'white knights' coming to the rescue of financial institutions in distress, yet others greeted the investments with skepticism and mounting concerns. A heated debate erupted on the nature of SWFs as benign investors or 'Trojan horses', calling for divergent regulatory proposals. Those in favor of SWF investments reiterated their countries' commitment to minimize any national restrictions on foreign investment, whereas those weary of SWF investments urged for a protectionist response and the raising of barriers towards SWF investments.

In such a climate, it was SWF recipient countries, most notably the United States, the European Union and Japan, who set in motion the regulation of SWF behavior by calling for "[...] a set of best practices to which funds would subscribe voluntarily. The practices would include pledges of nonpolitical governance structures and more disclosure of portfolio activities".[24] In a G-8 Summit meeting in 2007, the G8 assigned the task of drafting best practices in the areas of institutional structure, risk management, transparency and accountability to the IMF, the World Bank and the OECD.[25] The International Monetary and Finance Committee (IMFC) in its Communiqué of 20 October 2007 welcomed the initiative to develop SWF best practices as well as an analysis of issues crucial to SWF recipient and holder countries, so as to safeguard an open global financial environment while avoiding protectionist measures.[26] However, due to vehement protest on the part of influential SWFs to the IMF's proposed leading role in the drafting of best practices, the IMF was sidelined. Instead, a new body was formed – the International Working Group of SWFs (IWGSWF) – which was tasked with drafting SWF best practices. The IMF's role was reduced to that of providing secretarial and technical support to the IWGSWF.[27] The establishment of the IWGSWF was important for two reasons. First, it constituted a coordinated answer to the concerns of SWF recipient countries regarding SWFs investments. Second, it marked a shift in actors that participate in standard-setting. Whereas Western countries had been the ones that initially called for the

24 "Overseas Funds Resist Calls for a Code of Conduct", New York Times, 9 February 2008.

25 G7/8 Finance Ministers Meetings, "Statement of G7 Finance Ministers and Central Bank Governors", 19 October 2007, available at http://www.g8.utoronto.ca/finance/fm071019.htm, last accessed on 28 November 2011.

26 Communiqué of the International Monetary Financial Committee of the Board of Governors of the International Monetary Fund, 20 October 2007, available at http://www.imf.org/external/np/cm/2007/102007a.htm, last accessed on 4 November 2011.

27 According to statements made by the United Arab Emirates bank Governor Sultan bin Nassir Al Suwaidi, the IMF lacked the requisite experience in the areas of governance and transparency in order to lead an effort for the drafting of best practices. Al Suwaidi represented a number of SWF holder countries such as Bahrain, Egypt, Qatar, Jordan, Kuwait, Iraq, Lebanon, Libya, Oman, Syria and Yemen. For more information, see Emirates Business 24/7, "Suwaidi Critical of IMF Attempt to Monitor SWF Investments in West", 9 May 2008, available at http://www.emirates247.com/eb247/the-business-of-life/suwaidi-critical-of-imf-attempt-to-monitor-swf-investments-in-west-2008-05-09-1.226998, last accessed on 28 November 2011. For a more detailed account of the process leading to the establishment of the IWGSWF see Truman, 2010, pp. 121–139, see *supra* note 4.

development of SWF best practices, it was finally the SWF holder countries themselves that were dominant in the standard setting process.[28]

The IWGSWF was set up on 30 April – 1 May 2008. Its membership is composed of 26 SWF holder countries; Oman, Saudi Arabia, Vietnam, the OECD and the IMF enjoy observer status.[29] In September 2008, following its third meeting in Chile and after a relatively short period of time, the IWGSWF drafted and released the 'Generally Accepted Principles and Practices', commonly referred to as the 'Santiago Principles'. A subgroup of the IWG developed the Santiago Principles and in doing so, benefited from the IMF's findings from its Survey on SWF current structures and practices. These findings were presented before the IMFC. In the drafting of the Santiago Principles, the IWGSWF received input and feedback from SWF recipient countries, such as Australia, Brazil, Canada, France, Germany, India, Italy, Japan, South Africa, Spain, the United Kingdom and the United States, despite the fact that most of them are not IWGSWF members. Additional feedback was also provided from international organizations, namely the European Union, the OECD and the World Bank.[30]

The mandate of the IWGSWF was restricted to the drafting of the principles, so in 2009, it dissolved and gave its place to the International Forum of Sovereign Wealth Funds (IFSWF), which we address next.

### 7.3.2. IFSWF

In 2009, the IWGSWF met in Kuwait and issued the 'Kuwait Declaration'.[31] According to the 'Kuwait Declaration', the IWGSWF reiterated its commitment made before the IMFC to continue studying SWF activities.

---

28 Maurizia de Bellis, "Global Standards for Sovereign Wealth Funds: the Quest for Transparency", in *Asian Journal of International Law*, 2011, vol. 1, no. 2, p. 359.

29 IWGSWF's members are Australia, Azerbaijan, Bahrain, Botswana, Canada, Chile, China, Equatorial Guinea, Islamic Republic of Iran, Ireland, Korea, Kuwait, Libya, Mexico, New Zealand, Norway, Qatar, Russia, Singapore, Timor-Leste, Trinidad and Tobago, the United Arab Emirates and the United States.

30 IWGSWF, "Santiago Principles", 2008, see *supra* note 5.

31 International Working Group of Sovereign Wealth Funds, "Kuwait Declaration: Establishment of the International Forum of Sovereign Wealth Funds", 6 April 2009, available at http://www.iwg-swf.org/mis/kuwaitdec.htm, last accessed on 28 November 2011. [IWGSWF, "Kuwait Declaration"].

To this end, it announced the formation of the IFSWF. The IFSWF would take over and advance the work initiated by the IWGSWF.

The IFSWF's primary purpose is to provide for an informal platform facilitating the exchange of views between SWFs on issues of common interest and to promote understanding of the Santiago Principles and SWF activities to other relevant parties.[32] More specifically, the IFSWF is to serve three objectives. First, it is bestowed with the task of forming a communications platform between SWF and other relevant parties on a variety of SWF related issues such as new trends, investment regimes, *et cetera*. Second, it shall engage in view sharing on the application of the Santiago Principles. Third, it shall encourage cooperation with SWF recipient countries.

The mandate of the IFSWF reiterates the underlying objectives of the Santiago Principles: First, the maintenance of a stable global financial system and of the free flow of capital and investment; Second, compliance with regulatory and disclosure requirements foreseen in the SWF recipient country regulation; Third, investment on the basis of economic and financial considerations; and last, the establishment of a transparent and sound governance structure.

The IFSWF is to meet annually but the Kuwait Declaration also provides for the possibility of special meetings. So far, the IFSWF has met four times, in Kuwait in April 2009, Baku in October 2009, Sydney in May 2010 and in Beijing in May 2011.

Three sub-committees have been established within the framework of the IFSWF.[33] Sub-committee 1 is mandated to examine the practical application of the Santiago Principles in the territories of SWF host countries and report back to the IFSWF on the issues members face in their implementation as well as on ways to facilitate understanding of the Santiago Principles. The IFSWF stated in the most unequivocal manner, however, that such a report would not and does not amount to any attempt to create a regulatory, monitoring or evaluating body. Sub-committee 2 aims at reinforcing the existing dialogue with SWF recipient countries as well as international and regional investment and trade associations such

[32] *Ibid.*

[33] IWGSWF, "Working Group Announces Creation of International Forum of Sovereign Wealth Funds", Press Release, no. 09/01, 6 April 2009, available at http://www.iwg-swf.org/pr/swfpr0901.htm, last accessed on 28 November 2011.

as the Association of Southeast Asian Nations (ASEAN), the Asia-Pacific Economic Cooperation (APEC), the Golf Cooperation Council (GCC), the EU and the OECD. Through consultations with the above mentioned actors, it seeks for best methods for SWFs to demonstrate their commitment to abide by SWF recipient country rules on securities, tax and anti-monopoly as well as to disclose financial and non-financial information and to improve cooperation with SWF recipient countries investigations and regulatory actions.[34] Sub-committee 3 deals with investment and risk management practices.

The next part will introduce the IN-LAW framework and apply it to the IFSWF with a view to establishing whether it qualifies as an informal international lawmaking process.

## 7.4. The IN-LAW Framework and Its Application to the IFSWF

Informal International Lawmaking (IN-LAW) as a term depicts the rise of a phenomenon which is characterized by a triple informality of output, processes and actors. IN-LAW is defined as:

> Cross-border cooperation between public authorities, with or without the participation of private actors and/ or international organizations, in a forum other than a traditional international organization (process informality), and/ or as between actors other than traditional diplomatic actors (such as regulators or agencies) (actor informality) and/ or which does not result in a formal treaty or traditional source of international law (output informality).[35]

It is due to this triple informality, which detaches international lawmaking from the 'strictures of both domestic law as well as international law', that questions of an accountability deficit of IN-LAW arise.[36] This section will analyze the IN-LAW definition and apply it to the IFSWF. Two remarks are in order. For the purposes of this chapter and

---

34 International Forum for Sovereign Wealth Funds, "IFSWF Statement: Generally Accepted Principles and Practices (GAPP) Purpose and Objectives", Beijing May 2011, available at http://www.ifswf.org/pst/ifswfstatmt.pdf, last accessed on 28 November 2011. [IFSWF, "IFSWF Statement"].

35 Joost Pauwelyn, "Informal International Lawmaking: Framing the Concept and Research Questions", in Joost Pauwelyn, Ramses A. Wessel, Jan Wouters (eds.), *Informal International Lawmaking*, Oxford University Press, Oxford, 2012, p. 22.

36 *Ibid.*, p. 14.

since the IWGSWF has dissolved, only the IFSWF will be considered. Although the Santiago Principles were drafted by the IWGSWF, since the IFSWF succeeded the IWGSWF and has reaffirmed its commitment in adhering to and promoting the Santiago Principles, the Principles will be treated as an output of the IFSWF.

### 7.4.1. IN-LAW Process

Unlike traditional lawmaking, in IN-LAW process informality is understood as a loosely organized network or forum where lawmaking takes place. The notion excludes the *travaux préparatoires* leading to the adoption of an internationally legally binding text, as well as 'informal' or 'green room' meetings.[37] According to the IN-LAW framework, process informality is measured in terms of the legal personality of the forum, the structure of the forum, the regulation of meetings and the existence of procedural rules. These aspects will be analyzed in turn.

As concerns the legal personality of the IFSWF, "[...] the Forum shall not be a formal supranational authority and its work shall not carry any legal force".[38] The IFSWF lacks a detailed and declaratory constitutive document. The Kuwait Declaration comes close to such a document yet it lays down rudimentary rules as concerns the structure of the IFSWF, the meetings, the procedural rules and its mandate. The IFSWF is to be headed by a Chair and two Deputy Chairs, elected by the members through consensus and serving for a two years term. The work of the Forum will be facilitated by a Secretariat whose main task is to keep records and facilitate the activities of the IFSWF. The Kuwait Declaration also provides for the establishment of sub-groups to deal with special topics. Their establishment is entrusted to the Chair and Deputy Chairs, following consultations with the other IFSWF members. The IFSWF as a whole is to meet at a minimum once a year, whereas provision is made for special meetings, the necessity of which is to be determined by the Chair and Deputy Chairs. The sub-groups may meet more frequently.

As concerns procedural rules, the Kuwait Declaration is marked by an almost complete lack thereof. The decision-making process within the Forum is not delineated; the duties of the Chair and Deputy Chairs are not laid down. The only relevant rules mentioned are that the election of the

37 *Ibid.*, p. 17.

38 IFSWF, "Kuwait Declaration", see *supra* note 31.

Chair and Deputy Chairs will be made on the basis of consensus and that the IFSWF members are to finance themselves, whereas the organizational costs of the Forum meetings are to be borne by the SWF holder country/SWF member hosting the meeting.

The mandate of the IFSWF, as stated in the Kuwait Declaration, is first, the facilitation of communication between SWF holder countries on the one hand, and recipient countries, representatives of multilateral organizations and the private sector on the other; second, the contribution of the Forum to the development and maintenance of an open and stable investment environment. This is to be achieved by undertaking the guiding objectives of the Santiago Principles. They are namely, first, the maintenance of a stable global financial system and the free flow of capital and investment; second, compliance with SWF recipient countries regulatory and disclosure requirements; third, investment strategies guided by purely financial considerations; and last, the establishment of a transparent and sound governance structure.[39] The IFSWF's purpose is therefore to serve as an information network for the exchange of ideas on risk management, investment regimes and other issues pertaining to SWF activities as well as on the application of the Santiago Principles. Capacity building is also to be offered by the IFSWF in the application of the Santiago Principles by SWF holder countries. The IFSWF will additionally encourage cooperation with SWF recipient countries, relevant international organizations and private actors.

As mentioned above, the IFSWF in its mandate reiterates in essence its commitment to the Santiago Principles. The Santiago Principles purported to "identify a framework of generally accepted principles and practices that properly reflect appropriate governance, accountability, and arrangements as well as the conduct of investment practices by SWFs on a prudent and sound basis" with a view "to contribute to the stability of the global financial system, reduce the protectionist pressures, and help maintain an open and stable investment climate".[40]

The wording of the abovementioned stated purposes is rather lukewarm. This can be explained by keeping in mind that the Santiago Principles constitute a compromise document. It was a compromise on the part of SWF holder countries to come together and develop a common code of

39 IWGSWF, "Santiago Principles", p. 4, see *supra* note 5.

40 IWGSWF, "Kuwait Declaration", see *supra* note 31.

conduct in order to assuage the concerns of SWF recipient countries and in this way, protect SWF holder country investments. In essence, however, it seems that the underlying intent in drafting the Santiago Principles was to first, create customary norms through which SWFs would abandon any political considerations in the process of their investment activities; second, to provide a legal basis in laying down conformity standards; and third, to provide a basis for future legislation.[41]

Having examined the legal status, the structure, the regulation of meetings, the procedural rules as well as the mandate of the IFSWF, one can conclude that the IFSWF does satisfy the IN-LAW process informality element.

### 7.4.2. IN-LAW Actors

In terms of actor informality, IN-LAW does not refer to traditional diplomatic actors but rather to domestic regulators, ministries, independent or semi-independent agencies, private actors and/or international organizations. To evaluate whether the actor informality component of the IN-LAW definition is met, membership to both the IFWSF and the IWGSWF must be examined. Furthermore, the participation of any other actors is of equal importance.

The IFSWF includes the SWF holder countries participating in the dissolved IWGSWF as well as other SWFs who satisfy cumulatively two criteria: a) the definition of SWFs contained within the Santiago Principles and, b) they endorse the Santiago Principles. Representation of each member at the IFSWF is carried out by three senior level officials of the SWF, its owner or governing body. Membership in the IWGSWF is composed of 26 SWF holder countries and several countries/international organizations have permanent observer status (Oman, Saudi Arabia, Vietnam, the OECD and the IMF). Appendix II of the Santiago Principles contains a list of representatives from the IWG countries, SWFs and institutions. What can be concluded by looking at the Appendix is that representation per country differs. Although most SWF holder countries are represented by a combination of state officials employed by their ministries of finance and/or national bank, as well as a representative of their

41 Larry Catá-Backer, "Sovereign Investing in Times of Crisis: Global Regulation of Sovereign Wealth Funds, State-Owned Enterprises, and the Chinese Experience", in *Transnational Law and Contemporary Problems*, 2010–2011, vol. 19, no. 1, p. 93.

respective SWF, China and the Middle Eastern SWF holder countries are only represented by officials employed in their respective SWFs. Keeping in mind the governance structure of these specific SWF holder countries, one however should not immediately jump to the conclusion that public officials or public authority is not involved in the IWGSWF or the IFSWF for that matter.[42] Furthermore, the IFSWF takes the work of the IWGSWF forward by opening up and seeking contact with 'recipient country officials, and representatives of multilateral organizations and the private sector'.[43]

### 7.4.3. IN-LAW Output

As concerns output informality, the term denotes that any documents produced by the forum are neither a binding treaty nor any other traditional source of international law but rather a guideline, a standard, a declaration or even an informal policy coordination or exchange.[44] In order to assess the output informality of the IFSWF, two types of documents will be examined, namely first, the Santiago Principles and; second, the Communiqués and Statements issued by the Forum.

The Santiago Principles are a voluntary code of conduct which SWF holder countries have either implemented or aspire to implement.[45] As stated in the text of the Santiago Principles, the implementation of the generally accepted practices and principles contained within is subject to the SWF holder countries' legal and regulatory requirements.[46] Furthermore, despite their voluntary nature, the Santiago Principles are "to guide existing and future SWFs in various aspects of their activities",[47] steering in this way the future behavior of SWFs and their holder countries. It is this aforementioned aim of the Santiago Principles which ascribes to them the normative character of lawmaking that IN-LAW requires and which triggers accountability concerns.[48]

---

42 By way of example, one should note that the China Investment Corporation is directly accountable to the State Council.

43 IWGSWF, "Kuwait Declaration", see *supra* note 31.

44 Pauwelyn, 2012, see *supra* note 35, p. 15.

45 IFSWF, "IFSWF Statement", see *supra* note 34.

46 IWGSWF, "Santiago Principles", p. 5, see *supra* note 5.

47 *Ibid.*

48 Pauwelyn, 2012, see *supra* note 35, p. 21.

The Santiago Principles are not the only document that the IFSWF has produced. The IFSWF also issues Declarations or Communiqués and Statements. Their name seems to suggest that such documents are hortatory in nature and that they lack a binding character. Nevertheless, one can discern that the statements made in these documents are closely followed in practice.

The Kuwait Declaration sets out the structure of the IFSWF and allows the Chair and the Deputy Chairs to establish, in consultation with the IFSWF members, sub-groups on special topics.[49] On the same day that the Kuwait Declaration was issued, the Chair of the IFSWF also announced the formation of the three sub-committees.[50] At the conclusion of the IFSWF meeting in Sydney, the intention of the Members to undertake and publish a survey on the experiences of the Forum's members as concerns the application of the Santiago Principles was announced.[51] This initiative led to the publication of the Report on IFSWF Members' Experience in the Application of the Santiago Principles.[52] Further, the formation of a permanent Secretariat to the IFSWF was announced with the Beijing Communiqué.[53] To date this announcement has not yet materialized but judging from the previous record of compliance with the announcements made in statements and communiqués issued by the IFSWF, one should not expect any surprises.

What can be concluded from the aforementioned analysis on both the Santiago Principles and the IFSWF Declaration, Statements and Communiqués is that despite not being legally binding, they guide the be-

49 IWGSWF, "Kuwait Declaration", see *supra* note 31.

50 IWGSWF, "Working Group Announces Creation of International Forum of Sovereign Wealth Funds", see *supra* note 33. For details on the three sub-groups, see *supra* Part 7.3.

51 International Forum of Sovereign Wealth Funds, "Sydney Statement by the International Forum of Sovereign Wealth Funds", available at http://www.ifswf.org/pr/pr4.htm, last accessed on 28 November 2011.

52 International Forum of Sovereign Wealth Funds, "IFSWF Members' Experience in the Application of the Santiago Principles: Report prepared by the IFSWF Sub-Committee 1 and the Secretariat in collaboration with the Members of the IFSWF", 7 July 2011, p. 11, available at http://www.ifswf.org/pst/stp070711.pdf, last accessed on 28 November 2011. [IFSWF, "Report on the Application of the Santiago Principles"].

53 International Forum of Sovereign Wealth Funds, "Changes in the IFSWF Leadership and Steps towards Permanent Secretariat", available at http://www.ifswf.org/pr/pr7.htm, last accessed on 28 November 2011.

havior of the IFSWF members. The condition of output informality is therefore also met.

To sum up, the IFSWF is not a supranational forum but rather an informal communications-information platform between SWF holder countries and other relevant parties, which aims to promote the exchange of views between SWF holder countries on issues related to SWF activities, to encourage cooperation between SWF holder and recipient countries and to promote a better understanding of the Santiago Principles. The Santiago Principles have codified behavioral norms to be abided by in the exercise of SWF investment activities and have laid a basis for these norms as well as a basis for any future amendment. Members to the IFSWF are state officials of the SWF holder countries bearing no formal authority to bind their respective countries internationally and the work of the IFSWF does not carry any legal force. The IFSWF, accordingly, meets all three elements of IN-LAW informality.

The next part will examine the substantive content of the Santiago Principles in terms of accountability and transparency mechanisms. It needs to be stressed, however, that these mechanisms do not pertain to the IFSWF itself but to IFSWF members. Their examination is dictated in order to identify to whom SWFs, SWF holder countries and the IFSWF can and should be accountable to.

## 7.5. The Content of the Santiago Principles on Accountability and Transparency

The Santiago Principles form a voluntary code of conduct and consist of 24 principles accompanied by an explanatory note for each principle. The explanatory notes form an integral part of the principles. The IWGSWF Subgroup responsible for their elaboration was inspired by three sources: first, findings from the IMF commissioned voluntary SWF Survey on current structures and practices; second, related international principles and practices; and third, comments from SWF recipient countries as well as from the European Commission, the OECD and the World Bank.[54]

[54] International Forum of Sovereign Wealth Funds, "IFSWF Members' Experience in the Application of the Santiago Principles: Report prepared by the IFSWF Sub-Committee 1 and the Secretariat in collaboration with the Members of the IFSWF", 7 July 2011, p. 11, available at http://www.ifswf.org/pst/stp070711.pdf, last accessed on 28 November 2011. [IFSWF, "Report on the Application of the Santiago Principles"].

The Santiago Principles are structured into three thematic areas. The first part deals with the legal framework, objectives, and coordination with macroeconomic policies (Santiago Principles 1–5). The second part contains principles and practices on the institutional framework and governance structure (Santiago Principles 6–17), whereas the third part (Santiago Principles 18–23) sets out the investment and risk management framework.

Principle 24 provides for a periodic review mechanism of the Principles' implementation. As further elaborated in the explanatory note, the review can be conducted in either of the two following ways: either through self-assessment or through a third-party verification mechanism. It is desirable, however, to publicly disclose the content of the assessment to the extent that such disclosure is in compliance with applicable laws and regulations and to the extent that disclosure contributes to the stability of the international financial markets. The possibility of a peer review process is, however, not foreseen, as is for example in the case of the Financial Stability Board.[55]

Before proceeding with the actual analysis of the accountability principles and transparency requirements contained within the Santiago Principles, one must first examine what is meant by the term accountability.

The IN-LAW framework does not purport to define a commonly accepted definition of accountability. Instead, it purports to examine the efficiency of accountability mechanisms within an informal network, identify possible gaps and propose solutions which do not undermine the effectiveness of the informal network. Therefore, IN-LAW proceeds on the basis of a working definition of accountability which is defined as:

> [...] a relationship (at the domestic or international level) between an actor (exercising public authority in the context of IN-LAW) and a forum (internal to the IN-LAW process or an external stakeholder), in which the actor has an obligation (in particular, but not exclusively expressed in legal rules or procedures) to explain and to justify his or her conduct (*ex ante* leading up to a decision or *ex post* in the implementation of a decision), the forum can pose questions and pass judgment, and the actor may face consequences (in particu-

[55] Shawn Donnelly, Informal International Lawmaking: Global Financial Market Regulation, Chapter 5.

lar, but not exclusively, so as to enhance the democratic legitimacy of IN-LAW).[56]

Principles dealing with accountability and transparency relating to SWFs and their operations are scattered in all three parts of the Santiago Principle. Rather than examining the relevant principles one by one, this section will classify the relevant principles according to Gelpern's typology for accountability specific to SWFs. Gelpern identifies four axes of accountability relevant to SWFs on the basis of the actor to whom accountability is owed, namely internal public, internal private, external public and external private. As SWFs are investment vehicles operating transnationally within the territory of other states, the internal-external dichotomy refers to the territory of the SWF holder country and to the territory of the SWF recipient country respectively.[57] The private-public dichotomy denotes the complex nature of SWFs as government controlled or owned investment vehicles. SWFs are neither purely public nor purely private but rather combine elements of both. These four types of accountability will be analyzed in turn.

Internal public accountability is recognized towards the citizenry at large of the SWF holder country. By contrast to internal public accountability, internal private accountability by SWFs is owed to a designated subset of beneficiaries, such as the SWF holder country government and the shareholders of SWFs. External public accountability treats SWFs as state actors operating transnationally and thus bearing the duty to adhere to international norms. External private accountability deals with the accountability of SWFs when participating in the market of SWF recipient countries.

Gelpern's internal axes of accountability are equivalent to Grant and Keohane's delegation model of accountability and to Boven's democratic dimension of accountability, whereas the external axes are similar to Grant and Keohane's participation model.[58] Translated in the SWF context and seen through the lens of the delegation model, SWFs are accountable to the government of the SWF holder country and ultimately to the holder's country citizenry. Under the participation model, external ac-

56 Pauwelyn, 2012, p. 28, see *supra* note 35.

57 Gelpern, 2011, pp. 294–307, see *supra* note 4.

58 Ruth W. Grant and Robert O. Keohane, "Accountability and Abuses of Power in World Politics", in *The American Political Science Review*, February 2005, vol. 99, no. 1, pp. 30–33.

countability is owed to the SWF recipient countries and to their constituents.

The next paragraphs will attempt to classify the Santiago Principles under these four types of accountability, starting with internal private accountability and moving to internal public accountability. Next, external private accountability for SWFs will be examined, leaving for last the external public accountability.

### 7.5.1. Internal Private Accountability

The emphasis of the Santiago Principles seems to be on internal private accountability, that is, accountability owed to the government of the SWF holder country and the shareholders of the SWF. Such an emphasis was imperative in order to appease SWF recipient country concerns.

Principle 10 requires that an accountability framework for SWF operations be clearly defined in the relevant legislation, charter, other constitutive document or management agreement. The explanatory note to Principle 10 clarifies that accountability arrangements for the owner of the Fund, its governing body and the operational management should be in place. Further, these arrangements need be commensurate to their defined responsibilities.

For SWFs set up as a pool of assets, the owner can be accountable either to the legislature or to the public, whereas for SWFs established as separate legal entities, the governing body is accountable to the owner and the management is accountable to the governing body. The Principles further call on SWFs to establish appropriate evaluation methods for the performance of SWF managing bodies.

According to Principle 7, the owner of the SWF should set the objectives of the SWF, appoint the governing body members in accordance with clearly defined procedures, and exercise oversight over the SWF operations. Pursuant to a principal-agent relationship, the governing body of a SWF should act in the best interest of the Fund while having a clear mandate and adequate authority and competency in carrying out its tasks.[59] The roles and responsibilities of the governing body, their number, the procedural rules of their appointment and removal as well as their

[59] IWGSWF, "Santiago Principles", GAPP 8, p. 7, see *supra* note 5.

term of offices should be publicly disclosed in the SWF constitutive documents, relevant legislation or charter.[60]

The Santiago Principles further envisage the provision of an annual report on financial statements, operations and performance in accordance with internationally recognized or domestic accounting standards;[61] an annual audit in accordance with internationally recognized or national auditing standards;[62] and the existence of professional and ethical standards.[63]

Principle 21 reiterates the importance of ownership rights for SWFs and prescribes that in the exercise of ownership rights, SWFs should act consistently with their investment policy.

Furthermore, SWFs should publicly disclose their approach to voting rights. The assets and the performance of the SWF should be measured and reported to the owner of the SWF. This will enable the Fund managers to make informed decisions and the owners to evaluate the managers. As can be deduced, the above-mentioned principles remind us of corporate governance principles which enable SWF holder governments and SWF shareholders (principals) to hold the managing body of the SWF (agent) accountable.

### 7.5.2. Internal Public Accountability

In comparison with internal private accountability, there are far less principles within the Santiago document that pertain to internal public accountability. Nevertheless, there are some relevant principles.

The Santiago Principles envisage a clearly defined and publicly disclosed policy purpose for the SWFs.[64] Additionally, they provide for the public disclosure of sources of funding, withdrawal and spending rules and arrangements of SWFs in order to facilitate the understanding and promote awareness of the use of public monies and thus promote accountability. The Principles explicitly state that the SWF holder country's national budget documentation should explain the contribution made in light of the government's fiscal and monetary objectives. The Principles are,

---

60 *Ibid.*, p. 16.

61 *Ibid.*, GAPP 11, p. 8.

62 *Ibid.*, GAPP 12, p. 8.

63 *Ibid.*, GAPP 13, p. 8.

64 *Ibid.*, GAPP 2, p. 7.

however, silent on ways to achieve accountability. One can presume, however, that what the drafters had in mind was the exercise of an *ex post* control by the citizens of the SWF holder countries over their governments. A prerequisite for such an *ex post* control would be the availability of information to the citizenry of the SWF holder country.

### 7.5.3. External Private Accountability

The Santiago Principles address external private accountability as well. SWFs undertake investments in the territories of SWF recipient countries and are active in the recipient countries' private markets. The underlying objective of the principles addressing external private accountability is to safeguard SWF recipient countries from the possibility that SWFs pursue a geopolitical agenda in the territories of SWF recipient countries. Therefore, according to Principle 2, the policy purpose of the SWFs should be clearly defined and publicly disclosed in order to facilitate the adoption and application of appropriate investment strategies based on sound economic and financial criteria.[65] Similarly, Principle 19 calls for SWF investment decisions to aim at profit maximization and to be made solely on the basis of economic and financial criteria. Alternatively, should non-financial criteria be taken into consideration in the drawing up of the SWF's investment decisions, these should be clearly stated and publicly disclosed. Principle 20 deals with asymmetry of information and encourages SWFs not to take advantage of privileged information or inappropriate influence to the detriment of private entities. In this way it purports to promote fair competition. Finally, Principle 15 reiterates that SWFs operating in the territory of SWF recipient countries need to comply with all the regulatory and disclosure requirements applicable in SWF recipient countries, as set out in its legislation and regulations.

### 7.5.4. External Public Accountability

The Santiago Principles do not deal in detail with the notion of external public accountability, that is, the duty of SWFs to adhere to international norms when as state actors they operate transnationally. The Principles, however, touch upon two related themes:

[65] *Ibid.*

First, according to Principle 19, the SWF's aim should be profit maximization in accordance with economic and financial considerations. (More concrete formulations of this principle can be found in the text of other principles as well. For example, the instruction that SWF governance framework should establish – and publicly disclose – a clear division of roles between the owner and the governing body of the SWF so as to ensure that operational management and decisions are based on economic and financial considerations.[66]) As an exception to the rule formulated in Principle 19, SWFs may exclude investments for non-financial reasons, such as legally binding international sanctions and social, ethical, religious, environmental and other factors.[67] Factors that have been taken into consideration in excluding investments have been child labor, human rights abuses, construction of cluster bombs and others.

Second, the Principles seek to contribute to a stable global financial system. Accordingly, the Santiago Principles promote a number of information disclosure requirements such as concerning the Fund's policy purpose, funding, rules on withdrawal and spending operations, investment policy, asset allocations, rates of return, and exercise of ownership rights. The intention of the drafters in demanding the disclosure of this type of information was to give information on the SWFs' risk appetite and appease SWF recipient country concerns over the SWF's alleged ability to disrupt financial markets, demote national champions, *et cetera*.[68]

This section has attempted to present the accountability processes and transparency requirements contained within the Santiago Principles. It has, furthermore, classified such accountability processes either as internal private, internal public, external private, or external public, on the basis of the actor to whom SWFs could be held accountable to. The next section will proceed with a critical appraisal of the application of the above mentioned accountability and transparency mechanisms. The appraisal is based on a Report drawn up by the IFSWF Sub-Committee on the practical application of the Santiago Principles by IFSWF members.

---

66 *Ibid.*, GAPP 16 and GAPP 6, pp. 7–8.

67 *Ibid.*, GAPP Sub principle 19.1, p. 8.

68 *Ibid.*, Part II.B.

## 7.6. Experiences from the Application of the Santiago Principles

The IFSWF commissioned a report to examine the application of the Santiago Principles in SWF holder countries. The Report was based on a survey conducted by IFSWF Sub-Committee 1, a General Survey of the IFSWF Secretariat, additional information from SWF websites and public documents. Sub-Committee 1 in its presentation of the findings was adamant in clarifying that the report was neither intended to rate the members' transparency practices nor was it intended to rate the adequacy of the principles.[69] The next paragraphs will present the findings of the Report as concerns accountability (internal private, internal public, external private and external public) and transparency requirements mandated by the Santiago Principles. It needs to be clarified that the report is not extensive and does not cover in detail all of the Santiago Principles. An evaluation of the findings will follow in part B, identifying possible gaps and avenues of enhancement.

### 7.6.1. Findings of the Report

#### 7.6.1.1. Internal Private Accountability

Most SWFs are accountable either directly or indirectly to the parliament. When the SWF is constituted as a separate legal entity it is directly accountable to the parliament, but when it does not enjoy distinct legal personality it is indirectly accountable – through the Ministry of Finance, which in turn is accountable to the parliament. In few cases Ministers also respond to parliamentary questions and participate in reviews.[70]

Further, most members have confirmed that internal ethical and professional standards are in place for staff and management. These are set out in domestic legislation or in the Fund's internal rules.[71] Certain SWFs have extended the application of these standards to the governing bodies too.

---

69 IFSWF, "Report on the Application of the Santiago Principles", p. 9, see *supra* note 54.

70 *Ibid.*, p. 20.

71 *Ibid.*, p. 23. It seems therefore that the Santiago Principles have not made a valuable contribution in this aspect of internal private accountability.

#### 7.6.1.2. Internal Public Accountability

The findings on the disclosure of the SWFs' public policy, their sources of funding and the rules on withdrawal and spending are important. As regards the public disclosure of the Fund's policy purpose, most SWF holder countries submitted that their SWF's purpose is either typically available on the SWF's website or in annual reports.[72] As for the public disclosure of rules on sources of funding, withdrawal and spending, most SWFs meet the Principles' standard, as they are obliged to do so under their domestic legislation. The Report, however, does not clarify whether this domestic legislation pre-existed the Santiago Principles or not. Lastly, the Report reveals that members have found it challenging to remain consistent with their investment policy and the stated objectives of the SWF in times of financial crisis.[73]

#### 7.6.1.3. External Private Accountability

As concerns the obligation of SWFs to comply with SWF recipient country regulatory and disclosure requirements, the results of the Report are encouraging as only two out of the 20 responding members faced problems. The problems were related to the fact that the SWF recipient country regulation was either not transparent or unable to capture the activities of the SWF as it treated it as a purely private investor, and accordingly required legal documents appropriate for private corporations yet not for SWFs.[74]

#### 7.6.1.4. External Public Accountability

The practical application of Principle 19, which requires that SWF investment decisions should aim at profit maximization and should be based on economic and financial considerations, is of particular relevance. Subprinciple 19.1 mandates the public disclosure of any other considerations such as legally binding international sanctions and social, ethical or religious reasons. The survey provides an interesting insight into the SWF's perception of the content of this principle. Certain members assign a different meaning to it than that mandated in the explanatory notes to the

[72] *Ibid.*, p. 13.
[73] *Ibid.*, p. 26.
[74] *Ibid.*, p. 23.

Santiago Principles. They therefore include risk, transaction or concentration measures as non-financial considerations in their investment decisions. Others have identified solely environmental and humanitarian considerations, others responsible investment considerations, and yet others have linked the non-financial considerations to their SWF ethical guidelines.[75]

#### 7.6.1.5. Transparency

As regards transparency mechanisms, most SWFs revealed that they are under a domestic legal obligation to publicly disclose their operations and performance. Accordingly, almost all of them prepare audited financial statements[76] and most submit an annual report which includes the size, the allocations, the returns and the financial statements of the SWF. Regarding means chosen for public disclosure, these vary but the internet and the websites of the SWFs are the most widespread avenue. A few members are required by law to publish the above mentioned data in writing – such as in papers, parliament reports and official gazettes – so that they are publicly available to any interested party.[77] Regarding the public disclosure of investment policies, data such as investment objectives, risk tolerance, investment horizon, strategic asset allocation, investment constraints, use of leverage and use of external managers are disclosed to varying degrees. Only eight out of 23 members disclose information on all of these categories, whereas one member abstains from any disclosure on these issues.[78]

Principle 24 institutes a process of regular review of the implementation of the Santiago Principles. As concerns its implementation, 27% reported that the principle had been abided by before the inception of the Santiago Principles. The Report interprets this as meaning that 27% of SWF members had engaged in self-assessment prior to the Santiago Principles.[79]

75 *Ibid.*, pp. 30–31.
76 *Ibid.*, p. 20.
77 *Ibid.*
78 *Ibid.*, pp. 28–29.
79 *Ibid.*, p. 37.

### 7.6.2. Identification and Evaluation of Lacunas

The preceding section presented the findings of the first IFSWF commissioned report on the application of the Santiago Principles. The Report reaches the conclusion that 95% of IFSWF member practices are fully or partially consistent with the Santiago Principles. However, one should not immediately conclude that the Principles have been successful in holding SWF holder countries accountable at a domestic and/or an international level. Only relative conclusions can be drawn from a careful reading of the Report. The reasons contributing to the relative value of the Report will be analyzed in the following paragraph.

Whereas the initiative undertaken by the IFSWF is welcomed, the number of SWF holder countries participating in the IFSWF is relatively small in comparison to the existing SWFs.[80] Therefore, only relative and non-conclusive conclusions can be drawn regarding the Santiago Principles' success in instituting accountability mechanisms.

Moreover, it is impossible to draw definite conclusions on the efficiency of the Santiago Principles in holding the members accountable: The Santiago Principles constitute a compromise document through which SWF holder countries attempted to appease the concerns of SWF recipient countries. The content of the Santiago Principles encapsulated, however, practices that were already existing and carried out by the participating SWF holder country members. Therefore, from the beginning, in most cases, implementation was anyway rendered moot. The Report confirms this too – in particular where it refers to the principles on accountability and assurances of integrity operations.[81] Furthermore, the Report specifically states that its members are to a large extent partially or completely consistent with the Santiago Principles. However, 80% predates the inception of the Santiago Principles.

This does not mean that the Santiago Principles are deprived of any significant meaning and contribution. Advances have been made, mainly in the field of internal private accountability, with opaque SWFs providing publicly information, albeit to a limited degree. The Santiago Princi-

80 Only 23 SWF holder countries are participating in the IFSWF and of them only 21 participated in the Report. Keeping in mind that there is no commonly acceptable definition of SWFs, estimates of existing SWF are close to 50.

81 IFSWF, "Report on the Application of the Santiago Principles", p. 24, see *supra* note 54.

ples are also of value to newly established SWFs and to new members of the IFSWF which need to endorse the Santiago Principles in order to become members.

As concerns transparency mechanisms, it can be concluded that a delicate balance needs to be maintained. Due to the market sensitive character of the information or due to legal obligations that the SWFs have undertaken *vis-à-vis* contracted third parties, full disclosure might not be possible.[82] This conclusion seems to recapitulate a long held position of SWFs and SWFs have been extremely reluctant in publicly disclosing individual investments. A possible solution to this situation is to fully disclose information on a case-by-case basis, but only following a request from an affected SWF recipient country or an international organization, and under the precondition of confidentiality.[83] An alternative solution would be to disclose individual investments, but only if the proposed SWF investment would concern a particular type of investment.[84]

SWFs participating in the survey leading to the Report seem to value transparency although for different reasons. The majority of SWFs believe that transparency adds to the domestic legitimacy of SWFs. Others stress its role in providing a commercial advantage, a positive reputation, and assistance in communicating with stakeholders.[85] What can be concluded from the Report is that although SWFs see value in transparency, they stress that the purpose of the Santiago Principles was not the enforcement of transparency *per se*, but rather improving the understanding of SWF investments.

Bearing these limitations in mind, there are certain conclusions that can be drawn on the accountability of SWFs through the Santiago Principles, as well as the accountability of the IFSWF. These will be analyzed in turn.

As concerns accountability of SWFs through the Santiago Principles one can observe the following.

---

82 *Ibid.*, p. 29.

83 De Bellis, 2011, p. 376, see *supra* note 28.

84 Anthony Wong, "Sovereign Wealth Funds and the Problem of Asymmetric Information: the Santiago Principles and International Regulations", in *Brooklyn Journal of International Law*, 2009, vol. 34, no. 3, p. 1106.

85 IFSWF, "Report on the Application of the Santiago Principles", pp. 38–43, see *supra* note 52.

First, when the setting is not a typical democratic society, not all types of disclosure requirements serve internal private and internal public accountability equally. SWFs are not exclusively owned by Western-type democracies. Therefore, disclosure to the government does not automatically ensure that the disclosed information also reaches the public at large. This observation can of course be qualified depending on the type of disclosure requirements that are required and on the degree to which a country is not democratic. Moreover, even in non-democratic countries, SWFs as government-controlled or owned investment vehicles managing national wealth are subject to the scrutiny of the SWF holder country's population. The China Investment Corporation (CIC) incurred huge losses from its investments in Morgan Stanley and Blackstone. Following a public outcry, CIC had to modify its investment strategy. In a similar fashion, Temasek Holdings' losses in Merrill Lynch prompted a national uproar and the Minister of Finance had to defend Temasek's investment and divestment decision before the national parliament.[86] These examples support the conclusion that SWFs are responsive and need to justify their actions towards internal public stakeholders.

Second, a strong enforcement mechanism of voluntary behavioral standards does not guarantee the ability to hold SWFs accountable. The reply of an IFSWF member when asked why it does not comply with a public disclosure requirement is instructive. It replied that it was not legally obliged to do so. Therefore, the willingness to be bound is a *sine qua non* precondition when it comes to undertaking obligations prescribed either by hard or by soft law.

Third, the Report confirms the paramount significance of domestic legislation in transposing even soft law behavioral standards. The IFSWF members were found to be largely compliant with their obligations under the Santiago Principles. But it is impossible to know whether this would have been the case had domestic legislation prescribing these behavioral standards not been in place.

Finally, there is a link between the limited obligations in the areas of external public and private accountability and the IFSWF membership.

---

86 "Chinese Sovereign Wealth Fund Turning to Natural Resources", New York Times, 9 November 2009; "China's Sovereign Wealth Funds Set for Global Spending Spree", Sunday Times, 22 June 2008; "Judging Temasek's Growing Role in Merrill Lynch", Market Watch, 31 July 2008.

Membership is currently restricted to SWF holder countries and their SWFs. This limited membership has restrained the Santiago Principles from further formulating external public and private accountability processes. Only by expanding IFSWF's membership to SWF recipient countries and to private actors and by placing them on an equal footing with SWF holder countries, can meaningful accountability mechanisms also be foreseen at the external public and private level.

As concerns the accountability of the IFSWF as an entity, this issue has not received any attention so far – neither by SWF holder or recipient countries nor by international organizations. Civil society and private actors have not voiced any concerns in this regard. The constitutive document of the IFSWF, the Kuwait Declaration, is completely silent when it comes to the accountability of the Forum itself. This might be explained by the fact that the IWGSWF and the Santiago Principles constituted a compromise solution to bring together SWF holder and SWF recipient countries together in safeguarding the flow of SWF investments: SWF holder countries were primarily interested in the maintenance of an open investment environment for their SWF investments and SWF recipient countries were interested in receiving capital through the materialized SWF investment without jeopardizing their national or economic security.[87] The trade-off for SWF recipient countries in getting SWF holder countries involved in the IWGSWF process was to formulate the code of conduct in voluntary terms. Therefore, the process surrounding the adoption of the Santiago Principles had to be informal as well.

Moreover, since 2009 (when the IFSWF was set up) and up to date, we are still in the turbulence of a global financial crisis, in which cash fluidity is of utter importance. The parameters, therefore, have not changed in order to move to a more formalized setting. The IFSWF has, accordingly, also assumed a voluntary and informal character characterized by a lack of institutional mechanisms. As Smith observes, it is this lack of formal institutionalized accountability mechanisms within the voluntary framework of the IFSWF that negates any effort to hold the IFSWF accountable to either internal or external stakeholders.[88]

---

87 See *supra* 7.3.

88 Megan Smith, "The United Nations Principles for Responsible Investment from an IN-LAW Perspective", Chapter 8.

However, the fact that accountability of the IFSWF has not yet become a hot issue, does not preclude it from receiving attention in the future. Should this be the case, a few observations are in order. Despite the lack of formal accountability mechanisms, there might be ways to hold the Forum to account at an international level, indirectly through the SWF holder country members.

As concerns the international level, Norton observes that SWF holder countries maintain some level of accountability through the G20 or G7 and/or the IMFC. SWFs are domestically accountable to their respective Ministry of Finance and to their Central Bank.[89] To the extent that these SWF holder countries participate in the G20, G7 or the IMFC, they can be held accountable in those informal networks. Questions of legitimacy would of course arise in such a case since to date there exists no formal link between the IFSWF and the G20, G7 or IMFC. Alternatively, it might be possible to hold the IFSWF accountable, by pushing forward in the agenda the establishment of a peer review mechanism. That said, it is rather unlikely that SWF holder countries will at any time soon pave the way for peer review.

As concerns external pressure by NGOs or civil society or SWF recipient countries, the problem is that access to information is restricted to IFSWF members only. On the IFSWF's website, only documents and press releases that the IFSWF has decided to make public are available. Notes from IFSWF meetings, Sub-Committees, the agenda and other interesting information are only available to IFSWF Members on the provision of a password. However, one must reiterate and applaud the initiative undertaken by the IFSWF to approach SWF recipient countries, relevant international and regional organizations and the private sector. This might prove important in the future to pave the way towards the accountability of the IFSWF.

---

89 Joseph J. Norton, "The 'Santiago Principles' and the International Forum of Sovereign Wealth Funds: Evolving Components of the New Bretton Woods II Post-Global Financial Crisis Architecture and Another Example of Ad Hoc Global Administrative Networking and Related 'Soft' Rulemaking", in *Review of Banking and Financial Law*, 2009–2010, vol. 29, pp. 519, 525.

## 7.7. Concluding Remarks

The IFSWF is an informal group with no formal legal personality. It is composed of state officials from SWF holder countries, who do not have the ability to bind their respective countries. It has produced the Santiago Principles, a voluntary code of conduct for SWFs, and continues to issue Statements and Communiqués which guide the behavior of the IFSWF and its members. It, therefore, neatly falls under the IN-LAW definition. Its importance lies in the fact that it is an *informal* platform that attempts to bring together SWF host countries with SWF recipient countries, relevant multilateral organizations and the private sector. Only if its membership is broadened to include all relevant competing interests and counterparts on an equal footing, can all four types of accountability mechanisms (internal public and private, external public and private) provided for in the Santiago Principles be meaningfully reinforced and implemented. The value of the IFSWF as an informal lawmaking process is in coordinating the efforts of all SWF related stakeholders in promoting understanding of the SWF phenomenon and bridging their competing interests. For the time being, the IFSWF has not raised accountability concerns as it has not produced any new codes or regulations. The Santiago Principles, too, have not attracted any attention from an accountability perspective.

# 8

# The United Nations Principles for Responsible Investment from an IN-LAW Perspective

**Megan Smith***

## 8.1. Introduction

Recognizing a gap left by more traditional, state-centric international commitments and existing domestic regulations, many new governance initiatives seek to create and impose codes of conduct on businesses or investors as a means of regulating their impact on the environment, human rights, or other important areas. Like many non-state actors in our ever more globalized world, investors are both increasingly active and increasingly hard to regulate with domestic policy alone, since their operations and management are often split up across many countries and many jurisdictions. Launched in 2006, the UN Principles for Responsible Investment (UNPRI or PRI) seek to address this gap.

An excellent example of IN-LAW, PRI meets all three dimensions of 'informality': informal actors, informal process, and informal output.[1] Despite its connection with the United Nations (UN), an international organization (IO), most actors involved in PRI are informal, as they are not states. Actors include private and public pension funds, investment banks, and mutual funds among others. Furthermore, PRI itself is an informal process (a network or forum) rather than a formal IO. Finally, its output, non-binding principles as well as annual progress reports, is informal.

Among the many innovative aspects of PRI and IN-LAW more generally (the very important role of private actors, the diverse and unique forms that these organizations are taking, the limited or non-existent role of states), the most novel could be the fact that these new regulatory initiatives are often governed, in part or in whole, by businesses or industries

* **Megan Smith** is a recent graduate of the Master in International Affairs program at the Graduate Institute of International and Development Studies in Geneva.

1 Joost Pauwelyn, "Informal International Lawmaking: Framing the Concept and Research Questions", in Joost Pauwelyn, Ramses A. Wessel and Jan Wouters (eds.), *Informal International Lawmaking*, Oxford University Press, Oxford, 2012.

that are also the 'targets of regulation'.[2] Though one of the main benefits of the arrangement is that it includes private, non-state actors who would not otherwise be allowed to participate in formal governance processes, this arrangement is not without its disadvantages.[3]

Like many other examples of IN-LAW, there is great concern regarding the lack of accountability in PRI.[4] Using mainly primary and secondary source documents, including press releases, annual reports, and work programs, among other sources, I seek to explore the relationships both within PRI (between PRI and signatories and amongst signatories themselves) and between PRI and external stakeholders. Does PRI or its external stakeholders have the ability to ensure that signatories are honoring their commitment to the Principles? If accountability is being produced, what are the key factors or mechanisms that produce this accountability, and is it the result of *de jure* or *de facto* mechanisms?

In this chapter, I provide a background on the history and structure of PRI followed by an analysis of the relationships inside and outside PRI. I argue that there have been limited mechanisms for either PRI or external stakeholders to hold signatories accountable to the Principles, and thus there has been limited accountability to date, but that recent changes to the initiative could lead to greater accountability in the future. Furthermore, I would argue that while PRI has been accountable to its signatories, PRI has not been particularly accountable to external stakeholders. This is due to both a lack of institutionalized accountability mechanisms available to both internal and external stakeholders, such as mandatory consultations or sanctions for violating one's obligations, as well as the nature of the Principles themselves.

## 8.2. The History and Structure of PRI

What is responsible investment? Often interchangeably called socially responsible investment or sustainable and responsible investment (SRI), the concept lacks a common definition among academics and practitioners.

---

2 Kenneth Abbott and Duncan Snidal, "Strengthening International Regulation Through Transnational New Governance: Overcoming the Orchestration Deficit", in *Vanderbilt Journal of Transnational Law,* 2009, vol. 42, no. 2, pp. 505–506.

3 Pauwelyn, 2012, see *supra* note 1.

4 See among others in this volume Chapter 3 (Donnelly), Chapter 9 (Horna), Chapter 13 (Corredig) and Chapter 14 (Vidal).

Sparkes' definition does a good job of providing some common ground, defining socially responsible investment as a "combination of social and environmental goals with the financial objective of achieving a return on invested capital approaching that of the market".[5] Recently, the term responsible investment has tended to supplant SRI, since some stakeholders, most notably coming from the business world, feel that the term SRI implies a greater emphasis on social or environmental considerations at the possible expense of financial returns.[6] PRI itself does not employ an explicit definition of responsible investment; instead, there is an implicit description which has come about, subject to modification "through negotiations, compromise, and actions/inactions".[7]

### 8.2.1. The Principles

PRI consists of six Principles which are voluntary and aspirational in nature and "aim to help investors integrate the consideration of environmental, social and governance (ESG) issues into investment decision-making and ownership practices, and thereby improve long-term returns to beneficiaries".[8] Associated with the Principles is a series of actions, 35 in total, which can be undertaken by a signatory to implement each Principle. The Principles and associated actions espouse a strategy of engagement with corporations with rather than divestment. Also, while some responsible investment strategies focus on specific substantive rules, for example not investing in arms producers, the Principles largely stress a broad process for decision-making. PRI's lack of explicitness about actions to be taken and lack of a definition of responsible investment serve a political purpose, specifically "allow[ing] for more actors to participate without being constrained by an explicit definition with which they may not fully agree".[9] Since the goal of PRI has always been to mainstream the respon-

---

5 Many authors, including Sparkes, distinguish investment by religious groups whose investment is guided by a cohesive set of values and beliefs by calling it "ethical investment"; Russell Sparkes, "Ethical Investment: Whose Ethics, Which Investment?" in *Business Ethics: A European Review*, 2001, vol. 10, no. 3, p. 201.

6 Taylor R. Gray, "Investing for the Environment? The Limits of the UN Principles of Responsible Investment", 2009, p. 8, available at http://www.geog.ox.ac.uk/research/transformations/wpapers/wpg09-09.pdf, last accessed on 3 June 2011.

7 Gray, 2009, p. 7, see *supra* note 6.

8 Principles for Responsible Investment, "FAQ", available at http://www.PRI.org/faqs/, last accessed on 5 April 2011.

9 Gray, 2009, p. 7, see *supra* note 6.

sible investment ideology, recruiting a high number of signatories was key, and the lack of explicitness enabled it.[10] However, this vagueness has some downsides, which will be explored *infra*.

### 8.2.2. Before 2006: Lead-Up to and Motivations for PRI's Founding

> There is a disconnect between corporate responsibility as a broadly stated management imperative, and the actual behaviour of financial markets, which all-too-often are guided primarily by short-term considerations at the expense of longer-term objectives. With only rare exceptions, the financial community has not sufficiently recognized or rewarded corporate efforts to respond to environmental, labour or human rights challenges, even though such factors can be directly material to corporate performance.[11]

On 26 April 2006, PRI was launched by the UN Secretary-General (UNSG) Kofi Annan at the New York Stock Exchange. The initiative was able to attract 65 organizations in its first days, and its membership swelled to around 200 by the end of its first year in existence.[12] This seemingly rapid expansion, which has continued to this day, was the result of several years of preparatory work.

The focus on institutional investors began in 2002 when, due to the lack of initiatives for those actors, the United Nations Environmental Programme Finance Initiative (UNEP FI) established the Asset Management Working Group (AMWG) for fund managers.[13] In 2003, there was an Institutional Investor Summit on Climate Risk, which received the support and involvement of UNSG Annan and Ceres, a prominent non-profit known for its work on incorporating sustainable development considerations in business and investment decisions. In 2004, momentum continued with the launch of the 'Who Cares Wins'-Initiative. This initiative, the

[10] Gray, 2009, see *supra* note 6.

[11] Kofi Annan, "Remarks at the Launch of the Principles for Responsible Investment", available at http://www.un.org/apps/sg/sgstats.asp?nid=2006, last accessed on 3 February 2011.

[12] Principles for Responsible Investment, "PRI Report on Progress, 2007", p. 6, available at http://www.unpri.org/report07/PRIReportOnProgress2007.pdf, last accessed on 20 May 2011.

[13] "Interview with Dr. James Gifford, Executive Director of the UN Principles for Responsible Investment (PRI)", available at http://vimeo.com/9670817, last accessed on 15 May 2011.

combined effort of investors and several public sector actors such as the Global Compact (GC), the International Finance Corporation, and the Swiss Government, sought to help the financial community mainstream environmental, social, and governance (ESG) issues into its day-to-day operations.[14] Coinciding with the 2004 launch of Who Cares Wins, the presentation of an extensive study by the AMWG was vital to the eventual creation of PRI.[15] The formal path to PRI began in July 2004, when Dr. Klaus Töpfer, the executive director of UNEP, announced the plan for its creation. The actual drafting process of the Principles began in early 2005. In total, it took eight months and involved twenty investor organizations from twelve countries, with the support of seventy experts coming from all backgrounds, including civil society. The UNSG had been involved from the beginning and had "personally sent out the invitations to the largest pension funds" to participate.[16]

While PRI was clearly the result of several years of work and has its roots in a number of initiatives, this does not answer an important question: why was PRI created? Considering the existence of numerous voluntary initiatives geared towards investment and finance, some might question the necessity of PRI. There were already a number of IOs working on investment, such as the Organisation for Economic Cooperation and Development (OECD) and the UN via UNEP FI and the UN Conference on Trade and Development (UNCTAD). There were also a number of voluntary, public-private partnerships, which dealt with investment and/or ESG issues, such as the Ceres Principles. There was, however, little focus on public pension funds and other institutional investors up until this point. As these investors are influential and important to financial markets, their participation was considered an excellent way to internationalize the debate on responsible investment; at the other end of the spectrum, many investors, especially smaller ones, did not have the time or money to devel-

[14] Ivo Knoepfel and Gordon Hagar, "Future Proof? Embedding Environmental, Social and Governance Issues in Investment Markets. Outcomes of the Who Cares Wins Initiative 2004–2008", available at http://www.unglobalcompact.org/docs/news_events/8.1/who_cares_wins_29Jan09webversion.pdf, last accessed on 26 May 2011.

[15] James Gifford, "Financial markets and the Global Compact - the principles for responsible investment", in Andreas Rasche and Georg Kell (eds.), *The United Nations Global Compact: Achievements, Trends and Challenges*, 2010, Cambridge University Press, Cambridge, p. 197.

[16] Interview with Dr. James Gifford, see *supra* note 13.

op their own principles.[17] Additionally, there were other motivations, including the possibility that PRI would serve as an extension of or a complement to the work of the GC and UNEP FI and that it would facilitate the creation of a valuable network.[18]

### 8.2.3. Governance Structure

The Initiative describes itself as "a network of international investors working together to put the six Principles for Responsible Investment into practice".[19] In its own documents, PRI often stresses that it is investor-led and UN-backed, not the other way around. There are several entities which comprise PRI, including the PRI Advisory Council (PRIAC), the PRI Association (PRIA), and the PRI Foundation.

The most important body is the PRIAC, known as the PRI Board until 2010. The PRIAC, whose members are elected by signatories, is crucial, because it "determines the strategic direction of the PRI Association and advises the directors".[20] As part of a series of reforms to PRI and its operations, the PRIAC has undergone some changes in 2011. PRIAC used to have twelve members: nine representatives from asset owner signatory organizations, two non-elected representatives from the United Nations, and the chair. Now the Council has been expanded to include four positions meant for investment managers and service partner signatories.[21] These four representatives are elected by their peers, that is, other investment managers and service partners. Furthermore, one position on the PRIAC must now go to a service provider and another to an emerging

17 Gifford, 2010, p. 199, see *supra* note 15.

18 *Ibid.*

19 Principles for Responsible Investment, "About", available at http://www.PRI.org/about/, last accessed on 5 April 2011.

20 Principles for Responsible Investment, "PRI Strategy and Work Programme 2011-2013", p. 12, available at http://www.PRI.org/files/2011_PRI_SWP.pdf, last accessed on 7 May 2011.

21 Roughly, the three types of signatories are defined as follows: asset owners, the main type, are organizations that represent end-asset owners who hold long-term retirement savings, insurance and other assets, such as pension funds; investment managers are companies that manage the money of institutional or retail clients; professional service partners provide products or services to asset owners and/or investment managers, but do not own or manage money on their own. Principles for Responsible Investment, "FAQ", see *supra* note 8.

market organization.[22] The change in structure is closely linked to the change in funding, which is described in greater detail below.[23]

Decision-making processes are incredibly important to the functioning of and the dynamics within an organization. Though these may have been clear and available to signatories themselves, the decision-making processes of PRI, and the PRIAC in particular, have not been readily accessible to the public via either PRI's own publications or third-party sources until recently. In 2011, the PRIAC's constitution and operational framework were updated and added to PRI's public website.[24] The PRIAC tries to make decisions by consensus when possible, but it has the ability to decide matters with a simple majority.

The PRI Secretariat, also known as the PRI Association (PRIA), manages the initiative and is charged with helping investors achieve the Principles "by sharing best practice, facilitating collaboration and managing a variety of work streams".[25] The secretariat is small – currently having a staff of less than thirty people. Previously, financial and legal affairs were run from the Foundation for the Global Compact, based in New York.[26] As of 2010, however, a new entity, the PRI Association, was established and now runs most day-to-day work out of London. There is also a new associated entity called the PRI Foundation which will be a charity that works "to benefit the public in relation to education, environmen-

---

22 Principles for Responsible Investment, "PRI Strategy and Work Programme 2011-2013", p. 12, see *supra* note 20.

23 As Executive Director James Gifford said "Investment managers and service partners have always had a big input into the direction of the PRI, but on the move to fees, it was felt that formal representation from these signatories on the Council is essential to mainstreaming the PRI and responsible investment throughout the investment chain, and providing value for all signatories". David Brooksbank, "UN Principles for Responsible Investment Plans Radical Changes to Board", available at http://www.responsible-investor.com/home/article/unpri_radical_changes, last accessed at 1 June 2011.

24 The previous constitution and operational framework had been available by request only. While researching this topic, I requested copies of the former constitution and framework, but my request was denied.

25 Principles for Responsible Investment, "About", see *supra* note 19.

26 Principles for Responsible Investment, "PRI Strategy and Work Programme 2011-2013", p. 12, see *supra* note 20.

tal, social and corporate responsibility and the advancement of citizenship and community development".[27]

### 8.2.4. Membership

Signatories are defined as individuals or entities that have signed up to Principles and pay dues to the PRIA.[28] There are three main categories of signatory: asset owners (245), investment managers (543), and professional service partners (156) for a total of 944 signatories from approximately 50 countries as of November 2011. Though members generally self-select their category, PRIAC reserves the right to decide a signatory's category if it has characteristics of multiple categories.[29] It is also important to note that signatories agree to put the Principles in practice across their entire organizations, including subsidiaries, but there are no initial requirements to join related to current behavior or investment portfolio. There are also no penalties for leaving PRI voluntarily. Up to this point, however, only a few organizations have chosen to do so. Though little information has been made public regarding organizations leaving PRI, one can speculate that few organizations would choose to leave the initiative voluntarily given the relatively limited burden of PRI membership (financial, administrative, *et cetera*).

PRI has two partner organizations, both of which are slightly older than PRI itself: UNEP FI and the Global Compact. The latter is similar to PRI, in the sense that it is made up of a set of voluntary principles, though this initiative is aimed at businesses. To date there have been some cross-efforts with PRI and GC. For example, a subset of PRI signatories wrote to over 100 companies and urged them to join the GC in 2008.[30] Unfortunately,

---

27 Principles for Responsible Investment, "About", see *supra* note 19.

28 In the context of PRI, "member" has a specific meaning, which is narrower than the term signatory, referring only to asset owner signatories. Throughout this chapter, I use membership in the broader, everyday sense. UN Principles for Responsible Investment, "PRI Strategy and Work Programme 2011- 2013", p. 13, see *supra* note 20.

29 Arguably, the category of investors is relatively unimportant. The main reason it matters is that certain seats on the board are reserved for certain types of signatories. This may have been more of an issue pre-2011, when seats were not allotted to investment managers or service providers, just asset owner signatories. Also, it might also affect the amount of dues paid, since dues are calculated for investors based on assets under management and for service partners based on the number of employees.

30 Hugh Wheelan, "UN PRI Cuts its Teeth with First Public Investor Campaign: Supporters Say Boost to Global Compact Points the Way to More Sophisticated Collabo-

their actions are not always so coordinated. As critics have often pointed out, PRI signatories have blacklisted GC signatories in the past.[31]

### **8.2.5.** Funding

From 2006–2011, PRI was dependent on the voluntary support, both financial and in-kind, of signatories.[32] Each signatory was asked to contribute $10,000 annually, though only one-third of signatories contributed on average.[33] Furthermore, even fewer donated the whole amount with certain signatories, such as PGGM, the BT pension fund, and California Public Employees' Retirement System, donating hugely disproportionate amounts.[34] Starting in 2011, however, signatories were charged mandatory fees, payable to the PRIA, which vary depending on either assets under management, for investors, or number of employees, for service partners. The fees range from £330–£6,600 per year. Even with these new required contributions, PRI will continue to run on a relatively small amount of funds compared to other IOs; the indicative 2011–2012 budget, with expected contributions, is less than £4 million.[35]

### **8.2.6. Output and Activities**

PRI's work can be divided into three broad categories: strategic development, implementation support, and communications support. The first two are worth describing more extensively, as they are central to PRI's objectives.

rations", available at http://www.responsible-investor.com/home/article/un_pri/P0/, last accessed on 15 March 2011.

31 *Ibid.*

32 Additional support came and continues to come from institutional grants which fund particular projects.

33 Principles for Responsible Investment, "PRI Strategy and Work Programme 2011–2013", p. 14, see *supra* note 20.

34 Helen Fowler, "The Only Way Is Ethics", available at http://www.professionalpensions.com/professional-pensions/feature/2074084/ethics, last accessed on 7 May 2011.

35 Principles for Responsible Investment, "Annual Report of the PRI Initiative 2010", p. 20, available at http://www.unpri.org/files/annual_report2010.pdf, last accessed on 20 May 2011.

#### 8.2.6.1. Strategic Development

Under the strategic development banner, there are four main items. The first three are networks: the country networks, the academic network, and the public policy network, founded in 2007, 2008 and 2010 respectively. Under the new PRI strategy, there is an increased focus on country networks as well as a planned increase from five to seven country networks. The fourth item, which has been and continues to be a main goal of PRI, is signatory outreach and recruitment.

#### 8.2.6.2. Implementation Support

Implementation support is one of the most significant areas of work for PRI. The works streams, which help to identify asset-class-specific challenges, are central to this support. Currently, there are nine work streams, which are either established or in the process of being established. The following work streams are already established: listed equities (2006), small signatories (2007), private equity (2007), property (2008), ESG Alternatives/impact investing (2010), infrastructure (2011) and fixed income (2011). Hedge funds and commodities are currently being established.

In addition to work streams, two of the oldest and most important initiatives of PRI fall under the category of implementation support: the Clearinghouse and the Reporting and Assessment Process. The Clearinghouse, established in late 2006, is described as "PRI's flagship forum to help shareholders pool knowledge, resources and influence in order to engage with companies and policy makers on ESG issues" and "the hub of implementation support on active ownership activities both in terms of collaborative engagement and also assisting signatories in developing their own engagement capabilities".[36] The Clearinghouse has five full-time staff members, which represents a significant portion of PRI's total human resources. Over 80 collaborative engagements per year are launched through the Clearinghouse.

The other key initiative is the Reporting and Assessment Process, also established in 2006. Reporting is essential to PRI and, besides the newly-introduced fees, is the only mandatory obligation of signatories.[37]

36 UN Principles for Responsible Investment, "PRI Strategy and Work Programme 2011–2013", p. 6, see *supra* note 20.

37 A one-year grace period exists for new members before they are expected to participate in the reporting and assessment process.

At the beginning of the calendar year, each signatory is invited to complete the Reporting and Assessment survey within a two-month time frame. Then a portion of the signatories are contacted by telephone to verify responses and initiate a "sharing of ideas on different approaches to ESG issues".[38] While all responses are used to compile the annual progress report compiled by the secretariat, individual responses are confidential unless the organization chooses to make it public. In 2011, almost 45% of organizations who responded to the survey – 241 out of 545 – chose make their responses public.[39] Each signatory is also sent an individual, confidential feedback report comparing its results to those of its peers.

In 2009, PRI announced it would move to mandatory public reporting to be introduced in 2012. In summer 2011, more information was announced about this change and the associated timeline. Instead of continuing to use the current survey and requiring public disclosure, there will be a complete overhaul of the survey. Committees were formed to draft a new assessment tool, and input was sought from signatories. A draft version was released in September 2011 for a seven-week public consultation, with a second round of consultations planned for early 2012. The objective is to have the new framework in place for a voluntary pilot iteration in May 2012. After receiving feedback, the new framework will be finalized for a mandatory roll out in 2013.[40] The goals are to have a process that will be more transparent and better take into account the widely varied asset classes and investment activities that signatories represent.[41]

---

38 Principles for Responsible Investment, "Reporting and Assessment", available at http://www.unpri.org/reporting/, last accessed on 13 November 2011.

39 Principles for Responsible Investment, "2011 Report on Progress", pp. 4, 53, available at http://www.unpri.org/publications/2011_report_on_progress.pdf, last accessed on 13 November 2011.

40 Based on the most recent report, the mandatory public disclosure will likely be partial even in 2013 and beyond; Principles for Responsible Investment, "PRI Investor Reporting Framework – What Is Happening in 2012/2013; Project and Framework Outline", available at http://www.unpri.org/consultation/2011%2006%2015%20Reporting%20Framework%20project%20website.pdf, last accessed on 17 June 2011.

41 *Ibid.*

### 8.2.6.3. Implementation and Compliance

Since the Principles are voluntary and aspirational, most PRI efforts are focused on helping signatories comply with the Principles, via the implementation support outlined above, rather than punishing or shaming them for failing to live up to them. In fact, PRI has encouraged members to sign up even if they are currently far from target behaviors and in order to help them achieve behavior consistent with the Principles. Quoting the PRI website, "the commitments are, for most signatories, a work in progress and a direction to head in rather than a prescriptive checklist with which to comply. The initial focus is on innovation, collaboration and learning by doing".[42]

While there are "no legal or regulatory sanctions associated with the Principles", non-participation can lead to the organizations being publicly delisted.[43] This has happened to a few organizations in both 2009 and 2010, though the number might be higher in 2011. The small number is historically due in part to the fairly limited obligations on signatories. Before the fees were introduced in 2011, participation in the annual Reporting and Assessment survey was the only actual requirement.

From the beginning, reputational risks were stressed; during the launch event, for example, Annan reminded signatories that "in signing on to these principles, you are publicly committing yourselves to adopt and live up to them".[44] Though PRI has left naming and shaming to external actors up to this point, it is signaling a tougher stance towards laggards. The 2011 Report on Progress gives, for the first time, the number of signatories who, at the time of the Report, had not completed that year's survey ("not responded at list of being delisted").[45] Though the number of signatories delisted in 2011 remains to be seen, this reference seems to take a stronger position towards 'non-communicative' members. Furthermore, the recently adopted Administrative Rules state that even if signatories pay their dues and participate in the reporting and assessment process, they can still be delisted for behavior that could damage PRI's integrity.

[42] Principles for Responsible Investment, "FAQ", see *supra* note 8.

[43] *Ibid.*

[44] Kofi Annan, "Remarks at the Launch of the Principles for Responsible Investment", see *supra* note 11.

[45] Principles for Responsible Investment, "2011 Report on Progress", p. 53, see *supra* note 39.

Still, given the process-oriented and rather vague nature of the Principles, one might expect that this mechanism will only be used on the most egregious laggards.

### 8.3. Accountability

Whether one believes that accountability is a means to an end or an end in itself,[46] the general consensus is that accountability is both important and desirable. The IN-LAW project outlines three reasons for accountability's importance: democratic, that under a democratic system the power ultimately lies with individuals who have given power to others to govern; constitutional, that accountability prevents the abuse of power; and learning, that accountability leads to learning which is a way to make an organization more effective at achieving its goals.[47] In this section, accountability will be discussed inside and outside PRI as well as the mechanisms employed by internal and external stakeholders to achieve accountability. Adopting the type of pragmatic approach espoused by the IN-LAW project, a mix of mechanisms that have been identified by various authors, such as Zweifel, Keohane and Grant will be used;[48] mechanisms under consideration will not be limited to institutionalized mechanisms or *ex post* mechanisms. In addition to differentiating between internal and external stakeholders, there is a need to distinguish between the elaboration of the Principles, that is, their initial drafting, and implementation. Most of this case study will focus on the accountability in the latter, in part due to the greater amount of information available regarding implementation.

#### 8.3.1. Responsiveness Inside PRI: During their Elaboration

The main target of the Principles has always been institutional investors, such as pension funds, and they were involved long before the actual drafting of the Principles took place. Through UNEP FI's Asset Management Working Group and other lead-up discussions, investors began to

46 Or as Bovens (2010) has distinguished: 'as a virtue' or 'as a mechanism'; Pauwelyn, 2012, see *supra* note 1.

47 Pauwelyn, 2012, see *supra* note 1.

48 Ruth W. Grant and Robert O. Keohane, "Accountability and Abuses of Power in World Politics", in *American Political Science Review*, 2005, vol. 99, no. 01, p. 2; Thomas D. Zweifel, *International Organizations and Democracy: Accountability, Politics, and Power*, L. Rienner Publishers, Boulder, CO, 2006, p. 23.

shape the responsible investment discourse. Most importantly, institutional investors were central in the nearly year-long drafting process begun in 2005. Though there is limited public information about the drafting process, all available information suggests that investors had significant control over the Principles.

### 8.3.2. Responsiveness Inside PRI: In Their Implementation

Before delving into accountability mechanisms, it is important to consider the diversity of internal stakeholders. PRI's signatories are not a homogenous constituency, and thus do not have homogenous motivations for their involvement. Generally speaking, there are two distinct groups: a core group and a peripheral group. The core group, which represents a 'significant minority', has "fully internalized the responsible investment ideology of the UN PRI and rendered the strategies actionable".[49] Thus, membership in PRI is a way to pursue a strategy that they would have otherwise but with the benefit of cost-reducing collaboration.[50] The peripheral group, on the other hand, "ha[s …] yet to act on the ideology in a meaningful manner" and "appears to be free-riding on the efforts of the core group".[51] While benefiting the peripheral group, free-riding also threatens the whole organization, since much of its strength comes from its market authority and how it is perceived by external audiences.[52] Bearing in mind the heterogeneity of signatories, we can now examine accountability within PRI. In the relationship between PRI and its signatories to date, it appears that PRI has been more accountable to internal stakeholders, either the signatories themselves or their beneficiaries, than stakeholders have been to PRI. There seems to be a number of opportunities for signatories to engage with the Initiative such as the annual 'PRI in Person' event, discussions stemming from the survey verification process, and openness of staff to be contacted. Still, it is not entirely clear if the relative lack of complaints or problems is a testament to PRI and its activities or simply a function of PRI being of limited concern to interest to some signatories and/or their beneficiaries.

---

49 Gray, 2009, p. 10, see *supra* note 6.
50 *Ibid.*
51 *Ibid.*
52 *Ibid.*

Broadly speaking, some question the overall representativeness of PRI's membership; though membership is open to organizations from all countries and there are signatories from every region, certain regions are over-represented. Furthermore, among signatories "not all signatories are equally active in constructing, supporting, and promoting the UN PRI and the associated responsible investment ideology".[53] The disproportionate influence of certain signatories on PRI is in part due to having such an informal organization and process.

Similarly, the composition of the board, now known as PRIAC, could be an area of concern, specifically whether board itself and its actions are representative of signatories.[54] This was particularly true prior to 2011, since certain categories of signatories were not eligible to serve on the board. There is also a question of geographic representation. Among the nine asset owner slots, five must be filled by one member each from the five regions: Africa, Asia-Pacific, Eastern Europe, Latin America and Caribbean, and Western Europe and others; there are no geographic requirements for the non-asset owner slots, though an emerging market organization must be represented. Despite the institutional measures to ensure geographic diversity, the Board, at least in terms of composition, still tends to be dominated by members from Europe, North America, or Australia. Although this is most likely due to the simple fact that there are more signatories from developed countries, which means both more potential candidates and more votes, the lack of diversity in the board is troubling.[55] Beyond concerns about representing all signatories, this is also problematic for external stakeholders, since these developed country investors often have investments in developing countries and thus have opportunities to impact these countries through their behavior. In terms of operations, the release of governance documents in July 2011 has shed some additional light on the Board's activities and requirements – though perhaps this process has been clear to signatories all along. Given the Board's preference for consensus as stated in the Administrative Rules, one would expect that although the PRIAC would never make a decision that members staunchly opposed, that is, PRIAC is not likely to be a rogue actor, it may also lead to more conservative course of action over-

---

53 *Ibid.*, p. 12.

54 *Ibid.*

55 According to the 2011 Report on Progress, only 76 signatories come from developing and emerging countries, see *supra* note 39.

all, by mainly acting only on things that are agreed upon by everyone and thus representing the preferences of the 'lowest common denominator'.

Turning now to the ways in which PRI can ensure its members are held accountable, we must remind ourselves of the modest size of PRI's secretariat. Its first-year budget was around $150,000, and each year there was some budgetary uncertainty, due to a lack of a consistent revenue stream. Additionally, there were few staff members, and despite recent growth, the staff still remains relatively small today. Furthermore, PRI has always been developed and conceptualized as a network or a platform for collaboration rather than a hierarchical enforcement agency. While this may provide many benefits, such as the possibility of innovative peer-to-peer communication, it does not allow for PRI to enforce the Principles in a top-down manner.

Even if PRI was structured differently or the secretariat had more resources, there are few obligations to which signatories can be held accountable. Until the introduction of dues in 2011, the only specific requirement was participation in the annual Reporting and Assessment process. Though signatories could be delisted for being 'non-communicative', there were never lesser penalties at PRI's disposal and no sanctions for not following the Principles *per se*, simply means to assist with implementation.

Transparency is a key accountability mechanism because it serves an informational purpose, allowing others to see what actions are being taken, and possibly serving as a check on actors who may behave differently if they know they can be observed. The main mechanism for transparency in PRI is the Reporting and Assessment process, though up to this point it has not provided much transparency. Not only was there no requirement to make one's survey responses public, but it was also self-reported and relied on descriptive scales rather than concrete indicators. Furthermore, the verification component has been very weak. Due to a small budget, there are not enough staff members to follow up with every signatory or sufficient resources to hire an independent verifier; thus, only one-third of signatories have been verified each year. Furthermore, even if a signatory is contacted for verification, this process continues to place the burden on the signatory to be forthcoming.

In addition to requiring at least some public reporting, there are several changes to the survey which will aid transparency, including a new focus on capacity and differences in investment classes. The old survey was more general, obscuring differences across investors. Additionally, there was little focus on capacity, so it was difficult to determine who was making real progress. The new survey reduces the self-assessment aspect by moving away from descriptive scales and using both free-text and specific indicators, including binary (yes/no) and quantitative ones.[56] These changes to the survey will hopefully improve transparency, and thus provide PRI with a better picture of what its signatories are doing.

In many organizations, the budgetary process is an important realm for accountability. Historically, PRI has had a very small budget, due to its reliance on voluntary contributions. One would imagine that most of these donors were part of the core group and already on-board with PRI's work. The introduction of mandatory fees may lead to some important changes. Although the requirement of annual fees will certainly increase its budget, it may lead to some signatories leaving. In early 2011, PRI's executive director predicted that approximately one quarter of current signatories would leave PRI due to the new fees, but this has not occurred; as of summer 2011, shortly after the fees' introduction, over 90% of members had paid their dues.[57] In addition to giving PRI a more solid budget and removing uncommitted members, there is also a public reputational component, which seems to speak more to external stakeholders:

> The move to a fee-based structure will help remove accusations that members are merely paying lip service to PRI principles. The remaining signatories will inevitably look more committed to PRI and its principles. 'A number of people from our side and fund managers said it was about time, why did we not do this earlier', says [former Chair] MacDonald. 'People were concerned that having signatories not making any contribution damaged the brand'.[58]

Certainly, it will strengthen the organization, in that the increased budget will allow for PRI to conduct more programmatic activities. It may also change the *de facto* relationship with signatories. By instituting mandatory fees, PRI is increasing the minimum level of involvement for sig-

---

[56] Principles for Responsible Investment, "Scoping Document, Guiding the Drafting of the Reporting Framework", p. 6, available at http://www.unpri.org/consultation/2011_06_16_scoping%20document.pdf, last accessed on 17 June 2011.

[57] Principles for Responsible Investment, "2011 Annual Report", p. 22, available at http://www.unpri.org/publications/annual_report2011.pdf, last accessed on 13 November 2011.

[58] Fowler, "The Only Way is Ethics", see *supra* note 34.

natories. Thus, if an organization is not motivated enough to contribute financially to PRI, it must leave. Similarly, fees, though fairly small, may lead signatories to be more engaged in the initiative in order to make sure its money is spent in ways it agrees with. Even if an organization itself is indifferent to paying the fee, it could be made an issue of by its stakeholders, such as pensioners or investors.

One mechanism that has not been sufficiently addressed is the relationship of signatories to each other. As noted earlier, there exists a core and a periphery; some signatories have shown a strong interest in and a commitment to PRI by contributing financially to the budget, proposing and developing collaborative projects through the Clearinghouse, or allowing for its survey results to be publicly disclosed. At the other extreme, some signatories have not met even the minimal requirements of PRI membership and have been delisted. This huge range of behaviors by signatories damages the legitimacy of PRI and possibly the legitimacy of core members along with it. This dependent peer relationship, along with the reputational mechanism or the PRIAC's powers, could be the greatest accountability mechanism.

Like many new governance initiatives, most of the benefits of membership are not doled out by a central organization, but rather come from the market rewarding signatories for their membership and appropriate behavior.[59] Signatories who are active and follow the Principles in a meaningful way likely have an interest in making sure that PRI's reputation is good, because it reflects on all members. As a result, more active signatories can push laggards to be more involved and to follow through on their commitments and/or push PRIAC to apply pressure to them or delist them, since the strength of the brand can easily be diluted by the behavior of less-committed members.

### 8.3.3. Responsiveness to External Stakeholders

In the initial drafting phase, which began in 2005, some external stakeholders were invited for consultations. Around seventy experts were invited to participate and though we know that they came from a range of

[59] See John J. Kirton and Michael J. Trebilcock, (eds.), *Hard Choices, Soft Law: Voluntary Standards in Global Trade, Environment And Social Governance*, Ashgate Publishers, Farnham, 2004; David Vogel, *The Market for Virtue: the Potential and Limits of Corporate Social Responsibility*, Brookings Institution, Washington D.C., 2005.

backgrounds ("the investment industry, intergovernmental and governmental organisations, civil society and academia"), not much else is known about who these experts were, what countries they came from, how many experts came from each group, or how their feedback was, if at all, incorporated into the final Principles.[60] This lack of transparency has set the Principles up for criticisms that they were "effectively based on a compromise of international norms and values with no degree of ensured representative democracy".[61]

Though not usually meant to be an accountability mechanism for external stakeholders like NGOs, budgetary processes can be used as a monitoring process.[62] This has not happened to date, and there could be several reasons for this. First, PRI's funding and budget have always been small, particularly in its first few years, and thus there has not been much room for activities beyond modest set-up requirements. Second, PRI's publicly available budget is not broken down in great detail, so it is difficult to determine what exactly it is spending its money on. Furthermore, by their nature, the activities of PRI, such as survey administration and research, are fairly benign. Thus, it seems that individual signatories' investments are more likely to draw the scrutiny of external actors than PRI's activities.

Up until this point, there has been limited transparency, either in the Reporting and Assessment process or other activities, because much of the information is not available to external stakeholders. Access to many PRI resources is members-only, with a small number of publications made public, such as annual reports highlighting selected activities of signatories and networks. Limiting access is a response to the obvious free-rider problem: why would organizations join PRI and commit to reporting and paying the membership fees, no matter how big or small that commitment may be, if one of the major benefits, the access to information, best practices, *et cetera*, is open to everyone? Though understandable, there is a need for such discussions to be at least somewhat more open. For example, the fact that PRI is built on an implicit definition of responsible investment makes it important for external stakeholders to witness

60 Principles for Responsible Investment, "About", see *supra* note 19.

61 Gray, 2009, p. 12, see *supra* note 6.

62 Zweifel, 2006, p. 73, see *supra* note 48.

the ongoing construction of this ideology, since it will theoretically influence concrete investment decisions.

One positive change related to transparency is the set of announced changes to the Reporting and Assessment Process. Since the indicators and details are yet to be finalized, it is hard to say how significant this development will be. Since the current survey is not especially rigorous, due mostly to its reliance on self-assessment via descriptive scales, almost any change will be a welcome improvement. Of particular note is the move towards at least partial mandatory public reporting.

Despite any deficiencies it may have in its current version, the survey can be a great starting point for a dialogue between various stakeholders. Furthermore, although some organizations are under mandatory reporting requirements due to domestic legislation, many are not. For example, the filings for the also imperfect reporting requirements of the US Securities and Exchange Commission (SEC) are often used by campaigns such as the US-based campaign Investors Against Genocide, an organization which pushes for investors to divest in companies that have ties to Darfur, since SEC filings are more involved than the PRI reporting requirements. Hence, signatories' PRI reports may be more useful for stakeholders based in countries without reporting policies, or for stakeholders simply looking for a general starting point for dialogue, rather than a detailed information source.

Structurally, the PRI lacks the sort of explicit *de jure* mechanisms of other organizations, such as those of its partner institution, the Global Compact. For example, the GC has a dialogue facilitation process which allows external stakeholders to petition the GC if a company has not responded to their complaints within a certain amount of time; if the company then does not respond to GC overtures, it can be delisted from the initiative for non-communication.[63] There is also no representation for civil society in PRI, since, unlike the GC, PRI does not have a multi-stakeholder board. It seems that without major overhauls to the system, the sub-units of PRI are more suited to engagement with external stakeholders. This could include country networks and/or work streams, such as the Millennium Development Goal work stream.

[63] This is not to say that the dialogue facilitation process is not without its flaws; many have found the GC unwilling to side against businesses in these situations. Eric Cohen, "Telephone interview", 21 June 2011.

Beyond specific tools or channels, membership in the PRI can function as a starting point for external actors looking to change the behavior of investors. External actors, such as NGOs, can publicize behaviors of signatories which are not in line with the Principles and use their membership and the apparent disconnect between words and deeds to further shame them. Unfortunately, organizations can also invoke their own membership in PRI to deflect criticism from themselves, leading to perverse results.[64]

It is also important to look more broadly at the landscape of external actors and some inherent challenges that exist for an external actor trying to hold a signatory accountable for violating the Principles. One of the main challenges is the diversity of actors and diversity of issues. As previously noted the issues that fall under the category of ESG are extensive and varied. Furthermore, the number of people affected is also huge and varied: indigenous tribes, low skilled workers, *et cetera.* In addition to the fact that there are so many actors, many of whom have not historically had power either in their domestic society or global society, there is the challenge of having many groups that are interested in violations of the Principles in one country or in one issue area. There will be many external stakeholders who are less concerned with keeping signatories accountable as a whole and are more interested in specific signatories. Thus, we may see more one-on-one efforts to keep signatories accountable to the Principles.

Second, as compared to the relationship of multi-national corporations (MNCs) or a foreign direct investment (FDI)-type investor to external stakeholders, the chain linking these actors is much longer.[65] As a hypothetical example: an MNC builds a factory in a developing country, and its operations pollute nearby rivers and streams. For an NGO or an individual concerned by this action, the most obvious first point of engagement would likely be the company itself, since this is the organization most readily known to the public. Furthermore, it is likely easier and more effective to target one entity, since the decision is theirs alone. If one were to target a company's investors, there are likely to be hundreds of shareholders in a publicly traded company, who may or may not have voting rights. Furthermore, institutional investors may or may not control a large

64 *Ibid.*

65 Most signatories are portfolio investors, but there are some cases of direct investment.

enough portion to be able to effectuate change, either through shareholder resolutions or other means.

Though it may seem that PRI and its signatories' actions can have great effects on external stakeholders, it may be useful to consider the existence of a relationship in the opposite direction. Despite a lack of access "to any financial or political channels of direct governance" within PRI and the fact that external stakeholders support is not, strictly speaking, necessary for PRI's existence, " [external actors'] behavior could potentially have significant consequences for the organization".[66] Building on the work of Suchman, Gray points out that

> a non-state organization cannot resort to claims of sovereignty to establish rule-making authority but must do so by gaining legitimacy as dependent on how the organization is perceived by concerned external audiences.[67]

Thus, the size and diversity of PRI members, which is an advantage in gaining 'market authority', could also be a big weakness:

> As the signatory base is composed of both public and private institutional investors, the UN PRI has become of concern not only for financial audiences but also public and political audiences. Ultimately, the organization's degree of legitimacy will be determined by the culmination of the perceived legitimacy originating from each of these categories of external audience. The heterogeneity, both within and between, these broad categories of external audiences should not be underestimated.[68]

Essentially, PRI has a large and diverse external constituency whose support or lack thereof could significantly affect the organization. This is true for many reasons, especially since PRI relies on the market for reputational validation. Though these audiences have not exercised this power to date, that does not mean they will not do so in the future.

### 8.3.4. Challenges for All Involved

A major challenge in keeping signatories accountable, both for PRI and external stakeholders, is that the Principles have an escape clause of sorts.

---

66 Gray, 2009, p. 13, see *supra* note 6.
67 *Ibid.*, p. 14.
68 *Ibid.*

In the preamble, it reads: "Therefore, where consistent with our fiduciary responsibilities, we commit to the following".[69] Although this was likely necessary to attract and retain signatories, it poses a challenge for internal and especially external stakeholders to question decisions or actions taken by signatories. First, some of these organizations do not publicly disclose, either in part or in full, their financial information. And even if they did, one could imagine the argument arising that only the investor or the trustee can define and analyze its fiduciary responsibility. Perhaps more crucially, the main thrust of PRI is that one must take ESG issues into consideration, but that can be done in a myriad of ways. An inherent challenge with any procedural scheme or principles is that it is possible the requisite process is followed, but that the result is still substantively undesirable to many. Although there is nothing inherently wrong or illegitimate by focusing on inputs, the potential costs, especially to external stakeholders, could be great. Combine this with the broad nature of the Principles, and there is even more potential for results that do not meaningfully advance the responsible investment agenda.

## 8.4. Conclusion

Unique in the size of its membership and the scope of issues covered, the PRI is a relatively new but quickly growing initiative which has sought to mainstream responsible investment through voluntary and aspirational principles.[70] Like many new governance models, it relies heavily on the market, via reputational accountability, to be effective. Although PRI has had many successes in its first five years of existence, such as a growing membership and an increasingly high profile, it may be facing some challenges in the future.

To its harshest critics, PRI is a 'blue-washing' campaign which has allowed investors to use the UN's name to appear responsible and which has received little scrutiny up until now.[71] This uncritical reception may not last much longer, especially as PRI continues to grow. Further signatory growth will improve its market authority in the short term, but if, in trying to appeal to new organizations, PRI lowers current standards "of

69 Emphasis added by the author; Principles for Responsible Investment, "The Principles", see *supra* note 8.

70 Gray, 2009, p. 13, see *supra* note 6.

71 *Ibid.*, p. 14.

transparency, accountability, and enforcement", PRI will be opened up to further criticism.[72]

Though this is still a possibility given how much will remain the same, the recently proposed and implemented changes will likely have some impact on the dynamics between actors, improving the overall accountability of PRI. Because of introduction of mandatory membership dues as well as mandatory public reporting, PRI should become a stronger organization with more committed membership body over the next few years. Though it would still be short of a certification scheme that some might like to see, an increased membership burden could signal increased seriousness of the organization and represent some progress. At the same time, the mandatory fees will provide a more solid financial base, which will allow PRI to engage in far more programmatic activities. Regardless, additional scrutiny from outside actors, such as the media, civil society, or academia, is to be expected as the initiative grows older and larger, and attracts more attention.

Despite its obvious shortcomings, we must consider that this arrangement was purposely chosen by PRI's framers instead of a formal organization. Without knowing for certain why an informal scheme was chosen, one can surmise that there were certain reasons for choosing it, such as the desire to involve non-state actors as well as the impossibility of creating a binding commitment which would be acceptable to many parties.[73] Though some may find the Principles lacking in substance, they represent an international compromise; it is important to remember that responsible investment means many things to different people and finding common ground, even among its more fervent adherents, is difficult.

In terms of SRI, PRI is important for several reasons. First, it has the potential to become the go-to framework for institutional investors in responsible investment and influence many other actors in the process, due to its size, the scope of issues covered, and UN backing; there are few initiatives aimed specifically at institutional investors.[74] Furthermore, institutional investors have a unique role to play in financial markets. Whenever institutional investors have become interested in certain topics in the past, this has often led to the 'creation of a new mainstream finan-

72 *Ibid.*, p. 15.

73 Pauwelyn, 2012, see *supra* note 1.

74 Gray, 2009, p. 13, see *supra* note 6.

cial services industry' around those topics.[75] Additionally, "UN PRI signatories control sufficient capital [...] to require other actors to adjust their market strategies if they successfully implement the novel responsible investment strategies".[76]

From an IN-LAW perspective, PRI is significant, because it demonstrates many of the inherent challenges of accountability in these types of new governance schemes. Though it may be desirable to have formal, institutionalized roles for external stakeholders to address concerns or problems, there are ways for external stakeholders to impact the organization and its behavior even without formal channels. This, however, is difficult to do without good information, which in turn requires a certain amount of transparency.

Since PRI is in the midst of a number of important changes that will affect its funding, reporting, and governance structure among other things, there is great potential for changes in the dynamics between PRI and its signatories as well as PRI and external stakeholders. Only time will tell what the effects of the reforms on these dynamics will be.

---

[75] *Ibid.*, p. 12.

[76] *Ibid.*

# 9

# Can Accountability and Effectiveness Go Hand in Hand? Lessons from Two Latin American Competition Networks

**Pierre M. Horna**[*]

## 9.1. Introduction

> It is often presumed that, by definition, increased effectiveness requires a reduction in accountability or that more accountability will necessarily hamper effectiveness. We plan to further examine the relationship between effectiveness and accountability [...] there are certainly times where accountability and effectiveness go hand in hand. One such example is under the *learning dimension of accountability* whereby ex post accountability mechanisms that expose failures or mistakes can lead to improvement and more (rather than less) effectiveness of action.[1]

The functioning of two Latin American government networks to be assessed in the chapter proves, at least on the surface, that accountability has reduced network effectiveness and vice versa. Yet, as will be critically examined, both government networks can increase at the same time their accountability and effectiveness levels by strengthening the learning di-

---

[*] **Pierre M. Horna**, LL.M., is staff member of the Competition and Consumer Policies Branch at the United Nations Conference on Trade and Development (UNCTAD). This contribution represents the opinion of the author, and is the product of professional research. It is not meant to represent the position or opinions of the UNCTAD Secretariat or its Members, nor the official position of any staff members. The author would like to thank the valuable substantive comments of Professor Joost Pauwelyn and Edgar Odio on earlier drafts of the chapter as well as all the interviewed officials from the two networks assessed in Latin America. Any errors are the fault of the author.

[1] Joost Pauwelyn, "Informal International Lawmaking: Framing the Concept and Research Questions", in Joost Pauwelyn, Ramses A. Wessel and Jan Wouters (eds.), *Informal International Lawmaking*, Oxford University Press, Oxford, 2012 (emphasis added).

mension of accountability, one of the approaches that will be scrutinized throughout the chapter.

Since 2005, two government networks in Latin America[2] have attempted to deal with cross-border anti-competitive practices as a response to an increasingly globalized pattern of business practices across countries and markets.[3] The airline sector in Latin America offers a typical example of cross-border anti-competitive practices.[4] Initially, in response to the

---

2 Apart from the two government networks that will be analyzed in this chapter (Central American Group of Competition and the Andean Committee for the Defense of Competition), there are other networks in Latin America and the Caribbean, such as the Southern Cone Common Market-MERCOSUR (Brazil, Argentina, Paraguay, and Uruguay) and the Caribbean Community-CARICOM (Antigua and Barbuda, The Bahamas, Barbados, Belize, Dominica, Grenada, Guyana, Haiti, Jamaica, Montserrat, Saint Lucia, St. Kitts and Nevis, St. Vincent and the Grenadines, Suriname, and Trinidad and Tobago).

3 Cross-border anti-competitive practices develop when, for example, a jurisdiction encourages exporters to get together and fix minimum prices to increase revenues. This form of cross-border anti-competitive practice is defined as a classical export cartel, which has been traditionally excluded from national competition laws. A more complex example is that of the telecom industry, when a company receives a 'legal monopoly' after privatization of the telecom sector in different jurisdictions. In this regard, an abuse of the dominant position in the relevant regional market might take place and consumers across countries accessing mobile communications will face higher prices. Cross-border anti-competitive practices include international cartels which fix prices, for instance, in the airline and telecommunication sectors. These practices, engaged in by regional Latin American and international enterprises, can harm consumers' welfare and their freedom to have better end products. The response thus far has not been very effective. For instance, De Leon vividly suggests that: "These rules have traditionally reduced the scope of competition. Competition agencies have utterly failed to dismantle the anti-market institutions that have undermined competition in the region, as clearly shown by the failure of privatization to introduce a change in the competitive structure of markets. This is evidence of the lack of purpose of competition agencies, which is reinforced both in their misguided agenda against business restraints, as well as in their lack of legal power to challenge anti-competitive government rules. This is further evidence of their inability to challenge the anti-market institutions that ultimately are subject to their purview [...] Due to the role conventionally assigned to trade and professional associations in the region, it is not surprising that price fixing schemes organized through these associations are among the most prominent form of horizontal restraints on trade addressed by competition agencies". Ignacio De Leon, *An Institutional Assessment of Antitrust Policy - The Latin American Experience*, Kluwer Law International, Alphen aan den Rijn, 2009, pp. 35–37.

4 Central and South American consumers have been witnessing alliances and strategic partnerships between major airline companies with the purpose of increasing their

economic harm caused by these cross-border anti-competitive practices, Latin American governments enacted national competition laws inspired by the United States' (US) 'effects doctrine'.[5] However, national efforts were insufficient to deal with the growing impact of business practices on competition and consumer welfare. Hence, national governments in Latin America included initiatives to deal with cross-border anti-competitive practices within their already established and ongoing regional economic integration schemes. Two government networks were formed: The Central American Group of Competition (Central American Group)[6] and the Andean Committee for the Defense of Competition (Andean Committee).[7] Although these two networks show a different set of rules governing their genesis (since the Andean Committee is embedded within regional competition law and the Central American Group does not have a regional competition law), both adopted their own internal set of guide-

market shares in the region. There are high concerns in Central-America about the competitive conditions in the passenger airline industry when two dominant airlines coordinate themselves to fix airfare tariffs. Given that the effects are extra-territorial, they must be treated with the legal framework of the region. Two examples of airlines under scrutiny are: COPA and TACA. See Marcos Avalos, "The interface between trade, competition policy and development", Preliminary paper prepared for the Regional Seminar on Trade and Competition: Prospects and Future Challenges for Latin America and the Caribbean, Caracas, Venezuela 20–21 April 2009, Document No. SP/SRCC-PFDALC/DT N° 2-09, available at http://www.sela.org, last accessed on 27 November 2011.

5 With the US Antitrust jurisprudence in Alcoa Decision (1945), Judge Hand converted this line of authority into a general effects test, any anti-competitive behavior that takes place in the US market will be undergo legal consequences under US antitrust laws. See Einer Elhauge and Damien Geradin, *Global Antitrust Law and Economics*, Foundation Press, 2007, p. 1104. For further reference on this issue, see Jonathan T. Schmidt, "Keeping U.S. Courts Open to Foreign Antitrust Plaintiffs: A Hybrid Approach to the effective Deterrence of International Cartels", in *The Yale Journal of International Law*, 2006, vol. 31, no. 211, pp. 212–264.

6 The Central American Group was formed as a result of Central American governments deciding to establish an informal forum to discuss the effect of cross-border anti-competitive practices in the regional Central American market through their respective national regulators (competition authorities) in 2006.

7 The Andean Committee was established in 2005. In fact, South American countries part of the Andean Community integration scheme decided to strengthen the legal response to this type of regional business practice by adopting a regional competition law that will precisely tackle transnational anti-competitive practices.

lines/regulations[8] to practice and present important developments that are of relevance within the IN-LAW methodological framework. In addition, the two initiatives affect approximately 40% of the Latin American market, including Mexico, Brazil and Argentina, countries which are also part of regional initiatives such as NAFTA and MERCOSUR.

The ultimate goal of this contribution is to determine whether these two networks are accountable and effective according to the methodological framework of IN-LAW. In doing so, examples will be provided from the questionnaires and interviews conducted with the network participants. Based on these results, this chapter attempts to provide recommendations as to improve the accountability and effectiveness of the assessed networks and ultimately make a case for the need of IN-LAW, but also noting the limitations of the framework.

The contribution is structured as follows: Section 9.2. provides preliminary observations as to whether the two government networks fall within the scope of the methodological framework of IN-LAW. This section can be read in conjunction with the four appendixes to the chapter which provide detailed information about the objectives, life-cycle and other aspects of each network. Section 9.3. critically assesses the two government networks by using the accountability and effectiveness dimensions as set out in the IN-LAW framework. Based on the findings of Section 9.3., Section 9.4. examines whether accountability and effectiveness go hand in hand, particularly when strengthening the learning dimension of accountability in these networks. The final section provides recommendations on how to enhance the accountability and effectiveness of the two networks.

[8] For the Central American Group, the Internal Regulations for the functioning and organization of the Group were arguably approved. Document originally drafted in Spanish: "Lineamientos Internos de Organización y Funcionamiento del Grupo de Trabajo de Política de Competencia en la Integración Económica Centroamericana". Restricted circulation. In addition, the Andean Committee formally approved its Internal Regulations in its October 2005 second ordinary meeting. Minutes on 3 October 2005, "Acta de la Segunda Reunión Ordinaria del Comité Andino de Defensa de la Competencia" (CDC), 3 October 2005, Lima – Perú, SG/R.CDC/II/ACTA 2.17.28.

## 9.2. The IN-LAW Methodological Framework

### 9.2.1. Introduction

The purpose of this section is to set forth the methodology through which the critical assessment of Section 9.3. will be carried out. There has been a great increase in literature on network governance, particularly since 2004.[9] Scholars in global governance have done research on a rising phenomenon called transnational or trans-governmental regulatory networks as defined by P.H. Verdier.[10] Paraphrasing Slaughter's ideas, the proliferation of government networks shows common functions with the purpose: (i) to *expand regulatory reach*, allowing governments to close the gaps between their jurisdictions; (ii) to *build trust and establish relationships* among their participants, conditions which are essential for long-term cooperation; (iii) to *exchange information* regularly and develop databases of best practices; and (iv) to *offer technical assistance* and professional socialization to members from less developed nations.[11] Out of these functions, the tendency according to Anderson, is to focus on *expand[ing] the regulatory reach* and in the long-run, both Anderson and Slaughter agree that

> [T]he following phenomena constitute the sine qua non of government networks: the creation of common ties, personal

9 A comprehensive and detailed analysis was presented by Anne-Marie Slaughter in her book entitled *A New World Order*. This influential book baptized the regulators as new diplomats, vividly defining the concept of disaggregated State; Anne-Marie Slaughter, *A New World Order*, Princeton University Press, Princeton, 2004, p. 36. But Imelda Maher, "Competition Law in the International Domain: Networks as a New Forum Governance", in *Journal of Law and Society*, 2002, vol. 29, no. 1, pp. 111–136 and Oliver Budzinski, "The International Competition Network: Prospects and Limits on the Road Towards International Competition Governance", in *Competition and Change*, 2004, vol. 8, no. 3, pp. 223–242 suggested shortcomings of these type of networks. In this regard, Budzinski argued that there are linkages between networks, domestic policy change and convergence. Promoting regulatory convergence will come as a result of the network effects amongst network participants and subsequently, export-import regulation exercises will take place.

10 Pierre-Hugues Verdier, "Transnational regulatory networks and their limits", in *Yale Journal of International Law*, 2009, vol. 34, no. 113, p. 114.

11 Slaughter, 2004, see *supra* note 9. See also Kenneth Anderson, "Squaring the Circle? Reconciling Sovereignty and Global Governance Through Global Government Networks (Review of Anne-Marie Slaughter. A New World Order)", in *Harvard Law Review*, 2005, vol. 118, pp. 1255–1312.

> relationships, camaraderie, a shared professional and social outlook […] the most significant effect of global networks might be [...] the creation of a global bourgeoisie with a set of similar elite-class views as a process of socialization, rather than simply a network of one-off transactions […].[12]

In terms of network output, the working definition of informal international lawmaking (IN-LAW) notes that *informality* is approached through the (i) output of the network,[13] (ii) the process within the network life cycle,[14] and (iii) the actors involved.[15] In addition, the international aspect entails that there must be cooperation between two or more informal actors in different countries and this assumption should not prejudge whether domestic law might impose limitations and controls on the activity of regulators at the international level. Lastly, the *lawmaking* aspect refers to norm-setting or public policy-making, as broadly defined by public authorities. The literature on this particular point assesses whether the lawmaking feature is actually taking place in these types of networks.[16]

---

12 *Ibid.*, p. 1272.

13 Refers to the fact that network outputs do not lead to a formal treaty or any other traditional source of international law, but rather to guidelines, standards, declarations or even more informal policy coordination or exchanges.

14 In different degrees, activity occurs in loosely organized networks or forums that have a certain type of structure and, of course, that are different in an institutional framework as compared to a traditional international organization; Ramses A. Wessel and Ayelet Berman, "The Legal Form and Status of Informal International lawmaking Bodies", in Joost Pauwelyn, Ramses A. Wessel and Jan Wouters (eds.), *Informal International Lawmaking*, Oxford University Press, Oxford, 2012.

15 Not traditional diplomatic actors (heads of state, foreign ministers and embassies) but rather other ministries, domestic regulators, independent or semi-independent agencies. Some scholars have called them 'the new diplomats'. Slaughter, 2004, p. 36, see *supra* note 9. The traditional diplomats should not be involved in global technocracy. There are special issues in which they present a comparative advantage such as global security and human rights.

16 Joost Pauwelyn, "Informal International Public Policy Making: New International Law or Not International Law and Does it Even Matter?", in Joost Pauwelyn, Ramses A. Wessel and Jan Wouters (eds.), *Informal International Lawmaking*, Oxford University Press, Oxford, 2012.

### 9.2.2. Do "The Central American Group" and "The Andean Committee" Fall Under the Working Definition of IN-LAW?

| | | ***The Central American Group*** | ***The Andean Committee*** |
|---|---|---|---|
| ***Informality*** | *Output* | Informal policy-coordination and exchange of experiences as well as declarations after each annual forum. | Intended will to issue Internal Regulations for regional law of Bolivia and Ecuador. (that is, work plan adopted at 2nd meeting in October 2005). |
| | *Process* | The network is a forum as it was not officially set up under the premises of the Central American System of Integration (SICA) or any other economic integration scheme. | Relatively more formal than a forum. It has the legal nature of a technical group already endorsed by a regional competition law. It might be deemed as part of an international organization. |
| | *Actor* | Definitely domestic regulators which are independent from Ministries (in cases of Nicaragua, Honduras and El Salvador) and totally dependent from the willingness and hierarchy of the Ministers of Economy in the case of Costa Rica and Guatemala. | In the case of Peru and Colombia (Venezuela only during 2005), domestic regulators were completely independent from the influence of Ministers. In Ecuador, the under-secretary for Competition is part of the Ministry of Industry and Enterprises. Surprisingly, Bolivia has a completely independent competition authority which is not part of any ministry. |
| ***International*** | | Cooperation includes more than two actors from different countries. | Cooperation includes more than two actors from different countries. |
| ***Lawmaking*** | | Public policy recommendations by public authorities. | Public policy-making by public authorities. |

**Table 2**

As shown in the above classification, both government networks fall under the scope and definition of IN-LAW. Furthermore, these government networks, in accordance with Slaughter's classification, could be considered horizontal[17] and vertical networks.[18]

Further reflections on government networks are, in order, first, Slaughter sketches the common problems facing by government networks which account for: (i) global technocracy; (ii) distortion of national political processes; (iii) unrepresentative input into national judicial decision-making; (iv) unrepresentative input into global political processes; and (v) the ineradicability of power.[19] These problems can be addressed by the given IN-LAW methodological framework and, if the case merits, they will be covered in the following section regarding the critical assessment of the two networks.

Second, government networks may offer opportunities in order to tackle common problems amongst network participants. These are summarized as follows: (i) creating convergence and informed divergence[20] of, for instance, competition rules; (ii) improving compliance with international rules and sound principles of competition law; and (iii) increasing the scope, nature, and quality of international cooperation or absorptive capacity. A particular reference is made as to whether these government networks could be regarded as

> [P]rime mechanisms of regional governance, harnessing the capacity of government networks for self-regulation, thereby contributing to the development and enforcement of global standards of honesty, integrity, competence, and independ-

---

17 A horizontal network is defined as the interaction of peer government organizations that discuss common interest issues. As representatives of each Member State, they address regulatory issues such as telecom, finances, competition, *etc.* Slaughter, 2004, p. 25, see *supra* note 9.

18 Vertical networks consist of hierarchically connected network participants, for example, supranational vs. national authorities. This hierarchy results from either a treaty or an equivalent agreement. Regional grouping of institutions, such as the EU and its executive bodies, most notably the EU Commission, and its relation to the institutions of Member States, serves as a second example. *Ibid.*, page 25.

19 Anne-Marie Slaughter, "Disaggregated sovereignty: Towards the Public Accountability of Global Government Networks", in David Held and Mathias Koenig-Archibugi (eds.), *Global Governance and Public Accountability*, Blackwell Publishers, Oxford, 2005, pp. 40–47.

20 This issue of 'informed divergence' has been one of the major critiques made to Slaughter's book. See Anderson, 2004, p. 1274, see *supra* note 11.

> ence in performing the various functions that constitute a government [...].[21]

Third, a one-size-fits-all approach must be rejected. Rather, one should identify the building blocks that contribute to strengthening the accountability of IN-LAW.[22] While it is true that the very nature of informal networks raise additional problems regarding the mechanisms of accountability,[23] Corthaut, Demeyere, Hachez and Wouters provide three tools that may help improve accountability: (i) strengthening transparency; (ii) strengthening delegation of accountability and dealing with its limits; and (iii) strengthening participation (domestic democratic oversight and global democracy). These general recommendations will be discussed when providing insight on how to improve the accountability and effectiveness of the Central American Group and the Andean Committee.

## 9.3. Critical Assessment of Both Networks

### 9.3.1. Assessing the Degree of Accountability Through the Four IN-LAW Approaches

There is no unique definition of accountability. One description is "a relationship between an actor and a forum, in which the actor has an obligation to explain and to justify his or her conduct, the forum can pose questions and pose judgment, and the actor may face consequences". However, a critical point in the assessment of IN-LAW is to determine whether the two government networks suffer an accountability deficit. This situation might arise when neither domestic law nor international law has the ability to regulate this phenomenon precisely due to the informal nature of IN-LAW and the limited application of domestic rules in the lawmaking process.

---

21 Slaughter, 2004, p. 25, see *supra* note 9; Maher, 2002, pp. III-36, see *supra* note 9.

22 Tim Corthaut, Bruno Demeyere, Nicolas Hachez and Jan Wouters, "Operationalizing accountability in respect of informal international public policy making mechanisms", in Joost Pauwelyn, Ramses A. Wessel and Jan Wouters (eds.), *Informal International Lawmaking*, Oxford University Press, Oxford, 2012.

23 *Ibid.*

### 9.3.1.1. The Case of the Central American Group

A feature that has been scrutinized in the questionnaires sent to the founding members is the term 'accountability'. Only one of the three founding members interviewed said that there is an underlying commitment for all Group members to be accountable at domestic and regional levels. He added that it is of crucial importance to comply with the principle 'rendering of accounts' at both national and regional levels.[24] This statement implies that accountability does matter to the Group. Notwithstanding that it is not clear whether any accountability mechanisms previously envisaged in the Internal Guidelines have been implemented, either at the international level and/or at the domestic level. If the Group were to become formalized under the framework of SICA, the issue of accountability, at least at the regional level, may be covered. Consequently, at this stage, to ascertain whether the Group has been accountable ever since its inception in 2006, one should apply the four approaches to accountability and whether they have been addressed by the Group.[25]

#### 9.3.1.1.1 Accountability to Whom?

As the Council of Ministers of Economy of Central America (COMIECO) created the Group to deal with competition issues at the regional level, the Central American Group should theoretically report to COMIECO.[26] In practice, the Group regularly submits the minutes of the meetings to the Secretariat of the Central American Economic Integration Subsystem (SIECA) as the executive body of COMIECO.[27] Thus, COMIECO, being a part of the SIECA, delegated responsibility to the Central American

24 *Ibid.*

25 Four approaches of accountability: (1) Accountability to whom (delegation/internal v. participation/external; (2) Functions of accountability (why) – democratic, constitutional, learning; (3) Mechanisms of accountability (how) – international v. domestic; delegation v. legal; and (4) Timeline of accountability (when) – *ex ante* v. *ex post* activity. See Pauwelyn, 2012, see *supra* note 1.

26 The Creation of the Group. The Group was created by COMIECO, as the decision body of SIECA. Therefore, the Group stands before the COMIECO instance. In practice, every meeting (either virtual or not) will be reported to the SIECA Secretariat through the drafting of minutes.

27 The Group's decisions are expressed in minutes or even 'talking points' that are circulated after meetings for the members and its appropriate record to the SIECA Secretariat, the executive body of COMIECO.

Group to deal with competition issues at a regional level. However, given the relatively informal nature of the Group, there is no precise instruction on how each group is accountable to one another. There is a form of domestic accountability that can play a role, as the Group members individually report to their domestic constituencies in accordance with their respective legal system and domestic constraints. The domestic accountability lies in the legitimacy of competition policy enforcement at the local level gained through output legitimacy in the competition sphere, established by reputation among peers, and the quality of the legal and economic analyzes as represented in their decisions.[28]

#### 9.3.1.1.2 Functions of Accountability

First, regarding the democratic dimension of accountability, the Group appears not to be accountable to the constituency who originally conferred the decision making power, that is, the Group's creator: COMIECO. While it is true that the Central American Group could reach levels of accountability without necessarily having any democratic element – as there are other dimensions of accountability that should be taken into account – it should always aim at showing some level of responsiveness or representation. Otherwise, as the evidence shows, the fluctuating level of responsiveness has hampered the degree of accountability of the Group.[29]

Second, the constitutional dimension of accountability encompasses the prevention of the abuse of power and the need to impose checks and balances on power wielders. In the present case, COMIECO, the grantor of the Central American Group, is not sufficiently aware of the importance or the need to foster competition policy in the region and is consequently not exercising its power to implement its constitutional dimen-

[28] Imelda Maher, "The Rule of Law and Agency: The case of Competition Policy", IEP WP/06/01, International Economics Programme, London School of Economics, March 2006.

[29] Unfortunately this level of responsiveness often depends on the personal attitude of each of the members. Recently, the interviewees, as former founding members of the Group, have claimed that the level of responsiveness has changed during the lifespan of the Group due to specific attitudes based on just one or two members of the Network.

sion.[30] This observation can be attributed to the lack of an effective regional competition advocacy undertaken by the Central American Group.

Third, besides the analysis made *infra*[31] regarding the fundamental issue of confidentiality, essentially the Central American Group has learned from the mistakes and failures of other regional groupings with similar developments and circumstances. It appears that the Central American Group has taken into account the experience of the Andean Committee in terms of not enacting any regional competition norm before preliminary steps are observed to promote a competition culture, at the national level and then at the regional level.[32] In practice, the Central American Group has held its meeting and annual forums in a relatively closed manner which has allowed the members to speak freely about issues that are not spoken about in other forums. This particular feature justifies the alleged lack of transparency, accountability, formality (constitutional and democratic) of accountability that has been pointed out above.[33]

#### 9.3.1.1.3 Mechanisms of Accountability

To critically assess whether the Central American Group relies on domestic or international mechanisms to be accountable, it is important to ascertain the existing mechanisms available in this regard. As for the domestic mechanisms of accountability, it appears to be insufficient to address accountability of the Group by applying domestic rules because of the absence of empirical data that could sustain that all members of the Group

---

30 On the basis of the interviews with the Network participants and the author's personal experience, it appears that COMIECO and the SIECA Secretariat do not fully appreciate the extent of the minutes from all monthly virtual meetings.

31 See *infra* at Section 3: "Handling confidential information affects both accountability and effectiveness of networks: when the learning dimension of accountability may offer an opportunity" of the present critical assessment.

32 This strategy is precisely a recap of Section 6 in the IADB Project entitled "How the Group's activities are funded".

33 Members claim that the "secrecy" of their meetings is necessary due to the fact that there are different networks such as the International Competition Network (ICN), OECD Latin American Competition Forum and UNCTAD Intergovernmental Group of Experts on Competition Law and Policy, whereby Central American competition agencies do not have the opportunity to discuss freely their views on matters of relevance only to their markets. Hence, the Central American Group of Competition provides a distinctive forum in which all NCAs as exclusive members can exchange experiences and act as a unique voice before discussing issues at the different regional and worldwide networks on competition.

have a comparable degree of accountability. If evidence confirms that all network participants show an equivalent degree of domestic accountability, that assumption may ensure that the accountability of the Group as a whole is also addressed. In terms of the international sphere, the lack of legal status of the Group within the SIECA institutional framework hampers the redressing of SIECA mechanisms to ensure the accountability of the Group. The situation explained here sustains the accountability deficit present in the Group's activities as they fall outside the strictures of both domestic and international law.

Finally, the assessment whether the Group has devised, in a strict sense, institutionalized levels of accountability, governed by formal rules and procedures (and not, for example, accountability through markets or peer review), is crucial. On this particular point, the Internal Guidelines of the Group are deemed to be the main source of soft law that will govern the operation of the network. In practice, the Central American Group has observed relative adherence to the Internal Guidelines. The Group even continued into 2007 to assess whether the Internal Guidelines should be approved. It is therefore appropriate to ascertain that the Group does not have a formalized level of accountability with regards to the functioning of the network and how it is being managed.

#### 9.3.1.1.4 Timeline of Accountability

The IN-LAW methodology distinguishes between accountability of the decision-making process leading up to IN-LAW (*ex ante* activity), and accountability where judgments are made on activity that have already been addressed (*ex post* activity).[34] First, the accountability in the decision-making process is present in the Central American Group. Whilst the Group has not necessarily been involved in specific policy-making exercises, it is true that it has provided regulators with the necessary platform to freely exchange experiences on regional competition-related issues and sometimes even results in specific policy recommendations. The parties that are involved in this process are all network participants with a relatively high degree of influence on the decisions of other competition authorities that are more advanced than the others (that is, El Salvador and

[34] Pauwelyn, 2012, see *supra* note 1.

Costa Rica).[35] The principles guiding the decision-making process can be summarized as follows: (i) *Inclusiveness*, since, as any other network, the decision-making process has to include all members' views[36]; (ii) *Simple majority*: decisions are adopted on a simple majority basis having the necessary quorum to hold the meeting; (iii) *Flexibility in discussion topics;*[37] (iv) *Targeted binding effects only to relevant members*, those members that were not formally involved in the decision-making process will not be legally bound by the consequences, nor will they influence the outcome;[38] and (v) *Transparency*, which remains a delicate subject. While all members of the Group have access to all documentation such as minutes of the virtual and in-person meetings, technical background documents and public information is not easily accessible to outside members and the bulletin of the Group is the only information open to the public. Up to date, monthly virtual meetings are restricted and the Ministers of Economy were uncomfortable regarding the closeness involved in holding meetings.[39] The degree of transparency is further undermined by how the

---

35 In accordance with Article 18 of the Internal Guidelines, the decisions are adopted by simple majority (>50%) of the members attending the meeting. In case of a tie, the Pro tempore President has a deciding vote. There could be cases where the decisions will only have 'binding effects' for some member countries, in this particular assumption, the SIECA Secretariat will follow through for coherence with the overall objectives of the economic integration. The decisions that have a binding effect only for members will be gathered in official minutes by the Group member (apart from virtual meetings), and in other cases by the SIECA Secretariat.

36 However, Article 19 says that the minimum quorum for the meetings must use the 'half plus 1' formula.

37 It is, *e.g.*, possible to include additional topics prior to the meeting with a minimum of 48 hours notice.

38 There are some arguable comments on this point. As the Group is not a subsidiary organ of SICA, ergo, it does not have *erga omnes* effects elsewhere rather than the network itself. To this end, it is not clear what happens when a member is not in favor of a decision made by the Group or in the case that a member does not participate in the Group. Article 18 of the Internal Guidelines prescribes that "In the meetings, it could be possible to adopt decisions by some of the members. In this case, the decisions will be binding only to these members. In the latter, SIECA will have to follow-up the execution of the decisions in order to maintain and safeguard the objectives of the economic integration process". The decisions of the Group do not affect the states that are part of the Sub-System of Central American Economic Integration (SIECA), including their economic agents or institutions.

39 Celina Escolan, Former Head of the Salvadorian Competition Authority and one of the main founders of the Central American Group of Competition in 2006. Questionnaire respondent in August 2010.

Group reaches its decisions. This illustrates the 'power' granted to each member of the Group. For example, an outsider's request to view the agenda items at a virtual or annual meeting can be overturned by stating that the existing agenda (i) results from a decision taken on a consensus, and (ii) was circulated by the Rotating Presidency.

Second, in the *ex post* phase, as it regards judgments made upon activities of the Group, falls under the informal policy-making of the network under analysis related to the monitoring, compliance and enforcement mechanisms. The Pro Tempore President has the prerogative and authority to undertake monitoring and follow-up of decisions. In practice, all members of the Group are respectful towards the decisions made in the Group.[40] In addition, no reference is made to review mechanisms of decisions (feedback or regular updates). When referring to the role of domestic institutions in supporting the enforcement of these mechanisms, two dimensions are of interest: First, network participants are comprised of national institutions which have their own laws and regulations and thus they can be deemed as domestic institutions. Second, once the Group is legally formalized as a subsidiary body of SICA, which is a result of adopting the regional competition policy, then the domestic institutions will play a bigger role in enforcing the decisions taken by the Group. The reason is straightforward in this regard as the mere formalization of the Group as an instance of the economic integration process in Central America will have to be observed by member states.[41]

### 9.3.1.2. The Case of the Andean Committee

An underlying difference between the Andean Committee and the Central American Group is that the Committee has designed, at least from the reading of the Internal Regulations, a better degree of accountability. The

---

40 Throughout the Internal Guidelines, no reference is made with regard to administrative law-type principles (*e.g.*, access to information or review mechanisms for people affected or targeted, including transparency and reasoning, *etc.*). Nonetheless, the interviews of the founding members of the Group stated categorically that all decisions were made under strict consensus rule. Julio Bendaña, Oscar Lanza and Celina Escolán. Questionnaires sent in August 2010. However, evidence shows that at least in one case, the decision was made under simple majority, whereby the selection of a consultant to work under the technical assistance initiative described *supra* was not shared by all members of the Group (Minutes of 2010).

41 Lanza Rosales, *ibid.*

reason is that the Andean Committee, as part of the regional law enforcement scheme, has two primary and formal functions: (i) to assist in the investigations carried out by the Andean Community Secretariat and (ii) to undertake advocacy activities. The latter shows the different underlying approaches and intentions under which the Andean Committee was created. Its main purpose is to deal with cross-border investigations and assist the supranational authority in the investigations of cross-border anti-competitive behavior.

The case of the Central American Group shows a different scenario. The Group's major objective was merely to establish a forum of discussion and exchange experiences that may be geared towards the institutionalization of a regional competition authority in the future. Consequently, the degree of accountability in the Andean Committee was sound since its inception due to the ambitious objectives of cross-border competition case-handling in the region. This is discussed in detail in the following sections.

#### 9.3.1.2.1 Accountability to Whom?

The Andean Committee members are part of the Andean Community legal system and consequently have to report not only to the domestic constituencies but also to the regional institutions represented by the Andean Community Secretariat (ACS). The second paragraph of Article 4 of the Internal Regulations clearly states that in the case that any member of the Committee does not comply with the rights and obligations detailed in the first paragraph, the civil servant will incur functional liability in accordance with the domestic legislation of the Member State whose national authority is represented before the Committee. As the Committee has not yet been faced with any such situation, the application of the provision remains to be seen. However, it is the responsibility of the Committee to call upon and identify the civil servant that has incurred functional liability and therefore becomes subject to the enforcement of local punishing laws. Based on this particular provision, the Committee deals with the issue of accountability in both regional and domestic instances.

#### 9.3.1.2.2 Functions of Accountability

First, the Andean Committee, created by virtue of Article 38 of the Regional Competition Law Decision 608, is an essential part of the institutional mechanisms of the ACS. It institutionally interacts with the ACS by virtue of assistance in joint investigations. The Andean Committee, therefore, is accountable to the ACS as well as the Andean Community law and institutions. The Andean Committee is accountable to the constituency that originally conferred decision-making power to the Andean Community, which is essentially comprised of the Member States and its local or domestic institutions (democratic dimension of accountability). In this regard, the Andean Committee is responsive and representative of the national domestic constituencies that gave birth to the Andean Community of Nations in the 1960s.

Second, regarding the constitutional dimension, the agreed Internal Regulations provide the basis for this function in accordance with Article 4 in the case of any abuse of power or imbalances due to power wielders. In addition, the regional competition norm (Decision 608) prescribes a clear line of reporting and assistance between the Andean Committee and the ACS. This reveals the vertical network between these two institutions under the meaning of Slaughter's classification described *supra.*

Third, besides the issue of not effectively handling confidentiality issues examined *infra*[42] and from the primary sources of evidence, it appears that the learning dimension of accountability has not been taken into account during the operation of the Committee. The Andean Committee adopted ambitious objectives during the first three ordinary meetings that took place around the end of 2005. The Andean Community did not take into account the situation in two of the five members of the Community (Bolivia and Ecuador), as these two countries in 2005 did not have proper institutions to enforce competition laws in their domestic markets. The result of these two countries having poor national competition culture was that any advancement or action was irrelevant in terms of competition advocacy. The enforcement of competition laws at the regional level was not possible. The Andean Committee should have learned from the experiences of the EU establishing the European Competition Network during its period of legislation modernization. This network allocated cases and decentralized the investigation and enforcement of EU competition

[42] See *infra* in Section 9.3.3.: "Handling confidential information affects both accountability and effectiveness of networks: when the learning dimension of accountability may offer an opportunity".

rules.[43] The learning dimension in the case of Central American Group can prove usefulness in enhancing the responsiveness and effectiveness of the network. The Andean Committee should have reacted quickly towards the failure of not delivering results during the period 2005–2010 and learn their mistakes of the past.

#### 9.3.1.2.3 Mechanisms of Accountability

The use of the domestic legal systems to enforce accountability of the Committee serves the purposes of regional accountability of the Committee (dual accountability as explained *supra*). The legal mechanisms of accountability prescribed by Article 4 of the Internal Regulations are relevant to trigger any deviating conduct of the network participants.

#### 9.3.1.2.4 Timeline of Accountability

First, with regard to accountability within the policy-making process, the Andean Committee involves all members of the network and, as part of the Andean Community Law, member recommendations are fully endorsed and have legally binding effects not only on the members of the Committee but also at the domestic level.[44] Their strength is based on the legitimacy of policy recommendations endorsed by technical regulators (competition authorities) which are technically authorized to provide opinions at local and regional levels. Regarding the decision-making process, Article 15 of the Internal Regulations states that the Committee will

---

43 Frederic Jenny and Pierre M. Horna, "Modernization of the European system of Competition Law Enforcement: Lessons for other regional groupings", in Philippe Brusick, Ana Maria Alvarez and Lucian Cernat, *Competition Provisions in Regional Trade Agreements: How to Assure Development Gains*, United Nations, 2005, pp. 281–327. For a complete assessment of the ECN under accountability and effectiveness criteria, see Firat Cengiz, "Multi-level governance in Competition Policy: The European Competition Network", in *European Law Review*, 2010, vol. 35.

44 The legal effects at domestic and regional level are based on the particular dimension of regional competition law institutions of the Andean Community of Nations. The regional law has direct effect on member states. This is also endorsed by the technical discretionary feature of the Network participants, who are at the same time, competition authorities with domestic legitimacy. It is not possible to provide examples of this as there were only three ordinary meetings in 2005. The decisions should have bound the national authorities themselves to continue to meet but external circumstances had them resume their meetings in 2006 instead.

adopt its decisions under the consensus rule of the attendant members.[45] An important, distinct feature of the Andean Committee is the need to reach consensus on its decisions. In addition to its level of formality, as a formal network within the Andean Community legal system, the Committee's decisions have an *erga omnes* effect beyond its membership. Whereas the Central American Group upholds a simple majority rule, the Andean Committee requires unanimity as its decisions notably affect its members. In the Central American Group, binding effects are limited to the members who decide to vote; the informal nature of the Group shields outsiders from the effects of its decisions. In addition, the Internal Guidelines do not address administrative law-type principles (for example, access to information or review mechanisms for people affected or targeted transparency, reasoning, *et cetera*). Similarly, the regulations do not include action against stakeholders who, although not formally involved, may have substantial influence on the outcome but do not receive any repercussions. The regulation does not refer to the degree of the transparency in the decision-making process. However, it is noted that the minutes of the meetings should be made accessible to the public unless otherwise restricted by the authority to withhold documentation, especially in cases where Article 21 or 27 of the regional law are at stake.

Second, although the intent of the provisions was to foster a high level of accountability, the Andean Committee, unfortunately, has not been in operation since 2006. The reasons will be further examined *infra* when assessing the effectiveness of the Group and the issue of confidentiality.

### 9.3.2. Assessing the Level of Effectiveness in the Central American Group and the Andean Committee

Anderson convincingly states that real-world changes as a result of network effectiveness are what counts. He stresses that networks are merely a description of:

> bureaucratic outputs [where they] held meetings, wrote papers, made recommendations, and drafted statements. [...]

[45] An exception to this rule is when there are assumptions related to the application of Article 21 of the regional law (providing a formal opinion on case specific investigations handled by the Secretariat). In this case, it is mandatory for a qualified majority of at least three members to indicate a divergent opinion in writing.

> Yet unfortunately this is also precisely the procedure followed when networks create unsuccessful outcomes. Thus distinguishing between effective networks and bureaucratic black holes may prove difficult. [The] question [here is] whether horizontal networks achieve results, measured not by bureaucratic activity, but by real-world change.[46]

The above citation underpins the analysis of the effectiveness of these two government networks, and the following assessment thereof.

#### 9.3.2.1. Relatively Good Levels of Effectiveness and the Impact of the Central American Group

The effectiveness of the Central American Group may be regarded as a success. The informal forum of the classical horizontal government network of NCAs provided an important channel to share and exchange experiences amongst members during their monthly virtual meetings and annual discussion platforms. In addition, despite its lack of legal status, the Central American Group has acted as a single entity when interacting for fund-raising purposes. It has taken into account the experience of other regional groupings, such as the Southern American Government Network, and has been relatively effective during its first four years of existence.

##### 9.3.2.1.1 Does Cooperation Materialize?

The forum has created an excellent platform to exchange experiences on competition law enforcement and the possible application of the regional competition institutions in Central America. The fact that the number of member countries that had competition laws and institutions in 2006 (Costa Rica, El Salvador, and Honduras) increased to a majority of the members in 2012, shows the Group's impact.[47] After the creation of Procompetencia, the National Institute for the Promotion of Competition in Nicaragua in 2006,[48] it is expected that Guatemala will also be encour-

46 Anderson, 2004, pp. 1277, 1278, see *supra* note 11.

47 The first country in Central America to adopt a competition law was Costa Rica in 1995. A year later, Panama enacted its national law. El Salvador, Honduras, and Nicaragua adopted their competition laws in 2004, 2005, and 2006, respectively. Guatemala remains the only Spanish-speaking country in Central America to not have a competition law.

48 It must be noted that the real nomination of the Commissioners happened only on 11 May 2009.

aged to set up its national authority to deal with competition issues.[49] Next to this, it is important to note that even though Nicaragua did not have an established competition authority until 2009, in participated actively through the Directorate of Competition and Transparency of Market of the Ministry of Trade and Industry (MIFIC). Similarly, up to the present, Guatemala is represented in the Group by the Directorate of Competition of its Ministry of Economy.

#### 9.3.2.1.2 Does it Stick?

Despite the scarcity of resources, the Central American Group has held four annual forums since 2007 leading to three declarations. At the latest annual forum, held in Costa Rica from 21 to 22 October 2010, the importance of the forum's inputs and outcomes for the Central American region with regards to competition has been re-confirmed. In addition, the

49 In fact, several factors have led to the revival of the Central American Economic Integration process. Jorge Dominguez attempts to describe them as follows: "(i) Business firms led the revival of the Central American Common Market (CACM) in the late 1980s, taking advantage of the still-enduring 1960s CACM trade liberalization. Politicians followed business initiatives and re-started the CACM. CACM trade liberalization and central bank clearing would be the region's most lasting economic integration accomplishment. The CACM was reborn in the early 1990s lush with parchment institutions but the rules that worked were just those that had ever worked, namely, trade liberalization and central bank payments clearing, which were the most automatic and depended least on ongoing decision-making by politicians or CACM. Presidential initiative was a key reason for the flourishing of parchment institutions, and lack thereof for their weak institutional consolidation. No inter-state war broke out in the CACM after 1990 but militarized inter-state disputes were frequent. The CACM provided incentives to sustain inter-state peace but not enough to consolidate it; this failure probably hindered the deepening of regional economic integration. Structural asymmetries between CACM members remained the smallest in the Americas. For most of the 1990s and the 2000s, politically right-of-center parties governed throughout the CACM region. This political and economic regime homogeneity sustained market-oriented economic policies but did not prevent militarized inter-state disputes between like-minded governments. CACM dealt with its much more ambitious institutional agenda in the 1990s and 2000s by failing to ratify those most ambitious agreements or failing to implement them if ratified – the common external tariff was porous, the justices of the Central American Court were not busy. CACM countries had a mixed record of foreign economic policy coordination. Free trade with the US may weaken CACM and its institutions". Jorge I. Dominguez, "Regional Economic Institutions in Latin America: Politics, Profits, and Peace" (4 August 2010), available at http://ssrn.com/abstract=1653502, last accessed on 27 November 2011.

Group has followed the procedures set forth in the Internal Guides and held virtual monthly meetings. This is evidence of a strong and continued exchange of experiences among its members and its function as valid interface *vis-à-vis* international forums, including the OECD Latin American Forum, UNCTAD Intergovernmental Group of Experts (IGE) on Competition Law and Policy, and the Inter-American Development Bank (IADB).[50]

#### 9.3.2.1.3 Does it Solve the Problem?

The problem of effectively tackling cross-border anti-competitive practices has yet to be addressed.[51] One of the suggested approaches has been to closely examine the value added chain of cross-border markets such as the pharmaceutical sector. Another suggested approach has been to commission studies that would address finding the best institution within the existing regional integration schemes that may provide the facilities and infrastructure to deal with cross-border anti-competitive practices. The latter approach is the most important challenge to overcome in the Central American Group. In this regard, the Head of the Competition Authority in Honduras mentioned three important challenges of the Group: (i) the adoption of a Regional Competition Policy; (ii) the recognition of the Group as an instance (subsidiary body) of the Central American Integration System (SICA)[52]; and (iii) the passing of the competition law and institution in Guatemala.[53]

---

[50] The first annual forum was held in San Salvador on the occasion of the 4th meeting of the OECD Latin American Competition Forum from 11 to 12 July 2006, available at http://www.oecd.org/document/23/0,3343,en_40382599_40393122_40443671_1_1_1_1,00.html, last accessed on 27 November 2011.

[51] The Group has until this point only discussed the best route to approach this phenomenon.

[52] However, in an interview, Celina Escolán (Former Head of the El Salvador Competition Authority and advocate of the Group) suggests that it might not be convenient to formalize the instance of the Group under the SIECA because its headquarters is in Guatemala City and its bureaucrats do not understand the importance of adopting a competition regional policy. In addition, giving it a supranational nature is only possible under the Nicaraguan and Salvadorian Constitutional regimes. The remaining countries should be entering into constitutional reforms before creating a supranational entity under the SIECA regime. Furthermore, she added that SIECA Secretariat officials are interested in trade issues rather than competition issues. Mrs. Escolán, puts forward a 'coordinating regional office' whose objective should include fundraising activities, economic concentrations notifications at regional level (at least they should

#### 9.3.2.1.4 Does it Solve the Problem in a Cost-Effective Way?

Dealing with cross-border anti-competitive practices in Central America has been recognized as one of the most important challenges for the Group. However, the Group must take into account the importance of creating synergy and convergence of regional initiatives as to avoid the duplicity of efforts and to ensure that the ultimate goal of tackling international anti-competitive behavior is reached in a cost-effective way. The issue of promoting convergence and informed divergence should also be part of the outreach agenda of the Group. For instance, in the Central American region, regulators on economic issues and legislators have created their own network, the Forum of Presidents of Legislative Branches in Central America and the Caribbean (FOPREL).[54]

### 9.3.2.2. Lack of Effectiveness and Impact of the Andean Committee Since 2005: Identifying the Four Dimensions of Network Effectiveness

#### 9.3.2.2.1 Does Cooperation Materialize?

During the second half of 2005, ordinary meetings were held in September, October and November. As mentioned above, the Internal Regula-

inform all members as a fast-track mode), cartel investigations but not through mutual investigations (due to the confidential nature) but through regional studies on competition advocacy measures.

53 Lanza Rosales, *ibid.*

54 FOPREL has set out its own objectives: (a) To adopt holistic initiatives that aim at establishing and/or strengthening institutions supporting the development of a democratic culture, with emphasis on the public good; (b) To establish agile mechanisms based on consultations and initiative which lead to a common position based on solidarity, to protect the region's true interests in terms of social, economic and political growth in the region, when meeting with third-parties; and (c) To promote the development of legislative studies that can ensure regional exchanges and consultations, in order to efficiently enhance each country's handling of parliamentary exercises. In this regard, the participants in the recently organized UNCTAD Seminar on "Exchange of Experiences among Central American Competition Agencies, the Central American Court of Justice and Legislators with responsibilities on economic affairs" (25 June 2010) agreed to coordinate their activities of the different established networks and create synergies between its regional efforts, those from FOPREL parliaments, and the Central American Court of Justice. More information on the Managua Declaration see UNCTAD, "Managua Declaration, available at http://archive.unctad.org/templates/page.asp?intItemID=5509&lang=1, last accessed on 3 July 2012.

tions of the Committee were approved at the second meeting. Unfortunately, from 2006 to 2009, the Committee ceased operations as a result of several factors, including the change of political vision of the Bolivian government and the withdrawal of Venezuela as a member of the Andean Community, in 2006 and 2008, respectively.[55] However, from September to December 2005, the Committee did address several issues, including a cross-border investigation. The latter was conducted under Decision 285 and discussed at the request of the Colombian delegation.[56]

The output of the Committee was produced as envisaged in accordance with the work plan approved at the 2nd ordinary meeting of October 2005.[57] The Committee's work has gone beyond policy coordination. Had all the output been completed under this framework, it would have had legally binding consequences under the meaning of the regional law and the Andean Community legal system. Unfortunately, none of this work was carried out since no subsequent ordinary meetings took place. Nonetheless, the institutional framework and the legal provisions converged to promote an effective monitoring, compliance, and enforcement mechanism. In addition, the role of domestic institutions is envisaged in the en-

---

[55] "Increased domestic political heterogeneity weakened the prospects for the Andean Community and worsened inter-state disputes. The consolidation of the Hugo Chávez presidency upon surviving a failed coup attempt in 2002, and the forced departures from office of Bolivia's president Gonzalo Sánchez de Lozada and Ecuador's president Lucio Gutiérrez in 2003 and 2005, respectively, would leave the three countries with market-unfriendly governments. Colombia and Peru retained market-oriented economic policies and signed bilateral free-trade agreements with the United States"; Dominguez, see *supra* note 49.

[56] Minutes of the second ordinary meeting of the Committee on 3 October 2005; "Acta de la Segunda Reunión Ordinaria del Comité Andino de Defensa de la Competencia" (CDC) 3 de octubre de 2005, Lima–Perú, SG/R.CDC/II/ACTA 2.17.28, p. 11.

[57] *Ibid*, see Appendix III of the second ordinary meeting minutes, p. 10 referring to (i) Procedural Regulations of Decision 608 to apply the community competition law provisions; (ii) Procedural Regulations of Decision 608 as national law for Bolivia and Ecuador; (iii) Follow-up on the consultancy work undergone to evaluate the feasibility of adopting a community law on mergers and acquisitions; (iv) Proposal for a draft decision that will deal with unfair competition; and (v) Training workshops on recent regional legislation for Andean Community officials and Competition officials. In addition, it was envisaged to sensitize judges from the Andean Court of Justice. Particular reference to Bolivian and Ecuadorian government officials and Academics, Compilation of laws and jurisprudence on competition law in regulated sectors, and a Compilation of law and jurisprudence on competition law in order to continue the work of the EU Competition Project.

forcement of this internal regulation as the members of the Committee members have legal and domestic constraints which are sufficient to undertake the effective implementation of the Internal Regulations.

Regrettably, after the withdrawal of Venezuela from the Andean Community of Nations, the Committee went into a 'standstill situation' up to the present. However, with regards to real-world change, cooperation did take place under the basis of regional technical assistance program that attempted to bring together the Member countries of the Committee through different initiatives at regional level.

#### 9.3.2.2.2 Does it Stick?

No, it does not. Yet, the ongoing process of cooperation between NCAs of the Andean Community sub-region has been a major priority for the more established competition agencies in Colombia and Peru.

#### 9.3.2.2.3 Does it Solve the Problem?

Although the Committee did not serve its ultimate goal to investigate cross-border anti-competitive practices – since there is no case on record on the premises of the Andean Community of Law – there were competition related cases regarding the enforcement of IP laws and subsidies under regional laws.[58]

#### 9.3.2.2.4 Does it Solve the Problem in a Cost-Effective Way?

As it did not solve the problem of effectively tackling cross-border anti-competitive practices, this question cannot be answered.

58 The Tribunal of Justice of the Andean Community has ruled on a number of IP cases. Most of these cases have been related to prejudicial interpretations of national IP provisions raised by domestic judges. In this regard, the conclusion of these judgments is that the domestic judge should have the authority and competency to take into account the pre-judicial interpretation of the Andean Community Tribunal. See Jurisprudencia del Tribunal de Justicia de la Comunidad Andina XII, Tribunal de Justicia del Acuerdo de Cartagena, Quito, 2002, pp. 514–551. Gaceta Oficial del Acuerdo de Cartagena N° 1484 from 3 April 2007.

### 9.3.2.3. Promising Developments…

While the network effectiveness may be regarded as a failure from the perspective of the four dimensions of effectiveness, the regional competition law for the Andean Countries has been enforced at the domestic level. The situation has moreover dramatically changed as of 2010, with the emergence of vigorous Bolivian and Ecuadorian competition authorities. These authorities apply regional law at the national level by virtue of an authoritative regional provision of immediate effect at the national level. The Andean Committee is under re-activation, taking into account all the work carried out during the second half of 2005 and the willingness of international organizations to cooperate on this scheme.[59] The latter can be considered as a point of departure for the Andean Committee to re-start its operations. The institutional and legal framework are 100% implemented in Bolivia or Ecuador whereby effective competition law enforcement (using substantive regional law provisions) is taking place in these markets, fostering the consolidated competition culture in the remaining Andean countries: Colombia and Peru.[60] In summary, although it began its operations with challenging objectives and work plans, the Committee has had little success in terms of output and impact since its inception. An enormous effort took place to design the necessary institutional and legal structure of the Committee, and the creation of a supranational authority. Not only were there various external factors that undermined its work (withdrawal of Venezuela), but also the poor institutional development of Bolivia and Ecuador and network effectiveness issues, such as its inability to deal with confidentiality issues as explained *infra.*

59 With the Presidency of the Andean Community in Bolivia, the re-activation of the Andean Committee for the Defense of Competition is expected during the second half of 2010. In terms of impact during this assessment period, two new NCAs were established in the two most reluctant member countries towards the issue of regional competition law enforcement at the beginning of 2005. Also, applying a regional competition law at the national level boosted the Network's effectiveness in terms of reaching its ultimate goal; the spill-over effects of more advanced competition authorities to less advanced ones. With these two important premises, there is a promising future for the re-activation of the Committee.

60 For instance, prior to the enactment of the regional law, the international cooperation funded regional studies of the telecom market, surface transport, and agricultural market for Bolivia, Colombia, Ecuador, Peru and the Andean Community Secretariat.

### 9.3.3. Handling Confidential Information Affects Both the Accountability and Effectiveness of Networks: When the Learning Dimension of Accountability May Offer an Opportunity

The limitation imposed in most of the agreements with regard to the exchange of confidential information is a significant disadvantage for most Latin American countries. If confidential information located in a foreign jurisdiction is critical to a case, the constraint can be harmful. While several competition authorities consider this an area in need of improvement, it is noteworthy that the greatest limitation is the lack of specific conceptualization of the term 'confidentiality', since it carries a different definition depending on the legislation and/or competition authority. Regardless of the region where it operates (jurisdiction) and the level of institutional development of the networks, with or without a supranational authority dealing with cross-border anti-competitive practices, any competition authority has to face the issue of confidentiality. This major problem stems from having to handle confidential information that competition authorities become aware of when investigating anti-competitive business behavior.

Competition laws in many countries grant extensive power to competition authorities to facilitate the process of requesting different types of information from organizations under litigation. Nonetheless, competition authorities are cautious in exercising such powers. The power to collect economic information from businesses, particularly information of a strategic, competitive nature, has often been a matter of contention between enforcement agencies and the business community.[61] If the competition authority misuses confidential information received from businesses,[62] the competition authority might be subject to prosecution and legal liability. The issue of how to properly handle confidential information can affect the accountability and effectiveness of the networks involved. But moreover, it could lose its domestic reputation and legitimacy, thereby harming

[61] De Leon, see *supra* note 3.

[62] There is always a risk of misusing the information whenever the authority receives it. In addition, the risk increases when information is shared with other agencies of a given network. There will no doubt be more resistance to disclosure of information because activities can go from being legal in one country but illegal when it crosses the national boundary. Businesses have the right to sue their respective local authorities if they breach confidentiality by disclosing information with authorities abroad.

the constitutional and democratic dimensions of accountability under the meaning of IN-LAW. In turn, if the competition authority is unable to disclose confidential information to its peers within a transnational network of competition authorities during a joint investigation, then lack of information could undermine the effectiveness of the network due to incapacity to hold a thorough investigation. In this sense, it would not be possible to see whether cross-border anti-competitive practices are distorting competitive market conditions at a regional or international level.

The enforcement of competition laws between agencies at the international level is even more susceptible to coordination issues due to the lack of infrastructure/legal authority partnered with a lack of trust in other competition agencies abroad. Due to inexperience, these young agencies cannot monitor cartel activities or impose reasonable sanctions on businesses if found guilty of anti-competitive practices. Moreover, the process is complex and costly, a high burden for these developing countries.[63] Agencies often do not share confidential information with other jurisdictions because of restrictions in their own national laws. However, successful examples of coordination between agencies have led to a growing number of multilateral agreements between Central American countries to share confidential information across borders. The ease of process to share information has been established for countries such as Canada and the Republic of Costa Rica, which have agreed to a bilateral trade agreement (NAFTA) which states that both countries have an obligation to disclose confidential information, even if the exchange is not permitted by their national legislation. Other successful cases of bilateral agreements in Latin America that promote the application of competition laws and the exchange of confidential information include the agreement between the National Institute for the Defense of Competition and Intellectual Property Protection (INDECOPI) and the Superintendency of Industry and Commerce of Colombia (SIC). The agreement allows for the exchange of

[63] For example, the authority of Costa Rica has signed agreements on cooperation on competition with the Commission for the Defense and Promotion of Competition of the Republic of Honduras, the Institute for Promotion of Competition (Pro Competition) of the Republic of Nicaragua, the Superintendence of Competition of El Salvador and the Authority for Consumer Protection and Competition in Panama among others. While these agreements are intended to promote free competition last in the region, these efforts have been overshadowed by the lack of agreement on the exchange of confidential information between authorities, mainly due to the limitations of their domestic laws on the subject.

confidential information and requires both authorities to maintain the confidentiality of information shared between them and use this information solely for the purposes of application of competition law. In addition, agencies are not permitted to disclose any information to third parties by an agreement of mutual responsibility in matters of misuse of information.[64]

On the other hand, there are several countries like Guatemala who are still in the development phase of drafting legislation to face cross-border antitrust issues. When asked in an UNCTAD questionnaire to competition authorities in Central America, many of the countries indicated that they were not allowed to respond favorably when asked to cooperate with requests dealing with cross-border antitrust cases.[65] Another example includes Honduras, after it signed bilateral agreements with Costa Rica, El Salvador and Panama. Panamanian authorities noted that disclosure to transnational competition authorities is not necessary, stating that "Neither party is obliged to provide information to the other party if the disclosure of this information is prohibited by law or regulation of the party possessing the information or has been declared confidential".[66] The following paragraphs explore ways in which to approach the issue of confidentiality. In a specific scenario where both competition networks under assessment have not yet dealt with the issue of confidentiality, the learning dimension of accountability, as Pauwelyn suggests, "could offer an opportunity for learning through improvement upon earlier mistakes or public exposure of failure. Making a network more accountable in this sense can also make it more effective".[67]

#### 9.3.3.1. Timing: Formal Cooperation Implemented Too Early in the Andean Committee

The 2005 adoption of the regional law has bypassed necessary stages (advocacy, confidentiality, and building trust among competition authorities). This in turn has undermined the effectiveness and efficiency of the regional norm, thereby causing failure to tackle the ultimate goal of elimi-

64 UNCTAD, Commission on Trade and Development, Review of the experience gained so far in enforcement cooperation, including at the regional level, Geneva 2011, p. 11.

65 "Substantive analysis and case studies of national laws of Costa Rica, Honduras, Nicaragua, El Salvador and Guatemala" , UNCTAD Questionnaire – Primary source.

66 *Ibid.*

67 Pauwelyn, 2012, see *supra* note 1.

nating cross-border anti-competitive practices. The latter has brought about a 'regrettable' and 'paradoxical' situation of the Andean Committee within the Community Regional Competition Law Enforcement where the regional law (not having first solved the problem of confidentiality) became a 'barrier to cooperation' rather than a vehicle for sharing information and experience. Colombia might have an enormous resistance to cooperation with Bolivia and Ecuador regarding some case investigations as any commitment to cooperate might result in formal internal investigations against Colombia's own national enterprises.[68]

Critically, one should strike a balance between the levels of formality and informality when dealing with previous steps in order to build trust among peer authorities and, at the same time, to raise awareness of the need for convergence of domestic rules that deal with confidential information. While the experience of the Andean Committee (a relatively formal network) shows excessive optimism in terms of enforcing rules without observing necessary steps, the rules of the operation of the Central American Group (an informal network) evidences a great deal of caution in moving forward the institutional framework needed to undertake joint investigations or even cross-border investigations by a supranational authority. Each of these cases shows the advantages and disadvantages of formal and informal networks and there is evidence that an important issue should always be taken into account: timing. A further reflection on the issue of confidentiality is in order. Even if we solve the problem of confidentiality, there should be an additional level of convergence in investigation and on the imposition of sanctions and remedies. However, it is clear that securing confidentiality as a prerequisite to establishing trust between competition authorities should be dealt with first and thereby smoothen relations between the networks as a whole.

#### 9.3.3.2. The 'Division of Labor' between Formal and Informal Networks

The experiences and lessons learned from the assessed two networks is complex because high levels of formality have discouraged authorities

[68] The experience was shown in the minutes of 2005, when Colombia was requesting to withdraw the competence of the Andean Community Secretariat on a case that involved Colombian companies. Minutes of the 2nd ordinary meeting of the Committee on 3 October 2005, see *supra* note 56.

from cooperating together, as witnessed by the Andean Committee. But at the same time, this level of formality was needed in order to launch cross-border investigations. Therefore, an informal network would be limited when it comes to enforcing cross-border investigations. At best, it could have helped to launch joint case investigations but each authority would have been handling its investigations and rulings separately. A balance between formality and informality is actually needed between authorities to increase the effectiveness of the networks and in the learning dimension of accountability. The latter can offer scenarios as to when to increase or to decrease the 'intake' of formality of the competition networks.[69]

The above leads to establish a 'division of labor' between formal and informal networks. For instance, formal networks are appropriate to protect sensitive information gathered from investigations and to enforce the exchange of experiences when needed among network participants. In turn, informal networks should be designed to create convergence and inform divergent objectives (rationale of information in horizontal networks[70]) that do not require additional formalization of the actions and obligations of the network participants.

The evidence based on the Central American Group performance demonstrates the adverse effects and pitfalls of mixing together formal and informal networks. In other words, despite the Central American Group's relatively good effectiveness as assessed *supra*, its accountability performance under the meaning of IN-LAW did not reach optimal levels. The most important objection to be made to the Group concerns the transparency of its decision-making process and its excessive technocracy. In this regard, network participants suggested that this particular shortcoming has been the cause of the optimum level of network effectiveness, because technocracy allowed officials to come together off-shore, free from the usual intrusions of public representatives and private interest groups. At the same time, the Central American Group, acting as an informal network, has provided an excellent vehicle for sharing information that is not sensitive. If the network members wish to go further on this issue, they should be first formalized as an instance of the SIECA or COMIECO in order to force Central American businesses to disclose sensitive infor-

69 See *supra* sections on the functions of accountability of the two networks under assessment.

70 Slaughter, 2005, see *supra* note 19.

mation. Again, the issue of convergence of domestic laws on confidential information and business secrets should take place.

In conclusion, the built-in *effectiveness* and *accountability* criteria of informal and formal networks should respond to different objectives and strategies. One should not mix these objectives because they may be undermined by themselves. For example, formal networks may not fulfill their functions (that is, competition authorities cannot exchange confidential information for use in cross-border international cartels joint investigations) because of the levels of intrusion of informality that jeopardize the needed levels of formality. Similarly, informal networks may not achieve their ultimate objectives (*id est*, exchange of experiences and open discussion on topics of common concern) because there are certain levels of (unnecessary) formality that simultaneously undermine these objectives.

#### 9.3.3.3. Topics for Further Research on How to Improve the Level of Sharing Information When Dealing with the Issue of Confidentiality

To improve the level of information sharing among regulators in transnational networks and thereby improving its effectiveness, one could suggest disaggregating the type of information that is covered by confidentiality clauses.[71] For instance, when anti-competitive practices such as unilateral conduct (abuse of a dominant position in the market) or horizontal agreement occurs (price fixing among competitors) and protected information is illegally obtained, these business entities are not protected under

[71] It is of crucial importance to expressly determine which type of information should be protected. For instance, in Costa Rica, there is specific legislation with regards to the type of information that should be protected and which should not be protected. See the Article 2 related to the scope of protection of the "Ley de Información no divulgada". In addition, the types of information generated by competition authorities are generally: (i) responses to commission questionnaires; (ii) key arguments and views of the main parties; (iii) key arguments and views of third parties; (iv) the survey commissioned by main and third parties; (v) the survey commissioned by the commission; and (vi) information received during the course of hearings, meetings and telephone conversations. For more information see Brendan Sweeney, *The Internationalisation of Competition Rules,* Routledge Research in Competition Law, 2010, pp. 297–329.

any law or statute (that is, IP laws).[72] In this particular case, if networks were willing 'to disaggregate' the exchange-of-experience cooperation on certain types of information, then cooperation would be more effective. Different authorities are likely to handle this information in order to prosecute their own cases individually at the domestic level. In order to reach this level of 'disaggregated cooperation', network participants should be able to identify and define what confidential information is and what it is not. In addition, converging definitions of confidential information should also be part of their respective domestic legal systems. During issues related to merger notifications, one could think of types of information that could be shared among national regulators. This could be the basis for the analysis or assessment of mergers in each jurisdiction. The EU experience on this particular topic should be taken into account, particularly the experience of the European Competition Network (ECN).[73]

### 9.4. Lessons Learned and Recommendations

The evaluation of the life-cycle of these two government networks as assessed in the earlier sections shows that accountability and effectiveness are interdependent and cannot be assessed separately, since that would only reveal a partial landscape of reality.

On the surface, one could confirm the thesis that "increased effectiveness requires a reduction in accountability". The Central American

[72] The author believes that the existence of cartels should not be subject to the obligation of confidentiality, for instance, a recently discovered cartel in the market for wheat in El Salvador. In this particular market, allegations suggested that the business manager discovered information that was presumably covered by IP laws but indeed was completely illegal. In addition, in Costa Rica, a similar experience occurred regarding sacrosanct business information. Indeed, in the recent competition law reform process, the Costa Rican Parliament vetoed the possibility of sharing information with other competition authorities. The latter shows the complexity of the issue, since not only does the private sector seem naturally cautious about disclosing information to authorities but also legislators are extremely about sharing information with authorities that they do not trust. An example to illustrate this point can be seen when consultants encountered resistance when undertaking regional market studies in the pharmaceutical sector. They were unwilling to share price information, which is classified as a confidential trade secret. An interview carried out with the former head of the Salvadorian Competition Authority.

[73] Daniel Reichelt, "To What Extent Does the Cooperation Within the European Competition Network Protect The Rights of Undertakings?", in *Common Market Law Review*, 2005, vol. 42, pp. 745–782.

Group's low degree of accountability is offset by its higher level of effectiveness and its promising future negotiations toward the adoption of a Central American competition law. In turn, the assumption that "more accountability will hamper effectiveness" is demonstrated by the empirical evidence from the Andean Committee. Even in the case of the Committee's imminent re-activation, this fact might not be enough to start up a cross-border investigation because the issue of confidentiality would have to be dealt with first. To this end, there might be several ways to deal with the issue of confidentiality but that would start with existing domestic laws on the protection of sensitive information. The latter remains a topic for further research that goes beyond the scope of the present contribution.

Yet, this is only the tip of the iceberg. A more substantive point is that both accountability and effectiveness levels can eventually go hand in hand when the *learning dimension* of the mistakes from the past (a dimension of accountability related to responsiveness) can prompt actions that aim at increasing network effectiveness in the future. That could apply to the issue of confidentiality, which proves to be a major obstacle for further cooperation of these networks, as it could possibly undermine their effectiveness. As they build trust in each other's network, participants may also understand the need for public exposure and regional accountability with regards to the attainment of the overall objectives of the network, affirming the very existence of the networks. The empirical evidence shows, unfortunately, that neither of these networks has successfully handled the issue of confidentiality. The latter remains a serious constraint to further effectiveness improvement. Ideas for further research on means to strengthen confidentiality and disaggregated information at the regional level have been set forth above.

To foster both accountability and effectiveness, the assessed two government networks should focus on achievable objectives resulting from the competitive advantages for each network participant. They should refrain from setting unrealistic objectives from the onset, witness the failure of the Andean Committee to establish formal networks, and take the initiative to set the stage for regulators to freely share their experiences. For eventual effectiveness and impact of the network, trust must be built amongst the member participants (an internal aspect) first and this will strengthen the competition culture in the sub-regions covering the NCAs (external aspect). Regarding the latter, network participants should be aware of the limitations of the network[74] and be conscious of how and when the network can deal with the issue of confidentiality.

### 9.4.1. For the Central American Group

- Increase transparency to enhance accountability levels. Efforts should be made for these two government networks to be as visible as possible and in a position to link with other networks such as legislators and judges in Central American and the Southern subregions of Latin America.[75] In addition, to avoid technocracy at all levels and secrecy of the decision making process in the meetings, there should be a strategy to include key stakeholders and observers from the international arena. Regional businesses or NGOs should be involved once the institutional framework is set up in a later stage.[76]
- Raise awareness of the importance of regional competition law (effectiveness measure). These activities should be targeting the COMIECO and SIECA officers in order to sensitize the importance of regional competition policy for the Central American region. The ideal strategy would consist in undertaking regional sectoral, in-depth studies of key economic sectors common to at least three Central American countries.[77] In addition, there should be a detailed survey of all major alleged anti-competitive transnational practices.

---

[74] Indeed, the Network limitations raised here in addressing the first stage in this process (confidentiality) may not be attained through informal networks. With very unique examples in the world (the EU experience with the European Competition Network-ECN), a network in itself cannot necessarily address effective international cartels. For the comparison between ECN and other regional groupings, see Frederic Jenny and Pierre M. Horna, 2005, see *supra* note 43.

[75] See *supra* note 54 on FOPREL and the strategy presented by Kenneth Abbott in Kenneth W. Abbott and Duncan Snidal, "Strengthening International Regulation through Transnational New Governance: Overcoming the Orchestration Deficit", in *Vanderbilt Journal of Transnational Law*, 2009, vol. 42, no. 501, pp. 503–577.

[76] The issue of domestic democratic oversight and global democracy should be addressed when COMIECO decides to set up the institutional framework capable of investigating cases at the regional level.

[77] During the fourth annual forum of the Central American Group, findings of the study of pharmaceutical sector were presented to the audience. Observers from UNCTAD and IADB attended the meeting.

To carry out these studies, the Group should strengthen the participation of all market participants at the regional level.

- Create a supranational authority within COMIECO's institutional structure (effectiveness measure). The terms of reference for a study that will provide the institutional framework for the regional competition norm were discussed at the fourth annual forum of the Central American Group.[78] With the aim of investigating cross-border business behavior that distorts competition at the regional level, it seems that changes in the structure of COMIECO may take place in 2011.[79]
- Once the supranational authority is created, the issue of confidentiality can be subsequently dealt with. The idea of disaggregating cooperation, in sharing types of information that is normally handled by competition authorities, could be further explored in the event that the Central American Group would be institutionalized.

### 9.4.2. For the Andean Committee

- Re-activation of its operations of immediate effect (accountability and effectiveness). In view of the different institutional development of Bolivia and Ecuador from that of 2005, the re-activation of the Andean Committee should be the first priority in the short-run. Currently, Bolivia, holding the Andean Community Presidency, is about to call for a first meeting of the Andean Committee with the participation of observers from international organizations such as UNCTAD.
- Assistance in increasing the technical knowledge in the Andean Community Secretariat (accountability and effectiveness). Perhaps one of the weak points of the ACS was its low level of technical knowledge on competition law and policy. The reliance of major agencies such as Colombia and Peru (national constituencies) was a further drawback that will be addressed by the Andean Committee once it commences.

---

78 The annual forum was held recently in Costa Rica from 21 to 22 October 2010.

79 Recent interviews with the members of the Central American Group of Competition at the fourth Annual Forum of the Group held in Costa Rica from 21 to 22 October 2010.

- Update its Internal Regulations adopted in 2005. The Internal Regulations should be amended to provide a forum for the exchange of experiences and outreach activities in competition law at the regional level. To date, the regulations have focused on case-related assistance. The latter should come in a later stage.
- Once the Committee is operational, the issue of confidentiality can be dealt with to increase cooperation. The previous recommendation, related the re-activation of the Committee, will provide the basis for free discussion, including discussions on issues of confidentiality and how competition authorities can handle and share sensitive information amongst authorities. In this regard, important challenges will be faced such as whether informal networks present an alternative to more formal cooperation networks. Throughout this chapter, two government networks have been scrutinized through the use of accountability and effectiveness benchmarks. In view of the results, it appears that informal networks can indeed present an alternative, provided that network participants strike a coherent balance between appropriate levels of accountability (learning from past mistakes) and institutional effectiveness (establishing attainable objectives) within the framework of IN-LAW mechanisms.

# PART III

# HEALTH, FOOD AND SOCIAL STANDARDS

# 10

# Informal International Lawmaking in Medical Products Regulation

**Ayelet Berman**[*]

## 10.1. Introduction

In the past two decades, regulatory authorities have increasingly been in the business of harmonizing rules with their foreign counterparts.[1] This chapter focuses on three networks of regulatory authorities and industry that have been active in the business of harmonizing medical-products related rules: the International Conference on the Harmonization of Technical Requirements for Registration of Pharmaceuticals for Human Use (ICH), the International Cooperation on Harmonization of Technical Requirements for Registration of Veterinary Medicinal Products (VICH), and the Global Harmonization Task Force/International Medical Devices Regulators Forum (GHTF/IMDFR). These networks are informal at all three levels defined by Pauwelyn,[2] and as such fall within the category of IN-LAW bodies. This contribution's purpose is first, to provide an overview of these networks, and second, to derive some common features and characteristics that they share.

---

[*] **Ayelet Berman** is a Ph.D. Candidate in the International Law Unit at the Graduate Institute of International and Development Studies in Geneva and a Research Associate at the Centre for Trade and Economic Integration (CTEI). Before her Ph.D. studies, Berman was an Associate at Herzog, Fox and Neeman in Tel Aviv, Israel, and at Sidley Austin LLP in Geneva. Previously, she also held teaching and research assistantship positions in constitutional and administrative law at the Hebrew University of Jerusalem, Israel. She holds a LL.B. magna cum laude from the Hebrew University of Jerusalem, and a D.E.A. in International Law from the Graduate Institute. The author expresses thanks to the former and current employees of drug regulatory authorities, intergovernmental organizations, industry associations, and NGOs who have generously provided interviews.

[1] Anne-Marie Slaughter, *A New World Order*, Princeton University Press, Princeton, 2004.

[2] Joost Pauwelyn, "Informal International Lawmaking: Framing the Concept and Research Questions", in Joost Pauwelyn, Ramses A. Wessel and Jan Wouters (eds.), *Informal International Lawmaking*, Oxford University Press, Oxford, 2012, pp. 13–34.

The networks' main objective is to harmonize regulations and guidelines that set out the technical requirements for the registration of medical products. The medical products that are the subject matter of these networks are pharmaceuticals for human use (ICH), pharmaceuticals for animal use (VICH), and medical devices (GHTF/IMDFR). As a general rule, before a medical product can be sold, the responsible regulatory authority of the country where it will be used must authorize it. Normally, a law setting out the principal requirements for marketing authorizations should exist, and it will typically require that the safety, efficacy, and good quality of the medical product at hand be demonstrated. Regulatory authorities need to implement this legislation, and so many regulatory authorities have regulations and guidelines that outline the technical requirements (for example testing methods) underlying these principal requirements.

The three major markets for medical products have traditionally been the United States (US), Europe, and Japan. In the beginning of the 1990s they dominated 95% of the global market for medical products. At that time, trade in medical products was becoming increasingly international. And while all three had marketing authorization systems in place that were based on the same (safety, efficacy and quality) principles, the detailed technical requirements in each region differed. For the industry, this meant duplicating consuming and expensive test procedures and submitting different and burdensome applications to each region. The discrepancies in the technical requirements, hence, hampered trade and delayed the arrival of new products in different jurisdictions. From a public perspective, there were also growing expectations that there should be a minimum of such delay.

Against this backdrop, drug and medical device regulatory authorities and their respective industries decided to get together and harmonize such technical requirements. It was thought that harmonization would not only save producers time and costs, but would likewise benefit regulators that could more easily exchange information on complex scientific data. All this in turn would directly benefit patients who would have faster access to medical products.

As we shall see in this chapter, while dealing with different subject matters, the networks that were set up share several common features that, taken together, teach us about the state and problems of IN-LAW, at the very least in the context of medical product regulation. The networks are public-private bodies in which regulatory authorities and industry collaborate. They have administrative-like guideline development procedures, and fairly formal governance bodies. Moreover, from an institutional perspective, the networks were set up as clubs of developed countries, but they are now in the process of undergoing structural changes so as to better reflect the shift in the global medical products market that is taking place. In a related manner, the focus of the networks is also shifting from developing new guidelines towards encouraging non-member countries to adopt their guidelines. Further, we see the complementary relations between the networks and treaty-based intergovernmental organizations, as the latter have a supporting and at times active role in disseminating the networks' guidelines to non-members.

This chapter is organized as follows: Section 10.2. provides an overview of the ICH, Section 10.3. of the VICH and Section 10.4. of the GHTF/IMDRF. In each of these sections, the contribution addresses the following elements: (1) Background, (2) Legal Framework, (3) Members, (4) Other Participants, (5) Governance Structure, (6) Guideline Development Procedure, (7) Content of the Guidelines, (8) Globalization and Expansion of Participation, and (9) Adoption of Guidelines. Section 10.5. concludes and derives the network's common features and characteristics, thereby contributing to our understanding of how IN-LAW, at the very least in the regulation of medical products, works.

## 10.2. International Conference on the Harmonization of Technical Requirements for Registration of Pharmaceuticals for Human Use

### 10.2.1. Background

The ICH is a network of drug regulatory authorities and research-based industry associations from the US, EU, and Japan. It was established in 1991.[3] At the time, the pharmaceutical market had become increasingly international and the discrepancies in the technical requirements among the major trading partners – the US, the EU and Japan – was hampering

[3] Patrick F. D'Arcy and D.W.G. Harron, *Proceedings of the first International Conference on Harmonisation: Brussels 1991,* Queens University, Belfast, 1992.

trade and delaying the introduction of new drugs.[4] Given this background, and in light of the fact that the EU had successfully completed harmonization of European pharmaceutical technical requirements, the parties began discussions towards international harmonization. The discussions first began within the World Health Organization's (WHO) environment – particularly at the 1989 WHO Conference of Drug Regulatory Authorities. It quickly became clear, however, that most drug innovation was taking place in the 'triad', whereas developing countries did not have any particular interest in this topic (being mostly concerned with generic medicines) and also lacked resources to participate in such an initiative. Adopting the public-private network model, which Europeans had relied on for European harmonization, the parties set up the ICH.[5]

Traditionally, the ICH's main purpose has been the harmonization of technical requirements as to the safety, efficacy and quality of new drugs. Essentially, the work on the development of harmonized guidelines is almost complete, and the ICH's main focus nowadays is achieving global harmonization by supporting non-ICH countries in their adoption of ICH guidelines. This is discussed in greater length below.

### 10.2.2. Legal Framework

From a traditional international law perspective, the ICH lacks international legal personality. Nevertheless, the organization has several basic documents setting out the framework for its operations, such as the ICH's 'Terms of Reference'[6] and the Global Cooperation Group's (GCG) 'Terms of Reference'. Several documents are relevant for the guideline development procedure, such as the 'Formal ICH Procedure' (setting out the procedure for developing a new guideline),[7] the 'Question and Answer

4 ICH, "History", available at http://www.ich.org/about/history.html, last accessed on 21 November 2011.

5 For a detailed overview of the causes and events that led up to the ICH, see Ayelet Berman, "The Public-Private Nature of Harmonization Networks", Informal International Law Making Workshop, NIAS, the Hague, Netherlands, 2011, available at http://graduateinstitute.ch/ctei/home/working_papers.html, last accessed on 21 November 2011.

6 ICH, "Vision", available at http://www.ich.org/about/vision.html, last accessed on 21 November 2011.

7 ICH, "Formal ICH Procedure", available at http://www.ich.org/about/process-of-harmonisation/formalproc.html, last accessed on 21 November 2011.

Procedure' (a mechanism by which implementation advice may be requested),[8] the 'Revision Procedure' (revision of existing guidelines),[9] and 'Maintenance Procedure' (adding standards to existing guidelines).[10]

### 10.2.3. Members

The ICH is a public-private body and its members are drug regulatory authorities and research-based industry associations from the EU, Japan, and US. The regulatory authorities are the US Food and Drug Administration (FDA),[11] the European Commission DG Health and Consumers, the European Medicines Agency (EMA), the Japanese Ministry of Health, Labor & Welfare (JMHLW), and the Japanese Pharmaceuticals and Medical Devices Agency (JPMDA). The industry associations are the Pharmaceutical Research and Manufacturers Association of America (PhRMA), the European Federation of Pharmaceutical Industries' Associations (EFPIA), and the Japanese Pharmaceutical Manufacturers Association (JPMA).[12]

Such collaboration of regulatory authorities with industry associations has led to criticism that the ICH is a commercially driven process that has difficulty maintaining a public health-oriented approach.[13] On the other hand, the main argument in support of this joint structure has been that it provides regulators with direct access to expertise and the latest technological and scientific thinking.[14] Industry has much more resources,

---

8 ICH, "Q&A Procedure", available at http://www.ich.org/about/process-of-harmonisation/qa-procedure.html, last accessed on 21 November 2011.

9 ICH, "Revision Procedure", available at http://www.ich.org/about/process-of-harmonisation/revision-procedure.html, last accessed at 21 November 2011.

10 ICH, "Maintenance Procedure", available at http://www.ich.org/about/process-of-harmonisation/maintenance-procedure.html, last accessed on 21 November 2011.

11 Technical experts are drawn from FDA's Center for Drug Evaluation and Research (CDER) and the Center for Biologics Evaluation and Research (CBER).

12 ICH, "Steering Committee", available at http://www.ich.org/about/organisation-of-ich/steering.html, last accessed on 21 November 2011.

13 WHO, "Report of a WHO Meeting: The Impact of Implementation of ICH Guidelines in Non-ICH Countries", 2001, available at http://apps.who.int/medicinedocs/pdf/h2993e/h2993e.pdf, last accessed on 21 November 2011; John Abraham and Tim Reed, "Trading Risks for Markets: The International Harmonisation of Pharmaceuticals Regulation", in *Health, Risk and Society*, 2001, vol. 3, pp. 113–128.

14 EMA, "Overview of Comments Received on Draft Guideline Procedure for EU Guidelines and Related Documents within the Pharmaceutical Legislative Framework", Doc. Ref. EMEA/125817/2004, 24 June 2005, available at http://www.

manpower and expertise on technical issues than regulators, which are always short of resources. And so in keeping up with the newest developments and regulating effectively, regulators are dependent on industry.[15]

### 10.2.4. Other Participants

Besides members (that have decision-making power in the consensus based procedure – see below), there are additional participants that take part in the process, but are not (at least formally) among the decision makers: Observers and Interested Parties.

#### 10.2.4.1. Observers

The ICH has three formal observers: (i) Health Canada, the Canadian drug regulatory authority; (ii) the WHO, and (iii) EFTA countries (de facto represented by Swissmedic, the Swiss drug regulatory authority). The observers lack decision-making power but may attend the ICH meetings.[16]

The WHO acts as a link between ICH members and non–ICH members (particularly developing countries). It circulates ICH draft guidelines for comments by non-ICH countries, and disseminates the final guidelines too. Being a universal organization that encompasses both ICH members and non-ICH countries as its members, the WHO's role is to liaise between the conflicting interests of its members. ICH members are high-income countries, interested in new pharmaceutical innovation, whereas non-ICH countries are emerging and developing countries, interested in affordable pharmaceuticals, and generic medicines.[17] The WHO also has a role in facilitating training efforts aimed at strengthening regulator capacity and harmonization activities of non-ICH countries.

---

ema.europa.eu/docs/en_GB/document_library/Other/2009/10/WC500004015.pdf, last accessed on 21 November 2011.

15 Berman, 2011, see *supra* note 5.

16 Steering Committee, see *supra* note 12.

17 While the WHO encourages harmonization, it has, as its priority, the global access to essential medicines of good quality. See Dr. Lembit Rägo, "Mechanism for Outreach beyond ICH Participants", The Sixth ICH, Osaka, Japan, 12–15 November 2003, available at http://www.ich.org/LOB/media/MEDIA1383.pdf, last accessed on 21 November 2011.

### 10.2.4.2. Interested Parties

Interested Parties are those organizations that are expected to implement or to be regulated by the outcome of ICH efforts. These include the World Self-Medication Industry (WSMI) and the International Generic Pharmaceutics Alliance (IGPA). Originally, the purpose was for ICH guidelines to apply to the approval of new pharmaceuticals, but over time, some ICH guidelines (in particular those on quality) have been used to approve generic medicines. Consequently, the generic industry has an interest in the ICH process too. Other interested parties may also be determined by the Steering Committee over time. For example, the Over-the-Counter industry and pharmacopoeial authorities have also been invited to send representatives to some of the EWGs.[18]

## 10.2.5. Governance Structure

ICH conducts its business through several organs, in particular the Steering Committee, Informal Working Groups, Experts Working Groups, and Implementation Working Groups (as well as other specific working groups).[19] Furthermore, there is a Global Cooperation Group, a Regulators Forum and a Secretariat.

### 10.2.5.1. Steering Committee

The Steering Committee governs the ICH, determines its policies and procedures, selects topics for harmonization and monitors the progress of harmonization initiatives.[20] The six founding members each have two seats. Observers may attend too. The International Federation of Pharmaceutical Manufacturers and Associations (IFPMA) (which provides secretariat services) also participates as a non-voting member. In recent years, certain non-ICH drug regulatory authorities (DRAs) and regional harmonization initiatives (RHIs) have been invited to listen to technical topics (on the role of DRAs and RHIs see in greater detail the discussion under

[18] ICH, "FAQs", available at http://www.ich.org/about/faqs.html, last accessed on 21 November 2011.

[19] ICH, "Organisation of ICH", available at http://www.ich.org/about/organisation-of-ich/steering.html, last accessed on 21 November 2011.

[20] Steering Committee, see *supra* note 12.

'Globalization and Expansion of Participation' below). The Steering Committee meets at least twice a year.

### 10.2.5.2. Working Groups

An Informal Working Group is formed prior to any official ICH harmonization activity with the objective of developing/finalizing a Concept Paper, as well as developing a Business Plan. The Steering Committee creates an Expert Working Group when a new topic is accepted for harmonization, and charges it with developing a harmonized guideline. Topics are grouped under the general headings of 'Efficacy', 'Quality', 'Safety' and 'Multidisciplinary'. The Steering Committee may establish an Implementation Working Group to develop Q and As to facilitate the implementation of existing guidelines.[21]

As regards the participation in the working groups, each of the six official ICH members nominates official representatives and, unless otherwise specified by the Steering Committee, the official membership is limited to two officials per party per working group, one representative per observer, one for IFPMA, and if appropriate, one per interested party. In 2010, the ICH officially opened the working groups to active participation by non-ICH DRAs and RHIs.[22]

Two additional bodies are the Global Cooperation Group (GCG) and the Regulators Forum. In 1999, the ICH formed the GCG as a subcommittee of the Steering Committee. It is comprised of one representative from each of the six members, three observers, RHIs and DRAs. The Regulators Forum is a forum for regulatory agencies only and is comprised of ICH members, observers, RHIs and non-ICH DRAs (see discussion below).

The Secretariat is provided by IFPMA, an international industry association that represents national industry associations and companies and whose headquarters are located in Geneva.

---

[21] ICH, "Working Groups", available at http://www.ich.org/about/organisation-of-ich/working-groups.html, last accessed on 21 November 2011.

[22] ICH, "ICH Press Release, Fukuoka, Japan, 11 November 2010", available at http://www.ich.org/ichnews/press-releases/view/article/ich-steering-committee-fukuoka-japan-10-11-november-2010.html, last accessed on 21 November 2011.

### 10.2.6. Guideline Drafting Procedure

The development of a harmonized guideline undergoes a consultative five-step procedure.[23] All decisions in the working groups and the Steering Committee regarding the guidelines are reached by way of consensus among the members. A 'Concept Paper' put forward by one of the members or observers triggers the harmonization process. An Expert Working Group drafts a first guideline, and after its approval by the Steering Committee, the guideline leaves the ICH process and becomes the subject of regulatory consultation in the three regions (US, EU and Japan). In the US, for example, the guidelines undergo the notice and comment procedure set out in the FDA's Good Guidance Practices.[24] In the EU, they undergo EMEA's public consultation as set out in its Procedure for Guidelines.[25] Comments can also be submitted directly to the ICH. The WHO too circulates the draft guideline among its members for comments. Commenting is, hence, open to anyone from any country interested in doing so. The results of the consultations are forwarded to the ICH's working group and a renewed consensus building process takes place. The regulators will exchange the domestic comments they have received in order to arrive at a single, harmonized guideline. Once consensus is reached, the guideline will be adopted by the Steering Committee, and adopted as an ICH harmonized guideline. Consequently, while the guideline is not legally binding, each of the members adopts the guideline domestically.

### 10.2.7. The Content of the Guidelines

The guidelines set out the technical requirements as to the quality, safety, and efficacy of drugs – factors pharmaceutical manufacturers must demonstrate to the drug regulatory authorities in order for their drug to be approved for sale. The ICH also issues guidelines relating to multidisci-

23 Formal ICH Procedure, see *supra* note 7.

24 21 CFR 10.115; For a detailed overview of the domestic consultation procedures and oversight in the US, see Ayelet Berman, "The Role of Domestic Administrative Law in the Accountability of IN-LAW: The Case of the ICH", in Joost Pauwelyn, Ramses A. Wessel and Jan Wouters (eds.), *Informal International Lawmaking*, Oxford University Press, Oxford, 2012, pp. 468–499.

25 EMA, "Procedure for European Union Guidelines and Related Documents within the Pharmaceutical Legislative Framework", 2009, Doc. Ref. EMA/P/24143/2004 Rev. 1 corr., available at http://www.ema.europa.eu/docs/en_GB/document_library/Scientific_guideline/2009/10/WC500004011.pdf, last accessed on 21 November 2011.

plinary topics, such as on issues that support better and more effective collaboration and registration. So far about 50 guidelines have been issued.[26]

One of the ICH's biggest achievements is the Common Technical Document (CTD) and its electronic version (eCTD). The document sets out a harmonized structure and format for new drug applications, and it is considered to have revolutionized the submission procedure. The 'greatness' of the CTD is that it has immensely sped up and simplified the application for approvals in different regions. While the scientific data is developed in the same way for all three regions, the actual applications varied. A company would have to assemble the submission information for one drug regulatory authority, and then needed to reassemble it for another. The CTD assembles the building blocks of information intended for inclusion in a submission into a consistent harmonized format. Complex multiple submissions to different regulatory agencies are replaced by a single technical dossier to be submitted to all three ICH regions, thus facilitating simultaneous submission. This structure also significantly eases the communication between regulators in different countries.[27] It is, therefore, not surprising that the CTD has been the most widely adopted guideline, also beyond ICH regions.

Another important achievement of the ICH has been its guideline on Good Clinical Practice (GCP), as it too has become the global *de facto* standard for conducting clinical trials.

The scientific level of the guidelines is regarded as high and as incorporating state of the art technology. They are commonly considered to reflect the gold standard.[28] At the same time, looked at from a developing country perspective, the ICH guidelines have come under criticism. The WHO and other NGOs have raised the concern that the standards are unnecessarily high (that is, not justified by safety, efficacy, or quality concerns) for developing countries and small manufacturers, leading to a po-

---

26 ICH, "The Value and Benefits of ICH to Drug Regulatory Authorities – Advancing Harmonization for Better Health", 10 November 2010, available at http://www.ich.org/fileadmin/Public_Web_Site/News_room/C_Publications/ICH_20_anniversary_Value_Benefits_of_ICH_for_Regulators.pdf, last accessed on 21 November 2011.

27 *Ibid.*, pp. 1–6.

28 Report of a WHO Meeting, p. 9, see *supra* note 13.

tential squeeze out of local production.[29] There have similarly been claims that being too costly, the ICH standards on clinical trials are unattainable in developing countries, leading to a decrease in clinical trials in developing countries on pharmaceuticals that would benefit the local population.[30] Finally, despite harmonization, different regulatory authorities may reach different conclusions as regards the approval of a pharmaceutical.[31] This is related to the fact that in determining whether a product complies with the guideline, each agency will undertake its own scientific evaluation. Further, risk assessments are usually made regarding concrete populations, and so that too may lead to different conclusions. This is to say that the ICH should not be misunderstood to be a joint framework for the actual approval of new pharmaceuticals. Such decision-making remains within national sovereignty.

### 10.2.8. Globalization and the Expansion of Participation

Originally, the ICH was set up as a club, limited to the members and observers mentioned above. This club structure reflected the nature of the pharmaceuticals market that was almost exclusively dominated by the member regions at the time.[32] While the US remains the largest market, in the past 15 years, with globalization, the pharmaceuticals market is in the process of undergoing a major shift. The development and manufacture of drugs has shifted to developing and emerging economies including Asia, Eastern Europe, Central/South America, Gulf countries, and South Africa, with China and India becoming major players in this field.

---

29 *Ibid.*, pp. 21–24. See also "ICH: An Exclusive Club of Drug Regulatory Agencies and Drug Companies Imposing its Rules on the Rest of the World", in *Prescrire International*, 2010, no. 19; WHO, "Global Harmonization and the ICH", in *Essential Drugs Monitor*, 2001, available at http://apps.who.int/medicinedocs/en/d/Jh2977e/4.html, last accessed on 21 November 2011.

30 Trudie Lang, Phaik Yeong Cheah, and Nicholas J. White, "Clinical Research: Time for Sensible Global Guidelines", in *The Lancet*, 2011, vol. 377, pp. 1553–1554.

31 For example, the US FDA and EMA have taken different approaches with respect to GlaxoSmithKline's Avandia drug for the treatment of diabetes.

32 James F. Jr. Dobbins, "Opening Remarks by United States Ambassador to the European Communities", in Patrick F. D'Arcy and DWG Harron (eds.), *Proceedings of the first International Conference on Harmonisation,* Queen's University, Belfast, Brussels, 1992.

These developments have generated a growing interest of non-ICH countries in the ICH, and *vice versa*. We, hence, see an expansion of the participants that are allowed into the ICH process (though it falls short of full membership), as well as support on behalf of ICH to non-ICH countries in their adoption of ICH guidelines (we discuss the latter element in greater detail below under 'Adoption of Guidelines').

Interestingly, the globalization of the pharmaceutical market is having an effect on the institutional structure of the ICH, and is to some extent mirrored in the ICH's governance bodies. The ICH has set up two bodies to deal with these changing economic realities. Both the GCG and the Regulators Forum, as we shall see next, allow for greater communication with RHIs and non-ICH DRAs.

### 10.2.8.1. The Global Cooperation Group

The GCG is comprised of one representative from each of the six members, three observers, RHIs and as of recently, also DRAs.[33]

RHIs are "initiatives harmonizing drug regulation across a defined group of non-ICH countries".[34] The RHIs that are members of the GCG are the Asia-Pacific Economic Cooperation (APEC), the Association of Southeast Asian Nations Pharmaceutical Product Working Group (ASEAN PPWG),[35] the Gulf Cooperation Countries 'Gulf Central Committee for Drug Registration' (GCC-DR),[36] the Pan American Network on Drug Regulatory Harmonization (PANDRH),[37] the South African Devel-

---

33 ICH, "Global Cooperation Group", available at http://www.ich.org/about/organisation-of-ich/coopgroup.html, last accessed on 21 November 2011.

34 FAQs, see *supra* note 18.

35 ICH, "Association of Southeast Asian Nations Pharmaceutical Product Working Group", available at http://www.ich.org/about/organisation-of-ich/coopgroup/asean.html, last accessed on 21 November 2011. See also Dr. Mod. Zin Che Awang, "Regional Harmonization Initiatives – the Association of South-East Asian Nations", in *Proceedings, 10th ICDRA*, Hong Kong, available at http://whqlibdoc.who.int/hq/2003/a79903_(chp7).pdf, last accessed on 21 November 2011.

36 ICH, "Gulf Central Committee for Drug Registration", at http://www.ich.org/about/organisation-of-ich/coopgroup/gcc.html, last accessed 21 November 2011. Dr. Laila A. Rahman, "Centralized drug registration system in the Gulf Region", in *Proceedings 10th ICDRA*, Hong Kong, 2002, available at http://whqlibdoc.who.int/hq/2003/a79903_(chp7).pdf, last accessed on 21 November 2011.

37 ICH, "PANDRH", available at http://www.ich.org/about/organisation-of-ich/coopgroup/pandrh.html, last accessed on 21 November 2011.

opment Community (SADC),[38] and as of most recently the East African Community (EAC).[39]

The GCG's purpose has evolved over time.[40] When established in 1999, its role was predominantly perceived as enabling better communication between ICH members and other RHIs - but RHIs were not actually invited in yet. Then, in 2003, in view of improving participation and transparency towards non-ICH regions, RHIs were invited to become GCG members.[41] Since 2005, the ICH has become more ambitious, and has been conceiving of the GCG as a conduit for disseminating ICH guidelines globally.[42] It has also become much more proactive in this role, and undertakes activities to promote a better understanding of ICH guidelines and issues associated with their implementation.[43]

As time passed, the ICH felt that the GCG was not inclusive enough and was not properly reflecting the global face of drug development.[44]

---

38 ICH, "SADC", available at http://www.ich.org/about/organisation-of-ich/coopgroup/sadc.html, last accessed on 21 November 2011.

39 ICH, "EAC", available at http://www.ich.org/about/organisation-of-ich/coopgroup/apec0.html, last accessed on 21 November 2011.

40 For an overview of the GCG, see Mike Ward, "The Global Cooperation Group - A Bridge from ICH to the World Beyond", in *The Value and Benefits of ICH to Drug Regulatory Authorities—Advancing Harmonization for Better Health*, 2010, available at http://www.ich.org/fileadmin/Public_Web_Site/News_room/C_Publications/ICH_20_anniversary_Value_Benefits_of_ICH_for_Regulators.pdf, last accessed on 21 November 2011.

41 The 2003 GCG 'Terms of Reference' state that the GCG's purpose is to "act as the primary representative of ICH Steering Committee outside the ICH regions, and equally as such as a conduit for non-ICH parties to the ICH Steering Committee". ICH Global Cooperation Group, "Terms of Reference", November 2003, was withdrawn from the ICH's website.

42 A 2005 GCG mission statement is instructive, saying that the GCG's goal is: "To promote a mutual understanding of regional harmonisation initiatives in order to facilitate the harmonisation process related to ICH guidelines regionally and globally, and to facilitate the capacity of drug regulatory authorities and industry to utilise them".

43 Mike Ward, "Panel Discussion: Clinical Development in Asia and ICH: Implementation of ICH Guidelines in Asian Countries", in *Proceedings of ICH Tokyo Symposium: Hot Topics and Influence on Asia*, 2007, Tokyo, available at http://www.ich.org/fileadmin/Public_Web_Site/Meetings/E-ICH_Public_Meetings/ICH_Symposium__Tokyo__Japan__Nov_2__2007/Tokyo_Symposium_Proceedings_2007.pdf, last accessed on 21 November 2011.

44 ICH, "GCG Meeting Report", GCG 78F, 30 October 2007, Yokohama, Japan, available at http://www.ich.org/fileadmin/Public_Web_Site/Meetings/C-GCG_Reports/

The so-called 'pharmerging' countries – Brazil, China, India, and Russia[45] – were not members to the GCG. These countries have become major players in the pharmaceuticals market, and they produce many products that end up in the final product. For example, most active pharmaceuticals ingredients (APIs) are nowadays produced in China and India, or China conducts many clinical trials. In order to promote the use of relevant ICH standards by these countries, in 2007, the Steering Committee began inviting representatives from individual DRAs to participate in the GCG. The DRA's invited were either (i) countries with a tradition of using ICH guidelines or an intention to do so, or (ii) from countries that are a source of active pharmaceutical ingredients, medicinal products, or clinical data for the ICH regions. So far, eight DRA's have been invited to the GCG: Australia, Brazil, China, Chinese Taipei, India, Russia, Singapore, and South Korea. Brazil, China, and Russia participated for the first time in 2009.[46]

### 10.2.8.2. Regulators Forum

Not only was the GCG expanded to include DRAs, but the ICH also decided to set up a 'Regulators Forum'.[47] In 2008, it held its first meeting. The Regulators Forum consists of regulatory authorities only from the ICH member regions, the observers, the RHIs, as well as the other DRAs mentioned above (in accordance with the above selection criteria). Its purpose is to facilitate the implementation of ICH guidelines worldwide,

---

Oct_2007_Yokohama/Final_GCG_Report_Yokohama__October_2007.pdf, last accessed on 21 November 2011.

45 Raymond Hill and Mandy Chui, "The Pharmerging Future", in *Pharmaceutical Executive – The Business Magazine of Pharma*, IMS Health publication, 2009, vol. 29, no. 7, available at http://www.imshealth.com/imshealth/Global/Content/Document/Intelligence.360%20Documents/The_Pharmerging_Future.pdf, last accessed at 21 November 2011. They mention seven 'pharmerging' countries. The other three are Turkey, South Korea and Mexico.

46 Global Cooperation Group, see *supra* note 33.

47 Peter Arlett, "ICH Regulators Forum", at European Public ICH Meeting, 14 November 2008, Brussels, available at http://www.ema.europa.eu/docs/en_GB/document_library/Presentation/2009/11/WC500010483.pdf, last accessed at 21 November 2011; Kohei Wada, "Evolution and Achievements of ICH-GCG (Global Cooperation Group)", at European Public ICH Meeting, 14 November 2008, Brussels, available at http://www.ema.europa.eu/docs/en_GB/document_library/Presentation/2010/02/WC500070579.pdf, last accessed at 21 November 2011.

and to complement the work of the GCG.[48] So far, it has focused on the implementation of guidelines in areas of greatest interest, such as the CTD, good manufacturing practices (particularly of APIs), clinical trials, and product safety.[49]

### 10.2.9. Adoption of Guidelines

The ICH guidelines are considered voluntary, but they have all been implemented in the three ICH regions. Members will typically adopt the ICH guidelines as domestic (legally non-binding) guidance documents or guidelines.[50]

But ICH guidelines are considered *de facto* global standards and are adopted in many non-ICH countries, too.[51] Within these non-ICH countries we can roughly distinguish between three main groups. The first group is of countries that have a tradition of adopting ICH guidelines, and include Canada, EFTA countries, and Australia – as their pharmaceutical industries are closely linked with those of the ICH region. In Australia, for example, the Therapeutics Goods Administration as a rule uses exclusively ICH guidelines rather than domestic regulations.[52]

The second group concerns 'pharmerging' countries such as Brazil, China, and India. These countries either have an intention to use ICH guidelines or have become significant producers of pharmaceutical materials – in particular active pharmaceutical ingredients – or have become active in conducting clinical trials. Thus, such countries have or are in the process of adopting/adapting ICH guidelines, in particular those of rele-

---

[48] Petra Doerr, "The Regulators Forum", in *The Value and Benefits of ICH to Drug Regulatory Authorities – Advancing Harmonization for Better Health*, available at http://www.ich.org/fileadmin/Public_Web_Site/News_room/C_Publications/ICH_20_anniversary_Value_Benefits_of_ICH_for_Regulators.pdf, last accessed at 21 November 2011.

[49] Arlett, 2008, p. 10, see *supra* note 47.

[50] Berman, 2012, see *supra* note 24, p. 485.

[51] *E.g.*, Report of a WHO Meeting, see *supra* note 14; Roman Polap, "European Contribution to a Global Approach to Regulation", at 10th ICDRA, 2002, Hong Kong, available at http://whqlibdoc.who.int/hq/2003/a79903_(chp6).pdf, last accessed 21 November 2011.

[52] Leonie Hunt, "Use of ICH Guidelines in Prescription Medicine Regulation in Australia", available at http://www.ich.org/fileadmin/Public_Web_Site/Meetings/C-GCG_Reports/Nov_2008_Brussels/DRA_Australia_Presentation_in_Brussels.pdf, last accessed on 3 July 2012.

vance to manufacture of APIs, quality manufacture, clinical trials, and the CTD.[53] The RHIs mentioned above have also been actively encouraging the adoption of ICH guidelines in their region. For example, APEC has set up the APEC Harmonization Centre (AHC) in 2010, which promotes the implementation of ICH guidelines in the Asia-Pacific region.[54]

Moreover, with most export being to ICH countries, and most pharmaceutical companies in non-ICH countries dominated by ICH firms, developers and producers in these countries follow ICH guidelines even if they have not been formally adopted by the jurisdiction in which they operate. Bodies conducting clinical research will also normally follow the ICH Good Clinical Practice (GCP) guidelines to conduct a study, irrespective of whether the guideline has been formally adopted by the local regulatory authority.[55]

Finally, ICH guidelines also have an impact on developing countries. While the ICH guidelines were originally intended to apply to the evaluation and registration of new drugs,[56] the quality-related guidelines are now used as a basis to evaluate generic drugs too. They are, hence, of particular importance in developing countries.

To cater for this global interest in ICH guidelines and to encourage global adoption of ICH guidelines, the ICH undertakes various outreach

---

53 For example, China. See Jianhua Ding, "Panel Discussion: Clinical Development in Asia and ICH: Implementation of ICH Guidelines in Asian Countries", in *Proceedings of ICH Tokyo Symposium: Hot Topics and Influence on Asia*, 2007, Tokyo, available at http://www.ich.org/fileadmin/Public_Web_Site/Meetings/E-ICH_Public_Meetings/ICH_Symposium__Tokyo__Japan__Nov_2__2007/Tokyo_Symposium_Proceedings_2007.pdf, last accessed on 21 November 2011.

54 See Dawn Ronan, "Report on the Yokohama ICH Meeting", in *RAJ Pharma*, 27 August 2009. On the APEC Harmonization Centre, see AHC, "AHC, the APEC Harmonization Centre", available at http://www.apec-ahc.org/contents/page.jsp?mcode=1010101, last accessed on 21 November 2011; and DaiByung Kim, "Harmonization for a Healthier World: Establishing an APEC Harmonization Center in Seoul", 10 November 2008, available at http://www.ich.org/fileadmin/Public_Web_Site/Meetings/C-GCG_Reports/Nov_2008_Brussels/DRA_Korea_Presentation_in_Brussels.pdf, last accessed on 21 November 2011.

55 *E.g.*, PhRMA, "Principles on Conduct of Clinical Trials - Communication of Clinical Trial Results", PhRMA publication, available at http://www.phrma.org/sites/default/files/105/042009_clinical_trial_principles_final.pdf, last accessed on 21 November 2011. See also Lang et al., see *supra* note 30.

56 WHO Report on ICH Implementation in Non-ICH Countries, 2001, see *supra* note 13, p. 1.

activities. As mentioned above, it has set up the GCG and Regulators Forum, and one of their main objectives is to support non-ICH countries in implementing ICH guidelines. Training and capacity building support has become a major activity of the GCG.[57] The Regulators Forum, too, was set up with this purpose in mind. It provides a venue to discuss implementation challenges, to share experiences regarding implementation, and so forth.[58] As mentioned above, so far, it has focused on the implementation of guidelines in areas of greatest interest, such as the CTD, manufacturing (particularly of APIs), and clinical trials.[59]

## 10.3. The International Cooperation on Harmonization of Technical Requirements for Registration of Veterinary Medicinal Products

### 10.3.1. Background

The International Cooperation on Harmonization of Technical Requirements for Registration of Veterinary Medicinal Products (VICH) is a network of veterinary medicines regulatory authorities and animal health industries from the EU, the US, and Japan. It was launched in 1996, at first under the auspices of the World Animal Health Organization (OIE). At a later stage, the secretariat moved to the International Federation of Animal Health (IFAH), an industry association, which represents 95% of the animal health industry in the world.

The production, registration, and marketing of drugs are extremely expensive and time consuming for both industry and regulators. Thus, the good progress of the ICH encouraged the parties to set up a similar body that would harmonize technical requirements for registration of veterinary medicinal products relating to safety, efficacy, and quality. And indeed, the VICH's structure, members and working methods are very similar to that of the ICH.

The market for veterinary medicines is very small and is only about 5% of the human pharmaceuticals market. The VICH is, therefore, normally awarded much less attention than the ICH. Having said that, with

57 Wada, 2008, p. 15, see *supra* note 47; ICH, "ICH Training", available at http://www.ich.org/trainings/ich-trainings.html, last accessed on 21 November 2011.

58 Arlett, 2008, p. 8, see *supra* note 47.

59 *Ibid.*, p. 10.

the growing risk of zoonosis (diseases transferred from animals to humans and vice versa, such as avian flu, swine flu *et cetera*) due to the increased movement of goods and people, the importance of VICH has increased.

### 10.3.2. Legal Framework

The VICH lacks international legal personality. Its governance structure and guideline development procedure is set out in the 'Organisational Charter of VICH' (2007). Another important document is the 'VICH Strategy Paper Phase III (2011–2015)', though it is currently not publicly available.[60]

### 10.3.3. Members

Like the ICH, the VICH is a public-private network. Full members are animal drug regulatory authorities and industry representatives from the EU, the US, and Japan. The regulatory members from the EU are the EC DG Health and Consumers, and the European Medicines Agency; from the US they are the FDA[61] and the Department for Agriculture;[62] and for Japan the Ministry of Agriculture, Forestry and Fisheries. The industry members are the European Federation for Animal Health (IFAH–Europe), the US Animal Health Institute (AHI), and the Japanese Veterinary Products Association (JVPA).[63]

### 10.3.4. Other Participants

As with the ICH, the VICH lets non-members participate in the process: Associate Members, Observer Members, and Interested Parties. Formally, these participants do not have decision-making power but informally they presumably influence the guideline development process.

60 VICH, "VICH Process", available at http://www.vichsec.org/en/process.htm#3, last accessed on 21 November 2011.

61 Experts are drawn from the Center for Veterinary Medicine.

62 Experts are drawn from the Animal and Plant Health Inspection Service/Center for Veterinary Biologics.

63 VICH, "VICH Structure", available at http://www.vichsec.org/en/structure.htm#3, last accessed on 21 November 2011.

#### 10.3.4.1. Associate Members: The World Animal Health Organization

The World Animal Health Organization (OIE), an intergovernmental organization representing 174 member countries and territories, is an Associate Member. The VICH was initially established under the auspices of the OIE, but left that framework because OIE concerns animal health at large and pharmaceutical regulation concerns only a fraction thereof. Despite not being a full member, the OIE is considered a very important participant in VICH.

The OIE serves as a link between VICH and OIE's members. The OIE has an important role in disseminating VICH guidelines globally: It "circulates relevant VICH documents to OIE member countries for comments and circulates final VICH Guidelines",[64] and it "provides support to VICH and encourages its member countries to take into consideration the VICH results".[65]

The OIE, being an international organization focused on animal health issues (as well as public health issues related to animal health), considers VICH to be an important tool for achieving these goals. With the increased risk of zoonosis, the OIE would like non-VICH members to put certain regulatory safeguards in place, including on the basis of VICH guidelines. The OIE has recently enacted a 2011–2015 strategic plan to combat the problem of disease spread, and the VICH is an important pillar of that plan.[66] Further below, we discuss VICH's collaboration with OIE in view of encouraging adoption of VICH guidelines by developing countries.

#### 10.3.4.2. Observer Members

Observer members include regulatory authorities and industry representatives from Australia, New Zealand, and Canada. For each observer region, there is one delegate representing government authorities, and one representing industry associations. The regulators for Australia and New Zealand are the Australian Pesticides and Veterinary Medicines Authority

---

64 VICH, Article 5.2.4., "Organisational Charter of VICH", Revision 10, 2007, available at http://www.vichsec.org/en/process.htm, last accessed on 21 November 2011.

65 *Ibid.*

66 World Organisation for Animal Health (OIE), "Fifth Strategic Plan: 2011–2015", available at http://www.oie.int/fileadmin/Home/eng/About_us/docs/pdf/5th_StratPlan_EN_2010_LAST.pdf, last accessed on 21 November 2011.

(APVMA), and the New Zealand Food Safety Authority (NZFSA). For Canada, the regulators are Health Canada (Veterinary Drugs Directorate) and the Canadian Food Inspection Agency (Veterinary Biologics Section). The industry associations for Australia and New Zealand are the National Association for Animal Health Products (The Alliance) and the Agricultural Chemicals & Animal Remedies Manufacturer's Association of New Zealand (AGCARM). The Canadian industry is represented by the Canada Animal Health Institute (CAHI).[67]

#### 10.3.4.3. Interested Party

The Association of Veterinary Biologics Companies has been recognized as an Interested Party.[68] But others may be recognized from time to time.

### 10.3.5. Governance Structure

The VICH conducts its business through several organs, mainly the Steering Committee, Expert Working Groups, and the Secretariat. The structure is very similar to that of the ICH.

#### 10.3.5.1. Steering Committee

The Steering Committee is the executive organ of the organization, and it drives the harmonization process. It is comprised of two delegates of regulatory authorities and two delegates of industry associations for each region. Associate members and observer members have the opportunity to take part in the discussions of the Steering Committee, although they do not have any voting rights and do not sign-off any VICH draft or final guideline.[69] Nevertheless, in practice, their opinions are taken into account in the formation of the consensus. Interested parties may also attend some Steering Committee meetings but have no right to contribute to the discussions or intervene in the meetings as such in any way, unless requested by the chair to provide certain information.[70] The Steering Committee meets up to twice a year. Initially, the Steering Committee was chaired by

---

67 Article 5.1.4. Organisational Charter of VICH, 2004, see *supra* note 64.

68 *Ibid.*, Article 5.1.5.

69 *Ibid.*, Article 5.1.3. and 5.1.4.

70 *Ibid.*, Article 5.1.5.

the OIE, but now the Chair rotates between the three full member regions.[71]

#### 10.3.5.2. Expert Working Groups

The Expert Working Groups are in charge of the technical drafting of the guidelines.[72] Normally, they are comprised of six experts, one representing each full member. In addition, observers have the right to appoint one expert. The Steering Committee may also appoint additional experts from other regions.[73] In practice, the opinion of the observers may also be taken into account. There are several working groups, for example, on quality or on safety.[74] Minutes of the working group meetings are made available to the members only.

#### 10.3.5.3. Secretariat

The International Federation of Animal Health (IFAH), an association of veterinary medicine companies, located in Brussels, provides the Secretariat for VICH activities.[75] It has a supporting role in the organization's work, ensuring a smooth and continuous functioning of the process.

### 10.3.6. Guideline Drafting Procedure

The VICH develops guidelines in a consultation intensive nine-step procedure.[76] All decisions are reached by way of consensus. The VICH Steering Committee decides on any new topics for which a guideline is to be developed based on a detailed concept paper submitted by a VICH member. The concept paper should address the reasons for the proposed guideline (for example, the need for harmonization), the feasibility to achieve harmonization and the expected impact of the proposed guideline. Topics that are not considered to be domestically implementable by any of the members are also dropped at this initial stage.[77] Many of the rules

71 *Ibid.*, Article 5.1.6.
72 *Ibid.*, Article 6
73 *Ibid.*, Article 6.1.1.
74 VICH Structure, see *supra* note 63.
75 Article 5.1.6. Organisational Charter of VICH, 2004, see *supra* note 64.
76 *Ibid.*, Article 8. See also "VICH Process", *supra* note 60.
77 See also Berman, 2011, *supra* note 24, p. 477–479.

regarding pharmaceuticals for human use apply to pharmaceuticals for veterinary use too. Therefore, many of the topics covered by the ICH are copied by the VICH, with the necessary adaptations. Once the Steering Committee agrees on a new topic, the work is allocated to either an existing Expert Working Group, or a new one is formed.

The Expert Working Group develops a draft guideline in an internal consultative process involving face-to-face meetings, email exchanges, and/or teleconferences. The process for preparing the draft depends on the complexity of the topic and the existing level of harmonization. After the Expert Working Group has signed off on the draft guideline, it is submitted to the Steering Committee for approval and then published for consultation by the regulatory authorities in the VICH regions and published on the VICH website. Within each jurisdiction, consultations take place in accordance with the domestic rules on consultation. For example, in the US, they undergo the notice and comment procedures of the FDA's Good Guidance Practices.[78] Comments may be submitted directly to the VICH too. In view of the VICH's objective that its work provides a basis for wider international harmonization of registration requirements, also countries that are not part of the VICH can send comments during the public consultation. The OIE circulates the drafts to its members, and so also non-VICH countries are invited to comment. In practice, despite the possibility to comment, there is not much public input on the drafts, as the matters are very technical.

Following the close of the consultation period, the Expert Working Group reviews the comments received and finalizes the guideline taking into consideration these comments. The revised guideline is submitted to the Steering Committee for approval. After approval, the regulatory authorities implement the guideline in the VICH countries. While the VICH observer countries are not bound by the VICH recommendations, they are encouraged to take them into account in due course, and so are other countries – see the discussion further below.

[78] Code of Federal Regulations, Title 21, Volume 1: 21 CFR 10.115.

### 10.3.7. The Content of the Guidelines

To date there are 50 guidelines, including those that are in the development process.[79] This reflects a very low percentage of the total set of regulations for veterinary medicines. That is to say that the VICH is far from harmonizing everything and some areas will never be harmonized because the approaches in the different countries are too different.

The VICH guidelines set out harmonized data requirements, that is, standards for the scientific studies on quality, safety (for example toxicology, target animal safety, antimicrobial safety, and environmental impact assessment) and efficacy (for example GCP), that are required to obtain a marketing authorization of a veterinary medicinal product.

As with the ICH, the VICH does not normally develop guidance on how to carry out the assessment of the data or on the assessment approach. Assessments are done by the regulatory authorities of the VICH countries. Only in a few exceptional cases, for example, the guidelines on environmental impact assessment or the guideline on the establishment of the microbiological ADI, has the VICH produced guidelines covering the assessment approach.[80]

### 10.3.8. Globalization and Expansion of Participation

As with the ICH, VICH's membership structure is outdated and reflects the past rather than the present and the future. In view of adapting the VICH's institutional structure to the global pharmaceuticals market, the VICH is in the process of contemplating whether it should create a body such as the ICH's Global Cooperation Group. So far, the VICH has not yet determined what the appropriate governance structure should be.[81] In November 2011, the VICH has reached out to regional harmonization initiatives and several developing and emerging countries, in order to im-

79 VICH, "VICH Guidelines", available at http://www.vichsec.org/en/guidelines.htm#1, last accessed on 21 November 2011.

80 VICH, "VICH and its role for authorisation of veterinary medicinal products: Executive Summary", VICH/10/008, 5 May 2010, available at http://www.vichsec.org/index.htm, last accessed on 21 November 2011.

81 VICH, "VICH Global Outreach Strategy: Current thinking of the Steering Committee", VICH10/002, 20 May 2010, available at http://www.vichsec.org/index.htm, last accessed on 21 November 2011.

prove communication and to get a better understanding of their needs.[82] In the short term, VICH will consult non-VICH countries in its development of VICH guidelines.[83]

### 10.3.9. Adoption of Guidelines

Within the member countries most, if not all guidelines, have been implemented. In the US, they have been implemented as FDA guidance documents[84] and in the EU as EMEA guidelines.[85]

But the VICH's ambitions go beyond harmonization among its member countries. The VICH's 'Organisational Charter' clearly states in its objectives that it should "work towards providing a basis for wider international harmonization of registration requirements". As of late, however, the success of efforts to this end has been fairly limited.[86] It has proved rather difficult to gain an understanding and acceptance in non-VICH countries of the VICH principles, and particularly the guidelines and their implementation.[87]

This situation is supposed to change. With globalization and the increased risk of zoonosis, the OIE is encouraging OIE members, in particular developing countries, to adopt VICH guidelines. In fact, the OIE's strategic plan for 2011–2015 sets the promotion of VICH guidelines as one of its goals. According to the plan, the OIE will encourage its members to adopt VICH guidelines.[88] The FDA is even providing financial

---

82 VICH, "Press Release: VICH adopts Strategy 2011–2015", VICH/11/022, 24 February 2011, available at http://www.vichsec.org/en/news-and-meetings-press.htm, last accessed on 21 November 2011.

83 *Ibid.*

84 US FDA, "Veterinary International Conference on Harmonization (VICH) Guidance Documents", available at http://www.fda.gov/RegulatoryInformation/Guidances/ucm122050.htm, last accessed on 21 November 2011.

85 EMA, "Scientific Guidelines", available at http://www.ema.europa.eu/ema/index.jsp?curl=pages/regulation/general/general_content_000173.jsp&mid=WC0b01ac058002d89a, last accessed on 21 November 2011.

86 VICH Global Outreach Strategy, see *supra* note 81.

87 *Ibid.*

88 OIE, "Fifth Strategic Plan", see *supra* note 66. See also International Committee of the OIE, 77th General Session, "Resolutions", 24–29 May 2009, available at http://www.oie.int/fileadmin/Home/eng/About_us/docs/pdf/A_RESO_2009_PUB.pdf, last accessed on 21 November 2011.

support to the OIE to this end.[89] The OIE is further recommending that its member countries develop regional harmonization networks that will make it easier to harmonize their regulatory frameworks and adopt VICH guidelines.[90]

The background to the OIE's strong support of VICH is OIE's goal to ensure better provision of safe, efficacious, and good quality veterinary medicines in all of its member countries. Many developing countries lack a minimal infrastructure and regulatory framework. But a regulatory system is a precondition for the provision of medicines, and VICH guidelines would put part of this framework in place. Such tools must be in place so that if a disease breaks out in the future, action can be taken immediately to prevent global spread. For example, one of the OIE's goals is the eradication of the foot and mouth disease. To this end, animals need to be vaccinated, and there is, hence, a need to register vaccinations in all countries so as to make the vaccinations available. Such vaccinations cannot be registered without having a regulatory system in place.

Against this backdrop, the VICH has, since 2010, been in the process of developing the 'Global Outreach Initiative'.[91] This initiative, in very close collaboration with the OIE, aims at providing a basis for encouraging wider international harmonization of technical registration requirements in non-VICH countries, in particular in Africa, Asia, and South America.[92] The aim is to encourage non-VICH countries to use VICH guidelines as national or regional guidelines.[93] As mentioned, the idea is that adoption of VICH guidelines and the setting up of regulatory systems will enable broad access to high quality veterinary medicines to livestock producers, veterinarians, and pet owners in those countries (and in turn will reduce the global spread of diseases). To this end, the VICH will take on an active role and elaborate information and training materials, and through the OIE network will help with communicating and

89 US FDA, "Global Implementation of the Veterinary Medicinal Products Guidelines", 75 FR 61504–61505, available at http://www.regulations.gov/#!documentDetail;D=FDA-2010-N-0497-0001, last accessed on 21 November 2011.

90 VICH Global Outreach Strategy, see *supra* note 81.

91 *Ibid.*

92 VICH and its role for authorisation of veterinary medicinal products, see *supra* note 81.

93 *Ibid.*

providing assistance in implementation.[94] The VICH is, hence, becoming part of a global strategy for the governance of animal health, which is being orchestrated by the OIE.[95]

It should be noted, however, that at the time of writing, this initiative is still very much under development and many of the details are still unknown. There are also different concerns that will need to be addressed. For example, one of the concerns is that having been elaborated by developed countries and their industries, the guidelines do not cover topics that respond to the needs of developing countries (such as local diseases, storage conditions, *et cetera*).[96] A related concern is that VICH guidelines represent an unachievable highest common denominator between developed countries that may not be relevant for developing countries.[97] There will, accordingly, be a need for adaptation of VICH guidelines to local conditions. One of the proposed solutions has been that the VICH will establish mechanisms allowing consideration of the needs of non-VICH countries with regard to the revision of existing guidelines and the agreement on new topics for VICH guidelines.[98]

Another concern is that the needs of emerging and developing countries are not identical.[99] For some countries it will first be necessary for OIE to encourage the implementation of the basic infrastructure for a regulatory system ensuring registration and control of veterinary medicine. For countries that already have a basic regulatory system for veterinary medicinal products in place, the possibility for more interaction with VICH exists.[100] All of these issues will require further attention. How this will actually play out is still unknown at the time of the writing of this chapter.

---

94 VICH Global Outreach Strategy, see *supra* note 81.

95 *Ibid.* On intergovernmental organizations as orchestrators of transnational new governance, see Kenneth W. Abbott, "Strengthening International Regulation Through Transnational New Governance: Overcoming the Orchestration Deficit", in *Vanderbilt Journal of Transnational Law*, 2009, vol. 42, p. 501.

96 David Mackay, "Conclusions of the VICH 4 Conference", at VICH 4th Conference, 2010, OIE Paris, available at http://www.vichsec.org/en/8.%20Mackay%20conclusions.ppt, last accessed on 21 November 2011.

97 *Ibid.*

98 VICH Global Outreach Strategy, see *supra* note 81.

99 *Ibid.*

100 *Ibid.*

## 10.4. The Global Harmonization Task Force / The International Medical Device Regulators Forum

### 10.4.1. Background

Established in 1996, the Global Harmonization Task Force (GHTF) is a network of medical devices regulatory authorities and members of the medical device industry from the US, EU, Japan, Australia and Canada. The GHTF seeks the convergence of medical device regulatory practices related to ensuring the safety, effectiveness, performance and quality of medical devices through the development of harmonized guidelines.[101]

Essentially, the work on the GHTF guidelines or regulatory model is substantially complete and has allowed the founding members to construct regulatory systems largely aligned with the GHTF framework.[102] Against this backdrop, the GHTF has decided to move forward and focus on spreading the GHTF regulatory model internationally, as well as improving the implementation of the guidelines at the operational level.

To this end, the GHTF's founding regulatory authorities have now decided to transform the GHTF into a regulators-only network,[103] and have announced in October 2011, together with the medical devices regulatory authorities from Brazil and China, as well as the WHO, the establishment of the International Medical Device Regulators Forum (IMDRF), a regulators-only forum that will replace the GHTF.[104] The IMDRF will initially exist in parallel with the GHTF until work there is wrapped up and/or transferred to the new body. At the time of the writing of this chap-

---

[101] GHTF, Article 2.2 (B), "GHTF Guiding Principles", 20 May 2005, GHTF/SC/N1R8:2005, available at http://www.ghtf.org/about/guiding.pdf, last accessed on 21 November 2011.

[102] GHTF, "Statement from GHTF Chair: Update on Future Directions of GHTF", 28 March 2011, available at http://www.ghtf.org/documents/statement-future-2011.pdf, last accessed on 21 November 2011.

[103] *Ibid.*

[104] IMDRF, "Statement from the International Medical Device Regulators Forum", available at http://www.hc-sc.gc.ca/dhp-mps/md-im/activit/int/statement_imdrf_declar_fiacrmm-eng.php, last accessed on 21 November 2011.

ter, still very little is known about the IMDRF,[105] since its inaugural meeting only took place in February 2012.

### 10.4.2. Legal Framework

From a traditional international law perspective, the GHTF lacks international legal personality, though it has been internationally legally active, such as by being a party to Memoranda of Understanding with other international bodies (ISO). The members consider themselves a 'club of goodwill'. The governance and operational framework of its activities is set out in three constitutional-like documents: 'GHTF Roles and Responsibilities' (2008),[106] 'GHTF Guiding Principles' (2005),[107] and 'GHTF Operating Procedures'.[108] The IMDRF has not issued any governance documents so far.

### 10.4.3. Members

The GHTF, like the ICH and VICH, is a public-private network. The GHTF's founding members are medical device regulatory authorities and industry representatives from Europe, the US, Canada, Japan, and Australia. Regulatory authorities include the US FDA, the EU DG Health and Consumers, and the Japanese Pharmaceuticals and Medical Devices Agency. Industry representatives include the Advanced Medical Technology Association, Philips Healthcare, the European Coordination Committee of the Radiological, Electromedical and Healthcare IT Industry and others.[109]

---

105 The IMDRF has set up a website that at the time of the writing of this chapter is quite thin. Hopefully more information will be made available in the future; IMRDF website, available at http://www.imdrf.org, last accessed on 3 July 2012.

106 GHTF, "GHTF Roles and Responsibilities", 5 March 2008, GHTF/SC/N2R10 :2008, available at http://www.ghtf.org/documents/sc/sc_n2r10.pdf, last accessed on 21 November 2011.

107 GHTF Guiding Principles, see *supra* note 101.

108 See under "Governance: GHTF Procedural Documents", available at http://www.ghtf.org/about/governance.html, last accessed on 15 November 2011. In addition, the GHTF has also issued action plans and strategic direction documents.

109 For a full overview, see GHTF, "GHTF Steering Committee Membership List", available at http://www.ghtf.org/steering/steeringmembers.html, last accessed on 21 November 2011.

The GHTF is transforming now into a regulators-only forum, the IMDRF. The reasons for this transformation are essentially twofold. First, there had been criticism (especially within the US) that regulators are too close to industry. Second, in view of the pressures of a globalized manufacturing market for medical devices and increasing demands to streamline regulatory processes, harmonization is considered more important than ever, and the regulators group considered that the best way to achieve this would be on the basis of a regulators-only group. Such a group would allow for more detailed discussion on the optimum way to achieve harmonization at the operational level (which is currently not adequate – see discussion below).[110]

Not only is the IMDRF a 'regulators-only' network, but it is expanding to include new members: the medical regulatory authorities of Brazil (ANVISA), China, as well as the WHO.[111]

### 10.4.4. Other Participants

Besides the founding members, other parties may be entitled to participate in the GHTF process: Participating Members, Liaison Bodies, and Observers. Their participation falls short, however, of having (at least formally) a right to take part in the decision-making.

Participating Members are defined as "representatives of medical device regulatory authorities or medical device trade associations of countries other than the Founding Members". Liaison bodies are "public health organizations, international standard setting bodies or other groups who can contribute to or benefit from participation in GHTF".[112] Observers may be nominated too.[113]

To date, officially, there are three Liaison Bodies: (i) the Asian Harmonization Working Party (AHWP), an Asian regional network of medical devices regulatory authorities and industry associations that seeks harmonization of medical device regulations in its region. To this end it seeks to collaborate with the GHTF and make use of the work it devel-

110 Statement from GHTF Chair: Update on Future Directions of GHTF, see *supra* note 102.

111 IMDRF, "Management Committee Members and Alternates", available at http://www.imdrf.org/members.htm, last accessed on 1 December 2011.

112 Articles 2.2. and 2.3. GHTF Roles and Responsibilities, see *supra* note 106.

113 *Ibid.*, Article 3.

ops,[114] (ii) the International Organization for Standardization (ISO), and (iii) International Electrotechnical Commission (IEC). Collaboration between the GHTF and ISO is set out in several Memoranda of Understanding.[115]

Other organizations, such as the WHO (as well as PAHO, the WHO's Latin American regional organization), the Latin American Harmonization Working Party (LAHWP) as well as the Global Medical Device Nomenclature (GMDN) participate in certain GHTF bodies and collaborate with it,[116] though they are not formally acknowledged in the GHTF's governance documents mentioned above as liaison members.

### 10.4.5. Governance Structure

The GHTF conducts its business through several organs, the main ones being the Steering Committee, the Study Groups, and the Ad Hoc Working groups.

#### 10.4.5.1. Steering Committee / Management Committee

The Steering Committee is the GHTF's governing body and its role is "to provide policy and strategic direction" and to assign and provide oversight of technical work initiatives. Particularly, its role includes the adoption of GHTF guidance documents and the monitoring of their implementation. It is also in charge of internal oversight and review, and supports dispute resolution.[117] The Steering Committee includes four regulatory representatives and four industry representatives from each of the three founding geographic areas (North America, Europe, and Asia–Pacific). Only the Founding Members have a seat on the Steering Committee. However, Participating Members, Liaison Bodies and Observers may be invited to specific meetings.[118] In addition, at its discretion, the Steering Committee

---

[114] AHWP, available at http://www.ahwp.info/, last accessed on 3 July 2012.

[115] GHTF, "Memorandum of Understanding (MoU)", available at http://www.ghtf.org/mou/index.html, last accessed on 21 November 2011.

[116] Roland G. Rotter, "The Global Harmonization Task Force: Overview and Status", at 5th APEC-Funded Seminar on Harmonization of Medical Device Regulations, 14–16 May 2009, available at http://www.ghtf.org/meetings/conferences/5thapec/slides/slides-rotter.pdf, last accessed on 21 November 2011.

[117] Article 4.1. GHTF Roles and Responsibilities, see *supra* note 106.

[118] *Ibid.*, Article 3, 4.1.1.

"may consult members or outside parties in order to gather information and solicit external advice relevant to business matters pending before the Committee".[119] The Steering Committee meets not less than twice every 18 months.[120] As a rule, the Steering Committee meetings are closed sessions. However, open sessions may be convened.[121]

The chairmanship rotates among the national regulatory authorities of the three geographic regions every three years.[122] The chairmanship also serves as the dispute settlement mechanism. It is within the Chairman's responsibility to resolve "all disputes regarding GHTF decisions or actions brought forward by GHTF members or persons outside the GHT with the assistance of the Steering Committee as needed".[123] It is unknown whether disputes were ever brought before the chairman.

Within the IMDRF, a Management Committee will replace the Steering Committee. It will be composed of the regulatory officials, which "will provide guidance on strategies, policies, directions, membership and activities". The IMDRF will meet bi-annually.[124]

### 10.4.5.2. Study Groups / Ad Hoc Groups

The development of guidance documents takes place within five GHTF Study Groups,[125] as well as several Ad Hoc groups.[126] They are composed of founding members, but Participating Members and Liaison Bodies (such as AHWP) as well as Observers (such as the LAHWP) can be invited.[127] In addition, individuals who are not members of their Study Group or of the GHTF may be allowed to participate in their meetings as technical experts with observer status.[128]

---

119 *Ibid.*, Article 4.1.1.

120 *Ibid.*, Article 4.1.3.

121 *Ibid.*, Article 4.1.3.

122 *Ibid.*, Article 4.1.2.

123 *Ibid.*, Article 4.2.2.(B).

124 Statement from the International Medical Device Regulators Forum, see *supra* note 104.

125 GHTF, "Study Groups", available at http://www.ghtf.org/studygroups.html, last accessed on 21 November 2011.

126 GHTF, "Ad Hoc Working Groups", available at http://www.ghtf.org/steering/adhoc-groups.html, last accessed on 21 November 2011.

127 Article 4.4.2. GHTF Roles and Responsibilities Document, see *supra* note 106.

128 *Ibid.*, Article 4.6.

Study Groups must reflect an appropriate balance between the number of regulatory and industry experts representing device types, as well as across geographical areas.[129] In case of dispute over Study Group membership, the Steering Committee may be asked to arbitrate".[130]

Within the IMDRF, work will be conducted in Ad Hoc Working Groups, which "may draw upon expertise from various stakeholder groups such as industry, health care professionals, and consumer and patient groups".[131]

#### 10.4.5.3. Secretariat

Within the GHTF, the Secretariat rotated with the chairmanship, and it is currently not known whether a fixed secretariat will be set up under the IMDRF.

### 10.4.6. Guideline Drafting Procedure

The GHTF reaches all decisions by way of consensus. It develops the guidelines in a consultative seven-step procedure.[132] After a new topic is approved by the Steering Committee, the Study Group develops a working draft, which is disseminated to experts amongst the members' regulatory authorities and industry members or to external experts. The comments are then returned to the Study Group. Consequently, the Study Group concludes a final working draft, which, after approval by the Steering Committee, becomes subject to public consultation. All final working drafts are posted on the GHTF website, and the members also conduct consultations within their jurisdiction. These comments are then transferred back to the GHTF, which consequently issues a revised draft. Once endorsed by the Steering Committee, it becomes the final guideline, and is posted on the GHTF website. The members are expected to adopt the guideline within their domestic regulatory systems.

Whereas within the GHTF process, public interest stakeholders such as consumer or patients groups did not have a formal role (though

---

[129] *Ibid.*, Articles 4.4.2. and 4.5.2.

[130] *Ibid.*, Article 4.4.2.

[131] Statement from the International Medical Device Regulators Forum, see *supra* note 104.

[132] Article 3 GHTF Operating Procedures, see *supra* note 108.

they had a right to comment), there are some indications that they may have, if desired, a greater role in the IMDRF: the IMDRF has stated that it "may draw upon expertise from various stakeholder groups such as industry, academia, healthcare professionals, and consumer and patient groups".[133] At IMDRF's bi-annual meetings, "stakeholders will have an opportunity to learn of the work of the Forum, provide input on emerging issues and suggest potential new work items".[134] The details of such involvement are, however, currently unknown.

### 10.4.7. The Content of the Guidelines

GHTF guidelines provide a basis for comprehensive regulatory control of medical devices, or a regulatory model. The documents provide guidance as to ensuring the safety, effectiveness, performance, and quality of medical devices. These documents set out, *inter alia*, guidance as to premarket evaluation of medical devices (for example essential principles of safety, performance and labeling, *et cetera*), post market surveillance (for example adverse events reporting), quality system requirements, audit practices, and clinical safety of medical devices.[135]

### 10.4.8. Globalization and Expansion of Participation

At the time the GHTF was founded almost two decades ago, the three regions of North America, Europe, and Asia Pacific represented the major and dominant trading areas for medical devices. Expertise on medical devices was, hence, limited to the founding members. This is changing now, and medical device manufacturing is much more diverse, surging in a number of countries that are not participants in the GHTF. These countries are now developing new medical devices regulatory programs.

In order to prevent divergence between the advanced regulatory systems of the GHTF founding countries and non-GHTF countries that are in the process of developing such systems, and in order to give voice to the new expertise coming from more parts of the world, the GHTF has declared that it will allow broader participation in its work. In 2007, it

[133] Statement from GHTF Chair, see *supra* note 102.

[134] *Ibid.*

[135] GHTF, "GHTF Documents", available at http://www.ghtf.org/documents/, last accessed on 21 November 2011.

stated that inclusion is "the future hallmark of the GHTF",[136] and that "The Task Force will commit itself to increasingly welcome nations and regions wishing to be more active participants in the ongoing work of the organization".[137] In practice, however, the GHTF has been very cautious about expansion. The GHTF has been concerned, *inter alia*, that expansion could undermine the efficient and flexible manner in which the GHTF works.[138]

This has resulted in the criticism that the GHTF's structure does not allow regulators from emerging countries to have the voice they want and need.[139] And indeed, at the time of the GHTF's dissolution in 2011, the need for such expansion has been acknowledged again, with the chairman's statement that "the current GHTF membership is not reflective of the changing global market in 2011 and beyond".[140] He further declared that the IMDRF will "seek to include members from countries that are, or are likely to become, influential in medical device manufacture and/or regulation".[141]

While at the time of the writing of this chapter the details are still unknown, there are some indications that emerging economies such as Brazil and China will have a bigger role in the IMDRF than they did in the GHTF. Brazil will most likely become a member but the extent of the role China or other countries will have is currently unclear. Moreover, the WHO will also be sitting in the IMDRF's management committee, though its status – whether as member or observer – is yet to be discussed.

---

136 GHTF, "Action Plan for 2007–2010: Path Forward for the Global Harmonization Task Force", SG document, available at http://www.ghtf.org/about/GHTF_Action_Plan-Final_Version_2_.pdf, last accessed on 21 November 2011.

137 *Ibid.*

138 *Ibid.*

139 Maureen Kenny, "New regulators' only medtech harmonisation forum sets sights high but is thin on detail", 10 November 2011, available at http://www.rajpharma.com/productsector/medicaldevices/New-regulators-only-medtech-harmonisation-forum-sets-sights-high-but-is-thin-on-detail-323485?autnID=/contentstore/rajpharma/codex/f8422475-0ae8-11e1-bbe6-4d8e6a53eb99.xml, last accessed on 21 November 2011.

140 Statement from GHTF Chair, see *supra* note 102.

141 *Ibid.*

### 10.4.9. Adoption of Guidelines

The GHTF has issued over 30 guidance documents.[142] As we have seen above, with respect to the adoption of the guidelines, there are two main questions. The first question concerns the adoption by the founding regulatory authorities.

As in the case of the ICH and VICH, GHTF documents are not formally binding and so the members are not obliged to implement them in their jurisdictions. The members' agreement is to "take appropriate steps to implement GHTF guidance and policies within the boundaries of their legal and institutional constraints".[143] And it is "recognized that participating regulatory authorities retain the right to regulate according to their applicable sovereign regulations".[144]

In practice, while the regulatory systems of the founding members are largely aligned with the GHTF framework, uniform implementation of the GHTF model at an operational model amongst the founding member regulatory authorities has not been fully achieved.[145] In fact, founding members have been slow to adopt GHTF guidance within their domestic medical device regulatory systems.[146]

Against this backdrop, the regulatory authorities have decided to transform the GHTF into a regulators-only forum in the form of the IMDRF. Their thought has been that a regulators group would be the best way to achieve harmonization at the operational level as it would allow for more detailed discussion among members on the optimum ways to achieve such goal. The GHTF regulatory model and all of the GHTF documentation will serve as a springboard to this end.[147]

A second question concerns the adoption of GHTF guidelines by non-ICH countries. Many developing and emerging countries currently lack local medical device regulatory capacity. These countries will need

---

[142] *Ibid.*

[143] Article 2.1, GHTF Rules and Responsibilities, see *supra* note 106.

[144] Article 2.1, GHTF Guiding Principles, see *supra* note 101.

[145] Statement from GHTF Chair, see *supra* note 102.

[146] GHTF, "GHTF Retrospective Assessment: Key Findings and Recommendations", 11 January 2008, available at http://www.ghtf.org/about/, last accessed on 21 November 2011.

[147] Statement from GHTF Chair, see *supra* note 102.

to develop such a system, and one of the GHTF's main purposes is to contribute to building such capacity.

To this end, the GHTF aims to "foster international cooperation between countries with established and developing regulatory systems"[148] and to "serve as an information exchange forum through which countries with medical device regulatory systems under development can benefit from the experience of those with established systems and/or pattern their practices upon those of GHTF documents".[149] The GHTF is also "committed to collaboration with non-founding members, international standard-setting bodies and/or public health organizations in order to share experiences gained with its regulatory Member's regulatory systems [...]".[150]

The GHTF, accordingly, seeks to promote the implementation of GHTF guidelines, by regulatory authorities with developing regulatory systems. The goal is essentially that the latter pattern their regulatory systems upon the regulatory model developed by the GHTF.[151]

In order to support regulatory authorities in adopting the GHTF's model, bodies such as the WHO, AHWP, and LAHWP participate in some of the GHTF's work. Moreover, the GHTF also conducts training courses and conferences for non-members[152] for example, for APEC economies or other Latin American countries.[153] The GHTF's website is also an important tool for making its documents publicly available.[154]

Not only does the GHTF promote the use of its guidance documents, many non-members promote them too: PAHO (the WHO's Latin American arm) expressly urges its members to use GHTF guidelines in

---

[148] Article 2.2.(F) GHTF Guiding Principles, see *supra* note 101.

[149] *Ibid.*, Article 2.1.

[150] *Ibid.*, Article 3.4.

[151] GHTF, "Overview and Mission", available at http://www.ghtf.org/about/overview.html, last accessed on 21 November 2011; Michael Gropp, "Implementing GHTF Guidance", at GHTF Annual Conference, 12–14 May 2009, Toronto/Canada, available at http://www.ghtf.org/meetings/conferences/12thconference/slides/slides-gropp2.pdf, last accessed on 21 November 2011.

[152] GHTF Roles and Responsibilities, Article 5.2., see *supra* note 106.

[153] GHTF, "Meetings and Training", available at http://www.ghtf.org/meetings/, last accessed on 21 November 2011.

[154] Action Plan for 2007–2010, p. 5, see *supra* note 136.

their programs for the regulation of medical devices.[155] PAHO has also translated GHTF guidelines into Spanish and Portuguese to this end. The WHO similarly encourages all of its members, in particular those that are developing medical devices regulatory systems, to follow GHTF guidance.[156]

The AHWP similarly brings back GHTF guidance documents to discuss their adoption or adaptation in the Asian-Pacific region.[157] China, for example, accordingly adopts GHTF guidelines.[158] Also in Latin America and the Caribbean area, there is an interest in adopting/adapting GHTF documents.[159]

In the future, under the IMDRF we can expect even more active outreach to non-GHTF countries: the IMDRF has explicitly said that its

155 See PAHO, 42nd Directing Council, "S. CD 42.R10 Medical Devices", 52nd Session of the Regional Committee, CD 42/FR (29 September 2000), Final Report, available at http://www.paho.org/english/gov/cd/cd42_fr-e.pdf, last accessed on 21 November 2011.

156 PAHO/WHO, "A Guide for the Development of Medical Device Regulations", 2002, available at http://new.paho.org/hq/dmdocuments/2009/AguideforthedevelopmentofMedicalDevicesRegulations.pdf, last accessed on 21 November 2011; PAHO/WHO, "A Model Regulatory Program for Medical Devices: An International Guide", 2001, available at http://new.paho.org/hq/dmdocuments/2009/AmodelRegulatoryProgramforMedicalDevices_AnInternalGuide.pdf, last accessed on 21 November 2011; WHO, "Medical Devices Regulations: Global Overview and Guiding Principles", 2003, available at http://whqlibdoc.who.int/publications/2003/9241546182.pdf, last accessed on 21 November 2011.

157 Asian Harmonization Working Party, "Implementing GHTF Guidance in the Asia Pacific Region", at GHTF Annual Conference, 12–14 May, 2009, Toronto, Canada, available at http://www.ghtf.org/meetings/conferences/12thconference/slides/slides-ahwp.pdf, last accessed on 21 November 2011.

158 Hao Heping, "Introduction to Regulations for Medical Device in P.R. China", 9th GHTF Annual Conference, 27 June 2002, Singapore, available at http://www.ghtf.org/meetings/conferences/9thconference/presentations/chinese/haoheping.pdf, last accessed on 21 November 2011.

159 Antonio Hernandez, "Implementing GHTF Guidance in Latin America and Caribbean Region", at GHTF Annual Conference, 13 May 2009, Toronto, Canada, available at http://www.ghtf.org/meetings/conferences/12thconference/slides/slides-hernandez.pdf, last accessed on 21 November 2011.

goal is "to accelerate international medical device regulatory harmonization".[160]

## 10.5. Conclusion

The ICH, VICH, and GHTF are harmonization networks whose core members are the US FDA and the European Commission. Each of the networks deals with a different subject matter, but they share some common characteristics and features. These features teach us about the state and problems of IN-LAW – at the very least, within the area of medical product regulation.

First, despite lacking international legal personality and falling short of the formality of treaty based intergovernmental organizations, the networks have developed organized governance structures (that is, Steering Committees and Expert Working Groups), as well as detailed procedural rules as to the development of guidelines. These procedures also tend to be consultative, with consultation procedures at both the domestic level (that is, between the domestic regulatory authorities and their public) and the international level (that is, comments that may be submitted directly to the network, as well as inclusion of observers, interested parties and the like in the process). Decisions are by way of consensus. To conclude, despite being "informal" from an international law perspective, these networks have developed administrative-like formalities, and the participating regulators are also still bound by their domestic limitations. That being said, the networks lack an appeal process, though the GHTF, at least on paper, set up a complaints mechanism.

Second, due to the dependency of regulatory authorities on industry for information (concerning scientific matters as well as better understanding trade barriers), regulatory authorities have been collaborating with industry in developing standards – though we see a move away from this trend in the case of the GHTF. While public interest groups (such as patients, animal protection or consumer groups) have the right to comment – they do not participate at an equal footing with industry. This situation reflects the growing role of business in international relations and

160 Statement from the International Medical Device Regulators Forum, see *supra* note 104.

standard setting.[161] It also illuminates the need to find a way to adequately balance between effectiveness of standard setting on the one hand, and preventing regulatory capture and the protection of the public interest on the other.[162]

Third, from a (domestic) hierarchy of laws perspective, the networks harmonize rules that are essentially at the lowest level of the hierarchy pyramid. They are in most cases at the level of administrative (legally non-binding) guidance documents or in some cases, if at all, at the level of administrative (legally binding) regulations. While such guidance has significant meaning for companies and patients, principal issues (normally to be set out in law) are not dealt with in these harmonization networks. This suggests that IN-LAW among regulatory authorities is limited to topics that are within their authority to issue administrative regulations or guidance documents, whereas international collaboration on principal topics (that require adoption into primary law) will remain within the realm of traditional, formal intergovernmental relations. Hence, while IN-LAW among regulatory authorities may have proliferated in many areas of government regulation, the results here would suggest that we can grossly expect such collaboration to be limited to topics that do not require an amendment of a primary law.

Fourth, when the US, Europe, and Japan set up the networks in the 1990s, they rightfully reflected the global market of medical products. However, globalization and the shift of production to non-member countries have led to a rift between the market power realities and the institutional structure of the networks. We see in all of the networks a sense of unease with this situation, and a desire to integrate new countries into the institutional settings. As we have seen, the extent or the manner in which this is done varies among them, but all are in the process of adapting their institutional structures to this end. If we compare this development with formal intergovernmental organizations, integration of new powers is a much more complicated and slow process.[163] This flexibility that allows the relatively easy adaptation of institutional settings to global realities reflects the advantage of a network based cooperation model over a formal

[161] Tim Büthe and Walter Mattli, *The New Global Rulers: The Privatization of Regulation in the World Economy*, Princeton University Press, Princeton, 2011.

[162] Berman, 2011, see *supra* note 5.

[163] Stewart Patrick, "Irresponsible Stakeholders? The Difficulty of Integrating Rising Powers", in *Foreign Affairs*, 2010, vol. 89, no. 6, pp. 44–53.

treaty-based model.[164] It should be noted that the desire to involve the emerging markets in the process not only comes from them, but to a large extent also from the network members themselves: industry, seeking to expand their markets, want a global level playing field. And regulators will have an easier time controlling the products that enter their jurisdiction if all producers follow similar standards.

Fifth, in light of the shift of the supply chain to non-member countries, the focus of the networks has shifted to actively encouraging the adoption of their guidelines in non-member countries – by setting up supporting bodies (for example, ICH's Regulators Forum), collaboration with regional harmonization initiatives, collaboration with the WHO/OIE, training sessions, publicly available information, *et cetera*. Moreover, the regulatory framework developed by the networks is used as a source of information and expertise that developing countries or intergovernmental organizations (WHO, OIE) can rely on in developing their regulatory systems.

While the networks enjoy much epistemic legitimacy – with their guidelines considered 'state of the art' – the externalities the networks create towards non-members raise questions as to the extent to which the networks are responsive to the needs and interests of those affected by their guidelines. A common problem is the question of the appropriateness of 'western', commercially driven standards to the needs of emerging and developing countries. At this stage, it is unclear how this should or could be overcome. Possible ideas would be that the network set up special bodies to adapt the guidelines, or that the relevant IO would take charge of adapting the guidelines to local needs. Alternatively, local regulatory authorities would need to adapt them locally.

Sixth, formal intergovernmental organizations still have a role to play alongside IN-LAW. As we have seen, the WHO and OIE participate in the networks in observer-like roles. The purpose of this collaboration is for the intergovernmental organization, with its universal membership, to serve as a communication channel between the network members (being a club of developed countries) and non-members (mostly emerging and developing countries). The communication, however, appears to be in practice rather one-sided: as we have seen, the WHO and OIE circulate draft guidelines among their members and disseminate the final guidelines. The

164 Slaughter, 2004, see *supra* note 1.

WHO and OIE also expressly encourage their members to adopt the networks' guidelines. But it is questionable to what extent, if at all, the networks have taken the needs and interests of developing countries into account.[165]

To conclude, to a large extent the networks and the IOs complement each other.[166] While the IOs are in charge of broad fields – human health and animal health – the networks contribute by developing technical, scientific guidelines on specific topics. In fact, the IOs rely on the networks to fulfill a small part of their broader global strategies. This is evident in the case of the WHO and OIE. Both have been encouraging their members to adopt GHTF and VICH guidelines as part of their global strategy for regulatory governance in the field of medical devices and animal health, respectively.

[165] It is also unclear to what extent, if at all, the WHO/OIE have presented such interests before the networks. Very little public material about the discussions in the networks are available.

[166] This contrasts Slaughter's original prediction that networks would supersede IOs and represent the emerging "real new world order". Anne Marie Slaughter, "The Real New World Order", in *Foreign Affairs*, 1997, vol. 76, no. 5, pp. 183–197.

[illegible]

[illegible] the needs and interests of developing countries [illegible] crops.

[illegible] each other? [illegible] 1990s [illegible]
[illegible] guidelines [illegible]. In fact [illegible] the need [illegible]
[illegible] the use of the WHO [illegible]. Others [illegible] have been encouraging their [illegible]
[illegible] regulatory movements in the field of medical devices and [illegible]
health care [illegible].

[illegible]

# 11

# Food Safety Standards and Informal International Lawmaking

**Sanderijn Duquet**[*] **and Dylan Geraets**[**]

## 11.1. Introduction

Over the years, the rise of globalization processes in economy and technology has demanded ever-growing international governance responsibilities, including in the area of food safety.[1] National regulators have been setting food labeling, product and process standards which food processers and importers have to follow in order to ensure domestic food safety. The coordination of safety measures in globally integrated food chains and interconnected markets has proven to be by no means possible without international cooperation,[2] be it formal or informal.[3] Resulting from this, since the 1960s, standard-setting has also become an important international regulatory tool to ensure worldwide food safety. The current food

[*] **Sanderijn Duquet** (Master of Laws, Ghent U. and LL.M. International Legal Studies, American U. Washington College of Law) is a Ph.D. candidate at the Leuven Centre for Global Governance Studies and the Institute for International Law, University of Leuven, Belgium, where she works as a research fellow of the Policy Research Centre on Foreign Affairs, International Entrepreneurship and Development Cooperation for the Flemish Government.

[**] **Dylan Geraets** is a Ph.D. Candidate in Law and Research Fellow at the Leuven Centre for Global Governance Studies and the Institute for International Law, KU Leuven, Belgium.

[1] Michael A. Livermore, "Authority and Legitimacy in Global Governance: Deliberation, Institutional Differentiation, and the Codex Alimentarius", in *New York University Law Review,* 2006, vol. 81, p. 766; Ching-Fu Lin, "Global Food Safety: Exploring Key Elements for an International Regulatory Strategy" in *Virginia Journal of International Law*, 2011, vol. 51, p. 641.

[2] National food safety regulation and standards typically only address food produced or processed within their territory and imported foodstuff; Lee Ann Jackson and Marion Jansen, "Risk Assessment in the International Food Safety Policy Arena. Can the Multilateral Institutions Encourage Unbiased Outcomes?", in *Food Policy,* 2010, vol. 35, p. 538.

[3] Sandra Hoffmann and William Harder, "Food Safety and Risk Governance in Globalized Markets", in *Health Matrix: Journal of Law-Medicine,* 2010, vol. 20, pp. 7–8.

safety governance regime involves a multitude of actors – at the national, regional and international level – aiming to harmonize product and process standards to safeguard the quality of products for human consumption.[4]

The proliferation of food safety standard-setters goes hand in hand with various dynamics in food regulation. First, standard-setting seeks to reconcile a double objective: the protection of the health of consumers and the facilitation of trade in food products.[5] Domestic and regional measures to protect human safety and wellbeing can hinder trade.[6] The harmonization of international standards is crucial to facilitating market access[7] and the functioning of different markets – from production to distribution – in which powerful corporate capital is involved.[8] Second, public authorities controlling food chains are challenged by private actors (retailers, producers and suppliers) developing private food safety standards and practices.[9] Third, all standard-setters and regulative authorities are confronted with particular tensions between risk assessment and risk management, or, in more general terms, between science and policy.[10] Fourth, and of particular interest to this contribution, the rise of interna-

4 Lin, 2011, p. 650, see *supra* note 1.

5 Donna Roberts and Laurian Unnevehr, "Resolving Trade Disputes Arising From Trends in Food Safety Regulation: The Role of the Multilateral Governance Framework", in *World Trade Review,* 2005, vol. 4, no. 3, p. 470.

6 Standards can be used as non-tariff barriers to international trade; Spencer Henson and Steven Jaffee, "Understanding Developing Country Strategic Responses to the Enhancement of Food Safety Standards", in *The World Economy,* 2008, vol. 31, no. 4, p. 551; Jackson and Jansen, 2010, p. 538, see *supra* note 2. Sturm argues that the importing countries tend to set stricter food safety standards than the exporting countries. Daniel Sturm, "Product Standards, Trade Disputes, and Protectionism", in *Canadian Journal of Economics,* 2006, vol. 39, no. 2, p. 566.

7 Jan Wouters, Axel Marx and Nicolas Hachez, "In Search of a Balanced Relationship: Public and Private Food Safety Standards and International Law", Leuven Centre for Global Governance Studies Working Paper No. 29 – June 2009, available at http://ghum.kuleuven.be/ggs/publications/working_papers/new_series/wp21-30/wp29.pdf, at 3, last accessed on 27 November 2012.

8 Lin, 2011, p. 639, see *supra* note 1.

9 Steven Bernstein, "When is Non-State Global Governance Really Governance?", in *Utah Law Review*, 2010, vol. 91, p. 109; Jackson and Jansen, 2010, p. 539, see *supra* note 2.

10 Jackson and Jansen, 2010, pp. 540–544, see *supra* note 2.

tional informal lawmaking and cooperation has had particular influence on the development of food regulation.

After having introduced the concept of IN-LAW in a food safety context (11.2.), this contribution aims to map the current state of play of food standard-setting and the actors – public and private – involved at different levels, while measuring the extent to which they rely on informal law (11.3.). Subsequently, the use of informal law in food standard-setting will be assessed (11.4.) and more specifically the question whether informal law can be a full-grown regulatory element for effectively tackling global food safety issues. Finally, to conclude, the authors aim to look ahead at the likelihood of changes that could occur in the current architecture of the food governance regime, with a particular focus on the durability of the informal character of standard-setting (11.5.).

## 11.2. The Concept of Informal International Lawmaking

The notion of 'informal international lawmaking' (IN-LAW) is used in contrast to more 'traditional' forms of international lawmaking. This contribution therefore relies on the work of Joost Pauwelyn, who defines the IN-LAW mechanisms as

> Cross-border cooperation between public authorities, with or without the participation of private actors and/or international organizations, in a forum other than a traditional international organization (*process informality*), and/or as between actors other than traditional diplomatic actors (such as regulators or agencies) (*actor informality*), and/or which does not result in a formal treaty or traditional source of international law (*output informality*).[11]

It should be noted that this definition puts forward three distinctive elements to determine whether a form of international cooperation can be an IN-LAW mechanism which do not have to be cumulatively fulfilled.[12] Food standard-setters can be informal in any of the above three ways (actors, processes, output) and to different degrees.[13] Exclusively private

[11] This definition of IN-LAW has been presented in Joost Pauwelyn, "Informal International Lawmaking: Framing the Concept and Research Questions", in Joost Pauwelyn, Ramses A. Wessel and Jan Wouters (eds.), *Informal International Lawmaking*, Oxford University Press, Oxford, 2012, p. 22.

[12] *Ibid.*, p. 21.

[13] *Ibid.*

food safety cooperation mechanisms, which set standards, yet do not exercise public authority, are not covered under the IN-LAW definition.[14] Nevertheless, for means of comparison, a selection of these private mechanisms is assessed *infra* next to public informal international lawmaking (IN-LAW) mechanisms. This will further enable us to pinpoint substantial interactions between public and private standard-setters whose combined activities shape the regulatory system in food safety. This contribution also takes a broad view on the concept of lawmaking, which includes standard-setting, the proclamation of statements and guidelines, harmonization (when part of a broader normative process and joint international practice) and information-sharing that creates legal effects.[15] However, this assessment of lawmaking in an IN-LAW context does not automatically lead to the assumption that all of the mechanisms' output is law.[16]

### 11.3. Setting Food Safety Standards in a Multi-Actor Context

Transnational cooperation among national governments, agencies and private actors in the issuance and harmonization of food standards is characterized by variety in appearance. The starting point of this contribution is the observation that all cooperation systems in food standard-setting share an elementary level of 'output informality' as described by Pauwelyn – none of the created standards take the form of formal legally enforceable commitments or constitute a traditional source of international law.[17] As will be seen *infra*, due to external factors, the level of informality of the standards as the main output is not static.[18] Among the fora discussed in this contribution, the 'actor' and 'process informality' differ to an even greater extent. This leads to remarkable variances in the way IN-LAW serves as a common mode of lawmaking in food safety.

---

[14] *Ibid.*

[15] Our use of the concept of 'lawmaking' in a broad sense is inspired by Pauwelyn, 2012, p. 21, see *supra* note 11.

[16] *Ibid.*

[17] *Ibid.*, p. 15; See Aust who describes "an informal international instrument" as "an instrument which is not a treaty because the parties to it do not intend it to be legally binding"; Anthony Aust, The Theory and Practice of Informal International Instruments, in *The International and Comparative Law Quarterly*, 1986, vol. 35, p. 787.

[18] See *infra* "The Codex Alimentarius Commission", at 11.3.1.3.1.

### 11.3.1. Actors with a Public Character

#### 11.3.1.1. Bilateral Food Standard-Setting

For more than a century now, national authorities have been engaged in the setting of standards to regulate food products and processes that enter or circulate in their respective national markets.[19] While these national regulatory schemes differ from each other, bilateral initiatives on information exchanges and harmonization of food standards have become a pivotal part of international food safety governance. In 1991, Australia and New Zealand decided to integrate their food regulation and administrations and established the Australia and New Zealand Food Authority (ANZFA). The impact of this bilateral cooperation in food safety expanded as a result of the increasing institutionalization through the establishment of a joint Food Standards Australia-New Zealand Agency (FSANZ) in 2002.[20] The agency has been set up as a binational government administration and has the objective to develop and administer the Australia New Zealand Food Standards Code ('the Code').[21] The enforcement and interpretation of the Code remains the responsibility of state departments and food agencies of Australia and New Zealand.[22] Common standards are created that apply in both countries and are governed by the 'Agreement Between Australia and New Zealand Establishing a System for the Development of Joint Food Standards', signed on 5 December 1995.[23]

[19] In 1906, the Pure Food and Drug Act and the Beef Inspection Act were introduced in the United States of America, which had the objective of improving food safety conditions. In 1927, the US Food, Drug and Insecticide Administration (FDA) was established. Virtually all countries followed this example see, *e.g.*, the standard setting activities of the UK Food Standards Agency (FSA), the Food Safety Authority of Ireland (FSAI), the *Instituto Nacional de Alimentos* in Argentina and Canada Health.

[20] Roberts and Unnevehr, 2005, p. 473, see *supra* note 5.

[21] General food and food product standards listed in Chapter 1 and 2 of this Code apply in both Australia and New Zealand, while the food safety and primary production standards listed in Chapters 3 and 4 apply in Australia only.

[22] FSANZ, "Food Standards", available at http://www.foodstandards.gov.au/, last accessed on 27 November 2012.

[23] This treaty, which entered into force in 1996 and was amended in 2002 and 2010, established a joint Australian New Zealand Food Standards Code and the formation of the first truly binational government agency between Australia and New Zealand. See "History of FSANZ" at http://www.foodstandards.gov.au/scienceandeducation/, last accessed on 27 November 2012.

FSANZ contributes to global food safety governance through its participation in the Codex Alimentarius Commission,[24] WHO and FAO consultations and expert panels.[25]

The joint system adopted by Australia and New Zealand is a primary example of bilateral cross-border collaboration between public authorities in food standard-setting and information sharing. One of the consequences of the informal cooperation is that it may lead to lawmaking. The forum used in the Oceanic countries is an agency established with the specific purpose of exchanging information, developing and proclaiming food standards.[26] The Australian and New Zealand Food Regulation Ministerial Council is the executive body with the power to promulgate common food standards, but the FSANZ nevertheless allows the public to participate in amending the Code.[27] Individuals, organizations and corporations from Australia, New Zealand or any other country are given the opportunity to take part in the standardization processes. This significantly adds to the level of actor informality of the agency, although food agencies of both governments involved remain primary standard-setters.[28]

### 11.3.1.2. Regional Food Standard-Setting

Regional organizations that pursue free trade objectives, such as MERCOSUR and the European Union (EU), share the objective of identifying and reducing (non-tariff) barriers to food trade in their respective integrated markets. In pursuing these goals, both international organizations (IOs) have included the setting and harmonization of food standards in their activities. The EU and MERCOSUR also form important negotiation blocks in the Codex Alimentarius Commission.[29]

---

[24] See *infra* 11.3.1.3.1., The Codex Alimentarius Commission; Hoffmann and Harder, 2010, p. 44, see *supra* note 3.

[25] FSANZ, FAO/WHO Regional Conference on Food Safety for Asia and Pacific, Seremban, Malaysia, May 24–27, 2004, "The Application of Risk Analysis in Food Control - Challenges and Benefits", available at ftp://ftp.fao.org/docrep/fao/meeting/006/j1985e/j1985e00.pdf, last accessed on 27 November 2012.

[26] Hoffmann and Harder, 2010, p. 44, see *supra* note 3.

[27] "Changing the Code", available at www.foodstandards.gov.au/foodstandards/changingthecode/, last accessed on 27 November 2012.

[28] Hoffmann and Harder, 2010, p. 44, see *supra* note 4.

[29] See *infra*: Codex Alimentarius Commission, 11.3.1.3.1.

### 11.3.1.2.1 MERCOSUR

On 26 March 1991, Argentina, Brazil, Paraguay and Uruguay signed the Treaty of Asuncion, establishing the Common Market of the Southern Cone (MERCOSUR).[30] The reduction of trade barriers and the functioning of the common market have been the key objectives to harmonize the food regulation of these countries.[31] A Food Commission operates and manages harmonization activities in the Southern Common Market through a Technical Regulations Work Sub-Group. Food safety and food labeling standard-setting in MERCOSUR mainly relies on the adoption of the standards of the Codex Alimentarius Commission, which has been recognized as the international organization of reference. National standards[32] and private standards[33] also function as models for regulatory action in MERCOSUR.[34]

### 11.3.1.2.2 European Union

Following the BSE and dioxin contamination crises around the turn of the century, food safety laws underwent major reforms in both the EU and its Member States.[35] In the EU context, this brought about a formalization of the former policies and a movement towards centralization of the common

---

30 For more information on the economic and political integration, see the official MERCOSUR website, available at http://www.mercosur.int/, last accessed on 27 November 2012. Venezuela was accepted as a member in 2006 and is currently in the process of integrating into MERCOSUR. Bolivia, Chile, Colombia, Ecuador and Peru have associate member status. Jointly, these countries form one of the most important food producing blocks in the world.

31 Maria Cecilia de Figueiredo, "Southern Common Market Standards", in Naomi Rees and David Watson (eds.), *International Standards for Food Safety*, Aspen Publications, Gaithersburg MD, 2000, p. 80.

32 Of the member countries, but the EU and US Food and Drug Administration regulation are consulted too. *Ibid.*, p. 86.

33 Elizabeth Farina and Thomas Reardon, "Agrifood Grades and Standards in the Extended MERCOSUR: Their Role in the Changing Agrifood System", in *American Journal of Agricultural Economics*, 2000, vol. 82, no. 5, pp. 1172–1173.

34 De Figueiredo, 2000, p. 95, see *supra* note 31.

35 Robert Riedl and Christina Riedl, "Shortcomings of the New European Food Hygiene Legislation from the Viewpoint of a Competent Authority", in *European Food and Feed Law Review*, 2008, vol. 3, no. 2, p. 64; Hoffmann and Harder, 2010, pp. 30–31, see *supra* note 3.

food safety system.[36] The first European food safety regulations, containing a strategy to harmonize national laws at the European level by issuing common standards on the composition of food in pursuit of the reduction of trade barriers in the internal market,[37] had proven not to be effective enough.[38] In the mid-1980s policies moved towards a standardization of labeling of food products rather than of food substances.[39]

A new radical approach was therefore proposed by the European Commission when it determined food safety to be a key policy objective in its 2000 White Paper on this topic.[40] Current EU food strategies consist of three core elements: (1) scientific advice and risk assessment; (2) European food safety legislation; and (3) control and enforcement in Member States.[41] The majority of priorities put forward in the White Paper were given concrete form in the general 2002 European Food Safety Regulation adopted by the European Parliament and the Council.[42] This Regulation, binding upon all Member States, serves as the legal framework and model[43] for the EU's food safety policies and has the double objective of assuring a high level of protection of human health and consumers' interest in relation to food whilst ensuring effective functioning of the internal market through the free movement of food and feed.[44] The EU's policy is

36 In the aftermath of the BSE crisis, one important critique was that it was hard to determine which actor or policy level was to blame for it. Ellen Vos, "The EU Regulatory System on Food Safety: Between Trust and Safety", in Michelle Everson and Ellen Vos, *Uncertain Risks Regulated*, Routledge/Cavendish Publishing, London, 2009, p. 250.

37 Hoffmann and Harder, 2010, p. 30, see *supra* note 3.

38 Emilie H. Leibovitch, "Food Safety Regulation in the European Union: Toward an Unavoidable Centralization of Regulatory Powers", in *Texas International Law Journal*, 2007–2008, vol. 43, p. 432.

39 *Ibid.*

40 European Commission, White Paper on Food Safety, COM(1999) 719, 12 January 2000, p. 3.

41 *Ibid.* at 5.

42 Regulation (EC) No. 178/2002 of the European Parliament and of the Council of 28 January 2002, laying down the general principles and requirements of food law, establishing the European Food Safety Authority and laying down procedures in matters of food safety, *O.J.* 1 February 2002, L 31/1, amended by Regulation (EC) No. 1642/2003 and Regulation (EC) No 575/2006 ("European Food Safety Regulation").

43 Lin, 2011, p. 636, see *supra* note 1.

44 Art. 1 and 5 European Food Safety Regulation.

based on the prohibition to place unsafe food on the market[45] and four general principles – the use of risk analysis, the precautionary principle, the protection of consumers' interests and principles of transparency[46] – to govern all foodstuffs, rather than the setting of standards or regulations relating to specific products or processes.[47]

The Food Regulation functions as the point of reference and model law covering all aspects of the food chain process. The framework regulation has been criticized, however, for its vague character and the consequential inconsistencies in its interpretation and implementation by Member States.[48] The Regulation stipulates that international standards will be taken into account where these exist, with the exception of cases where international standards are an ineffective or inappropriate means for the fulfillment of the legitimate objectives of food law, where there is a scientific justification not to use them, or where they would result in a different level of protection from the one determined as appropriate in the EU.[49]

The EU and its Member States also aim to contribute to the development, consistency and coordination of international technical standards for food and feed.[50] Acting upon this, in 2003 the European Commission submitted a request for accession to the Codex Alimentarius Commission[51] and became its first Member Organization.[52] Similar to Codex's State members, the EU selectively implements Codex standards in its internal legal order. Codex standards are, however, an important part of European food safety lawmaking. On several occasions the Court of Justice referred to Codex standards in its case law.[53]

45 Art. 14 European Food Safety Regulation.

46 Arts. 6–10 European Food Safety Regulation.

47 Hoffmann and Harder, 2010, pp. 34–35, see *supra* note 3.

48 Lin, 2011, p. 657, see *supra* note 1.

49 Art. 5(3) European Food Safety Regulation.

50 Art. 13 European Food Safety Regulation.

51 Art. 1 Council Decision 2003/822/EC of 17 November 2003 on the accession of the European Community to the Codex Alimentarius Commission, *O.J.* 2003 L 309/14.

52 See "The Codex Alimentarius Commission", *infra* at 11.3.1.3.1.

53 Sara Poli, "The European Community and the Adoption of International Food Standards within the Codex Alimentarius Commission", in *European Law Journal,* 2004, vol. 10, no. 5, pp. 616–617; Hoffmann and Harder, 2010, p. 35, see *supra* note 3.

The 2002 Food Safety Regulation established the European Food Safety Authority (EFSA)[54] as an independent European agency funded by the EU budget, which began its activities by providing independent scientific and technical support and advice in 2003.[55] This primarily scientific body is not tasked with food management, a responsibility that remains with the Commission and the EU Member States.[56] Although EFSA creates scientific opinions rather than standards, its activities nevertheless have led to the *de facto* harmonization of European national food laws.[57]

Article 17 (1) of the Food Safety Regulation determines that primary responsibility for food safety in the Union rests with business operators.[58] Member States conduct official controls, enforce food regulations, and bear the duty to monitor and verify that the relevant requirements of food laws are fulfilled by food and feed business operators at all stages of production, processing and distribution.[59] The Commission, through the Directorate General for Health and Consumers (DG SANCO) and the Food and Veterinary Office (FVO) supervises this implementation of food safety law by national authorities.[60] FVO inspectors audit food production and processing establishments in Member States and third countries that export food and feed to the EU, to ensure compliance.[61] Non-compliance by Member States may result in infringement proceedings. The Commis-

54 See EFSA's website, available at http://www.efsa.europa.eu, last accessed on 27 November 2012. Art. 4 European Food Safety Regulation stipulates that the Authority consists of a Management Board, an Executive Director, an Advisory Forum, a Scientific Committee and Scientific Panels. For a more detailed assessment of these bodies, see Alberto Alemanno, "The European Food Safety Authority at Five", in *European Food and Feed Law Review*, 2008, vol. 3, no. 1, pp. 7–12.

55 Arts. 22 and 23 European Food Safety Regulation.

56 Alberto Alemanno describes the reluctance of the Member States of transferring the risk management tasks to an independent food agency instead of the Commission; Alemanno, 2008, p. 4, see *supra* at note 54. See Silvia Valtueña Martínez, Leng Heng, Wolfgang Gelbmann, Antoine Cuvillier and Pilar Rodríguez Iglesias, "The Regulation on Nutrition and Health Claims Made on Foods: Role of the European Food Safety Authority", in *European Food and Feed Law Review*, 2007, vol. 2, no. 2, p. 76.

57 Leibovitch, 2007–2008, p. 443, see *supra* note 38.

58 Art. 1 (a) Regulation (EC) No 852/2004 of the European Parliament and of the Council of 29 April 2004 on the hygiene of foodstuffs, *O.J.* 2004, L 139, corrigendum *O.J.* 2004, L 226/3 ("European Hygiene of Foodstuff Regulation").

59 Art. 17(2) European Food Safety Regulation.

60 Arts. 8 and 10 European Hygiene of Foodstuff Regulation.

61 Hoffmann and Harder, 2010, p. 36, see *supra* note 3.

sion is assisted by the Standing Committee on the Food Chain and Animal Health in the preparation of measures relating to foodstuffs and an Advisory Group on the Food Chain and Animal and Plant Health.[62] The Commission is also responsible for managing the network of national contact points in the Member States: the Rapid Alert System for Food and Feed (RASFF).[63] The RASFF is tasked with ensuring the uniform application of food safety law by public authorities in the EU Member States and facilitating the exchange of information on measures taken in response to serious food and feed risks.[64]

Turning to an IN-LAW assessment of the European food safety framework, it must first of all be emphasized that lawmaking in the European food safety system is founded on formal regulatory principles. There is a strict functional and institutional separation of science and policy laid down in the EU regulation.[65] The main actor involved in risk analysis and assessment is EFSA whilst risk management remains the political responsibility of the Commission at the supranational level and, even more important in the decentralized European system, the national food safety authorities.[66] EFSA reaches out to and works closely together with a variety of actors at the national level: from government officials, to scientific experts and even private actors such as business groups and NGOs. As to the processes used, it must be recalled that IN-LAW in the context of, or under the broader auspices of, a formal international organization is not excluded.[67] Elements of informal lawmaking are resembled in EFSA's functioning independently from the EU, constructed as a network of national authorities, though still being connected to the Union. Next to this, the Agency engages in informal harmonization processes through the organization of expert meetings. Regarding the output, EFSA issues opinions, guidelines, informal reports, scientific advice and recommendations

62 Art. 58 European Food Safety Regulation and Commission Decision 2004/613/EC of 6 August 2004 concerning the creation of an advisory group on the food chain and animal and plant health, *O.J.* 2004, L 275.

63 Art. 50 (1) European Food Safety Regulation.

64 Klaus. J. Henning, "Public Authority Communication on Consumer Protection", in *European Food and Feed Law Review*, 2009, no. 5, p. 333; RASFF website, available at http://ec.europa.eu/food/food/rapidalert/index_en.htm, last accessed on 27 November 2012.

65 Alemanno, 2008, p. 22, see *supra* at note 54.

66 Leibovitch, 2007–2008, pp. 434–435, see *supra* note 38.

67 Pauwelyn, 2012, p. 21, see *supra* note 11.

that serve as reference points, without being legally binding. Nevertheless, they have proven to have a considerable impact on 'harder' lawmaking activities.[68] These, for example, take the form of standards and principles to be implemented with the discretion of the Member States.[69] Although EFSA's output per se can therefore be described as informal, a certain re-formalization takes place when they are adopted in national regulation or by the Commission's management and control systems. Some consider EFSA to be part of a regulatory regime, arguing that its informal activities and soft harmonization can simply be labeled 'politics', having the primary purpose of strengthening formal EU lawmaking.[70] The RASFF system, intended to serve the internal notification of rapid alerts concerning food and feed and harmonization of laws, is based on informal cooperation in a network of national contact points. It can however be disputed whether this system actually holds rule-making powers.

#### 11.3.1.3. Global Food Safety Standard-Setting

##### 11.3.1.3.1 The Codex Alimentarius Commission

The Codex Alimentarius Commission (CAC or Codex) is an intergovernmental organization operating as a subsidiary of two UN Agencies: the Food and Agriculture Organization (FAO) and the World Health Organization (WHO).[71] The FAO Conference and the World Health Assembly jointly decided to establish Codex in 1963.[72] Codex designates itself as a

---

68 Art. 22 (7) European Food Safety Regulation; Leibovitch, 2007–2008, pp. 440–441, see *supra* note 38.

69 Leibovitch, 2007–2008, p. 443, see *supra* note 38.

70 Ed Randall, "Not That Soft or Informal: A Response to Eberlein and Grande's Account of Regulatory Governance in the EU with Special Reference to the European Food Safety Authority (EFSA)", in *Journal of European Public Policy,* 2006, vol. 13, no. 3, pp. 409–410.

71 Codex Alimentarius Commission, Secretariat, "Understanding Codex Alimentarius", Rome, 2006, available at ftp://ftp.fao.org/codex/Publications/understanding/Understanding_EN.pdf, and the official Codex Alimentarius website, available at http://www.codexalimentarius.org/, last accessed on 27 November 2012.

72 Neal D. Fortin, "Codex Alimentarius Commission" in Christian Tietje and Alan Brouder, *Handbook of Transnational Economic Governance Regimes*, Martinus Nijhoff Publishers, Leiden/Boston, 2009, p. 645; Ravi Alfonso Pereira, "Why Would International Administrative Activity be Any Less Legitimate, A Study of the Codex Alimentarius Commission", in *German Law Journal*, 2008, vol. 9, p. 1694.

science-based organization, which finances collaborative studies among individual scientists, laboratories, institutes and universities and participates in joint FAO/WHO expert committees and consultations.[73] The delegations of Member States in the Commission operate as risk managers in the standard-setting process.[74] The CAC has been successful in creating voluntary food standards and coordinating standard-setting activities of national, regional and multilateral authorities in the nourishment sector. Codex is considered to be the main actor in global food standard-setting: a 2002 Evaluation Report of the CAC concluded that Codex standards were seen by its Member States as a vital component of food control systems designed to protect consumer health and international trade.[75]

The Codex Commission and its Executive Committee are the central bodies in which Member States are represented.[76] The Commission established three types of subsidiary bodies: (1) General Subject Committees (Codex Committees) that prepare draft standards for submission to the Commission; (2) Commodity Committees whose activities concentrate on specific food commodities;[77] and (3) Regional Coordinating Committees through which regions or groups of countries coordinate food standard-setting activities in the region and develop regional standards. Decisions of the Committees and of the Commission are taken via a formal and institutionalized eight-step decision-making procedure and standards are adopted based on consensus.[78] However, in exceptional circum-

---

73 Codex Alimentarius Commission, 2006, pp. 21–22, see *supra* note 71.

74 Jackson and Jansen, 2010, pp. 543–544, see *supra* note 2. Wouters, Marx and Hachez rightly argue that deciding upon a food safety standard involves assessing the level of risk posed by a food product, and to make a policy choice (based on social preferences) about an acceptable level of that risk, to which society may be submitted. Wouters, Marx and Hachez, 2009, pp. 16–17, see *supra* note 7.

75 FAO and WHO, "Report of the Evaluation of the Codex Alimentarius and other FAO and WHO Food Standards Work", 15 November 2002, at para. 4, available at http://www.fao.org/docrep/meeting/005/y7871e/y7871e00.htm, last accessed on 27 November 2012.

76 Codex Alimentarius Commission, 2006, p. 15, see *supra* note 71.

77 Over time, 42 committees and task forces on specific themes (*e.g.*, food labeling, meat hygiene, milk products, food additives, *etc.*) were established by the CAC. For a complete list see the Codex website at http://www.codexalimentarius.org/committees-and-task-forces/en/, last accessed on 27 November 2012.

78 Codex Alimentarius Commission, 2006, p. 17, see *supra* note 71; Pereira, 2008, pp. 1698–1701, see *supra* note 72; Wouters, Marx and Hachez, 2009, p. 12, see *supra* note 7.

stances they can also be voted upon.[79] Non-binding Codex standards which Member States are encouraged to implement, are the output of this process.[80] Three types of standards are produced: (1) Codex Standards, relating to product characteristics; (2) Codex Codes of Practices, concerning production, processing, manufacturing, transport and storage practices; and (3) Codex Guidelines, which determine policies in key areas or serve interpretative purposes.[81]

To date, Codex brings together 182 Member States, one Member Organization (the European Union) and a number of Associate Members, who virtually represent the world's entire population.[82] The involvement of non-state actors in the multiple stages of the CAC administrative standard-setting procedure is reflected in the participation rules:[83] non-governmental organizations may apply to attend sessions of the Commission and of its subsidiary bodies as observers.[84] Aside from the phase of final adoption of the standard in which the right to speak is exclusively reserved to Member States, Codex rules of procedure allow non-state actors to put forward their points of view at every stage of the procedure.[85] Cur-

---

79 Elizabeth Smythe, "In Whose Interests? Transparency and Accountability in the Global Governance of Food: Agro-business, the Codex Alimentarius and the World Trade Organization", Paper presented at the annual meeting of the International Studies Association 48th Annual Convention, Hilton Chicago, Chicago, IL, USA, 28 February 2007, available at http://citation.allacademic.com/meta/p_mla_apa_research_citation/1/8/0/3/9/p180399_index.html, at 6, last accessed on 27 November 2012; Livermore, 2006, p. 781, see *supra* note 1.

80 A complete list of standards is available at http://www.codexalimentarius.org/standards/en/, last accessed on 27 November 2012.

81 Codex Alimentarius Commission, 2006, p. 11, see *supra* note 71.

82 Rule I and II, Rules of Procedure of the Codex Alimentarius Commission, adopted in 1963 at the first session of the Commission, available at http://www.fao.org/DOCREP/005/Y2200E/y2200e03.htm#bm03, last accessed on 27 November 2012; Neal D. Fortin, "Codex Alimentarius Commission", in Christian Tietje and Alan Brouder (eds.), *Handbook of Transnational Economic Governance Regimes*, Martinus Nijhoff, 2009, p. 646; Pereira, 2008, pp. 1696, see *supra* note 72. A complete list of members is available at http://www.codexalimentarius.org/members-observers/en/, last accessed on 27 November 2012. Territories and groups of territories not responsible for their international relations are listed as Associated Members.

83 Livermore, 2006, p. 781, see *supra* note 1.

84 Rule VII, Rules of Procedure of the Codex Alimentarius Commission, available at http://www.fao.org/DOCREP/005/Y2200E/y2200e03.htm, last accessed on 27 November 2012.

85 *Ibid.*, Rule VII, (1) Rules of Procedure.

rently, 150 NGOs, 49 International Governmental Organizations and 16 UN bodies are taking part in Codex processes. It is common for representatives of the food industry and to a lesser extent for consumer organizations to participate in Codex discussions as members of national delegations.[86] Still, the equal participation of all impacted stakeholders in Codex has been a concern for many years resulting in extensive discussions among scholars and commentators.[87] Civil society in general has a marginal impact on decision-making, as it only enjoys an observer status that allows it to present its views. The partaking of developing countries is questioned too. While, formally, they are members, in practice, they struggle to maintain an expensive team of scientists at the Codex headquarters in Rome and to send representatives to the many Codex meetings organized all over the world.[88]

The Codex Alimentarius Commission's mandate is formulated broadly. Its main objectives are the protection of health of consumers and the facilitation of international trade in food products through the removal of non-tariff barriers.[89] To accomplish these objectives, Codex supports

86 See the example of the US delegation in F. Edward Scarbrough, "Codex – What's All the Fuss?", in *Food and Drug Law Journal*, 2010, vol. 65, pp. 631–638. CAC is perceived to be one of the more industry-dominated IOs. The particular involvement of corporate actors is criticized as business interests make up the better part of observer NGOs and national delegations – most notably of developing countries – which are staffed by experts linked with industry. For further reading – Elizabeth Smythe, 2007, see *supra* note 79.

87 See amongst others: Wouters, Marx and Hachez, 2009, p. 13–14, see *supra* note 7; Michael A. Livermore, "Authority and Legitimacy in Global Governance: Deliberation, Institutional Differentiation, and the Codex Alimentarius", in *New York University Law Review*, 2006, vol. 81, pp. 783–785; Pereira, 2008, pp. 1708–1711, see *supra* note 72.

88 There have been efforts to improve the (more egalitarian) participation of all countries and civil society. An example is the establishment of the Codex Trust Fund. For a review of its functioning, see: Codex Trust Fund Mid-Term Review, Final Report, 30 April 2010, available at http://www.who.int/foodsafety/codex/cac33_14_Add1e.pdf , last accessed on 27 November 2012. This report concluded that although numerical participation of developing countries in Codex has increased resulting from the functioning of the Trust Fund, its new focus should be on the actual strengthening of participation and enhancing scientific/technical participation of those countries in Codex.

89 Art. 1 (a) Statutes of the Codex Alimentarius Commission, adopted in 1961 by the 11th Session of the FAO Conference and in 1963 by the 16th Session of the World Health Assembly, revised in 1966 and 2006; Pereira, 2008, p. 1694, see *supra* note 72.

the international harmonization of national food regulations.[90] Next to this, the CAC promotes the coordination of all other food standards activities carried out by national authorities,[91] and international governmental and non-governmental organizations. It also reaches out to regional food standards initiatives undertaken in, for example, the European Union and MERCOSUR.[92]

Codex standards are formally voluntary and non-binding. However, these standards indirectly acquired certain legal value in a number of international trade disputes.[93] Since 1994, one of the most important Codex features is its linkage with disciplines of the Agreement on Sanitary and Phytosanitary Measures (SPS Agreement) of the World Trade Organization (WTO). The SPS Agreement forms part of the Uruguay Round of multilateral trade negotiations, and makes explicit reference to the standards, guidelines and recommendations of three international bodies (The Three-Sisters), including Codex.[94] Article 3 of the SPS Agreement encourages WTO Members to base their SPS-measures on the standards, guidelines and recommendations of these IOs.[95] This has put further emphasis on the importance of Codex standards for two reasons.[96] First, the

---

90 "General Principle No. 1 of the Codex Alimentarius", in Codex Alimentarius Commission, Procedural Manual, available at ftp://ftp.fao.org/codex/Publications/ProcManuals/Manual_19e.pdf, at 17, last accessed on 27 November 2012; Thorsten Hüller and Leo Maier, "Fixing the Codex? Global Food-Safety Governance Under Review" in Christian Joerges and Ernst-Ulrich Petersmann (eds.), *Constitutionalism, Multilevel Trade Governance, and Social Regulation*, Hart Publishing, Oxford, 2006, p. 269.

91 To facilitate continuous contact with member countries, the Commission, in collaboration with national governments, has established country Codex Contact Points, and many member countries have National Codex Committees to coordinate activities nationally. Pereira, 2008, p. 1696, see *supra* note 72; Livermore, 2006, p. 774, see *supra* note 1.

92 Art. 1 (b) Statutes of the Codex Alimentarius Commission, adopted in 1961 by the 11th Session of the FAO Conference and in 1963 by the 16th Session of the World Health Assembly, revised in 1966 and 2006.

93 Fortin, 2009, p. 650, see *supra* note 72; Smythe, 2007, p. 4, see *supra* note 79.

94 In addition to the Codex Alimentarius Commission, these are the Office International des Epizooties (OIE) and the Secretariat of the International Plant Protection Convention (IPPC).

95 Henson and Jaffee, 2008, pp. 550–551, see *supra* note 6.

96 Art. 2 of the SPS Agreement, 1867 UNTS 493, signed on 15 April 1994, refers to Art. XX (b) GATT and recognizes the sovereign right of Members to provide the level of

Codex Alimentarius Commission is identified as a recognized international standard-setter for food safety and States are encouraged to base their food safety rules on Codex Standards.[97] Second, the SPS Agreement is subject to the very effective WTO dispute settlement mechanism which now indirectly also serves as a compliance mechanism for Codex standards.[98]

The exact legal nature of the Codex Alimentarius Commission remains a point of discussion in the literature since Codex has both formal and informal characteristics, and relies on public and private involvement.[99] That said, Codex cannot be defined as an informal international lawmaking body as understood in the sense of the definition put forward in this contribution.[100] Rather, it is an international organization with certain informal features.[101]

health protection they deem appropriate by taking sanitary and phytosanitary measures necessary for the protection of human, animal or plant life or health. Art. 3 establishes the principle that these SPS measures must be based on international standards, guidelines or recommendations, in particular those produced by the Codex Alimentarius Commission, the International Office of Epizootics, and the international and regional organizations operating within the framework of the International Plant Protection Convention. Members may introduce or maintain SPS measures which result in a higher level of protection than would be achieved by measures based on the relevant international standards, guidelines or recommendations, if there is a scientific justification, or when considered "necessary" following scientific risk assessment (Art. 3.3. SPS Agreement). The burden of proof therefore is on the nations wanting to depart from them. For a more detailed assessment, see David G. Victor, "The Sanitary and Phytosanitary Agreement of the World Trade Organization: An Assessment After Five Years", in *New York University Journal of International Law,* 2000, vol. 32, pp. 873–892.

97 Yoshiko Naiki, "Accountability and Legitimacy in Global Health and Safety Governance: the World Trade Organization, the SPS Committee, and International Standard-Setting Organizations", in *Journal of World Trade,* 2009, vol. 43, no. 6, pp. 1255–1279; Lukasz Gruszczynski, "The Standard of Review in International SPS Trade Disputes. Some New Developments", paper presented at the Standing Group on Regulatory Governance of the European Consortium for Political Research ECPR and the Regulation Network Third Biennial Conference from 17–19 June 2010, University College, Dublin, Ireland, p. 3, available at http://regulation.upf.edu/dublin-10-papers/7F4.pdf, last accessed on 27 November 2012.

98 Pereira, 2008, pp. 1703–1705, see *supra* note 72.

99 *Ibid*., p. 1697.

100 See *supra*: Introduction, 11.1.

101 IN-LAW processes can take place in the context of or under the broader auspices of a formal international organization, see *infra* the European Union.

In terms of output, Codex produces, legally speaking, non-binding standards. The output is formalized via national implementation of the standards and the linkage with the SPS Agreement and the WTO dispute settlement mechanism. The latter has modified the informal character of the Codex considerably: the use of political soft tools in deliberation and the use of consensus-based decision-making decreased, as trade interests (and therefore formality) increased.[102] Codex has been labeled a more politicized forum in which political compromises tend to reflect States' trade interests rather than public health.[103] Standards adopted short of consensus weaken both legitimacy and scientific authority.[104] One of the effects forthcoming from this evolution towards more formality is the increased academic attention devoted to the CAC as a responsive, legitimate and accountable standard-setter.[105]

Process formality exists because of the large involvement of FAO and WHO, the fairly high transparency, the institutionalized decision-making and the intergovernmental nature of Codex. Through an established decision-making process, three categories of Codex standards are adopted following a constraining eight-step procedure. These are published after adoption, in a well-defined form.

Actors involved are Member States who participate through food safety ministries, national contact points and national committees, one non-State member (the EU) and private actors who have obtained an 'observer status' or who participate in the national delegations.

#### 11.3.1.3.2 World Health Organization

The WHO is the directing and coordinating specialized agency for health within the United Nations system. Its responsibilities, among others, include the setting of norms and standards and the articulation of evidence-based policy.[106] The WHO's Constitution stipulates that the development,

[102] Livermore, 2006, p. 777, see *supra* note 1. Victor argues that Codex's work has been increasingly mired in controversy because it is viewed as more relevant because of the status its standards obtained in the SPS Agreement; Victor, 2000, p. 892, see *supra* note 96.

[103] Lin, 2011, p. 650, see *supra* note 1.

[104] *Ibid.*

[105] Livermore, 2006, pp. 777–781, see *supra* note 1.

[106] WHO, "About WHO", available at http://www.who.int, last accessed on 27 November 2012.

establishment and promotion of international standards with respect to food is one of the core functions of the WHO, with a view to attain the highest possible level of health by all peoples.[107] In May 1963, the 16th World Health Assembly approved the establishment of the Joint FAO/WHO Food Standards Program and the Codex Alimentarius Commission[108] was created to develop international food standards, guidelines and recommendations to protect the health of consumers.[109] The WHO nevertheless remained a relevant institution in global food safety: its key undertakings are international standard setting, facilitating risk assessments (for Codex and Member States) and providing technical assistance to governments.[110] The 2002 WHO Global Strategy for Food Safety identifies the availability of safe food as a basic human right. The reduction of foodborne diseases is, therefore, its top priority.[111]

WHO's central role is a normative one. Other than Codex's normative powers, WHO's supreme decision-making body, the World Health Assembly, has the authority to adopt conventions and agreements with respect to any matter lying within the competence of the Organization.[112] These will become binding upon the acceptance of Member States.[113] Article 21 grants the WHO Health Assembly authority to adopt binding reg-

[107] Arts. 1 and 2 (u) WHO Constitution, adopted by the International Health Conference held in New York from 19 June to 22 July 1946, signed on 22 July 1946 by the representatives of 61 States, in *Official Records of the World Health Organization*, vol. 2, 100, and entered into force on 7 April 1948. Amendments adopted by the 26th, 29th, 39th and 51st World Health Assemblies (resolutions WHA26.37, WHA29.38, WHA39.6 and WHA51.23) came into force on 3 February 1977, 20 January 1984, 11 July 1994 and 15 September 2005. See http://apps.who.int/gb/bd/PDF/bd47/EN/constitution-en.pdf, last accessed on 17 November 2011 ("WHO Constitution").

[108] See *supra*: "The Codex Alimentarius Commission", at 11.3.1.3.1.

[109] World Health Organization, Secretariat, "WHO Global Strategy for Food Safety: Safer Food for Better Health", Geneva, 2002, p. 11, available at http://www.who.int/foodsafety/publications/general/en/strategy_en.pdf, last accessed on 27 November 2012.

[110] *Ibid.*

[111] *Ibid.*, at p. 5 and p. 10.

[112] Art. 19 WHO Constitution.

[113] Art. 20 WHO Constitution stipulates that "each Member undertakes that it will, within eighteen months after the adoption by the Health Assembly of a convention or agreement, take action relative to the acceptance of such convention or agreement".

ulations on a limited number of topics,[114] even though the Member States are given an option to opt out by notifying the Director-General of a particular rejection or reservation. While the WHO Constitution enables WHO to act as a semi-legislator, the instruments in Articles 19 and 21 have not been used comprehensively throughout the years.[115] Legally non-binding and soft mechanisms as foreseen in Article 23 of the WHO Constitution[116] have been, on the other hand, used extensively. Most standards specifically relating to food safety are promulgated by Codex.[117] In conclusion, although the WHO has the power to conclude formal international lawmaking instruments, it favors flexible and informal instruments.[118]

With globalized food production and trade structures, the probability of the occurrence of international incidents involving contaminated food has demanded faster international information-exchange mechanisms.[119] WHO Member States cooperate through the International Food

---

114 These topics, pointed out in Art. 21 of the WHO Constitution, include (a) sanitary and quarantine requirements and other procedures designed to prevent the international spread of disease; (b) nomenclatures with respect to diseases, causes of death and public health practices; (c) standards with respect to diagnostic procedures for international use; (d) standards with respect to the safety, purity and potency of biological, pharmaceutical and similar products moving in international commerce; (e) advertising and labeling of biological, pharmaceutical and similar products moving in international commerce.

115 Lin argues that WHO Member States never seriously considered the treaty-making power under Art. 19 and only two international regulations under Art. 21 (a) and (b) have been promulgated; Lin, 2011, pp. 673–677, see *supra* note 1. The first and only WHO Convention (the 2003 Framework Convention on Tobacco Control) did not create food safety regulation.

116 Art. 23 of the WHO Constitution spells out: "The Health Assembly shall have authority to make recommendations to Members with respect to any matter within the competence of the Organization".

117 Lin, 2011, p. 677, see *supra* note 1. See, *e.g.*, the International Code of Marketing of Breastmilk Substitutes jointly adopted by WHO and UNICEF in 1981, adopted as a non-binding recommendation. For a more elaborate discussion on this Code, see Ina Verzivolli, "The Domestic Effectiveness of the International Code of Marketing of Breastmilk Substitutes" in this volume.

118 The WHO's "thin record of lawmaking" has been criticized; Lawrence O. Gostin, "Meeting Basic Survival Needs of the World's Least Healthy People: Toward a Framework Convention on Global Health", in *Georgetown Law Journal*, 2008, vol. 96, p. 375. Verzivolli argues that these WHO recommendations are characterized by process and actor formality and output informality, see *supra* note 117.

119 INFOSAN, "Food Safety", available at http://www.who.int/foodsafety/fs_management/infosan/en/, last accessed on 27 November 2012. Klaus Henning, "Pub-

Safety Authorities Network (INFOSAN), a joint initiative between WHO and FAO,[120] which has strong international informal characteristics. It must be noted that the pure lawmaking activities of the platform are limited, if existing at all. INFOSAN coordinates practical information-sharing without imposing legal obligations. Yet, Member States are 'expected' to follow relevant guidelines and principles and INFOSAN is involved in the formulation of recommendation and strategies.[121] Actors participating in this global network include food safety authorities and emergency and focal contact points located in 177 Member States.[122] An Advisory Group, consisting of experts from national food safety authorities across the globe, advises the Secretariat, reviews operations, formulates recommendations and provides input to INFOSAN strategies.[123] On the WHO website, INFOSAN publishes non-binding 'Information Notes' on a broad range of food safety topics.[124] INFOSAN therefore can be considered an informal public communication network.

### 11.3.2. Actors with a Private Character

Having assessed the actors involved in the public standard-setting process at the international level, we now turn to those international standard-setters that operate in the private sphere. In this part, we will shed light on

lic Authority Communication on Consumer Protection", in *European Food and Feed Law Review*, 2009, vol. 4, no. 5, p. 333.

120 Caroline Smith DeWaal and Gonzalo R. Guerrero Brito, "Safe Food International: A Blueprint for Better Global Food Safety", in *Food and Drug Law Journal*, 2005, vol. 60, p. 396. INFOSAN was officially inaugurated in October 2004 and has both routine and emergency activities. INFOSAN seeks to: (a) promote the rapid exchange of information during food safety-related events, (b) share information on important food safety-related issues of global interest, (c) promote partnership and collaboration between countries, (d) help countries strengthen their capacity to manage food safety risks. See WHO and FAO, "INFOSAN Background Information", October 2007, available at http://www.who.int/foodsafety/fs_management/infosan_1007_en.pdf, last accessed on 27 November 2012.

121 Lin, 2011, p. 679–680, see *supra* note 1.

122 World Health Organization and Food and Agriculture Organization of the United Nations, "INFOSAN Progress Report 2004–2010", Geneva, 2011, p. 11, available at http://whqlibdoc.who.int/publications/2011/ 9789241501286_eng.pdf, last accessed on 27 November 2012.

123 *Ibid.*

124 WHO, Food Safety, available at http://www.who.int/foodsafety/fs_management/ infosan_archives/en/index.html, last accessed on 27 November 2012.

three of these schemes: the International Organization for Standardization (ISO), the Global Partnership for Good Agricultural Practice (GLOBALG.A.P.) and the Global Food Safety Initiative (GFSI).

Having looked at the definition of IN-LAW, the question begs itself, why deal with private actors in this context at all? After all, IN-LAW requires at least some form of 'public involvement'.[125] In most cases, this 'public involvement' will not be present. We have opted to include these schemes by way of comparison and to assess whether they can provide guidance as to how the effectiveness of IN-LAW mechanisms can be improved. In dealing with these purely private mechanisms, we also discuss their weaknesses, especially in terms of (external) accountability. Additionally, including a number of these schemes provides a more accurate picture of the playing field in international food standard-setting. The International Organization for Standardization (ISO) is an interesting 'hybrid' form that incorporates both actors which have a public character, as well as actors with a purely private character.[126] GLOBALG.A.P. and GFSI have a purely private, commercial nature.

In recent years there has been a proliferation of private sector food standards. Fulponi submits that competition among retailers, firm reputation in terms of safety and quality and the use of private standards as a defense of due diligence with respect to mandatory legislation, were all reasons for the increase in the use of private standards.[127] A survey conducted by the United Nations Conference on Trade and Development (UNCTAD) revealed the presence of at least 400 private sector standard schemes.[128] Clapp and Fuchs note that private actors, and in particular corporations, play a larger role than ever before.[129]

---

125 Pauwelyn, 2012, p. 21, see *supra* note 11.

126 Spencer Henson and John Humphrey, "Understanding the Complexities of Private Standards in Global Agri-Food Chains as They Impact Developing Countries", in *Journal of Development Studies*, vol. 46, no. 9, p. 1632; Thomas Herzfeld, Larissa S. Drecher and Carola Grebitus, "Cross-National Adoption of Private Food Quality Standards", in *Food Policy,* vol. 36, no. 3, 2011, p. 401.

127 Linda Fulponi, Private Voluntary Standards in the Food System: the Perspective of Major Food Retailers in OECD Countries, in *Food Policy*, 2006, vol. 31, no. 1, pp. 1–13.

128 See World Trade Organization, Committee on Sanitary and Phytosanitary Measures, Note by the Secretariat, Private Standards and the SPS Agreement, dated 24 January 2007, Document G/SPS/GEN/746, p. 1; Margret Will and Doris Guenther, *Food Quality and Safety Standards – as required by EU Law and the Private Industry (A*

### 11.3.2.1. International Organization for Standardization (ISO)

The International Organization for Standardization (ISO) is a non-governmental organization. The National Standards Institutes and delegates from the public and private sectors of 162 countries formed it.[130] The aim of the organization is to promote the global development of standardization and related activities. ISO is currently made up of 162 members, divided into three categories: Member Bodies, Correspondent Members and Subscriber Members. The distinction is relevant as it indicates the level of involvement a certain member has in the standard-setting process.[131] Between 1947 and the present day, ISO has published more than 183,500 International Standards in hundreds of fields.[132]

As a result of its highly formalized standard-setting process and its linkage with the WTO's Technical Barriers to Trade Agreement, see *infra*, ISO is often regarded as a formal standard-setter. However, because of the high levels of output and actor informality, as well as process informality (as defined by Pauwelyn), we cannot speak of a formal lawmaker. There are several reasons for distinguishing ISO from traditional, formal, international lawmakers. First, the fact that its main output, international standards and standards-type-documents, are *ab initio* non-binding and voluntary, means that the organization is characterized by output in-

---

*Practicioners' Reference Book)*, Deutsche Gesellschaft fuer Technische Zusammenarbeit (GTZ), 2007, p. 162.

129 Jennifer Clap and Doris Fuchs, "Corporate Power and Global Food Governance: Lessons Learned" in Jennifer Clapp and Doris Fuchs (eds.), *Corporate Power in Global Agrifood Governance*, MIT Press, Cambridge, MA, 2009, pp. 285–296.

130 For a complete list, see: http://www.iso.org/iso/iso_members, last accessed on 27 November 2012.

131 A member body of ISO is the national body "most representative of standardization in its country". Only one such body for each country is accepted for membership of ISO. Member bodies are entitled to participate and exercise full voting rights in any technical committee and policy committee of ISO. A '*correspondent member*' is usually an organization in a country which does not yet have a fully-developed national standards activity. Correspondent members do not take an active part in the technical and policy development work, but are entitled to be kept fully informed about the work of interest to them. '*Subscriber membership*' has been established for countries with very small economies. Subscriber members pay reduced membership fees that nevertheless allow them to maintain contact with international standardization.

132 For a detailed discussion on a particular ISO standard in the IN-LAW context, see: Mary Footer, "Re-writing Global Social Responsibility the Corporate Way: ISO 26000 versus the UN Global Compact" in this volume.

formality, in the sense that the outcome is not a legally binding treaty in the traditional sense of international law. Second, actor informality is present as national bodies 'most representative of standardization' may encompass both public and private actors.[133] Third, in terms of process, ISO displays many formal characteristics. Its decision-making process, which we will describe *infra*, is a relatively detailed six-stage process that includes transparent and accessible rules, rules on voting as well as an appeals procedure. This decision-making process and the organization structure reflect the fact that ISO does not deal solely with food standards.[134] That said, ISO is not a treaty based international organization, and can hence, according to Pauwelyn's definition,[135] also be considered informal at the process level.

The ISO organizational structure has two main organs – the General Assembly and the Council.[136]

The General Assembly meets on an annual basis and consists of the Principal Officers of ISO and delegates nominated by the member bodies. The President, a prominent figure in standardization or in business, the Vice President, the Treasurer and the Secretary-General, are all Principal Officers. The Council is the ISO's governing body, which meets at least twice a year. Meetings are chaired by the President of the Council. The membership of the Council rotates to ensure that the ISO membership is adequately represented. All member bodies of ISO are eligible for appointment/election to the Council.[137] The operations of the Council are

---

133 For example, the Netherlands' member of ISO is the Nederlands Normalisatie-instituut (NEN), a private, non-profit organization founded in 1916. Mexico's Dirección General de Normas (DGN), on the other hand, is part of the Ministry of Economy and is thus a typical 'public' institution.

134 Spencer Henson and John Humphrey, "The Impacts of Private Food Safety Standards on the Food Chain and on Public Standard-Setting Processes", paper prepared for FAO/WHO, May 2009, at 17, available at http://ec.europa.eu/food/international/organisations/sps/docs/private_standards_codex_en.pdf, last accessed on 27 November 2012.

135 Pauwelyn, 2012, p. 22, see *supra* note 11.

136 A complete organizational chart is available at http://www.iso.org/iso/home/about/about_governance.htm, last accessed on 27 November 2012.

137 In 2011, member bodies elected to the Council are AFNOR (France), ANSI (USA), BSI (United Kingdom), DIN (Germany), DSM (Malaysia), GOST R (Russian Federation), ICONTEC (Colombia), IST (Iceland), JISC (Japan), KATS (Republic of Korea), KAZMEMST (Kazakhstan), MSA (Malta), SABS (South Africa), SAC (China),

managed and directed by the Central Secretariat which is headed by the Secretary-General.

ISO maintains cooperative relations with other IOs and in particular with the World Trade Organization (WTO).[138] Despite the fact that the ISO is not directly referred to in the Agreement on Technical Barriers to Trade (TBT Agreement), this agreement nevertheless makes reference to the ISO/IEC Guide 2, which contains a definition of 'standardizing bodies' that can be applied at the national level. ISO closely cooperates with the WTO to ensure that standards do not constitute barriers to trade.[139] ISO's commitment to reach different categories of stakeholders is also reflected in its cooperation with several UN agencies, such as the Codex Alimentarius Commission, the International Labour Organization (ILO) and the WHO.[140]

The decision-making process in ISO is a detailed and formalized six-stage process.[141] ISO national member bodies have a right of appeal in certain situations. In the decision-making process, consensus is preferred over voting;[142] it is defined as a:

SARM (Armenia), SASO (Saudi Arabia), SCC (Canada), SN (Norway), TSE (Turkey), UNI (Italy).

138 See World Trade Organization, Agreement on Technical Barriers to Trade (TBT Agreement), Article 2.4, which states: "Where technical regulations are required and relevant international standards exist or their completion is imminent, Members shall use them, or the relevant parts of them, as a basis for their technical regulations except when such international standards or relevant parts would be an ineffective or inappropriate means for the fulfillment of the legitimate objectives pursued, for instance because of fundamental climatic or geographical factors or fundamental technological problems."

139 WTO, "International intergovernmental organizations granted observer status to WTO bodies", available at http://www.wto.org/english/thewto_e/igo_obs_e.htm, last accessed on 27 November 2012.

140 For a complete list consult: ISO, "Organizations in cooperation with ISO", available at http://www.iso.org/iso/about/organizations_in_liaison.htm, last accessed on 27 November 2012.

141 ISO, "How does ISO develop standards?", available at http://www.iso.org/iso/home/standards_development.htm, last accessed on 27 November 2012.

142 ISO states, "because ISO standards are voluntary agreements, they need to be based on a solid consensus of international expert opinion. Consensus, which requires the resolution of substantial objections, is an essential procedural principle. Although it is necessary for the technical work to progress speedily, sufficient time is required before the approval stage for the discussion, negotiation and resolution of significant technical disagreements."

> general agreement, characterized by the absence of sustained opposition to substantial issues by any important part of the concerned interests and by a process that involves seeking to take into account the views of all parties concerned and to reconcile any conflicting arguments.[143]

The definition notes, "consensus need not imply unanimity". In case consensus is lacking, members may go to a vote. A draft document will be accepted as an ISO international standard when at least two-thirds of the ISO national members that participated in its development approve it.

Stakeholder involvement in ISO depends on the phase of the policy cycle. First, at the technical, standard-developing level, stakeholder participation is indirect through national delegations. These are usually composed of a mix of the stakeholder groups (industry/trade associations, science and academia, consumer associations, governments and regulators, societal and other interests). Second, beyond the purely technical level, ISO asks for input on new directions to be followed and on the setting of priorities.[144]

The main characteristic of ISO standards or standard-type documents is that they do not constitute a formal legal document in the traditional sense of international law. The outcome of the ISO decision-making process is not a legally binding treaty, but rather a document containing harmonized guidelines to be used in a particular production process. As ISO puts it: 'the agency neither regulates, nor creates laws'. Only once ISO standards are cited in national legislation and international conventions, do they acquire binding status. Intrinsically they are voluntary, however, they may become market requirements in some cases.[145]

ISO's output consists mainly of international standards and standards-type documents. Standards are developed on an incredibly wide variety of topics; from health care technology to telecommunications and

---

143 ISO, "How ISO Develops Standards", see *supra* note 141 and ISO/IEC Guide 2:2004

144 As an example, between May and October 2003, ISO organized a broad consultation of the ISO members, stakeholders, and major international partners to collect suggestions and expectations regarding ISO's strategy. In turn, extended consultations with their national stakeholders were organized. More concretely, a total of 41 consolidated national positions were received, with more than 40% of them coming from developing countries. Recommendations were also received from 13 IOs. These consultations formed the basis for the ISO Strategic Plan 2005–2010.

145 For example, the ISO 9000 Standards on Quality Management Systems or ISO 830 on Freight Container Dimensions.

clothing.[146] ISO standards related to the food sector are developed in ISO/TC 34 'Food Products'.[147] This technical committee currently provides 770 standards and related documents. The scope of this 'food' technical committee is described as follows:

> Standardization in the field of human and animal foodstuffs, covering the food chain from primary production to consumption, as well as animal and vegetable propagation materials, in particular, but not limited to, terminology, sampling, methods of test and analysis, product specifications, food and feed safety and quality management and requirements for packaging, storage and transportation.[148]

There are 53 countries active in ISO/TC 34 proceedings, whilst another 53 have observer status. ISO lists the main stakeholders as agricultural producers, food manufacturers, laboratories, merchants/retailers, consumers and regulators.[149] In recent years, ISO/TC34 has addressed several new areas related to the food sector; ranging from standards for the detection of genetically modified organisms (GMOs) and derived products in food, to ISO 22000 standards for safe food supply chains and quantitative ingredient declarations.[150] ISO 2200 aims to harmonize food safety management systems at a global level.[151] Moreover, ISO has developed a number of guidelines on third-party certification (ISO/IEC Guide 28:2004) and on the way certification bodies should operate (ISO/IEC Guide 65). General quality management standards such as ISO 9000 have,

---

146 A complete list is available at http://www.iso.org/iso/catalogue_ics.htm, last accessed on 27 November 2012.

147 ISO/TC 54 on Essential Oils, ISO/TC 93 on Starch and ISO/TC 234 on Fisheries and Aquaculture also develop food related standards, but will not be discussed in depth here.

148 ISO, TC 34 Food products, available at http://www.iso.org/iso/iso_technical_committee?commid=47858, last accessed on 17 November 2011.

149 ISO, "How ISO standards support objectives of World Food Day", available at http://www.iso.org/iso/news.htm?refid=Ref1084, last accessed on 27 November 2012.

150 One of the most recently adopted standards is ISO 12875:2011 on the "*Traceability of Finfish Products – Specification on the Information to be Recorded in Captured Finfish Distribution Chains*".

151 Consumer Goods Forum, "What is ISO 22000? GFSI Technical Committee Position Paper, 7/09/2009", available at http://www.ciesnet.com/pfiles/programmes/foodsafety/What%20is%20ISO%2022000%20September%202007.pdf, last accessed on 27 November 2012.

in a way, become global food safety norms.[152] In aiming to ensure coordination of issues related to food standards, ISO has established strong relations with a number of UN agencies that are concerned with food issues. These organizations include the WHO, the FAO and the CAC[153] (see above). ISO regularly reports to CAC on its activities when they are relevant for CAC's work.[154]

Accountability is sought after in a number of ways. The WTO Dispute Settlement Body, in a certain way, functions as a compliance mechanism for ISO standards in their relation to international trade.[155] Furthermore, ISO relies heavily on domestic institutions, as standards that gained legal power through national implementation are subject to national enforcement and review mechanisms.[156] Furthermore, according to the organization, there is broad participation (from both public and private actors as well as stakeholders), there are administrative rules that govern the decision-making processes, there are fixed-form procedures, and there is an appeal procedure for ISO standards. By publishing information on its standardization activities on its website, ISO tries to achieve a sufficient degree of transparency.

In sum, ISO displays informal characteristics at all three levels defined by Pauwelyn. We can consider ISO's output informal as the standards and standards-type-documents it produces are voluntary, and do not constitute in any way, shape or form a formal treaty under international law. Moreover, the wide variety of actors involved in the standard-setting process, ranging from representatives of national standard-setting bodies to private actors, is typical of actor informality. Actors involved are certainly not limited to actors traditionally associated with international law, such as diplomats, foreign ministers and Heads of State. ISO's detailed decision-making process includes rules on voting, transparency and appeals. Yet, it does not find its origins in a formally adopted international

---

152 Henson and Jaffee, 2008, p. 549, see *supra* note 6.

153 ISO has observer status.

154 See, for example, Codex Alimentarius Commission, "Communication from ISO (report of activities relevant to Codex work)", CAC/33 INF/6.

155 Its output is formalized because of the linkage with the WTO system.

156 On the implementation of food safety management systems in the UK, including ISO 22000, in the UK, see Lena Dzifa Mensah and Denyse Julien, "Implementation of Food Safety Management Systems", in *Food Control*, 2011, vol. 22, no. 8, pp. 1216–1225.

convention since ISO is an NGO rather than an IO. As Pauwelyn outlined, process informality does not prevent the existence of detailed procedural rules, permanent staff or a physical headquarter.

### 11.3.2.2. Global Partnership for Good Agricultural Practice (GLOBALG.A.P.)

As stated above, purely private mechanisms cannot be IN-LAW mechanisms. 'Public involvement', necessary to fulfill the conditions of IN-LAW is lacking in GLOBALG.A.P. Nevertheless, its operations show striking similarities with other food safety standard-setting mechanisms that can be labeled IN-LAW. In order to facilitate a comparison between the two types of mechanisms (IN-LAW and purely private systems), we now proceed with an analysis of two purely private actors in food safety standard-setting.

In 1997, the Euro-Retailer Produce Working Group (EUREP) founded EurepGAP. In 2007, it was re-branded 'GLOBALG.A.P.'. EurepGAP and its successor GLOBALG.A.P. are private initiatives that are owned by the food industry.[157] Food retailers, producers and suppliers that agree to the terms of reference of the organization are all eligible for membership. There are three groups of members: retailers, producers/suppliers and associates. We can thus speak of a relatively high degree of actor informality, as the actors are not diplomats, but rather representatives of private organizations, for example, businesses. Currently, the membership of GLOBALG.A.P. originates in a very large majority from developed, western countries.[158] Its terms of reference are:

> [t]o respond to consumer concerns on food safety, environmental protection, worker health, safety and welfare and animal welfare by:
>
> (i) Encouraging adoption of commercially viable farm assurance schemes, which promote the minimization of agrochemical and medicinal inputs, within Europe and worldwide.

[157] GLOBALG.A.P., History, available at http://www.globalgap.org/cms/front_content.php?idcat=19, last accessed on 27 November 2012.

[158] GLOBALG.A.P., Membership, available at http://www.globalgap.org/cms/front_content.php?idcat=4, last accessed on 27 November 2012.

(ii) Developing a Good Agricultural Practice (G.A.P.) framework for benchmarking existing assurance schemes and standards including traceability.

(iii) Providing guidance for continuous improvement and the development and understanding of best practice.

(iv) Establishing a single, recognized framework for independent verification.

(v) Communication and consulting openly with consumers and key partners, including producers, exporters and importers.[159]

GLOBALG.A.P.'s organizational structure is relatively straightforward. Leadership within the organization lies with the Board, which "agrees on the vision and short and long-term activity plan of the organization." Retailer and producers/supplier members elect the board. FoodPlus GmbH, which is registered as a private German company, takes care of the day-to-day management of the organization and the implementation of standards. The development and elaboration of standards takes place within 'Sector Committees', which, again, are elected by retailer and producer/supplier members. The 'Certification Committee' is composed of certification bodies that are members of the GLOBALG.A.P. Its role is to "harmonize the varying interpretations of the standard that may arise in the more than 100,000 yearly audits".

Over the years, GLOBALG.A.P. has produced four different types of standards.[160] For the purpose of this article, we will focus on the Integrated Farm Insurance Standard (IFA). The scope of IFA is separated into a modular structure and covers the production destined for human consumption of 'Crops, Livestock and Aquaculture'. Formally, GLOBALG.A.P. standards are voluntary in nature. There is no legal obligation requiring producers and retailers to use it. However, as with many stand-

[159] GLOBALG.A.P., "General Regulations – Integrated Farm Assurance", November 2009, available at http://www1.globalgap.org/cms/upload/The_Standard/IFA/English/GRs/PartI/GG_EG_IFA_GR_Part_I_ENG_V3-1_Nov09.pdf, last accessed on 27 November 2012.

[160] These are the GLOBALG.A.P. Integrated Farm Insurance Standard (IFA), the GLOBALG.A.P. Compound Feed Manufacturer Standard (CFM), the GLOBALG.A.P. Plant Propagation Material Standard (PPM) and the GLOBAL.G.A.P. Risk Assessment On Social Practice (GRASP). In addition, GLOBALG.A.P. currently develops a standard on Animal Transport (AT). This standard is scheduled for completion in 2011.

ard schemes that operate with the intention of becoming a harmonized benchmark, market access possibilities can be severely impeded without taking part in such a certification scheme. GLOBALG.A.P. gained great prominence and in a sense has become a 'norm', the significance of which extends throughout the supply chain and effectively "governs the wholesale and consumer markets in respect of food safety, but also of social and environmental issues, well beyond the individual contractual relations in which a retailer requires GLOBALG.A.P. certification from a producer".[161] Contrary to public standards, such as those developed under the CAC, the status of private sector standards is unclear under the WTO SPS Agreement.[162]

The decision-making procedure for the development of new standards under the GLOBALG.A.P. framework begins with the adoption of the project by consensus at the Board level. Subsequently, there is a public review phase and discussions at the Sector Committee level which take into account public comments. Decisions at the Sector Committee level are normally taken by consensus, but in the absence thereof, members may go to a vote. Once standards are approved by the relevant Sector Committee and by the Board, they are made subject to a second public comment phase, to correct 'technical errors'. Standards become final after this phase. Standards go through a revision process every four years to ensure continued relevance and effectiveness. Once a standard is implemented, producers of the relevant primary agricultural products may apply for GLOBALG.A.P. certification.[163] It can thus be said that at the process level, GLOBALG.A.P. displays many characteristics of a formalized and institutionalized non-state actor. Moreover, GLOBALG.A.P.'s IFA standard is, where possible, based upon public standards.[164]

---

[161] Nicolas Hachez and Jan Wouters, "A Glimpse at the Democratic Legitimacy of Private Standards – Democratic Legitimacy as Public Accountability: The Case of GLOBALG.A.P.", 14 April 2011, available at SSRN: http://ssrn.com/abstract=1809674, last accessed on 27 November 2012.

[162] Denise Prévost, "Private Sector Food-Safety Standards and the SPS Agreement: Challenges and Possibilities", in *South African Yearbook of International Law,* 2008, vol. 33, pp. 1–37.

[163] Certification will be given by approved certification bodies after several on-site inspections.

[164] Donal Casey, "Three Puzzles of Private Governance: Global GAP and the Regulation of Food Safety and Quality", in *University College Dublin Working Papers in Law, Criminology and Socio-Legal Studies Research Paper*, 2009, no. 22., available at

GLOBALG.A.P. claims that "[t]o ensure global acceptance GLOBALG.A.P. actively engages with many different stakeholders around the globe" and that it "welcomes proposals and recommendations from all relevant parties to feed into its standard development".[165] However, as noted by Hachez and Wouters, "the engagement of civil society by GLOBALG.A.P. is confined to discussion phases, and does not result in voting power in the decision-making process".[166]

### 11.3.2.3. Global Food Safety Initiative (GFSI)

The third case study centers on the Global Food Safety Initiative (GFSI), another private initiative in the food safety standard landscape. GFSI is a non-governmental non-profit organization that has been created under Belgian law. GFSI was launched in May 2000 in response to a number of major food safety scares. The goal of the network is to "provide continuous improvement in food safety management systems to ensure confidence in the delivery of safe food to consumers".[167] It tries to achieve this by pursuing the following objectives:

1. Promote convergence between food safety standards through maintaining a benchmarking-process for food safety management schemes.
2. Improve cost efficiency throughout the food supply chain through the common acceptance of GFSI recognized standards by retailers around the world.
3. Provide a unique international stakeholder platform for networking, knowledge exchange and sharing of best food safety practices and information.

GFSI's organizational structure consists of a day-to-day management that is performed by the Consumer Goods Forum (CGF) and a Board of Directors. In this governance structure, the Board provides stra-

---

http://regulation.upf.edu/utrecht-08-papers/dcasey.pdf, last accessed on 27 November 2012.

165 GLOBALG.A.P., Certification Body Committee, available at www.globalgap.org/cms/front_content.php?idcat=22, last accessed on 27 November 2012.

166 Hachez and Wouters, 2011, p. 18, see *supra* note 161.

167 GFSI FAQ, available at http://www.mygfsi.com/communication/frequently-asked-questions.html, last accessed on 27 November 2012.

tegic direction and oversees the daily management as performed by the CGF. The CGF, (formerly known as the CIES – The Food Business Forum), is an 'independent global parity-based Consumer Goods network'. Its function is to bring together the CEOs and senior management of around 400 retailer and manufacturer members of all sizes, across 150 countries.

The GFSI Board Members originate from retailers, producers and food service operators. The chair, a representative from the retail industry, is supported by two vice-chairmen from the producer and food service sectors. Membership works on an invitation basis and is limited to a maximum of 19 Board Members. The term of office is limited to three years, with the possibility of one renewal. The strategic direction is provided by the Board in cooperation with an Advisory Council and a group of stakeholders. In concrete terms the Board ensures progress is made against agreed timelines and deliverables, it coordinates communication activities and oversees that the tasks allocated to each Technical Working Group are attained. Furthermore, it assigns the Chairs of these Working Groups and it assigns one or two Board Member liaisons to each Technical Working Group to support and monitor their work and progress. The Advisory Council is made up of experts coming from academia, non-governmental organizations and governments. Their task is to provide further expertise to the GFSI Board. In 2006, GFSI formed a Technical Committee that is composed of retailers, producers, food service operators, standard owners, certification bodies, accreditation bodies, industry associations and other technical experts. In order to provide better feedback, the GFSI Board decided to restructure the Technical Committee into Technical Working Groups in 2009.[168] GFSI, like ISO and GLOBALG.A.P., is characterized by a high degree of actor informality. Any person who would like to provide input at the general meetings is invited to take part in the Stakeholder Group, which is an international forum[169] that currently attracts retailers,

[168] Currently there are working groups on Animal Handling, Auditor Competence, Global Markets, Guidance Document and Packaging. Available at http://www.mygfsi.com/structure-and-governance/gfsi-technical-committee.html, last accessed on 27 November 2012.

[169] The forum is held annually, usually prior to the Global Food Safety Conference. Issues raised at the meeting are subsequently considered by the GFSI Board and Advisory Council.

manufacturers, certification bodies, accreditation bodies, standard owners, food safety experts and consultants.

GFSI differs from GLOBALG.A.P. and ISO in that its output does not consist of standards or standard-type documents. Rather, GFSI occupies itself with a benchmarking process for food safety management schemes. Thus, it seeks convergence of differing food safety standards. The process of benchmarking entails that a particular food safety related scheme is compared to a document prepared by GFSI: the 'GFSI Guidance Document'.[170] As a result of its benchmarking activities, GFSI has been credited with achieving truly global harmonization of food safety standards.[171]

### 11.3.3. Coexistence of the Various Actors

A fundamental question is how these actors, and more specifically the public and private food safety standard-setters, coexist. Does the output overlap, complement, or even make the other standards redundant? One needs to be aware of the potential of private standards to undermine official food safety authorities. Concerns about legitimacy, authority and accountability have been raised, both regarding public and private standard-setters. The public wants to be governed by the 'right' institutions. Traditionally, only nation states were standard-setters and the question remains whether it is appropriate for private actors to be setting health rules instead of the public authorities. Henson and Humphrey assessed these questions in relation to the Codex Alimentarius and private standards, in their recent report to Codex. They rightly noted that Codex Standards do not exactly have the same nature as private standards, though ultimately both are intended to regulate the issue of food safety. CAC public standards are envisioned to become reference points for public legislation, whereas private standards such as GLOBALG.A.P. are destined to be used directly as such in private transactions.[172] Still, a risk exists that public standards are being sidelined progressively by much more dynamic

170 GFSI, Guidance Document, available at http://www.mygfsi.com/technical-resources/guidance-document.html, last accessed on 27 November 2012.

171 Bernd van der Meulen, "The Anatomy of Private Food Law", in Bernd van der Meulen (ed.), *Private Food Law*, Wageningen Academic Publishers, Wageningen, 2011, p. 105.

172 Henson and Humphrey, "Impact of Private Food Safety Standards", see *supra* note 134.

private standards. Nevertheless, this risk should not be overstated. As Henson and Humphrey have observed, where private food safety standards exist, they appear to take Codex guidelines as their point of departure. Moreover, in many market areas, private standards have not been developed (yet), and Codex remains the sole reference point.[173]

Other considerations focus on the coexistence and interaction of public and private international standard-setters, which is routine at the national level of most countries.[174] More concretely, food safety has been recognized as a shared responsibility. Public standard-setting processes, therefore, would benefit from inviting the private sector input and perspective.[175] Public and private standards complement each other, since, in general, private standards include a prerequisite that all relevant national standards have to be met which makes these standards never less stringent than official standards.[176] Both public and private food safety standard-setters seem to be able to operate side by side as the different sets of standards are not necessarily opposed. Moreover, they may be able to reinforce each other since private standards can be seen as a way to implement public standards. Lawmaking possibly also benefits from the expertise of a large pool of regulators when it leads to dynamic regulation, sensitive to changes concerning food safety and free trade.

## 11.4. The Use of Informal International Law in Food Safety Standard-Setting

Each of the actors exercising public authority discussed *supra* has, to a different extent, relied on informal mechanisms to set food safety standards. Some private standard-setters, such as ISO, can in our view also be considered IN-LAW mechanisms. The involvement of public actors in its activities leads to the conclusion that this organization also fulfills the requirements to be placed within the IN-LAW framework. Voluntary con-

173 Spencer Henson and John Humphrey, "Codex Alimentarius and Private Standards", in Bernd van der Meulen (ed.), *Private Food Law*, Wageningen Academic Publishers, Wageningen, 2011, pp. 170–71

174 Codex Alimentarius Commission, "Consideration of the Impact of Private Standards", 33rd session 5–9 July 2010, CX/CAC 10/3319, p. 3, available at ftp://ftp.fao.org/codex/Meetings/CAC/cac33/cac33_13e.pdf, last accessed on 27 November 2012.

175 *Ibid.*

176 Codex, "Consideration", p. 26, see *supra* note 174.

sensus standards such as GLOBALG.A.P. and GFSI cannot be placed within the IN-LAW framework. Yet, they have proven to be interesting case studies, which share a number of features with IN-LAW. In this section, it is our aim to moderately assess the grounds that motivated the standard-setting processes taking place outside the formal framework of public international decision-making structures (that is, the conclusion of treaties under the auspices of IOs). Subsequently, we will analyze why purely private food safety standard initiatives also play a considerable role in the food safety standard landscape.

Informal international lawmaking mechanisms active in the food sector share the objective of ensuring global food safety while enhancing international trade. There is a clear preference of all public standard-setting actors not to use classic public international law and its inherent formality. However, there is not a 'one model fits all' of informality. Moreover, a diverse range of motives explains the trend of public regulators to use informal lawmaking. Most of these motivations seem to be based on the idea that the specific theme of the regulation studied in this contribution – food safety – demands a certain level of informality at the international level. First, food law is characterized by a complexity that leads to seek alternatives to formal, binding lawmaking: there is a plethora of standards and standard-setters. Most national states and a number of public, private and hybrid networks have their own food safety standards. The need to harmonize these seems more pressuring than the desire to conclude a new legally binding treaty. Further, standards are based on scientific assessments that are detailed, sophisticated and subject to constant development. Their transformation into treaty articles would not be the most appropriate choice of regulation. Complications finally also arise from the different interests involved in food safety law – related to public health, agriculture, trade and internal market objectives. Second, often, novel and instant reactions are necessary to complement standard-setting undertakings. Both the EU and the WHO have established information sharing and rapid alert networks between national contact points. These too have resulted in certain lawmaking activities where they have led to harmonization of national procedures and processes. Here, it is interesting to compare the public food safety standard-setters with private initiatives. The food market replaces Codex Standards with more detailed and more stringent private standards precisely because these public standards risk being outdated and not responsive enough to the needs of the public.[177] The inclusion of private standard-setting practices and experience may therefore even be useful for IN-LAW mechanisms to keep being up to date.

Third, the use of informality also originates from practices at the domestic level at which most of the technical standard-setting is delegated to specialized authorities. On the international plain too, a central role is given to national food safety authorities that cooperate via a number of different networks at the bilateral, regional and international level. More than traditional international actors (heads of state, foreign ministers and embassies), these are engaged in day-to-day regulation both domestically and internationally. Moreover, if these national food safety authorities succeed to operate directly in all types of networks, IN-LAW tends to be a very effective way to cut costs otherwise associated with formal lawmaking.

Finally, it is unlikely that pure formal lawmaking on the international plain would succeed in producing similar output. As an example, the Codex Alimentarius Commission has been extremely successful in creating standards, which in turn has led to sensitizing the global community to the danger of food hazards and significantly helping to put food as an entity on political agendas. In 2005, the list of current official standards adopted by the Codex Alimentarius Commission included 214 standards, 52 recommended codes of practice and 45 principles and guidelines and domestic regulations. Codex also established more than 2000 maximum pesticide residue limits which can be considered as standards.[178] This mass-production of standards would not likely have occurred if formal state consent between all countries had to be reached instead of using its consensus-based decision making process.

As discussed *supra*, purely private food safety-standard initiatives are not IN-LAW mechanisms. Nevertheless, they are of substantial importance in the global food safety processes. These mechanisms are composed of private actors, such as producers and manufacturers, retailers, associates, exporters and sometimes even consumers and therefore cannot

177 It typically takes five to eight years to develop a Codex Standard.

178 See a current official standards list at http://www.codexalimentarius.org/standards/list-of-standards/en/, last accessed on 27 November 2012.

be considered as engaging in 'lawmaking'.[179] Unlike IN-LAW mechanisms, the focus is on internal accountability among members and includes stakeholders, rather than accountability to the general public and consumers.[180] Similar to IN-LAW food safety mechanisms, the private standard-setters' outcomes are not formal treaties but standard-type documents that may acquire binding legal status when implemented under national law. Because of the voluntary character of the private standards, the emphasis is on implementation at the national level. In this regard, indirectly, lawmaking processes are influenced by private actors setting standards.

These international private actors share the motives to use informality in standard-setting with their public counterparts.[181] A certain specific intention can nevertheless be distinguished: private standard-setters such as GLOBAL.G.A.P. opted to form networks to be able to better and more adequately respond to consumer demands and thus reflect a commercial interest. By 'establishing' a 'certified by GLOBALG.A.P.' label, retailers aim to gain a competitive edge, as consumers are increasingly interested in the source of their food.[182]

Some have argued that, in a way, private food safety standards may be more 'global' than 'public' international food standards.[183] What has become evident, at least, is that increased cooperation between the IN-LAW mechanisms identified above, and purely private actors, is a prereq-

---

179 Others, however, have argued in favor of the existence of a label of 'private food law' in which private actors do engage in lawmaking. Van der Meulen, 2011, p. 31, see *supra* note 171.

180 See the internal *versus* external accountability.

181 As discussed *supra* for the IN-LAW mechanisms: the very specific theme of food safety, the role of science, the need for instant reactions, and economic reasons all play a role in the private sector setting its own standards.

182 For example: Albert Heijn (a supermarket within the AHOLD concern) attempting to convince customers that their cucumbers were EHEC free, as they were certified by GLOBALG.A.P.

183 Van der Meulen, 2011, p. 108–9, see *supra* note 171. Van der Meulen states, "Contractual requirements, audits and certification can be applied across national borders. In this sense, private food law is more *global* than international food law (such as the SPS Agreement and the Codex Alimentarius). International (public) food law does not govern behavior of specific stakeholders, but sets a meta-framework for (national) food law that in turn applies to stakeholders' behavior. Private food law does govern stakeholders' behavior and in this sense private food law is more *law* than international food law".

uisite for responsive, accountable and affordable food safety standard-setting in the future.[184]

## 11.5. Concluding Remarks

Informality in international food safety regulation is here to stay. All public actors involved in standard-setting unquestionably opted for flexibility in their activities so as to produce informal output. Yet, nonc of the food safety standard-setters can be considered to be completely informal at all three levels of output, actors and process.

Where the public informal processes (IN-LAW) have not managed to answer the needs of the food market, these networks have been supplemented by forms of private cooperation. Assessing the durability of the informal character of food safety standard-setting, it can be concluded that in food safety the balance leans towards more informality and private regulation rather than a return to formality in international lawmaking. To a certain extent – regarding the output and process – a re-formalization can be observed. First, standards are often implemented in national legal orders and become legally binding under domestic law. Admittedly, this tends to facilitate the harmonization of national food standards. Second, the Codex and ISO case studies showed the changing nature of their former non-legally binding standards after the linkage with the WTO trade regime.[185] Third, formalized procedures are also observed in private standard-setting mechanisms. A certain formality and institutionalization is preferred to accomplish internal accuracy and the workability.

Given the visible shift in food safety regulation from the public domain to the private sphere, the need for cooperation between the public and private sector could not be more apparent. The possible gains of increased and enhanced interaction between public informal processes (IN-LAW) and private standards organizations should in our view not be underestimated.

---

[184] Spencer Henson and John Humphrey, "Codex Alimentarius and Private Standards", in Bernd van der Meulen (ed.), *Private Food Law*, Wageningen Academic Publishers, Wageningen, 2011, p. 170–1; Marinus Huige, "Private Retail Standards and the Law of the World Trade Organisation", in Bernd van der Meulen (ed.), *Private Food Law*, Wageningen Academic Publishers, Wageningen, 2011, p. 184.

[185] In Codex, more formal voting procedure on the adoption of standards replaced consensus based decision making, see *supra* 11.3.1.3.1.

# 12

# The Domestic Effectiveness of the International Code of Marketing of Breastmilk Substitutes

**Ina Verzivolli***

## 12.1. Introduction

This chapter focuses on the International Code of Marketing of Breastmilk Substitutes (the Code) as an element of international informal lawmaking (IN-LAW). The Code is a non-binding recommendation that sets minimum international standards on marketing and promotion of breastmilk substitutes, while demanding for implementation at the national level by States. With the aim of regulating the promotion and advertisement of infant foods used as substitutes for mother's milk, the World Health Organization (WHO) and the United Nations Children's Fund (UNICEF) jointly adopted the Code in 1981. The Code is a specific set of guidelines that regulates marketing and advertising practices of breastmilk substitutes without prohibiting their production and sale. It represents the basic minimum requirements to protect healthy practices in respect of infant and young child feeding. It demands a prohibition of all aggressive marketing practices including direct advertisement of breastmilk substitutes, distribution of free samples to mothers and the use of nurses and midwives to promote formula. It also sets rules for product labeling, among which is the requirement that these clearly acknowledge the superiority of breastfeeding. Additionally, it prohibits promotion of baby foods in health care facilities and donation of gifts or other donations to the health care professionals.

This chapter will analyze the effectiveness of IN-LAW through the case of the Code, focusing particularly on the issue of domestic effective-

* **Ina Verzivolli** is in charge of the Human Rights program of the Geneva Infant Feeding Association, the liaison office of the International Baby Food Action Network.

ness. While IN-LAW may be generally considered effective in triggering cooperation at the international level, it is more difficult to grasp its effectiveness at the domestic level.

In the first part, the chapter will assess whether IN-LAW makes it easier for international cooperation to take place, as opposed to formal international lawmaking. To this end, the first part of the chapter provides a historical overview of the international process that led to the creation of the Code, followed by an analysis according to the IN-LAW framework.

The second part will focus on domestic effectiveness of the Code, by analyzing the implementation of the Code by countries, the effectiveness of the implementation in terms of solving the problem, and the factors that may have played a role in this regard. Given the high variability of measures taken at the domestic level, one of the main factors considered will be the degree of 'strength'. Domestic variability will first be defined along the 'hardness' dimension. Following which, three particular case studies will be presented in order to analyze the factors that influence the effectiveness of the Code at the domestic level.

Finally, the chapter will also address the issue of accountability – as one of the prominent issues discussed in the IN-LAW research project. Furthermore, it will look at how effectiveness and accountability interplay in the case of the Code, both internationally and domestically.

## 12.2. International Effectiveness of the Code as IN-LAW

### 12.2.1. The Birth of the Code: International Awareness and the Problem with Artificial Feeding

#### 12.2.1.1. Introduction

Scientific research has shown that breastfeeding is vital for child survival, health and development, and is even beneficial for the mothers' health. Yet, it is a rare feeding practice in developed as well as developing countries.[1]

The Code, which regulates marketing practices of breastmilk substitutes, came as a result of a long process of public debate and criticism to-

[1] Lida Lhotska, "Whatever Happened to Health for All?", IBFAN-GIFA, Geneva, 2008, available at http://www.ibfan.org/art/Health_for_all.pdf, last accessed on 7 March 2012.

ward marketing practices of baby food industry. It became evident over the years that unethical advertising and marketing practices were causing disastrous consequences on infant health, especially in developing countries. Children were being denied what are considered the normative standards for infant feeding and nutrition for healthy growth and development, and were increasingly being exposed to the risks of artificial feeding.

Since the 1920s, doctors and pediatricians started registering a high level of infant mortality in developing countries which they related to widespread artificial feeding practices in these countries. The events that shed light on the issue of infant formula were a series of accusations from non-governmental organizations (NGOs) directed at baby food companies, first in the United States (US) and then in Europe, in the 1970s. Particularly important was the legal action, started by Nestlé against a Swiss activist group, for defamation. The organization War on Want had published a report "The Baby Killer" in 1974, which attracted widespread public attention. It was translated in several languages and published in a number of countries. In Switzerland, the German translation of the report's title meant "Nestlé kills babies" as a consequence of which, a lawsuit was filed against the publishing organization by Nestlé for libel. The process generated considerable public debate and media coverage. Plenty of evidence on the unethical marketing practices was presented during the trial, as a result of which Nestlé withdrew three out of four charges. War on Want was found guilty only with regards to the title of the publication. When delivering the final sentence, the judge publicly criticized Nestlé on its advertising policy and marketing practices.

Other events added to the public attention on the issue, especially in the US. In 1974, the company Bristol-Myers was sued in court by a religious organization, shareholder in the same company. The company's marketing practices and their effects were proven to be unethical and harmful. In 1976, several groups led by the Infant Formula Action Coalition (INFACT) started a consumers' boycott of all Nestlé's products, arguing that since it was the largest non-American corporation in the global baby formula market, direct pressure in the US could not be effective. The boycott was taken up in Canada, Australia, and the United Kingdom. As a result of increased public concern, in 1978, the US Senate held a hearing on the advertising, marketing, promotion, and use of infant formula in developing countries. Senator Edward Kennedy, who headed the hearings, was convinced of the necessity to find an international solution to an international problem. He asked Dr. Halfdan Mahler, Director-General (DG) of the WHO, to convene an international meeting on the subject.

The International Code was prepared by the WHO and UNICEF after a process of widespread consultation with governments and a wide range of actors including the infant feeding industry, professional associations, and NGOs. The Code was created over a period of 18 months and four different drafts had been prepared. This section resumes this initial period.[2]

### 12.2.1.2. The 1979 Meeting

The process of creating the Code started with a meeting on Infant and Young Child Feeding, which took place at the WHO headquarters in Geneva in October 1979. This meeting was unique in its kind, as it brought together a very wide range of actors: representatives from industry, international organizations, government representatives, and NGOs. It was a new experience for the WHO, which until then had engaged only in technical seminars with experts on a particular issue, or in conferences exclusively for government delegations.

The meeting approved a series of recommendations, which stressed the need to support breastfeeding and to control the marketing practices of the breastmilk substitutes industry to the public and to health workers. It generated general consent on the necessity of developing a code as a mechanism to define the principles and the controls to be put in place. This led to a public recognition that marketing practices of baby food companies interfere with breastfeeding and are detrimental to infant and young child health and nutrition.

### 12.2.1.3. 1980 WHA - First and Second Draft

In 1980, WHO and UNICEF drafted a first version of the Code based on the recommendations of the 1979 meeting. The draft, which was envisioned to be approved during the next WHA session, sparked many reac-

---

[2] See generally: Andy Chetley, *The Politics of Babyfood: Successful Challenges to an International Marketing Strategy*, Frances Pinter, London, 1986. See also Ellen Sokol, *The Code Handbook. A Guide to Implementing the International Code of Marketing of Breastmilk Substitutes*, IBFAN-ICDC, Penang, 2005.

tions. The industry was in complete opposition to the draft Code and considered it an illegitimate limitation to commercial activity. NGOs opposed some parts of the draft for being incomplete and asked for some further clarification in the definitions. Some countries (Belgium, Bulgaria, Finland, Greece and the Soviet Union) welcomed the draft initiative, while the major milk-exporting countries (Denmark, West Germany, France, Netherlands, New Zealand, Switzerland and the US) rejected the draft.

The US government sent a letter to the WHO, suggesting that the Code be voluntary or recommendatory. The letter warned that the US, which financed 25% of the WHO regular budget, would not accept a Code that was mandatory on governments. They also alerted that, "The decision to proceed with a 'code' or formal standards should be a deliberate step of the Assembly, one that can provide guidance for the approach to be taken. The contents of the document must then be subject to full intergovernmental negotiations".[3] This was a clear suggestion that WHO and UNICEF had overstepped their mandates, and reflected also the industry's position that the regulation of this domain should be left to the single countries to deal with.

At the 1980 WHA, countries discussed a second draft of the Code. The major milk-exporting countries continued rejecting the draft. Nevertheless, in a resolution, the States conferred to the WHO and UNICEF the duty of continuing to draft a Code, in the spirit of the 1979 meeting. The resolution also stated that the Code was to be submitted to the WHO Executive Board (EB) at its next session, and gave the Director-General (DG) the choice of submitting a regulation or recommendation.

### 12.2.1.4. WHA - The Third and Fourth Drafts

A third draft was prepared in 1980 and two consultation rounds were held with various actors. Even though the question of the final status of the Code was not officially discussed during these consultations, it was the main subject in the negotiations taking place in the corridors, as reported by those who participated.

The WHA had three options: adopting the Code as a convention (which creates a binding relationship between the signatory parties, requires a two thirds majority of the WHA and comes into force after Mem-

[3] Cited in Chetley, 1986, p. 77, see *supra* note 2.

ber States' ratification), a regulation (requiring a simple majority of the WHA and comes into force for all Member States after due notice of their adoption by the Assembly) or a recommendation (non-binding and requiring a simple majority). The option of adopting a convention was immediately abandoned, because it would have taken too long and the interests in play were many. Therefore, WHO could either adopt a Code in the form of a regulation or as a recommendation.[4]

The US delegation was initially lobbying for a recommendation and made it clear that in any other event it would not support the International Code. WHO staff was eager to please the US, as it contributed to a quarter of its budget. It was argued that a recommendation would receive global consensus, including from the US delegation. Also, WHO staff was hoping to receive the support from other industrialized countries through this move.

WHO and UNICEF prepared a fourth draft, which was presented at the EB in 1981.[5] Since the US' position was supportive of a recommendation, the EB approved the fourth draft without changes. In a resolution, the WHA was asked to adopt it as recommendation, with the clear understanding that this would generate a global consensus over the Code. However, in between the EB in January and the WHA in May 1981, the position of the US altered as a consequence of a change of administration. The new Reagan Administration took over in January 1981 and strong industry lobbying activity in the months preceding the WHA was witnessed. During the WHA of May 1981, the US casted the only vote against the Code.[6]

The International Code of Marketing of Breastmilk Substitutes was adopted through the resolution 34.22 by the 34$^{th}$ WHA in 1981, as "a minimum requirement to protect and promote appropriate infant and young child feeding". States were urged to implement the Code in its 'entirety'[7]

---

4 Sokol, 2005, see *supra* note 2.

5 Out of the 33 Members, 9 Members were strongly in favour of a regulation, while 8 others favoured a regulation but accepted a recommendation if this was to gain broader consensus. The rest favoured a recommendation.

6 The final voting results were: 118 in favor, 1 against (the US) and 3 abstentions (Argentina, Japan, Korea).

7 The primary responsibility to act on the Code lies with governments, which are encouraged to take measures "to give effect to the principles and aim of the Code at the national level, as appropriate to their social and legislative framework, including

and up to 2010 there have been 17 subsequent relevant WHA resolutions,[8] which enjoy the same status as the Code. The resolutions have expanded the scope of the Code and have specified additional standards of marketing for breastmilk substitute products. The Code must be read together with these subsequent resolutions as one single document.[9]

### 12.2.2. The International Informal Lawmaking Status of the Code

According to the definition of IN-LAW by Pauwelyn,[10] informality can be linked to *the process*, *the actors* or *the output* of the international cooperation between public authorities. From this analytical perspective, can the Code be considered a case of informal lawmaking at the international level?

*The process* that led to the adoption of the Code was characterized by the same degree of formality which qualifies traditional forms of international law. The international cooperation that gave rise to the Code was hosted by a traditional forum of an international organization (IO): the WHA, which is the decision-making body of the WHO.

Secondly, *the actors* involved at the international level represent traditional diplomatic actors: delegations or representatives appointed by Member States of the WHO to deliberate on health policies. Several other actors, especially public interest NGOs, were involved in bringing the issue to the attention of the public opinion. They lobbied to defend their interests and participated in the process of debate and consultation that preceded the final adoption. However, the final text was endorsed by the Member State delegations sitting in the WHA. These have the power to represent and bind their governments by adopting binding decisions.

---

adoption of legislation, regulations or other suitable measures" (Art. 11.1). World Health Organization, "International Code of Marketing of Breast-milk Substitutes", available at http://www.who.int/nutrition/publications/code_english.pdf, last accessed on 20 December 2011.

8 It integrates the subsequent resolutions, adopted by the WHA: 33.32; 34.22; 35.26; 37.30; 39.28; 41.11; 43.3; 45.34; 47.5; 49.15; 54.2; 59.21; 55.25; 58.32; 59.21; 61.20; 63.23.

9 Therefore, from now on, we will refer to the 1981 International Code of Marketing of Breastmilk Substitutes and the subsequent WHA resolutions as the Code.

10 Joost Pauwelyn, "Informal International Lawmaking: Framing the Concept and Research Questions", in Joost Pauwelyn, Ramses A. Wessel and Jan Wouters (eds.), *Informal International Lawmaking*, Oxford University Press, Oxford, 2012.

In terms of the *output*, the International Code is characterized by informality because it was not adopted as a convention or a binding regulation, but as a 'non-binding WHA resolution'. It represents minimum required standards that are non-binding and up to the State to implement at the national level using appropriate measures. The choice of a non-binding output was a result of the different political interests of States, as well as of other actors involved in the broader negotiation process.

Due to its non-binding character, the Code is not applicable before international courts or tribunals and has no direct application in the territory of States. Although baby food manufacturers and distributors should regard themselves as directly accountable under the International Code,[11] this presupposes the existence of national legal measures in order to hold them accountable. In practice, the Code has not brought about legal responsibility for transnational corporations at the international level.

### 12.2.3. Informality as a Compromise

When defining effectiveness of IN-LAW, the framing paper by Pauwelyn identifies four dimensions. According to the first one, in order to be effective, IN-LAW should enhance "the chances for international cooperation to occur".[12]

The process of Code drafting and the negotiations have shown that IN-LAW was a means to reach international cooperation on the regulation of marketing of breastmilk substitutes. The aspect of output informality was the most salient point of discussion during the negotiation process. Staff of the IOs involved, several governments, especially of developing countries that are net consumers of infant foods, and consumer groups supported a formal output (a regulation) as the safest way to protect the interest of consumers, the health of babies and control the perverse effects of marketing practices. While infant food industries and some governments, especially the ones that were net infant food producers, were not in favor of international regulations of transnational corporations and advo-

[11] Article 11.3 of the Code writes: "Independently from any other measure taken for implementation [...] manufacturers and distributers should regard themselves as responsible for monitoring their marketing practices according to the principles and aim of the Code". World Health Organisation, "International Code of Marketing of Breastmilk Substitutes", see *supra* note 7.

[12] Pauwelyn, 2012, p. 23, see *supra* note 10.

cated that the regulation of the marketing practices was to be left to each country to decide, it was clear that these governments and commercial actors did not want to create a treaty which would bind them to it.

Finally, many governments and staff from the WHO and UNICEF, judged that building universal consensus over the Code was more important than the formal status of the output. The choice of a non-binding output (a WHO recommendation) was a result of the different political interests of States, as well as of other actors involved in the broader negotiation process and represented a compromise between these interests. Thanks to this compromise it was possible to create a large, even though non-unanimous, consensus among the actors involved. Thus, the Code as IN-LAW proved effective in allowing for international cooperation to happen.

### 12.2.4. International Accountability Mechanisms

IN-LAW is said to suffer accountability gaps. This project borrows the definition of accountability by Bovens, which defines it as "a relationship between an actor and a forum, in which the actor has an obligation to explain and to justify his or her conduct, the forum can pose questions and pose judgment, and the actor may face consequences".[13] This form of accountability requires an institutionalized relationship between the forum and the actor and deals mostly with the accountability of the actors involved.

According to Article 11 of the Code, "monitoring of the application of this Code lies with the governments individually and collectively through the World Health Organization".[14] WHO Member States are required to communicate annually to the Director-General (DG) on the state of the actions taken to implement the Code. The DG examines these reports and prepares a biennial report for the World Health Assembly (WHA). Neither the DG, nor the WHA evaluate or emit judgments on the state of Code implementation by countries. It is up to the other Member

13 Cited in Tim Corthaut, Bruno Demeyere, Nicolas Hachez, Jan Wouters, "Operationalizing Accountability in Respect of International Informal Lawmaking Mechanisms", in Joost Pauwelyn, Ramses A. Wessel and Jan Wouters (eds.), *Informal International Lawmaking,* Oxford University Press, Oxford, 2012.

14 World Health Organisation, "The International Code of Marketing of Breastmilk Substitutes", see *supra* note 7.

States of the WHA to raise questions and criticisms or make suggestions with regards to the implementation of the Code. Through such open discussion, it is hoped that Member States will be incited or encouraged to implement the Code.[15]

The reality shows that this accountability mechanism is deficient. The 2004 report for the Executive Board (EB) of the DG showed that 23 years after the Code adoption by the WHA, the information on Code implementation by Member States had greatly reduced. Most of those Member States that have reported so far have done so only once.[16] The original information sent to the DG by governments is not publicly available and thus does not allow for public scrutiny of the information submitted by single Member States. Moreover, the regular GD reports to the WHA vary greatly in form and substance, with some reports containing only few paragraphs about the Code's implementation and others including numerous details.[17] No comprehensive monitoring plan or guidelines have been devised from the WHO and there are no clear indicators for the evaluation of the state of the Code's implementation by countries.[18]

This accountability mechanism relies on peer control[19] and is based on self-reported data by governments and suffers from lack of transparen-

---

15 Annelies Allain, *Fighting an Old Battle in a New World. How IBFAN Monitors the Baby Food Market*, Dag Hammarskjold Foundation, Uppsala, 2005.

16 The report reads, "With 162 (84 %) of WHO's 192 Member States having already reported (often more than once) the flow of new information has greatly reduced". Report by the Secretariat for the EB 113th Session, 2004, *Infant and Young Child Nutrition and Progress in Implementing the International Code of Marketing of Breastmilk Substitutes*, available at https://apps.who.int/gb/ebwha/pdf_files/EB113/eeb11338r2.pdf, last accessed on 4 December 2011.

17 World Health Organisation, "A Review of Nutrition Policies", available at http://apps.who.int/gb/ebwha/pdf_files/EB130/B130_1_annotated-en.pdf, last accessed on 8 December 2011.

18 The last comprehensive survey on nutrition policies at the country level carried out by WHO in 2009 relied on self-reporting by States. Only 97 States reported to the module of the survey on country implementation of the Code. Most of these countries did not provide the necessary legal documentation to support the responses, therefore the data reported is "based upon self-reporting without a systematic review of legal documents". See World Health Organisation, "A Review of Nutrition Policies", see *supra* note 17. For a critique of the WHO reporting process see Allain, 2005, p. 29, see *supra* note 15.

19 Grant and Keohane provide seven types of mechanisms for accountability: hierarchical, supervisory, fiscal, peer and public reputational. See Pauwelyn, 2012, p. 17, see *supra* note 10.

cy. States face no sanctions whenever they do not report or whenever they have taken no action to comply with the Code. This means that there is no independent monitoring system in place and even though the forum is able to pose questions, the actors (Member States) face no consequences. Thus if we take a narrow approach to accountability, the Code as IN-LAW suffers a deficit of accountability, which has produced a situation where only around 20% of WHO Member States have fully complied with the Code.[20]

## 12.3. Effectiveness at the Domestic Level

### 12.3.1. Implementation at Domestic Level

The second dimension of effectiveness identified by Pauwelyn concerns the implementation and compliance with the international cooperation materialized in the IN-LAW body. The third dimension recalls what is most commonly understood by effectiveness, which is whether or not the IN-LAW body contributes to solving the problem it addresses.[21] Both these dimensions relate to the domestic level and they are closely interrelated in the case of the Code. The second part of this chapter will analyze the factors that determine the implementation of the Code by countries and, secondly, it will turn to the questions of how effective implementation has been in terms of solving the problem and what factors have played a role in this regard.

Due to the informal character of the Code, States are not obliged to adopt it domestically and if they chose to do so, they have no obligation to implement it completely, even though WHO Member States are meant to consider it as a 'minimum requirement'.[22] Moreover, States are free to choose the type of measure (a voluntary code, a law, a decree, a regulation, *et cetera*) through which they will implement the Code,[23] which has led to a high variability of the types of measures adopted at the domestic

[20] International Baby Food Action Network, *State of the Code by Company*, IBFAN-ICDC, Penang, 2011

[21] The fourth dimension does not fall under the scope of this chapter.

[22] World Health Organisation, "International Code of Marketing of Breast-milk substitutes", see *supra* note 7.

[23] World Health Organisation, "International Code of Marketing of Breast-milk Substitutes. Frequently asked questions", available at http://www.who.int/maternal_child_adolescent/documents/9241594292/en/, last accessed on 20 December 2011.

level by States. This high variability is a direct consequence of the Code as an informal mechanism and will be analyzed as one of the key factors that may determine effectiveness at the domestic level. In particular, the next section will look at the influence that the 'the strength' of the domestic measures has on their effectiveness.

#### 12.3.1.1. The Strength of National Measures

In characterizing the strength of the national measures, the analysis will draw upon the definition of 'hardness' of Skjaerseth *et al.*,[24] according to whom hard laws are characterized by (i) a binding character,[25] (ii) precision[26] and (iii) delegation of authority.[27]

Translating this to the Code practices, the observations regarding the first criterion are that domestic measures range from hard laws (binding laws with clearly determined implementing regulations) to soft measures (non-binding such as voluntary initiatives often drafted and monitored in collaboration with industry). Second, implementation measures vary to the extent in which they integrate the provisions of the Code. Many States have not taken any measures at all to implement the Code. Among those countries that have taken steps, some have adopted laws that fully incorporate the Code or go even beyond it, while others have adopted measures that partially reflect Code provisions. Third, in the case of the Code, the delegation of authority means that a body or agency is identified and assigned the task of monitoring compliance according to specific procedures, filing complaints, and taking disciplinary action. Delegation of authority is usually specified in implementing rules and regulations which clearly spell out implementation responsibilities.

A close look at the data collected by the International Code Documentation Center (ICDC) on the state of the Code in national jurisdictions shows the uneven situation among countries. As of 2011, only 33 States

---

24 Jon Skjaerseth, Birger Olav, Schram Stokke and Jörgen Wettestad, "Soft Law, Hard Law, and Effective Implementation of International Environmental Norms", in *Global Environmental Politics*, 2006, vol. 6, pp. 104–120

25 Skjaerseth, Olav, Stokke and Wettestad explain that the binding character normally results from the adoptation by the legislative body (*e.g.*, the national parliament), and potentially can be used before a tribunal for settling disputes.

26 Meaning that the conduct required or prescribed is clearly determined.

27 Meaning that a third party has been delegated with the authority of interpreting and implementing the law.

have fully translated all provisions of the Code into national laws, while 17 countries have fully translated them into national voluntary codes. There are 81 countries that have partially integrated the Code provisions into their legislation, 47 of which have implemented only few provisions. European Union (EU) countries fall under this category as they have adopted the EU Directive on Infant Formulae and Follow-on Formulae, which covers few Code provisions. Another 23 countries have undertaken partial voluntary measures while 43 countries have so far taken no action in implementing the Code, among which are the US and North Korea. South Africa, Australia, Malaysia, China and others have adopted national voluntary measures which are not legally enforceable. Conversely, Brazil and India have national laws that translate the international soft law instrument into national hard laws and are considered as strong as or even stronger than the Code.[28]

Figure 1 shows the high variation of national implementation measures along the first two dimensions (binding character and precision) across different regions, according to the classification made by ICDC in 2010.

[28] The latest data collected by WHO in 2009, as a result of a survey on nutrition policies is not as accurate as the data provided by ICDC. The data only concerns 132 countries and is based on self-reporting from countries. Thus what some countries understand by the categories of 'full measure' or 'partial measure' may differ significantly. This set of data has been criticised by IBFAN and ICDC. World Health Organisation, "A Review of Nutrition Policies", see *supra* note 17. See also International Baby Food Action Network, 2011, see *supra* note 20.

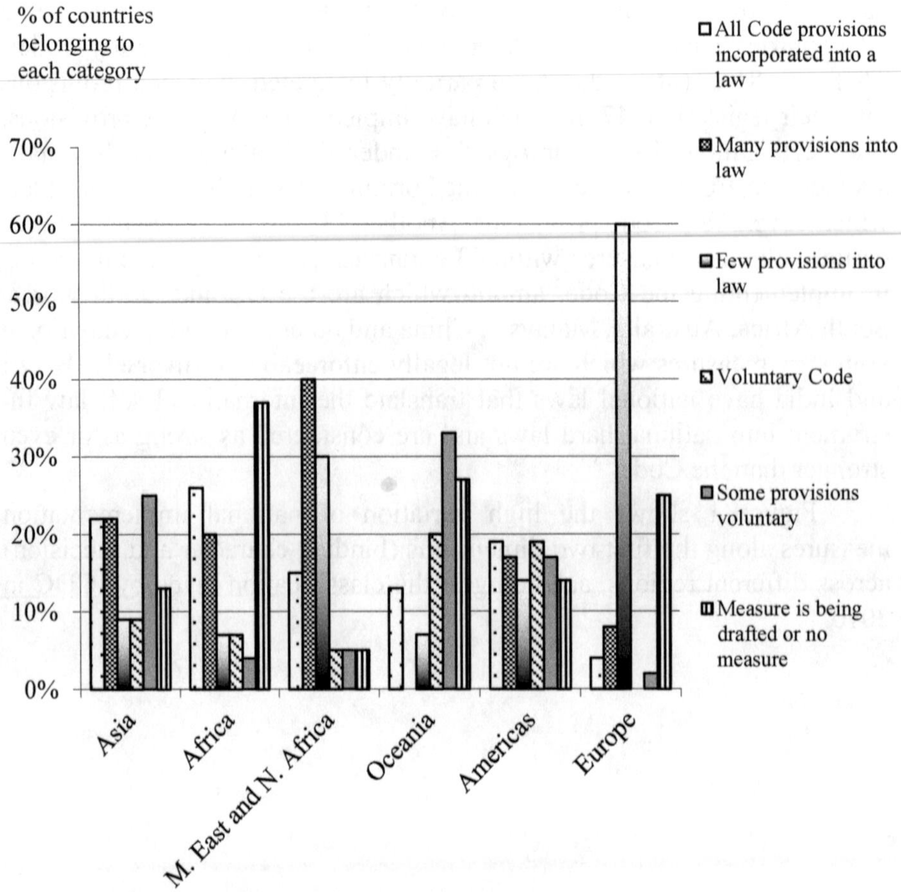


**Figure 1:** State of the Code's implementation at the national level.[29]

### 12.3.1.2. Defining Domestic Effectiveness

The Code aims to

> […] contribute to the provision of safe and adequate nutrition for infants, by the protection and promotion of breast-feeding, and by ensuring the proper use of the breastmilk

[29] The category 'Few provisions into law' gathers two of the original categories of ICDC: 1) Few provisions into law and 2) Some provisions into other laws. While the category "Measure is being drafted or no measure" gathers 3 of the original categories from ICDC: 1) Measure is drafted, 2) Being studied and 3) No information/no action. International Baby Food Action Network, 2011, see *supra* note 20.

substitutes, when these are necessary, on the basis of adequate information and through appropriate marketing and distribution (Article 1).[30]

Therefore, in order to analyze the effectiveness in terms of the problem being addressed, one would need to consider either the state of breastfeeding at the country level, or the marketing and distribution practices of baby food companies. The breastfeeding rates pose several analytical problems due to the fact that breastfeeding is related to several social, cultural, and economic factors including the influence of advertisement and promotion of formula products. Therefore, it is problematic to isolate the effect of the national implementation measures on the state of a country's breastfeeding rates. However, one should not eliminate it completely from the analysis. For example, an American study which examined the relationship between advertising in a parenting magazine and breastfeeding between 1972 and 2000 in the US, found that when the frequency of advertisements for artificial feeding increased, the percentage change in breastfeeding rates reported the next year tended to decrease.[31]

The second component consists of the marketing practices and conduct of baby food companies. In order to investigate this factor, the second section will analyze the evolution of baby food companies' conduct in relation to the Code's implementation history. Particular attention will be paid to key historical moments, that is, the moment of adoption of domestic measures, other events that have dictated a policy change in marketing regulation and the consequent positive change or lack thereof in company behavior.

### 12.3.2. Monitoring Domestic Implementation and Compliance with the Code

At the national level, according to the Code (Article 11.2), monitoring is a responsibility of every government.[32] The meaning of this article has not

30 World Health Organisation, "The International Code of Marketing of Breast-milk Substitutes", see *supra* note 7.

31 Katherine Foss, and Brian Southwell, "Infant Feeding and the Media: The Relationship between Parents' Magazine Content and Breastfeeding, 1972–2000", in *International Breastfeeding Journal*, 2006, vol. 1, pp. 1–10.

32 Article 11.2 of the Code reads "Monitoring the application of this Code lies with governments acting individually, and collectively through the World Health Organisation as provided in paragraphs 6 and 7 of this Article. The manufacturers and distributors

been explained in the Code. Each State decides separately what types of monitoring mechanisms are appropriate to monitor compliance with the Code within its national territory, in light of each national context. Individual State monitoring also means that it can be carried out only within the boundaries of a State and presupposes the existence of a national legal measure since the Code itself, as adopted by WHO, has no direct legal application in the States territories.

A great number of countries that have adopted the Code at the domestic level have not adopted regulations for translating it into effective measures. This means that no specialized body or agency has been conferred with the responsibility of monitoring, no clear guidelines and monitoring procedures have been set, and violations of the law have not been penalized. In some cases, a specific authority has been delegated by the law to monitor implementation of the domestic measures; however, these bodies are often left inactive due to a lack of resource allocation. In these cases, there is no effective implementation of the domestic law, as the law remains abstract and not applied effectively.

#### 12.3.2.1. Monitoring of State Action and Corporate Compliance by IBFAN

An important role in monitoring Code compliance worldwide is played by civil society. Article 11.4 of the Code gives NGOs, professional groups, institutions and concerned individuals the responsibility to draw the attention of manufacturers and distributors to activities that are incompatible with the Code so that appropriate action can be taken.[33] The major net-

of products within the scope of this Code, and appropriate nongovernmental organisations, professional groups, and consumer organisations should collaborate with governments to this end." Moreover, resolutions WHA 49.15 and 54.2 call upon governments to ensure proper and effective monitoring and reporting mechanisms and processes for effective implementation of the Code and subsequent relevant WHA resolutions. World Health Organisation, "International Code of Marketing of Breast-milk Substitutes. Frequently Asked Questions", see *supra* note 23.

[33] "Nongovernmental organisations, professional groups, institutions and individuals concerned should have the responsibility of drawing the attention of manufacturers or distributors to activities which are incompatible with the principles and aim of this Code, so that appropriate action can be taken. The appropriate governmental authority should also be informed." (Article 11.4). World Health Organization, "International Code of Marketing of Breast-milk Substitutes", see *supra* note 7.

work that has taken up this responsibility is the International Baby Food Action Network (IBFAN).

IBFAN was founded in October 1979 following the joint meeting of WHO and UNICEF, by the activist groups and consumer organizations that played an important role in putting the baby foods marketing onto the international health agenda. The network works toward universal and full implementation of the Code.

IBFAN pushed for strong monitoring guidelines in the Code negotiation process at WHA. Members of the network realized that although the Code was adopted, gaps in monitoring policy and practice still existed. The Code did not include monitoring guidelines, and no comprehensive monitoring policy was devised by the WHO. IBFAN members felt that if no one was given the responsibility to keep track of implementation, the Code might not produce the change for which it was conceived.[34] Therefore, IBFAN set as one of its main objectives, to monitor the compliance of governments with their commitment at the WHA in 1981 to implement the Code domestically, and the compliance of private sector companies to abide by the Code. IBFAN is the only actor that has so far developed indicators and a systematic and uniform strategy for monitoring and evaluating the implementation process by states and compliance with the Code by companies.

As a result of the lack of a comprehensive monitoring and evaluation strategy by the WHO and the Member States, IBFAN members founded the Code Documentation Centre (ICDC) in 1985.[35] This Centre organizes global monitoring, analyzes national measures and produces documents on the state of compliance at the domestic level. It keeps systematic track of measures taken at the national level with the goal of implementing the Code. At the same time, it supports IBFAN groups around the globe to monitor violations from corporations. For this purpose, ICDC offers training to IBFAN members, and often, when governments require their expertise, they also train public officials on how to effectively implement the Code domestically and how to monitor compliance.

34 Allain, 2005, see *supra* note 15.

35 In 1991, the Code Documentation Centre became an international foundation (International Code Documentation Centre) as a result of an international meeting organized by the Dutch government to celebrate the 10th anniversary of the Code. The meeting recommended that the documentation should be gathered and disseminated not only by WHO and UNICEF but also by the ICDC.

With the involvement of IBFAN country groups in the monitoring process, ICDC produces a periodical monitoring report: *Breaking the Rules, Stretching the Rules.*[36] This report shows how the main transnational baby food companies are complying with the Code. The organization also keeps track of Code implementation by country. The monitoring process carried out by IBFAN is the most comprehensive and transparent global monitoring on the Code. It shows that the Code is far from being effectively implemented, even though more than 30 years have passed since its adoption. It also proves that companies, despite being under direct obligation from the Code, continue violating its provisions.

### 12.3.3. Case Study Selection

Domestic effectiveness will be analyzed in three case studies: Malaysia, the Philippines and India. First, the selection is based on the different degrees of hardness of the national measures which implement the International Code to be observed: from a non-binding soft law in Malaysia, to a partially hard law in the Philippines, to a binding hard law in India. This variability in implementation measures is functional in analyzing the extent to which the strength of domestic measures influences their effectiveness.

Second, the case study selection is also based on the relevance breastfeeding has in terms of child mortality in the countries studied. Average exclusive breastfeeding rates in East Asia and the Pacific are just 61% at four months of babies' lives and even lower, at 35%, at six months of life.[37] As UNICEF's Regional Director for East Asia and Pacific puts it,

> [w]ithin the region, child survival is affected by poor water quality, hygiene and sanitation. Combine sanitary water with the replacement of breastfeeding by infant formula and the threat becomes even deadlier.[38]

---

36 See for example IBFAN-ICDC, "Breaking the Rules, Stretching the Rules 2007", available at http://www.ibfan.org/code_watch-btr.html, last accessed on 9 December 2011.

37 UNICEF, "WHO and UNICEF Call for Renewed Commitment to Breastfeeding", available at http://www.unicef.org/malaysia/media_6964.html, last accessed on 8 December 2011.

38 *Ibid.*

Third, in the case studies selection, a number of variables have been considered in order to avoid biased results. The three countries belong to the same geographical region. Malaysia and the Philippines are both insular countries and very similar in their biodiversity ('mega diverse' countries according to a UNESCO classification). Secondly, the penetration of the infant formula industry is similar in the three countries. The major baby food companies are present in all three of them: Nestlé, Danone, Abbott Ross, Wyeth and Mead Johnson.

Finally, the market for baby foods, in particular for infant formula, is a highly lucrative one. Most of the countries of the Asia and Pacific region have attractive markets for infant formula industries as the economies are very dynamic, with high annual growth rates and high fertility rates at the same time. As shown in the report from a business intelligence provider, the Euromonitor International of 2008, global sales of baby food (the bulk of which is comprised of artificial baby milks) are projected to grow by 37% from 2008 to 2013.[39] The region of Asia-Pacific is currently attributed the biggest share of the global baby food market (figure 2) and it is expected to contribute to almost two-thirds of the future growth of this market. Nestlé has announced double digit growth rates for its infant nutrition division in Asia and Oceania.[40] Considering the share of the baby food market in the region is necessary in order to avoid the bias of having high Code effectiveness in terms of company behavior due to the fact that infant formula industries are not particularly interested in the market of that country.

---

[39] Euromonitor International, *Global Packaged Foods: Market Opportunities for Baby Food to 201,* Euromonitor International, London, 2008.

[40] Nestlé, "Full Year Results 2010", available at http://www.nestle.com/Media/PressReleases/Pages/AllPressRelease.aspx?Name=Full-Year-Results-2010&PressReleaseYear=2010&Title=Full%20Year%20Results%202010&PageName=2010.aspx last accessed on 1 December 2011.

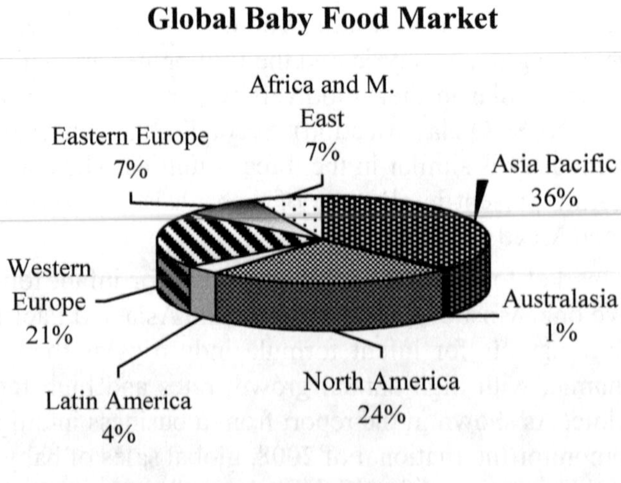


**Figure 2:** Global Baby Food Market.[41]

### 12.3.4. The Malaysia Case Study

Malaysia first introduced a voluntary Code to address the unethical promotion of formula products in 1979. The Code was revised in 1983, 1985, 1995, and finally in August 2008. Its official name is 'The Code of Ethics for the Marketing of Infant Foods and related Products' (Code of Ethics). The Ministry of Health worked closely with industry and civil society in drafting the Code of Ethics. Civil society has been one of the pushing factors behind the continuous revisions of the Code, with the purpose of making it stronger. The legal advice given by ICDC, which is situated in Penang, has strengthened the Code of Ethics. International organizations like UNICEF do not play an important role in the country, as Malaysia is not listed as a least developed country and local IOs' offices are relatively small.

The scope of the Malaysian Code of Ethics is similar to the International Code of Marketing of Breastmilk Substitutes. It applies to infant formula, follow-up formula, feeding bottles, teats, pacifiers, and any other products for infants up to the age of 6 months. It concerns their promotion in health facilities, retail outlets and media advertising. Free supplies are prohibited in the health care system and the baby food companies are pre-

41 Euromonitor International, 2008, see *supra* note 39.

vented from displaying products in public events. Even though the 2008 Code of Ethics prohibits 'incentives' to health professionals, it fails to explicitly prohibit sponsorships by baby food industry to the health care sector. The issue of labeling is included also in the Food Act Regulations, which ensures quality and appropriate labeling of products.

The government has been playing an increasingly important role in the process of revising, implementing, vetting and handling the complaints procedure for the national Code. There are two committees designated to implement the Code of Ethics: the Vetting Committee that vets labels and information materials produced by companies, and the Disciplinary Committee that handles complaints and decides on the disciplinary actions to be taken. These actions are to be implemented by the State Committee which is also in charge of the investigations. No representatives of the formula industry participate in any of these committees. Sanctions range from warnings, to suspension of vetting of new materials, press releases and blacklisting from government tenders. The Ministry of Health engages in a yearly exercise to publicly criticize the baby food companies for breaches of the Code and the results of monitoring and complaints are released to the press. In 2006, sanctions were imposed on eight out of the twelve companies that operate in the country.[42] These were banned from advertising or selling in the country for one year. Nevertheless, it remains unclear whether these penalties were fully applied or not. In 2010, the Ministry of Health sent a letter to the WHO and UNICEF reporting that the Disciplinary Committee had discussed seven cases of alleged violations. Only three of these were classified as violations of the Code of Ethics, but it is unknown whether any action has been taken, including public denunciation.

All main infant formula companies are found in the country, with Nestlé dominating the market. Two of the biggest formula companies – Nestlé and Abbott Ross – have both been found violating the Code of Ethics through wrongfully promoting in health care facilities and the use of misleading texts and pictures on their products.[43] According to one moni-

---

42 Nestlé, "WHO Code of Marketing", available at http://www.nestle.com/Common/NestleDocuments/Documents/Creating%20Shared%20Value/Products%20and%20Consumers/WHO_Code_Marketing.pdf, last accessed on 20 December 2011.

43 Abbott Ross was found in violation of articles concerning promotion to the public, labeling and through the use of aggressive promotional practices. International Baby

toring study commissioned by Nestlé, all other companies break the Code through providing health care facilities with free goods and samples.[44]

Violations in the country consist especially of free distribution of samples and supplies in private health facilities and other areas not clearly regulated by the Code of Ethics such as sponsorship. According to IBFAN, the lack of legal status of Code results in the non-prosecution of health operators and companies. This goes especially for medical professionals who are not subject to any sanctions since they are not required under the Medical Profession Act to comply with the Malaysian Code. The situation of companies is somewhat different, but the sanctions faced are much smaller than the profits to be collected from sample distribution.[45]

Although specific governmental authorities have been delegated the task of taking disciplinary actions upon violators, only a vague system of monitoring has been put in place by the government. Also, the fact that public criticizing happens only one week per year or even less undermines the credibility of this system of compliance. However, the annual public denunciation of violations may be effective in raising awareness. Nonetheless, violations persist, especially in relation to the high profit-making activities for companies that override the disadvantages of the sanctions and among private clinic staff because of gaps in the regulations. The sanctions have no legal power, cannot be claimed in court and thus their deterring function can be questioned.[46] Collaboration and monitoring by civil society is crucial for the monitoring and complaints mechanism to function properly. However, since NGOs depend on donor's funding, the system remains fragile and dependent upon the ability of these actors to find funding.

The Malaysian Code of Ethics is an example of a soft law with a non-binding character (voluntary code); it is quite clear in establishing guidelines for behavior (the scope of the Code of Ethics is close to that of

---

Food Action Network, *Asia-Pacific. Look what they are doing!*, IBFAN-ICDC, Penang, 2007.

44 Bureau Veritas, "Independent Assurance Statement", available at http://www.babymilk.nestle.com/news/Documents/Jan2009MalaysiaWHOCodeStatement.pdf, last accessed on 1 December 2011.

45 International Baby Food Action Network, Report to the Committee on the Rights of the Child on the Situation of Breastfeeding In Malaysia, IBFAN, 2006.

46 Sokol, 2005, see *supra* note 2.

the Code); and partially delegates authority (a vague and not very effective system of monitoring which has been put in place by the government).

### 12.3.5. The Philippines Case Study

The infant formula market in the Philippines is relatively large while the general situation of breastfeeding in the Philippines is poor. In 2003, WHO estimated that 16,000 children under the age of five died in the country as a result of improper feeding practices including infant formula.[47] While only about one third of Filipino children in the 0–5 month's age bracket are exclusively breastfed, the country spends at least $500 million annually on imported artificial infant formula and over $100 million in promoting these.[48] An advertising group in the Philippines announced that the total advertising expenditures for powdered milk products in the Philippines was around 2.3 billion Philippine Peso[49] in the first half of 2009 alone.[50]

In order to apply the Code domestically, the Philippines adopted the Filipino 'Milk Code', which was signed into law in 1986.[51] The adoption of the Milk Code was a result of five year long advocacy initiatives led by a coalition among various NGOs and the National Movement for the Promotion of Breastfeeding (NMPB); and was also supported by UNICEF.[52] The Milk Code Task Force, appointed by the Department of Health (DOH), became active in 1999 in proposing regulations for strict implementation of the law. These were overturned by a Health Secretary in close relation with the baby food industry in 2000, and were revised in

47 International Baby Food Action Network, Report to the Committee on the Rights of the Child on the Situation of Breastfeeding in the Philippines, IBFAN, 2009

48 David L. Clark, "Protecting breastfeeding through implementation of the international code: what's law got to do with it?", in *Breastfeeding Review,* 2011, vol. 19, no. 2, available at http://www.biomedsearch.com/article/Protecting-breastfeeding-through-implementation-international/267204158.html, last accessed on 20 March 2012.

49 2.3 billion Philippine Pesos amount to approximately US$ 50 million.

50 Vinia M. Datinguinoo, "Tempest in a (feeding) bottle", available at http://pcij.org/stories/tempest-in-a-feeding-bottle/, last accessed on 1 December 2011.

51 The full name of the Milk Code is: Philippine National Code on Marketing of Breast-milk Substitutes, Breast-milk Supplements and Related Products, 1986.

52 Baby Milk Action, "The Implementing Rules and Regulations for the Philippines Milk Code – Chronology", available at http://www.babymilkaction.org/pdfs/philippineschrono06.rtf, last accessed on 8 December 2011.

favor of baby food companies.[53] In 2006, new Implementing Rules and Regulations (IRR) were proposed by the Task Force and subsequently adopted by the Ministry of Health, in the view of changing market practices by baby food companies. The process of law enforcement of the Milk Code caused a strong resistance from the baby food industry and set up active lobbying against its adoption. The pressure exerted by industry was high, including a lawsuit by the Pharmaceutical Healthcare Association of the Philippines against the Filipino Secretary of Health, and threats to economic investments through visits and letters by the president of the American Chamber of Commerce to officials of the Department of Health and the President of the Philippines. Over the next three years, the government and civil society pursued a long and intense battle to defend the adoption of the IRR. Activist groups and international organizations, such as UNICEF and WHO, played an important role in sustaining the government initiative and denouncing the industry's lobbying activity. These groups showed their ability to activate national and international networking and support to the law enforcement process till the end. Finally, the Supreme Court decided in favor of the new Revised Implementing Rules and Regulations (RIRR) which eventually came into force in 2007.[54]

The Milk Code is a binding law and, together with the RIRR, it implements the provisions of the International Code in a high degree but not entirely.[55] The Department of Health (DOH) is responsible for its implementation, with the assistance of the Department of Justice, Social Work and Development, as well as the Department of Trade and Industry. Formally, it has a delegated authority for monitoring to the Inter-Agency

53 UNICEF, "Infant and Young Child Feeding Programme Review. Case Study: Philippines, 2009", available at http://www.aednutritioncenter.org/update_docs/IYCF_Feeding_Prog_Rev_Case_Study_Philippines.pdf, last accessed on 8 December 2011.

54 *Ibid.*

55 The Milk Code and subsequently also the RIRR only implement the Code and not the Subsequent WHA resolutions. This means that important recommendations such as the one on six months of exclusive breastfeeding which are contained in the WHA Resolutions, are not implemented through the domestic law in the Philippines. For an analysis of the decision by the Filipino Supreme Court on the IRR, see International Baby Food Action Network, "ICDC Legal Update, January 2008", available at http://www.ibfan.org/art/LU-Jan%202008.pdf, last accessed on 8 December 2011. See also Baby Milk Action, "Significant Protection for Infant Health in the Philippines Achieved as Court Rejects 'Restraint of Trade' Argument – But More Needed", available at http://www.babymilkaction.org/press/press10oct07.html, last accessed on 8 December 2011.

Committee (IAC). The IAC is in charge of pre-approving all advertisement and promotional materials for breastmilk substitutes. This Committee reviews marketing materials submitted by industry on a monthly basis. Nevertheless, the scope of action of this committee is limited due to the fact that review is applied only to promotional and marketing materials submitted on a voluntary basis by the baby food companies.

In order to ensure monitoring of compliance by these companies, the DOH issued 'Guidelines for Monitoring of Milk Code Activities' in 2009.[56] Virtually anyone can report a violation, although the Guidelines delegate the role of 'official monitors' to, *inter alia,* health offices in different levels, civil society organizations, and UNICEF and WHO, which then report to the Bureau of Food and Drug Administration. This mechanism does not guarantee a systematic and sustainable monitoring of violations, as official monitors are not required to undertake systematic monitoring activities and moreover the Guidelines suggest that NGOs and other official monitors should seek for funding from donor agencies, such as UNICEF or WHO.[57] From 2007–2009, only four out of 13 regions had reported any monitoring activities of the Milk Code and only three regions reported filing a complaint for the alleged violations.[58] Moreover, even if the RIRR provides for administrative sanctions or criminal penalties in cases of braches to the Milk Code, no sanctions have been applied up to date. Thus, even though the Milk Code has been clarified through the RIRR and several authorities are now tasked with its implementation, sustainable monitoring and effective enforcement of the law are still to be addressed in the Philippines.

In 2009, a documentary by UNICEF Philippines showed that violations of the Milk Code are very high and omnipresent. The influence of advertisement together with the influence that health workers have on mothers has created a situation where poor families who cannot afford in-

56 Department of Health, "Revised Implementing Rules and Regulations of Executive Order No. 51, Otherwise known as the 'Milk Code', Relevant International Agreements, Penalizing Violations Thereof and for Other Purposes", available at http://pcij.org/blog/wp-docs/ao2006-0012.pdf, last accessed on 8 December 2011.

57 Department of Health, "Guidelines for the Monitoring of Milk Code Activities", available at http://home.doh.gov.ph/dc/dc2009-0228.pdf, last accessed on 8 December 2011.

58 Department of Health, "Infant and Young Child Feeding: Strategic Plan of Action", available at http://www.doh.gov.ph/node/375, last accessed on 8 December 2011.

fant formula and do not have the hygienic conditions to properly prepare it, end up spending a considerable part of their income in what they believe is best for their newborns.[59] Given the lack of sanctions faced by industry in cases of breaches of the Milk Code, chances are that the situation continues being the same as the one described in this documentary.

The Filipino Milk Code is an example of a partially hard law with a binding character (voluntary code); quite clear in establishing guidelines for behavior (the scope of the Filipino law is close to that of the Code); and with partial delegation of authority (the RIRR identify the delegated authorities, however the system of monitoring has not shown to be effective up to date, with limited scope of work for the IAC, lack of systematic monitoring mechanisms, limited sustainability for the official monitors and lack of sanctions in cases of violations).

### 12.3.6. The India Case Study

In the wake of the adoption of the International Code, the Indian government responded positively and quickly by adopting the Indian National Code for Protection and Promotion of Breastfeeding in 1983. This Code, which was adopted as a resolution, was a temporary measure. While waiting for the legal enactment of the Indian Code, some rules for labeling of infant foods were included in the existing legislation Prevention of Food Adulteration Act (PFA) of 1954.

National activist groups forming the Voluntary Health Association of India (VHAI) and some individuals were not satisfied with this measure and they continuously lobbied policy makers to promulgate a bill that would incorporate the Indian Code. After some failed attempts within the Parliament, in 1992, a bill was introduced as a private member's bill by the opposition party. This was then taken over by the ruling party and introduced in the Parliament to be finally enacted as Infant Milk Substitutes Feeding Bottles, and Infant Foods (Regulation of Production, Supply and Distribution) Act 1992 (IMS Act). It takes the form of a criminal law with strict penal sanctions, including a minimum mandatory jail sentence of six months and with imprisonment up to three years for violation of some sections. In addition to government inspectors, the law authorizes citizens' groups to file criminal complaints in court for violations. Four or-

59 Andy Brown, "Formula for Disaster", available at http://www.youtube.com/watch?v=SNYDPKQOVUE, last accessed on 20 December 2012.

ganizations have been identified by the Government of India for this purpose: the Central Social Welfare Board (CSWB), the Indian Council for Child Welfare (ICCW), and the Association for Consumer Action on Safety and Health (ACASH) and the Breastfeeding Promotion Network of India (BPNI).[60]

Despite the strength of the 1992 IMS Act, activist groups were arguing that it contained several limitations. Mainly due to the fact that its application covered infant milk products which were used as breastmilk substitutes, but not other types of baby foods. Also, infant foods were defined as complementing mother's milk after four months, while the WHO recommends exclusive breastfeeding up to six months. Therefore, baby foods were being pushed for children at 4–6 months of age.

Violations continued even after the IMS Act was promulgated, mainly because of the lacunae identified above. In the first phase following the coming into force of the IMS Act, the advertisements continued to be shown on satellite and cable TV. These came to a stop in 2000, thanks to successful advocacy of BPNI with the ministry of information which resulted in an amendment to the Cable TV Network Regulation Act in 2000 that banned infant foods advertisements on cable and satellite networks. Sponsorship of health workers and their associations by baby food companies also persisted, together with other types of violations, which stemmed from loopholes in the Act.[61]

NGOs were convinced of the necessity to further strengthen the IMS Act and fill in the gaps left by the 1992 law. They drew up amendments to the law and brought them to the attention of the authorities. An inter-ministerial Task Force Group was constituted in 1995 with representatives from various ministries and some experts. In 1998, it recom-

---

60 ACASH and BPNI are part of the IBFAN network. For more information please read http://www.bpni.org, last accessed on 9 December 2011.

61 For example the definition of advertisement did not make it clear on whether TV and radio commercials were included and therefore there were TV ads on baby foods on all channels. Sponsorship for meetings and fellowships were offered to paediatricians, and research in nutrition also continued. Furthermore, while classifying the health care system, the pharmacies and drugstores were left out and free samples of infant formula were being given to doctors for "testing". In addition, educational materials were not clearly defined, and thus often advertisement passed through under the educational materials label. Radha Holla Bar, Arun Gupta, and Raj K. Anand, *Protecting, Promoting and Supporting Breastfeeding: The Indian Experience*. Breastfeeding Promotion Network of India, New Delhi, 2003, pp. 90–98.

mended amendments to the IMS Act to the government, which extended it to cover complementary foods and any foods for children up to the age of two. Meanwhile, BPNI lobbied with different ministers and parliamentarians and explained the amendment to different policy makers. On the other hand, industry lobbied hard against the Amendment and managed to delay the process by almost six years. Finally, in 2003, the IMS Amendment Bill was introduced in parliament and passed in both chambers.[62]

The 1992 IMS Act together with the 2003 Amendment Act constitutes the Indian implementation measure for the Code. This measure is stricter than the International Code. It integrates the Code provisions entirely and in addition it further establishes restrictions to the advertisement and promotion of breastmilk substitutes.[63]

After the amended Act, in 2003, violations have decreased. TV ads of infant and baby foods have disappeared, together with direct sponsorship of the health system. This means that the national law has been quite effective in preventing the advertisement of breastmilk substitutes to mothers, with repercussions on sales numbers for the baby food industry. The 2008 report of Euromonitor International, referred to above, shows the disparity in the retail value of milk formula between China and India, due to the differences in their domestic measures.[64] Baby food industry in China registers much higher profits mainly due to the fact that advertisement of breastmilk substitutes on television and the use of spokespeople are allowed.

Because of strict regulation, violations are deterred. However, companies have become more subtle and have found new ways to reach the health professionals.[65] For example, Nestlé provides sponsorships for health professionals' meetings indirectly through the Nestlé Nutrition In-

[62] Radha, Gupta, and Anand, 2003, p. 95–96, see *supra* note 61.

[63] Stringent rules are established for labeling including the prohibition of the use of pictures of infants and mothers. The domestic law includes regulation of marketing of complementary foods, has very strong restriction with regards to the promotion in the health system, and clearly determines the protection of breastfeeding up to the age of two years. It also requires the manufacturer to stress the financial and social implications of using infant formula and baby bottles and forbids manufacturers from offering inducements to or fixing salaries of employees on the basis of volumes of sales.

[64] Euromonitor, 2008, see *supra* note 39.

[65] For examples, see the last chapter of the IBFAN-ICDC, "Breaking the Rules, Stretching the Rules 2007", see *supra* note 36.

stitute.[66] Because the latter has been established as an independent entity, it may not be held legally accountable before the law, as it does not represent the company. However, the Indian government has interpreted this to be a violation of the national law and it has recently written to State governments and professional associations advising them to take note of such violations. Also, a premier health institution had to cancel the event sponsored by the Nestlé Nutrition Institute in December 2010.

Activist groups continue to play a watchdog role in India, also because of the role assigned to them by the IMS Act, as official monitors of violations. They have filed several lawsuits against companies.[67] One of these lawsuits has lasted 17 years and has just received the verdict. In this case BPNI filed a complaint against Nestlé in 1994 for allegedly violating the IMS Act, via their labeling policy and promotion activity. Nestlé challenged the constitutional validity of the IMS Act at the High Court of Delhi through a writ petition in 1995 and also asked for relief to quash the case against them. While the writ petition of Nestlé still awaits the final Court order any time, the case in lower Court has finally come to a conclusion in March 2012, and the court has charged Nestlé for violating the IMS Act.[68]

---

66 Baby Milk Action, "Nestlé Sponsors Doctors Conference – Breaking the Indian Law", available at http://info.babymilkaction.org/pressrelease/pressrelease30apr10, last accessed on 20 March 2012.

67 In 1993, ACASH filed a lawsuit filed against Johnson&Johnson on the grounds of unethical promotion of feeding bottles. The company finally apologized in the Court and voluntary agreed to withdraw completely from the bottle market in India. On the same year ACASH took to court Wockhardt, a manufacturer of pharmaceuticals and infant formula, due to violations of the labeling requirements of the IMS Act. Wockhardt also apologized in court and volunteered to stop using the name of its formula for other paediatric products. In 1994 Dr. Arun Gupta on behalf of ACASH filed a complaint in Delhi courts against Nestle. Radha, Gupta, and Anand, 2003, p. 115, see *supra* note 58.

68 The Times of India, "Nestlé hauled up for flouting advertisement norms", available at http://articles.timesofindia.indiatimes.com/2012-03-19/india/31210121_1_nestle-india-food-products-cerelac, last accessed on 22 March 2012.

## 12.4. Determinants of Effectiveness

### 12.4.1. Strong is More Effective

The table below summarizes the information on the measures adopted by Malaysia, the Philippines and India, along the three dimensions of 'strength' that were identified above.

| | Measure | 1.Binding Character | 2. Precision | 3. Delegation of Authority |
|---|---|---|---|---|
| **Malaysia** | 'The Code of Ethics for Infant Formula Products' (1995) | **Non-binding**: voluntary measure | **Partial:** weaker than the Code | **Partial**: monitoring only labels (Vetting Committee); and disciplinary actions in case of violations (Disciplinary Committee). |
| **The Philippines** | 'Philippine National Code on Marketing of Breastmilk Substitutes, Breastmilk Supplements and Related Products' (1986) – Filipino Milk Code | **Binding law** | **Almost full:** fully integrates provisions of the 1981 Code, but not the subsequent WHA resolutions. | **Partial**: delegated authority in charge of monitoring: IAC and designated official monitors. However, the monitoring is not systematic, is limited in scope and lacks sustainability. |

| India | 'Infant Milk Substitutes, Feeding Bottles and Infant Foods Act' (1992 IMS) | **Binding law** (criminal law) | **Full** (additional extra restrictions) | **Clear delegation of authority:** Four NGOs designated by law to monitor and file complaints; the cases are to be handled by tribunals. |
|---|---|---|---|---|

**Table 3**

Violations of the Code are found in all the countries that were considered in this chapter despite the different types of measures adopted by these countries. In Malaysia, violations are concentrated in the areas not regulated by the Code of Ethics. In the Philippines, violations of the national law are widespread, while in India, violations reported are few and they have been decreasing since the IMS Act came into effect.

The case of India shows that a strong law, along all three dimensions referred to above, is the most effective measure in generating compliance of companies with the Code. After the adoption of the amendments in 2003, evidence shows that marketing practices have changed: television commercials have disappeared, and the presence of baby food companies in the health care system is almost inexistent. Therefore, if the overall strength of the measures adopted in each of the countries is considered, one can clearly see that in the context of the strongest measure, the effectiveness of the Code appears to be at its highest level.

It is however, necessary to unravel the definition of 'strength' and consider the influence of its dimensions on the effectiveness of the national measures in terms of solving the problem of marketing of breastmilk substitutes. When the case studies of Malaysia and the Philippines are compared, the argument that stronger measures are more effective does not quite hold. Even if it is a soft measure, non-binding and less precise, the Malaysian voluntary Code of Ethics appears to be more effective than the Filipino law, due to the existence of effective mechanisms for monitoring and for disciplinary action against violators – therefore the existence of clearer accountability mechanisms at the domestic level. The binding character of the domestic measure and its precision appear to be less determining than the existence of effective mechanisms for monitoring and for disciplinary action against violators. The third dimension of the 'strength' of measures represents an important element whenever the effectiveness of laws or other normative measures is concerned. This is confirmed by the Indian case. In order for a certain rule to be effective, it is necessary that the authority that has the responsibility for systematically monitoring the compliance and the procedure to be followed in case of violations be clearly established. Effectiveness is thus closely interrelated with the enforcement of the domestic measure.

The precision of the norm – in other words, the scope of the Code covered by the domestic measure – also appears to be an important factor in determining compliance with the Code. As the Malaysian and Indian examples show, compliance will be higher for those parts of the International Code that are incorporated into the national measure and violations will tend to concentrate in the unregulated areas. A clear example is the case of TV commercials of baby foods in India. The 1992 Act did not clearly prohibit ads on television, therefore companies were using this gap to continue promotion. When the 2000 amendment clearly banned all types of promotion of baby foods, including television ads, these disappeared together with other forms of promotion. In Malaysia too, violations appear to be concentrated in areas not clearly regulated by the Malaysian Code of Ethics, such as the area of sponsorships to the health care system. On the other hand, the case of the Philippines shows that a highly precise national law and formal delegated authority does not by itself ensure compliance, if monitoring and follow up are not systematically carried out.

The case studies show that the binding character of the domestic measures does not explain Code compliance on its own. Whenever domestic measures, be it voluntary codes or laws, are accompanied by clear and effective delegation of authority, they appear to be more effective. Delegation of authority appears the most significant determinant of Code effectiveness from the case studies that were approached here. Moreover, the delegation of authority and the binding nature of the measure appear to mutually reinforce each other in determining effectiveness. A binding measure with clear delegation of authority, will guarantee a much higher effectiveness than a non-binding measure with established authorities responsible for its implementation. Finally, the precision of the norm will also shape the geography of Code effectiveness. Whenever domestic measures do not integrate some Code provisions, the effectiveness in those areas will be very weak despite the binding nature of the measure and the existence of clear implementation regulations and authorities.

The case study analysis has also shed light on other factors that influence the effectiveness of national measures, such as the type of sanctions and the role of civil society and of the baby food industry.

The severity of sanctions is an important factor. Malaysian sanctions against violators are weak, mainly rely on the public reputational mechanism, and it is not clear whether they are effectively implemented. They do not create a strong deterrent for violations, especially when the profits envisioned by companies are high. On the other hand, the Indian law criminalizes violations and imposes strict sanctions including imprisonment, which in comparison to the other cases create strong deterrents and ensure a good effectiveness of the Code. Many companies have been taken to court, and the risk for violators is high, including in terms of public image. It is expected that the recent charges against Nestlé will create a strong disincentive for future violations by companies. In the case of the Philippines, even if the law provides for administrative and penal sanctions for violations, there has been no application of these sanctions up to date, making the law ineffective, as it poses no real risks to companies.

### 12.4.2. Civil Society, Industry and Accountability

Civil society and the baby food industry influence the effectiveness of the Code, both in terms of its implementation domestically by governments and in terms of solving the problem of marketing of breastmilk substitutes.

The history of the Code at the international level and the three case studies discussed show that the role of actors representing societal interests, in other words the civil society, has been fundamental. The ability of NGOs, consumer groups, and professional organizations to advocate and organize themselves in national and international networks has been one of the influencing factors in adopting the Code, and it has been crucial in pushing governments to adopt and implement measures at the country level.[69] This is confirmed by the three case studies considered above.

69 UNICEF has also supported countries to implement measures that give effect to the Code. However, given the nature of these actors and the limited space for advocacy,

Networks such as IBFAN are still active and able to mobilize people and resources at the national and international level, especially during crucial historical moments when industry pressure has intensified and Code effectiveness put to risk. This is clearly demonstrated by the example of the Philippines in 2006–2007. Strong advocacy and pressure by civil society groups have been fundamental in the process of strengthening national measures. Thanks to persistent advocacy initiatives, sometimes strong and sometimes subtle, civil society groups have been important protagonists behind the process of strengthening the implementation of domestic measures in all the cases considered in this chapter.

Civil society actors have strengthened the accountability of the Code, if we consider the broader approach to accountability as described in Corthaut *et al.*[70] by enhancing participation, transparency and responsiveness to the people by the policy-makers. Enhanced accountability has in turn influenced the effectiveness of the Code domestically. Through its constant monitoring and documenting of both government measures to implement the Code, and of the industry practices that fail to comply with the Code requirements, NGOs and networks, such as IBFAN, have increased the transparency with regards to Code implementation processes and outcomes. Through denouncing violations as well as government inaction to comply with the Code, civil society actors have constituted themselves as a forum which continuously judges the effectiveness of the Code and are able to activate public reputational mechanisms for holding governments to account domestically and internationally on their commitments.

Secondly, the baby food industry has negatively affected the effectiveness of the Code. Not only does the domestic effectiveness of the Code depend on the behavior of the baby food companies by definition, but it is also affected by the way the baby food industry has impaired the ability of governments to be responsive to the general public and to com-

their role has been more of technical support for the drafting of laws and implementing regulations.

70 The broader approach to accountability as defined by Corthaut *et al.* represents "a dual relationship (operationalized through norms and procedure) between the public and a body, through which the latter 'takes account' of the interests, opinions and preferences of the former prior to making a decision (responsiveness), and through which it 'renders account' a posterior of its activities and decisions, with the possibility of facing sanctions (control)". Corthaut et al., 2012, p. 4, see *supra* note 13.

ply with their international commitments.[71] As identified by the 2008 Euromonitor International report referred to above, government regulation constitutes a barrier to the expansion of breastmilk substitutes markets. The report also notes that "the industry is fighting a rearguard action against regulation on a country-by-country basis".[72] The case studies show that the baby food industry has resisted and tried to stop the strengthening process of the domestic measures, in particular the implementation of rules and regulations for the enforcement of domestic measures. This is well illustrated by the case of the Philippines, where the baby food industry has adopted strategies of resistance in the face of the enforcement of national laws.

## 12.5. Conclusion

Even though the 1981 International Code of Marketing of Breastmilk Substitutes can be subsumed within the IN-LAW framework due to the nature of the informal outcome, at the same time, this output informality has been relevant considering its effectiveness.

The informal nature of the output increased effectiveness at the international level by making it possible for the international cooperation to materialize and for the actors involved to reach a political consensus during the process of the Code negotiation at the WHA. This confirms the expectation of the IN-LAW research project, according to which IN-LAW minimizes impediments to cooperation.

The Code remains an overarching standard on the marketing of breastmilk substitutes at the international level, which serves as a guide and map for action at the national level. Because of its informal nature, the Code has been implemented domestically through measures that vary according to their strength. Strong measures with a binding character, high precision and clear implementing authorities insure the highest effectiveness of the Code at the domestic level. This result is in line with the recommendation given to States by the Special Rapporteur on the right to

[71] The participation of the industry actors in implementing the Code domestically has only occurred in the case of Malaysia, where the domestic measure has a non-binding nature. However, participation in this case has not led to effectiveness (in terms of problem solved) as companies have been found to continue violating the Malaysian code.

[72] Euromonitor International, 2008, see *supra* note 39.

food in its 2012 report to the Human Rights Council. According to this report "[s]elf-regulation by the agrifood industry has proven ineffective" and therefore States are urged to "[t]ranspose into domestic legislation the International Code of Marketing of Breast-milk Substitutes and the WHO recommendations on the marketing of breastmilk substitutes and of foods and non-alcoholic beverages to children, and ensure their effective enforcement".[73]

The delegation of authority for both monitoring and disciplinary action is the element of the measure's strength which was found to foremostly influence domestic effectiveness. The binding character of the domestic measure and the precision also play a significant role.

The case of the Code shows that effectiveness is highly interrelated with accountability. At the domestic level, it is the accountability in the broader sense that positively influences effectiveness. Civil society actors and the baby food companies influence accountability in two different directions. Internationally organized civil society actors have played a key role in enhancing accountability through increasing the responsiveness of policy-makers, which in turn has translated into greater effectiveness of the Code. On the other hand, the baby food industry has negatively influenced the domestic effectiveness by continuously resisting government actions to adopt or strengthen national measures. This coupled with a deficit of accountability, in the narrow approach, has produced a situation where 31 years after the Code adoption, few countries have implemented it entirely.

Finally, this research chapter and the research design suffer several limitations in relation to the definitions, limited empirical research, possible selection bias, *et cetera*. Further research that would carefully consider these elements is required.

[73] Special Rapporteur on the Right to Food, "Report on the Right to Nutrition", available at http://www2.ohchr.org/english/bodies/hrcouncil/docs/19session/A.HRC.19.59_English.pdf, last accessed on 20 March 2012.

# 13

# Effectiveness and Accountability of Disaster Risk Reduction Practices: An Analysis through the Lens of IN-LAW

**Luca Corredig***

## 13.1. Introduction: A Strategy and a Framework for Disaster Risk Reduction

In an article published in 1977 in the Stanford Law Review, Robert L. Rabin stressed that our central fascination with natural disasters was not merely "an emotional reaction to the visual images of mass suffering and death" but more specifically a compulsion to explore the relational dimension of the scenario.[1] How do we relate with each other? Are the bonds of civility broken down by disasters? Or are they reinforced and strengthened? Perhaps most interestingly from the point of view of the present study, Rabin also noted that, if we move from the sphere of private reaction to that of public policy, we are taken to assess "the effectiveness of the legal system in serving one of its most ancient and fundamental goals: preserving a sense of community against the threat of chaos and disintegration".[2] This comment opens a broad range of questions not only related to the effectiveness of the institutional response to the disaster, but also to the institutional ability to avert the disaster itself. Over the centuries, there has been a tendency to wrongly classify such occurrences as unavoidable. Yet the risk factor created by natural hazards remains man-made: variables such as what we decide to build and where we decide to live strongly

* **Luca Corredig** holds a Master's degree in International Affairs from the Graduate Institute of International and Development Studies in Geneva. He served as an intern at the IFRC's International Disaster Response Laws, Rules and Principles programme (recently renamed the Disaster Law programme) in 2011 and at the United Nations International Strategy for Disaster Reduction in 2010.

1 Robert L. Rabin, "Dealing with Disasters: Some Thoughts on the Adequacy of the Legal System", in *Stanford Law Review*, 1997, vol. 30, p. 281.

2 *Ibid.*, p. 282.

condition our vulnerability to natural events.[3] Risk therefore – understood as our exposure to disasters – is configured over time through the interaction of the human environment and the natural environment.

The promotion of practices aimed at increasing community resilience through systematic efforts to manage the causal factors of disasters is nowadays known as disaster risk reduction (DRR). Such an approach is increasingly sustained across the world by specific policies and laws which, among others, define land-use planning, enforce building standards, promote community preparedness, support the adoption of early warning systems, and allocate resources. As it happens, in the same way many countries possess specialized institutions linked to the handling of emergencies and response activities, an increasing number of countries are adopting specialized institutions linked to DRR. What is most relevant from the point of view of the current study is nevertheless the fact that such process has, to a great extent, been promoted and driven by informal international lawmaking (IN-LAW).[4] Risk reduction clearly represents an area where governments increasingly rely upon a trans-governmental network designated for a specific public policy concern which, in the specific case of DRR, is known as the International Strategy for Disaster Reduction.

The International Strategy for Disaster Reduction (ISDR) was launched in December 1999 by the United Nations General Assembly as a successor to the International Decade for Natural Disaster Reduction, following the adoption of resolution 54/219.[5] As a whole, what is traditionally known as the ISDR system denotes in reality a loose 'alliance' of States, international organizations (IOs), nongovernmental organizations (NGOs), civil societies groups, financial institutions, and technical bodies working together and sharing information in the attempt to reduce disaster vulnerabilities of both communities and nations.[6] In this context, the Unit-

[3] ISDR, Global Assessment Report on Disaster Risk Reduction: Risk and Poverty in a Changing Climate, ISDR, Geneva, 2009, p. 5.

[4] See the introduction to this Volume as well as Joost Pauwelyn, "Informal International Lawmaking: Framing the Concept and Research Questions", in Joost Pauwelyn, Ramses A. Wessel and Jan Wouters (eds.), *Informal International Lawmaking*, Oxford University Press, Oxford, 2012, pp. 14–34.

[5] United Nations General Assembly, International Decade for Natural Disaster Reduction: successor arrangements, Res. 54/219, 1999.

[6] ISDR, "Mission and Objectives", available at http://www.unisdr.org/eng/about_isdr/isdr-mission-objectives-eng.htm, last accessed on 16 March 2011.

ed Nations International Strategy for Disaster Reduction Secretariat (UNISDR) – perhaps the better known face of the initiative – is mandated to act as a focal point, broker, and catalyst for DRR.[7]

The Global Platform for Disaster Risk Reduction, convened on a biannual basis in Geneva, acts as a mechanism through which stakeholders can exchange experiences, evaluate progress, and access information on best practices in the context of DRR. Beyond doubt, the Global Platform represents the main global forum in such issue area as well as the most visible expression of the international community's will to promote risk reduction.[8] Beyond the Global Platform, an array of less visible bodies such as National Platforms for Disaster Risk Reduction (NPs) and ad-hoc advisory groups can be observed. The former in particular represent an interesting feature of the ISDR system; the term loosely denotes "national mechanisms for coordination and policy guidance on DRR that are multi-sector and inter-disciplinary in nature"[9] which provide the means to enhance action at the State level.

But the peculiar features of the ISDR system do not stop here. The overall picture is rendered even more interesting from the point of view of IN-LAW by the adoption of a non-binding agreement, the Hyogo Framework for Action (HFA). The HFA – titled in full *Hyogo Framework for Action 2005–2015: Building the Resilience of Nations and Communities to Disasters* – was adopted in January 2005 in the attempt to further develop and strengthen existing institutions, mechanisms, and capacities.[10] As such, the HFA sets five priorities for action to guide governments into the adoption of practices conductive to disaster resilience, and for each it suggests key activities to be implemented by States "to their own circumstances and capacities".[11] The need to adopt such clause was dictated by the recognition that hazards and vulnerabilities – just as much as the funds

7 ISDR, *Hyogo Framework for Action 2005–2015 – Brochure*, ISDR, Geneva, 2007, p. 5.

8 Global Platform for Disaster Risk Reduction, "About the Global Platform – First session, 5–7 June 2007", available at http://www.preventionweb.net/globalplatform/2007/gp-abouth.html, last accessed on 16 March 2011.

9 UNISDR, *Terminology on Disaster Risk Reduction*, UNISDR, Geneva, 2009, p. 20.

10 United Nations General Assembly, *International Strategy for Disaster Reduction*, Res. 60/195, 2005.

11 ISDR, *Hyogo Framework for Action 2005–2015: Building the Resilience of Nations and Communities to Disasters*, ISDR, Geneva, 2005, pp. 3–6.

available to implement DRR measures – varied greatly across countries and hence no singular strategy could dictate specific overarching approaches. The five priorities for action were purposefully designed to allow flexibility and to encourage a certain amount of 'room for action', enabling countries to develop specific and pragmatic plans at the national level.[12]

In assessing the relative informality of cross-border cooperation in the context of DRR, it is important to consider different features of the mechanism that led to the adoption of the HFA. In particular, special attention must be given to the nature of the decision-making procedure (the process), the identity of those involved in it (the actors), as well as the character of the final document itself (the output). In this context, the ISDR system represents a perfect example of IN-LAW since it is informal in all of the above senses. In first place, ISDR did not lead to the adoption of a formal treaty or any other traditional source of international law. The HFA is a perfect example of soft law, as it is an instrument not intended to be legally binding. It is a collection of guidelines, a set of standards, and as a whole it denotes a declaration of intention rather than formal obligations. In line with Aust's analysis, the HFA can be considered an 'informal international instrument'[13] and therefore it represents a great example of output informality.

In second place, the HFA was drafted and adopted through a process organized by a loosely organized network of agents. It is important not to confuse the ISDR system with UNISDR, which, as mentioned above, is only the secretariat of the system as a whole. In spite of the fact that UNISDR is often the most visible face of risk reduction efforts at the international level, such a body mainly undertakes coordinative functions conducive to DRR advocacy and awareness-building, while enhancing communications and coordination mechanisms between ISDR parties. As stressed by von Oelreich, "the multi-stakeholder character of the ISDR

[12] Priorities, for example, invite States to "ensure that disaster risk reduction is a national and a local priority with a strong institutional basis for implementation", to "identify, asses and monitor disaster risks and enhance early warning", and to "use knowledge, innovation and education to build a culture of safety and resilience at all levels", *ibid*. pp. 6–9.

[13] Anthony Aust, "The Theory and Practice of Informal International Instruments", in *The International and Comparative Law Quarterly*, 1986, vol. 35, no. 4, p. 787.

system is evident"[14] and thus, even if UNISDR does possess a permanent staff, a physical headquarters in Geneva, and a number of regional offices, these only remain the tangible expression of a much larger and much less identifiable international network.

But who exactly are the actors operating within such a network? On one hand, a large part of members of the ISDR system belong to categories that are not traditionally involved in international lawmaking. Yet a quick look at the list of participants to the *World Conference on Disaster Reduction*, in the course of which the HFA was adopted, indicates that the network also comprises a wide variety of lesser-known State entities that seldom appear and interact outside of national borders.[15] The rationale behind the need to involve so many different actors in the creation of an international framework for the promotion of DRR practices is dictated by the nature of DRR itself; effective risk reduction is only achievable through the involvement and complementary work of diverse stakeholders. Hazards, for example, must be monitored and assessed in a wide range of fields, best practices need to be implemented in multiple areas and integrated in a country's development plan, and above all, change is required to happen at all levels of the system.

In a nutshell, resilience against disasters can only be improved by promoting vertical interaction between the international, national, and community level as well as horizontal cooperation across the different actors operating at each level. But is this happening? The HFA was specifically designed to promote such an approach, but as of today doubts still remain regarding the impact and potential of the Framework. Has the informal nature of the international lawmaking process in the context of DRR policies acted as a catalyst for change, or has it hindered their effective development? Before assessing the effectiveness of the HFA as an example of IN-LAW, it is important to make a subtle but crucial clarifica-

14 Eva von Oelreich, *In-depth Study on the United Nations Contribution to the Implementation of the Hyogo Framework for Action*, prepared for UNISDR, 2011, p. 10.

15 These include, for example, ministries of development, agriculture and forestry, civil engineering, public works and settlements, as well as departments for disaster preparedness, civil protection and disaster management agencies, and even hydrological or meteorological institutes. Moreover, the list also comprises a broad range of private actors and IOs, as already stressed above. United Nations, "World Conference on Disaster Reduction – Participants", available at http://www.unisdr.org/wcdr/intergover/official-doc/info/list-participants-WCDR-english.pdf, last accessed on 20 March 2011.

tion. This chapter – just as the other chapters in this book – is concerned with the question of whether informal cooperation at the international level effectively promotes change at the national and sub-national level. On the contrary, it is not concerned with the question of whether the specific provisions adopted at the international level reflect appropriate policies to tackle the issues at stake. The following subsection of this contribution will address these issues of effectiveness and accountability.

## 13.2. Evaluating Effectiveness

There is a heated debate in DRR circles regarding the appropriateness of the content of the HFA. Major discussions are taking place on the question of whether DRR policies should be mainstreamed into development policies or not, or whether climate change concerns should be further integrated into HFA implementation.[16] However, these questions are beyond the scope of this case study. Effectiveness in this context does not refer to the content of the HFA, but to the process that led to its adoption. Did IN-LAW allow for cooperation to materialize in the field of DRR? Did such kind of cooperation stick, or did it wither away? And did it ultimately solve the problem? These issues must be considered in order to assess the relevance of IN-LAW as a device for minimizing the impediments to cooperation. The 'problem' in this context is not represented by low levels of community resilience *per se*, but rather by an original lack of consideration for DRR. As such, in line with what is stressed above, the study does not directly attempt to evaluate the HFA, but rather the ability of the process that led to its adoption (IN-LAW) to trigger international cooperation conductive to changes in national policies. A major problem generally encountered when evaluating the impact of the HFA at the national level is the inability to clearly quantify progress. The five priorities for action are rather general; indeed, the lack of clear and measurable targets – such as those adopted by the Millennium Development Goals (MDGs) – makes any attempt to objectively assess the success of the HFA a difficult task.[17]

---

16 See, for example, UNISDR, "Summary of Mid Term Review Online Debate – Topic 2: Less Effective Elements of the HFA" and "Topic 3: Integration of Climate Change in HFA Implementation", available at http://www.preventionweb.net/english/professional/publications/v.php?id=18197, last accessed on 5 April 2011.

17 The framework for example, in relation to priority 4 (reduce the underlying risk factors), does not express the 'à la MDG' desire to increase by 50% the construction of

In order to address such an issue, the Secretariat proposed in 2008 a set of specific indicators for each priority, inviting States to evaluate their progress both qualitatively (by providing a description of the activities undertaken) and quantitatively (by assigning a value to the level of progress itself, with one representing minor achievements with "few signs of planning or forward action to improve the situation" and five denoting comprehensive achievements with "commitment and capacities to sustain efforts at all levels").[18] Progress in each priority for action is evaluated through the use of four to six indicators, and as a rule of thumb each State signatory to the HFA submits to UNISDR a National Progress Report on a biannual basis.[19] Moreover, every two years UNISDR oversees the publication of a Global Assessment Report whose objectives are to increase political and economic commitment to DRR as well as the effectiveness of risk reduction policy and strategies. The report – produced through a complex consultation process involving a large majority of ISDR partners – carefully reviews risk patterns and trends in DRR, while "providing

earthquake proof infrastructures by the year 2015; on the contrary, it merely articulates the commitment of States to "mainstream disaster risk consideration into planning procedures for major infrastructure projects". Similarly, in relation to priority 1, the HFA does not stress the responsibility of States to successfully implement specific legislation to support risk reduction, but rather it generally indicates their commitment to ensure that legislation is adopted or modified 'where necessary'. ISDR, 2005, pp. 6–12, see *supra* note 11.

18 UNISDR, *Indicators of Progress: Guidance on Measuring the Reduction of Disaster Risk and the Implementation of the Hyogo Framework for Action*, UNISDR, Geneva, 2008, p. 10.

19 In specific, each indicator takes the form of a statement of precise nature; for example, in relation to priority 2 (identify and monitor disaster risk), indicator iii) reads "early warning systems are in place for all major hazards, with outreach to communities". It is important to note that there are no specific guidelines clearly defining where the responsibility for monitoring and reporting on progress lies at the national level. The list of indicators is generally compiled for "nationally-designated HFA focal points, and officials in relevant sectors such as national development, civil protection, environment, education, agriculture, health and water resources". As such, reports received by UNISDR tend to be prepared by bodies or departments that vary across countries. French reports for example have been compiled by the Ministry of Sustainable Development, Pakistani ones by the National Disaster Management Authority, and Senegalese ones by the Civil Protection Unit. UNISDR, 2008, pp. 2–13 see *supra* note 18; and "HFA National Progress Reports", available at http://www.preventionweb.net/english/hyogo/progress/reports, last accessed on 20 March 2011.

strategic policy guidance" to both countries and the international community.[20] In order to evaluate specific progress on the status of HFA implementation, UNISDR also facilitated throughout the year 2010 a Mid-Term Review. The review process is overseen by an advisory group comprising DRR experts and representatives from governments, civil society, and grass-roots organizations. It promoted the collection of information through different tools such as in-depth studies, workshops, one-on-one interviews, and on-line debates.

As the literature review undertaken by UNISDR in the context of the Mid-Term Review highlights, there is little systematic material available that describes the state of DRR, articulates it along the broad structure of the Framework, and presents it in a manner comparable across countries.[21] This implies that establishing a firm baseline to evaluate the status of risk reduction practices at the national level prior to the adoption of the HFA is a difficult task. From the point of view of international cooperation on the other hand, it can safely be assumed that the launch of ISDR in 1999 represents the landmark event that led to the initial development of cross-country synergies in the field of DRR. Research did not find significant advocacy or informational material suggesting the existence of DRR-related international cooperation prior to ISDR. It could however be suggested that the *Yokohama Strategy and Plan of Action for a Safer World*, adopted in 1994 at the *World Conference on Natural Disaster Reduction*, did pave the way for the future creation of the ISDR system.[22] Even if such remains only the demonstration of existing political will rather than an example of pragmatic action, it is nevertheless important to highlight that it is through initiatives such as the Yokohama Strategy that interest for risk reduction was channeled towards the creation of ISDR, allowing for cooperation in the field of DRR.

But did such informal cooperation endure? Giving a final answer to this question is a complex issue due to the time-frame at stake. Consider-

[20] ISDR, "Global Assessment Report – Abstract", available at http://www.preventionweb.net/english/hyogo/gar/2011/?pid:34&pil:1, last accessed on 22 March 2011.

[21] Kamal Kishore, *Literature Review for the Mid-Term Review of the Hyogo Framework for Action*, prepared for UNISDR, 2011, p. 3, available at http://www.unisdr.org/files/18197_000kishore.literaturereview.pdf, last accessed on 14 March 2012.

[22] World Conference on Natural Disaster Reduction, "Yokohama Strategy and Plan of Action for a Safer World", available at http://www.preventionweb.net/files/8241_doc6841contenido1.pdf, last accessed on 27 April 2011.

ing the relatively new nature of the network, it is still too early to predict future trends. Cooperation has clearly 'stuck' up to today. Most importantly, as revealed below through an analysis of actors' involvement, cooperation seems to have increased since the adoption of the HFA, which prompted both the creation of special State-level institutions such as NPs for DRR and of *ad hoc* NGOs such as the Global Network for Disaster Reduction (GNDR).[23] From the substantial increase in the number of participants involved in the Global Platform for Disaster Risk Reduction, it can be observed that cooperation not only endures, but thrives. In 2007, the first Global Platform registered approximately 1200 participants, including representatives from 120 governments and 54 NGOs.[24] In 2009, the second session registered approximately 1600 participants, including representatives from 152 governments and 69 NGOs.[25] Numbers from the 2011 session are even more impressive as the event ultimately counted approximately 3000 participants.[26] These represented over 170 governments and 100 NGOs, and met throughout the week in high-level plenary sessions, multiple roundtables on pressing issues, and ad-hoc thematic panels.[27] The progressive involvement over the last decade of both States and NGOs in the ISDR network – as exemplified by the creation of NPs, DRR-specific NGOs, and the increasing attendance to the Global Platform – serves as a good indicator of sustained cooperation. But how can we evaluate the effectiveness of the HFA and cooperation in the

---

23 Such network, which groups national civil society organisations involved in risk reduction practices, was indeed absorbed in the ISDR system in the course of the 2007 Global Platform for DRR, in order to promote further cooperative practices especially at the local level. GNDR, "Who we are – About Global Network for Disaster Reduction", available at http://www.globalnetwork-dr.org/about-us.html, last accessed on 9 April 2011.

24 IISD, "Global Platform for Disaster Risk Reduction Bulletin", available at http://www.iisd.ca/ymb/gpdr1/html/ymbvol141num1e.html, last accessed on 25 April 2011.

25 ISDR, "Global Platform for Disaster Risk Reduction 2009 – List of Participants", available at http://www.preventionweb.net/globalplatform/2009/background/documents/GP09-Provisional-List-of-Delegates.pdf, last accessed on 25 April 2011.

26 Global Platform for Disaster Risk Reduction, "About the Global Platform – Third Session, 8–13 May 2011", available at http://www.preventionweb.net/globalplatform/2011/about/, last accessed on 25 April 2011.

27 IISD, "A Daily Report of the Third Session of the Global Platform for Disaster Reduction", available at http://www.iisd.ca/download/pdf/sd/ymbvol141num3e.pdf, last accessed on 14 May 2011.

ISDR system? If we consider – as previously stressed – a general lack of consideration for DRR at the national level as the central problem informal cooperation at the international level attempts to solve, than one way to evaluate the effectiveness of IN-LAW would be to assess its ability to trigger changes in national policies, laws and institutions. The HFA's Priority for Action 1 clearly states that

> countries that develop policy, legislative and institutional frameworks for disaster risk reduction and that are able to develop and track progress through specific and measurable indicators have greater capacity to manage risks and to achieve widespread consensus for, engagement in and compliance with disaster risk reduction measures across all sectors of society.[28]

As such, while the other priorities for action focus on more technical aspects of DRR, priority 1 strictly advocates for those fundamental 'modifications' that are *a priori* required to support any further action. It is difficult to imagine how priority 2 ("identify, assess and monitor disaster risk and enhance early warning") could be achieved without the creation of specific institutions in charge of the process; likewise the fulfillment of priority 3 ("use knowledge, innovation and education to build a culture of safety and resilience at all levels") would be impossible without the adoption and implementation of specific policies that for example promote the inclusion of DRR knowledge in school curricula.[29] In a nutshell, evaluating national progress towards the achievement of priority 1 represents the foremost important step in assessing the HFA's ability to promote change at the national and sub-national level.

## 13.3. Policies, Platforms and Laws

So how far have countries across the world gone towards the achievement of priority 1 since the adoption of the HFA? As a whole the 2009 Global Assessment Report noted that according to individual National Progress Reports "progress has been significant under HFA Priority for Action 1

---

[28] Priority Action 1, "Ensure that disaster risk reduction is a national and a local priority with a strong institutional basis for implementation", ISDR, 2005, p. 6, see *supra* note 11.

[29] UNISDR, *Words Into Action: A Guide for Implementing the Hyogo Framework*, UNISDR, Geneva, 2007, p. 21.

particularly in the development of policy and legislation, and in strengthening multi-sectoral institutional systems and platforms for disaster risk reduction".[30] In relation to the aforementioned quantitative scale ranging from 1 (minor achievements) to 5 (comprehensive achievements) countries have communicated an average level of progress of 3.5 for indicator 1 (existence of policy and legal frameworks), 3.1 for indicator 2 (availability of resources), 3.2 for indicator 3 (decentralization and community participation), and 3.3 for indicator 4 (existence of multi sectoral platform).[31] As such, by referring to the five-level assessment tool,[32] it could be assumed that in relation to priority 1 institutional commitment has generally been attained, yet deficiencies in areas such as operational capacities or financial resources still exist. The literature review carried out in the context of the Mid-Term Review of the HFA supports such findings through an analysis of national policy documents, and highlights that "over the last five years national level efforts have increasingly been framed using the HFA". It also reiterates that there appears to have been "notable progress in setting up institutional structures and developing plans", yet limited movement on "allocating resources from regular national budgets and encouraging broad-based participation in the process leading up to new institutional structures".[33]

Beyond doubt, a large number of States directly attribute progress in the development of different governance systems for DRR to the HFA. This is most evident in the increasing number of NPs and HFA Focal Points present across the world. These can be directly associated with the guidance provided in the Framework itself; on the contrary, it appears more difficult to link the development of more general policies to the HFA. Virtually all States display a variety of policies which could be considered conducive to DRR: a quick review of National Progress Reports highlights the existence of a myriad of disaster risk management policies, national disaster management policies, or emergency management policies. Moreover, States also report the existence of specific sectoral policies related to fire prevention, environmental protection, or water man-

30 ISDR, 2009, pp. 117, 120, 121, see *supra* note 3.

31 *Ibid.* p. 120.

32 UNISDR, 2008, p. 10, see *supra* note 18.

33 Kishore, 2011, pp. 3, 5, see *supra* note 21.

agement as examples of achievement in DRR.[34] While these are important features in evaluating the level of preparedness of a country, they cannot be considered direct examples of the impact an informal lawmaking process, such as the HFA, has had at the national level. Many of these policy frameworks have been established prior to the adoption of the HFA, and due to their variety in shape and purpose it is difficult to trace their evolution in connection to the Framework itself. It is therefore important to consider the arrangements, such as Focal Points, called into existence by the HFA. A Focal Point is merely the person officially designated by the State as the primary contact for the implementation of the HFA and, as the Mid-Term Review reports, the existence of such demonstrates "a clear interest by governments in complying with and implementing the provisions of this instrument". The growing number of focal points that went from 63 in 2006 to 192 in 2011 denotes in particular that "virtually all countries, with a few notable exceptions, have made an express commitment to the HFA".[35] But what appears to be even more relevant is the increase in the number of NPs across the world. As previously highlighted, these are multi-sectoral and inter-disciplinary mechanisms for policy guidance on DRR. In a nutshell, they act as the coordination mechanism to achieve the full integration of risk reduction policies in order to "contribute to the establishment and development of a comprehensive national DRR system".[36] Platforms as such are needed to integrate and coordinate the wide range of policies previously mentioned, and to eventually develop new ones in line with the indications contained in the HFA.

The primary task of a National Platform is therefore to represent itself as the institutional mechanism specifically created to advance the implementation of the HFA on a national level; indeed, such represents the fundamental pillar of the ISDR system within a State. While it is impossible to directly link the development of specific national policies to the implementation of the HFA, an association nevertheless can be observed between the creation and empowerment of NPs – charged with the task of

[34] PreventionWeb (the information portal on DRR), "HFA National Progress Reports", available at http://www.preventionweb.net/english/hyogo/progress/reports, last accessed on 1 May 2011.

[35] UNISDR, *Mid-Term Review of the Hyogo Framework For Action 2005–2015*, UNISDR, Geneva, 2011, pp. 21–22.

[36] UNIATF, *Summary for DRR National Platforms Guiding Principles*, UNITAF, 2004, p. 2.

coordinating such policies – and the guidance provided by the HFA. The HFA strongly advocates for the creation of such multi-sectoral NPs[37] and, as highlighted by indicator 4, assessing their existence is of primary concern for the ISDR system. But how effectively has the HFA promoted the creation of NPs? The Mid-Term Review of the HFA reported that the number of officially recorded NPs grew steadily since the adoption of the HFA in 2005. In particular platforms were recorded in 38 countries in 2007, which rose to 45 in 2008, and ultimately to 73 as of February 2011.[38] Approximately half of the signatories to the HFA have insofar created NPs during the relatively short time span since the adoption of the Framework. The trend clearly suggests that platforms are on the increase, and substantial progress could be forecasted over the remaining four years of its implementation.

Numbers again quite distinctly communicate that the HFA did indeed stimulate policy change at the national level. Nevertheless, before becoming too optimistic about the overall role of IN-LAW in the promotion of effective international cooperation, it is important to take a step back and consider more closely some of the features of those changes produced by the HFA. NPs are peculiar creatures; as highlighted by Sanahuja in the course of a study commissioned by IFRC and UNISDR, the link between platforms and the implementation of the HFA "probably constitutes the main common denominator that can be found in the vast diversity in formats and dynamics of existing NPs".[39] In other words, the fact that specific bodies called NPs were created at the national level in response to the adoption of the HFA is the only factor that ties such bodies together. Indeed, NPs exist in multiple shapes and colors, and their composition, concerns, and operating procedures appear to vary greatly depending on how they have developed across countries. Of great interest for the current study is the uneven participation in NPs of civil society and the private sector.[40] A large number of complaints were, for example, reported by the Mid-Term Review with regard to a lack of involvement of community level representatives in NPs, as well as a lack of transparency

[37] ISDR, 2005, p. 6, see *supra* note 11.

[38] UNISDR, 2011, pp. 21–22, see *supra* note 35.

[39] Haris E. Sanahuja, *National Platforms for Disaster Risk Reduction in the Americas*, prepared for IFRC and UNISDR, 2010, p. 10.

[40] Kishore, 2011, p. 6, see *supra* note 21.

in their membership and operations.[41] At the core of such a problem lies a rather simple issue of accountability; the general nature of the provisions contained in the HFA – coupled with the 'freedoms' associated with the informal nature of the process that supported its adoption – ultimately led to the creation of blurry governance mechanisms.

This is not surprising, considering that a large number of States failed to develop specific legislative mechanisms for the promotion of DRR. National legislation can help in setting the record straight by clearly allocating responsibilities, defining the scopes of different agencies, and laying explicit budgetary arrangement. Moreover, laws also allow individuals to base their arguments on recognized rights, making governments more accountable for eventual negligence in the implementation of risk reduction practices. Good governance for disaster risk reduction is indeed a matter of coordination and ultimately of accountability, and such could therefore be better promoted through specific formal legislative structures at the national level, rather than through informal policy mechanisms such as those generally promoted by NPs. The importance of national legal action is explicitly acknowledged in the HFA, which in Priority 1 recognizes legislative frameworks as key elements in the promotion of mitigation activities through "regulations and mechanisms that encourage compliance and that promote incentives".[42] On a secondary note, the adoption of specific laws can also be used – just as much as NPs – as a significant barometer of commitment to DRR directly associated with the guidance prescribed in the HFA.

It is relatively easy to find a compilation of recently enacted DRR legislation and, while a number of countries began adopting risk reduction laws independently already in the mid-1990s, several others appear to have developed new laws or updated existing ones by explicitly relying upon the principles included in the HFA.[43] This therefore represents another example of the tangible impact IN-LAW can have. Nevertheless, even if there has been a certain amount of progress in the adoption of

---

[41] UNISDR, 2011, p. 58, see *supra* note 35.

[42] ISDR, 2005, p. 6, see *supra* note 11.

[43] As the Mid-Term Review reports, countries with new or updated laws include for example India and Sri Lanka in 2005; El Salvador, Saint Lucia, Saint Vincent and Grenadines in 2006; Anguilla and Gambia in 2007; Indonesia in 2008; Egypt and Philippines in 2009; and Zambia and Papua New Guinea in 2010. UNISDR, 2011, p. 22, see *supra* note 35.

DRR specific laws, it is important not to overstate the trend, as it appears clear that not all laws are good laws. Legislative frameworks for disaster risk reduction differ widely on a number of fundamental issues related, for example, to the extent of the decentralization of authority, the promotion of community participation, the management of resources, and the development of liabilities for the failure to adopt and support established DRR practices.

The dichotomy between NPs and legislation is beyond doubt an oversimplification, as most States do ultimately rely upon mixed combinations of general and sectoral laws, variable policies, and multi-layered institutional mechanisms. Nevertheless, the use of such dichotomy appears to be extremely relevant for the purpose of the current study. It is not yet clear whether systems supporting increased accountability through the adoption and implementation of formal laws are ultimately more effective than those that do not. As it happens, many practitioners appear to be convinced that less formal mechanisms – such as those displayed by 'unregulated' NPs – are ultimately capable to better promote DRR. At the center of the debate lies therefore the traditional question of how accountability influences effectiveness. Does the former necessarily hamper the latter? Or is DRR one of those cases where the two go hand in hand? Giving an answer to such questions is not an easy task, as there appears to be a lack of sufficient empirical evidence regarding the effectiveness of different governance systems.[44] It is still too early to clearly ascertain the impact of policies and laws implemented following the adoption of the HFA. Disaster risk reduction is a long process, the results of which can be seen in time and – in some unfortunate cases – only when natural hazards strike again. Even so, a review of some of the features of the different 'systems' adopted at the national level could cast some light on how effectiveness links to accountability.

## 13.4. Four Interesting Cases

Across the world, signatories to the HFA have developed different mechanisms to promote the implementation of disaster risk reduction practices. While most of these approaches are in line with the recommendations included in the document, it appears clear that countries have ultimately favored some principles over others, in accordance with their specific na-

[44] Kishore, 2011, p. 5, see *supra* note 21.

tional realities and needs. Looking at the level of accountability of those mechanisms put in place at the national level in response to the adoption of the HFA, therefore, seems to be a simple but effective way to classify different approaches to DRR. At one hand of the spectrum sit those countries that established largely unregulated and unaccountable NPs, in a number of cases associated with low levels of transparency and community involvement. On the other hand of the spectrum lay those countries that adopted specific laws in the attempt to clearly define responsibilities and lines of accountability within their overall national mechanisms for DRR or their National Platform.

The case of the Dominican Republic serves as a first example. The country reported a level of progress of 4 under indicator 1 (national policy and legal framework for disaster risk reduction exists with decentralized responsibilities and capacities at all levels) in its latest national progress report, hence denoting 'substantial achievement' in line with the five level assessment tool.[45] Overall the country appears to have implemented a successful framework for the promotion of DRR, which includes specific policies for disaster prevention, mitigation and response, as well as sectoral legislation addressing sustainable development, climate change, territorial responsibility, public investment planning, and decentralization.[46] Moreover, in 2002, the country also adopted a specific act for risk management – the *Ley 147-02 Sobre Gestión de Riesgos* – defining the features of the coordination mechanism for DRR and disaster management in the country, which includes various entities such as the National Council of Prevention, Mitigation and Response and the National Emergency Commission, itself composed of multiple bodies. Nevertheless, throughout the text of the law[47] it appears that while responsibilities and accountabilities are clearly outlined in the context of disaster mitigation and response, such is not the case for disaster prevention. Indeed, the law de-

45 Luís Antonio Paulino, *República Dominicana: Informe Nacional del Progreso en la Implementación del Marco de Acción de Hyogo*, prepared for UNISDR, 2010, p. 5.

46 Gustavo Lara, Director General, Dominican Republic Red Cross, presentation given at the Third Session of the Global Platform for Disaster Risk Reduction, in the course of the side event "How can legislation promote disaster risk reduction at the community level?", 2011.

47 National Congress of the Dominican Republic, Ley 147-02 Sobre Gestión de Riesgos [Law 147-02 on the management of disaster risk], 2002, pp. 12, 17.

fines the protocol for situations of emergency, but fails to be specific about risk reduction efforts.

Due to the lack of clear and specific guidelines for the promotion of sustained DRR efforts, in 2008, the Dominican Republic empowered a National Technical Committee to serve as an advisory and coordinative body for DRR.[48] This body – that has often been presented at the international level as the country's National Platform in line with HFA's recommendations – appears to have achieved positive results since its validation. In particular, it identified for the first time the elements of a clear DRR strategy for the Dominican Republic, it elaborated project proposals for the formulation of the National Plan for Risk Management, it created a guide for municipal emergency planning, and it also secured budget to finance its activities.[49] The current status of such a body in terms of accountability is nevertheless vague: it is formed of 22 permanent representatives of different ministries and State bodies, as well as representatives of the Dominican Red Cross and the academic sector. Nevertheless, the selection of representatives is internally organized and the position of the Committee itself in relation to law 147-02 remains largely unclear.[50] Moreover, both its level of accountability *vis-à-vis* the broader society as well as the level of grassroots involvement in the consultation processes are rather low, as reported in the country's national progress report.

In relation to indicator 3 on community participation and decentralization, only small and incomplete achievements are to be observed.[51] In particular, the report stresses that in the Dominican Republic there appears to be little decentralization of DRR responsibilities and resources.[52] Both responsibilities and resources remain centralized within the National Technical Committee, which works rather effectively in promoting DRR despite the general provisions included in Law 147-02. The Dominican Republic, therefore, represents a good example of a country where risk reduction efforts have been successfully supported by a single central authority displaying low levels of accountability to local communities.

---

48 United Nations General Assembly, *Implementation of the International Strategy for Disaster Reduction*, report of the Secretary General A/64/280, 2009, p. 12.

49 GFDRR, *Disaster Risk Management in Latin America and the Caribbean Region*, GFDRR, 2010, p. 132.

50 Sanahuja, 2010, pp. 38–39, see *supra* note 39.

51 This reveals a level of progress of 2 for indicator 3.

52 Paulino, 2010, p. 7, see *supra* note 45.

The 'informal centralization' of DRR mechanisms does not appear to be the only existing strategy to enhance community resilience. Sweden has obtained positive results by supporting an approach to DRR that relies upon 'informal decentralization'. The municipality-based mechanism that the country has implemented throughout the years seems to work effectively even in the absence of DRR-specific legislation. Sweden does not possess an encompassing risk management act along the lines of the Law 147-02 of the Dominican Republic. The only law highlighted in the country's national progress report is the *2002 Civil Protection Act*, which provides for "equal, satisfactory and comprehensive protection for the whole country with responsibility given to local authorities".[53] Such provision is in line with the country's legislation on extraordinary events, which devolves responsibilities to the Country Administrative Boards in their geographical regions. The boards are responsible for acting as coordinators for DRR activities at the local level, which include the assessment of risks and vulnerabilities, as well as the monitoring of compliance with and implementation of national regulations. Since the adoption of the Civil Protection Act, the boards have been working closely with local governments: Chapter 3 of the act clearly defines the obligations of municipalities, which entail the development of plans of action, the implementation of preventive measures, and the dissemination of information.[54] At the top of the system sits the Swedish Civil Contingency Agency, a body recognized as the focal point for the country's National Platform. Charged with the task of improving "coordination of the work on preventing and reducing the effects of natural disasters", the agency expressly works towards the fulfillment of Sweden's commitments to the HFA.[55]

Risk reduction efforts in Sweden are supported by specific sectoral laws, referring, for example, to land use planning and building permission, crisis management, the environment, fire safety, and social welfare. The efforts are loosely coordinated by a central agency that promotes de-

---

53 Mette Lindahl-Olsson, *Sweden: National Progress Report on the Implementation of the Hyogo Framework for Action*, prepared for UNISDR, 2010, p. 7.

54 MSB, "Civil Protection Act: Government Bill 2002/03:119 – Reformed Rescue Services Legislation", available at https://www.msb.se/en/About-MSB/Legislative-areas/, last accessed on 24 April 2011.

55 Swedish National Platform for Disaster Risk Reduction, "Action Programme", available at http://www.preventionweb.net/files/13689_np158NP2010ActionProgramme1.pdf, last accessed on 25 April 2011, pp. 9–10.

centralization of responsibilities to municipalities and local authorities. Sweden strongly relies upon a 'bottom-up approach' that emphasizes the importance of 'proximity' in the attempt to manage risk directly at the community level.[56] Informality in this case refers to the fact that decentralization is not supported by a specific DRR law modeled after the HFA, but rather by general acts – such as the Civil Protection Act – and by governmental policies which empower local authorities over central ones. From this point of view, the difference between the system implemented in the Dominican Republic and the one adopted in Sweden is striking: while the former empowered a single central agency – the National Technical Committee – supporting little community-level involvement, the latter empowered local governments first, and only loosely coordinated their actions in the field of DRR through the national Civil Contingency Agency. In the Swedish case, it is important to stress that decentralization seems to support greater accountability to the people. As municipalities are directly in charge of writing local action plans for preparedness, undertaking vulnerability analysis and managing budget allocations, they are also directly subjected to the judgment and oversight of their residents.[57]

In either case, both systems seem to work rather effectively in implementing the provisions of the HFA; the National Progress Reports of each country highlight substantial progress across the whole spectrum of the five priorities of action even if – in line with the experience of most States across the world – limited financial resources is repeatedly singled out as a major issue. Sweden and the Dominican Republic therefore appear to be largely fulfilling their commitment to the HFA, even without the adoption of specific legislation that clearly defines the role and responsibilities of different national actors. In the former case, effectiveness is attained by decentralizing DRR tasks to the municipal level, while in the latter case it is attained by empowering a central authority. Nevertheless, in both examples, internal lines of accountability are not clearly institutionalized as national legislation fails to clearly define the roles of different agencies and levels of government in the implementation of risk reduction practices. The Swedish system appears more accountable to the

[56] Mette Lindahl-Olsson, Head of Natural Hazards and Critical Infrastructure Section, Swedish Civil Contingencies Agency, presentation given at the Third Session of the Global Platform for Disaster Risk Reduction, in the course of the side event "How can legislation promote disaster risk reduction at the community level?", 2011.

[57] Lindahl-Olsson 2010, p. 10, see *supra* note 53.

people: even so, such accountability is not institutionalized through specific mechanisms, but rather 'manifested' through the local electoral process. But what happens when decentralization of risk reduction responsibilities is supported by clear and encompassing central laws?

The case of Peru is highly relevant to the current debate: in the 1990s, the country transferred major responsibility for disaster management from the national government to the local governments, through a formal process clearly highlighting the role and duties of all actors involved in risk reduction activities. In particular, the authority of the National System for Civil Defence (SINADECI) – which since the adoption of *Law 19338 of the National System of Civil Defence* in 1972 had been charged with the task of promoting DRR and enhancing the country's emergency response mechanisms – was devolved to local Civil Defence Committees in a hierarchical manner: provincial committees supervise municipal ones, regional committees supervise provincial ones, and ultimately the National Institute of Civil Defence (INDECI) leads the planning and control of activities at the country level. However, while the overall coordination of the system and formulation of policies come under the responsibility of INDECI, municipalities and provinces are relatively autonomous in carrying out their plans, programs and projects, provided that such are in line with national policies.[58] Indeed, the intended purpose of the decentralization of DRR mechanisms was to increase risk management capacities at all administrative levels within the country, and was further supported in 2002 by the adoption of Law 27867 – the *Organic Law on Regional Governments* – which established both general and specific duties of local governments.[59]

Moreover, following the adoption of the HFA, Peru also instituted its National Platform in 2009. The launch of the platform arrived after a long and complex consultation process: indeed, the need to clearly allocate the role and responsibilities of the National Platform *vis-à-vis* both the HFA and the existing (and already complex) national mechanism for DRR led to expected complications and a number of setbacks. Eventually Peru's NP was established as a support forum for SINADECI, in which

[58] ISDR, "Peru: Institutional Settings", available at http://www.eird.org/wikien/index.php/Peru#HFA_P1_-_Institutional_and_legal_framework, last accessed on 3 March 2011.

[59] NDI, *Peru's Political Party System and the Promotion of Pro-poor Reform*, NDI, 2005, pp. 31–32.

representatives of public agencies and ministers, private entities and civil society meet to strengthen the organization's reach and broaden its institutional base. Overall, it is largely believed that the National Platform has promoted wide involvement of the aforementioned representatives in the overarching national DRR mechanism; most noticeably, the participation of civil society in the process is often deemed to be one of the most interesting aspects of the Peruvian case.[60] The National Platform links civil society with SINADECI – hence providing some level of citizen's oversight on the operation of the agency at the central and institutional level – while the decentralization of responsibilities of INDECI to the community level supports local accountability along the lines of the system adopted in Sweden, but with a greater degree of procedural formality.

The Peruvian mechanism for DRR, carefully designed to support central and local accountability to both citizens and governmental institutions, should be expected to yield positive results. Yet, this does not appear to be the case. As an IFRC review highlights, local governments "failed or were unable to assign resources or dedicated staff to the activities and designated committees, lacked adequate technical expertise and advice, and did not meet or carry out their expected tasks; moreover, local voters did not hold their mayor to account on this issue".[61] Similar issues are echoed by other studies which report difficulties in the country's ability to strengthen capacities at the local level, and to adopt functional budgetary approaches to effectively support local level action.[62] It is important to highlight that in the attempt to solve such issues, Peru adopted, at the end of January 2011, the *Law 29664 on the National System for Disaster Risk Management*. Such DRR-specific law, carefully drafted upon the recommendations included in the HFA, aims to strengthen the existing mechanism, increase available resources, and reinforce local capacities to reach the overall goal of "avoiding the creation of new risks".[63] It is too early to assess the effectiveness of the provisions contained in the bill;

---

60 Sanahuja, 2010, pp. 35–36, see *supra* note 39.

61 IFRC, *Desk Review on Trends in the Promotion of Community-Based Disaster Risk Reduction Through Legislation*, background paper prepared for the ISDR Global Assessment Report, 2010, pp. 3–4.

62 Sanahuja, 2010, p. 37, see *supra* note 39.

63 ISDR, "Peru: Institutional Settings", available at http://www.eird.org/wikien/index.php/Peru#HFA_P1_-_Institutional_and_legal_framework, last accessed on 3 May 2011.

nevertheless, before drawing the conclusion that more informality and less accountability – as in the case of Sweden and the Dominican Republic – lead to better results than the promotion of effective DRR practices through formal mechanisms and increased accountability.

The case of the Philippines is of paramount importance in this context. In 2010, the country adopted the *Republic Act 10121 on Disaster Risk Reduction and Management*, a comprehensive and encompassing act aimed at "strengthening the Philippine DRR and management system, providing for the DRR and management framework, institutionalizing the national plan, and appropriating funds".[64] The act reviews in details the powers and functions of the National Disaster Risk Reduction and Management Council (NDRRMC), as well as those of related institutions at both the regional and local levels. Overall, it supports decentralization of responsibilities not only vertically through the different levels of government, but also horizontally across different sectors by including environmental and development agencies in the process.[65] The act, as reported in the country's national progress report, seeks to "empower local governments and communities to enforce DRR measures to effectively address their respective risks", in line with both existing policies such as the Medium Term Philippine Development Plan and existing legislation, in the manner of the *Climate Change Act of 2009*. Thanks to the well-defined and comprehensive nature of Act 10121, the Philippines were able to report to UNISDR a level of progress of 4 under indicator 1,[66] also highlighting that current DRR mainstreaming efforts in different institutional spheres were paving the way towards the replication of efforts in other sectors, such as education.[67]

Strong support for decentralization and the involvement of numerous stakeholders nevertheless do not appear to have been conducive to institutional confusion in relation to lines of accountability. The NDRRMC – a national institution with a long legacy, known before the adoption of Act 10121 as the National Disaster Coordinating Council (NDCC) – re-

[64] Congress of the Philippines, Philippine Disaster Risk Reduction and Management Act of 2010, 2010, p. 1.

[65] *Ibid.* pp. 12–21.

[66] Indicator 1 deals with the existence of a national policy and legal framework for disaster risk reduction with decentralized responsibilities and capacities at all levels.

[67] Benito T. Ramos, *Philippines: National Progress Report on the Implementation of the Hyogo Framework for Action*, prepared for UNISDR, 2011, pp. 5–6.

mains firmly in charge of the process as the highest policy-making, coordinating and supervising body for DRR in the country. As spelled out in the recent act, such has the responsibility to monitor the development and enforcement of laws, guidelines, codes or technical standards by agencies and organizations, as well as promoting coordination mechanisms for a more coherent implementation of risk reduction policies. Most interestingly, the act also reiterates NDRRMC's responsibility to "coordinate or oversee the implementation of the county's obligations with disaster management treaties to which it is a party and see to it that the country's disaster management treaty obligations be incorporated in its DRR and management frameworks, policies, plans, programs and projects".[68] In spite of the fact that the system adopted in the Philippines resemble the one adopted in Peru, results on the ground appear to be radically different. Indeed, since the adoption of Act 10121 the Philippine DRR system has been regarded as a model example for governments across the world, as stressed by Margareta Wahlstrom, Special Representative of the Secretary-General for Disaster Risk Reduction and head of UNISDR.[69]

Above all, it appears that the specific DRR legislation adopted in the country is effectively promoting community empowerment, in line with the provisions contained in the HFA. As reported in a research study undertaken by Oxfam on the Philippine province of Albay, local governments can rely upon an effective and efficient DRR system backed up by adequate logistical and financial support.[70] Indeed, specific provisions contained in Act 10121 – which, for example, sets out minimal staffing levels for local disaster management secretariats, and mandates to reserve 5% of annual local revenues for risk reduction and preparedness activities – appear to mitigate some of the difficulties faced by other countries, such as those previously discussed in the case of Peru.[71] But how was this achieved? Priscilla Duque, Assistant Civil Defence Executive Officer at

[68] Congress of the Philippines, 2010, pp. 13–14, see *supra* note 63.

[69] Republic of the Philippines – Department of Foreign Affairs, "Philippines Joins International Disaster Risk Reduction Day Observance in Geneva", available at http://www.dfa.gov.ph/main/index.php/news-from-rp-embassies/1982-philippines-joins-international-disaster-risk-reduction-day-observance-in-geneva, last accessed on 10 May 2011.

[70] Preventionweb, "Philippines: Disaster Risk Reduction Practice Ideal Model in Disaster Management Says Study", available at http://preventionweb.net/go/14734, last accessed on 10 May 2011.

[71] IFRC, 2010, p. 4, see *supra* note 60.

the NDRRMC, stressed that the act was the product of a two decades long consultation process that took stock of an enabling policy environment, international guidance as contained in the HFA, as well as the participation of multiple stakeholders in the drafting process, and established institutions such as the NDCC.[72] In particular, the involvement of civil society's organizations such as the Philippine Red Cross, which played an important part in the creation of Act 10121, ensured support for the adoption of clauses providing for community integration in the national DRR framework.

Such clauses, which support grassroots input and spell out local responsibilities in relation to risk reduction practices, are indeed deemed to make the Philippine's approach "far more effective" than those of other countries.[73] Whether similar results will be achieved in Peru following the adoption of *Law 29664 on the National System for Disaster Risk Management* will therefore depend upon the specific provisions included in the new act, as well as the country's institutional capacity to implement it effectively. Legislation appears to be able to support positive DRR action, in particular when such spells out clear lines of accountability, soundly allocates responsibilities, and successfully empowers all actors with the necessary resources. Nevertheless, it is important to remember that the adoption of comprehensive DRR legislation does not appear to be the only way to fulfill national commitments to the Hyogo Framework for Action. Indeed, the "substantial reduction of disaster losses, in lives and in the social, economic and environmental assets of communities and countries"[74] appears to be an outcome that countries such as Sweden and the Dominican Republic are pursuing through strategies that support more informal – but similarly effective – approaches to DRR.

---

[72] Priscilla Duque, Assistant Civil Defence Executive Officer, National Disaster Risk Reduction and Management Council, Philippines, presentation given at the Third Session of the Global Platform for Disaster Risk Reduction, in the course of the side event "How can legislation promote disaster risk reduction at the community level?", 2011.

[73] IFRC, "Reducing Risk Through Law: The Case of the Philippines", available at http://www.youtube.com/user/IFRCIDRL#p/f/6/Bl1VhYGzU9Q, last accessed on 12 May 2011.

[74] ISDR, 2005, p. 3, see *supra* note 10.

## 13.5. Assessing Accountability

The brief review above highlights that there are marked differences in the way countries across the world have created, altered or maintained different policies, laws and institutions following the adoption of the HFA. The unbinding and voluntary nature of the Hyogo Framework was translated into a multitude of pragmatic national-level approaches. While the goal of such approaches is the same – supporting the implementation of the HFA's five priorities for action – specific 'paths' have been ultimately chosen by different countries. Indeed, it appears that governments have favored some principles over others, in accordance with their specific national realities and needs. Analyzing the level of accountability of mechanisms put in place at the national level therefore appears to be a simple but effective way to classify different approaches to DRR and, more specifically, different responses to the adoption of the HFA. The examples of Peru, the Dominican Republic, Sweden, and the Philippines – overall providing a good overview of global trends – denote that marked differences exist in relation to how much States support, in variable combinations, policies over laws, decentralization over strong central institutions, and ultimately accountability to their citizens.

Accountability beyond doubt is a troublesome term, and one for which there is no formal agreed-upon definition. Slaughter stresses that "in its broadest sense [...] accountability in a democratic society means responsiveness to the people" entailing "the responsiveness of the governors to the governed" through the creation of "exact rules designed to regulate the behavior of government institutions".[75] Legal approaches stemming from such an understanding of accountability generally single out the existence of two types of rules: substantive and procedural. The former, leading to what is known as output legitimacy, denotes that institutions should act in accordance with the values, goals and aspiration of the people they represent. The latter, leading to what is known as input legitimacy, denotes that institutions should also allow people to provide meaningful input in the decision-making process. The development and increasing influence of IN-LAW mechanisms in different policy sectors – such as in

[75] Anne-Marie Slaughter, "Agencies on the Loose? Holding Government Networks Accountable", in George A. Bermann, Matthias Herdegen, and Peter L. Lindseth (eds.), *Transatlantic Regulatory Cooperation*, Oxford University Press, Oxford, 2000, p. 523.

the case of DRR – carries important consequences in relation to these notions of accountability. Within the context of a system where international agencies and networks do influence decision-making at the national level, it is important to consider and examine issues of accountability at both the international and domestic level.

So what does the example of ISDR and the HFA tell us? Broadly speaking, IN-LAW in the context of disaster reduction appears to support, to a large extent, both the substantive and procedural meanings of accountability. While a large majority of scholars have traditionally criticized international networks for a lack of accountability – Alston for example wrote that these implied "the marginalization of governments as such and their replacement by special interest groups" suggesting "a move away from arenas of relative transparency into the back rooms"[76] – this does not appear to be the case in the current study. If anything, the transparency of the decision-making process at the international level in the context of DRR often appears to be superior to the transparency of the mechanisms successively adopted at the national level. As highlighted above, UNISDR strongly promotes the public diffusion of information on ISDR strategies, notably on the level of implementation of the HFA. Indeed, following the adoption of the framework – and in line with the specific requirement to monitor and report on its implementation[77] – it is the international network itself that plays the foremost important role in rendering information publicly available. This is especially true in the case of those developing countries that do not possess enough resources to rely upon information technologies. As stressed by Slaughter, these "may in fact hold the key to responding to the challenge of invisibility [...] offering a central site for the dissemination of information and the coordination of activities".[78]

Major DRR portals directly linked to the online ISDR system[79] are professionally maintained and regularly updated, and constitute the main point of access to information related to both national and international action. The ISDR system can be considered a 'transparency enhancer' op-

[76] Philip Alston, "The Myopia of the Handmaidens: International Lawyers and Globalization", in *European Journal of International Law*, 1997, vol. 8, pp. 435, 441.

[77] ISDR, 2005, pp. 14–15, see *supra* note 10.

[78] Slaughter, 2000, p. 528, see *supra* note 74.

[79] See references to websites such as www.preventionweb.net or www.unisdr.org, last accessed on 29 November 2011.

erating through a double feedback mechanism. The network actively collects information from the above-mentioned multitude of often unknown and hidden national authorities for disaster management, and renders such information available to people across the world. Simple on-line research shows that it is much easier to access information on specific national DRR policies through the monitoring process and information technologies supported by UNISDR, rather than directly through the websites of specific national agencies. With the exclusion of those States that created strong and effective national agencies – such as the Philippines' NDRRMC which, beyond doubt, directly supports public diffusion of information on its activities[80] – it is often impossible to find any information at all streaming directly from governments or their subsidiary bodies. In a nutshell, transparency on DRR policies largely exists precisely because of the empowerment of an informal international network, which possesses the resources to monitor and analyze national approaches: as such, information is not transferred directly from the State to its citizens, but first passed to the network that ultimately provides for its diffusion to the general public.

Transparency alone is obviously not all that it is needed in order to promote accountability. Nonetheless, transparency is a fundamental feature of both output legitimacy and input legitimacy. Without transparency it is impossible for people to assess whether a decision, policy, framework, or treaty reflects and supports their aspirations. Even more clearly, without transparency it is impossible for people to truly participate in a decision-making process. As already reported, civil society organizations are strongly involved and represented in the ISDR system. The HFA *per se* was drafted through the joint efforts of civil society organizations, governments, and IOs. The same applies to all the successive activities undertaken by ISDR including the different Global Assessment Reports and the final outcomes of the Global Platforms for Disaster Risk Reduction. Of course, as stressed by many, there is still not enough social demand for DRR.[81] The need to create more critical awareness at the grassroots level

---

80 See for example NDRRMC, "National Disaster Risk Reduction and Management Council", available at http://www.ndrrmc.gov.ph, last accessed on 29 November 2011.

81 UNISDR, "Summary of Mid-Term Review Online Debate – Topic 2: Less Effective Elements of the HFA", available at http://www.preventionweb.net/english/professional/publications/v.php?id=18197, last accessed on 5 April 2011.

is indeed obvious; Joseph Weiler, for example, expressed doubts regarding the usefulness of transparency on its own, reiterating that "if you do not know what is going on, which documents will you ask to see"?[82] But it is exactly this sort of action that ISDR is trying to promote. The need to create a culture of safety is of pivotal importance for the network, as reiterated in the HFA's third Priority for Action.

Provisions supporting civil society participation, mixed with transparency and continuous efforts to promote awareness at the community level, seem to support the view that 'the voices of the people' are in many cases better represented at the international level within the context of 'informal' mechanisms, rather than at the national level through the creation of more 'formal' institutions, as in the case of Peru. Such an observation nevertheless raises an important question: why is the level of output and input accountability displayed at the international level not necessarily replicated in the HFA-informed decision-making process at the national level? As it has already been reported, IN-LAW in the context of DRR allowed for cooperation to materialize, to endure, and ultimately to solve the problem (previously defined as a general lack of consideration for risk reduction policies). Nevertheless, it has also already been stressed that the provisions contained in the HFA have been implemented at the domestic level with a large degree of freedom, creating for example a dichotomy between those States empowering largely unaccountable NPs (as in the case of the Dominican Republic) and those favoring more accountable mechanisms through the adoption of specific DRR legislation (as in the case of the Philippines).

Part of the answer to the question why international informal lawmaking did not influence national policy-making in a more homogeneous fashion, is provided by Slaughter. She highlights that "network initiatives are subject to the normal political constraints on domestic policy-making processes once they are introduced at the domestic level".[83] ISDR was originally created around elements such as transparency, participation, and constant evaluation; yet, the decisions reached at the network level face specific features of national administrative, political and legislative systems during the implementation phase. Indeed, by looking at the final

[82] Joseph H.H Weiler, "To Be a European Citizen: Eros and Civilization", Working Paper Series in *European Studies*, 1998, p. 39, available at http://aei.pitt.edu/8990/1/weiler.pdf, last accessed on 23 June 2011.

[83] Slaughter, 2000, p. 526, see *supra* note 74.

status of HFA implementation in different countries, it appears clear that there are issues in relation to the 'timeline' of accountability. While the initial process through which international guidelines are adopted is, to a certain extent, accountable to the people, the latter process through which these guidelines are implemented at the national level often appears to display lower levels of accountability, especially in those cases where HFA recommendations are not embedded in clear domestic legal frameworks.

As such, it appears useful to distinguish between accountability in the decision-making process leading up to IN-LAW (*ex ante* activity), and accountability in relation to activities already taken or questions of implementation or compliance (*ex post* activity). At the international level *ex ante* activities of ISDR were, to a large extent, accountable: the decision-making process leading up to the adoption of a specific informal output (the HFA) was transparent and open. Nevertheless, *ex post* activities steaming from the HFA and undertaken at the national level are, at times, less accountable to the people. As reported, the transparent and multi-stakeholder character of the international DRR network is often lost at the national level, especially when States implement policies that do not directly support community involvement, specific institutional responsibilities, or clear revision procedures. It should however be kept in mind that such an observation does not entail a negative understanding of lack of accountability.

At the domestic level, *ex post* activities displaying low levels of accountability have proven to be just as successful as those strongly supporting accountability, as in the cases of the Dominican Republic and the Philippines. More interestingly, it is also fundamental to note that legislation – traditionally associated with greater process formality – is not necessary to support accountability, as alternative and less formal processes (as the decentralized system adopted in Sweden) can equally provide for it. On the contrary, poor and confusing legislative frameworks, as those in place in Peru prior to the adoption of Law 29664, can hamper accountability, in particular when the roles and responsibilities of different domestic agencies involved in DRR are not clearly defined. In a nutshell, ISDR and the HFA did support, in spite of their informal nature, *ex ante* accountability at the international level, and appear to have effectively triggered change at the national level. Nevertheless, the nature of *ex post* activities undertaken at the national level is marked by variety: while in some countries the HFA has brought along more accountable mechanisms, in others less accountable ones were triggered.

The nature of the link between accountability and effectiveness of national mechanism for risk reduction requires, beyond doubt, greater and more ad hoc attention. Nevertheless, there is still one last point that must be considered in the current debate: what is the status of *ex post* activities at the international level? UNISDR – and the ISDR system more in general – were not created with the sole scope of producing the HFA. The network endures beyond the adoption of the framework, and therefore activities related to the Framework are not simply 'passed on' to individual States, but also endure at the informal international level through the network. While the network was the only referent for *ex ante* activities (this being the only actor in the decision-making process leading up to IN-LAW), both the network and individual States alike are referents for *ex post* activities (as both can be judged for subsequent operations such as monitoring, planning and implementation). One simple way to 'dodge' the question would be to stress that we should not be concerned about the status of *ex post* activities of ISDR.

The informal nature of the network – just as much as the unbinding character of the HFA – entails that the State remains the final decision-maker, and hence the only agent that should be held accountable for the adoption of specific policies. As such, what ISDR does should not matter in relation to *ex post* accountability: it does not hold power over governments, and therefore governments' actions should only, ultimately, be considered and scrutinized by citizens. This should be kept in mind by those involved in the heated debate over the eventual creation of a binding instrument to follow-up to the HFA in 2015. As reported by the Mid-Term review of the HFA, there seems to be a clear distinction between the opinion of those coming from a government background, and the opinion of academic or civil society representatives: while the former appear reluctant to envisage a legally building framework, the latter often argue for a legal base "as offering a chance to make progress in meeting the needs of under-served or most vulnerable people".[84] Such a division obviously does not come as a surprise: on the one hand, we find traditional State concerns related to the adoption of binding international documents and the 'loss of sovereignty' that such an action entails. On the other hand, we

[84] UNISDR, 2011, p. 65, see *supra* note 34.

find that an increasing number of people positively recognize the action of the ISDR system, and invoke a *de facto* delegation of authority through a binding instrument.

On its own, such an observation goes a long way toward supporting previous findings of this paper. If civil society representatives largely solicit the adoption of a binding instrument to follow up to the HFA in order to 'meet the needs' of local communities, it could be assumed that such find themselves better represented at the international level (where the drafting of a binding instrument would take place) than at the national level (where internal mechanisms continue to raise questions of transparency and accountability). Nevertheless, it is important to keep in mind why DRR was originally promoted through IN-LAW, rather than through more formal international agreements. The practice of disaster risk reduction is a complex one, and one that requires the synergy of actions undertaken by a multitude of actors operating at different levels. As already reported, success strongly depends upon the cooperation of agencies belonging to different fields (environment, development, disaster management and infrastructures) and to different levels (international, regional, national and local). Indeed, it is the presence of so many actors that poses a first barrier militating against the adoption of a binding agreement: consensus would be difficult to reach under the umbrella of a framework capable of holding States accountable for eventual compliance failures.

But beyond the issue of consensus there are also a number of other barriers that are often overlooked by those in support of a binding DRR instrument. In first place, the multidisciplinary nature of effective DRR action is likely to clash with a plethora of existing sectoral laws at the national (but also at regional and municipal level – not to mention the State level in the case of federal systems) that regulate manifold issues such as budget allocations, building codes, education, as well as civil and criminal liabilities. National compliance with an international agreement affecting so many issue-areas would therefore require the amendment of numerous laws: as such, even if a DRR treaty could be adopted, its formal ratification would require a more complex process. In second place, the adoption of an effective binding instrument would also require the establishment of clear targets. DRR is not a matter of banning bad practices; on the contrary, DRR is an action-oriented approach. As such, a treaty that does not establish 'how much' should be achieved would be of little use. But how can we set uniform targets, when the resources individual States possess –

as well as national baselines of risk – are so uneven? At last, as previously reported, it is also important to remember that the adoption of a binding document would ultimately require the creation of clear institutional structures increasing the accountability of *ex post* activities at the international level. The adoption of a DRR treaty would be of little use without the formal empowerment of an international institution in charge of addressing issues of implementation and compliance. But as it is well understood, the *de facto* delegation of authority to a supranational body would ultimately raise recurrent questions linked to the issue of democratic deficit.

What is clearly at stake in this context is the informality of the ISDR system. Pure speculation tells us that a move to more formal arrangements at the international level could yield positive results, providing a solution for the lack of accountability of national institutions that is often perceived by the people at the community level. Nevertheless, it is important to remember that a move to increased formality could not only be difficult to realize, but also unnecessary. The informal nature of the ISDR system has already acted as a catalyst for change, and effectively promoted DRR through the agenda of governments in those years when risk reduction was of little concern to many.

## 13.6. Conclusion

The ISDR system represents an interesting example of network-based international cooperation. It fulfills the three main criteria of output, process and actor informality established by the IN-LAW project, as it supported the adoption of a non-binding document through activities that occurred outside of well-established channels involving, last but not least, uncommon entities not traditionally associated with lawmaking formalities. Overall, the informal nature of the network and the character of the framework it adopted seem to have effectively limited the impediment to cooperation in the field of disaster risk reduction. Indeed, within such specific context, IN-LAW appears to have been critical not only in supporting the emergence of consistent practices aimed at addressing pressing issues of common concern at the international level, but also in promoting observable change at the individual domestic level. As reported, in many cases, the adoption of the HFA has noticeably influenced national decision-making processes: key specifications included in the document –

such as the request to create NPs, define clear policies, and adopt specific laws – have often been complied with.

Although multiple gaps in areas such as operational capacities or financial resources militate against the effective implementation of national level provisions, and as such ultimately affect the success of DRR practices, it appears evident that the action of ISDR has altered and influenced governments' behavior. As it happens, ISDR actions are increasingly framing national efforts for risk reduction using the HFA, taking stock of its Priorities for Action in the development of plans and structures. The implementation of the Framework appears to be occurring on an *ad hoc* basis; the generality of the document, supporting a certain degree of freedom in relation to the specific practices to be adopted, ultimately allowed for the creation of both formal and informal arrangements at the domestic level. While some countries merely promoted a policy-based approach through the empowerment of a National Platform, others favored specific legislative mechanisms in the attempt to set the record straight. In spite of the fact that the dichotomy between policies and legislation is an over-simplification of the reality on the ground, such is nevertheless helpful for the purpose of the present study.

Different mechanisms implemented at the national level following the adoption of the HFA support variable levels of accountability and effectiveness. In some cases the empowerment of independent technical agencies working 'behind the curtain' and escaping traditional lines of accountability has gone a long way towards the promotion of effective DRR practices, as in the case of the Dominican Republic. Nevertheless, the adoption of specific laws clearly allocating responsibilities, laying explicit budgetary arrangements, and supporting citizens' participation has also led to positive results, as shown through the example of the Philippines. Overarching legislative frameworks for risk reduction do not appear to be the only way to increase the accountability of State institutions. On the contrary – while the adoption of poorly drafted laws has at times impeded both effectiveness and accountability – the more informal decentralization of responsibilities has also supported alternative bottom-up approaches promoting greater accountability to the people.

Answering the old question of how accountability impacts upon effectiveness at the domestic level, it is important to stress that overall IN-LAW, within the specific context of the ISDR system, should not raise concerns in relation to the question of accountability deficit. The actions of the network are transparent and largely influenced by civil society organizations. Indeed, this appears to be more responsive to the people than many domestic agencies. Far from moving the discussion away from arenas of relative transparency into back rooms, ISDR seems as a matter of fact to support exactly the inverse process. If anything, domestic back room discussion is often rendered public only through the action of the network, which does not only acts as a catalyst for change, but also as a transparency enhancer.

What requires more attention and greater concern is therefore the status of *ex post* activities undertaken at the national level. Domestic action in the field of risk reduction is often triggered by the HFA, but unfortunately, such is ultimately implemented by governments with varying degrees of success. In order to increase the accountability of *ex post* activities at the national level it would be necessary to increase the power of the network to hold governments accountable. This could be achieved by taking international cooperation in the field of DRR 'outside' of the realm of informality, adopting for example new binding instruments. But such an action would eventually raise concerns over the status of *ex post* activities at the international level, translating the existing problem to a new dimension.

Should we be concerned about the eventual lack of accountability of international mechanisms formally regulating DRR actions at the national level? Unfortunately there is not an easy answer to such a question. In line with domestic developments, it is difficult to predict the relationship between effectiveness and accountability. More in general, it is difficult to predict how easily the current system could support and adapt to an increased level of formality. Such a move can boost the system's capacity to promote effective practices at the ground level, but could also hamper its current efficiency, as such remains entrenched within output, process and actor informality.

# 14

# Informal International Lawmaking: The Kimberley Process' Mechanism of Accountability

**Victoria Vidal***

> Accountability is one of those terms about which there is a widespread sense of what it means, but difficulty in coming to any agreement about its definition.[1]

The importance of Informal International Lawmaking (IN-LAW) is constantly growing and the international community does not lack examples of this legal tendency. IN-LAW bodies are transnational networks producing legal effects that are generally well-respected by their members. Yet, they are not traditional international legal entities, and as such trigger a number of questions related to key issues of effectiveness and accountability. This chapter aims to assess one of these IN-LAW mechanisms, the Kimberley Process Certification Scheme (KP), using the IN-LAW framework introduced in this publication, and to study its accountability and effectiveness in an integrated way.[2] First, an overview of the KP is given to analyze its creation, functioning, and, more importantly, its functionality as an element of IN-LAW. Having understood the purpose of the KP, the second section and core of this chapter provides an in-depth analysis of how the Kimberley Process owes accountability to internal and external stakeholders. We first analyze accountability towards KP members in order to assess the KP's legitimacy and in a second step focus on the accountability of the KP owed to external stakeholders. This contribution, which is driven by empirical research and aims to be solution-oriented, provides the reader with a third section on the impact of the KP on the

---

* **Victoria Vidal** is Assistant at the Inter-Agency Unit of the Office of the United Nations High Commissioner for Refugees (UNHCR) in Geneva.

1 Hetty Kovach, Caroline Neligan, Simon Burall, "The Global Accountability Report 2003, Accountability Without Power?", One World Trust, p. 3.

2 Joost Pauwelyn, "Informal International Lawmaking: Framing the Concept and Research Questions", in Joost Pauwelyn, Ramses A. Wessel and Jan Wouters (eds.), *Informal International Lawmaking*, Oxford University Press, Oxford, 2012, p. 13–34.

field. A final part summarizes and discusses the KP's strengths, weaknesses, and potential solutions.

## 14.1. The Kimberley Process Certification Scheme

### 14.1.1. The Creation of the Kimberley Process

Marilyn Monroe used to sing that diamonds were a girl's best friend, and De Beers used to say that diamonds were forever. The horrific civil wars in Angola, Sierra Leone and Liberia showed us that diamonds were also a rebel's best friend.[3] Upon witnessing the horror and bloodshed of these wars, the international community started to react and the United Nations (UN) General Assembly adopted Resolution 55/56, which recognized the role of diamonds in fuelling conflict.[4] This Resolution was a milestone-moment and kicked off a number of initiatives. In 2000, diamond producing States symbolically met in Kimberley, South Africa, to eradicate the trade in conflict diamonds.[5] This meeting led to the creation in 2002, and the adoption in 2003, of the Kimberley Process Certification Scheme. The original creators were civil society organizations, the diamond industry (represented by the World Diamond Council) and the respective governments of the countries involved.[6] Their intention was to exclude diamonds that are used to fund wars from international trade, by controlling the origin of rough diamonds.[7] Most importantly, the KP imposes that "no shipment of rough diamonds is imported from or exported to a non-

[3] Ola Olsson, "Diamonds are a Rebel's Best Friend", in *The World Economy*, 2006, vol. 29, issue 8, pp. 1133–1150.

[4] United Nations General Assembly Resolution 55/56 entitled: "The role of diamonds in fuelling conflict: Breaking the link between the illicit transaction of rough diamonds and armed conflict as a contribution to prevention and settlement of conflicts".

[5] A conflict diamond is, according to the UN: "diamonds that originate from areas controlled by forces or factions opposed to legitimate and internationally recognized governments, and are used to fund military action in opposition to those governments, or in contradiction of the decisions of the Security Council", available at: http://www.un.org/peace/africa/Diamond.html, last accessed on 4 July 2012.

[6] Kimberley Process background, "KP Basics", available at: http://www.kimberleyprocess.com/web/kimberley-process/kp-basics, last accessed on 4 July 2012.

[7] "Kimberley Process Certification Scheme", available at http://www.kimberleyprocess.com/documents/10340/11192/KPCS%20Core%20Document, last accessed on 4 July 2012.

Participant".[8] In other words, Sweden for example, which is not a participant in the KP, cannot trade in diamonds. Despite the fact that this measure clearly violates article I.1 of the General Agreement on Tariffs and Trade (GATT), the World Trade Organization (WTO) granted a waiver to authorize this violation.[9] The KP is the first attempt at regulating the conflict diamond trade and is considered successful. Indeed, according to the Diamond Facts more than 99% of diamonds are conflict free since the implementation of the process.[10] Yet, certain weaknesses can also be observed, which are, however, not necessarily attributable to its IN-LAW status.

### 14.1.2. The IN-LAW Status of the Kimberley Process Certification Scheme

The Kimberley Process meets all three criteria of IN-LAW since it does not correspond to the traditional characteristics of formal international law. The KP did not promulgate a treaty or traditional instrument of international law that meets the criteria laid down in the Vienna Convention on the Law of Treaties. Indeed, plenipotentiaries did not formally negotiate the KP.[11] The 'informal' actors that were involved in its creation did not have the legal power to make it binding at the international level. Moreover, the actors decided not to sign the agreement,[12] traditionally an essential element of consent and part of the international law of treaties.[13] Also, these informal actors did not want to use the term 'agreement' in the negotiations and went to the negotiation with 'no mandate to approve anything'.[14] It appears obvious that members did not want to create a treaty and did not want to be bound by this treaty. However, this conclusion

8 "Kimberley Process Certification Scheme", see *supra* note 7.

9 Joost Pauwelyn, "WTO Compassion or Superiority Complex?: What To Make of the WTO Waiver for 'Conflict Diamonds'", in *Michigan Journal of International Law*, 2003, vol. 24, no. 4, pp. 1177–1207.

10 "Diamond Facts", available at http://diamondfacts.org/, last accessed on 4 July 2012.

11 Antonio Cassese, *International Law*, Oxford University Press, 2005, p.172.

12 Daniel Feldman, "Conflict Diamonds, International Trade Regulation and the Nature of Law", in *Journal of International Economic Law*, 2003, vol. 24, issue 4, p. 836.

13 Article 11 of the Vienna Convention states "The consent by a state to be bound by a treaty may be expressed by signature, exchange of instruments constituting a treaty [...]".

14 Frans Schram, *The Legal Aspects of the Kimberley Process*, International Peace Information Service, 2007, p. 7.

does not mean that the actors involved did not want to see negotiations resulting in an effective scheme. Moreover, they have bound themselves at the domestic level, via a sanction-system, and thus confirmed that the prime source of accountability of this IN-LAW body is national law.[15] States, civil society and the diamond industry did not want to sign a legally binding treaty for various reasons. Wright pointed out that a treaty could take years to be ratified and implemented and that it moreover would imply the need to set up a strict monitoring system.[16] Also, an international treaty entails the exclusion of non-State actors, which is undesired because of their crucial role as main producers and traders of diamonds.

The KP certificate is not part of international law, for better or for worse? IN-LAW and the Kimberley Process appear to be a rather successful marriage. Making echo of Pauwelyn's statement, the important question to raise is "does it even matter"?[17] What matters is the intent to be bound, expressed by the parties. This intent is demonstrated by the adopted binding measures at the domestic level. If the KP is not a traditional legal treaty, it is what is called a 'committing legal norms'.[18] The KP certificate allows international cooperation between different actors with different interests in order to achieve one common goal.[19]

### 14.1.3. The Functioning of the Kimberley Process

The Kimberley Process was created with the joint effort of governments, the diamond industry, and NGOs, all determined to establish effective control over the conflict diamond trade. Global Witness released a report prepared for the first meeting of the KP, entitled "Conflict Diamonds: Possibilities for the Identification, Certification and Control of Dia-

---

15 Pauwelyn, 2012, see *supra* note 2.

16 Clive Wright, "Tackling Conflict Diamonds: The Kimberley Process Certification Scheme", in *International Peacekeeping*, 2004, vol. 11, no. 4, p 703.

17 Joost Pauwelyn, "Is it International Law or Not And Does It Even Matter?", in Joost Pauwelyn, Ramses A. Wessel and Jan Wouters (eds.), *Informal International Lawmaking*, Oxford University Press, Oxford, 2012, pp. 125–161.

18 Dick Ruiter and Ramses A. Wessel, "The Legal Nature of Informal International Lawmaking: A Legal Theoritical Exercise", in Joost Pauwelyn, Ramses A. Wessel and Jan Wouters (eds.), *Informal International Lawmaking*, Oxford University Press, Oxford, 2012, pp. 162–181.

19 Pauwelyn, 2012, see *supra* note 2.

monds".[20] This report explains how the diamond industry works, how the quality and origin of a diamond can be recognized, and also shares case studies of national regulation to control the production, import and export of diamonds. This report appears to have been encouraging for the other actors involved and has been quoted in the main principles of the KP. The World Diamond Council initiated the writing of this report and passed a resolution, the 'Antwerp Resolution', which enacted national legislations to regulate the controlling of the origin of imported diamonds by a certificate and to impose sanctions on countries that buy diamonds from known illegal diamond companies.[21] Finally, the diamond industry and De Beers, fortunately or not, proposed a 'chain of warranties' that would regulate the commercial side of the diamond trade.[22] In other words, the diamond industry opted for self-regulation. All these propositions can be found in the Kimberley Process Certification Scheme and show the considerable effort made by different stakeholders with different interests to cooperate.

The KP works toward the goal of eliminating conflict diamonds by imposing on its members to control the origin of imported and exported rough diamonds. Such a control demands that all diamond traders provide a certificate of origin when exporting shipments of rough diamonds, including information such as the country of origin, the value of the shipment, the identification of the importer and exporter as well as the carat weight.[23] The KP also installed internal controls supervised by appropriate authorities. These controls will be made effective through the implementation of specific requirements into each Member State's national legislation. A violation of these requirements in its turn will incur sanctions trough dissuasive penalties. Finally, members are required to collect data and statistics of official import, export or production of diamonds, in order to assure transparency and cooperation.[24]

The acceptance of these rules on domestic regulation serves as a minimum threshold to be part of the KP. Since the prime source of accountability of the KP is domestic law, it is interesting to zoom in on how

---

20 Andrew Grant and Ian Taylor, "Global Governance and Conflict Diamonds: The Kimberley Process and the Quest for Clean Gems", in *Round Table: Commonwealth Journal of International Relations*, 2004, vol. 93, no. 375, p. 392.

21 Grant and Taylor, 2004, p. 393, see *supra* note 20.

22 Grant and Taylor, 2004, p. 394, see *supra* note 20.

23 "Kimberley Process Certification Scheme", p 12, see *supra* note 7.

24 "Kimberley Process Certification Scheme", Section III and IV, see *supra* note 7.

the European Union (EU) and the United States (US) implemented the KP in their national legislations. On one side, the EU implemented the Kimberley Process through EU Council Regulations.[25] This was achieved in the context of the EU's Common Foreign and Security Policy which is the mechanism used to implement UN Security Council Resolutions.[26] The 2002 Council Regulation aims at controlling the import and export of rough diamonds in accordance with the requirements laid down in the Kimberley Process.[27] The Council is the main decision-making body of the EU,[28] and has the power to pass laws which will have to be implemented in the legal system of each Member State. Next to its internal effects, the Council Regulation was a crucial step in the implementation of the KP worldwide since the EU is a major trade zone through which 70% to 80% of the global annual production of diamonds passes.[29] The EU's abovementioned Council Regulation states in Article 3 that the import of rough diamonds, not accompanied by a certificate, shall be prohibited and that every import of rough diamonds must be verified by a designated authority.[30] On the other side of the spectrum, the US implemented the Kimberley Process through a 2003 Congressional bill, the 'Clean Diamond Trade Act'.[31] Section 8 of this Act installs sanctions in case of non-compliance, to be enforced by the US Bureau of Customs and Border Protection and the US Bureau of Immigration and Customs Enforcement.[32] The European and American examples demonstrate that, viewed from a domestic law angle, the Kimberley Process is legally binding. As such, its accountability is organized along the same lines as other domestic regulations.

---

[25] Schram, 2007, p. 13, see *supra* note 14.

[26] Schram, 2007, p. 12, see *supra* note 14.

[27] European Union Council Regulation 2368/2002, chapter 1, Art. 1, available at http://eur-lex.europa.eu/LexUriServ/LexUriServ.do?uri=OJ:L:2002:358:0028:0048:EN:PDF, last accessed on 4 July 2012.

[28] The Council of the European Union, available at http://www.consilium.europa.eu/showPage.aspx?id=242&lang=en, last accessed on 4 July 2012.

[29] Schram, 2007, p. 12, see *supra* note 14.

[30] EU Council Regulation 2368, see *supra* note 27.

[31] Feldman, 2003, p. 837, see *supra* note 12.

[32] The Clean Diamond Trade Act, Section 8 (b), available at http://frwebgate.access.gpo.gov/cgi-bin/getdoc.cgi?dbname=108_cong_bills&docid=f:h1584enr.txt.pdf, last accessed on 4 July 2012.

An understanding of the procedural aspects of the KP is necessary and will assist in analyzing accountability issues related to its organizational structure. In other words: does the "process informality further limit normative strictures or control under both domestic and international law"?[33] The Kimberley Process structure comprises a Chair, Working Groups and Committees. The Chair is responsible for the overall supervision of the KP. Thus, it supervises the implementation of the KP, checks the operations of the Working Groups and the committees and finally, deals with general administration. The Chair rotates each year and is chosen among the participants.[34] There are five Working Groups: (i) a Monitoring Working Group, which checks if participants implement the scheme and makes visits to countries in order to assess their annual reports; (ii) a Working Group on Statistics, providing data on the production and trade of rough diamonds; (iii) a Working Group of Diamond Experts, which solves technical issues relevant to the implementation of the scheme; (iv) a Working Group on Rules and Procedures, which ensures the way in which decisions made are clear and consistent; and (v) a Working Group on Artisanal and Alluvial Production, which aims at promoting more effective internal controls.[35] The KP also has a Participation Committee to assist the Chair in the admission of new participants, and a Selection Committee to select the vice-chair.

## 14.2. The Accountability of the Kimberley Process Certification Scheme

A repeated concern regarding IN-LAW is the presumed accountability gap it creates, since it dispenses with the traditional mechanism of accountability inherent to international or national law.[36] At the national level, independent and impartial bodies that apply serve as sanction mechanisms and act when domestic laws are breached. The national independent judicial bodies keep accountability in a variety of ways, and in

[33] Joost Pauwelyn, Ramses A. Wessel and Jan Wouters, "Informal International Lawmaking: Framing the Concept and Research Questions", in Joost Pauwelyn, Ramses A. Wessel and Jan Wouters (eds.), *Informal International Lawmaking*, Oxford University Press, Oxford, 2012, p.18.

[34] "Kimberley Process Chair", available at http://www.kimberleyprocess.com/web/kimberley-process/chair, last accessed on 4 July 2012.

[35] All this information is found on the website aforementioned.

[36] Pauwelyn, 2012, p. 3, see *supra* note 2.

most cases, forms of hierarchical accountability and parliamentary oversight are in place. These accountability mechanisms are less clear at the international level. However, here, the concept of State Responsibility is well established. Indeed, a delinquent State under international law is under numerous obligations to cease, repair, as well as compensate for the wrongful act,[37] and most importantly, States are obliged and accountable under the concept of *jus cogens*. This is what can be called a traditional approach to accountability: holding an individual or an organization to account.[38] Dealing with non-traditional entities, the definition given by Bovens is also of relevance. Accountability is "A relationship between an actor and a forum, in which the actor has an obligation to explain and to justify his or her conduct, the forum can pose questions and pose judgment, and the actor may face consequences".[39] As mentioned in the introduction of this chapter, accountability and effectiveness will be studied together. In fulfilling the aspiration of the KP to be accountable, that is, responsive to the need of the people, it actually needs to take into account the views expressed by the people. The accountability of the KP will be measured at an internal and external dimension.

### 14.2.1. The Internal Accountability of the Kimberley Process

Internal stakeholders are those stakeholders who are directly and formally part of the organization: they can be staff, shareholders, member countries, or in some cases, NGOs.[40] This paragraph focuses on the member States composing the KP to test the level of accountability in relation to the main internal stakeholders. Relying on the definition given by Bovens, the KP should be transparent, involving members to participate in the decisions that affect them, and being responsive to their complaints. In the next section, a similar definition will be used to study the external accountability of the KP. It concentrates on elements of transparency (a prerequisite for accountability), the capacity of external stakeholders to file complaints, and the capacity of the KP to register complaints.

---

[37] Cassese, 2005, p. 259, see *supra* note 11.

[38] Kovach, Neligan, Burall, 2003, p. 3, see *supra* note 1.

[39] Mark Bovens, "Analysing and Assessing Public Accountability: A Conceptual Framework", in *European Law Review*, 2007, vol. 13, no. 4.

[40] Kovach, Neligan, Burall, 2003, p. 3, see *supra* note 1.

Members of the Kimberley Process have some degree of control over the KP scheme as they set the rules that will be binding on them. At the very beginning, the Kimberley Process lacked a system of checks and balances. It did not collect statistics nor had a functioning monitoring system to control its actions and activities. As mentioned in section one, members did not want to be bound by an international treaty precisely because this would imply a strict monitoring system. They were not comfortable with the idea of organizing 'intrusive inspections by outsiders'.[41] Nonetheless, in 2003, and following massive pressure stemming from civil society, inspection tools were installed by the Plenary Meeting together with a peer review mechanism, which is now under the control of the Working Group on Monitoring.[42] This Working Group on Monitoring is composed of members and observers designated by the Chair of the KP, and its main mandate is to check the implementation of the scheme by participants.[43] The Working Group reports directly to the Chair of the Kimberley Process. Yet, and interesting in light of accountability questions, the agenda of the Working Group is set by the Chair of the Working Group, and not by the KP itself, which allows members of the Working Group to maneuver. Also, in its report to the Chair, the Working Group is able to state any improvements it considers necessary to make the KP more effective. It is worth noting that participants can report to the Working Group when they deem a review visit to another participant advisable.[44] This reporting-function demonstrates the control the members of the KP have over the Working Group. For these reasons, the creation of the Working Group on Monitoring was applauded by civil society and its functioning first tested in 2004. In this case, the KP removed the Democratic Republic of the Congo (DRC) off its list of participants after a review report that concluded the incapacity of the DRC to explain the origin of its diamonds.[45] This example clearly demonstrates that members have an effective control over the KP, thus making the KP accountable to them.

41 Wright, 2004, p. 703, see *supra* note 16.

42 *Ibid.*

43 Kimberley Process Working Group on Monitoring, available at http://www.kimberley process.com/web/kimberley-process/monitoring, last accessed on 4 July 2012.

44 *Ibid.*

45 BBC News, "Congo Excluded From Diamond Trade", available at http://news.bbc.co.uk/2/hi/africa/3883047.stm, last accessed on 4 July 2012.

However, this success is also criticized due to concerns about the partiality and the ineffectiveness of the organ concerned. First of all, monitoring in the KP happens on a voluntary basis. Sanctions will be executed upon a member's request or will be completed with the consent of the country implied.[46] As such, the Working Group on Monitoring can be determined an organ composed of insiders and under the control of insiders. As a result, it is hard to call a system efficient wherein the monitoring system as well as the enforcement mechanism is not independent from the stakeholders.[47] In an interview with Mr. Kara, Director of the Diamonds and Human Security Program at Partnership Africa Canada, he noted that "all internal stakeholders do not have the same interests in KP".[48] Some will see it as a shield to the diamond industry, others as an instrument to fight conflict and poverty, and finally some will be indifferent. He thus argued, that "a conflict of interests emerges when those who commit the crimes also police themselves and their friends". This is, for example, illustrated by a Zimbabwean case. In 2008, the military took control over the Marangue diamond field in Zimbabwe, committing atrocious human rights violations. During the following June 2010 Intercessional meeting, the KP Monitor declared Zimbabwe compliant after holding private sessions with only a few members of the Working Group.[49] This process was repeated at the Annual Plenary meeting in Jerusalem in November 2010, where only the KP chair, USA and Zimbabwe were negotiating.[50] This example clearly demonstrates a political game of interest which cannot be eradicated without a well-functioning independent monitoring body. Moreover, it also demonstrates an unequal access to information to all the internal stakeholders and thus a lack of accountability.

---

46 Annie Wallis, "Data Mining: Lessons from the Kimberley Process for the United Nations, Development of Human Rights Norms for Transnational Corporations", in *Northwestern University Journal of International Human Rights*, 2005, vol. 4, issue 2, para. 43.

47 Wallis, 2005, para. 4, see *supra* note 46.

48 Director, Diamonds and Human Security Program at Partnership Africa Canada.

49 Information provided by Mr. Kara, see *supra* note 48.

50 Note: A draft agreement was presented the next day to all members who refused to sign it, as they were not part of the trilateral negotiations. A special meeting of the WGM was then held in Brussels in December to reach in agreement. This meeting, called the Brussels agreement, was not attended by Zimbabwe (information provided by Mr. Kara, see *supra* note 48.).

A last element that is worth examining when attempting to uncover the accountability of the KP is the possibility for a member to file a complaint. National or international law courts and dispute bodies are in place to hear these, unlike in the case of IN-LAW, where a grey area exists. Contrasting, for example, the WTO, there is no dispute settlement body that would allow the members of the Kimberley Process to complain about another member or about the activities of the KP. This being said, the KP process does recognize three types of complaints that can be filed by members internally. First, there is the procedural complaint that is brought to the Committee of Rules and Procedures. Second, as previously mentioned, participants can request that the Working Group on Monitoring visits another member.[51] It must be noted that this rarely happens and that, usually, these non-compliance concerns are raised by civil society. Since 2003, NGOs and some member States have been emphasizing the need to install an impartial monitoring system, the only tool to truly legitimize the Kimberley Process.[52] Third, at the domestic level, and contrasting the scarcity of complaints being filed at the international level, well-functioning compliance mechanisms are in place. Each KP member State has a competent authority to oversee the implementation of the Kimberley Process by ensuring that shipments of rough diamonds imported or exported carry a certification of origin. These authorities, typically, are members of the ministry of mines and energy or the ministry of finance and trade. A full list of designated authorities for each participant is to be found in Annex II of the KP scheme.[53] The authorities are in charge of issuing, validating, and verifying if a certificate accompanies shipments of rough diamonds. This implies that if a control is correctly applied, no shipments can enter or leave a member's territory without a valid certificate. If a suspicious parcel of rough diamonds is found, the competent authority notifies the KP Chair as a way of making a complaint. However, in reality, this international dimension of the complaint-mechanism is seldom applied. For example, in the US, the competent authority is the US Kimberley Process Authority (USKPA). This is the entity authorized by

---

51 Ian Smillie, *Comparative Case Study, The Kimberley Process Certification Scheme for Rough Diamonds*, Partnership Africa Canada, 2005, p. 5.

52 Wallis, 2005, para. 44, see *supra* note 46.

53 EC Council Regulation No. 2368/2002, available at http://eur-lex.europa.eu/LexUriServ/LexUriServ.do?uri=CONSLEG:2002R2368:20080528:EN:PDF, last accessed on 4 July 2012.

the US government to provide US Kimberley Process certificates to licensed entities for use in exporting rough diamonds from the US.[54] Through this authority the KP is accountable. Cecilia Gardner,[55] President and CEO of the Jewellers Vigilance Committee, underlined that the sanctions for non-compliance can include "seizure, fines, and potential criminal sanctions, including terms of imprisonment, depending on the circumstances" and that there are "at least four pending cases at this time in the US" between the USKPA and shippers of diamonds. Complaints involving, for example, shippers that did not comply with the KP requirements will only be dealt with at the domestic level since no direct complaint mechanism is in place at the international level. This example demonstrates the strength of the implementation of the KP. Yet, internal stakeholders cannot rely upon the KP to have their complaints heard, which shows a lack of responsiveness. It also reinforces the IN-LAW status of the KP, as the prime source of accountability of the KP in this case is domestic law.[56] Therefore, it can be concluded that the Kimberley Process' accountability towards internal stakeholders is oscillating between a real will to tackle conflict diamond trade and a mechanism that is not fully effective. This lack of effectiveness can be explained by the absence of a body that checks on members' activities and settles disputes between them. The reluctance to be controlled by an independent and outsider body endangers the legitimacy of the scheme.

### 14.2.2. The External Accountability of the Kimberley Process

By external accountability of the Kimberley process, we mean the capacity of entities external to the process to judge and sanction the effectiveness of this scheme or the lack thereof. This is reflected by the transparency level of the organization's activities, by the extent to which these stakeholders are part of the decision-making process and how the organization is able to register and respond to their complaints. Coming back to Bovens' words, we will measure to what extend the forum can pose questions and judgment and to what extent it will be taken into consideration.

---

54 USKPA, available at https://www.uskpa.org/default.aspx, last accessed on 4 July 2012.

55 President and CEO of the Jewellers Vigilance Committee.

56 Pauwelyn, 2012, see *supra* note 2.

As an example of external stakeholders this chapter looks at NGOs, the diamond industry and diamond miners affected by the KP. Despite the fact that NGOs and the diamond industry were part of the creation of the Kimberley Process, they do not have a vote in the decision-making process and thus are seen as external stakeholders. Even though they are part of working groups and committees, and are considered influential, they only act as observers.[57] Indeed, external stakeholders are affected by the organization's activities and decisions but are not officially part of it.[58] KP impacts upon NGOs working on conflict diamonds and human rights protection, individual miners, and the diamond industry. The latter is clearly affected by the KP as the effectiveness of the process will be reflected in the demand for these gems. Similar to the assessment of the accountability towards internal stakeholders, this section takes three elements to measure the level of accountability towards external stakeholders.

First, we will examine to what extent the Kimberley Process is transparent enough to be accountable. The Kimberley Process is increasingly transparent and allows participants and civil society to have access to the main activities and data of the KP. Some documents are made public, such as the reports of the Plenary Annual Meeting, the Third Year Review and the core documents setting up the scheme.[59] Also, statistics are made available to the public on the global production, import and export of rough diamonds by country. This is a crucial step forward in increasing the legitimacy of the KP, as it brings transparency not only towards the public but also to the other participants. As such, it provides external stakeholders with a manner to check the activity of members and gives to the public a way of being informed of the global movement of diamonds. This proved to be a useful tool in the accountability of the KP. In the period before the above-mentioned 2004 case of the DRC, for example, Canada, the then Chair of the Working Group on Statistics, carefully compiled data and found wrong information given by the DRC. A review

57 Information given by an interview with John Hall, General Manager of External Affairs of Rio Tinto. He is also responsible for key relationships with external stakeholders including governments, NGOs and industry bodies, as well as corporate responsibility programs such as the Extractive Industries Transparency Initiative and the Kimberley Process.

58 Kovach, Neligan, Burall, p. 3, see *supra* note 1.

59 "Kimberley Process Certification Scheme", see *supra* note 7.

visit in the country was carried out which eventually led to the exclusion of the DRC from the process.[60] As a security measure, only some data is available to the participants. Even though all KP participants must submit rough diamond production statistics on a semi-annual basis and rough diamond trade statistics,[61] no sanction exists for non-compliance. It is true that non-compliant members can eventually be expelled from the KP, which happened in the 2004 case of the DRC, but this procedure does not respond to defined rules and this sanction is far from systemically applied. Besides having no sanctions for non-compliance, it is reported that data given by countries is often delayed, missing, or based on different methodologies making it very difficult to compile a coherent and accurate database.[62] For example, Russia did not submit any data despite being one of the largest diamond producers[63] and Ghana and Venezuela submitted incomplete or limited data.[64] Neither of these members faced sanctions or was expelled. It is demonstrated that the main issue of the KP is not a lack of institutionalized transparency, which facilitates the *ex ante* accountability of this IN-LAW body, but rather the political will of participants in sharing the data. Thus, the accountability mechanism provided by the level of transparency is undermined by a lack of effectiveness, which could be achieved by the creation of an independent body on statistics. Indeed, even though in the DRC case Canada succeeded in analyzing the data that led to the expulsion of a member, it is not an independent body on statistics and operated as a member and – at the time – Chair of the Working Group. Indeed, according to Global Witness, independent and regular data analysis has been undermined whereas participants of the KP lack the will to provide the necessary funding.[65] As previously mentioned, when analyzing the accountability towards internal stakeholders, members and non-members do not have an equal level of access to information. Mr. Kara underlined that "access to information is highly uneven at the best of

[60] Smillie, p. 6, see *supra* note 51.

[61] "Kimberley Process Certification Scheme", see *supra* note 7.

[62] Wallis, 2005, para. 53, see *supra* note 46.

[63] *Ibid.*

[64] Global Witness and Partnership Africa Canada Report, "Implementing the Kimberley Process", p. 3, 2005, available at http://www.globalwitness.org/media_library_detail.php/136/en/implementing_the_kimberley_process, last accessed on 4 July 2012.

[65] Global Witness, Loopholes in the Kimberley Process Certification Scheme, "Summary of Results of Diamond Trade Statistics Review", October 2007, p. 5.

times and exclusive at the worst". Making data publicly available is an essential element in the accountability of the KP since it allows for the identification of irregularities in the legitimate diamond trade. Next to this, in order to be effective, the KP should include a cross-checking system with other external sources.[66]

The second element that will help us to measure the accountability of the KP towards external stakeholders is the capacity NGOs, the diamond industry, and miners have to judge the effectiveness of the certificate. NGOs seem to have some controlling power over State members.[67] The example of the organized campaign on the ineffectiveness of the KP and the need to have a monitoring system is of relevance: the voice of civil society was heard and the Working Group on Monitoring created. NGOs also influence the KP when performing their important role in releasing reports on human rights violations, on loopholes in the KP, on how to enhance the enforcement of the KP and so on. Another stakeholder in the KP is the diamond industry. Their main concerns relate to the need to create a positive image of the industry and to obey the law of demand and supply, rather than claiming the same sort of oversight powers NGOs claim. The diamond industry has a particular status within the scheme. Indeed, despite the fact that they act as observers in the working groups, they are self-regulating isolated actors and do not take up a role as watchdog or report companies. The latter role remains with the NGOs.[68]

As indicated above, it is in the interests of both the KP and the jewelry industry to maintain a good relationship and reputation, which will

---

66 Global Witness, p. 1, see *supra* note 65.

67 Indeed, it is thanks to them that the conflict diamond trade was brought to light in 1998 when Global Witness released the report titled "a Rough Trade" and pushed for the creation of an international certification scheme. See Global Witness, "A Rough Trade", available at http://www.globalwitness.org/media_library_detail.php/90/en/a_rough_trade, last accessed on 4 July 2012.

68 Indeed, how can one expect impartial control once realising the billions of dollars companies are making thanks to the diamond trade? On the ground, the diamond industry is asked to provide a warranty for "all buyers and sellers of both rough and polished diamonds must make the following affirmative statement on all invoices", it stipulates that: "The Diamonds herein invoiced have been purchased from legitimate sources not involved in funding conflict in compliance with United Nations Resolutions. The seller hereby guarantees that these diamonds are conflict free, based on personal knowledge and/or written guarantees provided by the supplier of diamonds". Also, how can a guarantee only be provided on 'personal knowledge'?

depend on NGOs campaigns and reports.[69] The Kimberley Process is composed of eminent personalities of the diamond industry like Eli Izhakoff, president of the World Diamond Council or Andrew Bone, Director of International Relations at De Beers.[70] The diamond industry had a deep economic stake in respecting the Kimberley Process requirements.[71] However, this NGO power is weakened by the predominant role of States in the KP, which tend to weaken the role of civil society and increase the power of the diamond industry.[72] In his interview, Mr. Kara argued in this respect, that the self-regulated industry is a "real joke in terms of credibility, legitimacy, effectiveness and accountability". To conclude, although we can state that various external stakeholders had some control over the Kimberley Process, this power is today threatened by the strong political interests involved in the KP.

The possibilities to participate in the KP are even more limited for artisanal miners, who are not given any formal role in the IN-LAW body. Yet, miners have a clear interest in being heard in proceedings, for example, of the Working Group on Artisanal and Alluvial production.

The mandate of the Group was deliberately limited to the promotion of more effective control over artisanal mines. So, while artisanal extraction of diamonds is a backbreaking job, the Group does not deal with issues relating to labor standards. The non-inclusion of miners, the prime external stakeholders, in the Group can be explained by the unwillingness to extend its mandate to the protection of human rights. NGOs proposed a draft to amend the Administrative Decision on Internal Controls to include the interests of citizens and miners.[73] In their opinion, stakeholders should be able to benefit from the KP in terms of human rights and economic profit. The situation in Botswana often serves as an example, since

---

69 Wallis, 2005, para. 30, see *supra* note 46.

70 World Diamond Council panel for the Plenary Meeting held in Jerusalem from 1 to 4 November 2010, available at http://www.worlddiamondcouncil.com/, last accessed on 4 July 2012.

71 Greg Campbell, in Grant and Taylor, 2004, p. 391, see *supra* note 20, argues that during the civil war it "made economic sense to trade with killers as it didn't threaten the demand for the goods" but now De Beers was respecting NGO pressure "as it made economic sense for the industry to condemn the trade and wash their hands".

72 Interview with Mr. Kara, see *supra* note 48.

73 Intersessional Meeting 2010, p. 12, available at http://www.kimberleyprocess.com/documents/plenary_intersessional_meeting_en.html.

Botswana succeeded in using diamond mining as a source of economic stimulus to provide free education for every child below the age of 13.[74] Full participation of the artisanal miners includes providing opportunities for having their voices heard and for filing complaints. The need for such participation rights was reflected in the DRC. When an association representing Congolese citizens brought a case to court against a mining company for human rights violations, one of the claimants stated "We have no option but to turn to the international community for justice".[75]

## 14.3. The Functioning of the Kimberley Process

This third section aims to shed light on the concrete effects of the KP on the protection of human rights. Diamonds are extraordinary gems; they are cherished for their physical properties and they embody the symbol of love. Diamonds are special because they are the tiniest and most concentrated form of wealth on the earth[76] and because they serve both as a medium of exchange and a store of value.[77] These characteristics at the same time make them ideal for smuggling and yielding huge profits. Over the years, the control of mines by rebel groups in Africa has brought about gross human rights violations that were particularly suffered by children. During the civil war in Liberia, known for being financed by the trade in blood diamonds, 15,000 children were recruited, beaten, tortured, and punished if they breached the rules dictated by the commanders.[78] Girls were probably the most affected by this conflict as they were "raped and sexually enslaved by the fighters".[79] Following these atrocities, when the KP members decided to generate a certificate of origin for diamonds, they

---

74 "Diamond Fact 5", available at http://diamondfacts.org/facts/fact_05.html, last accessed on 4 July 2012.

75 Global Witness, "Congolese Victims File Class Action Against Canadian Mining Compagny", 8 November 2010, available at http://www.globalwitness.org/library/congolese-victims-file-class-action-against-canadian-mining-company, last accessed on 4 July 2012.

76 Ingrid Tamm, "Diamonds in Peace and War: Severing the Conflict-Diamond Connection", World Peace Foundation Report, 2002, p. 5.

77 David Gold, "The Attempt to Regulate Conflict Diamonds", in *The Economics of Peace and Security Journal*, 2006, vol. 1, no. 1, p 49.

78 "How to Fight, How to Kill, Child soldier in Liberia", Human Rights Watch Report, p. 2, available at http://www.hrw.org/sites/default/files/reports/liberia0204.pdf, last accessed on 4 July 2012.

79 *Ibid.*

explicitly named "the systematic and gross human rights violations that have been perpetrated in such conflicts" as a reason for creating this system.[80] Yet, as mentioned above, the KP lacks the political will to extend the current mandate to the protection of human rights. Tackling the credibility and legitimacy of the KP, Jack Jolis, in a virulent report written for the Wall Street Journal, wrote that the Kimberley Process was an "Inspector Clouseau-like agglomeration of squabbling national boards and committees", and that it was still affecting the "most courageous and blameless in the entire diamond pipeline, that is, the independent, artisanal diamond diggers".[81] More recently, the incapacity to reach an agreement in the KP context has been observed in Zimbabwe. Indeed, in 2008, the military took control over the Marangue diamond field and killed around 200 miners. Gang rape, torture and forced enrollment of women and children was reported and attributed to the Zimbabwe's military.[82] Under the auspices of the KP, a Joint Work Plan was created, restricting the export of diamonds from this mine, while a credible agreement could not be reached.[83] The incapacity of the Kimberley Process to expel Zimbabwe and its ineffectiveness in general result from the fact that members remain incapable of reaching an agreement on political matters when too many various stakes and diplomatic issues are involved.

Another major problem undermining the accountability and output legitimacy of the KP is the difficulty of establishing the origin of diamonds. Diamonds are normally quite straightforward to identify, their physical characteristics "roughly correspond to their country of origin".[84] However, diamonds do not have a "legally dispositive geographical DNA"[85] and recognizing a rough diamond can be extremely difficult. The permeable boarders of African countries make it easy, for example, for Angolan diamonds to go through DRC or Rwanda before being sent to

80 "Kimberley Process Certification Scheme", see *supra* note 7.

81 Jack Jolis, "Naomi Campbell and the Blood Diamonds Hoax", Wall Street Journal, 10 August 2010.

82 James Melik, "Diamonds: Does the Kimberley Process Work?", BBC News, 28 June 2010.

83 Global Witness, "Conflict Diamond Scheme Must Resolve Zimbabwe Impasse", 5 November 2010, available at http://www.globalwitness.org/library/conflict-diamond-scheme-must-resolve-zimbabwe-impasse, last accessed on 4 July 2012.

84 Grant and Taylor, 2004, p. 395, see *supra* note 20.

85 Jolis, 2010, see *supra* note 81.

Lebanon or Anvers.[86] When they are mixed and "thrown together like coffee beans [...] they completely lose their lineage".[87] Also, it appears to be common that a diamond dealer would buy a parcel of diamonds from a Canadian mine, another from miners in Congo, mix them and sell them as a whole to an individual diamond cutter.[88] From there it is impossible to trace the origin of a diamond and also impossible for the KP to intervene as it only deals with rough diamonds and not cut gems. The mixing of diamonds demonstrates very clearly that some African countries have neither the means nor the will to control the export of rough diamonds. It also demonstrates that a self-regulating industry is an utopia at this point, an issue that weighs on the accountability of the KP. Some countries are just not willing to control the origin of their diamonds:[89] Ian Smilie[90] underlined in this sense that diamonds could come from Angola, Zimbabwe or even Mars.[91] However, other countries, like for example Sierra Leone, lack the resources "for monitoring large mining areas and highly porous borders"[92] or to fulfill their mission on conflict diamond trade.[93] Also, Sierra Leone's body responsible for licensing of mines and exporters, the Ministry of Mineral Resources, lacks the infrastructure to effectively control the origin of diamonds ready for export.[94] Thus, the KP is not at all accountable on this matter and needs to review its mechanism of internal control to be legitimate and have a positive impact on the conflict diamond trade.

---

86 Jean-Baptiste Naudet, "Diamants de sang: Le traffic continue", Le Nouvel Observateur, 9 to 15 September 2010, p. 56.

87 Jolis, 2010, see *supra* note 81.

88 *Ibid.*

89 Melik, 2010, see *supra* note 82.

90 Ian Smilie was a key actor in the creation of the KP and has been on the scene for years. However, very regrettably for the international community he left the KP as he did not believe in the KP anymore. He says "I could no longer in good faith contribute to pretence that failure is success". Quoted in the aforementioned article.

91 Melik, 2010, see *supra* note 82.

92 United States Government, *Conflict Diamonds: Agency Actions Needed to Enhance the Implementation of the Clean Diamond Trade Act, Report to Congressional Committees*, US Government Accountability Office, Washington D.C., 2006, p. 5.

93 Melik, 2010, see *supra* note 82.

94 Margo Kaplan, "Carats and Sticks, Pursuing War and Peace Trough the Diamond Trade", in *New York University of International Law and Politics*, 2003, vol. 35, no. 3, pp. 600–602.

## 14.4. Conclusion and Recommendations

This chapter aimed at analyzing the accountability of the Kimberley Process towards internal and external stakeholders. It first explained that this certificate was created with a real political will of tackling the conflict diamond trade and, even though it was never part of formal international law, considerable efforts were made to hinder trade in conflict diamonds. The Kimberley Process has a structure that at first glance looks like an IO, with a Chair, Committees, Working Groups, and Member States. Yet, it does not find its origins in a formally adopted international convention, and as Pauwelyn outlined, process informality does not prevent the existence of detailed procedural rules or a well-organized structure. Next to this, the informality of the actors involved and the reluctance of members to create a legally binding instrument makes the KP an excellent example of IN-LAW. The KP is often criticized for not being accountable towards affected people living in Africa, traders in diamonds, and the diamond industry. This chapter analyzed how internal and external stakeholders can hold the Kimberley Process to account. Towards internal stakeholders, accountability can be increased by improving transparency and by establishing a complaints mechanism. We concluded that in all matters, internal stakeholders are holders of significant powers at all stages of the process, and thus the Kimberley Process is accountable to them. Yet, this accountability is not in line with the desired level of effectiveness. The KP still lacks an independent body to enforce sanctions. Accountability towards external stakeholders is measured by the level of transparency of the KP and the capacity of external stakeholders to be part of the decision-making process and the complaints-mechanism. We concluded that the transparency element existed but is undermined as the data given by countries was not checked with external sources and thus posed a problem of veracity. The section then came to the conclusion that NGOs are involved in the KP scheme, although the States and the diamond industry remain the main actors. Also, other external stakeholders, such as diamond diggers, although most affected, are less involved in the KP. A final part aimed to provide some real life insights into the diamond problematic. The two main factors identified to be undermining the legitimacy of the KP certificate were, first, the exclusion of human rights matters from the KP's mandate and, second, the difficulties encountered to trace rough diamonds at source.

The diamond trade is a very sensitive issue and regulating it is far from evident. Some, like John Hall argue that the KP is involved in law-making because it is accepted as such by its members and backed by a United Nations Resolution. Moreover, the KP is legally binding at the domestic level and responds to the committing legal norms at the international level.[95] However, if the KP was a traditional legal instrument, it would have a legal personality, which would allow to hold it accountable as a separate entity through the independent body aforementioned. The IN-LAW status of the KP has certainly contributed to its success, if only for the fact that formal solutions could not be found to regulate the trade in conflict diamonds. Indeed, one must remember that over the years, the UN Security Council passed resolutions to embargo diamonds or weapons coming from Angola and Liberia,[96] which were not respected by countries or by companies.[97] We doubt that the KP would have been as effective if it was responding to the criteria of international law, as it would not allow this level of cooperation and informality desired by the members.

---

95 See Pauwelyn, Wessel and Wouters, 2012, see *supra* note 33.

96 See resolutions 1173 in 1998 / 1374, 1348, 1336 in 2001.

97 Lucinda Saunders, "Rich and Rare are the Gems They War: Holding De Beers Accountable for Trading Conflict Diamonds", in *Fordham Journal of International Law*, 2001, vol. 24, issue 4, pp. 1402–1476. See also Global Witness, "A Rough Trade", see *supra* note 67, who states that De Beers bought legally and illegally diamonds mined in Angola for the amount of US$ 500 millions in 1992.

# INDEX

## C



## D



## E

## F



## G



## H

## L



## M



## N



## O



## P

## R



## S



## T

## U



## V



## W



## Y

# TORKEL OPSAHL ACADEMIC EPUBLISHER

# ALSO IN THE LAW OF THE FUTURE SERIES

Sam Muller, Stavros Zouridis, Morly Frishman and Laura Kistemaker (editors):
*The Law of the Future and the Future of Law: Volume II*
Torkel Opsahl Academic EPublisher
The Hague, 2012
Law of the Future Series No. 1 (2012)
ISBN 978-82-93081-80-7

Sam Muller and Stavros Zouridis (editors):
*Law and Justice: A Strategy Perspective*
Torkel Opsahl Academic EPublisher
The Hague, 2012
Law of the Future Series No. 2 (2012)
ISBN 978-82-93081-82-1

www.ingramcontent.com/pod-product-compliance
Lightning Source LLC
Chambersburg PA
CBHW071337230926
51849CB00006B/511/J